INTRODUCTION TO BIBLICAL HEBREW

INTRODUCTION TO

BIBLICAL HEBREW

Thomas O. Lambdin

HARVARD UNIVERSITY

Charles Scribner's Sons • *New York*

15 17 19 K/P 20 18 16

Printed in the United States of America
ISBN 0-02-367350-8
Library of Congress Catalog Card Number 75-100128

PREFACE

This textbook is designed for a full year's course in elementary Biblical Hebrew at the college level. In its choice of vocabulary and grammar it is essentially an introduction to the prose, not the poetical language. While my aim has been to include only what I consider necessary for the grammatically intelligent reading of the texts on which the work is based, experienced teachers may nevertheless wish to expand or condense one portion or another according to the needs of their own courses and the problems of their particular students. By keeping the grammatical discussion at a relatively unsophisticated level I have tried to make the book as serviceable as possible to those who want to study the language without a teacher.

Although the present work clearly falls within the category of traditional grammars, there are several features in the presentation which require a brief comment. The generous use of transliteration is meant to serve three *Purpose* purposes: to enable the student to perceive Hebrew as a language, and not an exercise in decipherment; to remove the customary initial obstacle, wherein the student was required to master innumerable pages of rather abstract phonological and orthographic details before learning even a sentence of the language; and to facilitate the memorization of the paradigms, where the essential features are, in my opinion, set in greater relief than in the conventional script. The morphology of the verb is presented in a way that best exploits the underlying similarities of the various forms, regardless of the root type; this permits the introduction of the most common verbs at an appropriately early point in the grammar and also allows the discussions of the derived "conjugations" to be unhampered by restriction to examples from sound roots. As much space as possible has been given to the systematic treatment of noun morphology and to the verb with object suffixes; the simplification of this material attempted in many elementary grammars is actually a disservice to the student. When he turns to his first page of unsimplified reading, he finds that what he should have learned systematically must instead be learned at random, inefficiently and with no little difficulty. And finally, special attention has been given to an orderly presentation of prose syntax, beginning with a characterization of the various types of individual clauses and proceeding to sequences of interrelated clauses.

In the initial stages of preparing this book I was greatly aided in the selection of vocabulary by George M. Landes' *A Student's Vocabulary of Biblical Hebrew* (New York, 1961), furnished to me in page proof at that time by the author, to whom I now wish to acknowledge my thanks. In the nearly ten years since that time the innumerable suggestions and corrections submitted by my students and colleagues working with various drafts of the book have been of enormous help in improving the quality of the finished product. I am especially grateful, however, to Dr. Avi Hurwitz, now at the Hebrew University, for his great kindness in giving an earlier draft of this book a thorough and critical reading and in providing me with many corrections. The errors that remain are of course due to my own oversight.

The setting of pointed Hebrew with a special sign marking stress always proves to be a difficult job, even in this age of technological marvels. I wish to thank the publisher and the printer for their unstinting efforts to ensure correctness in this regard.

Cambridge, Mass.   THOMAS O. LAMBDIN
May 1971

CONTENTS

INTRODUCTION

The Hebrew Bible (Christian Old Testament) is a collection of writings whose composition spans most of the millennium from c. 1200 B.C. to c. 200 B.C. Because a spoken language does not remain constant over so long a period of time, we must recognize Biblical Hebrew as a form of the spoken language standardized at a particular time and perpetuated thereafter as a fixed literary medium. It is generally assumed that Biblical Hebrew, to the extent that it is linguistically homogeneous, is a close approximation to the language of the monarchic periods preceding the Babylonian Exile (thus, before 587 B.C.), during which a major portion of biblical literature was compiled and composed. The sparse inscriptional material of the ninth to seventh centuries B.C. corroborates this view, but does not permit us to establish more precise limits. In the post-exilic period spoken Hebrew came under the strong influence of other languages, especially Aramaic, but also Persian and, later, Greek. The literary language of biblical writings during this time remained relatively free of this influence, which shows up more clearly in post-biblical sources such as the Rabbinic Hebrew of the Mishna and other traditional works lying beyond the scope of this grammar. Exactly when Hebrew ceased to be a spoken language is difficult, if not impossible, to determine, but in all probability its demise was concurrent with the devastation of Judaea in the Jewish revolts against Roman rule in the first two centuries A.D.

Hebrew is a member of the extensive Semitic language family, whose principal divisions are as follows:

(1) Northeast Semitic: Babylonian and Assyrian (Akkadian);
(2) Southeast Semitic: Ancient South Arabic and the related modern languages of South Arabia and Ethiopia;
(3) Southwest Semitic: Classical Arabic and the host of related modern Arabic dialects;
(4) Northwest Semitic, comprising
    (a) Aramaic
    (b) Canaanite (Ugaritic, Phoenician, Hebrew)

Our knowledge of Biblical Hebrew is directly dependent on Jewish oral tradition and thus on the state of that tradition during and following the various dispersions of the Jews from Palestine. This dependence arises from the peculiarly deficient orthography in which the biblical text was written: it is essentially vowelless, or at most, vocalically ambiguous (see below, §8). The actual pronunciation of the language was handed down orally, and as the Jews left or were expelled from Palestine and formed new communities in Babylonia, Egypt, and eventually throughout most of the civilized world, the traditional reading of biblical texts diverged gradually from whatever norm might have existed prior to these dispersions. The written consonantal text itself achieved a final authoritative form around the end of the first century A.D. This text was successfully promulgated among all the Jewish communities, so that texts postdating this time do not differ from one another in any important particulars. Prior to the fixing of an authoritative text, however, the situation was quite different, and the reader is referred to the bibliography (Appendix E) for the names of a few works that will introduce him to the complex problems of ancient texts and versions.

Modern printed versions of the Hebrew Bible derive from several essentially similar sources, all reflecting the grammatical activity of Jewish scholars (or Masoretes, traditionalists) in Tiberias, who during the 9th and 10th centuries A.D. perfected a system of vowel notation and added it to the received consonantal text. Because the vowel system reflected in this notation is not exactly the same as that of the tradition used in other locales, we must recognize that Hebrew grammar, as based on the vocalized Tiberian Masoretic text, is no more or less authentic than that which would derive from other traditions: it is simply the best preserved and has received, by universal adoption, the stamp of authority. A treatment of the fragmentary evidence of the non-Tiberian traditions lies beyond the scope of an elementary grammar. The standard Masoretic text is also known as the Ben Asher text, after the family name of the Tiberian scholars identified with the final editing. The *Biblia Hebraica* (3rd edition, Stuttgart, 1937) used by most modern students and scholars is based on the copy of a Ben Asher manuscript now in Leningrad and dating from 1008/9 A.D. Most other printed Hebrew Bibles are based ultimately on the text of the Second Rabbinic Bible (Venice, 1524–25); the manuscript sources of this work have not been fully identified, but it does not differ substantially from the text of the *Biblia Hebraica*. A new and comprehensive edition of the Hebrew Bible is in progress in Israel; it will utilize the partially destroyed Aleppo Codex, which is convincingly claimed as an authentic manuscript of the Ben Asher family.

A limited number of variant readings are indicated marginally in the Masoretic text. These are commonly referred to as *kǝṯîḇ-qǝrē*, i.e. one word is written (*kǝṯîḇ*) in the consonant text itself but another, as indicated in the margin, is to be read (*qǝrē*).

SOUNDS AND SPELLING

[*Note: The material in this section has been presented as a unit for ready reference. After studying § § 1–3 the reader should begin Lesson 1 (p. 3). The reading of further paragraphs will be indicated as required.*]

1. The Sounds of Biblical Hebrew.

As stated in the Introduction, we cannot determine absolutely the sounds of Biblical Hebrew in the period during which the literary language was fixed. The pronunciation used in this book has been chosen to preserve as faithfully as possible the consonantal and vocalic distinctions recognized by the Masoretes, but, at the same time, to do the least violence to what we know of the earlier pronunciation. A uniform system of transliteration has been adopted which attempts to represent the Hebrew orthography simply and accurately.

a. Consonants

Type	*Transliteration*	*Pronunciation**
Labial	b	[b] as in bait
	p	[p] as in pay
	m	[m] as in main
	w	[w] as in well
Labio-dental	ḇ	[v] as in vase
	p̄	[f] as in face
Interdental	ṯ	[θ] as in thin
	ḏ	[δ] as in this
Dental or alveolar	t	[t] as in time
	d	[d] as in door
	s ⎫ ś ⎭	[s] as in sing
	z	[z] as in zone

* Square brackets enclose currently used phonetic symbols as a guide to those who are familiar with them. Do not confuse these with the transliteration.

	n	[n] as in noon
Prepalatal	š	[ʃ] as in show
	y	[y] as in yes
Palatal	k	[k] as in king
	g, ḡ	[g] as in go
	ḵ	[x] as in German Bach
Velar	q	[q]

There is no exact English equivalent of this sound. It is a type of [k], but with the contact between the tongue and the roof of the mouth as far back as possible.

Guttural	ʾ	[ʾ] the glottal stop
	h	[h] as in house
	ʿ	[ʿ] no Eng. equivalent
	ḥ	[ʜ] no Eng. equivalent

The glottal stop [ʾ] is used in English, but not as a regular part of its sound system. It is made by a complete stoppage of breath in the throat and may be heard in certain Eastern pronunciations of words like *bottle* and *battle*, in which the glottal stop replaces the normal *t*, thus [bɑʾl], [bæʾl]. The sound [ʜ] is an *h*-sound, but with strong constriction between the base of the tongue and the back of the throat, thus with a much sharper friction than ordinary *h*. The [ʿ] is similarly produced, but with the additional feature of voicing. Most modern readers of Biblical Hebrew do not use these two sounds, replacing them with [x] and [ʾ] respectively. Those making such a simplification should be careful not to confuse these four sounds in spelling.

The four sounds which we shall call gutturals throughout this book are more precisely described as laryngeals and pharyngealized laryngeals, but because the modern terminology is often inconsistently applied, we find no compelling reason to abandon the more traditional designation.

Liquids	r	[r] as in rope
	l	[l] as in line
Modified Dental	ṭ	[t] as in time
	ṣ	[ts] as in hits

The pronunciation indicated for *ṭ* and *ṣ* is a standard modern substitution for the original sounds, whose true nature can only be conjectured as [t] and [s] accompanied by constriction in the throat (pharyngealization or glottalization), thus producing a tenser, duller sound.

b. Vowels

It is customary in treating Hebrew vowels to speak of length as well as
Though this distinction is probably valid for the earlier pronunciati...,
doubtful whether vowel quantity played any important part in the original
Masoretic system. The diacritical marks used in our transcription are thus
to be taken as devices reflecting the Hebrew spelling and not necessarily as
markers of real length.

î, ī	[i] as in mach*i*ne	û, ū	[u] as in m*oo*d
i	[ɪ] as in *i*t	u	[ʊ] as in b*oo*k
ê, ē	[e] as in th*ey*	ô, ō	[o] as in n*o*te
e, ệ	[ɛ] as in b*e*t	o	[ɔ] as in b*ou*ght
a	[ɑ] as in f*a*ther or	ə	[ə] as in *a*bove, and
	[a] as in th*a*t		very brief in duration
ā, â	[ɑ] as in f*a*ther or		
	[ɔ] as in b*ou*ght		

Some distinction between the two vowels *a* and *ā* should be made, since they
must always be clearly distinguished in spelling. The choice is left to the
reader: either [a] as opposed to [ɑ] or [ɑ] as opposed to [ɔ].

In addition to the vowels listed above there are three others (*ă ě ŏ*) which,
together with *ə*, are known as reduced vowels. They are of very brief duration
but with the same quality as the corresponding full vowel: *ă* is a very short
a, *ě* a very short *e*, and *ŏ* a very short *o*.

The following diphthongal combinations of vowel + *y* or *w* occur
frequently at the ends of words:

îw	the vowel *î* + a very short [ŭ]. Also pronounced as [iv], as in English *eve*.
ēw, êw	*ē/ê* + [ŭ]. Also [ev], as in *save*.
āw, âw	*ā* + [ŭ] like the *ou* of *house*, or as [ɑw] or [ɑv]
aw	*a* + [ŭ], or as [ɑv] or [av]
āy	[ɑy] like the *y* of *sky*; or [ɔy], similar to the *oy* of *toy*.
ay	[ɑy] or [ay]
ôy, ōy	[oy], similar to the *owy* of *showy*, but without the *w*.
ûy, ūy	[uy] somewhat like the *uey* of *gluey*.

For descriptive purposes we shall refer to the vowels according to the following
classification, without prejudice to the actual length of the vowels involved:

(1) unchangeable long: *î ê ô û* and sometimes *ō*
(2) changeable long: *ē ā ō*
(3) short: *i e a o u*
(4) reduced: *ə ă ě ŏ*

2. Syllabification.

With very few exceptions a syllable must begin with a single consonant followed at least by one vowel. This rule alone will suffice for the accurate division of a word into syllables. Consider the following examples:

miḏbār (wilderness): *miḏ-bār*	pronounced	[mɪð'bɑr]
'āḇîw (his father): *'ā-ḇîw*		['ɑ'viw]
dəḇārîm (words): *də-ḇā-rîm*		[dəvɑ'rim]
mimménnî (from me): *mim-mén-nî*		[mɪm'mɛnni]
gibbôrîm (warriors): *gib-bô-rîm*		[gɪbbo'rim]
yišlāḥḗnî (he will send me): *yiš-lā-ḥḗ-nî*		[yɪʃlɑ'Heni]
malkəḵā (your king): *mal-kə-ḵā*		[malkə'xɑ]
malkêḵem (your kings): *mal-kê-ḵem*		[malxe'xɛm]

In none of these examples is any other division of syllables possible without violating the basic rule.

Syllables are of two types: *open* and *closed*. An open syllable is one which ends in a vowel; a closed syllable ends in a consonant. Syllables containing a diphthong may be considered as closed, taking the *y* or *w* as a consonant. The distinction is irrelevant in this case.

When determining syllabification note that a doubled consonant, such as –*bb*– or –*mm*–, is always to be divided in the middle. This does not mean that there is any perceptible pause between the syllables in pronunciation: a doubled consonant is simply held longer than a single one. Contrast the long *n* of English *meanness* with the normal short *n* of *any*. Examples are

libbəḵā (your heart): *lib-bə-ḵā*	[lɪbbə'xɑ]
mimməḵā (from you): *mim-mə-ḵā*	[mɪmmə'xɑ]
haššāmáyim (the heavens): *haš-šā-má-yim*	[haʃʃɑ'mayɪm]

3. Stress.

Words are stressed on the last syllable (ultima) or on the next to last (penultima). The former is more frequent.

ultimate stress: *dāḇār* (word); *dəḇārîm* (words); *nāḇî'* (prophet)
penultimate stress: *mélek* (king); *láylāh* (night); *nəḥóšeṯ* (bronze)

Only penultimate stress will be marked in this book.

The stressed syllable is often referred to as the *tonic* syllable, and the two preceding it as the *pretonic* and *propretonic* respectively.

4. The consonants known as the begadkepat.

Two sets of six sounds each are closely related to one another, both in sound and distribution. These are the six stops *b, g, d, k, p, t* on the one hand and their spirantized counterparts $\underline{b}$, $\bar{g}$, $\underline{d}$, $\underline{k}$, $\bar{p}$, and $\underline{t}$ on the other. Although no rule can be given for the choice between the sounds of one set and those of the other without important exceptions, the following observations will provide a safe guide for the majority of occurrences.

(a) Of the two sets, only the stops occur doubled. Thus we find -bb- (as in *habbáyit*, the house), -dd- (*haddélet*, the door), -kk- (*hakkəlî*, the vessel), etc., but never -ḇḇ-, -ḡḡ-, -ḏḏ-, etc.

(b) The stops *b, g, d, k, p, t* occur (excluding the doubling just mentioned) only at the beginning of a syllable when immediately preceded by another consonant:

malkî (my king): *mal-kî*

but   *mélek* (king): *mé-lek*.

Elsewhere one finds the spirantized counterpart, which, by a simple process of elimination, occurs (a) mainly at the close of a syllable, or (b) at the beginning of a syllable when the preceding sound is a vowel. Contrast, for example, the *b* of *midbār* (*mid-bār*) and the *ḇ* of *nāḇî'* (*nā-ḇî'*).[*]

When a word begins with one of these sounds, it usually has the stop when it occurs in isolation (thus: *báyit*, a house), but when some element ending in a vowel is prefixed, the stop is automatically replaced by the corresponding spirant. Be sure the following examples are clear:

báyit	a house	but	*kəḇáyit*	like a house
kəlî	a vessel		*ûḵəlî*	and a vessel
délet	a door		*lədélet*	to a door.

In a sentence the·mere fact that the preceding word ends in a vowel is enough to warrant the spirant; thus,

bānû ḇáyit   they built a house

not   *bānû báyit*.

There are, however, many exceptions to this, depending on the degree of grammatical relationship between the words in question.

It is best, at least hypothetically, to regard the stop *g* and the spirant *ḡ* as two distinct sounds, although no modern tradition except the Yemenite has preserved the difference.

5. Vowel Reduction.

Many of the changes that characterize Hebrew inflections follow distinct and predictable patterns, of which the most consistent is that of vowel reduction.

(a) *Propretonic reduction.* The vowels *ā* and *ē* are regularly reduced to *ə* in open *propretonic* syllables. That is, when in the course of inflection the

---

[*] Note that our statement does not preclude the possibility of a spirant occurring at the beginning of a syllable preceded by another consonant: *malḵêḵem* (your kings).

accent is shifted so as to place these two vowels in propretonic position, the replacement just mentioned is made. For example, when the plural ending -*îm* is added to the stem of the noun *nābî'* (prophet), the accent is on the ending, leaving the *ā* in propretonic position.

Thus,   *nābî'* + *îm* → **nā-ḇî-'îm* → *nəḇî'îm*

Similarly with *ē*:   *lēḇāḇ* + *ôt* → **lē-ḇā-ḇôt* → *ləḇāḇôt*

Other examples are   *māqôm* + *ôt* → **mā-qô-môt* → *məqômôt*
                       zāqēn + *îm* → **zā-qē-nîm* → *zəqēnîm*

This type of reduction is regularly found in the inflection of nouns and adjectives, but is less common among verbs other than those with object suffixes.

(b) *Pretonic reduction.* A second reduction pattern, often conflicting with the above, involves reduction of *ā* or *ē* in a *pretonic* open syllable. In noun inflections this is true mainly for those words whose first syllable (propretonic) is unchangeable (i.e. contains one of the unchangeable long vowels or is a closed syllable) and whose pretonic syllable would contain *ē*:

šōpēṭ + *îm* → *šōpəṭîm*

Pretonic reduction is very frequent in verbs, regardless of the vowel:

yiḵtōḇ + *û* → *yiḵtəḇû*   (they will write)
yittēn + *û* → *yittənû*   (they will give)
yišma' + *û* → *yišmə'û*   (they will hear).

Attention has been called to these two reduction patterns since one or the other figures in most of the inflections to be studied. Unfortunately, however, it is not always possible to predict accurately which pattern will be followed, so that each paradigm should be carefully analyzed.

THE RULE OF SHEWA. A sequence of two syllables each with *ə* (shewa) is not tolerated by Hebrew structure. When such a sequence would arise in the course of inflection or when combining various words and elements, the following replacement is made:

consonant + *ə* + cons. + *ə* → cons. + i + cons.

Thus: *lə* (to) + *nəḇî'î* (my prophet) → *linḇî'î* (not *lənəḇî'î*).

6. Special Features of the Guttural Consonants and R.

(a) The gutturals and *r* do not occur doubled.
(b) The gutturals are never followed immediately by *ə*.

These two characteristics account for certain regular deviations from an expected norm. For example, since the definite article before non-gutturals is *ha* + doubling of the following consonant, we should expect the article to be somewhat different before words beginning with a guttural or *r*. We shall see in the lessons that *hā-* occurs in some cases, *ha-* (without doubling) in others. Whenever a long vowel (*ā ē ō*) occurs before a guttural or *r* and corresponds formally to a short vowel before a doubled non-guttural, the vowel is said to be long by *compensatory lengthening*, i.e. to compensate for the non-doubling of the guttural. When a short vowel (*a i u o*) occurs before a guttural in similar situations, the guttural is said to be *virtually doubled*.

As for the second feature listed above, the presence of a guttural means a substitution of *ă* (less commonly of *ĕ* or *ŏ*) for an expected *ə*. This is illustrated by

ḥāḵām (wise person) + *îm* → *ḥăḵāmîm*   (not *ḥəḵāmîm*)
ḥāzāq (strong person) + *îm* → *ḥăzāqîm*   (not *ḥəzāqîm*).

It is convenient to think of *ă*, *ĕ*, and *ŏ* as varieties of *ə* to be used after gutturals and to see that a word like *ḥălôm* (dream) has essentially the same vowel pattern as *bəḵôr* (first-born).

When a word ends with ' , *ḥ*, or *h* (when this is not a vowel letter, see §8), a preceding *î ē û ô* is followed by a non-syllabic glide element *a*. Thus,

sûs (horse) but *lûᵃḥ* (tablet)
kōṯēḇ (writing) but *šōlēᵃḥ* (sending)
gāḏôl (big) but *gāḇôᵃh* (high).

THE RULE OF SHEWA as applied to sequences involving gutturals:
        cons. + *ə* + guttural + *ă* → cons. + *a* + gutt. + *ă*
E.g.   *bə* (in) + *ḥălômî* (my dream) → *baḥălômî*
Similarly with *ĕ* and *ŏ*. Another sequence arising from vowel reduction is illustrated by *ḥāḵām* + *ê* (which requires double reduction) → **ḥăḵəmê* → *ḥaḵmê*.
I.e.   gutt. + *ă* + cons. + *ə* → gutt. + *a* + cons.
N.B. Rules given in the grammar to account for the peculiarities of gutturals do not apply to *r* unless so stated.

7. The Hebrew Alphabet.

The alphabet used in writing all the traditional texts of the Old Testament is more properly Aramaic than Hebrew. The situation is summarized by the table on the following page.

Sometime during the first half of the second millennium B.C. the alphabet was invented in the Syro-Palestinian area. This alphabet was a new creation, not directly based on any other system of writing then in use, but it seems to have been most clearly influenced by certain features of Egyptian hieroglyphic writing, especially in the lack of symbols to represent vowels.

The most prolific branch of the alphabet was the Phoenician, attested in

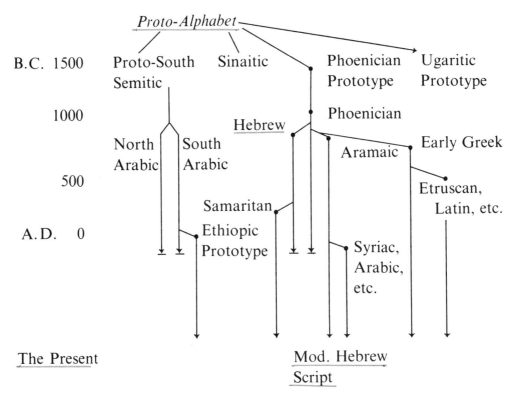

inscriptions from about the eleventh century onward. The Hebrews borrowed their script from the Phoenicians in the tenth century B.C., and this new "Hebrew" script, subsequently diverging from the parent Phoenician, was used in various types of inscriptions down to the beginning of the Christian Era. With the exception, however, of the manuscript traditions of the Samaritan sect, which still employs a form of this genuinely Hebrew script, the old script was replaced, especially in manuscript uses, by a cursive form of the Old Aramaic script, itself a daughter of the parent Phoenician of nearly the same age as the Hebrew.

It is this Aramaic manuscript hand which is already employed in Hebrew papyri and parchments of the second and first centuries B.C. and is attested as the normal alphabet for writing Hebrew from that time until the present.

THE HEBREW ALPHABET

NAME	LETTER	OUR TRANSCRIPTION	PHONETIC VALUE
ʾā́lep̄	א	ʾ	glottal stop or *zero*
bêṯ	בּ	b	[b]
	ב	ḇ	[v]
gîmel	גּ	g	[g]
	ג	ḡ	[g]
dā́leṯ	דּ	d	[d]
	ד	ḏ	[ð]
hē	ה	h	[h] or *zero*

NAME	LETTER		OUR TRANSCRIPTION	PHONETIC VALUE
wāw	ו		w	[w] or *zero*
záyin	ז		z	[z]
ḥēṯ	ח		ḥ	[H]
ṭēṯ	ט		ṭ	[t]
yōḏ	י		y	[y] or *zero*
kap̄	כ	ך	k	[k]
	כ	ך	ḵ	[x]
lắmeḏ	ל		l	[l]
mēm	מ	ם	m	[m]
nûn	נ	ן	n	[n]
sắmeḵ	ס		s	[s]
'áyin	ע		‘	[ᶜ]
pēh	פ	ף	p	[p]
	פ	ף	p̄	[f]
ṣāḏēh	צ	ץ	ṣ	[ts]
qōp	ק		q	[q]
rēš	ר		r	[r]
śîn	שׂ		ś	[s]
šîn	שׁ		š	[ʃ]
tāw	ת		t	[t]
	ת		ṯ	[θ]

8. Some Features of Hebrew Orthography (Spelling).

a. Hebrew is written from right to left.

b. Five of the letters have a special form used only at the end of a word: ך k, ם m, ן n, ף p, ץ ṣ.

c. In the earliest Hebrew and Phoenician inscriptions (10th cent. B.C.) no vowels were indicated in the writing. Thus the words *mélek* (king), *mōlēḵ* (ruling), *mālaḵ* (he ruled), *malkāh* (queen), *māləḵû* (they ruled), etc., would all be written simply as מלך *mlk*. From the ninth to the sixth centuries (i.e. pre-Exilic period, before the fall of Jerusalem in 587 B.C. and the Babylonian Exile) the consonants י y, ו w, and ה h were used at the end of a word to indicate final vowels:

> ו w = û   e.g. מלכו *mālaḵû*, they ruled
> י y = î   e.g. מלכי *malkî*, my king
> ה h = any other final vowel   e.g. מלכה *malkāh*, queen.

In the post-Exilic period י and ו were used as vowel indicators also inside a word, and values slightly different from those just cited were acquired:

> ו w = û or ô
> י y = ê, ệ, or î

The letter ה *h* was still used only at the end of a word as a vowel letter representing any vowel other than those just mentioned. The three letters י, ו, and ה in their function as vowel indicators are called *matres lectionis* (literally, mothers of reading), following traditional Hebrew grammatical terminology.

d. The MT in general reflects this stage of orthographic development. There are, however, some inconsistencies and irregularities to be noted:

(1) י and ו are sometimes missing when we should otherwise have expected them. The shorter spelling is called defective and the longer, full.

	Full			*Defective*	
יקום	*yāqûm*		יקם	*yāqūm*	he will arise
ירים	*yārîm*		ירם	*yārīm*	he will raise
גדול	*gāḏôl*		גדל	*gāḏōl*	big

Note that the only distinction between the vowels transcribed by *û*, *ū*; *î*, *ī*; and *ô*, *ō* is that the former of each pair is represented in the script by a *mater lectionis* while the latter is not.

(2) A final *ā* is not always indicated by ה: לְךָ *ləkā* (to you) תִּכְתֹּבְנָ *tiḵtōḇnā* (they shall write).

(3) א is unpronounced in many instances, but is always an integral part of the spelling: ראשׁ *rōš* (head), מצא *māṣā(')* (he found). It does not, however, belong to the category of *matres lectionis* discussed above since its appearance is limited mainly to words whose roots occur elsewhere in the language with the א retained in pronunciation. We have generally indicated quiescent א in our transliteration. Sometimes, for the sake of clarity, we have added the ' in parentheses, as in *māṣā(')* above.

Points (2) and (3) will be mentioned later in the section dealing with the grammatical forms in which these irregularities are commonly found.

9. The Daghesh

The Masoretes employed a dot or point within a letter to indicate

(a) that the consonant in question is doubled:

הַמֶּלֶךְ *hammélek* the king

(b) that, in the case of the ambiguous letters ב ג ד כ פ ת, the one with the point is the stop; the one without, the spirant:

ב	*b* or *bb*		ב	*ḇ*
ג	*g* or *gg*		ג	*ḡ*
ד	*d* or *dd*		ד	*ḏ*

(c) that a final ה is not to be taken as a vowel letter but as a morpho-logically significant consonant. Contrast

מלכה	malkā(h)	a queen	[ה is a *mater* for final -*ā*]
מלכה	malkāh	her king	[ה is part of the suffix meaning "her"]
בנה	bānāh	he built	[ה is a *mater*]
גבה	gāḇōᵃh	high	[ה is a root consonant, pronounced in this case]*

When the point indicates doubling, it is called *daghesh forte* (strong daghesh). When it indicates stop instead of spirant, it is called *daghesh lene* (weak d.). In a final ה it is known as *mappîq*.

The only use of daghesh where there is a possible source of confusion is in the *bǝḡaḏkǝp̄aṯ* letters. Technically we should expect two dagheshes when these represent doubled consonants, one to show the doubling (*d. forte*) and one to show *b* not *ḇ*. But since the spirant values for these six letters do not occur doubled, a second dot is superfluous and never written.

10. The Vowel Points.

Following their traditional pronunciation, the Masoretes added vowel points to the Hebrew text (see the Introduction). Because these points were superimposed on a text that already had a crude system for indicating vocalization, i.e. the *matres lectionis,* a large number of combinations were created (and hence the apparent complexity of our transliteration). The following table shows the form of the vowel signs and their position in relation to the consonants (here ב *b* and ה *ḥ*):

Name of Sign	Plain		With *mater* י *y*		With *mater* ו *w*		With *mater* ה *h* (final only)	
páṯaḥ	בַ	ba	—		—		—	—
qåmeṣ	בָ	bā or bo	בָי	bâ (rare)	—	—	בָה	bāh
hîreq	בִ	bi (or bī)	בִי	bî	—	—	—	—
ṣērê	בֵ	bē	בֵי	bê	—	—	בֵה	bēh
sǝḡōl	בֶ	be	בֶי	bê	—	—	בֶה	beh
ḥólem	בֹ	bō	—	—	בוֹ	bô	בֹה	bōh (rare)
qibbûṣ	בֻ	bu	—	—	בוּ	bû	—	—

And the reduced vowels:

בְ *bǝ*   חֲ *ḥă*   חֱ *ḥĕ*   חֳ *ḥŏ*

Remarks:

(1) In the case of defective writings, where *î* or *û* is meant but there is no *y* or *w* in the text, the vowel signs for *i* and *u* are used. The vowel ו (בֹ) is

---

* It is doubtful that every ה with *mappîq* is to be given a consonantal value [h]. The distinction between מלכה (queen) and מלכה (her king) was probably a graphic and not a phonological one.

called *šûreq*. Note that the reduced vowels *ă ĕ ŏ* are represented by a combination of the sign for *ə* and that of the corresponding non-reduced vowel. The names of the reduced vowels are *šəwā* (our Shewa), *ḥāṭēp páṭaḥ, ḥāṭēp səḡōl,* and *ḥāṭēp qắmeṣ* respectively.

(2) The distinction between $\underline{}$ = *ā* (*qắmeṣ*) and $\underline{}$ = *o* (*qắmeṣ ḥāṭûp*) is usually clear: $\underline{}$ = *o* in a closed, unaccented syllable (e.g. שָׁמְרִי *šomrî*; יִשְׁמַד *yošmaḏ*), but $\underline{}$ = *ā* elsewhere. There is ambiguity when a following consonant is pointed with $\underline{}$: should, e.g., מָלְכוּ be read *māləḵû* or *molḵû*? To resolve this ambiguity, a metheg is used (see §11).

(3) When a consonant closes a syllable (except at the end of a word), the Masoretes placed beneath it the Shewa sign: מַלְכִּי *mal-kî* (my king). For the beginning student this constitutes one of the biggest problems in reading Hebrew: when does the sign $\underline{}$ represent the vowel *ə* and when does it represent nothing (i.e. end of a syllable)? The answer to this question is not simple; in fact there are several schools of thought on the subject among the traditional Hebrew grammarians. Since it is completely immaterial to the understanding of the language and to translation, we shall not enter into the dispute, but rather adopt the following simple conventions:

(a) When two Shewa signs occur under consecutive consonants (except at the end of a word), the first represents zero and the second *ə*:

יִשְׁמְרוּ *yišmərû* (not *yišəmrû* or *yišəmərû*).

(b) When a preceding syllable has any one of the long vowels (*û/ū, ô/ō, î/ī, ê/ē, ệ, ā*), the Shewa sign represents *ə*:

הוּקְמוּ *hûqəmû* they were established
בֹּרְכוּ *bōrəḵû* they were blessed
יְשִׂימְךָ *yəśîməḵā* he will place you
יֵרְדוּ *yērəḏû* they will go down
שָׁתְתָה *šātətāh* she drank (see §11)

But after any other vowel it represents zero:

שִׁמְךָ *šimḵā* your name
מַלְכֵי *malḵê* kings
יִשְׁמָרְךָ *yišmorḵā* he will watch you

But under the first of two identical consonants the Shewa sign always represents the vowel *ə*, regardless of the type of vowel in the preceding syllable:

צְלָלֵי *ṣəlālê* shadows (not *ṣillê*).

(c) The Shewa sign under the first consonant of a word always represents *ə*:

בְּיָדוֹ *bəyāḏô* in his hand

[The various forms of the number two (fem.) are the only exceptions:

שְׁתַּ֫יִם *štáyim*   שְׁתֵּי *štê*]

(4) The glide vowel *a* (see §6) is represented by ‑ placed under the final guttural but pronounced before it: שְׁמֹעַ *šəmō^aʿ*; שָׂמֵחַ *śāmē^aḥ*. It is traditionally called *páṭaḥ furtivum*.

(5) The vowel sign *ḥólem* may coincide with one of the dots differentiating *śîn* and *šîn*; printed texts may vary. E.g. נָשֹׂא *nāśōʾ* (to lift); בֹּשׁ *bōš* (ashamed).

(6) The coincidence of a mater ׳ *y* and a consonantal ׳ *y* is frequent:

נָכְרִיָה   *nokrîyāh* (could also be transcribed as *nokriyyāh*)

(7) The consonant ך at the end of a word always has a shewa sign if it has no other vowel; thus לָךְ *lāk* (to you f.) but לְךָ *ləkā* (to you m.).

(8) In the rather rare situation where a final syllable of a word closes with two consonants, e.g. *wayyēḇk* (and he wept), the sign shewa is placed under both: וַיֵּבְךְּ.

11. Metheg.

The metheg is a short perpendicular stroke placed under a consonant and to the left of the vowel sign (if any). It serves several purposes in the orthography, of which the following are the most important:

(1) Since the vowels *ā* and *ē* are regularly replaced by *ə* in open syllables two or more places before the main stress, their appearance in such positions may be regarded as anomalous. They are usually marked with metheg:

אָנֹכִי *ʾānōkî* I

בֵּרַכְתַּ֫נִי *bēraktáni* you blessed me

(2) In fact, any long vowel occurring two or more syllables before the main stress may be so marked, although manuscripts are inconsistent in this. Compare

הוֹשַׁע *hôšaʿ* save!

הוֹשִׁיעֵ֫נִי *hôšî^ʿḗnî* save me!

This usage is particularly important with the vowel ‑, which is a short vowel *o* [ɔ] in closed, unaccented syllables and a long vowel *ā* elsewhere. The metheg is used with ‑ = *ā* in any doubtful position to ensure the correct reading:

יְבָרְכֵ֫נִי *yəḇārəkḗnî* he will bless me (not *yəḇorkḗnî*).

[Another device used in a word like the one just given to ensure correct reading is to point with ‑ instead of ‑:

יְבָרֲכֵ֫נִי *yəḇārăkḗnî*

This is an irregular use of *ă* for *ə*, since the consonant under which it appears need not be a guttural.]

(3) Short vowels before the main stress usually occur in closed syllables. Whenever the contrary occurs, the vowel may be marked with metheg:

תַּעֲמֹד *taʻămōd* she will stand

אָהֳלוֹ *'ohŏlô* his tent.

This last example, with ‑ָ = *o*, would seem to cancel out the usefulness of metheg for distinguishing between the two values of ‑ָ mentioned above. Actually, this is not often so, since ‑ָ = *ā* is very rarely followed by ‑ֳ *ŏ* in the next syllable, but rather by ‑ֲ *ă*: e.g. בָּחֲרוּ *bāḥărû* (they chose).

(4) Metheg with a short vowel in what appears to be a closed syllable indicates that the normal doubling of the following consonant has been given up: הַמְרַגְּלִים *hamraggəlîm* (the spies) for הַמְרַגְּלִים *hamməraggəlîm*. In this book metheg will be used consistently only with ‑ָ to mark the distinction between the o and ā values of the sign. Thus

אָכְלָה *'āḵəlāh* she ate

אָכְלָה *'oḵlāh* food

It is also employed sporadically to alert the reader to a syllabic division that might otherwise escape his notice.

INTRODUCTION TO BIBLICAL HEBREW

LESSON 1

[*Read §§ 1–3 of the section "Sounds and Spelling," pp. xv–xviii*]

12. The Noun: Gender.

Nearly all Hebrew nouns belong to one of two grammatical categories called gender: masculine and feminine. Nouns denoting animate beings usually have grammatical gender corresponding to natural gender (sex), but there is otherwise no clear correlation between gender and meaning. For example הַר *har* (mountain) is masculine, while גִּבְעָה *gibʿāh* (hill) is feminine.

There are some formal indications of gender: nouns ending in *-åh, -et,* and *-at* are nearly always feminine, such as

מַלְכָּה *malkåh*	queen	דַּעַת *dáʿat*	knowledge
בַּת *bat*	daughter	תִּפְאֶרֶת *tipʾéret*	glory

Nouns without these endings are usually masculine, but there are important exceptions, such as

אֶבֶן	*ébhen*	stone (fem.)
עִיר	*ʿîr*	city (fem.)
אֶרֶץ	*éreṣ*	earth (fem.)

Gender should therefore be learned for each noun, since it cannot be deduced safely from form or meaning. In the vocabularies of the lessons all nouns ending in *-åh, -et,* and *-at* are to be taken as feminine and all others as masculine unless there is a remark to the contrary. Typical listing will be

אִשָּׁה *'iššāh* woman   אֶרֶץ *'éreṣ* earth (f.)

דָּבָר *dābār* word   דֶּרֶךְ *dérek* way (m. or f.)

The last entry means that *dérek* may be used as either masculine or feminine; such words constitute a very small class.

13. Number.

Three categories of number are distinguished in Hebrew: singular, dual, and plural. The dual and plural are marked by special endings, but the singular is not:

Singular		Dual		Plural		
יָד	*yāḏ*	יָדַיִם	*yāḏáyim*	יָדוֹת	*yāḏôt*	hand
יוֹם	*yôm*	יוֹמַיִם	*yômáyim*	יָמִים	*yāmîm*	day
בֵּן	*bēn*	——		בָּנִים	*bānîm*	son
בַּת	*baṭ*	——		בָּנוֹת	*bānôṭ*	daughter

The dual is very restricted in use, being found mainly with the paired parts of the body and with set expressions of time or number, like "200," "twice," and "two years." For details, see below, §92.

The plural is indicated by the endings *-îm* and *-ôṭ* (or *-ōṭ*). Unfortunately, the plural is not always formed by simply adding one of these endings to the singular stem. In a very large number of nouns changes take place in the form of the stem:

מֶלֶךְ	*mélek* king	plural: מְלָכִים	*məlākîm*
אִישׁ	*'îš* man	אֲנָשִׁים	*'ănāšîm*
יוֹם	*yôm* day	יָמִים	*yāmîm*

The only general observation to be made concerning the plural endings is that most feminine nouns have plurals in *-ôṭ* and most masculine nouns in *-îm*. That this is only approximately true is clear from the following interesting exceptions:

אָב	*'āḇ* father	plural:	אָבוֹת	*'āḇôṭ*	(masculine)
אִשָּׁה	*'iššāh* woman		נָשִׁים	*nāšîm*	(feminine)

Note that a noun does not change its gender, regardless of the ending it has in the plural. During the next few lessons we shall take up the most important types of nouns and their plural forms. For use in the exercises the plural forms of a few very frequent (and often quite irregular) nouns will be introduced in the vocabulary before their general type has been studied in detail. It is advisable to learn these as they occur.

[4]

14. The Definite Article.

The definite article of Hebrew corresponds closely to the definite article of English in usage and meaning. The basic form of the article is *ha-* plus the doubling of the following consonant. It is prefixed directly to the noun it determines:

בַּיִת *báyiṯ* a house מֶלֶךְ *mélek* a king

הַבַּיִת *habbáyiṯ* the house הַמֶּלֶךְ *hammélek* the king

נַעַר *ná'ar* a youth

הַנַּעַר *hanná'ar* the youth

There is no indefinite article; *báyiṯ* may be translated as "house" or "a house." The noun with a definite article is used also to express the vocative: הַמֶּלֶךְ *hammélek* O king!

15. Prepositions.

From a purely formal point of view there are three types of prepositions in Hebrew:

a. Those joined directly to the following word and written as part of it. These are בְּ *bə* (in), לְ *lə* (to), and כְּ *kə* (like).

מֶלֶךְ *mélek* a king לְמֶלֶךְ *ləmélek* to a king

בְּמֶלֶךְ *bəmélek* in a king כְּמֶלֶךְ *kəmélek* like a king

When a noun is determined by the definite article, these three prepositions combine with the article into a single syllable having the same vowel of the article:

הַמֶּלֶךְ *hammélek* the king לַמֶּלֶךְ *lammélek* to the king

בַּמֶּלֶךְ *hammélek* in the king כַּמֶּלֶךְ *kammélek* like the king

b. Those joined (usually) to the following word with a short stroke called *maqqēp̄*. Among these are אֶל־ *'el-* (to, towards), עַל־ *'al-* (on, upon), and מִן־ *min-* (from):

עַל־הַבַּיִת *'al-habbáyiṯ* on the house

אֶל־הַבַּיִת *'el-habbáyiṯ* to the house

מִן־הַבַּיִת *min-habbáyiṯ* from the house

The *maqqēp̄* indicates that these words are proclitic, i.e. have no stress of their own, but are pronounced as the first syllable of the whole group taken as a single word.

c. The third and largest group consists of prepositions written as separate words:

אֵצֶל הַבַּיִת *'ēṣel habbáyiṯ* near the house

נֶגֶד הָעָם *néḡeḏ hā'ām* before the people

לִפְנֵי הַמֶּלֶךְ *lip̄nê hammélek* in the presence of the king

Many combinations of these types exist and will be noted in the vocabularies. Prepositions in the third group may on occasion be united with the following word with *maqqēp̄*. This optional proclitic pronunciation is dictated by rather complicated accentual rules which cannot be treated here. The reader should follow the example of the exercises, which will emphasize the more common usage.

16. Sentences with Adverbial Predicates.

A juxtaposed noun and prepositional phrase (or local adverb) constitute a predication in Hebrew.

הַנַּעַר בַּבַּיִת *hanná'ar babbáyit* The young man is in the house.

Such sentences contain no overt correspondent of the English verb "to be" and gain their tense from the context in which they occur. The isolated sentences of the exercises are best translated with the English present tense. The normal word order is subject (i.e. noun) — predicate (i.e. prepositional phrase or adverb), but an interrogative adverb, such as *'ayyēh* (where?), always stands first in the sentence:

אַיֵּה הַנַּעַר *'ayyēh hanná'ar* Where is the young man?

17. Vocabulary 1.

NOUNS:	נַעַר	*ná'ar*	young man, boy, lad; also used in the sense of "attendant, servant"
	זָקֵן	*zāqēn*	old man, elder (of a city)
	בַּיִת	*báyit*	house
	נָהָר	*nāhār*	river
	שָׂדֶה	*śāḏeh*	field
	דֶּרֶךְ	*dérek*	road, way (m. or f.)
PREPOSITIONS:	עַל־	*'al-*	on, upon, against, concerning, because of, over
	בְּ	*bə*	(see §15a) in, with (in the sense "by means of")
	אֵצֶל	*'éṣel*	near, beside, by
ADVERBS:	שָׁם	*šām*	there, in that place
	אַיֵּה	*'ayyēh*	where? in what place?
CONJUNCTION:	וְ	*wə*	and [prefixed directly to the following word: *wəhanná'ar*, and the young man]

Exercises:

(a) Divide each of the following words into syllables:

שְׁמָעֵנִי *šəmā'ēnî*   מִכּוֹכְבֵי *mikkôḵəḇê*

וַיְדַבְּרוּ *wayḏabbərû*   דְּבָרָיו *dəḇārâw*

בְּקַשְׁתִּיךָ	biqqaštîkā	שְׁלֹשִׁים	šəlōšîm
יִתְּנֵהוּ	yittənéhû	יִשְׁמְדוּ	yošmədû
בָּרְכֵנִי	bārăkḗnî	שְׂדוֹתֵיכֶם	śədôtêkem
הִגַּדְתַּנִי	higgadtánî	יַעַמְדוּ	ya'amdû
וַיָּמָת	wayyámot	זִקְנֵיהֶם	ziqnêhem

(b) Give the Hebrew for the following orally:

1. a house, the house, in the house, near the house
2. a field, in a field, in the field
3. a road, on a road, on the road
4. Where is the boy? — the old man? — the house?
5. The boy (old man, house) is there.
6. the old man and the boy; the house and the field.

(c) Translate:

1. 'ayyēh hanná'ar? hanná'ar babbáyit.
2. 'ayyēh hazzāqēn? hazzāqēn šām.
3. 'ayyēh habbáyit? habbáyit 'éṣel hannāhār.
4. haśśādeh ·éṣel hannāhār.
5. hanná'ar wəhazzāqēn baśśādeh.
6. 'ayyēh hazzāqēn? hazzāqēn 'al-haddérek.

1 אַיֵּה הַנַּעַר. הַנַּעַר בַּבַּיִת.
2 אַיֵּה הַזָּקֵן. הַזָּקֵן שָׁם.
3 אַיֵּה הַבַּיִת. הַבַּיִת אֵצֶל הַנָּהָר.
4 הַשָּׂדֶה אֵצֶל הַנָּהָר.
5 הַנַּעַר וְהַזָּקֵן בַּשָּׂדֶה.
6 אַיֵּה הַזָּקֵן. הַזָּקֵן עַל־הַדֶּרֶךְ.

(d) Write the following in Hebrew:

1. The house and the field are near the river.
2. The young man is on the road.
3. Where are the boy and the old man?
4. The boy is in the field.
5. The river is near the house.

[*Read §§4–6 of the section "Sounds and Spelling," pp. xviii-xxi*]

18. The Definite Article (cont.).

Before words beginning with a guttural consonant (א ʾ, ע ʿ, ה *h*, ח *ḥ*) or ר *r* the definite article has a form slightly different from that given in the preceding lesson.

a. Before א ʾ and ר *r* the article is הָ *hā-*

אִישׁ	ʾîš	a man	הָאִישׁ	*hāʾîš*	the man
רָעָב	rāʿāb	a famine	הָרָעָב	*hārāʿāb*	the famine

b. Before ע ʿ the article is normally הָ *hā-*, but if the ʿ is followed by an unaccented *ā*, the article is הֶ *he-*

עִיר	ʿîr	a city	הָעִיר	*hāʿîr*	the city
עָרִים	ʿārîm	cities	הֶעָרִים	*heʿārîm*	the cities
עָפָר	ʿāp̄ār	dust	הֶעָפָר	*heʿāp̄ār*	the dust

c. Before ה *h* and ח *ḥ* the article is normally הַ *ha-* (no doubling). But if ה *h* is followed by an unaccented *ā*, or if ח *ḥ* is followed by an accented or unaccented *ā*, the article is הֶ *he-*

הֵיכָל	*hêkāl*	a palace	הַהֵיכָל	*hahêkāl*	the palace
חֶרֶב	*ḥéreb*	a sword	הַחֶרֶב	*haḥéreb*	the sword
חָכָם	*ḥākām*	a wise man	הֶחָכָם	*heḥākām*	the wise man
הָרִים	*hārîm*	mountains	הֶהָרִים	*hehārîm*	the mountains

As noted in §15a the prepositions בְּ *bə*, לְ *lə*, and כְּ *kə* are joined immediately to the noun they govern, and before a noun with the definite article the consonant of the prepositon replaces the *h* of the article. The vowel of the article, chosen according to the rules just given, is in no way altered by this change:

| הָאִישׁ | *hāʾîš* | the man | לָאִישׁ | *lāʾîš* | to the man |
| הֶהָרִים | *hehārîm* | the mountains | בֶּהָרִים | *behārîm* | in the mountains |

19. Noun Plurals.

Consider the following sets of nouns:

a.	בְּכוֹר	*bəkôr*	plural:	בְּכוֹרִים	*bəkôrîm*	first-born	
	חֲלוֹם	*hălôm*		חֲלוֹמוֹת	*hălômôt*	dream	
b.	דָּבָר	*dābār*		דְּבָרִים	*dəbārîm*	word	
	זָקֵן	*zāqēn*		זְקֵנִים	*zəqēnîm*	old man	
	מָקוֹם	*māqôm*		מְקוֹמוֹת	*məqômôt*	place	

In the first set (a) the stems of the singular and plural are identical, but in the second set (b) the *ā* of the first syllable is reduced to *ə* in accordance with the principle given in §5. Note that in group (a) the vowel of the first syllable is already *ə* (or an equivalent) in the singular, so that there can be no further reduction in the plural.

A second, very frequent, type of two-syllable noun is represented by

מֶלֶךְ	*mélek*	plural:	מְלָכִים	*məlākîm*	king
זֶבַח	*zébah*		זְבָחִים	*zəbāhîm*	sacrifice
סֵפֶר	*sḗper*		סְפָרִים	*səpārîm*	book
נַעַר	*náʿar*		נְעָרִים	*nəʿārîm*	young man
עֶבֶד	*ʿébed*		עֲבָדִים	*ʿăbādîm*	servant

The singular form of these nouns is characterized by penultimate stress. All such nouns have the same pattern in the plural, as illustrated above. Note that the vowel of the singular is not significant for the vocalization of the plural form. Why is there an *ă* in the first syllable of עֲבָדִים *ʿăbādîm*?

20. Vocabulary 2.

NOUNS:
אִישׁ	*ʾîš*	(pl. irreg. אֲנָשִׁים *ʾănāšîm*)	man, husband
אִשָּׁה	*ʾiššāh*	(pl. irreg. נָשִׁים *nāšîm*)	woman, wife
בָּתִּים	*bāttîm*	the irreg. pl. of בַּיִת *báyit*, house
יֶלֶד	*yéled*	(pl. -*îm*)	boy, child
הֵיכָל	*hêkāl*	palace, temple
מֶלֶךְ	*mélek*	(pl. -*îm*)	king, ruler
סֵפֶר	*sḗper*	(pl. -*îm*)	book

	עֶבֶד	'ébeḏ	(pl. -îm) servant, slave
	עִיר	'îr	(pl. irreg. עָרִים 'ārîm) city (f.)
PRONOUNS:	הוּא	hû'	he, it (ref. to masc. noun)
	הִיא	hî'	she, it (ref. to fem. noun)
	מִי	mî	who? (no gender distinction)
ADVERBS:	פֹּה	pōh	here, in this place
	אֵיפֹה	'êp̄ōh	where? (a synonym of אַיֵּה 'ayyēh)

Exercises:

(a) Prefix the preposition לְ lə- (to) to the following nouns and pronounce the resulting combination (§4):

כֹּהֵן	kōhēn	(priest)	בָּבֶל	bāḇel	(Babylon)
כֶּרֶם	kérem	(vineyard)	בּוֹר	bôr	(pit)
כֶּלֶב	kéleḇ	(dog)	בָּקָר	bāqār	(cattle)
תּוֹרָה	tôrāh	(law)	גֵּר	gēr	(sojourner)
פָּרָשׁ	pārāš	(horseman)	פֶּסֶל	pésel	(idol)
דַּמֶּשֶׂק	damméseq	(Damascus)	דֶּרֶךְ	dérek	(way)
דּוֹר	dôr	(generation)	גּוֹרָל	gôrāl	(lot)
פֶּגֶר	péḡer	(corpse)	פִּיךָ	pîḵā	(your mouth)

(b) Add the plural ending as indicated to each of the following nouns in accordance with the rules given in §§5–6.

גְּבוּל	gəḇûl	(-îm)	boundary	עָנָן	'ānān	(-îm)	cloud
רְחוֹב	rəḥôḇ	(-ôṯ)	street	נָהָר	nāhār	(-ôṯ)	river
צָבָא	ṣāḇā'	(-ôṯ)	army	שָׁכֵן	šāḵēn	(-îm)	neighbor
קָהָל	qāhāl	(-îm)	assembly	חָצֵר	ḥāṣēr	(-ôṯ)	courtyard

(c) Give the proper form of the article for the following nouns:

הָדָר	hāḏār	splendor	אֲדָמָה	'ăḏāmāh	ground
עָפָר	'āp̄ār	dust	חָלָב	ḥālāḇ	milk
אָדָם	'āḏām	mankind	חָכְמָה	ḥokmāh	wisdom
רִיב	rîḇ	quarrel	הֵיכָל	hêḵāl	

(d) Form the plurals of the following nouns, using the ending indicated:

פֶּגֶר	péḡer	(-îm)	corpse	עֶבֶד	'ébeḏ	(-îm)	
שֶׁקֶל	šéqel	(-îm)	shekel	מֶלֶךְ	mélek	(-îm)	
קֶבֶר	qéḇer	(-îm)	grave	דָּבָר	dāḇār	(-îm)	
יֶלֶד	yéleḏ	(-îm)		זָקֵן	zāqēn	(-îm)	
עֶצֶם	'éṣem	(-ôṯ)	bone	דֶּרֶךְ	dérek	(-îm)	
אֶבֶן	'éḇen	(-îm)	stone	נֶפֶשׁ	népeš	(-ôṯ)	soul
נַעַר	ná'ar	(-îm)		חֶדֶר	ḥéḏer	(-îm)	room
נָהָר	nāhār	(-ôṯ)		חֶרֶב	ḥéreḇ	(-ôṯ)	sword

(e) Give the Hebrew for the following orally:

1. man, men, the men, in the men
2. woman, women, the women, in the women
3. king, kings, on the kings
4. elder, elders, on the elders
5. house, houses, near the houses
6. book, books, in the books
7. city, cities, in the cities

(f) Translate:

1. hā'ănāšîm bā'îr. הָאֲנָשִׁים בָּעִיר. 1
2. hannāšîm babbáyit. הַנָּשִׁים בַּבַּיִת. 2
3. hammélek wəhā'ăbādîm bahêkāl. הַמֶּלֶךְ וְהָעֲבָדִים בַּהֵיכָל. 3
4. hassəpārîm babbáyit. הַסְּפָרִים בַּבַּיִת. 4
5. 'ayyēh hannə'ārîm? hannə'ārîm baśśādeh. אַיֵּה הַנְּעָרִים. הַנְּעָרִים בַּשָּׂדֶה. 5
6. 'êpōh habbāttîm? habbāttîm bā'îr. אֵיפֹה הַבָּתִּים. הַבָּתִּים בָּעִיר. 6
7. 'êpōh hannəhārôt? hannəhārôt šām. אֵיפֹה הַנְּהָרוֹת. הַנְּהָרוֹת שָׁם. 7
8. he'ārîm šām wəhaddérek pōh. הֶעָרִים שָׁם וְהַדֶּרֶךְ פֹּה. 8

(g) Write in Hebrew:

1. The men and the women are in the city.
2. The king is in the palace.
3. The women are here.
4. Where are the young men and the servants?
5. The books are in the city.
6. The cities are near the rivers.

21. The Definite Article (concluded).

When a word begins with the syllables *yə-* or *mə-*, the definite article is usually
ה *ha-* without the doubling:

יְלָדִים	*yəlāḏîm*	הַיְלָדִים	*haylāḏîm*	the boys
יְאֹר	*yə'ōr*	הַיְאֹר	*hay'ōr*	the river, the Nile
מְרַגְּלִים	*məraggəlîm*	הַמְרַגְּלִים	*hamraggəlîm*	the spies

Note that in these words the prefixing of the article occasions the loss of a
syllable in pronunciation: *hay-lā-ḏîm*, not *ha-yə-lā-ḏîm*. Exceptions to the
preceding rule occur when the second syllable of the noun begins with ע '
or ה *h*:

יְהוּדִים	*yəhûḏîm*	הַיְּהוּדִים	*hayyəhûḏîm*	the Jews, Judaites

Several words have a slightly different form with the article. The following
are the most important:

אֶרֶץ	*'éreṣ*	הָאָרֶץ	*hā'áreṣ*	earth, land
הַר	*har*	הָהָר	*hāhār*	mountain
עַם	*'am*	הָעָם	*hā'ām*	people, nation
גַּן	*gan*	הַגָּן	*haggān*	garden
פַּר	*par*	הַפָּר	*happār*	steer, ox
חַג	*ḥaḡ*	הֶחָג	*heḥāḡ*	feast, festival
אֲרוֹן	*'ărôn*	הָאָרוֹן	*hā'ārôn*	box, chest, ark

Note that in הָהָר *hāhār* the form of the article does not follow the rule given in the preceding lesson.

22. Adjectives.

Adjectives agree in number and gender with the noun they modify. Unlike the noun, where gender need not be related to form, the distinction between masculine and feminine in the adjective is clearly and uniformly marked:

	SINGULAR		PLURAL	
masc.	טוֹב	*ṭôḇ* (good)	טוֹבִים	*ṭôḇîm*
fem.	טוֹבָה	*ṭôḇāh*	טוֹבוֹת	*ṭôḇôt*

Adjectives of two syllables with *ā* in the first syllable show a change in the stem before the endings of the fem. sing. and of the plural. The *ā* is replaced by *ə* (as described in §5 above):

גָּדוֹל *gāḏôl*	גְּדוֹלִים *gəḏôlîm*	חָכָם *ḥāḵām*	חֲכָמִים *ḥăḵāmîm*
גְּדוֹלָה *gəḏôlāh*	גְּדוֹלוֹת *gəḏôlôt*	חֲכָמָה *ḥăḵāmāh*	חֲכָמוֹת *ḥăḵāmôt*

The forms of קָטֹן *qāṭōn* (small) are unusual in that there is a different stem before the endings:

קָטֹן *qāṭōn*	קְטַנִּים *qəṭannîm*
קְטַנָּה *qəṭannāh*	קְטַנּוֹת *qəṭannôt*

Monosyllabic adjectives, a relatively small group, show the following typical forms. The principles underlying the change in the stem will be discussed in a later lesson:

רַב *rab*	רַבָּה *rabbāh*	רַבִּים *rabbîm*	רַבּוֹת *rabbôt*	much, many
מַר *mar*	מָרָה *mārāh*	מָרִים *mārîm*	מָרוֹת *mārôt*	bitter
רַע *ra'*	רָעָה *rā'āh*	רָעִים *rā'îm*	רָעוֹת *rā'ôt*	evil
עַז *'az*	עַזָּה *'azzāh*	עַזִּים *'azzîm*	עַזּוֹת *'azzôt*	strong
חַי *ḥay*	חַיָּה *ḥayyāh*	חַיִּים *ḥayyîm*	חַיּוֹת *ḥayyôt*	living
דַּל *dal*	דַּלָּה *dallāh*	דַּלִּים *dallîm*	דַּלּוֹת *dallôt*	poor

Adjectives ending in *-eh* have the following forms:

יָפֶה *yāp̄eh*	יָפָה *yāp̄āh*	יָפִים *yāp̄îm*	יָפוֹת *yāp̄ôt*	beautiful
קָשֶׁה *qāšeh*	קָשָׁה *qāšāh*	קָשִׁים *qāšîm*	קָשׁוֹת *qāšôt*	hard, difficult

Other types of adjectives will be commented upon as they occur.

23. The Use of Adjectives.

Adjectives occur in two functions, attributive and predicative. By attributive is meant an adjective which forms a phrase with the noun it modifies, and this phrase as a whole has a single function in the sentence. For example, in I read a good book, good modifies book and the phrase a good book is the object of the verb read. The attributive adjective in Hebrew follows its noun and agrees with it in number, gender, and definiteness.

אִישׁ טוֹב	'îš ṭôḇ	a good man
הָאִישׁ הַטּוֹב	hā'îš haṭṭôḇ	the good man
אֲנָשִׁים טוֹבִים	'ănāšîm ṭôḇîm	good men
הָאֲנָשִׁים הַטּוֹבִים	hā'ănāšîm haṭṭôḇîm	the good men
אִשָּׁה טוֹבָה	'iššāh ṭôḇāh	a good woman
הָאִשָּׁה הַטּוֹבָה	hā'iššāh haṭṭôḇāh	the good woman
נָשִׁים טוֹבוֹת	nāšîm ṭôḇōt	good women
הַנָּשִׁים הַטּוֹבוֹת	hannāšîm haṭṭôḇōt	the good women
עִיר גְּדוֹלָה	'îr gədôlāh	a great city (f.)
הָעִיר הַגְּדוֹלָה	hā'îr haggədôlāh	the great city
עָרִים גְּדוֹלוֹת	'ārîm gədôlōt	great cities
הֶעָרִים הַגְּדוֹלוֹת	he'ārîm haggədôlōt	the great cities

Note that the adjective agrees with the gender of the preceding noun and not with its ending.

A juxtaposed noun and articleless adjective usually constitute a predication, the adjective being taken as the predicate and the noun as the subject. In the predicate function the adjective may stand before or after its noun subject. There is agreement in number and gender, but the predicate adjective does not, by definition, have the definite article:

טוֹב הָאִישׁ	ṭôḇ hā'îš	The man is good.
הָאִישׁ טוֹב	hā'îš ṭôḇ	
טוֹבָה הָאִשָּׁה	ṭôḇāh hā'iššāh	The woman is good.
הָאִשָּׁה טוֹבָה	hā'iššāh ṭôḇāh	
טוֹבִים הָאֲנָשִׁים	ṭôḇîm hā'ănāšîm	The men are good.
טוֹבוֹת הַנָּשִׁים	ṭôḇōt hannāšîm	The women are good.

A series of adjectives may occur in either function:

הָעִיר הַגְּדוֹלָה וְהַטּוֹבָה hā'îr haggədôlāh wəhaṭṭôḇāh the great and good city
הָעִיר גְּדוֹלָה וְטוֹבָה hā'îr gədôlāh wəṭôḇāh The city is great and good.

An adjective may be modified by a prepositional phrase in the predicate usage:

טוֹבָה הָעִיר לָעָם ṭôḇāh hā'îr lā'ām The city is good for the people.

When a subject noun is indefinite, there is a chance of ambiguity:

חָכְמָה טוֹבָה good wisdom or Wisdom is good.

This is uncommon and can usually be resolved from the context.

[14]

Adjectives may be used as nouns (i.e. in noun functions) in two ways: (1) the adjective, usually with the definite article, may mean "the one who is...," as הֶחָכָם *heḥākām* the wise one, the wise man; (2) both the masc. and fem. singular forms of some adjectives may be used as abstract nouns, "that which is...," as הָרַע *hāra'* or הָרָעָה *hārā'āh*, evil, wickedness.

24. Vocabulary 3.

NOUNS: דָּבָר *dābār* (pl. -îm) word, matter, thing, affair

רָעָב *rā'āb* famine

אֶרֶץ *'éreṣ* (pl. -ôt) land, earth (f.)

הַר *har* mountain

עַם *'am* people, nation

גַּן *gan* garden

ADJECTIVES: טוֹב *ṭôb* good

גָּדוֹל *gādôl* great, big

קָטֹן *qāṭōn* small, little, unimportant

יָפֶה *yāpeh* beautiful, handsome

רַע *ra'* evil, bad, wicked

ADVERBS: מְאֹד *mə'ōd* much, very (follows the adjective it modifies, as in טוֹב מְאֹד *ṭôb mə'ōd*, very good)

Exercises:

(a) Give all four forms (masc., fem.; sing., pl.) of the following adjectives:

קָדוֹשׁ *qādôš*	holy	כָּבֵד *kābēd*	heavy
רָחוֹק *rāḥôq*	distant	צָמֵא *ṣāmē'*	thirsty
קָרוֹב *qārôb*	near	שָׁלֵם *šālēm*	whole, sound

(b) Give the Hebrew for the following orally:

1. the good man, the small man, the evil man
2. the large city, the small city, the evil city
3. the beautiful woman, the small woman, the good woman
4. a good boy, a big city, a small field, a large house
5. in the city, in the large city, near the large city
6. in the great palace, near the large river
7. cities, the cities, in the cities, in the great cities
8. men, the men, the evil men, in the evil men
9. women, the women, concerning the evil women
10. land, the land, the great land

(c) Translate:

1. hā'iššāh rā'āh mə'ōd.   הָאִשָּׁה רָעָה מְאֹד. 1
2. hû' yāpeh.   הוּא יָפֶה. 2

[15]

3. hā'îš wəhā'iššāh yāp̄îm mə'ōḏ.   3 הָאִישׁ וְהָאִשָּׁה יָפִים מְאֹד.

4. 'ayyēh hā'ănāšîm haṭṭôḇîm?   4 אַיֵּה הָאֲנָשִׁים הַטּוֹבִים.
   hā'ănāšîm haṭṭôḇîm bā'îr   הָאֲנָשִׁים הַטּוֹבִים בָּעִיר הַקְּטַנָּה.
     haqqəṭannāh.

5. 'êp̄ōh hanná'ar hāra'?   5 אֵיפֹה הַנַּעַר הָרָע.
   hû' babbáyiṯ haggāḏôl.   הוּא בַּבַּיִת הַגָּדוֹל.

6. 'ayyēh hammélek?   6 אַיֵּה הַמֶּלֶךְ.
   hû' bahêkāl haggāḏôl.   הוּא בַּהֵיכָל הַגָּדוֹל.

7. mî ṭôḇ? ṭôḇāh hā'iššāh hayyāp̄āh.   7 מִי טוֹב. טוֹבָה הָאִשָּׁה הַיָּפָה.

8. haddāḇār ṭôḇ mə'ōḏ.   8 הַדָּבָר טוֹב מְאֹד.

9. gāḏôl hārā'āḇ bā'îr.   9 גָּדוֹל הָרָעָב בָּעִיר.

10. hā'ăḇāḏîm rā'îm mə'ōḏ.   10 הָעֲבָדִים רָעִים מְאֹד.

11. hazzəqēnîm 'ēṣel habbáyiṯ.   11 הַזְּקֵנִים אֵצֶל הַבַּיִת.

12. he'ārîm haqqəṭannôṯ 'ēṣel hannāhār   12 הֶעָרִים הַקְּטַנּוֹת אֵצֶל הַנָּהָר הַגָּדוֹל.
     haggāḏôl.

(d) Write in Hebrew:

1. The women are very beautiful.
2. The city is very large.
3. The house is near a small field.
4. The men and the women are on the road.
5. The large houses are in the city.
6. The women are wicked.
7. The matter is unimportant (lit. small).
8. The small garden is near the road.

LESSON 4

[*Read § 7 in the section "Sounds and Spelling," pp. xxi-xxiii*]

25. Noun Plurals (cont.).

Nouns of two syllables whose first syllable is either closed or contains an unchangeable long vowel and whose second syllable has either $\bar{a}$ or $\bar{e}$ form their plurals in two ways: the first syllable remains unchanged, but in the second $\bar{e}$ is reduced to ∂, while $\bar{a}$ is generally retained. The following nouns illustrate most of the important types:

(a) with a closed first syllable:

מִשְׁפָּט	*mišpāṭ*	pl.	מִשְׁפָּטִים	*mišpāṭîm*	judgment
מַלְאָךְ	*malʾāk*		מַלְאָכִים	*malʾākîm*	messenger
מִזְבֵּחַ	*mizbēᵃh*		מִזְבְּחוֹת	*mizbəhôṯ*	altar

(b) with an unchangeable long vowel in the first syllable:

אֹיֵב	*ʾōyēb*		אֹיְבִים	*ʾōyəbîm*	enemy
כֹּהֵן	*kōhēn*		כֹּהֲנִים	*kōhănîm*	priest
כּוֹכָב	*kôkāb*		כּוֹכָבִים	*kôkābîm*	star
הֵיכָל	*hêkāl*		הֵיכָלִים	*hêkālîm*	temple

A special situation is encountered in a few words such as

| עִוֵּר | *ʿiwwēr* | | עִוְרִים | *ʿiwrîm* | blind (adj.) |
| כִּסֵּא | *kissēʾ* | | כִּסְאוֹת | *kisʾôṯ* | throne |

in which the doubled consonant of the singular is simplified in the plural with the resulting loss of a syllable: not *'iwwərîm*, *kissə'ôt*. Such irregularities will always be noted in the vocabularies.

26. The Active Participle.

All verb forms and most nouns in Hebrew can be analyzed into at least two parts: a root and a formative vowel pattern. In the group of words

בָּרוּךְ	*bārûk*	blessed (adj.)
מְבָרֵךְ	*məbārēk*	blessing (verb)
בֹּרַךְ	*bōrak*	he was blessed
בֵּרֵךְ	*bērēk*	he blessed
בְּרָכָה	*bərākāh*	blessing (noun)

the sequence of consonants *BRK* carries the basic notion of "bless." Such a sequence is called the root of the forms given above. Note that the root is a grammatical abstraction from the given words and not *vice versa*; that is, because a root has no existence apart from its incorporation into words, it leads to misunderstanding the nature of language to say that the words are derived from the root.

The pattern of vowels associated with a given word may or may not have a specific meaning of its own. For example, from the words *mélek* (king), *malkāh* (queen), *malkût* (kingdom), *mālak* (he ruled), *homlak* (he was made to rule), etc., we may certainly abstract a root *MLK* having to do with kings and ruling. Nevertheless, we cannot find any but the most meager support for taking the word *mélek* as the root *MLK* plus a meaningful formant pattern *e-e* (as one who does what the root specifies). The vowel pattern *e-e* is not a normal one for the formation of agent nouns. But consider the following set of words:

כֹּתֵב	*kōtēb*	writing	הֹלֵךְ	*hōlēk*	walking, going
יֹשֵׁב	*yōšēb*	sitting	יֹרֵד	*yōrēd*	descending

The vowel pattern *ō-ē* is a regular one for the formation of the active participle with roots of the triconsonantal type illustrated. Thus, while it is always analytically legitimate to isolate roots and formative patterns, one must exercise caution about assigning specific meaning to the latter.

We shall begin our study of the Hebrew verb with the participial form mentioned above. The participle is in nearly all respects an adjective so far as its syntax and inflection are concerned:

masc.	יֹשֵׁב	*yōšēb*	יֹשְׁבִים	*yōšəbîm*	sitting
fem.	יֹשֶׁבֶת	*yōšébet*	יֹשְׁבוֹת	*yōšəbôt*	

The first vowel is unchangeably long; the vowel of the second syllable is *ē*

and therefore changeable. Note the feminine singular form with *-et* and a corresponding change in the vowel of the final stem syllable; the form יֹשְׁבָה *yōšəḇāh* is also found, but less frequently.
The participle may be used attributively,

הָאִישׁ הַכֹּתֵב   *hā'îš hakkōṯēḇ*   the writing man or
                                     the man who is writing

or predicatively,

הָאִישׁ כֹּתֵב   *hā'îš kōṯēḇ*   The man is writing.

These differ in no way from the adjectival syntax of the preceding lesson.

The participle, both as an attribute and as a predicate, usually indicates a continuing action, one in progress, and is best translated with the English progressive tenses. Tense, as in the adjectival sentences of the preceding lesson, must be gained from the context. The participial sentences in the exercises should be translated in the present tense or in the immediate future (he is going to..., he is about to...):

הָאִישׁ נֹתֵן לֶחֶם לַדַּלָּה   *hā'îš nōṯēn léḥem laddallāh*
The man is giving (is going to give) bread to the poor woman.

27. The Object Marker אֶת- *'eṯ-*.

When the direct object of a verb is a definite noun (i.e. has the definite article) or is a proper name, it is usually preceded by the object marker אֶת- *'eṯ-* (or, without *maqqēp̄*, אֵת *'ēṯ*):

הָאִישׁ שֹׁמֵר אֶת־הַתּוֹרָה   *hā'îš šōmēr 'eṯ-hattôrāh*
             The man is observing the Law.
הָעָם אֹהֵב אֶת־דָּוִד   *hā'ām 'ōhēḇ 'eṯ-Dāwīḏ*
             The people love David.

But if the object is indefinite, it is not marked:

הָאִישׁ כֹּתֵב דָּבָר   *hā'îš kōṯēḇ dāḇār*
             The man is writing a word.

אֶת may be repeated before each member of a compound object:
הָאֲנָשִׁים שֹׁמְרִים אֶת־הַתּוֹרָה וְאֶת־הַמִּצְוֺת   *hā'ănāšîm šōmərîm 'eṯ-hattôrāh*
                                 wə'eṯ-hammiṣwōṯ
             The men are observing the Law and the
                 commandments.

28. Vocabulary 4.

NOUNS: שֹׁפֵט *šōp̄ēṭ* (pl. *-îm*) judge
        מַלְאָךְ *mal'āḵ* (pl. *-îm*)   messenger, angel
        כִּסֵּא *kissē'* (pl. irreg. כִּסְאוֹת *kis'ôṯ*)   throne
VERBS: כֹּתֵב *kōṯēḇ* writing

אֹכֵל   *'ōḵēl*   eating

נֹתֵן   *nōṯēn*   giving, setting, placing

הֹלֵךְ   *hōlēḵ*   going, walking

יֹשֵׁב   *yōšēḇ*   sitting, dwelling, inhabiting

PREPOSITIONS: אֵת   *'ēṯ* or אֶת־ *'eṯ-*   direct object marker (see §27)

לְ   *lə-*   to, for (in dative sense); as

אֶל־   *'el-*   to, toward (motion or traversing of space usually implied, but often synonymous with לְ *lə-*)

בְּעֵינֵי   *bə'ênê*   in the eyes of, in the opinion of, as far as — is concerned

Exercises:

(a) Form the plurals of the following nouns:

סֹפֵר	*sōp̄ēr* (-îm) scribe	גַּנָּב	*gannāḇ* (-îm) thief
מוֹעֵד	*mô'ēḏ* (-îm) appointed time	שֻׁלְחָן	*šulḥān* (-ôṯ) table
מִשְׁכָּן	*miškān* (-îm) tabernacle	מִקְדָּשׁ	*miqdāš* (-îm) sanctuary

(b) Give the Hebrew for the following orally:

1. the judge is sitting
2. the king is writing
3. the boy is going
4. the woman is giving
5. the messenger is going
6. the man is giving
7. the slave is eating
8. the woman is going

(c) Pluralize each of the items in the preceding exercise. E.g. the judges are sitting, etc.

(d) Transform the items of exercise (b) into noun + modifier, as "the judge who is sitting," etc.

(e) Translate:

1. haššōp̄ēṭ nōṯēn 'eṯ-hassép̄er lā'îš.   הַשֹּׁפֵט נָתַן אֶת־הַסֵּפֶר לָאִישׁ.
2. hā'iššāh yōšéḇeṯ wə'ōḵélet babbáyiṯ.   הָאִשָּׁה יֹשֶׁבֶת וְאֹכֶלֶת בַּבַּיִת.
3. hā'ănāšîm hōləḵîm 'el-hahêḵāl haggāḏôl.   הָאֲנָשִׁים הֹלְכִים אֶל־הַהֵיכָל הַגָּדוֹל.
4. hammélek yōšēḇ wəḵōṯēḇ bassép̄er.   הַמֶּלֶךְ יֹשֵׁב וְכֹתֵב בַּסֵּפֶר.
5. hammal'āḵîm hōləḵîm 'el-hahêḵāl.   הַמַּלְאָכִים הֹלְכִים אֶל־הַהֵיכָל.
6. ra' haddāḇār bə'ênê hā'ām.   רַע הַדָּבָר בְּעֵינֵי הָעָם.
7. hannə'ārîm hōləḵîm 'el-hannāhār.   הַנְּעָרִים הֹלְכִים אֶל־הַנָּהָר.
8. hammélek yōšēḇ 'al-hakkissē' bahêḵāl.   הַמֶּלֶךְ יֹשֵׁב עַל־הַכִּסֵּא בַּהֵיכָל.
9. hā'ām yōšēḇ bā'áreṣ haggəḏôlāh.   הָעָם יֹשֵׁב בָּאָרֶץ הַגְּדוֹלָה.
10. hā'îš wəhā'iššāh yōšəḇîm bā'îr hārā'āh.   הָאִישׁ וְהָאִשָּׁה יֹשְׁבִים בָּעִיר הָרָעָה.
11. haššōp̄əṭîm hōləḵîm 'el-hannāhār.   הַשֹּׁפְטִים הֹלְכִים אֶל־הַנָּהָר.

12. haylāḏîm yōšəḇîm ʼéṣel hannāhār   12 הַיְלָדִים יֹשְׁבִים אֵצֶל הַנָּהָר הַקָּטֹן.
     haqqāṭōn.

13. hûʼ kōṯēḇ ʼet-haddəḇārîm   13 הוּא כֹּתֵב אֶת־הַדְּבָרִים עַל־הַסֵּפֶר.
     ʻal-hassép̄er.

14. ʼêp̄ōh yōšəḇôṯ hannāšîm?   14 אֵיפֹה יֹשְׁבוֹת הַנָּשִׁים.

15. ṭôḇîm hāʻăḇāḏîm bəʻênê hammélek.   15 טוֹבִים הָעֲבָדִים בְּעֵינֵי הַמֶּלֶךְ.

(f) Write in Hebrew:

1. The boys are going to the city.
2. The slaves are sitting near the small houses.
3. The boy is giving the book to the man.
4. The man and the woman are living in the garden.
5. The men are giving the small field and the garden to the king.
6. The people are dwelling in a good land.

LESSON 5

[Read §§ 8-9 in the section "Sounds and Spelling," pp. xxiii-xxv]

29. The Prepositions בְּ bə-, לְ lə-, and כְּ kə-.

The form of these three prepositions is determined by the first consonant or syllable of the word to which they are prefixed:

a. If the noun begins with the syllable יְ yə, the anticipated forms *bəyə, *ləyə, and *kəyə are replaced by bî, lî, and kî:

יְרוּשָׁלַ֫ם	yərûšāláim	Jerusalem
בִּירוּשָׁלַ֫ם	bîrûšāláim	in Jerusalem
לִירוּשָׁלַ֫ם	lîrûšāláim	to Jerusalem
כִּירוּשָׁלַ֫ם	kîrûšāláim	like Jerusalem

b. If the noun begins with any other consonant followed by ə, the prepositions have the vowel i:

שְׁמוּאֵל	šəmû'ēl	Samuel
בִּשְׁמוּאֵל	bišmû'ēl	in Samuel
לִשְׁמוּאֵל	lišmû'ēl	to Samuel
כִּשְׁמוּאֵל	kišmû'ēl	like Samuel

Note that the ə of the noun is dropped in pronunciation: biš-mû-'ēl, not bi-šə-mû-'ēl.

c. If the noun begins with a guttural followed by a reduced vowel (ă, ĕ, or ŏ), the prepositions have the corresponding full short vowel:

[22]

חֲלוֹם	ḥălôm	a dream	אֱמֶת	'ĕmét	truth
בַּחֲלוֹם	baḥălôm	in a dream	בֶּאֱמֶת	be'ĕmét	in truth
לַחֲלוֹם	laḥălôm	to a dream	לֶאֱמֶת	le'ĕmét	to truth
כַּחֲלוֹם	kaḥălôm	like a dream	כֶּאֱמֶת	ke'ĕmét	like truth
אֳנִיָּה	'ŏnîyāh	a ship			
בָּאֳנִיָּה	bo'ŏnîyāh	in a ship, etc.			

d. Before words stressed on the first syllable (thus mainly monosyllabic words) the prepositions are optionally vocalized with *ā*. Instances of this rather restricted form will be noted as they occur.

e. As we have stated previously, these three prepositions combine with the definite article, which loses its initial ה *h*. The vowel of the article remains unchanged.

f. Aside from the special circumstances given in the preceding paragraphs, the prepositions occur simply as בְּ * bə-*, לְ *lə-*, and כְּ *kə-*:

בְּעִיר	*bə'îr*	in a city
כְּמֶלֶךְ	*kəmélek*	like a king
לְאִישׁ	*lə'îš*	to a man.

30. The Preposition מִן *min.*

a. Before the definite article this preposition may have either the form מֵ *mē-*, which is joined directly to the following word, or מִן *min-*, which is usually joined to the following word with *maqqēp̄*:

from the king	*min-hammélek*		מִן־הַמֶּלֶךְ
or	*mēhammélek*.		מֵהַמֶּלֶךְ

b. Before nouns beginning with a guttural or *r*, the preposition takes the form מֵ *mē-*, joined directly:

עִיר	*'îr*	a city	מֵעִיר	*mē'îr*	from a city
רֹאשׁ	*rō(')š*	a head	מֵרֹאשׁ	*mērō(')š*	from a head

c. Before all other nouns the form is מִ *mi* + the doubling of the first consonant:

מֶלֶךְ	*mélek*	a king	מִמֶּלֶךְ	*mimmélek* from a king.

The sequence *miyyə-* is commonly contracted to *mî-*, as in

מִיהוּדָה *mîhûdāh* (for *miyyəhûdāh*) from Judah.

31. The Comparative.

The adjective is not altered in form to express the comparative. Instead, the preposition מִן *min* is used before the noun which is the basis of comparison.

הָאִישׁ חָכָם מֵהַנַּעַר *hā'îš ḥāḵām mēhanná'ar*
The man is wiser than the boy.

Other sentence orders are possible and not unusual:

יָפָה הָאִשָּׁה מֵהַנַּעֲרָה *yāpāh hā'iššāh mēhanna'ărāh*
The woman is more beautiful than the girl.

The same construction may be translated "too...for:"

קָשָׁה הָעֲבוֹדָה מֵהָאִישׁ *qāšāh hā'ăḇôḏāh mēhā'îš*
The work is *too* hard *for* the man.

The choice between the comparative and "too" translations depends on which makes the better sense.

32. The Relative Word אֲשֶׁר *'ăšer*.

Unlike English, the prepositional phrase in Hebrew does not commonly stand next to a noun as a modifier. Thus, while we may speak of *the book on the table* or *the fountain in the park*, where *on the table* and *in the park* modify *book* and *fountain* respectively, in Hebrew such modification is more frequently introduced by the word אֲשֶׁר *'ăšer*, which is usually the equivalent of the English relative pronouns *who, which,* and *that.*

הָאִישׁ אֲשֶׁר בָּעִיר *hā'îš 'ăšer bā'îr*   the man in the city, or
the man who is in the city

הָעָם אֲשֶׁר בָּאָרֶץ *hā'ām 'ăšer bā'áreṣ* the people in the land, or
the people which is in the land.

The word אֲשֶׁר *'ăšer* is not affected by the gender or number of the antecedent:

הָאִשָּׁה אֲשֶׁר בַּהֵיכָל *hā'iššāh 'ăšer bahêḵāl* the woman in the temple.

אֲשֶׁר *'ăšer* is not commonly employed before adjectives or participles. Thus, English *the man who is wise* is simply הָאִישׁ הֶחָכָם *hā'îš heḥāḵām*, or הֶחָכָם *heḥāḵām* alone. *The man who is sitting* is הָאִישׁ הַיּשֵׁב *hā'îš hayyōšēḇ*. The participle may be used alone, even without the definite article, as an equivalent of English *one who, anyone who, whoever, he who*:

הֹלֵךְ בֶּאֱמֶת *hōlēḵ be'ĕmét*   he who (or whoever) walks in truth.

33. Vocabulary 5.

NOUNS:
זָהָב	*zāhāḇ*	gold
חָכְמָה	*ḥokmāh*	wisdom
כֶּסֶף	*késep*	silver, money
עֲבוֹדָה	*'ăḇôḏāh*	work, task, servitude (cf. *'éḇeḏ*)
עֵצָה	*'ēṣāh*	counsel, advice

ADJECTIVES: יָקָר *yāqār* precious

יָשָׁר *yāšār* just, upright

צַדִּיק *ṣaddîq* righteous

קָשֶׁה *qāšeh* difficult, hard, harsh

רָשָׁע *rāšā'* evil, bad, criminal

PROPER NAMES: דָּוִד *Dāwīd* David

שְׁמוּאֵל *šəmû'ēl* Samuel

יְרוּשָׁלַ͏ִם *Yərûšāláim* Jerusalem [Note that in the Hebrew spelling the second י is missing. This spelling may point to an early dialectal variant pronunciation *Yərûšālêm*]

OTHER: מִן *min-* (prep.) from; also used partitively:

מֵהָאֲנָשִׁים *mēhā'ănāšîm*, some of the men.

אֲשֶׁר *'ăšer* (rel. pronoun) who, which, that

Exercises:

(a) Prefix the preposition בְּ *bə-* to the following words, first without the article, then with it. Example: *késep, bəkésep, bakkésep.*

מְלָכִים	*məlākîm*	יְלָדִים	*yəlādîm*	חֲדָרִים	*ḥădārîm* (rooms)
עֲבָדִים	*'ăbādîm*	דְּרָכִים	*dərākîm*	אֲדָמָה	*'ădāmāh* (ground)
עָרִים	*'ārîm*	נְעָרִים	*nə'ārîm*	אֳנִיָּה	*'ŏnîyāh* (ship)

(b) Give the Hebrew for the following orally. Use the adjective in the masculine singular form.

1. better than the boy
2. larger than the house
3. larger than the river
4. smaller than a field
5. worse than the men
6. more precious than gold
7. more just than the king

(c) Give the Hebrew for the following orally. Then transform them into phrases using *'ăšer*. Example:

The city is in the land → the city which is in the land

hā'îr bā'áreṣ → *hā'îr 'ăšer bā'áreṣ*

1. The boy is in the large field.
2. The words are in the book.
3. The woman is on the road.
4. The gold is in the temple.
5. The silver is in the house.

(d) Translate:

1. *yəqārāh ḥokmāh mizzāhāb.*   יְקָרָה חָכְמָה מִזָּהָב. 1

2. *qāšāh hā'ăbôdāh mēhā'ănāšîm.*   קָשָׁה הָעֲבוֹדָה מֵהָאֲנָשִׁים. 2

3. yəšārîm hā'ăḇāḏîm mēhamməlāḵîm. יְשָׁרִים הָעֲבָדִים מֵהַמְּלָכִים. 3

4. Dāwiḏ yāšār mə'ōḏ. דָּוִד יָשָׁר מְאֹד. 4

5. hû' nōṯēn ḥokmāh lammélek hayyōšēḇ 'al-hakkissē'. הוּא נֹתֵן חָכְמָה לַמֶּלֶךְ הַיֹּשֵׁב עַל־הַכִּסֵּא. 5

6. rā'îm haddəḇārîm 'ăšer bassḗp̄er. רָעִים הַדְּבָרִים אֲשֶׁר בַּסֵּפֶר. 6

7. ṭôḇāh ḥokmāh mikkésep̄. טוֹבָה חָכְמָה מִכֶּסֶף. 7

8. yəšārîm hā'ănāšîm. יְשָׁרִים הָאֲנָשִׁים. 8

9. Dāwiḏ wəhā'ănāšîm yōšəḇîm bîrûšāláim. דָּוִד וְהָאֲנָשִׁים יֹשְׁבִים בִּירוּשָׁלַ͏ם. 9

10. mî ṣaddîq miššəmû'ēl? מִי צַדִּיק מִשְּׁמוּאֵל. 10

11. hā'ēṣāh rā'āh mə'ōḏ. הָעֵצָה רָעָה מְאֹד. 11

12. 'ayyēh hayšārîm wəhaṣṣaddîqîm? אַיֵּה הַיְשָׁרִים וְהַצַּדִּיקִים. 12

(e) Write in Hebrew:

1. The king is giving the gold and the silver to the men who are in the palace.
2. Wisdom is more precious than silver.
3. The messengers in Jerusalem are very bad.
4. Samuel and David are just and righteous.
5. The task is too difficult for the boy.
6. The field is larger than the garden near the house.
7. The judges are more evil than the kings.

[*Read* § *10 in the section "Sounds and Spelling," pp. xxv-xxvii*]

34. Noun Plurals (cont.).

There are, in general, two types of monosyllabic nouns in terms of changes in the plural stem: (a) those with no change, and (b) those having a doubling of the final consonant:

(a)	שִׁיר	*šîr*	שִׁירִים	*šîrîm*	song
	סוּס	*sûs*	סוּסִים	*sûsîm*	horse
	אוֹת	*'ôṯ*	אוֹתוֹת	*'ôṯôṯ*	sign
	דָּם	*dām*	דָּמִים	*dāmîm*	blood
	עֵץ	*'ēṣ*	עֵצִים	*'ēṣîm*	tree
(b)	עַם	*'am*	עַמִּים	*'ammîm*	people
	חֵץ	*ḥēṣ*	חִצִּים	*ḥiṣṣîm*	arrow
	חֹק	*ḥōq*	חֻקִּים	*ḥuqqîm*	statute

Note the following particulars:

(1) Nouns with the stem vowels *û, î, ô,* and usually *ā* do not alter the stem before the plural ending.

(2) Nouns with stem vowel *ē* behave in one of two ways:

      (a) the stem is unchanged, as in *'ēṣ – 'ēṣîm*

      (b) the final stem consonant is doubled and *ē* is replaced by *i,* as in *ḥēṣ – ḥiṣṣîm.*

(3) Nouns with *a* are similar to the above:

      (a) When the final stem consonant is a guttural or *r*, the stem
      vowel is "lengthened" to *ā*, as in *har – hārîm*.

      (b) Otherwise the final stem consonant is doubled and the stem
      vowel remains the same, as in *'am – 'ammîm*.

(4) Nouns with the stem vowel *ō* usually follow the pattern of *ḥōq –
ḥuqqîm*. Often, however, *ō* is a defective writing for *ô*, so that care must be
taken not to confuse the type *ḥōq* with that of *'ôṭ* in group (a).

Because of irregularities and minor unpredictable deviations, the plurals
will be given with the singulars in the vocabularies. The following nouns are
irregular in that the plural stems do not conform to the types just enumerated:

רֹאשׁ	*rō(')š*	head	plural:	רָאשִׁים	*rā(')šîm*
יוֹם	*yôm*	day		יָמִים	*yāmîm*
בֵּן	*bēn*	son		בָּנִים	*bānîm*
עִיר	*'îr*	city		עָרִים	*'ārîm*
אִישׁ	*'îš*	man		אֲנָשִׁים	*'ănāšîm*

35. Participles (cont.).

When the second or third consonant of a verbal root is a guttural (א ', ע ',
ה *h*, ח *ḥ*) the forms of the participle are slightly modified. When the second
consonant is a guttural, we find *ă* for *ə* in the plural stem:

צֹעֵק	*ṣō'ēq*	צֹעֲקִים	*ṣō'ăqîm*	crying out
צֹעֶקֶת	*ṣō'éqeṭ*	צֹעֲקוֹת	*ṣō'ăqôṭ*	

When the third consonant is an ע ' or ח *ḥ*, the feminine singular has *a* instead
of *e* in the last two syllables:

בֹּרֵחַ	*bōrē^aḥ*	בֹּרְחִים	*bōrəḥîm*	fleeing
בֹּרַחַת	*bōráḥaṭ*	בֹּרְחוֹת	*bōrəḥôṭ*	

When the third consonant is א ', which is not pronounced when it would
close a syllable, the fem. sing. has *ē*:

קֹרֵא	*qōrē'*	קֹרְאִים	*qōrə'îm*	calling
קֹרֵאת	*qōrē(')ṭ*	קֹרְאוֹת	*qōrə'ôṭ*	

36. Vocabulary 6.

NOUNS: קוֹל *qôl* (pl. -ôṭ) voice, sound; *bəqôl gāḏôl*: aloud, in a loud voice

           עֵץ *'ēṣ* (pl. *'ēṣîm*) tree, wood

           כֶּרֶם *kérem* (pl. -îm) vineyard

VERBS: צֹעֵק *ṣō'ēq* crying out (in distress)

           שֹׁלֵחַ *šōlē^aḥ* sending

           נֹטֵעַ *nōṭē^a'* planting

           יֹצֵא *yōṣē'* going forth, leaving

OTHER: תַּחַת *táḥat* (prep.) under; instead of

כִּי *kî* (conj.) because, since, for; that

רַב *raḇ* (adj.) much, many, numerous (forms in §22)

Exercises:

(a) Give the Hebrew for the following orally:

1. The old man is going forth.
2. The woman is planting.
3. The judge is sending.
4. The people is crying out.
5. The servant is going forth.

(b) Pluralize each of the sentences in (a).

(c) Translate:

1. hā'ănāšîm nōṭə'îm 'ēṣîm rabbîm 'al-hāhār.   הָאֲנָשִׁים נֹטְעִים עֵצִים רַבִּים עַל־הָהָר. 1

2. hanná'ar yōšēḇ táḥat hā'ēṣ 'ăšer baggān.   הַנַּעַר יֹשֵׁב תַּחַת הָעֵץ אֲשֶׁר בַּגָּן. 2

3. gədôlîm hā'ēṣîm 'ăšer behārîm mēhā'ēṣîm 'ăšer 'éṣel hannāhār.   גְּדוֹלִים הָעֵצִים אֲשֶׁר בֶּהָרִים מֵהָעֵצִים אֲשֶׁר אֵצֶל הַנָּהָר. 3

4. 'ammîm rabbîm yōšəḇîm bā'áreṣ kî hā'áreṣ ṭôḇāh mə'ōd.   עַמִּים רַבִּים יֹשְׁבִים בָּאָרֶץ כִּי הָאָרֶץ טוֹבָה מְאֹד. 4

5. hā'ām ṣō'ăqîm bəqôl gādôl kî qāšāh mə'ōd hā'ăḇôdāh.   הָעָם צֹעֲקִים בְּקוֹל גָּדוֹל כִּי קָשָׁה מְאֹד הָעֲבוֹדָה. 5

6. mî yōṣē' min-hā'îr hārā'āh?   מִי יֹצֵא מִן־הָעִיר הָרָעָה? 6

7. rā'îm haddəḇārîm bə'ênê hammélek hayyāšār.   רָעִים הַדְּבָרִים בְּעֵינֵי הַמֶּלֶךְ הַיָּשָׁר. 7

8. hā'iššāh yōṣē(')t mēhabbáyit.   הָאִשָּׁה יֹצֵאת מֵהַבַּיִת. 8

9. hā'ăḇādîm nōṭə'îm kérem qāṭōn 'éṣel haśśādeh.   הָעֲבָדִים נֹטְעִים כֶּרֶם קָטֹן אֵצֶל הַשָּׂדֶה. 9

(d) Write in Hebrew:

1. The king is sending the messengers to the judge who is in the city.
2. The people are going out of Jerusalem because the famine is very great.
3. Who is crying out in the house?
4. The vineyard and the garden are near the house.
5. He is sitting under a large tree.
6. The men are good, but the servants are bad.
7. The servants are better than the messengers.

LESSON 7

[Read § 11 of the section "Sounds and Spelling," pp. xxvii-xxviii]

37. Predication of Existence.

In order to state that something exists, Hebrew employs the word יֵשׁ *yēš*, commonly translated "there is (are)."

יֵשׁ אִישׁ	*yēš 'îš*	There is a man.
יֵשׁ אִשָּׁה	*yēš 'iššāh*	There is a woman.
יֵשׁ אֲנָשִׁים	*yēš 'ănāšîm*	There are men.

There is no change in the word for number or gender of the object predicated. The negative expression, for non-existence, is אֵין *'ên*:

אֵין אִישׁ	*'ên 'îš*	There is no man.
אֵין אִשָּׁה	*'ên 'iššāh*	There is no woman.

This sentence type figures largely in expressing possession:

אֵין לָאִישׁ כֶּסֶף	*'ên lā'îš késep̄*	The man has no silver.
יֵשׁ אִישׁ לָאִשָּׁה	*yēš 'îš lā'iššāh*	The woman has a husband.

In the preceding lessons we dealt with sentences having an adverbial predicate. All of the examples used, both in the lesson and in the exercises, had definite nouns as subjects. When one constructs a similar sentence with an indefinite subject, such as "A man is in the house," we find that this is virtually equivalent to the existential sentence "There is a man in the house."

Thus, the sentences expressing existence and those having adverbial predicates are sometimes identical:

subj. definite	הָאִישׁ בַּבַּיִת	*hā'îš babbáyiṯ*	The man is...
subj. indef.	יֵשׁ אִישׁ בַּבַּיִת	*yēš 'îš babbáyiṯ*	A man is ...
			There is a man...
	אֵין אִישׁ בַּבַּיִת	*'ēn 'îš babbáyiṯ*	No man is...
			There is no man...

38. The Prepositions בְּ *bə-*, לְ *lə-*, and אֶת־ *'eṯ-* with Pronominal Suffixes.

When a personal pronoun is the object of a preposition, it is appended as a suffix directly to the preposition:

לִי	*lî*	to me	לָנוּ	*lánû*	to us
לְךָ	*ləkā*	to you (m. s.)	לָכֶם	*lākém*	to you (m. pl.)
לָךְ	*lāk*	to you (f. s.)	[לָכֶן	*lākén*	to you (f. pl.)]
לוֹ	*lô*	to him	לָהֶם	*lāhém*	to them (m. pl.)
לָהּ	*lāh*	to her	לָהֶן	*lāhén*	to them (f. pl.)

Here, as elsewhere in the language, a distinction between genders is made in the second person as well as in the third. There are thus four Hebrew pronouns corresponding to English "you."

The preposition בְּ *bə* with suffixes is exactly like the above. An alternate form בָּם *bām* for בָּהֶם *bāhém* is also used.

The pronouns as objects of the verb may occur as suffixes on the object marker, as follows:

אֹתִי	*'ōṯî*	me	אֹתָנוּ	*'ōṯắnû*	us
אֹתְךָ	*'ōṯəkā*	you (m. s.)	אֶתְכֶם	*'eṯkem*	you (m. pl.)
אֹתָךְ	*'ōṯāk*	you (f. s.)	[אֶתְכֶן	*'eṯken*	you (f. pl.)]
אֹתוֹ	*'ōṯô*	him	אֹתָם	*'ōṯām*	them (m. pl.)
אֹתָהּ	*'ōṯāh*	her	אֹתָן	*'ōṯān*	them (f. pl.)

The 3rd pers. pl. forms also occur as אֶתְהֶם *'eṯhem* and אֶתְהֶן *'eṯhen.*

Some examples of usage:

הָאִישׁ נֹתֵן לָנוּ לֶחֶם	*hā'îš nōṯēn lánû léḥem*
	The man is giving (to) us bread.
אֵין לִי כֶּסֶף	*'ēn lî késep*
	I have no silver.
יֵשׁ לָהֶם מֶלֶךְ	*yēš lāhem mélek*
	They have a king.
הַמֶּלֶךְ שֹׁלֵחַ אֹתָם אֶל־הָעִיר	*hammélek šōlēªḥ 'ōṯām 'el-hā'îr*
	The king is sending them to the city.

39. Vocabulary 7.

NOUNS: צֹאן *ṣō(')n* (no pl.) a collective term for small cattle (sheep and goats)

בָּקָר *bāqār* (no pl.) a collective term for large cattle (bulls, steers, cows, etc.)

גָּמָל *gāmāl* (pl. irreg. גְּמַלִּים *gəmallîm*) camel

לֶחֶם *léḥem* (no pl.) bread, food

VERBS: יֹרֵד *yōrēḏ* descending, going down

ADJECTIVES: עָשִׁיר *'āšîr* rich

דַּל *dal* poor

PARTICLES: יֵשׁ *yēš* there is, there are

אֵין *'ên* there is not, there are not

Exercises:

(a) Give the Hebrew for the following orally:

1. I have a _____. (house, garden, field, vineyard)
2. She has no _____. (husband, slaves, money, books)
3. We have no _____. (king, judge, city, camels)
4. The man has no wife.
5. They (m. pl.) have _____. (small-cattle, camels, gold, silver)
6. There are no trees on the mountain.
7. There are many houses in the city.
8. There are many messengers here.
9. He is sending us.
10. He is writing to us.
11. He is giving us bread.
12. He is dwelling in it.
13. She is sending them.
14. She is planting it for them.

(b) Translate:

1. *'ên 'îš yōšēḇ 'al-hakkissē'.*   אֵין אִישׁ יֹשֵׁב עַל־הַכִּסֵּא.

2. *yēš sḗp̄er šām.*   יֵשׁ סֵפֶר שָׁם.

3. *'ên šōp̄ēṭ yāšār bā'îr.*   אֵין שֹׁפֵט יָשָׁר בָּעִיר.

4. *hammal'āḵîm yōrəḏîm mēhāhār kî 'ên lāhem léḥem šām.*   הַמַּלְאָכִים יֹרְדִים מֵהָהָר כִּי אֵין לָהֶם לֶחֶם שָׁם.

5. *hā'ăšîrîm nōṭənîm léḥem laddallîm hayyōšəḇîm šām.*   הָעֲשִׁירִים נֹתְנִים לֶחֶם לַדַּלִּים הַיֹּשְׁבִים שָׁם.

6. *hā'ănāšîm yōṣə'îm min-hā'îr wəhōləḵîm 'el-hāhār.*   הָאֲנָשִׁים יֹצְאִים מִן־הָעִיר וְהֹלְכִים אֶל־הָהָר.

7. *hannāšîm yōṣə'ôṭ mēhā'îr wəyōrəḏôṭ 'el-hannāhār.*   הַנָּשִׁים יֹצְאוֹת מֵהָעִיר וְיֹרְדוֹת אֶל־הַנָּהָר.

8. yēš lā́nû báyit gāḏôl wəḡan qāṭōn.   יֵשׁ לָנוּ בַּיִת גָּדוֹל וְגַן קָטֹן. 8

9. mî hā'ănāšîm haholəkîm 'el-hā'îr?   מִי הָאֲנָשִׁים הַהֹלְכִים אֶל־הָעִיר? 9

10. haylāḏîm yōšəḇîm wə'ōḵəlîm bakkérem.   הַיְלָדִים יֹשְׁבִים וְאֹכְלִים בַּכֶּרֶם. 10

11. hû' 'āšîr mə'ōḏ; yēš lô ḵéseṗ wəzāhāḇ.   הוּא עָשִׁיר מְאֹד. יֵשׁ לוֹ כֶּסֶף וְזָהָב. 11

(c) Write in Hebrew:

1. The king has no city and he has no land.
2. Where are the young men sitting and eating?
3. The rich have bread but the poor have no bread.
4. The poor are crying out because they have no food.
5. The judges are sending the books to the king, for there are many good things in them.
6. The king is sending me to the judge because he has a difficult problem (= thing).
7. There are many camels here.

LESSON 8

40. The Demonstrative Adjectives and Pronouns.

	SINGULAR			PLURAL		
masc.	זֶה	*zeh*	this	אֵלֶּה	*'élleh*	these
fem.	זֹאת	*zō(')t*	this			
masc.	הוּא	*hû'*	that	הֵם	*hēm*	those
fem.	הִיא	*hî'*	that	הֵנָּה	*hénnāh*	those

These words have a usage parallel to that of the adjective.

הָאִישׁ הַזֶּה	*hā'îš hazzeh*	this man
הָאִשָּׁה הַזֹּאת	*hā'iššāh hazzō(')t*	this woman
הָאֲנָשִׁים הָאֵלֶּה	*hā'ănāšîm hā'élleh*	these men
הַנָּשִׁים הָאֵלֶּה	*hannāšîm hā'élleh*	these women
הָאִישׁ הַהוּא	*hā'îš hahû'*	that man
הָאִשָּׁה הַהִיא	*hā'iššāh hahî'*	that woman
הָאֲנָשִׁים הָהֵם	*hā'ănāšîm hāhēm*	those men
הַנָּשִׁים הָהֵנָּה	*hannāšîm hāhénnāh*	those women

The demonstrative stands last in a series of adjectives:

הָאִישׁ הַטּוֹב הַזֶּה	*hā'îš haṭṭôb hazzeh*	this good man
הָאִשָּׁה הַטּוֹבָה הַזֹּאת	*hā'iššāh haṭṭôbāh hazzō(')t*	this good woman

The form without the article has the status of a pronoun (compare the use of the predicate adjective):

זֶה הָאִישׁ	zeh hā'îš	This is the man.
זֹאת הָאִשָּׁה	zō(')ṯ hā'iššāh	This is the woman.
אֵלֶּה הַדְּבָרִים	'élleh haddəḇārîm	These are the words.

Note that agreement in number and gender is present, as with the adjective.

41. Participles (cont.).

masc.	בֹּנֶה	bōneh	בֹּנִים	bōnîm
fem.	בֹּנָה	bōnāh	בֹּנוֹת	bōnôṯ
	(בֹּנִיָּה	bōnîyāh)		

The final ה *h* of the form בֹּנֶה *bōneh* is a *mater lectionis* for the final vowel and is not a third root consonant. The root in this class of verbs must be considered as variable in form, sometimes *BN-*, sometimes *BNY*. Note that the feminine has two forms in the singular; either may be used, but *bōnîyāh* is quite rare.

42. Vocabulary 8.

NOUNS: בִּינָה *bînāh* understanding, perceptiveness
צֶדֶק *ṣédeq* righteousness (cf. *ṣaddîq*)
אֵשׁ *'ēš* (no. pl.) fire (f.)
נָבִיא *nāḇî'* (pl. -*îm*) prophet
VERBS: בֹּנֶה *bōneh* building
עֹלֶה *'ōleh* ascending, going up
נֹפֵל *nōp̄ēl* falling

Exercises:

(a) Give the Hebrew for the following orally:

1. this famine
2. these houses
3. that city
4. this money
5. that task
6. this advice
7. these cities
8. these mountains
9. those peoples

(b) Transform the phrases of (a) into sentences according to the model:

this famine → This is the famine.

(c) Translate:

1. dal hannāḇî' hazzeh wə'ên
   lô léḥem.

   דַּל הַנָּבִיא הַזֶּה וְאֵין לוֹ לֶחֶם. 1

2. hā'anāšîm hā'élleh 'ōlîm
   'el-hehārîm.

   הָאֲנָשִׁים הָאֵלֶּה עֹלִים אֶל־הֶהָרִים. 2

3. hannəḇî'îm hayšārîm hōləkîm
   bəṣédeq.

   הַנְּבִיאִים הַיְשָׁרִים הֹלְכִים בְּצֶדֶק. 3

4. bînāh wǝḥokmāh ṭôḇôṯ
   mizzāhāḇ.

בִּינָה וְחָכְמָה טוֹבוֹת מִזָּהָב. 4

5. hā'ēš nōpélet 'al-habbáyiṯ 'ăšer
   'éṣel hahêḵāl.

הָאֵשׁ נֹפֶלֶת עַל־הַבַּיִת אֲשֶׁר אֵצֶל 5
הַהֵיכָל.

6. hā'ănāšîm bōnîm báyiṯ gāḏôl
   bā'îr hahî'.

הָאֲנָשִׁים בֹּנִים בַּיִת גָּדוֹל בָּעִיר הַהִיא. 6

7. rā'îm hā'ām kî 'ên lāhem bînāh.

רָעִים הָעָם כִּי אֵין לָהֶם בִּינָה. 7

8. hû' šōlē°ḥ lánû nāḇî' ṣaddîq.

הוּא שֹׁלֵחַ לָנוּ נָבִיא צַדִּיק. 8

9. 'ên mélek bîrûšāláim.

אֵין מֶלֶךְ בִּירוּשָׁלַֽם. 9

(d) Write in Hebrew:

1. These camels are mine (lit. to me) and those camels are yours.
2. You have no understanding.
3. He is going up to the cattle which are in the mountains.
4. She is falling.
5. The boys are building a small house near the garden.
6. The people are dwelling in this land because it is great and beautiful.
7. He is placing (lit. giving) fire upon that wicked city.

LESSON 9

43. The Perfect of כָּתַב *kāṯaḇ*.

There are two full verbal inflections for person, number, and gender for each Hebrew verb. The first, called the perfect, is formed by adding subject suffixes to a relatively fixed stem, as illustrated by

כָּתַב *kāṯaḇ*   he wrote

כָּתַ֫בְתִּי *kāṯáḇtî*   I wrote.

The second, called the imperfect, uses a different stem and has person, number, and gender marked by both prefixes and suffixes, as in

יִכְתֹּב *yiḵtōḇ*   he will write

תִּכְתֹּ֫בְנָה *tiḵtóḇnāh*   they (fem. pl.) will write.

We shall begin our study of the verb with the perfect, the full inflection of which is as follows:

כָּתַב	*kāṯaḇ*	he wrote	כָּתְבוּ	*kāṯəḇû*	they wrote
כָּתְבָה	*kāṯəḇāh*	she wrote			
כָּתַ֫בְתָּ	*kāṯáḇtā*	you (m. s.) wrote	כְּתַבְתֶּם	*kəṯaḇtem*	you (m. pl.) wrote
כָּתַבְתְּ	*kāṯaḇt*	you (f. s.) wrote	כְּתַבְתֶּן	*kəṯaḇten*	you (f. pl.) wrote
כָּתַ֫בְתִּי	*kāṯáḇtî*	I wrote	כָּתַ֫בְנוּ	*kāṯáḇnû*	we wrote

The following particulars should be noted:

(1) The traditional arrangement of a verbal paradigm in Hebrew begins with the third person and proceeds to the first.

(2) In the perfect, there is a distinction in form for gender in the second and third persons of the singular and the second person plural. The others, including the first person singular and plural and the third person plural, do not reflect the gender of the subject.

(3) The endings given in the paradigm above are standard for nearly all the verbs in the language. Many variations will be seen to occur in the stems of various verb types, but the endings themselves remain fairly constant. The 2nd pers. masc. sing. also appears with a final *mater lectionis*: כָּתַבְתָּה *kātábtāh*.

(4) The stem of the verb *kātab* changes in accordance with the shape of the suffix added:

    (a) Before the unstressed endings -*tā*, -*t*, -*tî*, and -*nû* the stem remains the same as in the third person masculine singular.

    (b) The addition of the endings -*āh* and -*û*, both stressed and consisting of a vowel, opens the final syllable of the stem. Before these endings the second stem vowel is regularly replaced by (reduced to) *ə*.

    (c) The endings -*tem* and -*ten* are always stressed. Because they begin with a consonant the second stem syllable remains closed and unchanged. The first stem vowel, if in an open syllable as in the paradigm under study, is reduced to *ə*.

(5) When the final root consonant is the same as that which begins the suffix, only one letter is written, but with daghesh *forte*; thus, from כָּרַת (he cut) we have כָּרַתִּי *kāráttî* (I cut), and from שָׁכַן (he settled), שָׁכַנּוּ *šākánnû* (we settled).

Verbs whose roots contain a guttural consonant, or whose roots have other phonological peculiarities, such as that of *bōneh*, deviate from the paradigm given above and will be dealt with in the following lessons. Verbs whose roots have no phonological peculiarities are sometimes referred to as "sound" or "regular" triliteral verbs.

44. The Meaning of the Perfect.

We shall see in the course of this book that the translation value of Hebrew tenses is very largely dependent on the kind of sentence or clause in which the verb is used. In the isolated sentences of the following exercises there are only two or three values possible for the translation of the perfect:

    (1) With all verbs, regardless of their meanings, the Hebrew perfect may be translated as the English simple past (I wrote) or the present perfect (I have written).

    (2) With verbs signifying perception, or the attitude or disposition of the subject toward an object, rather than a direct action performed on the object, the perfect may be translated by the general present tense:

אָהַ֫בְתִּי 'āhábtî I love (or, as above, I loved, have loved)

יָדַ֫עְתִּי yādá'tî I know (or, I knew, have known).

(3) With verbs signifying the mental or physical state of the subject, and which consequently do not occur with a direct object, the perfect may be translated by the English present of the verb "to be" + an adjective:

זָקַ֫נְתִּי zāqántî I am old (or I have become old, I grew old)

(4) Rarely in prose, but rather frequently in poetry and proverbial expressions, the perfect is used to denote habitual activity with no specific tense value. Such uses are translated by the English general present (I write).

45. Word Order in the Verbal Sentence.

The verb usually stands first, then the subject, object, and various adverbial elements in that order.

זָכַר הָאִישׁ אֶת־הַדְּבָרִים zāḵar hā'îš 'et-haddəḇārîm
The man remembered the words.

כָּתַב הָאִישׁ אֶת־הַדָּבָר בַּסֵּ֫פֶר kāṯab hā'îš 'et-haddāḇār bassḗp̄er.
The man wrote the word in the book.

It is by no means unusual to find the subject or some other element before the verb, but such sentence order is often conditioned by interclause relationships (taken up below) or by emphasis on the element which is placed first.

The verb agrees in person, number, and gender with its subject. Pronominal subjects are inherent in the verb form itself.

זָכַר אֶת־הַדְּבָרִים zāḵar 'et-haddəḇārîm
He remembered the words.

זָכְרָה אֶת־הַדְּבָרִים zāḵərāh 'et-haddəḇārîm
She remembered the words.

זָכְרָה הָאִשָּׁה אֶת־הַדְּבָרִים zāḵərāh hā'iššāh 'et-haddəḇārîm
The woman remembered the words.

The particle אֶת־ 'et- is used before definite objects, as previously explained.

The perfect is negated with לֹא lō', which is always placed immediately before the verb:

לֹא זָכַ֫רְתִּי אֶת־הַדָּבָר lō' zāḵártî 'et-haddāḇār
I did not remember the word.

The indirect object, always marked by the preposition lə-, tends to precede the direct object when the former is pronominal and the latter nominal:

נָתַן לוֹ אֶת־הָאִשָּׁה   *nāṯan lô 'eṯ-hā'iššāh*
He gave him the woman.

Otherwise, direct object + indirect object may be considered the normal order:

נָתַן אֹתָהּ לוֹ לְאִשָּׁה   *nāṯan 'ōṯāh lô lə'iššāh*
He gave her to him as a wife.

נָתַן אֶת־הָאִשָּׁה לָאִישׁ   *nāṯan 'eṯ-hā'iššāh lā'îš*
He gave the woman to the man.

46. The Forms of the Conjunction וְ *wə-*.

Like the prepositions *bə-*, *lə-*, and *kə*, the conjunction וְ *wə-* (and) differs in form before various word beginnings:

(a) Before a labial consonant בּ *b*, פּ *p*, or מ *m*, its form is וּ *û-*:

בַּיִת	*báyiṯ*	a house	וּבַיִת	*ûbáyiṯ*	and a house
פֹּה	*pōh*	here	וּפֹה	*ûpōh*	and here
מַיִם	*máyim*	water	וּמַיִם	*ûmáyim*	and water

(b) Before a word beginning with יְ *yə-*, the conjunction and the first syllable of the word contract to וִי *wî-*:

יְהוּדָה	*yəhûḏāh*	Judah	וִיהוּדָה	*wîhûḏāh*	and Judah
יְדַעְתֶּם	*yəda'tem*	you knew	וִידַעְתֶּם	*wîda'tem*	and you knew

(c) Before a word beginning with any consonant (except י *y*) + ə, the form is וּ *û-*:

שְׁמוּאֵל *šəmû'ēl* Samuel   וּשְׁמוּאֵל *ûš(ə)mû'ēl* and Samuel

(d) Before a guttural + ă, ĕ, or ŏ, the conjunction is respectively וַ *wa-*, וֶ *we-*, or וָ *wo-*:

אֲרָצוֹת	*'ărāṣôṯ*	lands	וַאֲרָצוֹת	*wa'ărāṣôṯ*	and lands
אֱדֹם	*'ĕdōm*	Edom	וֶאֱדֹם	*we'ĕdōm*	and Edom
אֳנִי	*'ŏnî*	a fleet	וָאֳנִי	*wo'ŏnî*	and a fleet

47. Vocabulary 9.

NOUNS: יוֹם *yôm* (pl. irreg. יָמִים *yāmîm*) day; note הַיּוֹם *hayyôm*, today.

לַיְלָה *láylāh* (pl. rare) night [Note position of stress; masculine.]

מָקוֹם *māqôm* (pl. -ôṯ) place, locale

שָׁמַיִם *šāmáyim* (pl.) heaven(s), sky

VERBS: יָלַד *yālaḏ* to bear, give birth to

קָבַץ *qāḇaṣ* to gather

	זָכַר	*zākar*	to remember
ADJECTIVE:	אֶחָד	*'eḥāḏ*	one (fem. irreg. אַחַת *'aḥat*); אֶחָד מִן *'eḥāḏ min* one of
PREPOSITIONS:	בֵּין	*bên*	between; "between A and B" may be expressed as *bên A ûḇên B* or *bên A wǝB.*
	בְּתוֹךְ	*bǝṯôḵ*	in the midst of
	מִתּוֹךְ	*mittôḵ*	from the midst of
ADVERBS:	גַּם	*gam*	also, even, too [Placed directly before the word it modifies, as in *gam-hammélek,* the king too, even the king.]
	לֹא	*lō'*	no, not; general negative placed before the word it negates

Exercises:

(a) Give orally the full paradigm of the perfect for each of the following verbs: זָכַר יָשַׁב יָרַד

(b) Write out the following phrases in Hebrew with special attention to the form of the conjunction "and":

(1) gold and silver
(2) wisdom and understanding
(3) advice and work
(4) small cattle and large cattle
(5) servants and camels; camels and servants
(6) a great and rich man
(7) a poor and unimportant woman
(8) one man and one woman

(c) Translate:

1. yāšaḇ hā'îš bên-hannāhār ûḇên-haśśāḏeh.

יָשַׁב הָאִישׁ בֵּין־הַנָּהָר וּבֵין־הַשָּׂדֶה. 1

2. qāḇaṣ hannāḇî' 'eṯ-hā'ām 'ēṣel hahêḵāl haggāḏôl.

קָבַץ הַנָּבִיא אֶת־הָעָם אֵצֶל הַהֵיכָל הַגָּדוֹל. 2

3. bayyôm hahû' nāp̄ǝlāh 'ēš min-haššāmáyim.

בַּיּוֹם הַהוּא נָפְלָה אֵשׁ מִן־הַשָּׁמַיִם. 3

4. hālǝḵû hā'ām 'el-haššōp̄ēṭ hayyāšār wǝlō' hālǝḵû 'el-hannāḇî' hārāšā'.

הָלְכוּ הָעָם אֶל־הַשֹּׁפֵט הַיָּשָׁר וְלֹא הָלְכוּ אֶל־הַנָּבִיא הָרָשָׁע. 4

5. mî hannǝḇî'îm hahōlǝḵîm 'el-hā'îr?

מִי הַנְּבִיאִים הַהֹלְכִים אֶל־הָעִיר. 5

6. balláylāh hahû' yārǝḏû hā'ǎnāšîm mēhehārîm.

בַּלַּיְלָה הַהוּא יָרְדוּ הָאֲנָשִׁים מֵהֶהָרִים. 6

7. yāšábnû bətôk hā'îr wəlō'
   hāláknû min-hammāqôm
   hahû'.

7 יָשַׁבְנוּ בְּתוֹךְ הָעִיר וְלֹא הָלַכְנוּ מִן־הַמָּקוֹם
   הַהוּא.

8. yālədāh hā'iššāh yəlādîm
   rabbîm wəyāp̄îm.

8 יָלְדָה הָאִשָּׁה יְלָדִים רַבִּים וְיָפִים.

9. ləmî qāḇáṣtā 'et-hakkésep̄
   wə'et-hazzāhāb?

9 לְמִי קָבַצְתָּ אֶת־הַכֶּסֶף וְאֶת־הַזָּהָב.

10. lō' nāp̄al 'eḥād mēhannə'ārîm.

10 לֹא נָפַל אֶחָד מֵהַנְּעָרִים.

(d) Write in Hebrew:

1. He gave wisdom and understanding to the prophets.
2. They sent the gold and the silver to the men in the temple.
3. This work is very hard because we have no understanding.
4. Today the men are building a house in the city.
5. Where did they write those words?
6. I remember that he gave me the book.
7. There is evil in this place.
8. One of the women is leaving the city.

LESSON 10

48. The Perfect of Verbs with Guttural Root Consonants.

The presence of guttural consonants in the root of a verb occasions slight modifications in the inflection of the perfect. All of these are simple and predictable variations, with the exception of roots whose third consonant is א (hereafter designated simply as verbs III-*Aleph*),* whose inflection will be considered separately from those given here.

3 m. s.	עָמַד	'āmaḏ	בָּחַר	bāḥar	שָׁמַע	šāma'
3 f. s.	עָמְדָה	'āməḏāh	בָּחֲרָה	bāḥărāh	שָׁמְעָה	šāmə'āh
2 m. s.	עָמַ֫דְתָּ	'āmáḏtā	בָּחַ֫רְתָּ	bāḥártā	שָׁמַ֫עְתָּ	šāmá'tā
2 f. s.	עָמַדְתְּ	'āmaḏt	בָּחַרְתְּ	bāḥart	שָׁמַעְתְּ	(šāma't)
1 s.	עָמַ֫דְתִּי	'āmáḏtî	בָּחַ֫רְתִּי	bāḥártî	שָׁמַ֫עְתִּי	šāmá'tî
3 pl.	עָמְדוּ	'āməḏû	בָּחֲרוּ	bāḥărû	שָׁמְעוּ	šāmə'û
2 m. pl.	עֲמַדְתֶּם	'ămaḏtem	בְּחַרְתֶּם	bəḥartem	שְׁמַעְתֶּם	šəma'tem
2 f. pl.	עֲמַדְתֶּן	'ămaḏten	בְּחַרְתֶּן	bəḥarten	שְׁמַעְתֶּן	šəma'ten
1 pl.	עָמַ֫דְנוּ	'āmáḏnû	בָּחַ֫רְנוּ	bāḥárnû	שָׁמַ֫עְנוּ	šāmá'nû

In verbs I-gutt. (i.e. whose first root consonant is a guttural) the only variation from the standard paradigm is the replacement of ă for ə in the 2nd pers. pl. forms. This replacement should by now be familiar to the reader

---

* Most Hebrew grammars employ the letters פ, ע, and ל to designate the first, second, and third root consonants respectively. Thus, our III-*Aleph* corresponds to the more usual designation *Lamedh-Aleph*.

from previous examples. The same is true for verbs II-gutt., where we find *ă* for *ə* in the forms *bāḥărāh* and *bāḥărû*.

The only form in the paradigm of *šāmaʿ* (III-gutt.) that requires comment is שָׁמַעַתְּ, which, as it stands, is anomalous. It is likely that such spellings were meant by the punctators to show an option: we should read either שָׁמַעַתְ *šāmáʿat*, ignoring the daghesh, or שָׁמַעְתְּ *šāmaʿt*, ignoring the second *a*.

49. The Perfect of נָתַן *nātan*.

This verb has a peculiarity in its inflection: the second *n* of the stem is always assimilated to the initial consonant of the subject suffixes. Note carefully the following forms; the daghesh is *forte*, indicating doubling.

נָתַן	*nātan*	he gave	נָתְנוּ	*nātənû*	they gave
נָתְנָה	*nātənāh*	she gave			
נָתַתָּ	*nātáttā*	you (m. s.) gave	נְתַתֶּם	*nətattem*	you (m. pl.) gave
נָתַתְּ	*nātatt*	you (f. s.) gave	נְתַתֶּן	*nətatten*	you (f. pl.) gave
נָתַתִּי	*nātáttî*	I gave	נָתַנּוּ	*nātánnû*	we gave

50. Noun Plurals (continued).

(a) Dissyllabic nouns with the sequence *-áyi-* show a regular contraction in the plural stem:

זַיִת	*záyit*	olive tree	pl.	זֵיתִים	*zêtîm*
אַיִל	*ʾáyil*	ram		אֵילִים	*ʾêlîm*

The noun בַּיִת *báyit* (house) is irregular: בָּתִּים *bāttîm*. Note the *ā* in a closed unaccented syllable; this is virtually unique with this word.

(b) There are many nouns of two syllables whose singular and plural stems are identical. These include nouns both of whose syllables are not susceptible to the changes presented in the preceding sections dealing with the noun. Examples are

אֶבְיוֹן	*ʾebyôn*	poor	pl.	אֶבְיוֹנִים	*ʾebyônîm*
גִּבּוֹר	*gibbôr*	warrior		גִּבּוֹרִים	*gibbôrîm*
צַדִּיק	*ṣaddîq*	righteous man		צַדִּיקִים	*ṣaddîqîm*
עַמּוּד	*ʿammûd*	column		עַמּוּדִים	*ʿammûdîm*

Note that both syllables of such nouns are either closed or contain an unchangeable long vowel.

(c) A small group of nouns ends in *-eh* in the singular. Although this is not a suffix, but an integral part of the root word, it does not occur on the plural stem:

שָׂדֶה	śāḏeh	field	pl.	שָׂדוֹת	śāḏôṯ
מַחֲנֶה	maḥăneh	camp		מַחֲנוֹת	maḥănôṯ

Nouns originally participles of verbs III-*Hē* (i.e. whose third root consonant is given as ה) also belong to this class: רֹעֶה *rō'eh*, pl. רֹעִים *rō'îm*, shepherd.

51. Vocabulary 10.

NOUNS:
גִּבּוֹר   *gibbôr* (pl. -îm) warrior, hero, valiant man

גִּבְעָה   *gibʿāh* hill

מַֽיִם   *máyim* water [Like שָׁמַֽיִם, a plural without a singular]

מַחֲנֶה   *maḥăneh* (pl. -ôṯ) camp

מִלְחָמָה   *milḥāmāh* battle, war

פְּרִי   *pərî* fruit

VERBS:
בָּחַר   *bāḥar* to choose [May take object with אֶת- *'eṯ-*, but more commonly with בְּ *bə*: בָּחַר בִּי *bāḥar bî* he chose me.]

הָרַג   *hāraḡ* to kill, slay

יָדַע   *yāḏaʿ* to know

לָקַח   *lāqaḥ* to take

עָמַד   *ʿāmaḏ* to stand

PREPOSITION:
לִפְנֵי   *lip̄nê* before, in front of, in the presence of

Exercises:

(a) Inflect in the perfect: הָלַךְ   אָכַל   צָעַק   שָׁלַח   נָטַע

(b) Give the Hebrew for the following orally:

1. They planted many trees.
2. She stood near the houses.
3. You chose me.
4. They did not choose you.
5. I took the money.
6. They killed the young man.
7. You (f. s.) took the water.
8. You (m. pl.) have eaten the bread.
9. We sent the messengers to the judge.

(c) Translate:

1. nāṭəʿû hāʾănāšîm kérem gāḏôl   נָטְעוּ הָאֲנָשִׁים כֶּֽרֶם גָּדוֹל עַל־הַגִּבְעָה.   1
    'al-haggibʿāh.

2. lōʾ yāḏáʿtî kî hûʾ hāraḡ   לֹא יָדַֽעְתִּי כִּי הוּא הָרַג אֶת־הַנָּבִיא.   2
    'et-hannābîʾ.

3. ʿāmᵊḏû hāʿăḇāḏîm hārəšāʿîm   עָמְדוּ הָעֲבָדִים הָרְשָׁעִים לִפְנֵי הַמֶּֽלֶךְ.   3
    lip̄nê hammélek.

4. bāḥártî bəḵā ləmélek 'al-hā'ām haggādôl hazzeh.

בָּחַרְתִּי בְּךָ לְמֶלֶךְ עַל־הָעָם הַגָּדוֹל הַזֶּה. 4

5. nāpəlû gibbôrîm rabbîm bammilḥāmāh hahî'.

נָפְלוּ גִבּוֹרִים רַבִּים בַּמִּלְחָמָה הַהִיא. 5

6. yēš maḥăneh bên-hannāhār ûḇên-hehārîm.

יֵשׁ מַחֲנֶה בֵּין־הַנָּהָר וּבֵין־הֶהָרִים. 6

7. mî šālaḥ 'ōṯəḵā 'el-hammāqôm hazzeh?

מִי שָׁלַח אֹתְךָ אֶל־הַמָּקוֹם הַזֶּה. 7

8. mî hāraḡ 'eṯ-hā'ănāšîm hā'élleh?

מִי הָרַג אֶת־הָאֲנָשִׁים הָאֵלֶּה. 8

9. lāqəḥāh hā'iššāh mēhappərî wənāṯənāh 'ōṯô lā'îš.

לָקְחָה הָאִשָּׁה מֵהַפְּרִי וְנָתְנָה אֹתוֹ לָאִישׁ. 9

10. bāḥărû hā'ām 'eṯ-Dāwiḏ lāhem ləmélek.

בָּחֲרוּ הָעָם אֶת־דָּוִד לָהֶם לְמֶלֶךְ. 10

(d) Write in Hebrew:

1. He planted a tree in the midst of this garden.
2. They cried out in a loud voice because of this hard work.
3. They chose for them(selves) a land and dwelt there.
4. The men took the gold and silver from the temple. They also slew the prophets who (were) there.
5. She knew that those words (were) very bad.
6. One of the young men fell in that battle.
7. They gave me bread and water, but I did not give them the money.

LESSON 11

52. The Perfect of Verbs III-Aleph: מָצָא māsā'.

מָצָא	*māsā(')*	he found	מָצְאוּ	*māsə'û*	they found
מָצְאָה	*māsə'āh*	she found			
מָצָאתָ	*māsā́(')ṯā*	you (m. s.) found	מְצָאתֶם	*məsā(')ṯem*	you (m. pl.) found
מָצָאת	*māsā́(')ṯ*	you (f. s.) found	מְצָאתֶן	*məsā(')ṯen*	you (f. pl.) found
מָצָאתִי	*māsā́(')ṯî*	I found	מָצָאנוּ	*māsā́(')nû*	we found

In verbs III-*Aleph* the second syllable of the stem in the perfect has *ā* instead of *a* in those forms to which a suffix beginning with a consonant is added. In other words, whenever א originally closed a syllable, it was lost and the lengthening of the vowel took place as a consequence. The ' is preserved when it begins the syllable, as in *māsə'āh* and *māsə'û*. Remember, however, that the א is always found in the spelling, even when not pronounced. Note too that there is no *daghesh lene* in the ת of the suffixes, since they are now preceded in pronunciation by a vowel instead of a consonant.

53. Noun Plurals (continued).

The majority of feminine nouns in -*āh* show no change in the stem before the plural ending:

שָׁנָה	*šānāh*	year	pl.	שָׁנִים	*šānîm*	
תּוֹרָה	*tôrāh*	law		תּוֹרוֹת	*tôrôṯ*	
אַמָּה	*'ammāh*	cubit		אַמּוֹת	*'ammôṯ*	
בְּרָכָה	*bərākāh*	blessing		בְּרָכוֹת	*bərākôṯ*	

בְּהֵמָה	bəhēmāh	beast	בְּהֵמוֹת	bəhēmôṯ
תְּבוּאָה	təḇû'āh	product	תְּבוּאוֹת	təḇû'ōṯ
תְּפִלָּה	təp̄illāh	prayer	תְּפִלּוֹת	təp̄illōṯ
מִשְׁפָּחָה	mišpāḥāh	family	מִשְׁפָּחוֹת	mišpāḥōṯ

But nouns of the general pattern *CvCCāh*,* like מַלְכָּה *malkāh* (queen), where the two contiguous consonants are different (thus not *'ammāh* above), have a different plural stem:

מַלְכָּה	malkāh	queen	pl.	מְלָכוֹת	məlāḵōṯ	[Note the ā.]
גִּבְעָה	giḇ'āh	hill		גְּבָעוֹת	gəḇā'ōṯ	
חֶרְפָּה	ḥerpāh	reproach		חֲרָפוֹת	ḥărāp̄ôṯ	

But note מִצְוָה *miṣwāh*, pl. מִצְוֹת *miṣwōṯ*, where the מ is a prefix and not part of the root.

54. Interrogative הַ hă-.

Any sentence may be converted into a question by prefixing a form of the particle הַ *hă-* to the first word:

הֲשָׁלַח הָאִישׁ	hăšālaḥ hā'îš ...	Did the man send ...?
הֲטוֹבָה הָאָרֶץ	hăṭôḇāh hā'āreṣ	Is the land good?

Before gutturals the form is normally הַ *ha-*:

הַעֹמֵד הָאִישׁ	ha'ōmēḏ hā'îš	Is the man standing?

But if the guttural is followed by ā or o, the form used is הֶ *he-*:

הֶאֲכַלְתָּ	he'ăḵáltā	Have you eaten?

Before non-guttural consonants followed by ə the form is also הַ *ha-*:

הַכְּתַבְתֶּם	hak(ə)ṯaḇtem	Did you write?

Rarely one encounters the same doubling of the following consonant that we met in the definite article:

הַכְּתַבְתֶּם	hakkəṯaḇtem	Did you write?

55. More on אֲשֶׁר 'ăšer.

We saw above (§32) that אֲשֶׁר *'ăšer* indicates that a following phrase modifies as a unit the preceding word. This is true also for clauses, as the following examples show:

---

* C = consonant; v = a, i, e, o.

הַכֹּהֵן אֲשֶׁר כָּתַב אֶת־הַדָּבָר   *hakkōhēn 'ăšer kātab 'et-haddābār*
the priest *who* wrote the word

הַמַּלְאָךְ אֲשֶׁר שָׁלַח הַמֶּלֶךְ   *hammal'āk 'ăšer šālaḥ hammélek*
the messenger *whom* the king sent

56. Vocabulary 11.

NOUNS: שֶׁמֶשׁ   *šémeš*   sun
   יָרֵחַ   *yārē*[a]*ḥ*   moon
   כּוֹכָב   *kôkāb* (pl. -*îm*)   star
   עָנָן   *'ānān*   cloud
   בְּרָכָה   *bərākāh* (pl. -*ôt*)   blessing
   שָׁנָה   *šānāh* (pl. -*îm*)   year
   תּוֹרָה   *tôrāh* (pl. -*ôt*)   law, The Law

VERBS: מָצָא   *māṣā'*   to find
   בָּרָא   *bārā'*   to create
   קָרָא   *qārā'*   to call, name; to summon; to declare, read aloud [+ *'el*: to call unto (someone); + *lə*: to summon (someone)]
   אָמַר   *'āmar*   to say, speak

CONJUNCTION: לֵאמֹר   *lē(')mōr*   introduces a direct quotation after verbs of saying; it has no translation value in English)

Exercises:

(a) Form the plurals of the following nouns, as described in §53:

צָרָה   *ṣārāh* (-*ôt*) distress   עֵצָה   *'ēṣāh* (-*ôt*) counsel
עוֹלָה   *'ôlāh* (-*ôt*) burnt-offering   חֻקָּה   *ḥuqqāh* (-*ôt*) statute
מִנְחָה   *minḥāh* (-*ôt*) gift, offering   שִׂמְלָה   *śimlāh* (-*ôt*) cloak
עֶגְלָה   *'eḡlāh* (-*ôt*) heifer   עֲרָבָה   *'ărābāh* (-*ôt*) desert, steppe
קְלָלָה   *qəlālāh* (-*ôt*) curse   בְּתוּלָה   *bətûlāh* (-*ôt*) virgin
מְסִלָּה   *məsillāh* (-*ôt*) highway   מְגִלָּה   *məḡillāh* (-*ôt*) scroll
מַמְלָכָה   *mamlākāh* (-*ôt*) kingdom

(b) Give the Hebrew for the following orally. Then convert each into a question by prefixing the appropriate form of הֲ *hă-*:

1. He stood before the king.
2. They slew the warriors in the battle.
3. You (m. pl.) knew that the city (was) on a hill.
4. I took the fruit.
5. You chose us.
6. We have no water.
7. The rich man has large cattle and camels.

8. You went down to the river.

9. You (m. sing.) ate the bread.

(c) <u>Translate</u>:

1 אֵלֶּה הַדְּבָרִים אֲשֶׁר כָּתַב הַנָּבִיא בַּסֵּפֶר הַהוּא.

2 הָלְכוּ אֶל־הָעִיר וְלֹא מָצְאוּ אֶת־הַיֶּלֶד הַקָּטֹן.

3 הַשֶּׁמֶשׁ בַּשָּׁמַיִם וְגַם־הַיָּרֵחַ שָׁם, הַשֶּׁמֶשׁ בַּיּוֹם וְהַיָּרֵחַ בַּלַּיְלָה.

4 גַּם־בַּלַּיְלָה יֵשׁ כּוֹכָבִים רַבִּים וְיָפִים.

5 בַּשָּׁנָה הַהִיא נָפְלוּ גִבּוֹרִים רַבִּים.

6 שָׁלַח עָנָן גָּדוֹל אֲשֶׁר עָמַד לִפְנֵי הָעָם.

7 אָמַר לוֹ הַמֶּלֶךְ לֵאמֹר הֲשָׁלַחְתָּ אֶת־הָאִישׁ אֶל־הָהָר.

8 מִי בָרָא אֶת־הָאָרֶץ וּמִי בָרָא אֶת־הַשָּׁמַיִם.

9 טוֹבָה הַתּוֹרָה וְטוֹבִים הַדְּבָרִים אֲשֶׁר בָּהּ.

10 יָצָא קוֹל מִתּוֹךְ הֶעָנָן.

11 הֲיְצָאתֶם מֵהָעִיר הָרָעָה.

12 קָרָא הַנָּבִיא אֶל־הָעָם בְּקוֹל גָּדוֹל לֵאמֹר רָעִים מְאֹד הַדְּבָרִים אֲשֶׁר אֲמַרְתֶּם.

(d) <u>Write in Hebrew</u>:

1. He created the sun, the moon, and the stars.
2. Did you find the book in the house?
3. Did he say to them that (kî) the law is just?
4. This blessing is for us and for those who dwell in the midst of this people.
5. The cloud stood over the earth.
6. Where did he find the small cattle?
7. The king summoned the prophet, but the prophet did not go to the palace.
8. Have you (m. pl.) remembered this law and the words which I have written in it for you?

LESSON 12

57. The Perfect of Verbs III-Hē: בָּנָה bānāh.

בָּנָה	*bānāh*	he built	בָּנוּ	*bānû*	they built
בָּנְתָה	*bānəṯāh*	she built			
בָּנִיתָ	*bānîṯā*	you (m. s.) built	בְּנִיתֶם	*bənîṯem*	you (m. pl.) built
בָּנִית	*bānîṯ*	you (f. s.) built	בְּנִיתֶן	*bənîṯen*	you (f. pl.) built
בָּנִיתִי	*bānîṯî*	I built	בָּנִינוּ	*bānînû*	we built

Note that the stem vowel in the first syllable behaves quite normally. The stem itself is variable (*bānāh, bānəṯ-, bānî-, bənî-, bān-*), and we must again point out that the ה of the 3rd masc. sing. is not a real root consonant but a *mater lectionis* for the final vowel. It is convenient, however, to follow traditional grammar and to speak of this class of verbs as III-*Hē*.

When a verb III-*Hē* is also I-gutt., the regular substitution of ă for ə is found in the 2nd pers. pl. forms:

עֲלִיתֶם   *'ălîṯem*   you (m. pl.) went up

עֲלִיתֶן   *'ălîṯen*   you (f. pl.) went up

The verb הָיָה *hāyāh* (to be) is inflected regularly as a member of this class; only the 2nd pers. pl. shows a slight peculiarity, with ĕ for ă:

הֱיִיתֶם   *hĕyîṯem*   you (m. pl.) were

58. Directive ה ָ -āh.

The suffix -āh added to a noun indicates motion toward. It occurs on both proper nouns and common nouns, the latter with or without the article.

This ending is never stressed and may thus be distinguished from the feminine ending -āh. Because directive -āh cannot be added to all nouns, each form is best learned individually, without a lengthy analysis of the minor changes that take place in the stem. The following list contains the most important of the words using this suffix:

אֶ֫רֶץ	'éreṣ	land, earth	אַ֫רְצָה	'árṣāh	to the earth, to the land, onto the ground
בַּ֫יִת	báyiṯ	house	הַבַּ֫יְתָה	habbáytāh	to the house, home
			בַּ֫יְתָה	báytāh	
הַר	har	mountain	הָהָ֫רָה	hāhárāh	to the mountain,
			הֶ֫רָה	hérāh	mountainward
מִדְבָּר	miḏbār	wilderness	מִדְבָּ֫רָה	miḏbárāh	toward the wilderness
עִיר	'îr	city	הָעִ֫ירָה	hā'îrāh	toward the city
שָׁמַ֫יִם	šāmáyim	heaven	הַשָּׁמַ֫יְמָה	haššāmáymāh	heavenward
מִצְרַ֫יִם	miṣráyim	Egypt	מִצְרַ֫יְמָה	miṣráymāh	toward Egypt
יְרוּשָׁלַ֫ם	yərûšālá(y)im	Jerusalem	יְרוּשָׁלַ֫מָה	yərûšālá(y)māh	toward Jerusalem
נֶ֫גֶב	néḡeḇ	Negev (the southern part of Palestine; the south in general)	נֶ֫גְבָּה	néḡbāh	toward the Negev, southward
שְׁאֹל	šə'ōl	Sheol (residence of the dead)	שְׁאֹ֫לָה	šə'ólāh	to Sheol

Note especially its use on the directional adverbs:

אָ֫נָה	'ánāh	whither? to what place (contrast אַיֵּה)
שָׁ֫מָּה	šámmāh	thither, to that place (contrast שָׁם)
הֵ֫נָּה	hénnāh	hither, to this place (contrast פֹּה)

Similarly on the terms for the directions:

צָפוֹן	ṣāp̄ôn	north	צָפ֫וֹנָה	ṣāp̄ônāh	northward
קֶ֫דֶם	qéḏem	east	קֵ֫דְמָה	qéḏmāh	eastward
תֵּימָן	têmān	south	תֵּימָ֫נָה	têmánāh	southward
יָם	yām	sea, west	יָ֫מָּה	yámmāh	seaward, westward

59. Vocabulary 12.

Special Note: The two most frequent designations of God in the OT are אֱלֹהִים *'ĕlōhîm* and יהוה *Yhwh*.

(1) אֱלֹהִים is a plural word, generally construed as a singular. It may mean "gods" when used as a plural and "God" when used as a singular or a plural, with or without the article.

(2) יהוה is the name of God. For pious or superstitious reasons יהוה was

read as אֲדֹנָי 'ăḏōnāy (lit. my lords, my Lord). Just when this practice began is not certain, but it may predate the Christian Era. The Masoretes indicated this substitution by applying the vowel points of 'ăḏōnāy, slightly modified, to יהוה, hence יְהֹוָה. The literal interpretation of this latter form as Yəhōwāh = Jehovah dates from modern times.

Both of these words behave erratically after the prefixed prepositions: the initial א is lost in pronunciation:

בֵּאלֹהִים	bē(')lōhîm	בַּיהוה	ba(')ḏōnāy
לֵאלֹהִים	lē(')lōhîm	לַיהוה	la(')ḏōnāy
כֵּאלֹהִים	kē(')lōhîm	כַּיהוה	ka(')ḏōnāy

Those who wish to read יהוה as Yahweh, the most likely original pronunciation, must remember to repoint these prepositions as bəYahweh, ləYahweh, etc.

When the name יהוה occurs in conjunction with אֲדֹנָי, the former is read as אֱלֹהִים and pointed יֱהֹוִה. This is to avoid the repetition in reading 'ăḏōnāy 'ăḏōnāy.

NOUNS:
בְּרִית bərîṯ covenant, treaty (f.)
חֵן ḥēn grace, favor
יְשׁוּעָה yəšû‘āh (pl. -ôṯ) salvation, deliverance, victory
שִׂמְחָה śimḥāh (pl. -ôṯ) joy

VERBS:
עָשָׂה ‘āśāh to do, make, act, perform, bring about
רָאָה rā'āh to see
כָּרַת kāraṯ to cut; כָּרַת בְּרִית to make a treaty
נָסַע nāsa‘ to set out, travel, journey

PREPOSITIONS:
עִם ‘im with, together with
כְּ kə like, as, according to
אֵת 'ēṯ
אֶת־ 'eṯ- } with, together with

Note the idiom מָצָא חֵן בְּעֵינֵי as in

מָצָא דָוִד חֵן בְּעֵינֵי הַמֶּלֶךְ David found favor with the king.
          (or, The king became fond of David.)

Exercises:

(a) Give the Hebrew for the following orally:

1. On that day he made a treaty with the king.
2. The prophet grew fond of the boy.
3. A great sound ascended heavenward.
4. They went up toward-the-city with the people.
5. They built a house in that place.
6. Who did this evil thing?
7. Did you act according to the words which are there?

8. The woman fell to-the-ground.
9. They traveled from the midst of the city toward-the-mountain.
10. Those men also did not remember.

(b) Translate:

1 עָשָׂה הַגִּבּוֹר יְשׁוּעָה גְדוֹלָה לָעָם.

2 אֵין יְשׁוּעָה בֵּאלֹהִים לָאִישׁ הָרָע.

3 הֶעָשִׂיתָ אֶת־הַדָּבָר הַזֶּה.

4 הַזְכַּרְתֶּם אֶת־הַבְּרִית אֲשֶׁר כָּרַת יהוה אֶת־הָעָם.

5 יֵשׁ שִׂמְחָה גְדוֹלָה בִּירוּשָׁלַ‍ִם כִּי יהוה שָׁם.

6 גְּדוֹלָה הָעִיר אֲשֶׁר בָּנִינוּ בָּאָרֶץ הַזֹּאת.

7 רָאִיתִי אֵשׁ יֹרֶדֶת מֵהַשָּׁמַיִם וְנֹפֶלֶת אַרְצָה.

8 נָסַע הַזָּקֵן הָעִירָה.

9 עָשָׂה אֱלֹהִים אֶת־הַשָּׁמַיִם וְאֶת־הָאָרֶץ.

10 עָלְתָה הָאִשָּׁה יְרוּשָׁלַ‍ְמָה כִּי שָׁם הַשֹּׁפֵט.

11 לֹא זָכַרְתְּ אֶת־הַבְּרִית אֲשֶׁר כָּרַתְנוּ עִם־הָעָם.

(c) Write in Hebrew:

1. Who said to you that the camp is near the river?
2. The man is a just judge.
3. Did you see the moon and the stars?
4. God did not find a righteous man in the evil city.
5. These are the words which we saw in the law.
6. Great and good is the earth which the Lord created.
7. The people came forth from that land in that year.
8. The king was pleased with the woman (lit. the woman found favor etc.).

LESSON 13

60. Sentences with a Nominal Predicate.

One of the simplest of all sentence types in Hebrew is that in which two nouns (or noun phrases) are juxtaposed to indicate a predication:

דָּוִד מֶלֶךְ טוֹב   *Dāwīd mélek̲ t̲ôb̲*   (1)
David is a good king.

The demonstrative pronouns הוּא *hû'*, הִיא *hî'*, and their plurals are often used in sentences of this type in the following way:

דָּוִד הוּא מֶלֶךְ טוֹב   *Dāwīd hû' mélek̲ t̲ôb̲* (2)
דָּוִד מֶלֶךְ טוֹב הוּא   *Dāwīd mélek̲ t̲ôb̲ hû'* (3)

Although it is probable that the use of the demonstrative pronoun places a greater emphasis on one or another of the sentence elements, it is impossible for us to determine this nuance with any accuracy, since there are no informants available who speak Biblical Hebrew. It is likely that (2) answers the question "Who is a good king?" and that (3) answers "What is David?", while the first type (1) is a neutral statement of fact without a question in mind.

61. The Verb הָיָה hāyāh (to be).

In the preceding lessons we have studied four types of non-verbal sentences:

    (1) with adjectival predicate: טוֹב הָאִישׁ   *t̲ôb̲ hā'îš*

[55]

(2) with adverbial predicate: הָאִישׁ בַּבַּיִת   *hā'îš babbáyit*

(3) with existential predicate: יֵשׁ אִישׁ   *yēš 'îš*

(4) with nominal predicate: דָּוִד מֶלֶךְ טוֹב   *Dāwīd mélek ṭôb*

None of these has any specific tense value, which must rather depend on the context in which the sentence occurs. All of these sentences, however, may be converted into verbal sentences by using the verb הָיָה *hāyāh*, which in the perfect has the normal tense values of that form:

(1)   הָיָה הָאִישׁ טוֹב   *hāyāh hā'îš ṭôb*   The man was good.

(2)   הָיָה הָאִישׁ בַּבַּיִת   *hāyāh hā'îš babbáyit*   The man was in the house.

(3)   הָיָה כֶּסֶף   *hāyāh késep*   There was silver.

(4)   דָּוִד הָיָה מֶלֶךְ טוֹב   *Dāwīd hāyāh mélek ṭôb*   David was a good king.

Each is negated with לֹא *lō'*. Note that יֵשׁ is replaced by הָיָה in (3) and that a negative existential sentence like אֵין כֶּסֶף becomes לֹא הָיָה כֶּסֶף .

In sentences of the type

הָיָה דָוִד לְמֶלֶךְ טוֹב   *hāyāh Dāwīd ləmélek ṭôb*

the preposition adds the nuance of "becoming" to the verb of being. Although such a sentence equates two nominal elements, it is nevertheless of type (2).

Note the following use of לְ :

הָיְתָה שָׂרָה לְאַבְרָהָם לְאִשָּׁה   *hāyətāh Śārāh lə'Abrāhām lə'iššāh*

which may be translated "Sarah became Abraham's wife" or "Sarah became a wife of Abraham's" or "Sarah was Abraham's wife." If we replace לְ with כְּ , the idea is that of "acting in the place or capacity of, but not actually being":

הָיָה הָאִישׁ לַנַּעַר כְּאָב   *hāyāh hā'îš lanná'ar kə'āb*

> The man was like a father to the youth, or
> The man became the youth's father, as it were.

Of course הָיָה לְ , as the past tense of יֵשׁ לְ , may be used to translate possession in past time:

הָיָה צֹאן לְאַבְרָהָם   *hāyāh ṣō(')n lə'Abrāhām*   Abraham possessed cattle.

Sentences with a participial predicate, such as הָאִישׁ כֹּתֵב , the man is (was) writing, are seldom converted with הָיָה . Why this is so will become clearer when we have taken up the syntax of Hebrew narrative below.

62. Noun Plurals (concluded).

Feminine nouns ending in *-et, -at, -āt, -ît, -ôt,* or *-ût* show much variety in the plural. The words given below are a sufficient sampling of this group, whose forms must be learned singly as they occur. None of these words represents a frequent type.

בַּת	*baṯ*	daughter	pl.	בָּנוֹת	*bānôṯ*	
עֵת	*'ēṯ*	time		עִתִּים	*'ittîm*	
דֶּלֶת	*déleṯ*	door		דְּלָתוֹת	*dəlāṯôṯ*	
מִשְׁמֶרֶת	*mišméreṯ*	office		מִשְׁמָרוֹת	*mišmārôṯ*	
חַטָּאת	*ḥaṭṭāṯ*	sin		חַטָּאוֹת	*ḥaṭṭā'ôṯ*	
חֲנִית	*ḥănîṯ*	spear		חֲנִיתִים	*ḥănîṯîm*	
מַלְכוּת	*malkûṯ*	kingdom		מַלְכֻיּוֹת	*malkûyôṯ*	

63. Vocabulary 13.

NOUNS: חַטָּאת *ḥaṭṭā(')ṯ* (pl. חַטָּאוֹת) sin (f.)

חֲלוֹם *ḥălôm* (pl. -ôṯ) dream

בַּת *baṯ* (pl. בָּנוֹת) daughter

אֵימָה *'êmāh* fear, terror, dread

שִׁפְחָה *šip̄ḥāh* (pl. -ôṯ) maidservant, female slave

אָמָה *'āmāh* (pl. irreg. *'ămāhôṯ* אֲמָהוֹת) maidservant, female slave

VERBS: הָיָה *hāyāh* to be, become (+ לְ)

חָטָא *ḥāṭā'* to sin (against: לְ)

חָלַם *ḥālam* to dream

לָכַד *lāḵaḏ* to capture, take captive

Exercises:

(a) Give the Hebrew for the following sentences orally:

1. Samuel is a just judge.
2. Jerusalem is a great city.
3. This servant is a righteous man.
4. The sun and moon are in the heavens.
5. The blessing which he spoke is good.
6. The cloud is very large.
7. There are many stars in the sky.
8. He has many daughters.
9. The warriors are in the camp.

(b) Transform the sentences of (a) into past tense with the appropriate form of the verb הָיָה.

(c) Translate:

1 לָכְדוּ אֶת־הֶעָרִים אֲשֶׁר בָּאָרֶץ הַהִיא וְגַם־אֶת־הָעָם אֲשֶׁר בָּהֶן.

2 בַּלַּיְלָה חָלַמְתִּי חֲלוֹם וְזֶה הַחֲלוֹם אֲשֶׁר חָלָמְתִּי.

3 שָׁלְחָה הָאִשָּׁה אֶת־הַשִּׁפְחָה אֶל־הַנָּבִיא.

4 נָפְלָה אֵימָה גְדוֹלָה עַל־הָעָם כִּי חָטְאוּ לַיהוה.

5 יֵשׁ לִי בָּנוֹת רַבּוֹת וְיָפוֹת.

6 לֹא הָיִינוּ רָעִים בְּעֵינֵי הַנָּבִיא.

7 אֵימָה נָפְלָה עַל־הָאָרֶץ כִּי לָכַדְנוּ אֶת־הֶעָרִים.

8 רַבּוֹת הַחַטָּאוֹת אֲשֶׁר חָטָאתָ לֵאלֹהִים.

9 כָּתַב בַּסֵּפֶר אֶת־הַדְּבָרִים אֲשֶׁר רָאָה בַּחֲלוֹם אֲשֶׁר חָלַם.

(d) <u>Write in Hebrew</u>:

1. We made no treaty with these people.
2. There was no joy in the city that day.
3. We did not find favor in the eyes of the prophet.
4. Where did they find you?
5. These words are a great blessing for the people.
6. The king is a just and righteous man.

LESSON 14

64. The Perfect of קָם qām and בָּא bā'.

The two verbs קָם *qām* (he arose) and בָּא *bā'* (he came) represent a new type of root not mentioned previously. These verbs have essentially biconsonantal roots so far as their verbal inflections are concerned, but because there are sometimes associated with them nouns exhibiting a second form of the same root with *Waw* or *Yodh* in the middle, these roots are classified as II-*Waw* or II-*Yodh* in traditional grammar. They are also spoken of as Hollow Verbs. In the standard lexicon of Biblical Hebrew קָם and בָּא are listed under the roots קום and בוא respectively. The distinction between roots II-*Waw* and II-*Yodh* will become clear only when certain forms are taken up later; for the present the distinction is immaterial. קָם will be taken as the norm of this class:

קָם	*qām*	he arose	קָ֫מוּ	*qắmû*	they arose
קָ֫מָה	*qắmāh*	she arose			
קַ֫מְתָּ	*qắmtā*	you (m. s.) arose	קַמְתֶּם	*qamtém*	you (m. pl.) arose
קַמְתְּ	*qámt*	you (f. s.) arose	קַמְתֶּן	*qamtén*	you (f. pl.) arose
קַ֫מְתִּי	*qắmtî*	I arose	קַ֫מְנוּ	*qắmnû*	we arose

Note that the stem vowel is short in all persons other than the 3rd. The length of the stem vowel is almost completely dependent on whether or not the stem syllable is open or closed. Unlike verbs previously learned, the accent remains on the stem in the forms of the 3rd fem. sing. and the 3rd common plural.

Because בָּא has א as its final root consonant, we find the same kind of deviation here as with מָצָא. The full paradigm of this important verb is

בָּא	*bā'*	he came	בָּאוּ	*bā'û*	they came
בָּאָה	*bā'āh*	she came			
בָּאתָ	*bá(')tā*	you (m. s.) came	בָּאתֶם	*bā(')tem*	you (m. pl.) came
בָּאת	*bá(')t*	you (f. s.) came	בָּאתֶן	*bā(')ten*	you (f. pl.) came
בָּאתִי	*bá(')tî*	I came	בָּאנוּ	*bá(')nû*	we came

The stem of the participle in these verbs is the same as that of the 3rd masc. sing. perfect:

	SINGULAR		PLURAL	
masc.	קָם	*qām*	קָמִים	*qāmîm*
fem.	קָמָה	*qāmāh*	קָמוֹת	*qāmôṯ*

Stress is normal in these forms, being on the ultima (final syllable). Note that the fem. sing. part. is distinguished from the 3rd fem. sing. perf. only by the position of the stress: קָ֫מָה *qámāh* she arose, but קָמָ֫ה *qāmáh* arising. Given a sentence such as

הָאִישׁ קָם   hā'îš qām,

we may, unless we have the context in which the sentence occurs, translate "the man arose" (perfect) or "the man is arising" (participle). The only criterion that can be applied to an isolated sentence is that the perfect more frequently precedes its subject, while the participle follows it. The above sentence, then, without further information, is *more probably* participial.

65. The Prepositions מִן *min* and כְּ *kə* with pronominal suffixes.

מִמֶּ֫נִּי	*mimménnî*	from me	מִמֶּ֫נּוּ	*mimménnû*	from us
מִמְּךָ	*mimməkā*	from you (m. s.)	מִכֶּם	*mikkem*	from you (m. pl.)
מִמֵּךְ	*mimmēk*	from you (f. s.)	מִכֶּן	*mikken*	from you (f. pl.)
מִמֶּ֫נּוּ	*mimménnû*	from him	מֵהֶם	*mēhem*	from them (m. pl.)
מִמֶּ֫נָּה	*mimménnāh*	from her	מֵהֶן	*mēhen*	from them (f. pl.)
			מֵהֵ֫נָּה	*mēhénnāh*	

כָּמֹ֫ונִי	*kāmônî*	like me	כָּמֹ֫ונוּ	*kāmônû*	like us
כָּמֹ֫וךָ	*kāmôkā*	like you (m. s.)	כָּכֶם	*kākem*	like you (m. pl.)
כָּמֹ֫וךְ	*kāmôk*	like you (f. s.)	כָּכֶן	*kāken*	like you (f. pl.)
כָּמֹ֫והוּ	*kāmôhû*	like him	כָּהֶם	*kāhem*	like them (m. pl.)
כָּמֹ֫והָ	*kāmôhā*	like her	כָּהֶן	*kāhen*	like them (f. pl.)

The forms of the suffixed pronouns with these two prepositions are somewhat different from those already studied. Although a comparison is helpful, it is best to learn these forms as a new paradigm.

The forms *kāmônî* etc. may be used in a quasi-pronominal sense "anyone like me" etc.

אֵין כָּמֹוהוּ בָּאָרֶץ   *'ên kāmôhû ḇā'áreṣ*
> There is no one like him in the land, or
> There is not his like (or equal) in the land.

66. כֹּל **kōl.**

The word כֹּל *kōl* in one form or another corresponds variously to English "each, every, all, the whole." The uninflected form precedes the noun it modifies and may be joined with *maqqēp̄* as כָּל- *kol-* or stand independently as כֹּל *kōl*. The following examples represent typical usage. Note carefully the constructions translated with "each, every," as opposed to "all."

כָּל־יֹום	*kol-yôm*	each day, every day
כָּל־הַיֹּום	*kol-hayyôm*	all the day, the whole day, all day
כָּל־הַיָּמִים	*kol-hayyāmîm*	all the days
כָּל־עִיר	*kol-'îr*	each city, every city
כָּל־הָעִיר	*kol-hā'îr*	all the city, the whole city
כָּל־הֶעָרִים	*kol-he'ārîm*	all the cities.

The expression כָּל־אֲשֶׁר *kol-'ăšer* is used as a compound relative "everything which (or that)." As the object of a verb it is preceded by *'et-*:

נָתַן לֹו אֶת־כָּל־אֲשֶׁר קָנָה   *nātan lô 'et-kol-'ăšer qānāh*
> He gave him everything that he had acquired.

With an adjective כָּל has an indefinite pronominal sense:

כָּל־חָדָשׁ   anything new

67. Vocabulary 14.

NOUNS: כְּלִי *kəlî* (pl. irreg. כֵּלִים) vessel, utensil
     עֶרֶב *'éreḇ* evening
     שֻׁלְחָן *šulḥān* (pl. -ôt) table
     בֹּקֶר *bóqer* morning
VERBS: קָם *qām* to arise
     שָׂם *śām* to put, set, place
     בָּא *bā'* to come, enter (may be followed by a noun of place without a preposition)
     צָם *ṣām* to fast
     גָּר *gār* to sojourn
     שָׁתָה *šātāh* to drink
OTHER: עַד *'ad* (Prep.) to, as far as, by, until
     כֹּל *kōl* all, each, every

Exercises:

(a) Give the Hebrew for the following orally:

1. He is better than I.
2. There is none like us.
3. He took the money from us.
4. Have you seen a woman like her?
5. in the whole land which is before the people
6. every joy and every deliverance which I have given to you
7. all the sins which you have sinned
8. each treaty which I have made with the people
9. all the gold and all the silver
10. everything I own (lit. everything which is to me).

(b) Translate:

1. נָפַל הַמֶּֽלֶךְ אַֽרְצָה וְלֹא קָם כָּל־הַיּוֹם הַהוּא עַד־הָעֶֽרֶב.

2. שַֽׂמְנוּ אֶת־הַכֵּלִים עַל־הַשֻּׁלְחָן, הֲלֹא מְצָאתֶם אֹתָם שָׁם.

3. עָשׂוּ אֶת־הַכֵּלִים מִזָּהָב וּמִכֶּֽסֶף כִּי הֵם הָיוּ לַהֵיכָל הַגָּדוֹל אֲשֶׁר בִּירוּשָׁלַֽם.

4. בָּֽאוּ הָעָם הָעִֽירָה בְּשִׂמְחָה גְדוֹלָה כִּי לָהֶם הָיְתָה יְשׁוּעָה בַּמִּלְחָמָה.

5. צַֽמְנוּ כָל־הַיּוֹם וְלֹא אָכַֽלְנוּ לֶֽחֶם וְלֹא שָׁתִֽינוּ·מָֽיִם.

6. אֵֽלֶּה הָאֲנָשִׁים הַגָּרִים בְּתוֹךְ הָעָם הַזֶּה.

7. אֵיפֹה שַֽׂמְתָּ אֶת־הַפְּרִי אֲשֶׁר לָקַֽחְתָּ מֵהָעֵץ.

8. בָּֽאוּ כָל־הַגִּבּוֹרִים הֵֽנָּה כִּי יָדְעוּ כִּי פֹה הַמֶּֽלֶךְ.

9. שָׁתוּ הָאֲנָשִׁים מַֽיִם וְגַם־אָכְלוּ לֶֽחֶם.

10. זֶה הָאִישׁ אֲשֶׁר בְּחַרְתֶּם לָכֶם לְמֶֽלֶךְ.

(c) Write in Hebrew:

1. She did not see the men who were coming on the road toward the city.
2. The righteous are fasting day and night.
3. God has given us a great victory today.
4. He set out for Jerusalem in the evening.
5. The Lord is God, and there is none like Him in the earth and in the heavens.
6. They set a large table before the king.
7. They sat there all that night until morning.
8. Many and great are the sins that we have committed.

68. The Perfect of סָבַב sābab.

The root of this verbal type is peculiar in having identical second and third root consonants. The Perfect is as follows:

סָבַב	sābab	he went around	סָבֲבוּ	sābăbû	they went around
סָבֲבָה	sābăbāh	she went around			
סַבּוֹתָ	sabbôtā	you (m. s.) "	סַבּוֹתֶם	sabbôtem	you (m. pl.) "
סַבּוֹת	sabbôt	you (f. s.) "	סַבּוֹתֶן	sabbôten	you (f. pl.) "
סַבּוֹתִי	sabbôtî	I went around	סַבּוֹנוּ	sabbônû	we went around

Here we find a new feature: before all suffixes beginning with a consonant the stem is sabbô-. Otherwise the forms are relatively normal, but note ă for ə, in accordance with §11 (2).

When the last two root consonants are a guttural or r, the forms where we should expect doubling are replaced with ones showing compensatory lengthening.

אָרַר	'ārar	he cursed	אָרֲרוּ	'ārărû	they cursed
אָרֲרָה	'ārărāh	she cursed			
אָרוֹתָ	'ārôtā	you (m. s.) cursed	אֲרוֹתֶם	'ārôtem	you (m. pl.) cursed
אָרוֹת	'ārôt	you (f. s.) cursed	אֲרוֹתֶן	'ārôten	you (f. pl.) cursed
אָרוֹתִי	'ārôtî	I cursed	אָרוֹנוּ	'ārônû	we cursed

69. The Prepositions עִם 'im and אֶת- 'et̲ with Pronominal Suffixes.

עִמִּי	'immî	with me		עִמָּ֫נוּ	'immā́nû	with us
עִמְּךָ	'immək̲ā	with you (m. s.)		עִמָּכֶם	'immāk̲em	with you (m. pl.)
עִמָּךְ	'immāk̲	with you (f. s.)		עִמָּכֶן	'immāk̲en	with you (f. pl.)
עִמּוֹ	'immô	with him		עִמָּם	'immām	with them (m. pl.)
עִמָּהּ	'immāh	with her		עִמָּן	'immān	with them (f. pl.)

An equally common variant of the 1st pers. sing. is עִמָּדִי 'immād̲î, with me; and of עִמָּם 'immām: עִמָּהֶם 'immāhem, with them.

אִתִּי	'ittî	with me		אִתָּ֫נוּ	'ittā́nû	with us
אִתְּךָ	'ittək̲ā	with you (m. s.)		אִתְּכֶם	'ittək̲ém	with you (m. pl.)
[אִתָּךְ	'ittāk̲	with you (f. s.)]		[אִתְּכֶן	'ittək̲én	with you (f. pl.)]
אִתּוֹ	'ittô	with him		אִתָּם	'ittām	with them (m. pl.)
אִתָּהּ	'ittāh	with her		[אִתָּן	'ittān	with them (f. pl.)]

Note the curious contrast between עִמָּכֶם with ā and אִתְּכֶם with ə.

70. Final Remarks on אֲשֶׁר.

Since אֲשֶׁר is not normally governed by a preposition in Hebrew, the counterparts of English "to whom," "for whom," and the like must be expressed differently. This is accomplished by using a resumptive pronoun within the relative clause itself, as the following examples will make clear:

the man *to whom* I gave the silver → the man *who* I gave the silver *to him*
הָאִישׁ אֲשֶׁר נָתַ֫תִּי לוֹ אֶת-הַכֶּ֫סֶף   hā'îš 'ăšer nāt̲áttî lô 'et̲-hakkésep̲

the city *from which* they came → the city *which* they came *from it*
הָעִיר אֲשֶׁר יָצְאוּ מִמֶּ֫נָּה   hā'îr 'ăšer yāṣə'û mimménnāh

the man *with whom* they sat → the man *who* they sat *with him*
הָאִישׁ אֲשֶׁר יָשְׁבוּ אִתּוֹ   hā'îš 'ăšer yāšəb̲û 'ittô

If appropriate, the adverbs שָׁם and שָׁ֫מָּה may be used instead of a pronoun:

the city in which he dwelt → the city which he dwelt there
הָעִיר אֲשֶׁר יָשַׁב שָׁם   hā'îr 'ăšer yāšab̲ šām

the city to which he went → the city which he went thither
הָעִיר אֲשֶׁר הָלַךְ שָׁ֫מָּה   hā'îr 'ăšer hālak̲ šámmāh

The resumptive pronoun is optional when אֲשֶׁר refers to the direct object of the verb:

the man whom I sent → the man *who* I sent *him*
הָאִישׁ אֲשֶׁר שָׁלַ֫חְתִּי אֹתוֹ   hā'îš 'ăšer šāláḥtî 'ōt̲ô

or simply (and normally)

הָאִישׁ אֲשֶׁר שָׁלַ֫חְתִּי

In this and previous paragraphs (§§ 32, 55) we have outlined the more or less normative uses of אֲשֶׁר as a close correspondent of the English relative pronouns. Many instances of אֲשֶׁר are met, however, which do not tally with the simple treatment given here. Most of these uses can be dealt with as they are met if two general tendencies are kept in mind:

(1) אֲשֶׁר tends to take on a compound relative meaning "that which." As such, it may stand as a conjunction at the head of a clause with the force "the fact that…" and further may require the translation value of "since, because," or some other English subordinating conjunction. The exhaustive classification of all these independent pronominal and quasi-conjunctional uses is beyond the scope of an elementary grammar.

(2) Because אֲשֶׁר acquires an independent pronominal status ("that which"), it may occasionally be found with a preceding preposition, quite contrary to common usage.

Resulting from these tendencies and *in regular use as conjunctions are*

יַ֫עַן אֲשֶׁר	*yá'an 'ăšer*	because (lit. because of the fact that)
אַחֲרֵי אֲשֶׁר	*'aḥărê 'ăšer*	after
כַּאֲשֶׁר	*ka'ăšer*	as, according as, when

Finally, although most relative clauses are signalled with אֲשֶׁר, it is possible to use a clause to modify a preceding noun with no formal mark of the relationship whatever (the term asyndetic is used to describe this):

Gen. 15:13	בְּאֶ֫רֶץ לֹא לָהֶם	in a land (which is) not theirs
I Sam. 6:9	מִקְרֶה הוּא הָיָה לָּ֫נוּ	It was a chance thing (that) happened to us.

This type of relative clause in more frequent in poetry than in prose, and more frequent after an indefinite antecedent than a definite one.

71. Vocabulary 15.

NOUNS:	מִצְוָה	*miṣwāh* (pl. -ōṯ)	commandment
	אוֹר	*'ôr* (pl. -îm)	light
	חֹ֫שֶׁךְ	*ḥōšek*	darkness
	אֹיֵב	*'ōyēḇ* (pl. -îm)	enemy
VERBS:	סָבַב	*sāḇaḇ*	to surround, go around
	אָרַר	*'ārar*	to curse
	עָזַב	*'āzaḇ*	to abandon
	עָבַר	*'āḇar*	to cross (a place); to transgress (a commandment)
	יָרַשׁ	*yāraš*	to inherit
	שָׁכַח	*šāḵaḥ*	to forget
CONJUNCTION:	כַּאֲשֶׁר	*ka'ăšer*	as, according as, when

Exercises:

(a) Give the Hebrew for the following orally:

1. the vessel in which there is water
2. the man whom the king summoned
3. the house in which we found a table
4. the evening in which we ate and drank
5. the people with whom he is sojourning
6. the day during (lit. in) which we fasted
7. the cloud from which fire came forth
8. the year in which many fell in battle
9. the law in which there are blessings and wisdom
10. the heavens in which he created the sun, moon, and stars

(b) Translate:

עָבַרְנוּ אֶת־הַמִּצְוֹת אֲשֶׁר שָׁם הַנָּבִיא לִפְנֵי הָעָם. 1

הֶעָזַבְתָּ אֹתִי וְאֶת־הָעָם אֲשֶׁר אִתִּי. 2

זֹאת הָאָרֶץ אֲשֶׁר יְרַשְׁנוּ כַּאֲשֶׁר אָמַר לָנוּ הָאֱלֹהִים. 3

בַּלַּיְלָה הַהוּא חָלַמְתִּי חֲלוֹם וּבוֹ רָאִיתִי אֶת־הַכּוֹכָבִים אֲשֶׁר בַּשָּׁמָיִם. 4

הָעָם הֹלְכִים בְּחֹשֶׁךְ כִּי אֵין לָהֶם אוֹר. 5

קָרָא אֱלֹהִים לַחֹשֶׁךְ לַיְלָה וְלָאוֹר קָרָא יוֹם. 6

הָאֹיְבִים סָבְבוּ אֹתִי וְאֵין לִי יְשׁוּעָה מֵיהוה כִּי חָטָאתִי חַטָּאוֹת רַבּוֹת לַיהוה וְהוּא אָרַר אֹתִי וְאֶת־הָעָם אֲשֶׁר עִמִּי. 7

עָמַדְנוּ עַל־הַגִּבְעָה וּמִשָּׁם רָאִינוּ כִּי סָבְבוּ הָאֹיְבִים אֶת־הָעִיר וְהָרְגוּ אֶת־כָּל־הָעָם. 8

לָכְדוּ אֶת־הָעִיר וְגַם־לָקְחוּ אֶת־כָּל־הַכֵּלִים מֵהַהֵיכָל. 9

בַּבֹּקֶר עָבַר אֶת־הַנָּהָר הוּא וְכָל־הָעָם אִתּוֹ כַּמִּצְוָה אֲשֶׁר אָמַר אֱלֹהִים לָהֶם. 10

(c) Write in Hebrew:

1. Light is better than darkness.
2. Have you forgotten the words which I wrote for you in the book?
3. I have transgressed all the laws and all the commandments which you gave to me.
4. The Lord cursed the evil city and all the wicked people who were in it.
5. There are no enemies in this land.
6. The old man gave me good advice, for he knew that I had not done those evil things.

LESSON 16

72. The Construct Chain.

There is in BH no preposition having the same range of meaning expressed by English "of." The of-relationship, the genitive case of the classical languages, has its correspondent in the construct chain:

קוֹל הַנָּבִיא   *qôl hannābî'*   the voice of the prophet

מֶלֶךְ הָאָרֶץ   *mélek hā'áreṣ*   the king of the land

As these examples show, the simple juxtaposition of two nouns serves to mark a modifying relationship. The first noun in such a chain is said to be in the construct state. In more modern terminology, the first noun occurs in a bound form as opposed to the normal or free form (absolute) used elsewhere.

The construct or bound form of a noun is frequently different from the absolute. This difference has arisen mainly because of the stress situation involved: the first noun loses its primary stress and becomes proclitic to the second noun. Loss of stress may be complete, as commonly with בֶּן (note the *maqqēp̄*):

בֶּן־הַמֶּלֶךְ   *ben-hammélek*   the son of the king

but more commonly the first noun retains its stress:

מֶלֶךְ הָאָרֶץ   *mélek hā'áreṣ*   the king of the land

More important than stress difference, however, is the change in vocalization found in many words:

דְּבַר הַמֶּלֶךְ   *dəḇar hammélek*   the word of the king

This will be taken up below.

Only the final noun in a construct chain may have the definite article. The definiteness of the entire expression depends on the second noun; if it is made definite with the article or is a proper name, the first noun is also definite:

קוֹל הַנָּבִיא   *qôl hannāḇî'*   *the* voice of *the* prophet
קוֹל שְׁמוּאֵל   *qôl šəmû'ēl*   *the* voice of Samuel

as contrasted with

קוֹל נָבִיא   *qôl nāḇî'*   *a* voice of *a* prophet

Thus, the nouns of a construct chain will correspond generally to English "the ... of the ..." or "a ... of a ..." In order to express explicitly "a ... of the ...," the preposition לְ is used (often with אֲשֶׁר) with the normal (absolute) form of the noun:

דָּבָר (אֲשֶׁר) לַמֶּלֶךְ   *dāḇār ('ăšer) lammélek*   a word of the king
מִזְמוֹר לְדָוִד   *mizmôr ləDāwīḏ*   a psalm of David

Either noun of a construct chain may be pluralized. The special forms of the plural construct will be dealt with in Lesson 18. For the present note that דִּבְרֵי *diḇrê* is the construct form of דְּבָרִים:

דְּבַר הַנְּבִיאִים   *dəḇar hannəḇî'îm*   the word of the prophets
דִּבְרֵי הַנָּבִיא   *diḇrê hannāḇî'*   the words of the prophet
דִּבְרֵי הַנְּבִיאִים   *diḇrê hannəḇî'îm*   the words of the prophets

Any adjective modifying either noun must follow the entire chain. Some ambiguity may occur here, but agreement in number and gender or the general context is usually a sufficient guide. Be sure all of the following examples are clear (אֵשֶׁת and נְשֵׁי are the construct forms of אִשָּׁה and נָשִׁים respectively):

דְּבַר הַנָּבִיא הָרַע   the word of the evil prophet
                        or, the evil word of the prophet
דִּבְרֵי הַנָּבִיא הָרָעִים   the evil words of the prophet
דְּבַר הַנְּבִיאִים הָרָעִים   the word of the evil prophets
אֵשֶׁת הָאִישׁ הַטּוֹב   the wife of the good man
אֵשֶׁת הָאִישׁ הַטּוֹבָה   the good wife of the man
נְשֵׁי הָאִישׁ הַיָּפוֹת   the beautiful wives of the man
נְשֵׁי הָאֲנָשִׁים הַיָּפִים   the wives of the handsome men

The use of two adjectives, one modifying each noun, is avoided. But two adjectives may modify either noun, as in

דִּבְרֵי הַמֶּלֶךְ הַטּוֹב וְהַיָּשָׁר the words of the good and just king

דִּבְרֵי הַמֶּלֶךְ הַטּוֹבִים וְהַיְשָׁרִים the good and just words of the king

The construct chain may be extended to three or more nouns, but examples of four or more are very rare:

אֵשֶׁת בֶּן־הַנָּבִיא the wife of the son of the prophet

The same rules for definiteness and adjectival modification apply.

Occasionally, and usually with fixed expressions, the first or second noun of a construct chain may be replaced by a longer phrase. The following types are considered anomalous and should not be used in the exercises:

מֶלֶךְ הַשָּׁמַיִם וְהָאָרֶץ the king of heaven and earth
(second noun replaced by noun + noun)

דִּבְרֵי וּמַעֲשֵׂי הַמֶּלֶךְ the words and deeds of the king
(first noun replaced by noun + noun)

שִׂמְחַת בַּקָּצִיר the joy of (or in) the harvest
(preposition used with second noun; possibly a contamination with the verbal idiom *sāmē*[a]*ḥ bə* to rejoice in)

Active participles may be construed with a following object (1) as verbs

הַשֹּׁמֵר אֶת־הַתּוֹרָה the one who is (now actually) keeping the law

or (2) in a construct relationship as nouns

שֹׁמֵר הַתּוֹרָה the one who (in general) keeps the law.

As indicated, there is frequently a difference in meaning: as a verb, the reference is real and particular; as a noun, general and non-particular.

The precise meaning of the construct chain is difficult to define. While a rough translation using "of" or the possessive, as in "the king's son," will often suffice, there are many instances where an adjective or prepositional phrase is better:

לוּחַ אֶבֶן a stone tablet
לוּחַ הָאֶבֶן the stone tablet
הַר קֹדֶשׁ a holy mountain
כְּלִי מַיִם a vessel for water

The student should keep in mind the fact that in a construct chain the second noun modifies or restricts the first in some way; from this general rule he may proceed to a correct translation as demanded by the context and by proper English usage. Slavish adherence to a single translation pattern should be avoided.

73. The Form of the Construct Singular.

The construct form of a singular noun (exclusive of feminines in *-āh* and a few others) may be derived from the absolute by the application of the following rules:

(1) Unstressed *ē* and *ā* are replaced by *ə*.
(2) *ā* in a final closed syllable is replaced by *a*.
(3) *ē* in a final closed syllable usually remains unchanged, but in a small group of words is replaced by *a*.

Below are listed examples of the most frequent noun types:

	Absolute		*Construct*	*Rule applied*
יָד	*yāḏ*	יַד	*yaḏ*	2
מָקוֹם	*māqôm*	מְקוֹם	*məqôm*	1
נָבִיא	*nābî'*	נְבִיא	*nəbî'*	1
כּוֹכָב	*kôkāḇ*	כּוֹכַב	*kôkaḇ*	2
הֵיכָל	*hêkāl*	הֵיכַל	*hêkal*	2
מִשְׁפָּט	*mišpāṭ*	מִשְׁפַּט	*mišpaṭ*	2
גַּנָּב	*gannāḇ*	גַּנַּב	*gannaḇ*	2
דָּבָר	*dāḇār*	דְּבַר	*dəḇar*	1 and 2
זָקֵן	*zāqēn*	זְקַן	*zəqan*	1 and 3 (with change)
שֹׁפֵט	*šōpēṭ*	שֹׁפֵט	*šōpēṭ*	3 (without change)
לֵבָב	*lēḇāḇ*	לְבַב	*ləḇaḇ*	1 and 2
מֶלֶךְ	*mélek*	מֶלֶךְ	*mélek*	none
סֵפֶר	*sḗper*	סֵפֶר	*sḗper*	none (the *ē* is stressed)
נַעַר	*náʿar*	נַעַר	*náʿar*	none

74. Vocabulary 16.

Nouns: אֶבֶן *'éḇen* (pl. *-îm*)   stone (f.)

דָּג *dāḡ* (pl. *-îm*)   fish [The fem. דָּגָה *dāḡāh* is used as a collective term.]

חֲצִי *ḥăṣî* (no. pl.)   half

יָם *yām* (pl. יַמִּים *yammîm*) sea; note יָמָּה *yámmāh* seaward, westward.

לוּחַ *lûᵃḥ* (pl. *-ôṯ*)   tablet

מְלָאכָה *məlā(')ḵāh*   occupation, work

עוֹף *'ôp̄* (coll., no pl.)   birds, fowl

עֵשֶׂב *'ésẹḇ* (coll.)   grass, herbage

צֶלֶם *ṣélem* (pl. *-îm*)   image, likeness

VERBS: שָׁבַר šāḇar to break, smash

שָׁמַע šāma‘ to hear; + אֶל or ל to heed, listen to; + בְּ/לְקוֹל to obey.

שָׁבַת šāḇaṯ to cease, rest

OTHER: לָמָּה lámmāh Why? [Before the gutturals א, ה, and ע the form לָמָה lāmáh is preferred.]

Exercises:

(a) Form the construct singular of the following nouns (all according to rule):

אֹיֵב	אוֹר	אֶרֶץ	אִישׁ
גִּבּוֹר	גָּמָל	גַּן	בֹּקֶר
הַר	הֵיכָל	דָּבָר	דֶּרֶךְ
חֲלוֹם	חֵן	זָהָב	זָקֵן
כֶּסֶף	כִּסֵּא	יוֹם	יֶלֶד
לֶחֶם	כְּלִי	כּוֹכָב	כֶּרֶם
נָהָר	מָקוֹם	מַלְאָךְ	מֶלֶךְ
עִיר	עֶבֶד	סֵפֶר	נָבִיא
עֶרֶב	עָנָן	עֵץ	עַם
קוֹל	פְּרִי	צֹאן	צֶדֶק
	שֻׁלְחָן	שֹׁפֵט	רָעָב

(b) Give orally the Hebrew for the following:

1. a vessel of silver
2. the mountain of the Lord
3. the man's camel
4. the woman's garden
5. the temple of the city
6. the boy's dream
7. the men's silver
8. the servant's voice
9. the light of the stars
10. the child's bread
11. the river of that land

(c) Translate:

(1) פְּרִי הָעֵץ
(2) עֵץ הַגָּן
(3) גַּן הָאִישׁ הַקָּטֹן
(4) אִישׁ הָאִשָּׁה הָרַע
(5) אִישׁ הָאִשָּׁה הָרָעָה
(6) שֹׁפֵט הָעָם הַיָּשָׁר

(7) קוֹל הַנָּבִיא
(8) עֶבֶד הַמֶּלֶךְ הַטּוֹב
(9) אִישׁ הָעִיר הֶעָשִׁיר
(10) רְעַב הַדַּלִּים
(11) עֲנַן הַשָּׁמַיִם הַגָּדוֹל
(12) זְהַב הַהֵיכָל הַיָּקָר

(d) Translate:

(1) לֹא שָׁמְעוּ הָעָם לְקוֹל הַנָּבִיא כִּי הָיוּ רְשָׁעִים מְאֹד.
(2) שָׁבַר הַנָּבִיא אֶת־לוּחַ הָאֶבֶן וְלֹא נָתַן אֹתוֹ לָעָם.
(3) לָמָּה שְׁבַתֶּם מֵהַמְּלָאכָה.
(4) בָּעִיר הָרָעָה רָאִינוּ צֶלֶם גָּדוֹל וְלֹא יָדַעְנוּ מִי הוּא.

(5) הַאֲכַלְתֶּם אֶת־הַדָּגִים אֲשֶׁר נָתְנוּ לָכֶם.

(6) עוֹף הַשָּׁמַיִם יָפֶה מְאֹד.

(7) יָצָא חֲצִי הַמַּחֲנֶה לַמִּלְחָמָה.

(8) בָּאנוּ הָעִירָה וְלֹא מָצָאנוּ שָׁם אֶת־נְבִיא הָאֱלֹהִים.

(9) שָׂם הַכֹּהֵן אֶת־סֵפֶר הַתּוֹרָה עַל־הַשֻּׁלְחָן.

(10) קַמְתִּי בַבֹּקֶר וְלֹא זָכַרְתִּי אֶת־הַצֶּלֶם אֲשֶׁר רָאִיתִי בַחֲלוֹם אֲשֶׁר חָלַמְתִּי.

(11) זֶה הַמֶּלֶךְ אֲשֶׁר שָׁם הָעָם עַל־הַכִּסֵּא.

(12) בָּאָה הָאִשָּׁה לִפְנֵי הַמֶּלֶךְ וְהַמֶּלֶךְ לֹא שָׁמַע אֶל־קוֹל הָאִשָּׁה.

(13) בַּלַּיְלָה וּבְאוֹר הַיּוֹם הָעָם שֹׁמְעִים אֶל־קוֹל הָאֱלֹהִים וְהֹלְכִים בְּדֶרֶךְ יהוה כַּמִּצְוָה אֲשֶׁר נָתַן לָהֶם.

(e) <u>Write in Hebrew</u>:

1. He crossed the road of the city.
2. Why have you abandoned me to the enemy?
3. Who broke this vessel?
4. He cursed us because we forgot the word of the law.
5. The wicked king took captive the people of Jerusalem.
6. He abandoned me because I sinned against him and did not listen to him.
7. They did not rest until the evening.

LESSON 17

75. The Construct Singular: Minor Types.

(a) The two words אָב and אָח show a suffixed -*î* in the construct, with regular reduction of the stem vowel: אֲבִי *'ăḇî*, אֲחִי *'ăḥî*.

(b) All nouns of the patterns בַּיִת and מָוֶת show a regular contraction in the construct (*ayi* → *ê* and *āwe* → *ô*):

בַּיִת *báyiṯ*   constr. בֵּית *bêṯ*

מָוֶת *máweṯ*   מוֹת *môṯ*

(c) The construct form of בֵּן is commonly proclitic to the following word as ־בֶּן (with *e*). A similar form occurs for שֵׁם but is much less frequent.

(d) A few nouns outwardly identical to the type זָקֵן (constr. *zəqan*) have an unusual construct form; these include

כָּתֵף *kāṯēp̄*   constr. כֶּתֶף *kéṯep̄*   shoulder

יָרֵךְ *yārēḵ*   יֶרֶךְ *yéreḵ*   thigh

(e) Nouns ending in -*eh* have construct forms in -*ēh*. Other changes are in accordance with the rules given:

שָׂדֶה *śāḏeh*   constr. שְׂדֵה *śəḏēh*

מַחֲנֶה *maḥăneh*   מַחֲנֵה *maḥănēh*

There are quite a few other apparent exceptions to the basic rules given in

Lesson 16. None of these, however, is frequent enough to represent a type; such individual deviations will be noted in the vocabularies when necessary.

76. The Construct Singular of Feminine Nouns in -āh.

After the replacement of the ending *-āh* by *-at*, these nouns normally conform to the rules given in the preceding lesson.

שָׁנָה	*šānāh*	year	constr.	שְׁנַת	*šənat*	Rule 1
עֵצָה	*'ēṣāh*	advice		עֲצַת	*'ăṣat*	Rule 1
מַלְכָּה	*malkāh*	queen		מַלְכַּת	*malkat*	No further change
תְּבוּאָה	*təbû'āh*	produce		תְּבוּאַת	*təbû'at*	,,
תְּפִלָּה	*təpillāh*	prayer		תְּפִלַּת	*təpillat*	,,
בְּרָכָה	*bərākāh*	blessing		בִּרְכַּת	*birkat*	Rule 1 and the Rule of Shewa (§5)*
נְבֵלָה	*nəbēlāh*	corpse		נִבְלַת	*niblat*	As above.

These last two examples should be clear: the reduction of *a* to *ə* by Rule 1 would have led to *bərəkat, which, by the Rule of Shewa, becomes *birkat*.

Two types of variations from the norm are common:

(1) Most trisyllabic nouns beginning with a closed syllable have pen-ultimately stressed construct forms:

מִלְחָמָה	*milḥāmāh*	war	constr.	מִלְחֶמֶת	*milḥémet*
מִשְׁפָּחָה	*mišpāḥāh*	family		מִשְׁפַּחַת	*mišpáḥat*

(2) Sometimes the expected reduction of *ē* or *ā* to *ə* does not take place. This is by and large unpredictable and will require special note.

בְּרֵכָה	*bərēkāh*	pond	constr.	בְּרֵכַת	*bərēkat*
צָרָה	*ṣārāh*	distress		צָרַת	*ṣārat*

Most feminine nouns ending in *-at, -et, -ût, -ît*, etc., in the absolute are not susceptible to further change in the construct form. Those that are follow the rules. The construct form of אִשָּׁה is quite irregular: אֵשֶׁת *'ēšet*.

77. Vocabulary 17.

NOUNS: רָקִיעַ   *rāqîaʻ*   the firmament (apparently considered as a solid barrier by the cosmographers of Genesis)

         יַבָּשָׁה   *yabbāšāh*   dry ground

         אָב   *'āb* (pl. *-ôt*) father

         אָח   *'āḥ* (pl. irreg. אַחִים *'aḥîm*) brother

---

* Note the reversion of *k* to *k*. This is unusual; one would expect בִּרְכַת without *daghesh lene*.

בֵּן   *bēn* (pl. irreg. בָּנִים *bānîm*)   son

מַלְכָּה   *malkāh* (pl. -ôṯ)   queen

שֵׁם   *šēm* (pl. -ôṯ)   name

ADJECTIVES: רִאשׁוֹן   *rišôn*   first (fem. רִאשׁוֹנָה *rišônāh*)

שֵׁנִי   *šēnî*   second (fem. שֵׁנִית *šēnîṯ*)

שְׁלִישִׁי   *šəlîšî*   third (fem. שְׁלִישִׁית *šəlîšîṯ*)

רְבִיעִי   *rəḇî'î*   fourth (fem. רְבִיעִית *rəḇî'îṯ*)

חֲמִישִׁי   *ḥămîšî*   fifth (fem. חֲמִישִׁית *ḥămîšîṯ*)

OTHER: עַל־פְּנֵי   *'al-pənê* (prep.)   on the surface of, up against

כֵּן   *kēn* (adv.)   thus, so (referring to what has been mentioned)

Exercises:

(a) Translate:

(1) בֵּית הַנָּבִיא	(8) עֲבוֹדַת הָאִישׁ הַקָּשָׁה
(2) עֲצַת הַמֶּלֶךְ	(9) יְשׁוּעַת הַגִּבּוֹרִים
(3) שְׁנַת הַמִּלְחָמָה הַגְּדוֹלָה	(10) גִּבְעַת הָאָרֶץ הַהִיא
(4) בִּרְכַת הָאָבוֹת	(11) בֶּן־הַשֹּׁפֵט
(5) מַלְכַּת הַשָּׁמַיִם	(12) בַּת הָאִישׁ הַדַּל
(6) תּוֹרַת הָאֱלֹהִים	(13) שֵׁם הָאָרֶץ הַזֹּאת
(7) שִׂמְחַת הָעָם הַגְּדוֹלָה	(14) מַחֲנֵה הָאֹיְבִים

(b) Give orally the Hebrew for the following:

1. The rich man's field
2. the father of the king
3. the third battle of the year
4. the youngest (= small) brother of the prophet
5. the fifth word of the law
6. the blessing of the Lord
7. the wisdom of the king
8. the first house of the city
9. the firmament of the heavens
10. the image of God

(c) Reading: The Creation

[N.B. Genuine BH narrative requires the use of a verb form we shall not study until Lesson 22. The reading selections of Lessons 17 to 22 should therefore be regarded as simply sequences of isolated sentences, related in meaning but not in syntax.]

בַּיּוֹם הָרִאשׁוֹן בָּרָא אֱלֹהִים אֶת־הַשָּׁמַיִם וְאֶת־הָאָרֶץ. הָאָרֶץ הָיְתָה תֹהוּ וָבֹהוּ*וְחֹשֶׁךְ הָיָה עַל־פְּנֵי הַמָּיִם. בָּרָא אֱלֹהִים אֶת־הָאוֹר. קָרָא לָאוֹר יוֹם וְלַחֹשֶׁךְ קָרָא לַיְלָה. כֵּן עָשָׂה אֱלֹהִים בַּיּוֹם הָרִאשׁוֹן.

בַּיּוֹם הַשֵּׁנִי עָשָׂה אֱלֹהִים רָקִיעַ בְּתוֹךְ הַמַּיִם וְהָרָקִיעַ עָמַד בֵּין הַמַּיִם אֲשֶׁר תַּחַת הַשָּׁמַיִם וּבֵין הַמַּיִם אֲשֶׁר עַל־הַשָּׁמָיִם. קָרָא לָרָקִיעַ שָׁמָיִם. כֵּן עָשָׂה בַיּוֹם הַשֵּׁנִי.

בַּיּוֹם הַשְּׁלִישִׁי קִבַּץ אֱלֹהִים אֶת־הַמַּיִם אֲשֶׁר תַּחַת הַשָּׁמַיִם אֶל־מָקוֹם אֶחָד. לַיַּבָּשָׁה קָרָא אֱלֹהִים אֶרֶץ וְלַמַּיִם קָרָא יַמִּים. גַּם־בַּיּוֹם הַשְּׁלִישִׁי בָּרָא אֶת־כָּל־עֵשֶׂב הָאָרֶץ וְאֶת־כָּל־עֵץ.

(d) Write in Hebrew:

1. The house of stone did not fall.
2. The joy of the people is in the law of the Lord.
3. Half of the young men fell in the battle that day.
4. I drank the water from a stone vessel and I ate the food which was on a wooden table.
5. I sojourned with the people of that land (for) many years.
6. In the morning he set out toward-the-west.
7. The name of this king is David.

---

* *tôhû wābōhû:* a designation of the primordial chaos; "formlessness and void" is an acceptable translation for this rather obscure phrase.

78. The Construct Forms of Plural Nouns in -îm.

In the construct form of nouns having plurals in -îm, this ending is replaced by -ê. Vowel reductions take place as usual in accordance with the rules given in §73.

	Absolute		*Construct*	*Rules applied*
יָמִים	yāmîm	יְמֵי	yəmê	1
בָּנִים	bānîm	בְּנֵי	bənê	1
חִצִּים	ḥiṣṣîm	חִצֵּי	ḥiṣṣê	
עַמִּים	ʻammîm	עַמֵּי	ʻammê	
סוּסִים	sûsîm	סוּסֵי	sûsê	
זֵיתִים	zêtîm	זֵיתֵי	zêtê	
בְּכוֹרִים	bəkôrîm	בְּכוֹרֵי	bəkôrê	
גְּבוּלִים	gəbûlîm	גְּבוּלֵי	gəbûlê	
גְּמַלִּים	gəmallîm	גְּמַלֵּי	gəmallê	
דְּבָרִים	dəbārîm	דִּבְרֵי	dibrê	1 and rule of ə
אֲנָשִׁים	ʼănāšîm	אַנְשֵׁי	ʼanšê	1 and rule of ə
זְקֵנִים	zəqēnîm	זִקְנֵי	ziqnê	1 and rule of ə
כֵּלִים	kēlîm	כְּלֵי	kəlê	1
כּוֹכָבִים	kôkābîm	כּוֹכְבֵי	kôkəbê	1
הֵיכָלִים	hêkālîm	הֵיכְלֵי	hêkəlê	1
מִשְׁפָּטִים	mišpāṭîm	מִשְׁפְּטֵי	mišpəṭê	1
כֹּהֲנִים	kōhănîm	כֹּהֲנֵי	kōhănê	

Dissyllabic nouns with penultimate stress (the general type *mélek*) must be singled out for particular attention. Although all these nouns have a common *absolute* plural pattern, the *construct* form cannot be obtained by normal rules:

(a) Nouns like מֶלֶךְ (with *é*) have *a* or *i* in the stem syllable of the plural construct. The correct vowel must be learned with each word. Following is a list of all words of this group that have been introduced to this point. Hereafter the characteristic vowel of each word will be noted in the vocabularies.

מְלָכִים	מַלְכֵי	*malkê*
עֲבָדִים	עַבְדֵי	*'abdê*
כְּרָמִים	כַּרְמֵי	*karmê*
יְלָדִים	יַלְדֵי	*yaldê*
דְּרָכִים	דַּרְכֵי	*darkê*
אֲבָנִים	אַבְנֵי	*'abnê*
נְעָרִים	נַעֲרֵי	*na'ărê*

(b) Nouns like סֵפֶר (with *é*) have *i* (sometimes *e*):

סֵפֶר	סְפָרִים	סִפְרֵי	*siprê*
שֵׁבֶט	שְׁבָטִים	שִׁבְטֵי	*šibṭê* tribes
עֵדֶר	עֲדָרִים	עֶדְרֵי	*'edrê* herds

(c) Nouns like שֹׁרֶשׁ (with *ō*) have *o*:

שֹׁרֶשׁ	שָׁרָשִׁים	שָׁרְשֵׁי	*šoršê* roots

There are several nouns with irregularities in the plural construct which should be noted here:

רָאשִׁים	*rāšîm*	רָאשֵׁי	*rāšê*	No reduction
עָרִים	*'ārîm*	עָרֵי	*'ārê*	No reduction
הָרִים	*hārîm*	הָרֵי	*hārê*	No reduction

The construct forms of שָׁמַיִם and מַיִם are שְׁמֵי *šəmê* and מֵי *mê* respectively.

79. The Construct Form of Plural Nouns in -ôṯ.

The ending *-ôṯ* remains in the construct form, which is subject to the same rule (1) of reduction already cited. Here again, if nouns of the types *mélek*, *séper*, *šóreš* (or *ná'ar*, *zéra'*, *'órah*) have plurals in *-ôṯ*, the stem vowel cannot be predicted on the basis of rules.

שֵׁם	שֵׁמוֹת	שְׁמוֹת	*šəmôṯ*	Rule 1
לֵב	לִבּוֹת	לִבּוֹת	*libbôṯ*	
נֶפֶשׁ	נְפָשׁוֹת	נַפְשׁוֹת	*napšôṯ*	Unpredictable
חֶרֶב	חֲרָבוֹת	חַרְבוֹת	*ḥarbôṯ*	"

אֶרֶץ	אַרְצוֹת	אַרְצוֹת	'arṣôṯ	"
אֹרַח	אָרְחוֹת	אָרְחוֹת	'orḥôṯ	
מָקוֹם	מְקוֹמוֹת	מְקוֹמוֹת	məqômôṯ	
בְּרָכָה	בִּרְכוֹת	בִּרְכוֹת	birkôṯ	1 and rule of ə
שָׂדֶה	שְׂדוֹת	שְׂדוֹת	śəḏôṯ	1

The construct plurals of feminine nouns like גִּבְעָה and מַלְכָּה take the same vowel as the singular: גִּבְעוֹת but מַלְכוֹת.

80. Vocabulary 18.

NOUNS: אָדָם 'āḏām (1) the proper name Adam; (2) a collective term (no pl.) mankind; (3) a singular noun (no pl.) a man ['āḏām characterizes a man as opposed to what is not human, while 'îš is man as opposed to woman or child.]

אֲדָמָה 'ăḏāmāh earth, ground, soil, landed property [sometimes synonymous with 'ereṣ, which retains more of a geographical or political rather than agricultural sense]

בְּהֵמָה bəhēmāh (constr. בֶּהֱמַת behĕmaṯ) (pl. -ôṯ) beast, animal, often used collectively

רֶמֶשׂ rémeś (no pl.) a collective term for all creeping things

זָכָר zāḵār (pl. -îm) a male

נְקֵבָה nəqēḇāh a female

שַׁבָּת šabbāṯ (pl. irreg. שַׁבָּתוֹת) sabbath (f.)

ADJECTIVES: שִׁשִּׁי šiššî sixth (fem. שִׁשִּׁית šiššîṯ)

שְׁבִיעִי šəḇî'î seventh (fem. שְׁבִיעִית šəḇî'îṯ)

אַחֵר 'aḥēr other, another (fem. אַחֶרֶת 'aḥéreṯ; m. pl. אֲחֵרִים 'ăḥērîm, f. pl. אֲחֵרוֹת 'ăḥērôṯ)

VERBS: יָצַר yāṣar to form, fashion

Note: Three words often confused are

(1) חַי ḥay, an adjective whose forms are given in §22; "alive, living"

(2) חַיָּה ḥayyāh, a noun (pl. -ôṯ), used as a general term for any "living thing or animal."

(3) חַיִּים ḥayyîm, a noun used only in the plural form but with the singular meaning "life, lifetime."

Exercises:

(a) Translate the following phrases. Make sure that all construct forms are clearly understood.

(1) אַנְשֵׁי הָעִיר　　(3) אֹיְבֵי הָעָם
(2) נְשֵׁי הַמֶּלֶךְ　　(4) בָּתֵּי הָעִיר

INTRODUCTION TO BIBLICAL HEBREW

(5) גִּבְעוֹת הָאָרֶץ	(17) צַלְמֵי הָאֱלֹהִים
(6) דִּבְרֵי הַסֵּפֶר	(18) בְּנוֹת הָעָם
(7) הֵיכְלֵי הָעִיר	(19) דַּרְכֵי הֶהָרִים
(8) הָרֵי הָאָרֶץ	(20) בִּרְכוֹת הַנְּבִיאִים
(9) מַלְכֵי הָאָרֶץ	(21) גְּמַלֵּי הֶעָשִׁיר
(10) כּוֹכְבֵי הַשָּׁמַיִם	(22) גִּבּוֹרֵי הָעָם
(11) בֶּהֱמַת הַשָּׂדֶה	(23) זִקְנֵי הָעִיר
(12) חַיַּת הָאָרֶץ	(24) חֲלוֹמוֹת הַנַּעַר
(13) חַיֵּי הָאִישׁ	(25) יַלְדֵי הַנָּשִׁים
(14) אַבְנֵי הָהָר	(26) יְמֵי הַמְּלָכִים
(15) דְּגֵי הַיָּם	(27) כְּלֵי הַהֵיכָל
(16) לוּחוֹת הַתּוֹרָה	(28) מַלְאֲכֵי הַמֶּלֶךְ

(b) Give first the plural of each noun; then use the construct plural form in the given phrase.

(1) place, the places of the land
(2) camp, the camps of the enemy
(3) commandment, the commandments of the Lord
(4) river, the rivers of the land
(5) prophet, the prophets of that city
(6) book, the books of the prophets
(7) servant, the servants of the king
(8) city, the cities of the land
(9) tree, the trees of the garden
(10) judge, the judges of the people
(11) father, the fathers of the children
(12) son, the sons of the elders

(c) Reading: The Creation (concluded).

בַּיּוֹם הָרְבִיעִי בָּרָא אֱלֹהִים אֶת־הַשֶּׁמֶשׁ וְאֶת־הַיָּרֵחַ. הַשֶּׁמֶשׁ הוּא הָאוֹר הַגָּדוֹל אֲשֶׁר לַיּוֹם וְהַיָּרֵחַ הוּא הָאוֹר הַקָּטֹן אֲשֶׁר לַלָּיְלָה. עָשָׂה גַם־אֶת־הַכּוֹכָבִים וְנָתַן אֹתָם בִּרְקִיעַ הַשָּׁמָיִם.

בַּיּוֹם הַחֲמִישִׁי בָּרָא אֱלֹהִים אֶת־הַדָּגִים אֲשֶׁר בַּיַּמִּים וּבַנְּהָרוֹת וּבְכָל־הַמַּיִם הָאֲחֵרִים אֲשֶׁר עַל־הָאָרֶץ. עָשָׂה אֶת־הָעוֹף אֲשֶׁר עַל־הָאָרֶץ וְעַל־פְּנֵי רְקִיעַ הַשָּׁמָיִם.

בַּיּוֹם הַשִּׁשִּׁי עָשָׂה אֱלֹהִים אֶת־חַיַּת הָאָרֶץ אֶת־כָּל־בְּהֵמָה וְאֶת־כָּל־רֶמֶשׂ. יָצַר אֶת־הָאָדָם מֵהָאֲדָמָה בְּצֶלֶם אֱלֹהִים. זָכָר וּנְקֵבָה בָּרָא אֹתָם.

בַּיּוֹם הַשְּׁבִיעִי שָׁבַת אֱלֹהִים מִכָּל־הַמְּלָאכָה אֲשֶׁר עָשָׂה.
(הַיּוֹם הַשְּׁבִיעִי אֲשֶׁר שָׁבַת אֱלֹהִים בּוֹ הוּא יוֹם הַשַּׁבָּת.)

(d) Write in Hebrew:

1. These are the names of the children of the people who came to Jerusalem.

[80]

2. He slew the evil sons of the prophet because they had transgressed the laws of the Lord.
3. He gave money to the first woman, but to the other he gave nothing.
4. Have you seen the stars of the heaven which God placed in the firmament?
5. Where are the tablets of stone which the prophet smashed?
6. The Lord is the salvation of all peoples.

LESSON 19

81. The Independent (Subject) Form of the Personal Pronoun.

אֲנִי	'ănî	I	אֲנַ֫חְנוּ	'ănáḥnû	we
אָנֹכִי	'ānōkî	I			
אַתָּה	'attāh	you (m. s.)	אַתֶּם	'attem	you (m. pl.)
אַתְּ	'att	you (f. s.)	אַתֶּן / אַתֵּ֫נָּה	'atten, 'attḗnnāh	you (f. pl.)
הוּא	hû'	he, it (m. s.)	הֵם / הֵ֫מָּה	hēm, hḗmmāh	they (m. pl.)
הִיא	hî'	she, it (f. s.)	הֵ֫נָּה	hḗnnāh	they (f. pl.)

Remarks: Both forms of the 1st pers. sing. pronoun are very frequent, with no clear difference in meaning or range. A rare alternate of the 2nd fem. sing. is attested: אַתִּי, with final î. נַ֫חְנוּ and אָ֫נוּ occur as very rare variants of אֲנַ֫חְנוּ. The 2nd pers. fem. pl. forms are too infrequent to determine preferences; אַתֶּן is vocalized אַתֵּן in some texts. In the Pentateuch the 3rd pers. fem. sing. is spelled הוּא, i.e. the masculine form is written but the feminine form is read; the reason for this is obscure. הֵם and הֵ֫מָּה are both frequent, but show slightly different distributions: הֵם dominates in the Pentateuch, while הֵ֫מָּה is commoner in Samuel and several of the poetic books.

The independent forms of the personal pronoun are used mainly as the subjects of sentences, and mostly of non-verbal sentences:

אֲנִי טוֹב	I am good.
אֲנִי הֹלֵךְ	I am walking.
אֲנִי אִישׁ	I am a man.
אֲנִי בַּבַּ֫יִת	I am in the house.

They may be used in a variety of disjunctive ways and may stand before the verb in a verbal sentence to give emphasis to the subject. This emphasis need not be strong; it may be merely that the discourse has had a shift in subject, which would not entail any special emphasis in the English translation.

82. The Interrogative Pronouns.

(a) מִי *mî* who? Not inflected for number or gender.

מִי עָשָׂה אֶת־הַדָּבָר הַזֶּה	Who did this thing?
מִי אַתְּ	Who are you?
בַּת מִי אַתְּ	Whose daughter are you?
לְמִי נָתַתָּ אֶת־הַכֶּסֶף	To whom did you give the money?

(b) מַה *mah* what? Not inflected for number or gender.

The form of this word depends on the beginning of the following word, but in a less consistent way than was the case with the definite article or the conjunction *wə-*. The following simplified rule will cover most instances met:

(1) Before א ה ר use מָה *māh*.
(2) Before ע ח use מֶה *meh*.
(3) Elsewhere, before non-guttural consonants, use מַה *mah* plus the doubling of the first consonant of the following word.

Any of these forms may be followed by *maqqēp̄*.

Both מִי and מַה are sometimes followed by a demonstrative pronoun, better left untranslated, as in

מַה זֹּאת עָשִׂיתָ	What have you done?
מִי זֶה הוּא	Who is he?

83. The Prepositions אֶל, עַל, תַּחַת and אַחֲרֵי with Pronominal Suffixes.

These four prepositions, among others, take a set of pronominal endings quite different from those already studied.

1 c. s.	אֵלַי	*'ēlay*	עָלַי	*'ālay*
2 m. s.	אֵלֶ֫יךָ	*'ēlêḵā*	עָלֶ֫יךָ	*'ālêḵā*
2 f. s.	אֵלַ֫יִךְ	*'ēláyiḵ*	עָלַ֫יִךְ	*'āláyiḵ*
3 m. s.	אֵלָיו	*'ēlâw*	עָלָיו	*'ālâw*
3 f. s.	אֵלֶ֫יהָ	*'ēlêhā*	עָלֶ֫יהָ	*'ālêhā*
1 c. pl.	אֵלֵ֫ינוּ	*'ēlênû*	עָלֵ֫ינוּ	*'ālênû*
2 m. pl.	אֲלֵיכֶם	*'ălêḵem*	עֲלֵיכֶם	*'ălêḵem*
2 f. pl.	אֲלֵיכֶן	*'ălêḵen*	עֲלֵיכֶן	*'ălêḵen*
3 m. pl.	אֲלֵיהֶם	*'ălêhem*	עֲלֵיהֶם	*'ălêhem*
3 f. pl.	אֲלֵיהֶן	*'ălêhen*	עֲלֵיהֶן	*'ălêhen*

1 c. s.	תַּחְתַּי	*taḥtay*	אַחֲרַי	*'aḥăray*
2 m. s.	תַּחְתֶּ֫יךָ	*taḥtêḵā*	אַחֲרֶ֫יךָ	*'aḥărêḵā*
2 f. s.	תַּחְתַּ֫יִךְ	*taḥtáyiḵ*	אַחֲרַ֫יִךְ	*'aḥăráyiḵ*
3 m. s.	תַּחְתָּיו	*taḥtâw*	אַחֲרָיו	*'aḥărâw*
3 f. s.	תַּחְתֶּ֫יהָ	*taḥtêhā*	אַחֲרֶ֫יהָ	*'aḥărêhā*
1 c. pl.	תַּחְתֵּ֫ינוּ	*taḥtênû*	אַחֲרֵ֫ינוּ	*'aḥărênû*
2 m. pl.	תַּחְתֵּיכֶם	*taḥtêḵem*	אַחֲרֵיכֶם	*'aḥărêḵem*
2 f. pl.	תַּחְתֵּיכֶן	*taḥtêḵen*	אַחֲרֵיכֶן	*'aḥărêḵen*
3 m. pl.	תַּחְתֵּיהֶם	*taḥtêhem*	אַחֲרֵיהֶם	*'aḥărêhem*
3 f. pl.	תַּחְתֵּיהֶן	*taḥtêhen*	אַחֲרֵיהֶן	*'aḥărêhen*

84. Vocabulary 19.

NOUNS: נָחָשׁ *nāḥāš* (pl. -îm) snake, serpent

עֵ֫זֶר *'ézer* help, assistance

צֵלָע *ṣēlā'* (pl. -îm or -ôṯ) rib, side; the construct form is irregular: צֶ֫לַע *ṣéla'*

שִׁיר *šîr* (pl. -îm) song

בָּשָׂר *bāśār* flesh, meat; כָּל־בָּשָׂר *kol-bāśār* mankind

מָ֫וֶת *máweṯ* death

ADJECTIVES: אָרוּר *'ārûr* accursed

נֶחְמָד *neḥmāḏ* pleasant

חָכָם *ḥāḵām* wise; as noun: a wise man

VERBS: שָׁר *šār* to sing (cf. שִׁיר above)

OTHER: אֶתְמוֹל *'eṯmôl* or תְמוֹל *təmôl* (adv.) yesterday

אַחֲרֵי *'aḥărê* (prep.) after, behind; (conj.) + אֲשֶׁר after

אַחַר *'aḥar*

Exercises:

(a) Translate:

(1) אֲנַ֫חְנוּ הֹלְכִים הָעִ֫ירָה	(7) מַה־יָּצַר אֱלֹהִים מֵהָאֲדָמָה
(2) הַאַתֶּם עֹלִים יְרוּשָׁלַ֫מָה	(8) מִי זָכַר וּמִי נֶקֶבָה
(3) לָ֫מָּה אַתָּה צֹעֵק	(9) מַה־יּוֹם הַשַּׁבָּת
(4) מָה אַתְּ שֹׁתָה וּמָה אַתְּ אֹכֶ֫לֶת	(10) אֲנַ֫חְנוּ צְמֵאִים וְהֵם אֹכְלִים
(5) אֲנִי כֹתֵב אֶת־הַדְּבָרִים הָהֵם	(11) הַהֵם קֹרְאִים אֶל־הַנָּבִיא
(6) הַאַתֶּן גָּרוֹת בְּתוֹךְ הָעָם הַזֶּה	

(b) Give orally the Hebrew for the following:

1. What is the name of this man?
2. Who is the son of the rich woman?
3. What did he do on the sixth day?
4. What did he call the dry ground?

5. What did you do yesterday?
6. Did you see him yesterday?

(c) Translate:

(1) שָׁמְעוּ הַנְּעָרִים אֶל־קוֹל הַגִּבּוֹר כִּי הוּא הָיָה חָכָם מִכָּל־הָאֲנָשִׁים.

(2) יָפֶה וְנֶחְמָד הַגַּן אֲשֶׁר נָטַעְתָּ בַּמָּקוֹם הַזֶּה.

(3) אֲרוּרִים הָאֲנָשִׁים הָהֵם כִּי חָטְאוּ לַיהוה אֱלֹהִים.

(4) אָכַלְנוּ מִבְּשַׂר הַבָּקָר וּמִמֵּי הַנָּהָר שָׁתִינוּ.

(5) לָמָה לֹא נָתַתָּ אֶת־חֲצִי הַבָּשָׂר לַדַּלִּים כִּי הָיָה לָהֶם רָעָב.

(6) אַיֵּה שַׂמְתָּ אֶת־הָאֶבֶן הָאַחֶרֶת.

(7) מִי שָׁבַר אֶת־הַכֵּלִים הָאֵלֶּה אֲשֶׁר יָצַרְתִּי אֶתְמוֹל.

(8) אֵלֶּה דִּבְרֵי הַשִּׁיר אֲשֶׁר שָׁר הַמֶּלֶךְ עַל־מוֹת הַגִּבּוֹרִים הַגְּדוֹלִים.

(9) אָכְלָה הַבְּהֵמָה מֵעֵשֶׂב הַשָּׂדֶה.

(10) מָה הַמְּלָאכָה אֲשֶׁר עֲשִׂיתֶם אֶתְמוֹל.

(11) יָשְׁבוּ שָׁם כָּל־יְמֵי חַיֵּי הַנָּבִיא.

(d) Write in Hebrew:

1. God made woman from the rib of the man.
2. Who are the enemies of this people?
3. These are the words concerning the life of the great king.
4. He made the fish of the seas and the birds of the heavens.
5. In whose image (lit. in the image of whom) did God fashion man?
6. What did he place in the firmament of the heavens on the fourth day?

(e) Reading: In the Garden of Eden

קָרָא הָאָדָם שֵׁמוֹת לְכָל־הַבְּהֵמָה וּלְעוֹף הַשָּׁמַיִם וּלְכָל־חַיַּת הַשָּׂדֶה וְלָאָדָם לֹא הָיָה עֵזֶר כְּנֶגְדּוֹ.[1] בָּנָה יהוה אֱלֹהִים אֶת־הַצֵּלָע אֲשֶׁר לָקַח מִן־הָאָדָם לְאִשָּׁה.[2] הָיְתָה הָאִשָּׁה אֶת־הָאִישׁ בַּגָּן.

הַנָּחָשׁ הָיָה עָרוּם[3] מִכָּל־חַיַּת הַשָּׂדֶה אֲשֶׁר עָשָׂה יהוה אֱלֹהִים. שָׁמְעָה הָאִשָּׁה אֶל־קוֹל הַנָּחָשׁ וּמִפְּרִי[4] הָעֵץ אֲשֶׁר בְּתוֹךְ הַגָּן אָכְלָה כִּי רָאֲתָה כִּי טוֹב וְנֶחְמָד הָעֵץ. אָכַל גַּם־הָאָדָם אֶת־הַפְּרִי אֲשֶׁר נָתְנָה לוֹ הָאִשָּׁה.

אָמַר אֱלֹהִים אֶל־הָאָדָם לֵאמֹר הֲמִן־הָעֵץ אֲשֶׁר בְּתוֹךְ־הַגָּן אָכַלְתָּ. אָמַר הָאָדָם לֵאמֹר הָאִשָּׁה אֲשֶׁר נָתַתָּ עִמָּדִי הִיא נָתְנָה לִי מִן־הָעֵץ. אָמַר יהוה אֱלֹהִים לָאִשָּׁה: מַה־זֹּאת עָשִׂית. וְהִיא אָמְרָה לוֹ אֶת־כָּל־אֲשֶׁר אָמַר הַנָּחָשׁ אֵלֶיהָ. אָמַר יהוה אֶל־הַנָּחָשׁ: כִּי עָשִׂיתָ זֹּאת אָרוּר אַתָּה מִכָּל־הַבְּהֵמָה וּמִכָּל־חַיַּת הַשָּׂדֶה. יָצְאוּ הָאָדָם וְהָאִשָּׁה מִן־הַגָּן כִּי חָטְאוּ לַיהוה אֱלֹהִים.

Notes to Reading:

1. "suitable for him"
2. בָּנָה ... לְ in the sense "to build or make something into something else"
3. "crafty, shrewd"
4. Note the frequent partitive use of מִן: "some of the fruit"

85. The Noun with Pronominal Suffixes.

Pronominal possession, such as "my book," "his king," etc., is indicated in Hebrew by suffixation of the pronominal element. The forms of the pronoun attached to the singular noun are more or less the same as those used with the prepositions already studied. The major difficulty lies, as usual, in the alterations of the nominal stem rather than in the endings. Here is the paradigm of סוס (horse), the stem of which remains unchanged throughout:

סוּסִי	*sûsî*	my horse		סוּסֵנוּ	*sûsénû*	our horse
סוּסְךָ	*sûsəkā*	your (m. s.) horse		סוּסְכֶם	*sûsəkem*	your (m. pl.) horse
סוּסֵךְ	*sûsēk*	your (f. s.) horse		סוּסְכֶן	*sûsəken*	your (f. pl.) horse
סוּסוֹ	*sûsô*	his horse		סוּסָם	*sûsām*	their (m. pl.) horse
סוּסָהּ	*sûsāh*	her horse		סוּסָן	*sûsān*	their (f. pl.) horse

Special note should be made of the following points:

(1) The 2nd pers. fem. sing. and the 1st pers. com. pl. always have -ē-. Recall that the prepositions are mixed in this regard, with $\bar{a}$ in some cases (*bāk*, *lāk*, *'immāk*) and $\bar{e}$ in others (*mimmēk*). ⟨τ and ..⟩

(2) The ə of סוּסְךָ *sûsəka* should be thought of as properly part of the suffix (*sûs* + *əkā*) and not part of the noun stem. On the contrary, the ə of סוּסְכֶם *sûsəkem* and סוּסְכֶן *sûsəken* should be taken as part of the noun stem (*sûsə* + *kem*). The reason for this apparently arbitrary distinction will become clear below.

Let us next look at these same suffixes on a noun like דָּבָר:

דְּבָרִי	dəbārî	דְּבָרֵנוּ	dəbārḗnû
דְּבָרְךָ	dəbārəkā	דְּבַרְכֶם	dəbarkem
דְּבָרֵךְ	dəbārēk	דְּבַרְכֶן	dəbarken
דְּבָרוֹ	dəbārô	דְּבָרָם	dəbārām
דְּבָרָהּ	dəbārāh	דְּבָרָן	dəbārān

The shift of the stress from the noun stem to the suffix has produced the same kind of reduction we encountered in the plural and construct forms, namely, $\bar{a}$ and $\bar{e}$ in propretonic (two before the main stress) open syllables are replaced by $ə$. The 2nd pers. forms are the only ones that require comment. As suggested above, the $ə$ of -əkā is taken as part of the suffix; this leaves the final stem syllable open (də-bā-rə-kā), and the noun stem before this suffix will accordingly have in most cases the same form as the 1st pers. sing. The endings of the 2nd pers. pl., however, are -kem and -ken (without $ə$); the final syllable of the noun stem is closed (də-bar-kem) and the vowel, if possible, is shortened. The noun stem before these two suffixes is most often identical to the construct form. To understand the stem changes, then, the suffixes must be considered as of two kinds: (1) those beginning with a consonant, often called "heavy" (-kem and -ken), and (2) those beginning with a vowel (all the rest), often called "light."

Feminine nouns in -āh have -āt before the light suffixes and -at before the heavy suffixes:

תּוֹרָתִי	tôrātî my law etc.	תּוֹרָתֵנוּ	tôrātḗnû
תּוֹרָתְךָ	tôrātəkā	תּוֹרַתְכֶם	tôratkem
תּוֹרָתֵךְ	tôrātēk	תּוֹרַתְכֶן	tôratken
תּוֹרָתוֹ	tôrātô	תּוֹרָתָם	tôrātām
תּוֹרָתָהּ	tôrātāh	תּוֹרָתָן	tôrātān

Nouns with penultimate stress, like mélek and ná'ar, and certain other irregular types will be treated separately in later lessons. The following table includes most of the remaining common types of singular nouns illustrated with light and heavy suffixes. Be sure that the phonetic changes noted in the comments are clear.

Sing. Abs.		w. suff. 1 s.		w. suff. 2 pl.		Comments

Sing. Abs.	w. suff. 1 s.	w. suff. 2 pl.	Comments
1. Monosyllabic nouns:			
יָד yād	יָדִי yādî	יֶדְכֶם yedkem	Irregular; we expect yadkem.
עַם 'am	עַמִּי 'ammî	עַמְּכֶם 'amməkem	Cf. pl. stem in 'ammîm.
אֵם 'ēm	אִמִּי 'immî	אִמְּכֶם 'imməkem	Cf. pl. stem in 'immôt.
שִׁיר šîr	שִׁירִי šîrî	שִׁירְכֶם šîrəkem	

אִישׁ	'îš	אִישִׁי	'îšî	אִישְׁכֶם	'îšəkem
עִיר	'îr	עִירִי	'îrî	עִירְכֶם	'îrəkem
קוֹל	qôl	קוֹלִי	qôlî	קוֹלְכֶם	qôləkem
יוֹם	yôm	יוֹמִי	yômî	יוֹמְכֶם	yôməkem
רֹאשׁ	rō(')š	רֹאשִׁי	rō(')šî	רֹאשְׁכֶם	rō(')šəkem
סוּס	sûs	סוּסִי	sûsî	סוּסְכֶם	sûsəkem

2. Nouns with -áyi- and -áwe-:

בַּיִת	báyiṯ	בֵּיתִי	bêṯî	בֵּיתְכֶם	bêṯəkem	Note -áyi- → -ê-.
מָוֶת	máweṯ	מוֹתִי	môṯî	מוֹתְכֶם	môṯəkem	Note -áwe- → -ô-.

3. Dissyllabic nouns:

רְכוּשׁ	rəḵûš	רְכוּשִׁי	rəḵûšî	רְכוּשְׁכֶם	rəḵûšəkem	
חֲלוֹם	ḥălôm	חֲלוֹמִי	ḥălômî	חֲלוֹמְכֶם	ḥălôməkem	
דָּבָר	dāḇār	דְּבָרִי	dəḇārî	דְּבַרְכֶם	dəḇarkem	Propretonic reduction.
זָקֵן	zāqēn	זְקֵנִי	zəqēnî	זְקַנְכֶם	zəqankem	Propretonic reduction.
נָבִיא	nāḇî'	נְבִיאִי	nəḇî'î	נְבִיאֲכֶם	nəḇî'ăkem	Propr. red.; ă after gutt.
מָקוֹם	māqôm	מְקוֹמִי	məqômî	מְקוֹמְכֶם	məqôməkem	Propr. red.
כּוֹכָב	kôḵāḇ	כּוֹכָבִי	kôḵāḇî	כּוֹכַבְכֶם	kôḵaḇkem	
מִשְׁפָּט	mišpāṭ	מִשְׁפָּטִי	mišpāṭî	מִשְׁפַּטְכֶם	mišpaṭkem	
אֹיֵב	'ōyēḇ	אֹיְבִי	'ōyəḇî	אֹיִבְכֶם	'ōyiḇkem	
צַדִּיק	ṣaddîq	צַדִּיקִי	ṣaddîqî	צַדִּיקְכֶם	ṣaddîqəkem	

4. Feminine nouns in -āh:

שָׁנָה	šānāh	שְׁנָתִי	šənāṯî	שְׁנַתְכֶם	šənaṯkem	Propretonic reduction.
עֵצָה	'ēṣāh	עֲצָתִי	'ăṣāṯî	עֲצַתְכֶם	'ăṣaṯkem	Propretonic reduction.
תּוֹרָה	tôrāh	תּוֹרָתִי	tôrāṯî	תּוֹרַתְכֶם	tôraṯkem	
בִּינָה	bînāh	בִּינָתִי	bînāṯî	בִּינַתְכֶם	bînaṯkem	
חֻקָּה	ḥuqqāh	חֻקָּתִי	ḥuqqāṯî	חֻקַּתְכֶם	ḥuqqaṯkem	
גִּבְעָה	giḇ'āh	גִּבְעָתִי	giḇ'āṯî	גִּבְעַתְכֶם	giḇ'aṯkem	
אֲדָמָה	'ăḏāmāh	אַדְמָתִי	'aḏmāṯî	אַדְמַתְכֶם	'aḏmaṯkem	Propretonic reduction and Rule of Shewa.
בְּרָכָה	bərāḵāh	בִּרְכָתִי	birkāṯî	בִּרְכַתְכֶם	birkaṯkem	Propretonic reduction and Rule of Shewa.
עֲבוֹדָה	'ăḇôḏāh	עֲבוֹדָתִי	'ăḇôḏāṯî	עֲבוֹדַתְכֶם	'ăḇôḏaṯkem	
תְּפִלָּה	təp̄illāh	תְּפִלָּתִי	təp̄illāṯî	תְּפִלַּתְכֶם	təp̄illaṯkem	

The suffixes attached to the plural noun have the forms given in the preceding lesson for אֶל and עַל. When a noun plural ends in -îm, these suffixes replace the plural ending. They should thus be thought of as a fusion of the plural ending and the pronominal element:

סוּסַי	*sûsay*	my horses etc.	סוּסֵינוּ	*sûsênû*	
סוּסֶיךָ	*sûsệkā*		סוּסֵיכֶם	*sûsêkem*	
סוּסַיִךְ	*sûsáyik*		סוּסֵיכֶן	*sûsêken*	
סוּסָיו	*sûsâw*		סוּסֵיהֶם	*sûsêhem*	
סוּסֶיהָ	*sûsệhā*		סוּסֵיהֶן	*sûsêhen*	
דְּבָרַי	*dəbāray*		דְּבָרֵינוּ	*dəbārênû*	
דְּבָרֶיךָ	*dəbārệkā*		דִּבְרֵיכֶם	*dibrêkem*	
דְּבָרַיִךְ	*dəbāráyik*		דִּבְרֵיכֶן	*dibrêken*	
דְּבָרָיו	*dəbārâw*		דִּבְרֵיהֶם	*dibrêhem*	
דְּבָרֶיהָ	*dəbārệhā*		דִּבְרֵיהֶן	*dibrêhen*	

Note the stress difference when the endings of the 2nd pers. and 3rd pers. pl. are added. Here a noun with two changeable vowels will undergo the double reduction met in the plural construct form.

Nouns with plurals in -ôt add these same suffixes, but directly to the plural ending without replacement.

תּוֹרוֹתַי	*tôrôtay*	my laws etc.	תּוֹרוֹתֵינוּ	*tôrôtênû*	
תּוֹרוֹתֶיךָ	*tôrôtệkā*		תּוֹרוֹתֵיכֶם	*tôrôtêkem*	
תּוֹרוֹתַיִךְ	*tôrôtáyik*		תּוֹרוֹתֵיכֶן	*tôrôtêken*	
תּוֹרוֹתָיו	*tôrôtâw*		תּוֹרוֹתֵיהֶם	*tôrôtêhem*	
תּוֹרוֹתֶיהָ	*tôrôtệhā*		תּוֹרוֹתֵיהֶן	*tôrôtêhen*	
בִּרְכוֹתַי	*birkôtay*		בִּרְכוֹתֵינוּ	*birkôtênû*	
בִּרְכוֹתֶיךָ	*birkôtệkā* etc.		בִּרְכוֹתֵיכֶם	*birkôtêkem* etc.	

The suffix -êhem is occasionally replaced by -ām, as in אֲבֹתָם for אֲבוֹתֵיהֶם their fathers.

A complete list of noun types, under which all nouns used in this book are classified, will be found in Appendix A. When in doubt about the behavior of a noun stem before the pronominal suffixes the reader should locate the noun in the glossary and refer to the number indicated for the reference list.

The following selection of the most frequent plural types should prove adequate for most purposes:

abs. pl.		w. suff. 1 s.		w. suff. 2 m. pl.		
דָּמִים	*dāmîm*	דָּמַי	*dāmay*	דְּמֵיכֶם	*dəmêkem*	blood
בָּנִים	*bānîm*	בָּנַי	*bānay*	בְּנֵיכֶם	*bənêkem*	sons
יָמִים	*yāmîm*	יָמַי	*yāmay*	יְמֵיכֶם	*yəmêkem*	days
שָׁנִים	*šānîm*	שָׁנַי	*šānay*	שְׁנֵיכֶם	*šənêkem*	years

נָשִׁים	nāšîm	נָשַׁי	nāšay	נְשֵׁיכֶם	nəšêkem	wives
עַמִּים	'ammîm	עַמַּי	'ammay	עַמֵּיכֶם	'ammêkem	peoples
חִצִּים	ḥiṣṣîm	חִצַּי	ḥiṣṣay	חִצֵּיכֶם	ḥiṣṣêkem	arrows
שִׁירִים	šîrîm	שִׁירַי	šîray	שִׁירֵיכֶם	šîrêkem	songs
סוּסִים	sûsîm	סוּסַי	sûsay	סוּסֵיכֶם	sûsêkem	horses
עָרִים	'ārîm	עָרַי	'āray	עָרֵיכֶם	'ārêkem	cities
בָּתִּים	bāttîm	בָּתַּי	bāttay	בָּתֵּיכֶם	bāttêkem	houses
דְּבָרִים	dəbārîm	דְּבָרַי	dəbāray	דִּבְרֵיכֶם	dibrêkem	words
אֲנָשִׁים	'ănāšîm	אֲנָשַׁי	'ănāšay	אַנְשֵׁיכֶם	'anšêkem	men
זְקֵנִים	zəqēnîm	זְקֵנַי	zəqēnay	זִקְנֵיכֶם	ziqnêkem	elders
נְבִיאִים	nəbî'îm	נְבִיאַי	nəbî'ay	נְבִיאֵיכֶם	nəbî'êkem	prophets
מִשְׁפָּטִים	mišpāṭîm	מִשְׁפָּטַי	mišpāṭay	מִשְׁפְּטֵיכֶם	mišpəṭêkem	judgements
אֹיְבִים	'ōyəbîm	אֹיְבַי	'ōyəbay	אֹיְבֵיכֶם	'ōyəbêkem	enemies
בָּנוֹת	bānôt	בְּנוֹתַי	bənôtay	בְּנוֹתֵיכֶם	bənôtêkem	daughters
תּוֹרוֹת	tôrôt	תּוֹרוֹתַי	tôrôtay	תּוֹרוֹתֵיכֶם	tôrôtêkem	laws
מְלָכוֹת	məlākôt	מַלְכוֹתַי	malkôtay	מַלְכוֹתֵיכֶם	malkôtêkem	queens
גְּבָעוֹת	gəbā'ôt	גִּבְעוֹתַי	gib'ôtay	גִּבְעוֹתֵיכֶם	gib'ôtêkem	hills
מִצְוֹת	miṣwôt	מִצְוֹתַי	miṣwôtay	מִצְוֹתֵיכֶם	miṣwôtêkem	command-ments
בְּרָכוֹת	bərākôt	בִּרְכוֹתַי	birkôtay	בִּרְכוֹתֵיכֶם	birkôtêkem	blessings

Note that -ôt plurals have the same stem as the construct plural before all the suffixes, while -îm plurals have the construct plural stem only before -kem, -ken, -hem, and -hen.

A noun with a pronominal suffix is definite. Therefore

(1) a modifying adjective has the definite article:

סוּסִי הֶחָזָק   my strong horse

דְּבָרָיו הַטּוֹבִים   his good words

(2) when it is the direct object of a verb, the preposed 'et is required:

רָאִיתִי אֶת־סוּסוֹ   I saw his horse.

But when the noun refers to a part of the body 'et is frequently omitted:

שָׁלַח יָדוֹ   He put forth (lit. sent) his hand.

86. Vocabulary 20.

NOUNS: חוּץ   ḥûṣ the outside; חוּצָה ḥûṣāh and הַחוּצָה haḥûṣāh to the outside, outwards; מִחוּץ לְ miḥûṣ lə- on the outside of

      חַיִל   ḥáyil (pl. חֲיָלִים) strength; army; wealth. Very frequent in the phrase גִּבּוֹר חַיִל a warrior, fighter

      מִסְפָּר   mispār number, enumeration; אֵין מִסְפָּר לְ (are) without number, innumerable; from this idiom מִסְפָּר comes to be used alone in the sense of "numerable," i.e. "few" — e.g. אַנְשֵׁי מִסְפָּר a few men (lit. men of number)

מֶרְכָּבָה   *merkā<u>b</u>āh* (pl. מַרְכָּבוֹת) chariot

סוּס   *sûs* (pl. -îm) horse

פָּרָשׁ   *pārāš* (constr. פָּרָשׁ ; pl. פָּרָשִׁים) horseman, rider

צָבָא   *ṣā<u>b</u>ā'* (constr. צְבָא ; pl. -ôt) army, host (of soldiers, angels, celestial bodies). Also in the frequent designations of God as אֱלֹהֵי צְבָאוֹת or יהוה צְבָאוֹת

רוּחַ   *rû^aḥ* (pl. -ôt) breath, wind, spirit (f.)

צוּר   *ṣûr* (pl. -îm) rock, cliff; fig. support, defence

קָהָל   *qāhāl* assembly, congregation

קִיר   *qîr* (pl. -ôt) wall

ADJECTIVES: חָדָשׁ   *ḥā<u>d</u>āš* new

חָזָק   *ḥāzāq* strong, firm, hard

VERBS: רָכַב   *rā<u>k</u>a<u>b</u>* to ride

Exercises:

(a) Translate. Be sure you understand why the stems appear as they do.

9 זְהָבְךָ זְהַבְכֶם		1 קוֹלְךָ קֹלָהּ	
10 חָכְמָתוֹ חָכְמָתָהּ		2 זְקֵנֶיהָ זְקַנְכֶם	
11 מִצְוֺתֶיךָ מִצְוָתְךָ		3 שְׁנָתֵנוּ שָׁנֵינוּ	
12 יְשׁוּעָתֵנוּ יְשׁוּעַתְכֶם		4 שִׂמְחָתִי שִׂמְחוֹתַי	
13 נְהָרָהּ נַהֲרוֹתֶיהָ		5 כִּסְאִי כִּסְאוֹ	
14 מוֹתִי מוֹתוֹ		6 כּוֹכְבֶיהָ כּוֹכְבֵיכֶם	
15 שֻׁלְחָנְךָ שֻׁלְחָנֶךָ		7 אוֹרוֹ אוֹרָיו	
		8 אַדְמַתְכֶם אַדְמָתָם	

(b) Give the Hebrew for the following orally:

1. your (m. s.) people, your tree, your birds
2. your (m. pl.) song, your advice, your (small) cattle
3. my places, my camps, my hunger, my commandments
4. my voice, my law, my messengers, my prophet
5. his firmament, his tablet, his throne, his palace
6. his words, his fish (pl.), his camels, his blessings
7. their (f. pl.) enemies, their warriors, their death

(c) Translate:

(1) אֵין מִסְפָּר לְחֵיל הָאֹיֵב. יֵשׁ לָהֶם גִּבּוֹרִים כְּמִסְפָּר כּוֹכְבֵי הַשָּׁמָיִם.

(2) אֵין כָּל־חָדָשׁ תַּחַת הַשָּׁמֶשׁ.

(3) קָם מֶ֫לֶךְ חָדָשׁ עַל־הָאָ֫רֶץ.

(4) חָזָק הוּא מִמֶּ֫נִּי.

(5) אָנֹכִי בָא אֵלֶ֫יךָ בְּשֵׁם יהוה צְבָאוֹת.

(6) שָׁלַח הַמֶּ֫לֶךְ אֶת־סוּסָיו אֶת־מַרְכְּבוֹתָיו וְאֶת־פָּרָשָׁיו.

(7) שָׁ֫רוּ אֶת־שִׁירָם הֶחָדָשׁ לַיהוה.

(8) רָאִ֫יתִי אֶת־הַשֶּׁ֫מֶשׁ וְאֶת־הַיָּרֵ֫חַ וְאֶת־הַכּוֹכָבִים וְאֶת־כָּל־צְבָא הַשָּׁמָ֫יִם.

(9) אֵ֫לֶּה שְׁמוֹת כָּל־גִּבּוֹרֵי הַחַ֫יִל אֲשֶׁר נָפְלוּ בַּמִּלְחָמָה הַהִיא.

(10) בָּנוּ בַ֫יִת חָדָשׁ בְּעִירָם.

(11) הָרָעָב הָיָה חָזָק בָּאָ֫רֶץ וְלֹא הָיָה לֶ֫חֶם לְעָם.

(12) אָמַר אֵלָיו הַמַּלְאָךְ: יהוה עִמְּךָ גִּבּוֹר הֶחָ֫יִל.

(13) שָׁבְרָה רוּחַ גְּדוֹלָה וַחֲזָקָה אֶת־צוּרֵי הֶהָרִים.

(14) אֲרוּרִים אֲנָשֶׁ֫יךָ כִּי חָטְאוּ בְּעֵינֵי יהוה.

(15) רְאִינוּ אֶת־הָאֲנָשִׁים רֹכְבִים עַל־סוּסֵיהֶם.

(16) מִי גִבּוֹר הַחַ֫יִל הָרֹכֵב עַל־הַמֶּרְכָּבָה.

(d) Write in Hebrew:

1. He took a rib from the man and from it he made a woman.
2. The song which they sang was pleasant and good.
3. The enemy is too strong for our warriors.
4. They slew the beast and ate (from) its flesh.
5. This is a new song about horsemen, chariots, and war.
6. There is no help for our congregation.
7. The wall of their great city fell.

LESSON 21

87. Stative Verbs.

In addition to verbs like those already studied there is a much smaller group with *ē* or *ō* in the final stem syllable of the perfect. The majority of these verbs are stative, i.e. they denote the state of the subject rather than describing an action, and are translated in English mainly by adjectives:

כָּבֵד *kābēd* he is heavy, was heavy, has become heavy

זָקֵן *zāqēn* he is old, was old, has become old

There are other verbs of the regular *a*-perfect type which belong to this category on the basis of their meaning and which, to judge from other inflectional forms they exhibit, originally belonged to the stative inflectional category as well, but in the course of time have been assimilated to the dominant *a*-perfect type because their meaning shifted from a purely stative one to an action, such as

קָרַב *qārab* he is (was, has become) near; he approached.

Then too, there are verbs with perfects in *ē* which are treated as transitive active, with a direct object, such as

שָׂנֵא *śānē'* he hated.

Formally, there are *ē*-verbs in the uncomplicated triliteral class (כָּבֵד *kābēd*), in the class III-*Aleph* (מָלֵא *mālē'* to be full), and in the class of Hollow Verbs (מֵת *mēt* he died); there are *ō*-verbs in the uncomplicated triliteral class and in the hollow class (בֹּשׁ *bōš* he was ashamed). The inflection of these verbs is given below in parallel columns to facilitate comparison. The most frequent type, that of *kābēd*, is given in full as a model. The others are given with conjectured forms in parentheses since not all the forms are attested in BH.

	to be heavy		to be afraid
כָּבֵד	*kābēd*	יָרֵא	*yārē'*
כָּבְדָה	*kābǝdāh*	יָרְאָה	*yārǝ'āh*
כָּבַ֫דְתָּ	*kābádtā*	יָרֵ֫אתָ	*yārḗtā*
כָּבַדְתְּ	*kābádt*	יָרֵאת	*yārēt*
כָּבַ֫דְתִּי	*kābádtî*	יָרֵ֫אתִי	*yārḗtî*
כָּבְדוּ	*kābǝdû*	יָרְאוּ	*yārǝ'û*
כְּבַדְתֶּם	*kǝbadtem*	יְרֵאתֶם	*yǝrētem*
כְּבַדְתֶּן	*kǝbadten*	[יְרֵאתֶן]	*yǝrēten*]
כָּבַ֫דְנוּ	*kābádnû*	יָרֵ֫אנוּ	*yārḗnû*

	to die		to be able		to be ashamed
מֵת	*mēt*	יָכֹל	*yākōl*	בֹּשׁ	*bōš*
מֵ֫תָה	*mḗtāh*	יָכְלָה	*yākǝlāh*	בֹּ֫ושָׁה	*bôšāh*
מַ֫תָּה	*máttā*	יָכֹ֫לְתָּ	*yākóltā*	[בֹּ֫שְׁתָּ	*bốštā*]
[מַתְּ	*mátt*]	יָכֹלְתְּ	*yākólt*	בֹּשְׁתְּ	*bốšt*
מַ֫תִּי	*máttî*	יָכֹ֫לְתִּי	*yākóltî*	בֹּ֫שְׁתִּי	*bốštî*
מֵ֫תוּ	*mḗtû*	יָכְלוּ	*yākǝlû*	בֹּ֫שׁוּ	*bốšû*
[מַתֶּם	*mattem*]	יְכָלְתֶּם	*yǝkoltem*	[בָּשְׁתֶּם	*boštem*]
[מַתֶּן	*matten*]	יְכָלְתֶּן	*yǝkolten*	[בָּשְׁתֶּן	*bošten*]
מַ֫תְנוּ	*mátnû*	יָכֹ֫לְנוּ	*yākólnû*	בֹּ֫שְׁנוּ	*bốšnû*

Because of their non-action meaning stative verbs rarely appear in a participial form like כֹּתֵב. There is often an adjective associated with each of these verbs, frequently identical in stem form to the 3rd pers. masc. sing. of the perfect, with which it can be easily confused.

VERB			ADJECTIVE		
כָּבֵד	*kābēd*	to be heavy	כָּבֵד	*kābēd*	heavy
זָקֵן	*zāqēn*	to be old	זָקֵן	*zāqēn*	old
רָעֵב	*rā'ēb*	to be hungry	רָעֵב	*rā'ēb*	hungry
טָהֵר	*ṭāhēr*	to be pure	טָהוֹר	*ṭāhôr*	pure
קָרֵב	*qārab*	to be near	קָרֵב	*qārēb*	approaching; קָרוֹב *qārôb* near

מֵת	*mēṯ*	to die		מֵת	*mēṯ*	dead
מָלֵא	*mālē'*	to be full		מָלֵא	*mālē'*	full
קָטֹן	*qāṭōn*	to be small		קָטֹן	*qāṭōn,* קָטָן *qāṭān* small

Only in the masc. sing. is there any formal ambiguity. An isolated sentence such as

זָקֵן הָאִישׁ

may be translated verbally, "The man grew old (was old, has become old)," or adjectivally, "The man (is) old." But when the subject is feminine or plural, the distinction is clear:

זָקְנָה הָאִשָּׁה	(verbal) The woman grew old.
זְקֵנָה הָאִשָּׁה	(adjectival) The woman is old.
זָקְנוּ הָאֲנָשִׁים	(verbal) The men became old.
זְקֵנִים הָאֲנָשִׁים	(adjectival) The men are old.

There is no ambiguity, of course, when the verbal and adjectival stems are different in form.

Both verbs and adjectives may, because of their meaning, be construed with מִן in a comparative sense:

כָּבֵד הָאִישׁ מִמֶּֽנִּי   The man became more important than I.

Stative verbs from geminate roots (cf. §68) are inflected as follows in the third person:

תַּם   tam   תַּֽמּוּ   támmû   to be complete, finished
תַּֽמָּה   támmāh

The remainder of the inflection is like that of סָבַב.

88. The Nouns אָב, אָח and פֶּה.

These three nouns are similar in having *-î* in the construct singular and before suffixes. Note also the variant form of the suffixes:

abs.	אָב	*'āḇ*	father	אָח	*'āḥ*	brother	פֶּה	*peh*	mouth
constr.	אֲבִי	*'ăḇî*		אֲחִי	*'ăḥî*		פִּי	*pî*	
	אָבִי	*'āḇî*		אָחִי	*'āḥî*		פִּי	*pî*	
	אָבִֽיךָ	*'āḇîḵā*		אָחִֽיךָ	*'āḥîḵā*		פִּֽיךָ	*pîḵā*	
	אָבִיךְ	*'āḇîḵ*		אָחִיךְ	*'āḥîḵ*		פִּיךְ	*pîḵ*	
	אָבִֽיהוּ	*'āḇîhû* }		אָחִֽיהוּ	*'āḥîhû* }		פִּֽיהוּ	*pîhû* }
	אָבִיו	*'āḇîw* }		אָחִיו	*'āḥîw* }		פִּיו	*pîw* }
	אָבִֽיהָ	*'āḇîhā*		אָחִֽיהָ	*'āḥîhā*		פִּֽיהָ	*pîhā*
	אָבִֽינוּ	*'āḇînû*		אָחִֽינוּ	*'āḥînû*		פִּֽינוּ	*pînû*

אֲבִיכֶם	*’ăḇîḵem*	אֲחִיכֶם	*’ăḥîḵem*	פִּיכֶם	*pîḵem*
אֲבִיכֶן	*’ăḇîḵen*	אֲחִיכֶן	*’ăḥîḵen*	פִּיכֶן	*pîḵen*
אֲבִיהֶם	*’ăḇîhem*	אֲחִיהֶם	*’ăḥîhem*	פִּיהֶם	*pîhem*
אֲבִיהֶן	*’ăḇîhen*	אֲחִיהֶן	*’ăḥîhen*	פִּיהֶן	*pîhen*

The plural forms of אָח are noteworthy:

abs.	אַחִים	*’aḥîm*	אַחַי	*’aḥay*	אַחֵינוּ	*’aḥênû*
constr.	אֲחֵי	*’ăḥê*	אַחֶיךָ	*’aḥêḵā*	אֲחֵיכֶם	*’ăḥêḵem*
			אַחַיִךְ	*’aḥáyiḵ*	אֲחֵיכֶן	*’ăḥêḵen*
			אֶחָיו	*’eḥâw*	אֲחֵיהֶם	*’ăḥêhem*
			אַחֶיהָ	*’aḥêhā*	אֲחֵיהֶן	*’ăḥêhen*

89. Vocabulary 21.

NOUNS: פֶּה *peh* (pl. rare) mouth. Note the prepositional phrases כְּפִי, לְפִי, and עַל־פִּי with the meaning "in proportion to, according to." These may be used as conjunctions with אֲשֶׁר: כְּפִי אֲשֶׁר "according as." Note the phrase פֶּה אֶחָד "unanimity"

יָד *yāḏ* (du. יָדַיִם; pl. -ôṯ) hand, side, (fig.) force (f.)

דָּם *dām* (pl. -îm) blood

כָּבוֹד *kāḇôḏ* glory, honor, wealth

מִנְחָה *minḥāh* (pl. מְנָחוֹת) offering

VERBS: כָּבֵד *kāḇēḏ* to be heavy, important, serious; adj. כָּבֵד *kāḇēḏ*.

מָלֵא *mālē’* to be full, filled, fulfilled. No preposition is required in Hebrew: מָלְאָה הָאָרֶץ רָעָה The earth was filled *with* wickedness. Adj. מָלֵא *mālē’*, full.

מֵת *mēṯ* to die; adj. מֵת *mēṯ* dead

בֹּשׁ *bōš* to be ashamed (no corresponding adj.)

שָׁמַר *šāmar* to watch, keep, observe

עָבַד *‘āḇaḏ* to serve, work; till (the ground)

חָרָה *ḥārāh* to become angry, used impersonally with לְ: חָרָה לָאִישׁ The man became angry.

רָעָה *rā‘āh* to tend (flocks), to shepherd (+ dir. obj. or + בְּ); to graze; רֹעֶה *rō‘eh* a shepherd

PROPER NAMES: קַיִן *Qáyin* Cain

הֶבֶל *Héḇel* Abel

חַוָּה *Ḥawwāh* Eve

Exercises:

(a) Translate and identify each of the following sentences as verbal or non-verbal. Which are ambiguous?

(7) בֹּשְׁנוּ כִּי חָטָאנוּ   (1) אָבִיו מֵת

(8) הָאֲנָשִׁים מֵתִים   (2) הַכְּלִי מָלֵא דָם

(9) כָּבְדָה הָאֶבֶן מִמֶּנִּי   (3) מָלֵא הַהֵיכָל כְּבוֹד יהוה

(10) הַמַּיִם מָלְאוּ דָגִים   (4) מֵתוּ הָאֲנָשִׁים

(11) מָלֵאנוּ שִׂמְחָה   (5) הָאִשָּׁה מֵתָה

     (6) כָּבֵד הָרָעָב

(b) Translate:

(5) כְּפִי אֲשֶׁר אָמַרְתְּ   (1) כְּפִי דְבָרֶיךָ

(6) עִם־אָחִיו   (2) מִפִּי אָבִיהוּ

(7) מִתּוֹךְ אָחִי   (3) דִּבְרֵי פִּיךָ

(8) אֲחֵי אָבִינוּ   (4) לְפִי דִבְרֵי אָחִיךָ

(c) Give the Hebrew for the following orally:

1. the law of our fathers
2. the year of the death of our brother
3. The sky is full of clouds.
4. The field was full of chariots and horsemen.
5. The new vessel is full of water.
6. They were ashamed.
7. The heavens are in his hand.

(d) Write in Hebrew:

1. They served the just king many years.
2. The shepherd became angry because the men had killed his brother.
3. We have observed the law which you gave to our fathers and we have not transgressed the commandments which are therein.
4. The man's hand was full of blood.
5. The army sat outside the city, and inside the city the people cried out: "We are (as) dead (men)."
6. This matter is too serious for us.

(e) Reading: Cain and Abel.

יָדַע¹ הָאָדָם אֶת־חַוָּה. יָלְדָה חַוָּה בֵּן לְאִישָׁהּ וְקָרְאָה אֶת־שֵׁם הַיֶּלֶד קָיִן. יָלְדָה גַם־אֶת־ הֶבֶל אֲחִי קָיִן. קַיִן הָיָה עֹבֵד אֶת־הָאֲדָמָה וְהֶבֶל הָיָה רֹעֵה צֹאן. הֵבִיא² קַיִן מִפְּרִי הָאֲדָמָה מִנְחָה³ לַיהוה וְהֶבֶל הֵבִיא² גַּם־הוּא מִבְּכֹרוֹת⁴ צֹאנוֹ. הָיְתָה מִנְחַת הֶבֶל טוֹבָה בְּעֵינֵי יהוה וּמִנְחַת קַיִן לֹא הָיְתָה טוֹבָה. חָרָה לְקַיִן מְאֹד. הָרַג קַיִן אֶת־הֶבֶל אָחִיו בַּשָּׂדֶה.

אָמַר יהוה אֶל־קָיִן: אַיֵּה הֶבֶל אָחִיךָ.

אָמַר קַיִן: לֹא יָדַעְתִּי. הֲשֹׁמֵר אָחִי אָנֹכִי.

אָמַר יהוה: מֶה־עָשִׂיתָ. קוֹל דְּמֵי אָחִיךָ צֹעֲקִים⁵ אֵלַי מִן־הָאֲדָמָה, וְאַתָּה אָרוּר אַתָּה⁶ מִן־ הָאֲדָמָה אֲשֶׁר לָקְחָה אֶת־דְּמֵי אָחִיךָ מִיָּדֶךָ.

אָמַר קַיִן אֶל־יהוה: עֲוֹנִי⁷ גָּדוֹל מִמֶּנִּי.

Notes to the Reading.

1 in a sexual sense
2 "(he) brought"
3 supply "as"
4 "from the first-born of"
5 pl. by attraction to דְּמֵי ; the real subject is קוֹל .
6 repetition for emphasis: "and as for you, you are cursed (or banned)"
7 "my guilt"

LESSON 22

90. The Imperfect.

We come now to the second main inflection of the Hebrew verb, the imperfect. The imperfect, in contrast to the perfect, is primarily a prefixal conjugation, although suffixal elements are also present.

SING.	יִכְתֹּב	yiktōb	he will write
	תִּכְתֹּב	tiktōb	she will write
	תִּכְתֹּב	tiktōb	you (m. s.) will write
	תִּכְתְּבִי	tiktəbî	you (f. s.) will write
	אֶכְתֹּב	'ektōb	I shall write
PLURAL	יִכְתְּבוּ	yiktəbû	they (m. pl.) will write*
	תִּכְתֹּבְנָה	tiktóbnāh	they (f. pl.) will write
	תִּכְתְּבוּ	tiktəbû	you (m. pl.) will write
	תִּכְתֹּבְנָה	tiktóbnāh	you (f. pl.) will write
	נִכְתֹּב	niktōb	we shall write

Note that the reduction of the stem vowel from ō to ə is regular before a suffixal element consisting of a vowel. In the plural there is a formal difference in the 3rd pers. pl. (contrast the perfect) between the two genders, but the fem. pl. of the 3rd and 2nd persons are formally the same.

We shall see that in the study of the imperfect it is necessary to make

---

* A not uncommon variant has the ending -ûn with or without the reduction of the stem vowel: יִכְתְּבוּן yiktəbûn or יִכְתֹּבוּן yiktōbûn they will write.

more subdivisions among the root types than was necessary with the perfect. For example, verbs with נ, א, or י in first root position have forms which diverge considerably from those just given for the sound triliteral verb. Verbs introduced thus far in the vocabularies and inflected exactly like כָּתַב are the following:

יִזְכֹּר זָכַר	*yizkōr*	to remember	יִלְכֹּד לָכַד	*yilkōḏ*	to capture
יִכְרֹת כָּרַת	*yikrōṯ*	to cut	יִקְבֹּץ קָבַץ	*yiqbōṣ*	to gather
יִשְׁבֹּר שָׁבַר	*yišbōr*	to break	יִשְׁבֹּת שָׁבַת	*yišbōṯ*	to cease
יִשְׁמֹר שָׁמַר	*yišmōr*	to observe	יִכְתֹּב כָּתַב	*yiktōḇ*	to write

91. The Meaning of the Imperfect.

(a) Future: יִכְתֹּב he will write

(b) Habitual or customary action: יִכְתֹּב he writes (as a matter of custom), he used to write (as a matter of custom), or he will write (idem). In this usage tense is not explicit and must be gained from the context in which the verb occurs.

(c) Modal: the imperfect must frequently be translated in one of several modally modified ways, using the English equivalents "may, might, would, could, can, should." Precise directions for this translation are virtually impossible to give, since it is conditioned by the entire syntactic structure in which the verb is imbedded (conditional clause, final clause, etc.). The most important of these syntactic patterns will be considered in later lessons. In an isolated sentence the future or habitual translation is more appropriate.

With the exception of the future usage, where the action described may be quite specific, the imperfect is otherwise used to described action conceived by the speaker as general, non-specific, habitual, potential, or to some degree probable. It is not entirely accurate, however, to describe such action as incomplete or unfinished, as is often done (hence the name imperfect for the form).

The imperfect is negated with לֹא:

לֹא יִכְתֹּב   he will not write, does not write, was not accustomed to write, wouldn't write etc.

In poetry the negative אַל־ is also found: אַל יִכְתֹּב.

92. The Dual.

Nouns denoting objects which naturally occur in pairs are frequently used in a dual form, the endings of which are *-áyim*, constr. *-ê*. When suffixes are added to the dual, the resulting form is the same as that of the *-îm* plurals: e.g. יָדַי my (two) hands. Following is a list of the nouns most often encountered in the dual, with a sampling of suffixed forms.

Sing.	Dual Abs.	Constr.	With Suffixes:	
יָד	יָדַ֫יִם	יְדֵי	יָדָיו יָדֶ֫יךָ יָדַ֫יִךְ יָדַי	hand (f.)
רֶ֫גֶל	רַגְלַ֫יִם	רַגְלֵי	רַגְלֵיכֶם רַגְלֶ֫יךָ רַגְלַי	foot (f.)
[מֹתֶן]	מָתְנַ֫יִם	מָתְנֵי		loins (m.)
עַ֫יִן	עֵינַ֫יִם	עֵינֵי	עֵינָיו עֵינֶ֫יךָ עֵינַ֫יִךְ עֵינַי	eye (f.)
אֹ֫זֶן	אָזְנַ֫יִם	אָזְנֵי	אָזְנָיו אָזְנֶ֫יךָ אָזְנַ֫יִךְ אָזְנַי	ear (f.)
כָּנָף	כְּנָפַ֫יִם	כַּנְפֵי	כְּנָפָיו כְּנָפֶ֫יךָ כְּנָפַ֫יִךְ	wing (f.)
קֶ֫רֶן	קַרְנַ֫יִם/קְרָנַ֫יִם	קַרְנֵי	קַרְנָיו/קַרְנָיו	horn (f.)
שֵׁן	שִׁנַּ֫יִם	שִׁנֵּי		teeth (f.)
				(two rows)

Also the following expressions of time and measurement:

יוֹמַ֫יִם two days (יוֹם)   עַרְבַּ֫יִם two evenings (עֶ֫רֶב)

שְׁנָתַ֫יִם two years (שָׁנָה)   צָהֳרַ֫יִם noon (not *two* noons)

שְׁבוּעַ֫יִם two weeks (שָׁבוּעַ)   אַמָּתַ֫יִם two cubits (אַמָּה)

פַּעֲמַ֫יִם twice (פַּ֫עַם once)

Adjectives modifying the dual are found in the plural:

יָדַ֫יִם חֲזָקוֹת (two) strong hands (rem. יָד is feminine)

93. Vocabulary 22.

NOUNS: אֹ֫זֶן *'ózen* (du. אָזְנַ֫יִם; pl. -ôṯ) ear (f.)

רֶ֫גֶל *régel* (du. רַגְלַ֫יִם; pl. -îm) foot (f.); note the phrase בְּרַגְלֵי "belonging to, in the following of"

קֶ֫בֶר *qéber* (pl. -îm) grave, sepulchre

עַ֫יִן *'áyin* (du. עֵינַ֫יִם; pl. -ôṯ) eye; spring, well (f.)

צָהֳרַ֫יִם *ṣohŏráyim* (du. only) noon

מִצְרַ֫יִם *miṣráyim* Egypt; מִצְרַ֫יְמָה *miṣráymāh* to Egypt.

VERBS: קָבַר *qābar* (imperf. יִקְבֹּר) to bury

מָכַר *mākar* (imperf. יִמְכֹּר) to sell

שָׂרַף *śāraṗ* (imperf. יִשְׂרֹף) to burn

דָּרַשׁ *dāraš* (imperf. יִדְרֹשׁ) to inquire, seek, require

ADVERBS: פַּעֲמַ֫יִם *pa'ămáyim* twice

Exercise:

(a) Translate:

(1) יִשְׂרְפוּ אֶת־הַבַּ֫יִת   (6) תִּשְׁמְרִי אֹתִי

(2) נִזְכֹּר אֹתוֹ   (7) תִּמְכְּרוּ אֹתוֹ

(3) יִקְבְּרוּ אֹתָ֫נוּ   (8) תִּכְרְתוּ בְרִית אִתָּ֫נוּ

(4) תִּמְכֹּרְנָה אֹתָם   (9) תִּכְתְּבִי אֵלֵ֫ינוּ

(5) אֶדְרֹשׁ כֶּ֫סֶף מִמֶּ֫נּוּ   (10) יִשְׂרֹף אֹתָהּ

(b) Give the Hebrew for the following orally:

1. My (two) ears have heard.
2. Your (m. s.) (two) eyes have seen.
3. He put forth (= sent) his (two) hands.
4. Her (two) eyes are beautiful.
5. I placed them under my (two) feet.
6. The people who belong to him (lit. are in his feet) are standing.

(c) Translate:

(1) הָיָה יהוה עִם־הַמֶּלֶךְ כִּי אֶת־אֱלֹהֵי אָבִיו דָּרַשׁ וּבְמִצְוֺתָיו הָלָךְ.

(2) יִשְׂרְפוּ אֶת־הָאִשָּׁה הָרָעָה בָּאֵשׁ מִחוּץ לָעִיר.

(3) יִמְכְּרוּ אֶת־אֲחִיהֶם הַקָּטֹן בְּיַד הָאֲנָשִׁים הַיֹּרְדִים מִצְרַיְמָה.

(4) עָשָׂה הָאִישׁ אֶת־כָּל־מְלֶאכֶת עֲבוֹדַת בֵּית יהוה.

(5) בַּיּוֹם הַהוּא תִּשְׁבֹּת מִכָּל־מְלָאכָה אֲשֶׁר אַתָּה עֹשֶׂה כִּי יוֹם הַשַּׁבָּת הוּא.

(6) אֶדְרֹשׁ אֶת־יהוה כָּל־יְמֵי חַיַּי כִּי צוּרִי וִישׁוּעָתִי הוּא.

(7) הֲתִמְכְּרוּ אֹתִי בְּיַד אֹיְבָי.

(8) מַה־מְּלֶאכֶת אָחִיךָ.

(9) שָׂרְפוּ אֹיְבָיו אֶת־בֵּית יהוה וְאֶת־בֵּית הַמֶּלֶךְ וְאֶת־כָּל־בֵּית גָּדוֹל שָׂרְפוּ בָּאֵשׁ.

(10) לַיּוֹם הַהוּא קָרְאוּ שַׁבָּת כִּי בוֹ שָׁבַת יהוה מֵהַמְּלָאכָה.

(d) Write in Hebrew:

1. He will break them like a vessel.
2. I shall remember your (m. s.) commandments all the days of my life.
3. They will bury their father in the grave of his fathers.
4. What do my brothers require of (= from) me?
5. The evil sons did not (customarily) remember the words of their old father.
6. Will our enemies capture the city and its people?

LESSON 23

94. Imperfect in a.

Stative verbs of the types כָּבֵד and קָטֹן, as well as all verbs with a guttural consonant in second or third root position, have *a* instead of *ō* in the stem of the imperfect.

יִכְבַּד	yikbaḏ	יִשְׁמַע	yišmaʿ	יִבְחַר	yibḥar
תִּכְבַּד	tikbaḏ	תִּשְׁמַע	tišmaʿ	תִּבְחַר	tibḥar
תִּכְבַּד	tikbaḏ	תִּשְׁמַע	tišmaʿ	תִּבְחַר	tibḥar
תִּכְבְּדִי	tikbəḏî	תִּשְׁמְעִי	tišmə'î	תִּבְחֲרִי	tibḥărî
אֶכְבַּד	ʾekbaḏ	אֶשְׁמַע	ʾešmaʿ	אֶבְחַר	ʾebḥar
יִכְבְּדוּ	yikbəḏû	יִשְׁמְעוּ	yišmə'û	יִבְחֲרוּ	yibḥărû
תִּכְבַּדְנָה	tikbáḏnāh	תִּשְׁמַעְנָה	tišmáʿnāh	תִּבְחַרְנָה	tibḥárnāh
תִּכְבְּדוּ	tikbəḏû	תִּשְׁמְעוּ	tišmə'û	תִּבְחֲרוּ	tibḥărû
תִּכְבַּדְנָה	tikbáḏnāh	תִּשְׁמַעְנָה	tišmáʿnāh	תִּבְחַרְנָה	tibḥárnāh
נִכְבַּד	nikbaḏ	נִשְׁמַע	nišmaʿ	נִבְחַר	nibḥar

A small group of verbs, exactly like כָּתַב in the perfect, and which are neither stative nor with guttural root consonants, are nevertheless inflected with *a* in the imperfect. The most important of these are:

שָׁכַב	šākab	יִשְׁכַּב	yiškab	to lie down
לָמַד	lāmad	יִלְמַד	yilmad	to learn
רָכַב	rākab	יִרְכַּב	yirkab	to ride

[103]

95. Verbs III-Aleph: the Imperfect.

As in the perfect, the quiescence of א at the end of a syllable has led to the lengthening of the stem vowel:

יִקְרָא	*yiqrā'*	יִקְראוּ	*yiqrə'û*
תִּקְרָא	*tiqrā'*	תִּקְרֶ֫אנָה	*tiqré(')nāh*
תִּקְרָא	*tiqrā'*	תִּקְראוּ	*tiqrə'û*
תִּקְרְאִי	*tiqrə'î*	תִּקְרֶ֫אנָה	*tiqré(')nāh*
אֶקְרָא	*'eqrā'*	נִקְרָא	*niqrā'*

96. The Nouns בֵּן and שֵׁם.

These two nouns are similar in the singular before suffixes in that the stem vowel is reduced to *ə*:

בְּנִי	*bənî*	בְּנֵ֫נוּ	*bənénû*	שְׁמִי	*šəmî*	שְׁמֵ֫נוּ	*šəménû*
בִּנְךָ	*binkā*	[בִּנְכֶם	*binkem*]	שִׁמְךָ	*šimkā*	שִׁמְכֶם	*šimkem*
בְּנֵךְ	*bənēk*	[בִּנְכֶן	*binken*]	שְׁמֵךְ	*šəmēk*	[שִׁמְכֶן	*šimken*]
בְּנוֹ	*bənô*	[בְּנָם	*bənām*]	שְׁמוֹ	*šəmô*	שְׁמָם	*šəmām*
בְּנָהּ	*bənāh*	[בְּנָן	*bənān*]	שְׁמָהּ	*šəmāh*	[שְׁמָן	*šəmān*]

Remember that the plural of בֵּן is בָּנִים and that of שֵׁם is שֵׁמוֹת. There is no irregularity in these plural forms before the pronominal suffixes.

97. Vocabulary 23.

NOUNS: רְכוּשׁ   *rəkûš*   moveable property

כְּנַעֲנִי   *kəna'ănî*   Canaanite (adj. or noun)

מִזְבֵּחַ   *mizbēªḥ* (constr. מִזְבַּח ; pl. -ôt)   altar

קֶ֫דֶם   *qédem* east; מִקֶּ֫דֶם לְ   on the east of

VERBS: שָׁכַב   *šākab* (יִשְׁכַּב)   to lie down

בָּטַח   *bāṭaḥ* (יִבְטַח)   to trust, rely

גָּאַל   *gā'al* (יִגְאַל)   to redeem

שָׂמַח   *śāmaḥ* (יִשְׂמַח)   to rejoice

ADVERBS: אָז   *'āz*   then, at that time

מִשָּׁם   *miššām* = מִן + שָׁם   from there, thence

אָ֫נָה   *'ánāh*   whither? to what place?

מֵאַ֫יִן   *mē'áyin*   from where? whence?

Proper Names in the Reading:

אַבְרָם   *'Abrām*   an alternate form of אַבְרָהָם *'Abrāhām*

אוּר כַּשְׂדִּים   *'Ur Kaśdîm*   Ur of the Chaldaeans, a city in southern Mesopotamia

תֶּ֫רַח   *Téraḥ*   the father of Abraham

חָרָן   *Ḥārān*   (1) a son of Terah
(2) a city in northern Mesopotamia

שָׂרַי   *Śāray*   an alternate form of שָׂרָה *Śārāh*, the wife of Abraham

לוֹט   *Lôṭ*   Abram's nephew

כְּנַעַן   *Kənáʿan*   Canaan, a designation of the area later comprising Palestine and Phoenicia.

שְׁכֶם   *Šəkem*   Shechem, a city about 40 m. north of Jerusalem

בֵּית־אֵל   *Bêṯ-'ēl*   Bethel, a city about 15 m. north of Jerusalem

Exercises:

(a) Translate:

(1) אָנָה תִּשְׁלַח אֹתִי
(2) אֶל־מִי תִּקְרָאוּ
(3) אֵיפֹה תִּמְצֶּאנָה הַנָּשִׁים לֶחֶם לִבְנֵיהֶן וְלִבְנוֹתֵיהֶן
(4) לָמָּה תִּשְׂמַחְנָה בְּנוֹת יְרוּשָׁלַ͏ִם
(5) יִבְחֲרוּ לָהֶם בְּמֶלֶךְ

(6) לֹא אֶבְטַח בְּךָ וּבְדִבְרֵי פִיךָ
(7) מִי יִגְאַל אֹתִי מִידֵי אֹיְבִי
(8) מֵאַיִן בָּאתָ בְּנִי
(9) מִקֶּדֶם לָעִיר בָּאתִי אָבִי
(10) אָנָה אַתָּה הֹלֵךְ

(b) Give the Hebrew for the following orally:

1. our sons and our daughters
2. our little brother
3. our names
4. our father and our brother
5. our army and our horsemen
6. our congregation and our people
7. our blood
8. our offering; our offerings

(c) Translate:

(1) יִשְׂמַח כָּל־בֹּטֵחַ בְּךָ כִּי יְשׁוּעַת עַמֵּנוּ אַתָּה.
(2) יִשְׁכְּבוּ הָאֲנָשִׁים שָׁם עַד־הַבֹּקֶר.
(3) טוֹב הָאִישׁ אֲשֶׁר יִבְטַח בְּשֵׁם יהוה.
(4) יִכְבַּד שֵׁם הָאִישׁ הַזֶּה מִשֵּׁם כָּל־אִישׁ יֹשֵׁב בָּאָרֶץ הַזֹּאת.
(5) לֹא יִשְׁמְעוּ בְּנֵי הַזָּקֵן אֶל־קוֹל אֲבִיהֶם כִּי רָעִים הֵם מְאֹד.
(6) יָדַעְתִּי כִּי הוּא יִגְאַל אֶת־עַמִּי.
(7) שָׂמַחְתִּי כַּאֲשֶׁר רָאִיתִי אֶת־כָּל־אֲשֶׁר עָשָׂה לָנוּ יהוה.
(8) מִי יִגְאַל אֹתָנוּ מִיַּד הָאֹיְבִים.
(9) תִּכְבַּד הָעֲבוֹדָה עָלֶיךָ וְתִצְעַק אֵלַי בְּקוֹל גָּדוֹל וְלֹא אֶשְׁמַע לְקוֹלֶךָ.
(10) אֶבְחַר מִכֶּם אִישׁ לִי לְנָבִיא.

(d) Write in Hebrew:

1. His enemies will not find him in Egypt.
2. He will create a new heaven (m. pl.) and a new earth.
3. We have seen that his hands are strong and we know that our deliverance is in him.
4. His brothers went in-the-following-of the wicked king.

5. Our eyes have seen the glory of the Lord.
6. The stars of heaven were without number.
7. The heavens were filled with a great light.

(e) Reading: Abraham

יֵשְׁבוּ אַבְרָם בֶּן־תֶּרַח וְלוֹט בֶּן־חָרָן בֶּן־תֶּרַח בְּאוּר כַּשְׂדִּים. יָצָא תֶּרַח אֶת־אַבְרָם בְּנוֹ וְאֶת־
לוֹט בֶּן־בְּנוֹ וְאֶת־שָׂרַי אֵשֶׁת אַבְרָם לָלֶכֶתּ¹ אַרְצָה כְּנַעַן.² יֵשְׁבוּ בְחָרָן וְשָׁם מֵת תֶּרַח אֲבִי אַבְרָם.
הָלַךְ אַבְרָם מֵחָרָן כַּאֲשֶׁר אָמַר לוֹ יהוה. לָקַח אַבְרָם אֶת־שָׂרַי וְאֶת־לוֹט בֶּן־אָחִיו אִתּוֹ וְגַם־
אֶת־כָּל־הָרְכוּשׁ אֲשֶׁר הָיָה לָהֶם בְּחָרָן.

בָּאוּ אַרְצָה כְּנַעַן. עָבַר אַבְרָם בָּאָרֶץ עַד־מְקוֹם שְׁכֶם. הָיָה הַכְּנַעֲנִי אָז בָּאָרֶץ. אָמַר יהוה
אֶל־אַבְרָם בִּשְׁכֶם: אֲנִי נֹתֵן אֶת־הָאָרֶץ הַזֹּאת לְזַרְעֶךָ.³ בָּנָה אַבְרָם מִזְבֵּחַ לַיהוה שָׁם.

נָסַע מִשָּׁם הָהָרָה⁴ מִקֶּדֶם לְבֵית־אֵל. גַּם־שָׁם בָּנָה מִזְבֵּחַ וְקָרָא שָׁם בְּשֵׁם⁵ יהוה.

Notes to the Reading:

1. "to go"
2. The directive *-āh* may, as here, appear on the first member of a construct chain: "toward the land of Canaan."
3. "your progeny"
4. See §58
5. קָרָא בְּ "to call *on* the name of"

98. The Narrative Sequences.

Peculiar to Hebrew among the Semitic languages, the narrative sequences, as we shall call them, involve a complementary use of the two verbal conjugations, the perfect and the imperfect. The translation values given for the perfect (§44) and imperfect (§91) are in no way altered by the following discussion as long as the verb in question does not stand in one of the sequences we shall describe.

(a) The *Perfect + Imperfect* sequence is used mainly for past tense narration and is extremely common throughout the OT. The mark of this sequence is a special form of the conjunction, *wa* + doubling, joining the verbs in the sequence. Such sequences may continue for dozens of clauses, each of which, if it is a part of the main narrative, *begins with the verb* in the imperfect with the conjunction prefixed:

קָם הָאִישׁ וַיִּדְרשׁ... The man arose and sought...

עָמַד וַיִּקְרָא... He stood and called...

The subject need not be the same in each clause:

יָשַׁב אֵצֶל הַהֵיכָל וַיִּקְרְאוּ אֵלָיו הָעָם He sat down near the temple and the people
וַיִּשְׁמַע אֶל־קוֹלָם... called to him and he hearkened unto their
                       voice...

The form of the conjunction is illustrated by

וַיִּכְתֹּב *wayyiktōb* and he wrote   וַיִּכְתְּבוּ *wayyiktəbû* and they (m.) wrote

וַתִּכְתֹּב *wattiktōb* and she wrote, etc.   וַתִּכְתֹּבְנָה *wattiktōbnāh* and they (f.) wrote, etc.

וָאֶכְתֹּב *wā'ektōb* and I wrote   וַנִּכְתֹּב *wanniktōb* and we wrote

All past tense narrative in which each verb is temporally or logically consequent upon the preceding verb employs this sequence. The imperfects so used take on the tense value of the perfect and are said to be converted. The "perfect" value of the form *wa* + imperfect became so commonplace that it may be employed even without a perfect to begin the sequence:

וַיִּכְתֹּב הָאִישׁ אֶת־הַדְּבָרִים   (And) The man wrote the words.

The conjunction used in the narrative sequences is called the *waw*-conversive or the *waw*-consecutive, after its function.

Because every Hebrew narrative, then, contains a series of clauses beginning with "and" plus a verb, it is obviously impossible to translate literally and have acceptable English. The student should make generous use of subordinating constructions, such as adverbial clauses and participial modifiers, in his English translation, taking care only to preserve the proper logical or temporal sequence of the Hebrew.

(b) The *Imperfect + Perfect* sequence is used with all the meanings of the imperfect, whether future or habitual/durative. The conjunction before the perfect is normal and pointed according to the regular rules given in §46.

יִמְצָא אֹתוֹ וְנָתַן לוֹ אֶת־הַכֶּסֶף   He will find him and give him the money.

יִשְׂרְפוּ אֶת־הָעִיר וְלָכְדוּ אֶת־הָעָם   They will burn the city and take captive the people.

If the first imperfect is used in the habitual sense, this is carried through the sequence:

יִקְרָא אֶל־הַנָּבִיא וְאָמַר: He used to call to the prophet and say:

Note that when a negative clause is inserted in the sequence, the verb is no longer first. The verb of the negative clause is then in its normal, non-converted form:

הָלְכוּ וַיִּקְרְאוּ אֵלָיו וְלֹא שָׁמַע   They went and called to him but he did not hear.

After such an interruption the original sequence may be resumed by reverting to the converted forms. This and other complications will be dealt with below.

In the converted perfect the stress is usually shifted to the final syllable in the 1st pers. sing. and the 2nd pers. masc. sing.:

וְכָתַבְתִּי *wəkātabtî* and I shall write
וְכָתַבְתָּ *wəkātabtá* and you shall write

Pointing (vocalization) is unaffected by this shift in stress, which does not take place in all instances, especially the corresponding forms of verbs III-*Aleph* and III-*Hē*.

99. The Segholates.

Nouns with penultimate stress, like מֶלֶךְ, are collectively called segholates because of the presence of the vowel seghol (e) in one or both syllables. These nouns revert to an original one-syllable stem in the singular when a suffix is added: מַלְכִּי *malkî* my king. The vowel of the suffixal form, in this instance *a*, is the characteristic vowel of the word and also occurs in the construct plural. The four main types of segholate nouns are represented by

	Absolute	Construct	w. suff.	pl. Abs./Constr.	Pl. w. suff.	
(a)	מֶלֶךְ	מֶלֶךְ	מַלְכִּי	מְלָכִים	מְלָכַי	king
			מַלְכְּךָ	מַלְכֵי	מַלְכֵיהֶם	
			מַלְכְּכֶם			
(b)	קֶבֶר	קֶבֶר	קִבְרִי	קְבָרִים	קְבָרַי	grave
			קִבְרְךָ	קִבְרֵי	קִבְרֵיכֶם	
			קִבְרְכֶם			
(c)	סֵפֶר	סֵפֶר	סִפְרִי	סְפָרִים	סְפָרַי	book
			סִפְרְךָ	סִפְרֵי	סִפְרֵיכֶם	
			סִפְרְכֶם			
(d)	קֹדֶשׁ	קֹדֶשׁ	קָדְשִׁי	קָדָשִׁים	קָדָשַׁי	holiness
			קָדְשְׁךָ	קָדְשֵׁי	קָדְשֵׁיכֶם	
			קָדְשְׁכֶם			

Nouns with *ē* have a characteristic *i*; those in *ō* have *o*. But those with *e* may have either *a* or *i*, which must accordingly be learned with each noun. Of the nouns of this type which have occurred thus far all have a characteristic *a* (thus אֶרֶץ, דֶּרֶךְ, חֶסֶד, כֶּסֶף, כֶּרֶם, יֶלֶד, מֶלֶךְ, עֶבֶד, אֶבֶן, צֶלֶם) except קֶבֶר and צֶדֶק, which have *i* (קִבְרִי, צִדְקִי).

100. Remarks on Some Prepositions.

(a) The noun פָּנִים (face), found only in the plural (with sing. meaning) forms a part of several important prepositions:

לִפְנֵי	*lipnê*	in the presence of, before
מִפְּנֵי	*mippənê*	from the presence of, from before, because of
מִלִּפְנֵי	*millipnê*	
עַל־פְּנֵי	*'al-pənê*	on the surface of, up against

When suffixes are added the noun behaves normally (cf. the plural בָּנִים with suffixes):

לְפָנַי	ləp̄ānay	before me	לְפָנֵ֫ינוּ	ləp̄ānênû	before us
לְפָנֶ֫יךָ	ləp̄ānêḵā	before you etc.	לִפְנֵיכֶם	lip̄nêḵem	before you etc.

(b) Many prepositions, like the preceding, are compounded from a simple preposition plus a noun. Suffixes are attached according to the rule applying to the noun type in question, e.g.

עַל־דְּבַר	'al-dəḇar	because of	עַל־דְּבָרִי	'al-dəḇārî	etc.
בְּתוֹךְ	bətôḵ	in the midst of	בְּתוֹכוֹ	bətôḵô	in the midst of it
בְּקֶ֫רֶב	bəqéreḇ	in the midst of	בְּקִרְבּוֹ	bəqirbô	in the midst of it

(c) Even the simple prepositions may be compounded with one another for greater clarity. Most of these are self-explanatory:

מֵעַל	mē'al	from on	מִתַּ֫חַת	mittáḥat	from under
מֵאֵת	mē'ēt	from with, from at			

101. Vocabulary 24.

NOUNS:

קֶ֫רֶב   qéreḇ (w. suff. קִרְבִּי) inward part, midst; בְּקֶ֫רֶב (prep.) within

חֶ֫סֶד   ḥésed (w. suff. חַסְדִּי; pl. -îm) kindness; a proper act

מִדְבָּר   miḏbār (no pl.) wilderness, desert; land for grazing, not necessarily uninhabited, but away from the larger urban centers

פָּנִים   pānîm (pl. only) face

מַרְאֶה   mar'eh appearance

מִצְרִי   miṣrî (pl. מִצְרִים) Egyptian (adj. or noun); fem. מִצְרִית

מִקְנֶה   miqneh cattle, property

חֲמוֹר   ḥămôr (pl. -îm) donkey, he-ass

אָתוֹן   'ātôn (pl. -ôt) donkey, she-ass (f.)

מַגֵּפָה   maggēp̄āh (pl. -ôt) stroke, plague, affliction

נֶ֫גֶב   néḡeḇ the Negev, the southern part of Palestine; הַנֶּ֫גְבָּה toward the Negev

אָחוֹת   'āḥôt (pl. abs. not attested) sister

כֹּהֵן   kōhēn (pl. -îm) priest

VERBS: נָגַף   nāḡap̄ to strike, plague, afflict

OTHER: לְמַ֫עַן   ləmá'an (conj.) so that, in order that (+ the imperfect)

בַּעֲבוּר   ba'ăḇûr (prep.) for the sake of, because of

עַל־דְּבַר   'al-dəḇar (prep.) for the sake of, because of

Exercises:

(a) Translate:

(1) הָרְגוּ אֶת־מַלְכֵּ֫נוּ וַיִּקְבְּרוּ אֹתוֹ מִחוּץ לָעִיר.

(2) נָגַף אֱלֹהִים אֶת־הָעָם וַיִּשְׁלַח אֶת־נְבִיאוֹ אֲלֵיהֶם.

(3) לָכְדוּ אֶת־רְכוּשׁוֹ וַיִּשְׂרְפוּ אֶת־בֵּיתוֹ.

(4) יִקְרְאוּ אֵלָיו וְלָקְחוּ אֹתוֹ וּמָכְרוּ אֹתוֹ בִּידֵי אֹיְבָיו.

(5) בָּאוּ אֶל־בֵּית הָאִשָּׁה וַיִּשְׁכְּבוּ שָׁם כָּל־הַלַּיְלָה.

(6) שָׁמַעְנוּ אֶל־קוֹלֶךְ וַנִּבְטַח בִּדְבָרֶיךָ.

(7) קָמוּ וַיִּבְחֲרוּ לָהֶם מֶלֶךְ.

(8) בַּצָּהֳרַיִם נִרְכַּב עַל־חֲמוֹרֵינוּ הַמִּדְבָּרָה.

(9) תִּקְרְאוּ בְּקוֹל גָּדוֹל וְסַבּוֹתֶם אֶת־הָעִיר פַּעֲמָיִם.

(10) הֲלֹא שָׁמַעְתָּ בְּאָזְנֶיךָ אֶת־דִּבְרֵי נְבִיאִי.

(11) טוֹבָה אַרְצֵנוּ וְטוֹבִים כְּרָמֵינוּ.

(12) נִשְׁבֹּר אֶת־צַלְמוֹ.

(13) זָכַרְנוּ אֶת־חַסְדְּךָ אֲשֶׁר עָשִׂיתָ אִתָּנוּ.

(14) הָאֵלֶּה יְלָדָיִךְ.

(b) <u>Give the Hebrew</u> for the following orally:

    1. his book, his books
    2. his money, his gold
    3. his ear, his foot
    4. his way, his ways
    5. his enemy, his judges

Repeat the preceding with "her" for "his."

(c) <u>Translate</u>:

(1) נָגַף יהוה אֶת־מֶלֶךְ־מִצְרַיִם כִּי עָשָׂה אֶת־הָרַע בְּעֵינָיו.

(2) בָּעֶרֶב שָׂמָה הָאִשָּׁה לֶחֶם וּמַיִם לְפָנָיו עַל־הַשֻּׁלְחָן וְלֹא אָכַל וְלֹא שָׁתָה.

(3) בָּאוּ הַבַּיְתָה וַיִּשְׁכְּבוּ שָׁם עַד־הַבֹּקֶר.

(4) לָקְחוּ הַכֹּהֲנִים אֶת־הַבָּשָׂר מֵעַל־הַמִּזְבֵּחַ.

(5) קָבְרוּ אֶת־אֲבִיהֶם בַּמָּקוֹם אֲשֶׁר קָבַר בּוֹ אֲבִיהֶם אֶת־אָבִיהוּ.

(6) הָלְכוּ הָאֲנָשִׁים אֶל־הַהֵיכָל וַיִּקְרְאוּ בְּקוֹל גָּדוֹל לִפְנֵי הַמֶּלֶךְ וַיִּשְׁמַע הַמֶּלֶךְ אֶל־קוֹלָם.

(7) אֶשְׁלַח אֶת־הַכֶּסֶף אֵלֶיךָ בַּעֲבוּר בִּנְךָ הַקָּטֹן.

(8) עָשִׂיתָ חֶסֶד עִמָּנוּ וְעִם־עַמֵּנוּ.

(9) לָקְחוּ אֶת־אֲחִיהֶם וַיִּמְכְּרוּ אֹתוֹ בִּידֵי הָאֲנָשִׁים הַיֹּרְדִים מִצְרַיְמָה וְהֵם מָכְרוּ אֹתוֹ בִּידֵי הַמִּצְרִים.

(10) רָכַב עַל־חֲמוֹרוֹ הָעִירָה וּבְנוֹ אִתּוֹ.

(d) Write in Hebrew:

    1. She became angry and smashed all the vessels which were in the house.
    2. He went outside the city to the fields and sought his brothers there and he found them near the river.
    3. You have not observed the treaty which you made with us.
    4. We are fasting that God may hear our words and give (seq. with "hear") us deliverance from the enemy.
    5. He will capture the nations with a strong hand and the wise men of the earth will come in order to hear his words.

(e) Reading: Abraham in Egypt

יָרַד אַבְרָהָם מִצְרַיְמָה כִּי כָבֵד הָרָעָב בְּאֶרֶץ כְּנָעַן. אָמַר אַבְרָהָם לְשָׂרָה כַּאֲשֶׁר בָּאוּ מִצְרָיְמָה: יָדַ֫עְתִּי כִּי אִשָּׁה יְפַת מַרְאֶה[1] אָתְּ. יִרְאוּ[2] אֹתָךְ הַמִּצְרִים וְאָמְרוּ אֵשֶׁת הָאִישׁ הַהוּא זֹאת וְהָרְגוּ אֹתִי וְלָקְחוּ אֹתָךְ. אִמְרִי[3] כִּי אֲחוֹתִי אָתְּ לְמַ֫עַן יִיטַב לִי[4] בַּעֲבוּרֵךְ.

כֵּן עָשְׂתָה שָׂרָה כַּאֲשֶׁר בָּאוּ מִצְרָיְמָה. אָמְרָה אֶל־הַמִּצְרִים כַּדְּבָרִים אֲשֶׁר אָמַר לָהּ אִישָׁהּ. לָקְחוּ הַמִּצְרִים אֹתָהּ אֶל־בֵּית פַּרְעֹה וְלֹא הָרְגוּ אֶת־אַבְרָהָם. נָתְנוּ לְאַבְרָהָם צֹאן וּבָקָר וַחֲמוֹרִים וַעֲבָדִים וּשְׁפָחוֹת וַאֲתֹנוֹת וּגְמַלִּים בַּעֲבוּר שָׂרָה.

נָגַף יהוה אֶת־פַּרְעֹה מַגֵּפוֹת גְּדֹלוֹת[5] עַל־דְּבַר שָׂרָה אֵשֶׁת אַבְרָהָם וַיִּקְרָא פַרְעֹה לְאַבְרָהָם לֵאמֹר: מַה־זֹּאת עָשִׂיתָ לִּי. לָמָה אָמַ֫רְתָּ אֲחוֹתִי הִיא. וַיְשַׁלַּח[6] אֶת־אַבְרָהָם וְאֶת־שָׂרָה וְאֶת־כָּל־אֲשֶׁר לוֹ. עָלָה אַבְרָהָם מִמִּצְרַיִם הוּא וְשָׂרָה וְכָל־אֲשֶׁר־לוֹ וְלוֹט עִמּוֹ הַנֶּ֫גְבָּה. אַבְרָהָם כָּבֵד מְאֹד בַּמִּקְנֶה בַּכֶּ֫סֶף וּבַזָּהָב.

Notes to the Reading:

1. Note the adj. in construct with a specifying noun: "beautiful in appearance."
2. "They will see". Note the beginning of an imperfect sequence.
3. "Say" (imperative)
4. "it will go well for me"
5. Note the use, very frequent in Semitic, of a cognate object, "to strike a striking." It is best to translate: "struck the Pharaoh *with* great plagues"
6. "and he expelled"

LESSON 25

102. The Imperative.

The basic stem of the Imperative is always closely related to that of the imperfect and can be deduced from it.

	IMPERFECT		IMPERATIVE
יִכְתֹּב	*yiktōb*	כְּתֹב	*kətōb*
יִשְׁכַּב	*yiškab*	שְׁכַב	*šəkab*
יִשְׁמַע	*yišmaʿ*	שְׁמַע	*šəmaʿ*
יִבְחַר	*yibḥar*	בְּחַר	*bəḥar*
יִקְרָא	*yiqrāʾ*	קְרָא	*qərāʾ*

The endings of the imperative are the same as those on the second person forms of the imperfect:

	SING.	PLURAL
masc.	—	-û
fem.	-î	-nāh

But when -î and -û are added to the stem, it is altered as follows:

כְּתֹב	*kətōb*	כִּתְבִי	*kitbî*	כִּתְבוּ	*kitbû*	כְּתֹבְנָה	*kətōbnāh*
שְׁכַב	*šəkab*	שִׁכְבִי	*šikbî*	שִׁכְבוּ	*šikbû*	שְׁכַבְנָה	*šəkábnāh*
שְׁמַע	*šəmaʿ*	שִׁמְעִי	*šimʿî*	שִׁמְעוּ	*šimʿû*	שְׁמַעְנָה	*šəmáʿnāh*
בְּחַר	*bəḥar*	בַּחֲרִי	*baḥărî*(!)	בַּחֲרוּ	*baḥărû*(!)	בְּחַרְנָה	*bəḥárnāh*
קְרָא	*qərāʾ*	קִרְאִי	*qirʾî*	קִרְאוּ	*qirʾû*	קְרֶאנָה	*qəré(ʾ)nāh*(!)

[113]

The suffix -āh occurs frequently on the masc. sing. imperative with no striking modification of meaning. The stem usually appears with o before this suffix:

כָּתְבָה   *koṯbāh*   write! (m. s.)

but verbs with a-imperfects often have i, as in שִׁכְבָה lie down; שִׁלְחָה send. The negative of the imperative is

(a) אַל + imperfect: for immediate, specific commands, such as "Don't go!" "Don't wait!" etc.

(b) לֹא + imperfect: for durative, non-specific: "you shall not do such-and-such (ever)."

The particle נָא may follow any imperative form, as in

קְרָא נָא   שִׁמְעִי נָא   שְׁלַח נָא

It is frequently joined with *maqqēp̄*, which means that the verb surrenders its primary stress to the particle. The pattern of שְׁמֹר נָא with *maqqēp̄* is

שְׁמָר־נָא   *šəmor-nā'*

נָא may also be added to the אַל of the negative imperative:

אַל־נָא תִּשְׁלַח   Do not send!

This particle may be translated as "please", "I pray," or the like, but is most often best ignored.

103. Verbs I-guttural: Imperfect and Imperative.

The two basic types of imperfect for this class are represented by

(a) עָבַד imperf. יַעֲבֹד *ya'ăḇōḏ* imperat. עֲבֹד *'ăḇōḏ* to serve

(b) חָזַק יֶחֱזַק *yeḥĕzaq* חֲזַק *ḥăzaq* to be strong

Verbs with ō-imperfects have a in the prefixal element (except in 1st pers. sing.); those with a-imperfects have e. The imperfect in each of these main types has developed a secondary vowel after (under) the guttural root consonant. In inflection the *Rule of Shewa* must apply: thus, expected יַעֲמְדוּ *ya'ămədu* becomes יַעַמְדוּ *ya'amdû* (note retention of *ḏ*), and similarly elsewhere:

יַעֲמֹד	*ya'ămōḏ*	יַעַמְדוּ	*ya'amdû*	יֶחֱזַק	*yeḥĕzaq*	יֶחֶזְקוּ	*yeḥezqû*
תַּעֲמֹד	*ta'ămōḏ*	תַּעֲמֹדְנָה	*ta'ămōḏnāh*	תֶּחֱזַק	*teḥĕzaq*	תֶּחֱזַקְנָה	*teḥĕzáqnāh*
תַּעֲמֹד	*ta'ămōḏ*	תַּעַמְדוּ	*ta'amdû*	תֶּחֱזַק	*teḥĕzaq*	תֶּחֶזְקוּ	*teḥezqû*
תַּעַמְדִי	*ta'amdî*	תַּעֲמֹדְנָה	*ta'ămōḏnāh*	תֶּחֶזְקִי	*teḥezqî*	תֶּחֱזַקְנָה	*teḥĕzáqnāh*
אֶעֱמֹד	*'e'ĕmōḏ*	נַעֲמֹד	*na'ămōḏ*	אֶחֱזַק	*'eḥĕzaq*	נֶחֱזַק	*neḥĕzaq*

The inflection of the imperative offers no special problems:

עֲבֹד *'ăḇōḏ*	עִבְדִי *'iḇḏî*	עִבְדוּ *'iḇḏû*	עֲבֹדְנָה *'ăḇōḏnāh*		
חֲזַק *ḥăzaq*	חִזְקִי *ḥizqî*	חִזְקוּ *ḥizqû*	חֲזֹקְנָה *ḥăzáqnāh*		

There are several verbs where no secondary vowel is present. The inflection, except for the vowel of the preformative, follows the regular pattern of יִכְתֹּב or יִכְבַּד. E.g.

יַחְשֹׁב *yaḥšōḇ*   he will reckon   תֶּהְדַּר *tehdar*   you will honor

יַחְשְׁבוּ *yaḥšəḇû*   they will·reckon

The verb חָטָא, both I-gutt. and III-*Aleph*, combines the features of each type:

יֶחֱטָא *yeḥĕṭā'*			יֶחֶטְאוּ *yeḥeṭ'û*	
תֶּחֱטָא *teḥĕṭā'*			תֶּחֱטֶאנָה *teḥĕṭé(')nāh*	
תֶּחֱטָא *teḥĕṭā'*			תֶּחֶטְאוּ *teḥeṭ'û*	
תֶּחֶטְאִי *teḥeṭ'î*			תֶּחֱטֶאנָה *teḥĕṭé(')nāh*	
אֶחֱטָא *'eḥĕṭā'*			נֶחֱטָא *neḥĕṭā'*	

104. The Segholates (cont.)

The main types of segholates are slightly modified when gutturals occur in the root.

(a) Guttural in first position: only the type סֵפֶר is affected; the characteristic vowel is *e* instead of *i*:

עֶדֶר	עֶדֶר	עֶדְרִי	עֲדָרִים	עֲדָרַי	flock
		עֶדְרְךָ	עֲדָרֶי		
		עֶדְרְכֶם			

(b) Guttural in second root position:

נַעַר	נַעַר	נַעֲרִי	נְעָרִים	נְעָרַי	young man
		נַעַרְךָ	נְעָרֶי	נַעֲרֵיכֶם	
		נַעַרְכֶם			
תֹּאַר	תֹּאַר	תָּאֳרִי	no pl. attested		form
		תָּאָרְךָ			
		תָּאָרְכֶם			

Note especially the forms before the heavy suffixes and -*kā*.

(c) Guttural in third root position:

זֶרַע	זֶרַע	זַרְעִי	זְרָעִים	זְרָעַי	seed
		זַרְעֲךָ	זְרָעֶי	זַרְעֵיכֶם	
		זַרְעֲכֶם			
זֶבַח	זֶבַח	זִבְחִי	זְבָחִים	זְבָחַי	sacrifice
		זִבְחֲךָ	זְבָחֶי	זִבְחֵיכֶם	
		זִבְחֲכֶם			

way (f.)	אָרְחוֹתַי	אָרְחוֹת	אָרְחִי	אֹרַח	אֹרַח
	אָרְחוֹתֵיכֶם	אָרְחוֹת	אָרְחֲךָ		
			אָרְחֲכֶם		

105. Vocabulary 25.

NOUNS: צָרָה ṣārāh (pl. -ôṯ) distress, trouble [The first vowel is not reduced; constr. צָרַת]

גְּבֶרֶת gəḇéreṯ (pl. not attested) mistress, lady [With suff. גְּבִרְתִּי]

עֵדֶר 'éḏer (pl. -îm) flock, herd

זֶרַע zéra' (pl. -îm) seed, offspring, progeny, descendants

VERBS: יָרֵא yārē' (§ 87) to be afraid (of מִן or מִפְּנֵי or with simple object construction)

בָּרַח bāraḥ (יִבְרַח) to flee

שָׁב šāḇ to return, go or come back

הָרָה hārāh to conceive, become pregnant

OTHER: אֵי־מִזֶּה 'ê-mizzeh (adv.) from what place? from where? [May also be used adjectivally: אֵי־מִזֶּה עִיר from what city?]

פֶּן־ pen- (conj.) lest, so that not [followed by imperfect]

כַּיּוֹם kayyôm today, this day

נָא nā(') particle used after imperatives, cohortatives, and jussives; see §§ 102, 136.

Exercises:

(a) Translate:

(7) אַל־תַּעֲזֹב אֶת־כֹּהֲנֶיךָ	(1) דִּרְשׁוּ אֶת־יהוה
(8) עִבְרוּ אֶת־הַשָּׂדֶה עַד־הַכֶּרֶם	(2) קְבֹץ נָא אֶת־הָעָם לְפָנַי
(9) דְּרָשׁ־נָא כַּיּוֹם אֶת־דְּבַר יהוה	(3) לִכְדוּ אֶת־עָרֵי אֹיְבֵיכֶם
(10) לֹא תַעַבְרוּ אֶת־מִצְוֺת יהוה	(4) קְבֹר אֹתָם שָׁם
(11) אַל־תַּעֲמְדִי שָׁם	(5) רְכְבִי אֵלָיו עַל־סוּסֵךְ
(12) שִׁלַּחְנָה אֶת־הָאָתוֹן אֵלַי	(6) אַל־תִּכְרְתוּ בְרִית אִתָּם

(b) Give the Hebrew for the following orally:

1. Where is your sister?
2. Do not sin against the Lord.
3. Do not kill those men.
4. Send me my books.
5. Gather the priests and the prophets.
6. Do not cross over toward the Negev.
7. Sell these vessels.
8. Redeem your servant.
9. Send your maidservants to me.
10. Abandon your sinful ways.

(c) Translate:

(1) תִּשְׁמַע אֶל־קוֹלִי וְשַׁבְתָּ הָעִירָה פֶּן־יַהַרְגוּ אֹתְךָ אֹיְבֶיךָ.

(2) תַּעַמְדוּ פֹה וּשְׁמַעְתֶּם אֶת־דִּבְרֵי גְבִרְתְּכֶם.

(3) נַעֲבֹר אֶת־הָאָרֶץ וְיָשַׁבְנוּ עַד־הַיָּם.

(4) אֶרְכַּב הָהָרָה וְהָרַגְתִּי אֶת־הָאֲנָשִׁים הָרָעִים הַיֹּשְׁבִים שָׁם.

(5) תִּקְבֹּץ אֶת־הָעָם לְפָנַי וְאָמַרְתִּי אֲלֵיהֶם כַּדְּבָרִים הָאֵלֶּה.

(6) שָׁכַב הַנַּעַר וַיַּחֲלֹם חֲלוֹם.

(7) לֹא תֶחֶטְאוּ לַיהוה אֱלֹהֵיכֶם.

(d) Write in Hebrew:

1. I shall abandon my flock and return to the city.
2. They will serve the Lord all the days of their life.
3. I shall ride to the city on my donkey so that I may sell this property.
4. Because of you they will kill me and take my possessions for them (selves).
5. His sister is beautiful in appearance.
6. At that time the Canaanite dwelt east of this place up to the desert.
7. He is an old man and has no offspring.
8. I am afraid of you and your men.

(e) Reading: Sarah and Hagar

שָׂרָה אֵשֶׁת אַבְרָהָם לֹא יָלְדָה לוֹ וְלָהּ שִׁפְחָה מִצְרִית וּשְׁמָהּ הָגָר.¹ נָתְנָה שָׂרָה אֶת־הָגָר שִׁפְחָתָהּ הַמִּצְרִית לְאַבְרָהָם אִישָׁהּ לוֹ לְאִשָּׁה.² בָּא אַבְרָהָם אֶל־הָגָר³ וְהִיא הָרָתָה. חָרָה לְשָׂרָה כַּאֲשֶׁר רָאֲתָה כִּי הָרָתָה הָגָר.

יָרְאָה הָגָר מִפְּנֵי שָׂרָה גְבִרְתָּהּ וַתִּבְרַח הַמִּדְבָּרָה.

מַלְאַךְ יהוה מָצָא אֹתָהּ עַל־עֵין הַמַּיִם⁴ בַּמִּדְבָּר. אָמַר הַמַּלְאָךְ: הָגָר שִׁפְחַת שָׂרָה אֵי־מִזֶּה בָאת וְאָנָה אַתְּ הֹלֶכֶת. אָמְרָה הָגָר: מִפְּנֵי שָׂרָה גְבִרְתִּי אָנֹכִי בֹּרַחַת. אָמַר לָהּ מַלְאַךְ יהוה: שׁוּבִי⁵ אֶל־גְּבִרְתֵּךְ. אֶת־שֵׁם הַבֵּן אֲשֶׁר אַתְּ יֹלֶדֶת תִּקְרְאִי יִשְׁמָעֵאל כִּי שָׁמַע יהוה אֶל־צָרָתֵךְ. שָׁבָה הָגָר אֶל־שָׂרָה גְבִרְתָּהּ. יָלְדָה הָגָר לְאַבְרָהָם בֵּן וַיִּקְרָא אַבְרָהָם שֵׁם בְּנוֹ אֲשֶׁר יָלְדָה הָגָר יִשְׁמָעֵאל.

Notes to the Reading:

1. Note the series of non-verbal (thus non-consecutive) clauses taking their tense value from the general context.
2. The לוֹ is superfluous in translation, since it simply reinforces לְאַבְרָהָם. It could, however, be retained thus: "...(to act) as a wife for him."
3. בָּא אֶל־ is frequently used of a man approaching a woman for sexual intercourse.
4. The definite article frequently appears where the narrator has a specific object in mind even though it has not been previously mentioned.
5. "return" (imperative)

LESSON 26

106. The Jussive and Cohortative.

The imperfect, with or without slight modifications, may be used in an indirect imperative sense in all persons. For example,

יִשְׁלַח he will send or let him send

תִּשְׁלַח you will send or may you send

אֶשְׁלַח I shall send or let me send

The third person forms, singular and plural, so used are called jussives. In the verbs we have studied thus far these are identical in form to the imperfect. The first person indirect imperative, called the cohortative, is usually marked with a suffix -āh on the imperfect:

אֶשְׁלַח	ʾešlaḥ	I shall send	נִשְׁלַח	nišlaḥ	we shall send
אֶשְׁלְחָה	ʾešləḥāh	let me send	נִשְׁלְחָה	nišləḥāh	let us send

Note that the vowel of the imperfect is regularly reduced to ə before this suffix. The cohortative form may replace the normal imperfect in a perfect + imperfect narrative sequence with no apparent change in meaning.

107. Sequences involving the Imperative, Jussive, and Cohortative.

In meaning these three form a single paradigm: jussive = 3rd pers., imperative = 2nd pers., cohortative = 1st person. The sequences involving one are usually similar to or the same as sequences involving the others. The following three sequences are the most frequently met:

(a) *Imperative + Imperative.* Imperatives may be simply listed one after the other and joined by the required regular form of the conjunction:

שְׁמַע... וּשְׁלַח... וַעֲמֹד...   hear ... and send ... and stand ...

Verbs joined in this way may or may not be consequent on one another.

(b) *Imperative + Perfect.* Explicit consecution is expressed by this sequence, which is the analog of the *imperfect + perfect* narrative sequence:

שְׁמַע וְשָׁלַחְתָּ וְעָמַדְתָּ   hear ... and (then) send ... and (then) stand ...

(c) Imperative
   Jussive   } + { Imperfect
   Cohortative   Cohortative   This important sequence

usually has a special translation value, which should be carefully noted. The second clause expresses a purpose or result (Eng. "so that"):

שְׁמַע... וְאֶשְׁלַח   Hear ... so that I may send
כְּתֹב... וְאֶשְׁמַע   Write ... so that I may hear
נֵלְכָה...וְיִמְצָא   Let us go ... so that he may find

Note that the conjunction *wə-* has its normal, non-converting form here.

108. Verbs I-Aleph: Imperfect and Related Forms.

Verbs I-*Aleph* fall into two groups in the imperfect:

(a) Five verbs regularly have *ō* in the preformative, with quiescence of the א:

אָכַל	'ākal	יֹאכַל	yō(')kal	to eat
אָמַר	'āmar	יֹאמַר	yō(')mar	to say
אָבַד	'ābad	יֹאבַד	yō(')bad	to perish

The other two, אָפָה (to bake) and אָבָה (to be willing), will be treated under verbs III-*Hē*. The inflection of the imperfect is otherwise normal:

יֹאכַל	yōkal	יֹאכְלוּ	yōkəlû
תֹּאכַל	tōkal	תֹּאכַלְנָה	tōkálnāh
תֹּאכַל	tōkal	תֹּאכְלוּ	tōkəlû
תֹּאכְלִי	tōkəlî	תֹּאכַלְנָה	tōkálnāh
אֹכַל	'ōkal	נֹאכַל	nōkal

Note that only one א is written in the 1st pers. sing.
When preceded by *waw*-conversive the forms תֹּאמַר, יֹאמַר, and נֹאמַר are replaced by forms with *e*, with a retraction of the stress:

[119]

וַיֹּאמֶר *wayyṓmer* and he said

וַתֹּאמֶר *wattṓmer* and she (or you, m. s.) said

וַנֹּאמֶר *wannṓmer* and we said

But when these stand at the end of a clause, immediately preceding what is said, the regular form with *a* may be used. Contrast:

וַיֹּאמֶר אֵלָיו: שְׁמַע And he said to him: "Hear."

וַיֹּאמַר: שְׁמַע And he said: "Hear."

(b) Other verbs I-*Aleph* resemble the class of I-guttural verbs, e.g.

אָסַר *'āsar* יֶאֱסֹר *ye'ĕsōr* (or יֶאְסֹר *ye'sōr*) to bind

but with *e* in the preformative regardless of the stem vowel. In the inflection the *e* is replaced by *a* when the *Rule of Shewa* is applied. This is in contrast to verbs I-guttural with *e*:

יֶחֱזַק *yeḥĕzaq* but יֶאֱסֹר *ye'ĕsōr*

יֶחֶזְקוּ *yeḥezqû* יַאַסְרוּ *ya'asrú*

A few verbs show conflicting forms due to mixing. Among the most frequently met are אָחַז (to hold), which has imperfect יֶאֱחֹז and יֹאחֵז (note the anomalous *ē*), and אָהַב (to love), whose attested forms are

יֶאֱהַב *ye'ĕhab* ——

תֶּאֱהַב *te'ĕhab* ——

תֶּאֱהַב *te'ĕhab* תֶּאֱהֲבוּ read *tēhăbû*

אֱהַב אֹהַב *'ĕhab* or *'ōhab* ——

All regular verbs I-*Aleph*, whether of type (a) or (b), have the same forms in the imperative:

אֱסֹר *'ĕsōr* אִסְרִי *'isrî* אִסְרוּ *'isrû* אֱסֹרְנָה *'ĕsṓrnāh*

אֱמֹר *'ĕmōr* אִמְרִי *'imrî* אִמְרוּ *'imrû* אֱמֹרְנָה *'ĕmṓrnāh*

109. Vocabulary 26.

NOUNS: בֶּגֶד *bégeḏ* (בִּגְדִי; pl. -*îm*) garment

שַׁעַר *šá'ar* (pl. -*îm*) gate (of a city or large building); also refers to the space inside the city gate used by officials for public meetings.

אָסִיר *'āsîr* (pl. -*îm*) prisoner

VERBS: אָבַד *'āḇaḏ* (יֹאבַד) to perish, be destroyed, die

אָחַז *'āḥaz* (יֹאחֵז) or (יֶאֱחֹז) to seize, grasp, take hold of

אָסַר *'āsar* (יֶאֱסֹר) to bind, fetter, take prisoner

אָהַב *'āhaḇ* (יֶאֱהַב) to love

קָרַע *qāra'* (יִקְרַע)   to tear, rend
פָּתַח *pātaḥ* (יִפְתַּח)   to open
סָגַר *sāḡar* (יִסְגֹּר)   to close
גָּדַל *gāḏal* (יִגְדַּל)   to be/become great; to grow up, reach maturity

Exercises:

(a) Translate:

אֶשְׁכְּבָה (1)		וּסְגֹר . . . פְּתַח (6)	
נִדְרְשָׁה (2)		וְכִתְבִי . . . קִרְאִי (7)	
יִזְכֹּר (3)		וּשְׂרַפְתֶּם . . . שִׁבְרוּ (8)	
נִשָּׁבְרָה (4)		וִידַעְתֶּם . . . שִׁמְעוּ (9)	
אֶשְׁבְּתָה (5)		וְתִשְׁמְעוּ . . . עִמְדוּ (10)	

(b) Give the Hebrew for the following orally:

1. Let us make a treaty.
2. Let him eat the fish.
3. Let us seize their property.
4. Let him smash the tablets of stone.
5. Let us chose a king for ourselves (= us).
6. May his name become great throughout (= in) the entire land.
7. May they hear our words and know that we are good men.
8. Let me hear the words which the prophet spoke.

(c) Translate:

(1) קָרַע הַמֶּלֶךְ אֶת־בְּגָדָיו וַיֹּאמַר: תֹּאבַד הָעִיר וְאָסְרוּ הָאֹיְבִים אֶת־עַמָּהּ.

(2) בַּבֹּקֶר יִפְתְּחוּ אֶת־שַׁעַר הָעִיר וּבְרַחְתֶּם עִמָּנוּ הָהָרָה פֶּן־יִמְצְאוּ אֶתְכֶם וְהָרְגוּ אֶתְכֶם.

(3) נִשְׁלָחָה אֹתוֹ אֶל־הַמִּלְחָמָה וְיֹאבַד שָׁם.

(4) אִסְרוּ אֹתָם וּלְקַחְתֶּם אֹתָם הַחוּצָה.

(5) סִגְרוּ אֶת־שַׁעַר הָעִיר כִּי בָא הָאֹיֵב עָלֵינוּ.

(6) תֶּאֱהַב אֶת־אִמְּךָ וְאֶת־אָבִיךָ.

(7) יֹאבְדוּ הָרְשָׁעִים כִּי אֵין לָהֶם יְשׁוּעָה.

(8) וַיֹּאמֶר הַנָּבִיא: יוֹם רַע בָּא וְנָגַף אֱלֹהִים אֶתְכֶם וְאֶת־בְּנֵיכֶם כִּי לֹא שְׁמַעְתֶּם אֶל־קוֹל נְבִיאוֹ וְלֹא שְׁמַרְתֶּם אֶת־מִצְוֹת הַתּוֹרָה.

(9) אֱחֹז אֶת־חֲצִי הַכֶּסֶף לְךָ וְנָתַתָּ לִי אֶת־הַחֲצִי הָאַחֵר.

(10) לֹא תֹאכְלוּ מֵעוֹף הַשָּׁמָיִם.

(11) נֹאמְרָה אֶל־הַמֶּלֶךְ כִּי הָעֲבוֹדָה קָשָׁה מִמֶּנּוּ.

(12) יֹאחֲזוּ אֶת־הַזָּהָב וְנָתְנוּ אֹתוֹ לַאֲחֵרִים.

(d) Write in Hebrew:

1. Let us close the gates and remain (= dwell) in the city until morning.
2. Why did he break the tablets and say that we had sinned against the Lord?

3. Remember (m. pl.) these words lest you sin.
4. He loved the woman because she was beautiful in appearance.
5. They will tear their garments on that day, for the enemy will bind them and they will go with the other prisoners to another country and dwell there (for) many years.

110. Temporal Clauses and Phrases.

Within a narrative sequence temporal modifiers are very frequently placed before the clause they modify and are introduced by *waw-conversive* + a form of the verb הָיָה. In the past tense narrative this is uniformly וַיְהִי *wayhî* (יְהִי *yəhî* is the imperfect form of הָיָה) and in the future (or habitual/durative) narrative it is וְהָיָה *wəhāyāh*. The temporal clause is then followed by the expected sequential form of the main narrative. Study the following examples carefully (all are to be taken as though imbedded in a narrative):

וַיְהִי בַבֹּקֶר וַיִּשְׁלַח...	and in the morning he sent...
וַיְהִי אַחֲרֵי הַדְּבָרִים הָאֵלֶּה וַיִּשְׁמַע קוֹל..	and after these things he heard a voice...
וַיְהִי כַּאֲשֶׁר רָאָה אֹתָם וַיִּקְרָא...	and when he saw them he cried out...
וְהָיָה כִּי תִשְׁמְעוּ אֶת־הַדְּבָרִים הָאֵלֶּה וּזְכַרְתֶּם...	and whenever you hear these words you shall remember...
וְהָיָה בַבֹּקֶר וִיצָאתֶם...	and in the morning you shall go forth...

Note that either a clause or prepositional phrase may occur in this position. The most frequently met conjunctions are כַּאֲשֶׁר (when, as), and כִּי (when, whenever). Time words such as עֵת , שָׁנָה , יוֹם (time) are common with the preposition בְּ ; also מִקֵּץ (at the end of, after). Rarely a participial clause occurs, requiring the English conjunction "while":

וַיְהִי הֵם עֹמְדִים שָׁם וַיִּשְׁמְעוּ...	and while they were standing there they heard...

111. Feminine Nouns Ending in -et̪ and -at̪.

These behave much like the segholates in the singular before suffixes:

גְּבֶ֫רֶת	גְּבִרְתִּי	my mistress (cf. קִבְרִי)
דַּ֫עַת	דַּעְתִּי	my knowledge
בֹּ֫שֶׁת	בָּשְׁתִּי	my shame (cf. קָדְשִׁי)

Also to this group belong those nouns with penultimately stressed construct forms:

מִלְחָמָה	constr.	מִלְחֶ֫מֶת	w. suff.	מִלְחַמְתִּי.
מְלָאכָה		מְלֶ֫אכֶת		מְלַאכְתִּי

The noun בַּת has the stem בִּתּ *bitt-* before the suffixes: בִּתִּי my daughter.

אִשָּׁה before suffixes appears as אִשְׁתִּי, אִשְׁתְּךָ, etc.

The attachment of suffixes to the plural stems of these nouns offers no special problems.

112. Nouns of the Type פְּרִי.

It is difficult to formulate rules for this small class of nouns other than to note the replacement of the final long vowel by a consonantal *y* before the light suffixes in the singular. There is, however, much inconsistency, especially in the formation of the plural. The following sampling of attested forms should enable the student to identify nouns of this class when encountered:

כְּלִי	w. suff.	כֶּלְיְךָ	כְּלֵיכֶם		(pl. | כֵּלִים)	vessel
פְּרִי		פִּרְיִי	פֶּרְיְךָ	פִּרְיֶ֫ךָ	פִּרְיוֹ	פִּרְיָהּ	fruit
			פֶּרְיְכֶם		פִּרְיֵהֶם	פִּרְיָן	
עֳנִי		עָנְיִי			עָנְיֶ֫ךָ		affliction
חֳלִי		חָלְיוֹ			(pl. חֳלָיִים)		sickness
חֲצִי		חֶצְיוֹ	חֲצִים				

113. Vocabulary 27.

NOUNS: זְקוּנִים *zəqûnîm* (pl. only in sing. sense) old age

בְּאֵר *bə'ēr* (pl. -ôt̪; constr. pl. בְּאֵרוֹת) well, pit

עֳנִי *'ŏnî* (see §112) affliction

VERBS: פָּקַד *pāqad̪* (יִפְקֹד) to keep one's promise or commitment toward; to pay attention to; to visit; to appoint; to pass in review, muster

רַע *ra'* to be bad (cf. תַּם, §87; root is רעע)

תָּעָה *tā'āh* to wander about lost

כָּלָה *kālāh* to be depleted, finished, at an end

ADVERB: אַחֲרֵי כֵן *'aḥărê kēn* afterwards, after this

Note the idiom: מַה־לְּךָ What is the matter with you?

Exercises:

(a) Translate:

(1) וַיְהִי אַחֲרֵי מוֹת אָבִינוּ וַנַּעֲזֹב אֶת־עִירֵנוּ וַנַּעֲבֹר אֶת־הָאָרֶץ עַד־הַיָּם.

(2) וְהָיָה בַיּוֹם הַבָּא וְשָׁלַחְתִּי אֶת־אֲמָתִי אֵלֶיךָ כַּאֲשֶׁר אָמַרְתָּ לִי אֶתְמוֹל.

(3) וַיְהִי בַבֹּקֶר וַיִּשְׁכַּח אֶת־הַחֲלוֹם אֲשֶׁר חָלַם בַּלָּיְלָה.

(4) וְהָיָה כִּי תִשְׁמְעוּ אֶל־קוֹל נְבִיאַי וְזָכַרְתִּי אֶתְכֶם כִּי עַמִּי אַתֶּם.

(5) וַיְהִי כַּאֲשֶׁר רָאָה אֶת־בְּאֵר הַמַּיִם וַיִּשְׂמַח.

(6) וַיְהִי כַּאֲשֶׁר שָׁמַע אֶת־קוֹלָהּ וַיִּשְׁלַח אֶת־מַלְאָכוֹ אֵלֶיהָ.

(7) וְהָיָה בַיּוֹם הַהוּא וְרָעִיתָ אֶת־עֶדְרְךָ פֹּה פֶּן־יַאַסְרוּ אֹיְבֵינוּ אֹתָךְ וְלָקְחוּ אֶת־הָעֵדֶר.

(8) וְהָיָה כִּי אֶקְרָא אֵלֶיךָ וּבָרַחְתָּ מִן־הַמָּקוֹם הַזֶּה וְשַׁבְתָּ הַבָּיְתָה.

(9) וְהָיָה בַשָּׁנָה הַהִיא וְסָבְבוּ אֹיְבֵיכֶם אֶת־עִירְכֶם כִּי אָרַר יהוה אֶתְכֶם בַּעֲבוּר הַחַטָּאוֹת אֲשֶׁר חֲטָאתֶם לוֹ.

(10) וַיְהִי בַיּוֹם הַשְּׁבִיעִי וַיִּשְׁבֹּת אֱלֹהִים מִמְּלַאכְתּוֹ.

(b) Translate:

(6) דִּבְרֵי גְּבִרְתִּי   (1) קוֹל עָנֶיךָ

(7) אֲמָהוֹת וּשְׁפָחוֹת   (2) חֲצִי פִּרְיוֹ

(8) אֲחוֹת הַכְּנַעֲנִי   (3) שְׁנַת מִלְחַמְתֵּנוּ

(9) רְכוּשׁ הַמִּצְרִים   (4) יוֹם מְלַאכְתְּךָ

(10) מִזְבַּח הַהֵיכָל   (5) יְמֵי זְקוּנֶיךָ

(c) Write in Hebrew:

1. When they saw him they called to him.
2. When his life came to an end, they buried him in the grave of his fathers.
3. When you cross the river you will see the land which I am about to give (use participle) to you.
4. Afterward they sent men to Egypt, for there was a famine in the land.
5. On that day you will see him standing before you.
6. When she found the tree she ate some of (lit. from) its fruit.
7. In the evening you shall go out of the city and flee toward the mountain.

(d) Reading: Sarah and Hagar (cont.)

יהוה פָּקַד אֶת־שָׂרָה כַּאֲשֶׁר אָמַר. יָלְדָה שָׂרָה לְאַבְרָהָם בֵּן לִזְקוּנָיו וַיִּקְרָא אַבְרָהָם אֶת־שֵׁם בְּנוֹ אֲשֶׁר יָלְדָה לוֹ שָׂרָה יִצְחָק וַיִּגְדַּל הַיֶּלֶד עִם־בֶּן־הָגָר הַמִּצְרִית וַיְהִי כַּאֲשֶׁר רָאֲתָה שָׂרָה אֶת־בֶּן־הָאָמָה עִם־בְּנָהּ יִצְחָק וַתֹּאמֶר לְאַבְרָהָם אִשָּׁה לֵאמֹר: גָּרֵשׁ[1] אֶת־הָאָמָה הַזֹּאת וְאֶת־בְּנָהּ.

רַע הַדָּבָר מְאֹד בְּעֵינֵי אַבְרָהָם עַל־דְּבַר בְּנוֹ יִשְׁמָעֵאל וַיֹּאמֶר אֱלֹהִים אֶל־אַבְרָהָם: כָּל־אֲשֶׁר תֹּאמַר אֵלֶיךָ שָׂרָה שְׁמַע בְּקוֹלָהּ כִּי בְיִצְחָק יִקָּרֵא לְךָ[2] זֶרַע וְגַם אֶת־בֶּן־הָאָמָה לְגוֹי גָּדוֹל אֲשִׂימֶנּוּ[3] כִּי זַרְעֲךָ גַּם־הוּא.

וַיְהִי אַחֲרֵי־כֵן וַיְשַׁלַּח⁴ אַבְרָהָם אֶת־הָגָר וְאֶת־בְּנָהּ. תָּעֲתָה הָאָמָה בַּמִּדְבָּר וַיְהִי כַּאֲשֶׁר כָּלוּ הַמַּיִם וְהַלֶּחֶם אֲשֶׁר נָתַן לָהּ אַבְרָהָם וַתִּשְׁכַּב עַל־הָאֲדָמָה וַתֵּבְךְּ⁵ וַיִּשְׁמַע אֱלֹהִים אֶת־קוֹל הַנַּעַר וַיִּקְרָא מַלְאַךְ אֱלֹהִים אֵלֶיהָ מִן־הַשָּׁמַיִם לֵאמֹר: מַה־לָּךְ הָגָר. אַל־תִּירְאִי⁶ כִּי שָׁמַע אֱלֹהִים אֶת־קוֹל הַנַּעַר.

וַיְהִי אַחֲרֵי הַדְּבָרִים הָאֵלֶּה וַתִּמְצָא הָגָר בְּאֵר מָיִם. הָיָה אֱלֹהִים אֶת־הַנַּעַר וַיִּגְדַּל הַנַּעַר בַּמִּדְבָּר עִם־אִמּוֹ.

Notes to the Reading:

1. "drive away" (imperative)
2. "your descendants will be named"
3. "I shall make him into a great nation *(gôy)*"
4. "expelled"
5. "and wept"
6. "fear not!"

LESSON 28

114. The Infinitive Construct.

Each Hebrew verb has two forms to which the name infinitive is given. One of these, the infinitive absolute, functions more as an adverb and will be dealt with in a later lesson. The other, the infinitive construct, corresponds more closely to the traditional view of an infinitive. The form of the infinitive construct is more or less uniform for those verb classes whose imperfects we have studied up to this lesson. The vowel of the first syllable is *ə* (or with gutturals *ă* or *ě*) and that of the second is *ō*. The infinitive is frequently used with pronominal suffixes, before which the stem is variable.

	Perfect	Imperfect	Imperative	Inf. Construct	w. suff.
Sound trilit.	כָּתַב	יִכְתֹּב	כְּתֹב	כְּתֹב	כָּתְבִי
I-guttural	עָמַד	יַעֲמֹד	עֲמֹד	עֲמֹד	עָמְדִי
II-guttural	בָּחַר	יִבְחַר	בְּחַר	בְּחֹר	בָּחֳרִי
III-guttural	שָׁמַע	יִשְׁמַע	שְׁמַע	שְׁמֹעַ	שָׁמְעִי
I-*Aleph*	אָכַל	יֹאכַל	אֱכֹל	אֱכֹל	אָכְלִי
III-*Aleph*	מָצָא	יִמְצָא	מְצָא	מְצֹא	מָצְאִי

Some inconsistency is found among those verbs which have *a*-imperfects but which are neither II/III-guttural; this includes stative verbs like כָּבֵד and the small group represented by יִשְׁכַּב שָׁכַב. These are poorly attested for the infinitive construct, but they usually follow the pattern given above. Occasionally there is a form with *a*, such as שְׁכַב (to lie down), but even here, before suffixes, the normal pattern emerges: שָׁכְבִי *šokbî*.

[127]

115. Some Uses of the Infinitive Construct.

The infinitive is by definition a form having both nominal and verbal functions. In the latter role it may have subjects and objects as well as other typically verbal adjuncts. The infinitive, together with its adjuncts, then occupies a nominal function in the total clause. When pronouns form the subject of an infinitive, they are suffixed:

כָּתְבִי	*kotbî*	my writing	כָּתְבֵ֫נוּ	*kotbḗnû*	
כָּתְבְךָ	*kotbəkā*	your (m. s.) writing	כָּתְבְכֶם	*kotbəkem*	
כָּתָבְךָ	*kotobkā*		כָּתְבְכֶן	*kotbəken*	
כָּתְבֵךְ	*kotbēk*	etc.	כָּתְבָם	*kotbām*	
כָּתְבוֹ	*kotbô*		כָּתְבָן	*kotbān*	
כָּתְבָה	*kotbāh*				

When the infinitive construct stands before a following noun, that noun may be either the subject or object of the infinitive, although the former is more likely:

כְּתֹב הָאִישׁ	the man's writing (i.e. act of writing)
הֲרֹג אִישׁ	killing a man
	(or) a man's killing

The ambiguity of the second example is grammatical as well as semantic. The infinitive is in construct (hence its name) with its subject, as in the first example, but in the second the word אִישׁ should probably be regarded as an object noun (not construct) when it is the object, especially since it requires אֵת when made definite:

הֲרֹג אִישׁ	to kill a man
הֲרֹג אֶת־הָאִישׁ	to kill the man

When pronouns are involved with the infinitive construct, the arrangement of subject and object is a little more complicated, but the following examples should make the situation clear:

הָרְגִי אֶת־הָאִישׁ	my killing the man
הֲרֹג הָאִישׁ אֹתִי	the man's killing me
שָׁמְרִי אֶת־הַתּוֹרָה	my observing the law
שָׁמְרִי אֹתוֹ	my observing him
שָׁמְרוֹ אֹתִי	his observing me
כְּתֹב דָּבָר	to write a word
כְּתֹב אֶת־הַדָּבָר	to write the word
כָּתְבְךָ אֶת־הַדָּבָר	your writing the word

As a unit the infinitival phrase may be

sentence subject: טוֹב שָׁמְרְךָ אֶת־הַתּוֹרָה   your observing the law is good or it is good that you observe the law object of a prep.:   עַד־מָצְאַךָ אֹתוֹ   until you find him

object of verb: לֹא יָכֹלְתִּי שְׁמֹעַ   I was not able to hear

But the most frequent use of the infinitive construct is with the pre-positions בְּ, כְּ, and לְ :

(a) With בְּ and כְּ the infinitive is the equivalent of an adverbial (mostly temporal) clause in English:

     כְּשָׁמְעוֹ אֶת־הַדָּבָר   when he heard the word

     בְּעָמְדִי לְפָנָיו   when (or while) I stood before him

Both prepositions are common in this usage, but with certain verbs, especially שָׁמַע and רָאָה, כְּ is by far the preferred preposition. There are reasons, founded in the aspectual nature of these verbs, which govern this choice, but a catalog of uses would serve no purpose in an elementary grammar of this sort.

The infinitive with בְּ or כְּ is very frequent in the construction treated in §110:

     ...וַיְהִי כִּשְׁמֹעַ אַבְרָהָם   and when Abraham heard...

     ...וְהָיָה כְּשָׁמְעֲךָ אֶת־קוֹלִי   and when you hear my voice...

(b) With לְ the inf. construct occurs in a wide variety of complementary and explanatory uses, often with the meaning of purpose, goal, or result:

     ...בָּאוּ ... לִשְׁמֹעַ   They came ... to hear ...

     ...לֹא יָכְלוּ לִלְכֹּד   They could not capture ...

   תִּשְׁמֹר אֶת־דֶּרֶךְ יהוה לַעֲשׂוֹת   You shall observe the way of the Lord

     ...צֶדֶק   by doing (inf. of עָשָׂה) righteousness ...

(1) הָיָה + לְ + Inf. expresses (a) "to be about to" or (b) "to be compelled to": הָיָה הַשַּׁעַר לִסְגֹּר The gate was about to close.

(2) עַל + noun or pron. + לְ + Inf. expresses obligation or respon-sibility: עָלַי לִמְצֹא אֹתוֹ I must find him.

(3) אֵין + לְ + Inf. = "it is not possible (permitted) to": אֵין לָבוֹא Entering is forbidden.

The infinitive construct is negated with בִּלְתִּי :

     לְבִלְתִּי אֲכֹל אֶת־הַפְּרִי   not to eat the fruit

     לְבִלְתִּי שְׂרֹף אֶת־הַמְּגִלָּה   not to burn the scroll

116. Final Remarks on Some Noun Types.

The only important group of nouns not included in our previous discussions is that comprising nouns ending in -eh. Most of these are derived from roots found in verbs III-*Hē* and which in an earlier stage of the language were either III-*Yodh* or III-*Waw*. Subsequent contractions and loss have obscured the origins of these forms, and certain coincidental developments within the language have led to some formal confusion between singular and plural. In the singular these nouns:

(1) may follow regular inflection with complete loss of the *-eh*:

שָׂדֶה	field	שָׂדִי	שָׂדְךָ	etc.
מַטֶּה	staff		מַטְּךָ	

(2) may exhibit a partially distinct set of suffixes, especially *-ēhû* in the 3rd pers. sing.

מַעֲשֶׂה	deed	מַעֲשֵׂהוּ
מִקְנֶה	cattle	מִקְנֵהוּ

(3) or may have suffixal forms like the *-îm* plurals:

מִקְנַי	my cattle	מַעֲשַׂי	my deed

For nouns having plurals in *-ôṯ*, such as שָׂדֶה and מַחֲנֶה, the occurrence of such forms as שָׂדַי and מַחֲנַי as plurals is suspect. Although these may be listed as plurals in concordances and grammars, many such forms are more likely singulars.

117. Vocabulary 28.

VERBS: יָכֹל *yāḵōl* to be able; (+ לְ) to prevail over

חָפֵץ *ḥāpēṣ* (יַחְפֹּץ) to take delight in; to desire (to do something: + inf.)

חָדַל *ḥāḏal* (יֶחְדַּל) to cease, stop (intr.); to stop (doing something: + inf.)

תַּם *tam* (see §87) to finish, be at an end; to finish (doing something: + inf.)

אָסַף *'āsap̄* (יֶאֱסֹף) to gather

NOUNS: תֹּאַר *tō'ar* form, appearance

מִשְׁתֶּה *mišteh* banquet

אַהֲבָה *'ahăḇāh* love [used as the inf. constr. of אָהַב]

אֵם *'ēm* (w. suff. אִמִּי ; pl. *-ôṯ*) mother

Prepositions frequently used before the infinitive construct:

עַד	until	כְּ	when, as
אַחֲרֵי	after	לְמַ֫עַן	so that, so as to
בְּ	when, while	יַ֫עַן	because

Exercises:

(a) Translate:

(1) לְמַ֫עַן שָׁמְרְךָ אֶת־הַתּוֹרָה   (2) בְּהָרְגוֹ אֶת־אֹיְבָיו

(3) כְּשָׁלַח הַמֶּלֶךְ אֶת־עֲבָדָיו   (10) בִּשְׂרֹף אוֹיְבֵינוּ אֶת־הָעִיר

(4) כְּשָׁמֹעַ הָאִישׁ אֶת־קוֹלֵנוּ   (11) בְּקָרְאוּ שֵׁמוֹת לַחַיּוֹת

(5) בְּכָרְתֵנוּ בְרִית   (12) בְּקָרְעִי אֶת־בִּגְדִי

(6) בְּבָרְאוֹ אֶת־הָרֶמֶשׂ   (13) יַעַן סָגְרָם אֶת־הַשַּׁעַר

(7) לַהֲרֹג אֶת־כָּל־הַזְּכָרִים   (14) עַד־מָצְאָם אֹתוֹ

(8) בְּצַעֲקָם אֵלַי   (15) לְבִלְתִּי אֱכֹל־אֶת־בַּהֲמוֹת הַשָּׂדֶה

(9) בְּכָתְבְךָ אֶת־דְּבָרָיו   (16) לְבִלְתִּי עֲבֹר אֶת־מִצְוֹתָיו

(b) Give the Hebrew for the following orally:

1. when you forget this law
2. while I stood there
3. after we gathered them
4. when they buried him
5. until they bind us
6. after they lie down
7. not to ride on the horse
8. until you call to us
9. until I break the tablets
10. while he was eating
11. so that he send you to us
12. so that you observe them

(c) Translate:

(1) וְהָיָה בְּבָחֳרָם בּוֹ לְמֶלֶךְ וְיָשַׁב עַל־הַכִּסֵּא.

(2) לָמָה עָשִׂיתָ הָרַע בְּעֵינַי לְבִלְתִּי שְׁמֹעַ בְּקוֹלִי.

(3) וַיְהִי בְּמָצְאוֹ אֶת־הַיֶּלֶד וַיַּהֲרֹג אֹתוֹ.

(4) וַיְהִי כְּשָׁמְעֵנוּ אֶת־הַקּוֹל וַנִּשְׂמַח.

(5) לֹא יָכֹלְתִּי אֱכֹל אֶת־הַלֶּחֶם הַזֶּה.

(6) חָפְצוּ לַהֲרֹג אֶת־יֹשְׁבֵי הָעִיר וְלֹא יָכְלוּ לִמְצֹא אֹתָם.

(7) וְהָיָה אַחֲרֵי אָסְפוֹ אֶת־הָאֲנָשִׁים אֵלָיו בְּבֵיתוֹ וְעָשָׂה מִשְׁתֶּה גָּדוֹל.

(8) טוֹב אַתָּה כִּי זָכַרְתָּ אֶת־מִצְוֹתַי לְבִלְתִּי חֲטֹא לִי.

(9) וַיְהִי כַּאֲשֶׁר רָאָה אֹתָהּ כִּי יְפַת תֹּאַר וִיפַת מַרְאֶה הִיא מְאֹד וַיֶּאֱהַב אֹתָהּ וַיַּחְפֹּץ אֹתָהּ לוֹ לְאִשָּׁה.

(10) וְהָיָה בִּפְקֹד יהוה אֶת־שָׂרָה וְהָרְתָה וְיָלְדָה בֵּן לְאִישָׁהּ.

(11) מִי יַחְפֹּץ לִגְאֹל אֹתָךְ.

(12) יָצְאוּ מֵהַהֵיכָל לְבִלְתִּי שָׁמְעָם אֶת־דִּבְרֵי הַמֶּלֶךְ הָרָשָׁע.

(13) וַיְהִי אַחֲרֵי חָדְלוּ לִשְׁמֹעַ בְּקוֹל הַנָּבִיא וַיֶּחֶטְאוּ חַטָּאוֹת רַבּוֹת.

(14) תַּמּוּ הָעָם לַעֲבֹר אֶת־הַנָּהָר.

(15) הָיוּ הַשָּׁנִים כְּיָמִים בְּעֵינָיו בְּאַהֲבָתוֹ אֹתָהּ.

(16) וַיְהִי בֶּאֱחֹז הָאִשָּׁה אֶת־בִּגְדוֹ וַיַּעֲזֹב אֶת־בִּגְדוֹ וַיִּבְרַח מִן־הַבָּיִת.

(d) Write in Hebrew:

1. When they killed the prisoners we fled from there and crossed over hither.
2. You have sinned in not loving your father and your mother.
3. They sat in her house until the men opened the gate.
4. We wish to remember both the living and the dead.
5. It is not permitted to eat the flesh of these animals.

6. When he saw (use perf.) the dry ground, he rejoiced, for he knew that the waters had ceased from the face of the earth.
7. We were not able to write, nor were we able to read.

LESSON 29

118. Verbs I-Nun: Imperfect and Related Forms.

The following two verbs are the most typical of this class:

	Perfect	Imperfect	Imperative	Inf. Constr.	w. suff.
ō-imperf.	נָפַל	יִפֹּל	נְפֹל	נְפֹל	נָפְלִי
a-imperf.	נָסַע	יִסַּע	סַע	נְסֹעַ	נָסְעִי

In the imperfect of both types the *nûn* is assimilated to the second root consonant throughout the inflection, which is otherwise quite regular:

יִפֹּל	*yippōl*	יִפְּלוּ	*yippəlû*
תִּפֹּל	*tippōl*	תִּפֹּלְנָה	*tippṓlnāh*
תִּפֹּל	*tippōl*	תִּפְּלוּ	*tippəlû*
תִּפְּלִי	*tippəlî*	תִּפֹּלְנָה	*tippṓlnāh*
אֶפֹּל	*'eppōl*	נִפֹּל	*nippōl*

Verbs with *a*-imperfects have a short imperative, inflected as follows:

סַע	*sa'*	סְעִי	*sə'î*	סְעוּ	*sə'û*	סַעְנָה	*sá'nāh*
סְעָה	*sə'āh*						

The infinitive construct of verbs with *a*-imperfects may be of two different types, both of which occur for most of these verbs: (1) a regular form, like נְסֹעַ *nəsō[a']*, (2) a short form with the suffix -*t*: סַעַת

Perfect	Imperfect	Imperative	Inf. Construct	w. suff.	
נָגַע	יִגַּע	גַּע	גַּעַת	——	to strike
			נִגְעַ	נָגְעִי	
נָטַע	יִטַּע	טַע	טַעַת	——	to plant
			נְטֹעַ	——	
——	יִגַּשׁ	גַּשׁ	גֶּשֶׁת	גִּשְׁתִּי	to approach

Special Remarks:

(a) Note that יִגַּשׁ is not used in the perfect.

(b) The forms of נָשָׂא (to raise up), which is also III-*Aleph*, are

נָשָׂא	יִשָּׂא	שָׂא	שְׂאֵת / שֵׂאת	שְׂאֵתִי
			נְשֹׂא	——

(c) The verb נָתַן has an imperfect etc. with *ē*:

נָתַן	יִתֵּן	תֵּן	תֵּת	תִּתִּי

(d) The verb לָקַח behaves as though I-*Nun* in the imperfect etc.:

לָקַח	יִקַּח	קַח	קַחַת	קַחְתִּי

(e) The doubling of the second root consonant of the imperfect is given up in some verbs when followed by ə:

יִסְעוּ *yisʿû* (they will set out) not יִסְּעוּ *yissəʿû*

Below are the full paradigms of לָקַח and , נָתַן , נָשָׂא , נָסַע.

Imperfect:	יִסַּע	יִשָּׂא	יִתֵּן	יִקַּח
	תִּסַּע	תִּשָּׂא	תִּתֵּן	תִּקַּח
	תִּסַּע	תִּשָּׂא	תִּתֵּן	תִּקַּח
	תִּסְעִי	תִּשְׂאִי	תִּתְּנִי	תִּקְחִי
	אֶסַּע	אֶשָּׂא	אֶתֵּן	אֶקַּח
	יִסְעוּ	יִשְׂאוּ	יִתְּנוּ	יִקְחוּ
	תִּסַּעְנָה	תִּשֶּׂאנָה	תִּתֵּנָּה	תִּקַּחְנָה
	תִּסְעוּ	תִּשְׂאוּ	תִּתְּנוּ	תִּקְחוּ
	תִּסַּעְנָה	תִּשֶּׂאנָה	תִּתֵּנָּה	תִּקַּחְנָה
	נִסַּע	נִשָּׂא	נִתֵּן	נִקַּח
Imperative:	סַע	שָׂא	תֵּן	קַח
	סְעִי	שְׂאִי	תְּנִי	קְחִי
	סְעוּ	שְׂאוּ	תְּנוּ	קְחוּ
	סַעְנָה	שֶׂאנָה	תֵּנָּה	קַחְנָה

The preposition ל appears as לָ before the infinitives with a stressed first syllable unless the infinitive is in construct with a following noun. E.g.

לָטַעַת   לָשֶׁת   לָשֵׂאת   לָקַחַת   לָתֵת

119. Vocabulary 29.

NOUNS: מְגוּרִים   *məḡûrîm* (pl. only)   the place where one sojourns, residence

כֻּתֹּנֶת   *kəṯṓneṯ* ⌐ (pl. -ôṯ) tunic

כֻּתֹּנֶת   *kuttṓneṯ* ⌐

נֶ֫דֶר   *néḏer* or נֵ֫דֶר   *nḗḏer* (w. suff. נִדְרִי ; pl. -îm)   vow

תּוֹלְדוֹת   *tôləḏôṯ*   history, genealogy (pl. only)

VERBS: יִגַּשׁ   *yiggaš* (perf. not used)   to approach [usually with אֶל]

נָדַר   *nāḏar* (יִדֹּר)   to vow

גָּעַר   *gā'ar* (יִגְעַר)   to rebuke

שָׂנֵא   *śānē'* (יִשְׂנָא)   to hate

הַב   *haḇ*   A defective verb found only in the imperative forms: הָבוּ הָבִי הָבָה הַב give! come now ... let's ...!

נָשָׂא   *nāśā'* (יִשָּׂא) to raise, lift up, carry

ADJECTIVE: צָעִיר   *ṣā'îr*   small, young

NUMBERS: שְׁנַ֫יִם   *šənáyim* (masc.)   two; constr. שְׁנֵי *šənê*

שְׁתַּ֫יִם   *štáyim* (fem.)   two; constr. שְׁתֵּי *štê*

The absolute form of the number "two" may stand before or after the noun it modifies, which is in the plural:

אֲנָשִׁים שְׁנַ֫יִם   or   שְׁנַ֫יִם אֲנָשִׁים

נָשִׁים שְׁתַּ֫יִם   שְׁתַּ֫יִם נָשִׁים

The construct form is used only before the noun:

שְׁתֵּי נָשִׁים   שְׁנֵי אֲנָשִׁים

PROPER NAMES: רָחֵל   *Rāḥēl*   Rachel

לֵאָה   *Lē'āh*   Leah

לָבָן   *Lāḇān*   Laban

יַעֲקֹב   *Ya'ăqōḇ*   Jacob

Exercises:

(a) Translate:

(1) תֵּן לִי שְׁנֵי סְפָרִים

(2) קְחִי אֶת־כַּסְפֵּךְ

(3) יִגַּשׁ אֵלַי הָאִישׁ

(4) וַתִּדֹּר הָאִשָּׁה נֶ֫דֶר

(5) אַל־תִּשְׂנְאוּ אֶת־אֲחִיכֶם.

(6) וַיִּגַּף אֹתָם מַגֵּפוֹת רַבּוֹת וּכְבֵדוֹת

(7) וַיִּקְחוּ אֶת־כֻּתָּנְתּוֹ וַיִּקְרְעוּ אֹתָהּ

(8) שְׁנַ֫יִם זְקֵנִים הֹלְכִים עַל־הַדֶּ֫רֶךְ

(9) גְּשִׁי אֵלַי בִּתִּי

(10) סְעוּ מִצְרַ֫יְמָה

(11) תֶּן לָ֫נוּ עֵ֫זֶר

(12) יִפֹּל אַ֫רְצָה בְּגִשְׁתְּךָ אֵלָיו

(13) טוֹב תִּתְּךָ לִי אֶת־הַכֶּ֫סֶף

(14) שָׂא אֶת־עֵינֶ֫יךָ הַשָּׁמַ֫יְמָה

(b) Give the Hebrew for the following orally:

1. Give (m. pl.) us your help.
2. Kill (m. pl.) the snake.

3. Do not eat (m. pl.) its flesh.
4. Take (m. s.) two stones.
5. Plant (m. s.) the tree here.
6. Approach (f. s.) him.
7. and he struck him
8. and they gave him their sons
9. and I fell to the ground
10. and he traveled toward the wilderness
11. we shall give them food
12. we shall set out in the morning

(c) Translate:

(1) לֹא יָכֹלְתִּי לָשֵׂאת הָאֲבָנִים הָאֵלֶּה כִּי כְבֵדוֹת הֵנָּה מִשְּׂאֵתִי אֹתָן.

(2) לֹא יַחְפֹּץ לָגֶשֶׁת אֵלֶיךָ בְּקָרְאֲךָ אֵלָיו.

(3) אֱסֹף אֶת־הָעָם הֵנָּה פֶּן־יֹאבְדוּ בִּידֵי הָאֹיְבִים.

(4) בְּרַח הָהָרָה לְבִלְתִּי קַחְתָּם אֹתוֹ וְאֶת־מִקְנֵהוּ.

(5) סְגֹר אֶת־שַׁעַר הָעִיר פֶּן־יִגְּשׁוּ הָאֲנָשִׁים וְהָרְגוּ אֹתָנוּ.

(6) וַיִּטְּעוּ שָׁם כֶּרֶם וְעֵצִים רַבִּים.

(7) וַיְהִי בְגִשְׁתּוֹ אֵלַי וָאֶשָּׂא אֶת־עֵינַי אֵלָיו וָאֹמַר: לָמָה בָאתָ אֵלַי בְּנִי.

(8) תֵּעָתָה הָאִשָּׁה עִם־שְׁנֵי בָנֶיהָ וְלֹא יָכְלָה לִמְצֹא לָהֶם מָיִם.

(9) חָפַצְתִּי לִנְסֹעַ אֶתְמוֹל וְלֹא יָכֹלְתִּי לִמְצֹא אֶת־בְּגָדַי וְאֶת־כְּתָנְתִּי.

(10) וְהָיָה כְּפִתְחָם אֶת־הַשַּׁעַר וִיצָאתֶם הַחוּצָה.

(11) הָבָה נִשְׁמְעָה בְקוֹלוֹ כִּי צַדִּיק הוּא בְּעֵינֵינוּ.

(12) קְחוּ אֶת־רְכוּשְׁכֶם וְאֶת־כָּל־אֲשֶׁר־לָכֶם וּנְסַעְתֶּם אֶל־הָאָרֶץ הַהִיא וִישַׁבְתֶּם גַּם־אַתֶּם בְּאֶרֶץ מְגוּרֵי אֲבוֹתֵיכֶם.

(d) Write in Hebrew:

1. When he approached us, we called to our servants.
2. And he set out and crossed over as far as the river.
3. And he raised his hands heavenward and cried out in a loud voice.
4. Take (f.s.) your sons and go forth (perf.) from this place.
5. We could not bear (= carry) the affliction which he set upon us.
6. His song is pleasant and his words are good in our ears.
7. And afterward they set out each (= a man) to his land.

(e) Reading: Jacob and Rachel

וּלְלָבָן הָיוּ שְׁתֵּי בָנוֹת, שֵׁם הַגְּדוֹלָה לֵאָה וְשֵׁם הַקְּטַנָּה רָחֵל וְרָחֵל הָיְתָה יְפַת תֹּאַר וִיפַת מַרְאֶה
וַיֶּאֱהַב יַעֲקֹב אֶת־רָחֵל וַיֹּאמֶר אֶל־לָבָן: אֶעֱבָד אֹתְךָ שֶׁבַע שָׁנִים בְּרָחֵל² בִּתְּךָ הַקְּטַנָּה.
וַיֹּאמֶר לָבָן: טוֹב תִּתִּי אֹתָהּ לָךְ מִתִּתִּי אֹתָהּ לְאִישׁ אַחֵר.

וַיַּעֲבֹד יַעֲקֹב בְּרָחֵל שֶׁבַע שָׁנִים אֲשֶׁר הָיוּ בְעֵינָיו כְּיָמִים אֲחָדִים³ בְּאַהֲבָתוֹ³ אֹתָהּ וַיֹּאמֶר יַעֲקֹב
אֶל־לָבָן: הָבָה אֶת־אִשְׁתִּי כִּי מָלְאוּ יָמָי. וַיֶּאֱסֹף לָבָן אֶת־כָּל־אַנְשֵׁי הַמָּקוֹם וַיַּעַשׂ מִשְׁתֶּה וַיְהִי
בָעֶרֶב וַיִּקַּח אֶת־לֵאָה בִּתּוֹ הַגְּדוֹלָה וַיִּתֵּן אֹתָהּ לְיַעֲקֹב וְהוּא בָּא אֵלֶיהָ בַּלָּיְלָה.

וַיְהִי כַאֲשֶׁר רָאָה יַעֲקֹב בַּבֹּקֶר כִּי לֵאָה אִתּוֹ וַיֹּאמֶר אֶל־לָבָן: מַה זֹּאת עָשִׂיתָ לִּי. הֲלֹא בְרָחֵל
עָבַדְתִּי עִמָּךְ וְלָמָּה רִמִּיתָנִי.⁵ וַיֹּאמֶר לָבָן: בִּמְקוֹמֵנוּ אֵין לָתֵת הַצְּעִירָה לִפְנֵי הַבְּכִירָה.⁶
אַתֶּן גַּם־אֶת־זֹאת בַּעֲבוֹדָה² אֲשֶׁר תַּעֲבֹד עִמָּדִי שֶׁבַע שָׁנִים אֲחֵרוֹת. וַיִּתֵּן לָבָן אֶת־רָחֵל לְיַעֲקֹב
לְאִשָּׁה וַיַּעֲבֹד יַעֲקֹב אֶת־לָבָן שֶׁבַע שָׁנִים אֲחֵרוֹת בְּרָחֵל.

Notes to the Reading:

1. "seven"
2. There are three idiomatic uses of בְּ in this selection:

עָבַד בְּ   to serve someone *for* a reward or compensation

בְּאַהֲבָתוֹ אֹתָהּ   *because* he loved her

בַּעֲבוֹדָה   *in exchange for* the labor

3. The pl. of אֶחָד has the sense of "several, a few"
4. "and he prepared"
5. "have you deceived me?"
6. "first-born" hence "eldest" (feminine)

LESSON 30

120. Verbs I-Yodh: Imperfect, Imperative, and Infinitive Construct.

Just as in the class of verbs I-*Nun* there are two distinct types of verbs I-*Yodh* depending on the stem vowel of the imperfect:

	Perfect	Imperfect	Imperative	Inf. Constr.	w. suff.	
ē-imperfects:	יָשַׁב	יֵשֵׁב	שֵׁב	שֶׁבֶת	שִׁבְתִּי	dwell
a-imperfects:	יָשֵׁן	יִישַׁן	[יְשַׁן]	יְשֹׁן	[יָשְׁנִי]	sleep

Verbs with *ē*-imperfects have *ē* in the preformative and have short imperative and infinitive stems. Exactly like יָשַׁב are

יָלַד	יֵלֵד	לֵד	לֶדֶת	לִדְתִּי	bear
יָרַד	יֵרֵד	רֵד	רֶדֶת	רִדְתִּי	descend

The verb יָדַע belongs to this group, even though it has an *a*-imperfect due to the final root guttural:

יָדַע	יֵדַע	דַּע	דַּעַת	דַּעְתִּי	know

The verb יָצָא has slightly different forms because it is also III-*Aleph*:

יָצָא	יֵצֵא	צֵא	צֵאת	צֵאתִי	go forth

The verb הָלַךְ is irregular in also belonging here:

הָלַךְ	יֵלֵךְ	לֵךְ	לֶכֶת	לֶכְתִּי	go

To the second group, represented by יָשֵׁן above, belong the verbs

יָרַשׁ	יִירַשׁ	רֵשׁ	רֶשֶׁת	רָשַׁתִּי	inherit
יָעַץ	יִיעַץ	—	—	—	advise
יָקַץ	יִיקַץ	—	—	—	wake up
יָבֵשׁ	יִיבַשׁ	—	יְבֹשֶׁ(ת)	—	dry up

and the III-*Aleph* verb

יָרֵא	יִירָא	יְרָא	יְרָא	—	fear

[Note: the noun יִרְאָה (fear) is normally used as the inf. construct for this verb.] The imperatives and inf. constructs of this group are poorly attested in BH but show the same mixture of the two possible types which we encountered with verbs I-*Nun*.

The verb יָכֹל has irregular forms with *û* in the preformative of the imperfect:

תּוּכְלִי   תּוּכַל   יוּכַל   etc.

In the class of verbs I-*Yodh* and in those classes to be treated in the following lessons there is frequently a difference in the imperfect form used with waw-conversive, particularly in the 3rd pers. sing. masc. and fem., the 2nd pers. sing. masc., and the 1st pers. pl. In general the accent on these forms is retracted to an *open* preformative syllable; *ē* in the stem is replaced by *e*. A similar instance was met with יֹאמַר versus וַיֹּאמֶר. There are, however, inconsistencies:

(a) The change is regular for *ē*-imperfects other than יֵצֵא:

וַיֵּשֶׁב	וַתֵּלֶד	וַיֵּרֶד	וַיֵּלֶךְ	but	וַיֵּצֵא
וַתֵּשֶׁב		וַתֵּרֶד	וַתֵּלֶךְ		וַתֵּצֵא
וַנֵּשֶׁב		וַנֵּרֶד	וַנֵּלֶךְ		וַנֵּצֵא

(b) It is *not* found with the *a*-imperfects other than יֵדַע:

וַיֵּרַשׁ   וַיִּישַׁן   וַיִּיקַץ   but   וַיֵּדַע

Several verbs have imperfects formed on the analogy of roots I-*Nun*:

יָצַר	to fashion	imperf. יִצֹּר	(but also, irregularly, וַיִּיצֶר)
יָצַק	to pour	יִצֹּק	(but also, irregularly, וַיִּצֶק)
יָצַת	to kindle	יִצַּת	

Given below are the full paradigms of the most frequent types of the class

I-*Yodh*:				
יֵשֵׁב	יֵלֵךְ	יֵצֵא	יֵדַע	יִירַשׁ
תֵּשֵׁב	תֵּלֵךְ	תֵּצֵא	תֵּדַע	תִּירַשׁ
תֵּשֵׁב	תֵּלֵךְ	תֵּצֵא	תֵּדַע	תִּירַשׁ
תֵּשְׁבִי	תֵּלְכִי	תֵּצְאִי	תֵּדְעִי	תִּירְשִׁי

אִירַשׁ	אֵדַע	אֵצֵא	אֵלֵךְ	אֵשֵׁב
יִירְשׁוּ	יֵדְעוּ	יֵצְאוּ	יֵלְכוּ	יֵשְׁבוּ
תִּירַשְׁנָה	תֵּדַעְנָה	תֵּצֶאנָה	תֵּלַכְנָה	תֵּשַׁבְנָה
תִּירְשׁוּ	תֵּדְעוּ	תֵּצְאוּ	תֵּלְכוּ	תֵּשְׁבוּ
תִּירַשְׁנָה	תֵּדַעְנָה	תֵּצֶאנָה	תֵּלַכְנָה	תֵּשַׁבְנָה
נִירַשׁ	נֵדַע	נֵצֵא	נֵלֵךְ	נֵשֵׁב

רַשׁ	דַּע	צֵא	לֵךְ	שֵׁב
רְשִׁי	דְּעִי	צְאִי	לְכִי	שְׁבִי
רְשׁוּ	דְּעוּ	צְאוּ	לְכוּ	שְׁבוּ
רַשְׁנָה	דְּעֶנָה	צֶאנָה	לֵכְנָה	שֵׁבְנָה

121. Vocabulary 30.

NOUNS: שָׁלוֹם *šālôm* peace, well-being; state of one's health. Note the idiom: שָׁאַל לְשָׁלוֹם לְ to inquire about the health of

עֵמֶק *ʿēmeq* (w. suff. עִמְקִי , pl. -*îm*) valley, lowland

בַּעַל *báʿal* (pl. -*îm*) lord, master, owner, husband. Frequent in idioms as "one invested with, endowed with," as בַּעַל חֲלוֹמוֹת a dreamer. Also members (pl.) of a guild or profession, as בַּעֲלֵי הַפָּרָשִׁים professional horsemen. Also a proper name or epithet of a Canaanite deity, rarely applied to God.

ADJECTIVES: רָחוֹק *rāḥôq* distant, far; מֵרָחוֹק at a distance, from afar

קָרוֹב *qārôb* near, close (to: אֶל)

VERBS: קָרַב *qārab* (יִקְרַב) to be near, draw near; approach (+ בְּ, לְ, אֶל)

יָשֵׁן *yāšēn* (יִישַׁן) to sleep

שָׁאַל *šāʾal* (יִשְׁאַל) to ask, inquire, request (a thing: אֶת ; a person מִן , לְ , אֶת)

עָנָה *ʿānāh* to answer (a person: אֶת); + בְּ to testify against

CONJUNCTION: טֶרֶם *ṭérem* or בְּטֶרֶם *baṭérem* before, not yet. Usually followed by the imperfect, regardless of the tense required in English: טֶרֶם יִשְׁכַּב before he had lain down, or he not yet having lain down.

PROPER NAMES: יִשְׂרָאֵל *Yiśrāʾēl* (1) = Jacob; (2) the name of a people

יוֹסֵף *Yôsēp* Joseph

Exercises:

(a) Translate:

(7) תִּירְשׁוּ אֶת־הָאָרֶץ הַזֹּאת   (1) רְדָתֵנוּ מִצְרַיְמָה

(8) רֵד הָעִירָה   (2) שֵׁב פֹּה

(9) שְׁבוּ בְּבֵיתְכֶם   (3) בְּלִדְתֵּךְ בֵּן

(10) נוּכַל לָלֶכֶת בַּבֹּקֶר   (4) דְּעוּ כִּי הַמֶּלֶךְ בָּא

(11) צְאוּ מֵהָעִיר   (5) אַל־תִּירְאִי

(12) בְּרִשְׁתְּכֶם אֹתָהּ   (6) לֹא תוּכַל לִישֹׁן

(b) Give the Hebrew for the following orally:

1. Go forth (m. s.) today.
2. and when we knew
3. She will bear a son.
4. We shall not inherit this land.
5. He will fashion a new vessel.
6. We shall not be afraid of them.
7. and as he went forth
8. Do you know all these things?
9. Let us go down to the Negev.
10. And they went to their country.
11. Let us sit down and eat.
12. And he slept the whole night.

(c) Translate:

(1) לֹא יִישַׁן שֹׁמֵר יִשְׂרָאֵל.

(2) וַיִּקְרְבוּ הָאֲנָשִׁים אֵלָיו לִשְׁאֹל לוֹ לְשָׁלוֹם.

(3) וְהָיָה בִקְרֹא הָעָם אֵלַי וְעָנִיתִי אֹתָם.

(4) וַיְהִי בִישֹׁן הַיֶּלֶד וַיַּחֲלֹם חֲלוֹם.

(5) רָחוֹק מְאֹד מֵהַמָּקוֹם הַזֶּה הָעֵמֶק אֲשֶׁר אַתֶּם הֹלְכִים שָׁמָּה.

(6) הָרְגוּ אֶת־בַּעַל הַבַּיִת וַיִּקְחוּ אֶת־כָּל־רְכֻשׁוֹ אִתָּם וַיֵּצְאוּ מֵהָעִיר.

(7) וַיִּשְׁאַל הָאִישׁ וַיֹּאמַר: מֶה עָשִׂיתִי כִּי תִשְׂנָא אֹתִי.

(8) בְּשָׁלוֹם אֶשְׁכַּב וְאִישַׁן כִּי אַתָּה עִמִּי יהוה אֱלֹהִים.

(9) קְרַב אֶל־הַהֵיכָל וּשְׁמַע אֶת־דִּבְרֵי הַנָּבִיא.

(10) לָמָּה לֹא עָנִיתָ כַּאֲשֶׁר שָׁאַלְתִּי לְךָ לְשָׁלוֹם.

(11) לֹא תִקְרַב הָרָעָה בְּבֵיתְךָ כִּי נָתַן יהוה אֶת־מַלְאָכָיו לִשְׁמֹר אֹתְךָ וְאֶת־כָּל־דְּרָכֶיךָ.

(12) מַה־תִּשְׁאַל מִמֶּנִּי.

(13) לָכְדוּ אֶת־הָעִיר בְּטֶרֶם יִבְרְחוּ יֹשְׁבֶיהָ הַמִּדְבָּרָה.

(d) Write in Hebrew:

1. Who is the husband of that beautiful woman standing near the gate?
2. They came to the city from afar to inquire after the health of the king.
3. The owner of the field came and told us to go to our (own) house(s).

4. They set out and traveled many days until they found a large and pleasant valley in which they might dwell in peace.

5. Let us hear his words so that we might know the place from which he has come.

(e) Reading: Joseph and His Brothers (1)

יָשַׁב יַעֲקֹב בְּאֶרֶץ מְגוּרֵי אָבִיו בְּאֶרֶץ כְּנָעַן. אֵלֶּה תּוֹלְדוֹת יַעֲקֹב. יוֹסֵף בֶּן־שְׁבַע עֶשְׂרֵה[1] שָׁנָה הָיָה רֹעֶה אֶת־אֶחָיו בַּצֹּאן וְיִשְׂרָאֵל אָהַב אֶת־יוֹסֵף מִכָּל־בָּנָיו כִּי בֶן־זְקֻנִים הוּא לוֹ וְעָשָׂה לוֹ כְּתֹנֶת פַּסִּים.[2] רָאוּ אֶחָיו כִּי אֹתוֹ אָהַב אֲבִיהֶם מִכָּל־אֶחָיו וַיִּשְׂנְאוּ אֹתוֹ וְלֹא יָכְלוּ דַבְּרוֹ[3] לְשָׁלוֹם.

וַיַּחֲלֹם יוֹסֵף חֲלוֹמוֹת וּבַחֲלוֹמֹתָיו יִשְׁתַּחֲווּ[4] אֶחָיו וְאָבִיו וְאִמּוֹ לְפָנָיו. וַיַּגֵּד[5] אֶת־הַחֲלוֹמוֹת לְאֶחָיו וַיִּשְׂנְאוּ אֹתוֹ עַל־חֲלוֹמֹתָיו וְעַל־דְּבָרָיו וַיַּגֵּד[5] גַּם־אֶל־אָבִיו וַיִּגְעַר בּוֹ אָבִיו וַיֹּאמֶר לוֹ: מָה הַחֲלוֹם הַזֶּה אֲשֶׁר חָלָמְתָּ. הֲבוֹא נָבוֹא[6] אֲנִי וְאִמְּךָ וְאַחֶיךָ לְהִשְׁתַּחֲוֹת[7] לְפָנֶיךָ אָרְצָה.

אֶחָיו שָׂנְאוּ אֹתוֹ וְאָבִיו שָׁמַר אֶת־הַדָּבָר.

Notes to the Reading:

1. "seventeen"
2. meaning unknown. Perhaps "a full garment with long sleeves."
3. "to speak to him"
4. "(they) would bow down"
5. "and he told"
6. "Shall we indeed come"
7. "to bow down"

LESSON 31

122. Verbs III-Hē: Imperfect, Imperative, and Infinitive Construct.

This class of verbs is quite uniform in its inflection. The imperfect ends in *-eh* except where this is replaced by an inflectional ending; the imperative ends in *-ēh*; and the inf. constr. in *-ôt*. Below are the paradigms of בָּנָה, which may be taken as a norm of this class, and several verbs which have other peculiarities in addition to being III-*Hē*: עָלָה, also I-guttural; הָגָה, also I-guttural but differing in the preformative vowel from עָלָה; נָטָה, also I-*Nun*; and the slightly irregular verb הָיָה.

	to build	to ascend	to meditate	to extend	to be
Imperfect:	יִבְנֶה	יַעֲלֶה	יֶהְגֶּה	יִטֶּה	יִהְיֶה
	תִּבְנֶה	תַּעֲלֶה	תֶּהְגֶּה	תִּטֶּה	תִּהְיֶה
	תִּבְנֶה	תַּעֲלֶה	תֶּהְגֶּה	תִּטֶּה	תִּהְיֶה
	תִּבְנִי	תַּעֲלִי	תֶּהְגִּי	תִּטִּי	תִּהְיִי
	אֶבְנֶה	אֶעֱלֶה	אֶהְגֶּה	אֶטֶּה	אֶהְיֶה
	יִבְנוּ	יַעֲלוּ	יֶהְגּוּ	יִטּוּ	יִהְיוּ
	תִּבְנֶינָה	תַּעֲלֶינָה	תֶּהְגֶּינָה	תִּטֶּינָה	תִּהְיֶינָה
	תִּבְנוּ	תַּעֲלוּ	תֶּהְגּוּ	תִּטּוּ	תִּהְיוּ
	תִּבְנֶינָה	תַּעֲלֶינָה	תֶּהְגֶּינָה	תִּטֶּינָה	תִּהְיֶינָה
	נִבְנֶה	נַעֲלֶה	נֶהְגֶּה	נִטֶּה	נִהְיֶה
Imperative:	בְּנֵה	עֲלֵה	הֲגֵה	נְטֵה	הֱיֵה

[143]

בְּנִי	עֲלִי	הַגִי	נְטִי	הָיִי
בְּנוּ	עֲלוּ	הַגוּ	נְטוּ	הָיוּ
בְּנֶינָה	עֲלֶינָה	הַגֶּינָה	נְטֶינָה	—
Inf. Constr. בְּנוֹת	עֲלוֹת	הֲגוֹת	נְטוֹת	הֱיוֹת

The verb חָיָה (to live) is inflected like הָיָה, except that the inf. constr. is vocalized with *ă* in the first syllable: חֲיוֹת.

The two verbs אָפָה (to bake) and אָבָה (to be willing) have imperfects יֹאפֶה and יֹאבֶה, following the I-*Aleph* patterning in conjunction with the III-*Hē*.

There is a distinct form for the jussive in the singular. It may be thought of as a shortened (or apocopated) form of the imperfect, without the final *-eh*, but the development of a secondary vowel to resolve the resulting final consonant cluster has produced inconsistencies. Here, for reference, is a list of the most important verbs III-*Hē* with their attested short forms:

	Perfect	Imperfect	Jussive 3 m. s.	3 f. s./2 m. s.	1 c. s.	1c. pl.
build	בָּנָה	יִבְנֶה	יִבֶן			
despise	בָּזָה	יִבְזֶה	יִבֶז	תִּבֶז		
weep	בָּכָה	יִבְכֶּה	יֵבְךְ	תֵּבְךְ		
reveal	גָּלָה	יִגְלֶה	יִגֶל			
be harlot	זָנָה	תִזְנֶה		תִּזֶן		
be done	כָּלָה	יְכַלֶּה	יְכֶל	תֵּכֶל		
turn	פָּנָה	יִפְנֶה	יִפֶן	תֵּפֶן	אֶפֶן	נֵפֶן
acquire	קָנָה	יִקְנֶה	יִקֶן			
be many	רָבָה	יִרְבֶּה	יֶרֶב	תֵּרֶב		
drink	שָׁתָה	יִשְׁתֶּה	יֵשְׁתְּ	תֵּשְׁתְּ	אֶשְׁתְּ	
capture	שָׁבָה	יִשְׁבֶּה	יִשְׁבְּ			
II-*guttural*:						
pasture	רָעָה	יִרְעֶה	יִרַע			
see	רָאָה	יִרְאֶה	יֵרֶא	תֵּרֶא	אֶרֶא	
be lost	תָּעָה	יִתְעֶה		תֵּתַע		
I-*guttural*:						
answer	עָנָה	יַעֲנֶה	יַעַן	תַּעַן	אַעַן	
ascend	עָלָה	יַעֲלֶה	יַעַל	תַּעַל	אַעַל	נַעַל
do	עָשָׂה	יַעֲשֶׂה	יַעַשׂ	תַּעַשׂ	אַעַשׂ	נַעַשׂ
conceive	הָרָה			תַּהַר		
camp	חָנָה	יַחֲנֶה	יִחַן			
be angry	חָרָה	יֶחֱרֶה	יִחַר			
I-*Nun*:						
extend	נָטָה	יִטֶּה	יֵט	תֵּט		

Anomalous:

| be | הָיָה | יִהְיֶה | יְהִי | | תְּהִי | אֱהִי | נְהִי |
| live | חָיָה | יִחְיֶה | יְחִי | | | | |

The importance of these forms lies not so much in their use as jussives but rather in the fact that these short forms are used regularly with *waw-*conversive in the past narrative sequence:

וַיַּֽעַשׂ   and he made

וַתֵּֽבְךְּ   and she wept

The short forms of the 3rd and 2nd persons are nearly always used; in the first person there is an option between the short and normal forms:

וָאֶבְכֶּה or וָאֵבְךְּ and I wept

Note the sequence form וַיַּרְא (and he saw), which differs from the jussive יֵ֫רֶא. There are no cohortatives in *-āh* for verbs III-*Hē*. The stem of the inf. construct undergoes no changes with the addition of the pronominal suffixes:

בְּנוֹתִי my building

בְּנוֹתְךָ your building

etc.

123. Vocabulary 31.

NOUNS: בּוֹר *bôr* (pl. -ôṯ) pit, cistern; fig. the grave

רֵעַ *rēaʿ* (pl. -îm) friend, companion [the stem vowel is not changeable: pl. constr. רֵעֵי; the singular with the 3rd pers. masc. sing. suffix is רֵעֵ֫הוּ]

שִׂמְלָה *śimlāh* (pl. -ôṯ) outer garment, cloak

VERBS: שָׁפַךְ *šāp̄ak* (יִשְׁפֹּךְ) to pour, shed (blood)

תָּפַשׂ *tāp̄aś* (יִתְפֹּשׂ) to seize, grab

נָטָה *nāṭāh* (יִטֶּה) to extend; pitch (tent); turn aside (intr.)

בָּכָה *bāḵāh* (יִבְכֶּה) to weep, mourn

שָׁחַט *šāḥaṭ* (יִשְׁחַט) to slaughter (usu. of animals)

OTHER: עַתָּה *ʿattāh* (adv.) now, and so then, then

רֵיק *rêq* (adj.) empty, worthless, idle

PROPER NAMES: דּוֹתָן *Dôṯān* Dothan, a city about 13 m. north of Shechem

רְאוּבֵן *Rəʾûḇēn* Reuben, first-born son of Jacob (by Leah)

IDIOMS: (1) A plural verb followed by אִישׁ and a correlated singular suffix is to be taken distributively or reciprocally:

הָלְכוּ אִישׁ אֶל־בֵּיתוֹ Each man went to his (own) house.

וַיֹּאמְרוּ אִישׁ אֶל־רֵעֵ֫הוּ And they said to one another.

(2) The imperative of הָלַךְ is frequently used before another imperative or cohortative in a sense difficult to translate. It is more or less an

invitation or inciting to action, like English "*Come on*, let's . . ." It may therefore be omitted often from translation.

לְכוּ וְנַהַרְגֵהוּ אֹתוֹ   Come on, let's kill him.

(3) An imperative, especially of הָלַךְ and other verbs of motion, may be followed by the dative pronoun which has no translation value in English:

לֵךְ לְךָ Go!   סְעוּ לָכֶם Travel!

Exercises:

(a) Translate:

(1) יִבְנוּ עִיר חֲדָשָׁה	(11) אַל־תֵּתַע
(2) יְהִי אוֹר	(12) טֵט אֶת־יָדְךָ
(3) וַיֵּחַר לוֹ מְאֹד	(13) לָמָּה תִבְכֶּה
(4) וַיִּכְלוּ הַמַּיִם מֵעַל פְּנֵי הָאָרֶץ	(14) וַיְכַלּוּ לַעֲשׂוֹת אֶת־הַמְּלָאכָה
(5) וַנַּעַל יְרוּשָׁלָ֫מָה	(15) וַיַּעֲלוּ הָהָרָה לִרְאוֹת אֶת־הַחַיּוֹת
(6) כִּרְאוֹתִי אֹתָם	(16) יִרְעֶה אֶת־עַמּוֹ כִּרְעֹה
(7) נַעֲשֶׂה אֱלֹהֵי עֵץ	(17) וַנֵּשֶׁב וַנֹּאכַל וַנִּשְׁתֶּה
(8) בִּרְעוֹתָם אֶת־צֹאנָם	(18) אַל־תִּבְכֶּה עַל־הָרְשָׁעִים
(9) וַיַּעַן וַיֹּאמֶר	(19) אֲטֶה אֶת־יָדִי הַשָּׁמָ֫יְמָה
(10) אַל־תִּשְׁתֶּה אֶת־הַמַּ֫יִם	(20) וַתֵּתַע הָאִשָּׁה בַּמִּדְבָּר
	(21) וַיִּשְׁחֲטוּ מֵהַבָּקָר וּמֵהַצֹּאן

(b) Give the Hebrew for the following orally:

1. Don't pour the water.
2. Why are you crying?
3. You ask and he will answer.
4. before he created the earth
5. They were afraid to approach.
6. Remember the history of your people.
7. His house is close to the city.
8. I slept the whole night.
9. Her husband left her.
10. The place is too far away for us to see.

(c) Translate:

(1) וַתִּדֹּר הָאִשָּׁה נֶ֫דֶר וַתֹּאמַר: אֶתֵּן לַיהוה אֶת־הַיֶּ֫לֶד הַזֶּה אֲשֶׁר אֵלֵד וְהוּא יֵשֵׁב בְּהֵיכַל יהוה וְעָבַד אֹתוֹ כָּל־יְמֵי חַיָּיו.

(2) וַיֹּאמֶר הָאִישׁ: לָמָּה בָחַ֫רְתָּ בִּי וְאָנֹכִי הַצָּעִיר בְּבֵית אָבִי.

(3) וַיַּעַן אֹתוֹ יהוה לֵאמֹר: אֶהְיֶה עִמְּךָ בְּכָל־אֲשֶׁר אַתָּה עֹשֶׂה.

(4) סָבְבוּ אֹתִי שֹׂנְאַי וְעָזְבוּ אֹתִי אֹהֲבַי.

(5) לָמָּה תַעַזְבוּ אֶת־אֶ֫רֶץ מְגוּרֵי אֲבִיכֶם וִישַׁבְתֶּם אֶל־הָאָ֫רֶץ הַהִיא.

(6) בֹּ֫שְׁנוּ כִּי לֹא לָקַח אֶת־הַמִּנְחָה אֲשֶׁר נָתַ֫נּוּ לוֹ.

(7) וַיֹּאמֶר יהוה אֶל־מֹשֶׁה: נְטֵה אֶת־יָדְךָ עַל־הַשָּׁמַיִם וִיהִי חֹשֶׁךְ עַל־אֶרֶץ מִצְרָיִם וַיֵּט מֹשֶׁה אֶת־יָדוֹ עַל־הַשָּׁמַיִם וַיְהִי חֹשֶׁךְ בְּכָל־אֶרֶץ מִצְרָיִם וְלֹא רָאוּ אִישׁ אֶת־אָחִיו וְלֹא קָמוּ אִישׁ מִמְּקֹמוֹ.

(d) Write in Hebrew:

1. The men of the city rebuked him because he had not heeded the words of the elders.
2. They are evil men because they have shed blood and sinned against the Lord.
3. And he raised his eyes and saw two men standing near the well.
4. And when she heard these words, she fell to the ground and wept.
5. You shall see and you shall know that the Lord is with us.
6. Heaven and earth are full (of) your (m. s.) glory.
7. Eat and drink for in the morning we shall go forth to battle.

(e) Reading: Joseph and his Brothers (2)

וַיֵּלְכוּ אֶחָיו לִרְעוֹת אֶת־צֹאן אֲבִיהֶם בִּשְׁכֶם וַיֹּאמֶר יִשְׂרָאֵל אֶל־יוֹסֵף: הֲלֹא אַחֶיךָ רֹעִים בִּשְׁכֶם, לְכָה וְאֶשְׁלַח אֹתְךָ אֲלֵיהֶם, לֶךְ נָא רְאֵה אֶת־שְׁלוֹם אַחֶיךָ וְאֶת־שְׁלוֹם הַצֹּאן, וַיִּשְׁלַח אֹתוֹ מֵעֵמֶק חֶבְרוֹן וַיָּבֹא¹ שְׁכֶמָה.²

וַיְהִי אַחֲרֵי אֲשֶׁר לֹא מָצָא אֹתָם בִּשְׁכֶם וַיֵּלֶךְ וַיִּמְצָא אֹתָם בְּדוֹתָן וַיִּרְאוּ אֹתוֹ אֶחָיו מֵרָחוֹק וּבְטֶרֶם יִקְרַב אֲלֵיהֶם וַיֹּאמְרוּ אִישׁ אֶל־אָחִיו: בַּעַל הַחֲלוֹמוֹת בָּא וְעַתָּה לְכוּ וְנַהַרְגָה אֹתוֹ וְשָׁמְנוּ אֹתוֹ בְּאַחַד הַבֹּרוֹת וְאָמַרְנוּ כִּי חַיָּה רָעָה אֲכָלָה אֹתוֹ.

וַיִּשְׁמַע רְאוּבֵן אֶת־דִּבְרֵיהֶם וַיֹּאמֶר אֲלֵיהֶם: אַל־תִּשְׁפְּכוּ דָם, וְיָד אַל־תִּשְׁלְחוּ בוֹ. וַיְהִי כַּאֲשֶׁר בָּא יוֹסֵף אֶל־אֶחָיו וַיִּתְפְּשׂוּ אֹתוֹ וַיִּקְחוּ אֶת־כֻּתָּנְתּוֹ מִמֶּנּוּ וַיַּשְׁלִיכוּ³ אֹתוֹ הַבּוֹרָה וְהַבּוֹר הָיָה רֵיק אֵין בּוֹ מָיִם.⁴

Notes to the Reading:

1. "and he came"
2. שְׁכֶם with directive -āh
3. "and they threw"
4. Note the asyndetic clause beginning with אֵין.

LESSON 32

124. Hollow Verbs (II-Waw/Yodh): Imperfect, Imperative, and Infinitive Construct.

In the inflection of the perfect (§64) the lexical distinction between verbs II-*Waw* and II-*Yodh* is irrelevant. In the imperfect, however, the stem vowel reflects this distinction and is, indeed, responsible for the classification of the verbs under their respective consonantal types: verbs with *û*-imperfects are considered II-*Waw*, and those with *î*-imperfects as II-*Yodh*. Neither the *waw* nor the *yodh* has a consonantal value in the main inflections of these forms. The two basic types are

		Perfect	*Imperfect*			*Imperative*	*Inf. Construct*	
II-*Waw*	קָם	*qām*	normal	יָקוּם	*yāqûm*	קוּם *qûm*	קוּם *qûm*	
			jussive	יָקֹם	*yāqōm*			
			converted	וַיָּקָם	*wayyā́qom*			
II-*Yodh*	שָׂם	*śām*	normal	יָשִׂים	*yāśîm*	שִׂים *śîm*	שׂוּם *śûm*	⎫
			jussive	יָשֵׂם	*yāśēm*		שִׂים *śîm*	⎬
			converted	וַיָּשֶׂם	*wayyā́śem*			⎭

Verbs of the second type are unstable, in that the vowel of the infinitive construct varies between *û* and *î*. Some verbs have *î* consistently, such as שִׂית (to place), while others have either vowel: לִין or לוּן (to pass the night). Because of this variation they may be listed in the lexicon under either root form.

Note that the jussive and the form used with *waw*-conversive are distinct. Remember that the jussive forms are limited to the 3rd pers. sing. masc. and fem. The distinctive converted form, with retraction of the accent to the preformative syllable, is commonly found only in these same persons, plus the 2nd pers. masc. sing.; otherwise the converted form is the same as the normal imperfect.

Imperfect:

יָקוּם	*yāqûm*	יָקוּמוּ	*yāqûmû*	יָשִׂים	*yāśîm*	יָשִׂימוּ	*yāśîmû*
תָּקוּם	*tāqûm*	תְּקוּמֶ֫ינָה	*təqûmênāh*	תָּשִׂים	*tāśîm*	תְּשִׂימֶ֫ינָה	*təśîmênāh*
תָּקוּם	*tāqûm*	תָּק֫וּמוּ	*tāqûmû*	תָּשִׂים	*tāśîm*	תָּשִׂ֫ימוּ	*tāśîmû*
תָּק֫וּמִי	*tāqûmî*	תְּקוּמֶ֫ינָה	*təqûmênāh*	תָּשִׂ֫ימִי	*tāśîmî*	תְּשִׂימֶ֫ינָה	*təśîmênāh*
אָקוּם	*'āqûm*	נָקוּם	*nāqûm*	אָשִׂים	*'āśîm*	נָשִׂים	*nāśîm*

Jussive:

יָקֹם	*yāqōm*	יָשֵׂם	*yāśēm*
תָּקֹם	*tāqōm*	תָּשֵׂם	*tāśēm*

Converted:

וַיָּ֫קָם	*wayyā́qom*	וַיָּ֫שֶׂם	*wayyā́śem*
וַתָּ֫קָם	*wattā́qom*	וַתָּ֫שֶׂם	*wattā́śem*
וַתָּ֫קָם	*wattā́qom*	וַתָּ֫שֶׂם	*wattā́śem*
וַתָּק֫וּמִי	*wattāqûmî*	וַתָּשִׂ֫ימִי	*wattāśîmî*
	(etc.)		(etc.)

Cohortative:

אָק֫וּמָה	*'āqûmāh*	אָשִׂ֫ימָה	*'āśîmāh*
נָק֫וּמָה	*nāqûmāh*	נָשִׂ֫ימָה	*nāśîmāh*

Imperative:

קוּם	*qûm*	שִׂים	*śîm*
ק֫וּמִי	*qûmî*	שִׂ֫ימִי	*śîmî*
ק֫וּמוּ	*qûmû*	שִׂ֫ימוּ	*śîmû*
קֹ֫מְנָה	*qṓmnāh*	[שֵׂ֫מְנָה	*śḗmnāh*]

Inf. Construct with Suffixes

קוּמִי	*qûmî*	שׂוּמִי	*śûmî*
קוּמְךָ	*qûməkā*	שׂוּמְךָ	*śûməkā*
קוּמֵךְ	*qûmēk*	שׂוּמֵךְ	*śûmēk*
	(etc.)		(etc.)

Remarks:

1. Imperfect fem. pl. of the form תָּקֹ֫מְנָה *tāqṓmnāh* (instead of תְּקוּמֶ֫ינָה) also occur.

2. Several verbs, mainly with gutturals or ר as the final root consonant, have *a* instead of *o* or *e* in the converted form. E.g. יָסוּר *yāsûr*, but וַיָּ֫סַר *wayyā́sar* (and he turned aside); יָנוּחַ *yānû*ʰ, but וַיָּ֫נַח *wayyā́naḥ* (and he rested).

The following verbs belonging to these two principal types have occurred thus far in this text:

גָּר	יָגוּר	to sojourn	מֵת	יָמוּת	to die
צָם	יָצוּם	to fast	שָׂם	יָשִׂים	to set
קָם	יָקוּם	to arise	שָׁר	יָשִׁיר	to sing
שָׁב	יָשׁוּב	to return			

A few verbs occur with *ô* as the characteristic vowel of the imperfect and related forms. The following are the most important of these:

Perfect			Imperfect		Imperative		Inf. Construct	
בָּא	*bā'*	normal	יָבוֹא	*yābô'*	בֹּא	*bō'*	בּוֹא	*bô'*
		jussive	יָבֹא	*yābô'*				
		converted	וַיָּבֹא	*wayyābô'*				
בֹּשׁ	*bōš*		יֵבוֹשׁ	*yēbôš*	בּוֹשׁ	*bôš*	בּוֹשׁ	*bôš*
אֹר	*'ōr*		[יָאוֹר	*yā'ôr*]	אוֹר	*'ôr*	אוֹר	*'ôr*

Inflection proceeds as above. The variation between *ô* and *ō* in these forms is not grammatically significant. Note that the accent is not retracted in וַיָּבֹא .

125. Vocabulary 32.

NOUNS: בֶּצַע   *béṣaʿ* (w. suff. בִּצְעִי) profit, gain, advantage. Note the idiom: מַה־בֶּצַע What profit is there?

סָרִיס   *sārîs* (pl. irreg. סָרִיסִים) eunuch, officer.

אָדוֹן   *'ādôn* (pl. -îm) lord, master. Often used in the plural with singular meaning.

VERBS: שָׁת   *šāṯ* (יָשִׁית) to put, place, set. A synonym of שָׂם .

רָץ   *rāṣ* (יָרוּץ) to run

נָס   *nās* (יָנוּס) to flee

רָדַף   *rādap̄* (יִרְדֹּף) to pursue, chase, persecute (object with אֶת־ or אַחֲרֵי)

קָנָה   *qānāh* (יִקְנֶה) to acquire, purchase, buy

OTHER: לִקְרַאת   *liqra(')ṯ* (prep., with suff. לִקְרָאתִי etc.) toward, to meet, against

הִנֵּה   *hinnēh* An introductory particle, customarily translated "behold," emphasizing the immediate presence of an object or a fact. In its idiomatic use with רָאָה it is best omitted from translation: רָאָה וְהִנֵּה אֲנָשִׁים בָּאִים He saw men coming. (or) He saw that men were coming. But *not* "He saw, and behold men were coming."

PROPER NAMES: פַּרְעֹה   *parʿōh* the title of the king of Egypt, the Pharaoh

פּוֹטִיפַר   *pôṭîp̄ar* Potiphar

גִּלְעָד   *gilʿād* Gilead, a region east of the Jordan River

יְהוּדָה   *yəhûḏāh* Judah: (1) the fourth son of Jacob, by Leah; (2) the tribe bearing his name; (3) the southern kingdom, as opposed to Israel, the northern kingdom, during the period of the divided monarchy.

- יִשְׁמְעֵאלִים ·   *yišmə'ē(')lîm*   Ishmaelites, a term applied to various little known nomadic groups several times in the OT.

Exercises:

(a) Translate:

(1) וְהָיָה בִּשְׁאֹל הָעָם אֹתוֹ וְלֹא יַעֲנֶה אֹתָם.

(2) נֹוּסוּ כִּי אֹיְבֵיכֶם רֹדְפִים אַחֲרֵיכֶם.

(3) מִי הָאִישׁ הָרָץ לִקְרָאתֵנוּ.

(4) מָכְרוּ אֶת־הַמִּקְנֶה אֲשֶׁר קָנוּ שָׁם.

(5) אֵיפֹה שַׂתָּ אֶת־כְּלִי הַמַּיִם.

(6) וַיְהִי אִישׁ יָשָׁר בְּכָל־אֲשֶׁר עָשָׂה.

(7) וַיַּרְא וְהִנֵּה סָרִיס הַמֶּלֶךְ בָּא לִקְרָאתוֹ.

(8) וַיָּקָם וַיֵּלֶךְ עִמּוֹ הַמִּדְבָּרָה.

(9) וַיָּשֶׂת אֶת־הַסְּפָרִים לִפְנֵי אִמּוֹ.

(10) וַיְהִי בַּצָּהֳרַיִם וָאֵרֶא אִישׁ בָּא לִקְרָאתִי.

(11) וָאָקוּם וָאָנוּס מִלְּפָנָיו.

(12) אֶשְׁכַּב וְיָשַׁנְתִּי פֹּה עַד־הַבֹּקֶר.

(13) בֵּיתֵנוּ קָרוֹב אֶל־הַהֵיכָל.

(14) רְדֹף אַחֲרֵיהֶם כִּי לָקְחוּ אֶת־רְכוּשֵׁנוּ.

(b) Give the Hebrew for the following orally:

1. Run to the field.
2. They will flee from their houses.
3. Who will inherit his garden?
4. Where will you buy the cattle?
5. Where did you put my money?
6. Did they chase you?
7. The king's official is very rich.
8. There is no advantage in weeping.
9. We left because of the famine.
10. You shall run and find him.
11. We fled when they burned our houses.

(c) Translate the following:

(8) וַיִּגַּר שָׁם   (1) יָדֵנוּ תִּהְיֶה בֹּו בְּהָרְגֵנוּ אֹתוֹ

(9) וַיָּשֶׂם אֹתוֹ בְּקִבְרוֹ   (2) קֹוּמִי וְשׁוּבִי הַבַּיְתָה

(10) יָרוּץ הַיֶּלֶד אֶל־הַשָּׂדֶה   (3) לֹא חָפַצְנוּ לָצוּם

(11) הַנְּעָרִים שָׁבִים אִישׁ אֶל־בֵּיתוֹ   (4) מַה־בֶּצַע כִּי נָגוּר פֹּה

(12) נוּס כִּי אֹיִבְךָ בָּא   (5) נָשִׂימָה אֶת־אָחִינוּ עַל־הַכִּסֵּא

(13) חָפְצוּ לָשׁוּב וְלֹא יָכֹלוּ   (6) לֹא יָכֹלְתִּי לָרוּץ

(14) מִי יַחְפֹּץ לָשֶׁבֶת שָׁם   (7) תֶּחְדַּל לָצוּם

(d) Write in Hebrew:

1. And in the morning his companion arose and went to the city.
2. They will slaughter our cattle and burn our vineyards.
3. It is bad to shed blood.
4. They arose and pursued him, but they could not find him.
5. And now, let us choose a king for ourselves (= us).
6. Where did you put his cloak?
7. Did you know that this vessel is empty?

(e) Reading: Joseph Is Taken to Egypt

וַיֵּשְׁבוּ אֲחֵי יוֹסֵף לֶאֱכָל לֶחֶם וַיִּשְׂאוּ עֵינֵיהֶם‎[1] וַיִּרְאוּ וְהִנֵּה אֹרְחַת‎[2] יִשְׁמְעֵאלִים בָּאָה מִגִּלְעָד וְהֵם הֹלְכִים לָרֶדֶת מִצְרָיְמָה.

וַיֹּאמֶר יְהוּדָה אֶל־אֶחָיו לֵאמֹר: מַה־בֶּצַע כִּי נַהֲרֹג אֶת־אָחִינוּ, לְכוּ וְנִמְכְּרָה אֹתוֹ לַיִּשְׁמְעֵאלִים וְיָדֵנוּ אַל־תְּהִי בוֹ כִּי אָחִינוּ בְשָׂרֵנוּ הוּא.

וַיִּשְׁמְעוּ אֶחָיו וַיִּמְכְּרוּ אֶת־יוֹסֵף לַיִּשְׁמְעֵאלִים וַיֵּרֶד יוֹסֵף אִתָּם מִצְרָיְמָה.

וַיִּקֶן אֹתוֹ פּוֹטִיפַר סְרִיס פַּרְעֹה אִישׁ מִצְרִי מִיַּד הַיִּשְׁמְעֵאלִים וַיְהִי יהוה אֶת־יוֹסֵף וַיְהִי אִישׁ מַצְלִיחַ‎[3] בְּבֵית אֲדֹנָיו הַמִּצְרִי.

Notes to the Reading:

1. The omission of אֶת־ here and often in the readings to follow is in accord with the usage found in the text underlying the reading.
2. אֹרְחָה a caravan
3. "successful"

LESSON 33

126. Geminate Verbs: Imperfect, Imperative, and Infinitive Construct.

Geminate Verbs or Double Ayin Verbs

No single class of verbs shows as much variety in the formation of the imperfect as that of geminate verbs, i.e. whose second and third root consonants are identical. No one of these verbs occurs frequently enough to offer a complete paradigm; the following tables, therefore, represent a compilation from the available data. On historical grounds, the more original forms of the imperfect system are

	Perfect	*Imperfect*		*Imperative*		*Inf. Constr.*	
ō-imperfects	סָבַב *sābab*	normal	יָסֹב *yāsōb*	סֹב *sōb*		סֹב *sōb*	
		jussive	יָסֹב *yāsōb*				
		converted	וַיָּסָב *wayyásob*				
a-imperfects	קַל *qal*	normal	יֵקַל *yēqal*	——		[קֹל *qōl*]	
		jussive	יֵקַל *yēqal*				
		converted	וַיֵּקַל *wayyēqal*				

In the normal inflection of these forms the original doubling of the final stem consonant shows up before any suffixed vowel. The accent, except in the case of the ending -ênāh, remains on the stem:

יָסֹב	*yāsōb*	יָסֹבּוּ	*yāsóbbû*	יֵקַל	*yēqal*	יֵקַלּוּ	*yēqállû*
תָּסֹב	*tāsōb*	תְּסֻבֶּינָה	*təsubbênāh*	תֵּקַל	*tēqal*	[תְּקַלֶּינָה	*təqallênāh*]
תָּסֹב	*tāsōb*	תָּסֹבּוּ	*tāsóbbû*	תֵּקַל	*tēqal*	תֵּקַלּוּ	*tēqállû*

[153]

תָּסֹֽבִּי	*tāsóbbî*	תְּסֻבֶּֽינָה	*təsubbênāh*	תְּקַלִּי	*tēqállî* [תְּקַלֶּֽינָה	*təqallênāh*]
אָסֹב	*'āsōb*	נָסֹב	*nāsōb*	אֶקַל	*'ēqal*	נֵקַל	*nēqal*

A second type of imperfect, not infrequent, follows the pattern of verbs I-*Nun* in the formation of the stem, but there are several optional forms in the inflection:

יִסֹּב	*yissób*	יִסֹּֽבּוּ or יִסְּבוּ	*yissóbbû* or *yissəbû*
תִּסֹּב	*tissób*	תִּסֹּֽבְנָה	*tissóbnāh*
תִּסֹּב	*tissób*	תִּסֹּֽבּוּ or תִּסְּבוּ	*tissóbbû* or *tissəbû*
תִּסֹּֽבִּי or תִּסְּבִי	*tissóbbî* or *tissəbî*	תִּסֹּֽבְנָה	*tissóbnāh*
אֶסֹּב	*'essób*	נִסֹּב	*nissób*

And similarly throughout for יִקַּל *yiqqal* etc.

The following further oddities in the inflection of the imperfect are mentioned for reference only:

(1) Assimilation to the Hollow Verb inflection is not unknown: thus, e.g., יָשׁוּד *yāšûd*, from the root שׁדד .

(2) Inflections like the first given above also have such alternate forms as יֶקְלוּ *yēqəlû* (with reduction) instead of יֵקַלּוּ *yēqállû*. E.g. יָזְמוּ *yāzəmû* (they will consider) for expected יָזֹֽמּוּ *yāzómmû*.

(3) Rarely one encounters forms belonging to the paradigm of still other types, such as יֵחֵמּוּ *yeḥĕmû* (they will be warm, root חמם), or תִּישַֽׁמְנָה *tîšámnāh* (you will be devastated, root שׁמם).

The imperative and infinitive construct show similar deviations, but the following should be taken as the norm:

	Imperative		Inf. Construct	
ō-imperfects	סֹב	*sōb*	סֹב	*sōb*
	סֹֽבִּי	*sóbbî*	סֻבִּי	*subbî*
	סֹֽבּוּ	*sóbbû*	סֻבְּךָ	*subbəkā*
	סֹֽבְנָה	*sóbnāh*	סֻבֵּךְ	*subbēk*, etc.
a-imperfects	קַל	*qal*		
	קַלִּי	*qallî*		
	קַלּוּ	*qallû*		
	קַֽלְנָה	*qálnāh*		

The fem. sing. imperative also occurs with ultimate stress: גֻּזִּי *gozzî* (shear), רָנִּי *ronnî* (jubilate). Occasionally the inf. construct appears in the pattern of the regular triliteral verb: שָׁדֹד *šədōd* (to devastate), שָׁלֹל *šəlōl* (to plunder), גָּזֹז *gəzōz* (to shear).

Note the imperfects of תַּם (to be finished): יִתַּם or יִתֹּם .

רַע (to be bad): יֵרַע

127. Vocabulary 33.

NOUNS: מְאוּמָה mə'ûmāh (no pl.)   anything; with negative: nothing

אַף 'ap (w. suff. אַפִּי ; dual אַפַּֽיִם)   nose, face, anger. Used as the subject of חָרָה ; thus חָרָה אַפּוֹ = חָרָה לוֹ. The object of the anger is expressed by the preposition בְּ .

VERBS: חָשַׂךְ ḥāśak (יַחְשֹׂךְ)   to withhold, keep back for oneself

חָנַן ḥānan (יָחֹן)   to favor, be gracious toward

שָׁמֵם šāmēm (יִשֹּׁם or יֵשַׁם)   to be desolated (of places), to be appalled (of persons); act. part. שָׁמֵם desolated.

דַּם dam (יִדֹּם)   to be silent, astonished

מָדַד mādad (יָמֹד)   to measure

OTHER: עִבְרִי 'ibrî (pl. עִבְרִים ; fem. sing. עִבְרִיָּה)   Hebrew, as adj. or noun.

כִּי אִם kî 'im (conj.)   unless, except (that); but rather

אֵיךְ 'êk (interrog. adv.)   how, in what manner? Also used in exclamations.

אֵיכָה 'êkāh idem

Exercises:

(a) Translate:

(1) תָּחֹן אֹתוֹ וְאַל־תִּשְׁפֹּךְ אֶת־דָּמוֹ

(2) תֵּשַׁם הָעִיר וְיִשְׁבֶּֽיהָ יִדֹּֽמּוּ

(3) מִי יָכֹל לָמֹד אֶת־הַשָּׁמַֽיִם

(4) יֵרַע הַדָּבָר בְּעֵינָיו

(5) תַּֽמּוּ לַעֲבֹר אֶת־הַנָּהָר

(6) דָּֽמּוּ כַּאֲשֶׁר רָאוּ אֹתָֽנוּ

(7) אַחַר מָדְךָ אֶת־הַשָּׂדֶה

(8) וַיֵּרְעוּ הַדְּבָרִים בְּעֵינַי

(9) אֵיךְ תַּעֲשֶׂה אֶת־הַמְּלָאכָה

(10) וַיִּתַּֽמּוּ לֶאֱכֹל

(11) וְעַתָּה חֹן אֹתִי כִּי אֲנִי עַבְדֶּֽךָ

(12) בְּטֶֽרֶם תָּסֹֽבּוּ אֶת־הָעִיר

(13) וַתֵּדַּם הָאָרֶץ בִּנְטוֹתוֹ אֶת־יָדָיו

(14) מַדֹּֽנוּ אֶת־הַכֶּֽסֶף

(15) וַיְהִי כְּשָׁמְעוֹ אֶת־דְּבָרַי וַיִּֽחַר אַפּוֹ בִי

(b) Give the Hebrew for the following orally. Use infinitival constructions where possible:

1. and when he lay down
2. and when I shall have finished building
3. and when they had become silent
4. so that he might redeem us
5. and when I measured the vessels
6. until our work is finished
7. and when they had chosen a king
8. lest he withhold his blessing from us
9. lest they smash the altar
10. when we came from east of the city
11. because we sinned against the Lord
12. after he had gone forth from the camp

(c) Write in Hebrew:

1. There was a war between the Israelites (lit. sons of Israel) and the Canaanites who were in the land at that time.
2. We will not be able to go forth unless you go forth with us.
3. Let us rejoice in his being gracious toward us and in his giving us deliverance from our enemies.
4. Where will you go and where will you dwell and what will you do?
5. After he had seized our money he ran out of the house.
6. He will give help to those who trust in him, but those who have sinned against him will perish.

(d) Reading: Joseph and Potiphar's Wife

וַיְהִי אַחַר הַדְּבָרִים הָאֵלֶּה וַתִּשָּׂא אֵשֶׁת פּוֹטִיפַר אֶת־עֵינֶיהָ¹ אֶל־יוֹסֵף כִּי הוּא הָיָה יְפֵה מַרְאֶה וַתֹּאמֶר אֵלָיו: שִׁכְבָה עִמִּי, וַיְמָאֵן² יוֹסֵף וַיֹּאמֶר אֵלֶיהָ: אֲדֹנִי נָתַן בְּיָדִי אֶת־כָּל־אֲשֶׁר יֶשׁ־לוֹ, אֵין אִישׁ גָּדוֹל מִמֶּנִּי בַּבַּיִת הַזֶּה, וְלֹא חָשַׂךְ מִמֶּנִּי מְאוּמָה כִּי אִם אוֹתָךְ בַּאֲשֶׁר³ אַתְּ אִשְׁתּוֹ וְאֵיךְ אֶעֱשֶׂה הָרָעָה הַגְּדוֹלָה הַזֹּאת וְחָטָאתִי לֵאלֹהִים.

וַיְהִי כְּדַבְּרָהּ⁴ אֶל־יוֹסֵף⁴ יוֹם יוֹם⁵ וְלֹא שָׁמַע אֵלֶיהָ לִשְׁכַּב אֶצְלָהּ לִהְיוֹת עִמָּהּ וַיְהִי כְּהַיּוֹם הַזֶּה⁶ וַיָּבֹא הַבַּיְתָה לַעֲשׂוֹת מְלַאכְתּוֹ וְאֵין אִישׁ מֵאַנְשֵׁי הַבַּיִת שָׁם בַּבַּיִת וַתִּתְפֹּשׂ אֹתוֹ בְּבִגְדוֹ לֵאמֹר: שִׁכְבָה עִמִּי, וַיַּעֲזֹב בִּגְדוֹ בְּיָדָהּ וַיָּנָס וַיֵּצֵא הַחוּצָה.

וַיְהִי כִּרְאוֹתָהּ כִּי עָזַב אֶת־בִּגְדוֹ בְּיָדָהּ וַיָּנָס הַחוּצָה וַתִּקְרָא לְאַנְשֵׁי בֵיתָהּ וַתֹּאמֶר לָהֶם לֵאמֹר: רְאוּ בָּא אֵלַי הָעֶבֶד הָעִבְרִי לִשְׁכַּב עִמִּי וָאֶקְרָא בְּקוֹל גָּדוֹל וַיְהִי כְּשָׁמְעוֹ אֶת־קוֹלִי וַיַּעֲזֹב בִּגְדוֹ אֶצְלִי וַיָּנָס וַיֵּצֵא הַחוּצָה.

וַיְהִי בְּבוֹא אִישָׁהּ הַבַּיְתָה וַתֹּאמֶר גַּם־אֵלָיו כַּדְּבָרִים הָאֵלֶּה וַיְהִי כְּשָׁמְעוֹ אֶת־דִּבְרֵי אִשְׁתּוֹ וַיִּחַר אַפּוֹ וַיִּקַּח אֶת־יוֹסֵף וַיִּתֵּן אֹתוֹ בַּמָּקוֹם אֲשֶׁר אֲסִירֵי הַמֶּלֶךְ שָׁם.

Notes to the Reading:

1. Obviously an amatory gesture.
2. "(he) refused"
3. "because"
4. "when she spoke"
5. Repetition of a noun to express distributive notion: every day, day after day.
6. "on a certain day." The unusual form of the preposition *kə* is due to its idiomatic usage in this phrase, where it means literally "about, approximately."

LESSON 34

128. The Passive Participle.

The passive participle, a verbal adjective, is formed on the pattern $\bar{a}$–$\hat{u}$ with all verbal root types except those II-*Waw/Yodh*.

Perfect	Passive Participle			Infinitive Absolute	
כָּתַב	כָּתוּב	*kātûb*	written	כָּתוֹב	*kātôb*
עָזַב	עָזוּב	*'āzûb*	abandoned	עָזוֹב	*'āzôb*
בָּחַר	בָּחוּר	*bāḥûr*	chosen	בָּחוֹר	*bāḥôr*
שָׁלַח	שָׁלוּחַ	*šālûᵃh*	sent	שָׁלוֹחַ	*šālôᵃh*
אָכַל	אָכוּל	*'ākûl*	eaten	אָכוֹל	*'ākôl*
נָטַע	נָטוּעַ	*nāṭûᵃ'*	planted	נָטוֹעַ	*nāṭôᵃ'*
נָשָׂא	נָשׂוּא	*nāśû'*	raised up	נָשׂוֹא	*nāśô'*
יָדַע	יָדוּעַ	*yādûᵃ'*	known	יָדוֹעַ	*yādôᵃ'*
סָבַב	סָבוּב	*sābûb*	surrounded	סָבוֹב	*sābôb*
בָּנָה	בְּנוּי	*bānûy*	built	בָּנֹה	*bānōh*
קָם	(קוּם)	*(qûm)*	_____	קוֹם	*qôm*
שָׂם	(שִׂים)	*(śîm)*	placed	שׂוֹם	*śôm*

Because of semantic incompatibility the form is not usually found with verbs having stative or intransitive meanings. The generally intransitive character of verbs II-*Waw/Yodh* makes the occurrence of a passive participle in that class rare and open to question; the forms מוּל *mûl* (circumcised) and שִׂים *śîm* (placed) are often quoted as examples.

The stem forms as given above call for little comment. Note the furtive *pátah* in roots III-guttural and the final *yodh* in roots III-*Hē*.

As an adjective the participle is tenseless, but bears the connotation of completed action. In English, therefore, a relative clause with a perfect or preterite verb is often required in translation:

הָאִישׁ הֶהָרוּג the slain man, the man who was slain

הַסֵּפֶר הַכָּתוּב the written book, the book which was written

The participle as a predicate adjective has the same properties as other adjectives in this position (§23). E.g.

הָאִישׁ הָרוּג   The man is/was/has been slain.

gains its tense from the context in which it occurs and not from the participle itself.

The addition of a prepositional phrase to express an agent, as in "the man who was slain by his enemies," is virtually unknown in Hebrew, but like any adjective it may be in construct with a following qualifying noun:

עִיר שְׂרוּפַת אֵשׁ   a city which has been burned with fire

The participle need not be in the construct state:

אִישׁ חָגוּר כְּלֵי הַמִּלְחָמָה   a man girded with the weapons of war

129. The Infinitive Absolute.

The infinitive absolute, whose forms are given in the preceding paragraph, is not inflected. It is primarily an adverb whose main uses are as follows:

(1) It is placed before or after a finite verbal form to emphasize the verbal idea in some way. The English translation of this construction will vary from context to context, often requiring the use of adverbs such as "surely, certainly, indeed" or the like. E.g.

שָׁמוֹר תִּשְׁמְרוּ אֶת־מִצְוֹתַי   You shall indeed observe my commandments.

אִם רָאֹה תִרְאֶה בָּעֳנִי אֲמָתֶךָ   If you will indeed look upon the affliction
                                          of your maidservant . . .

The more usual position is before the verb, as above. If the verb is used intransitively the inf. absolute may follow:

שִׁמְעוּ שָׁמוֹעַ . . . וּרְאוּ רָאֹה . . .   Listen carefully . . . and look carefully . . .

(2) Similar to the preceding is a sequence of two inf. absolute complementing a finite verb; the two infinitives are often antithetical in meaning:

וַיֵּלֶךְ הָלוֹךְ וְאָכוֹל   And he walked along eating.
                              (lit.) And he walked, walking and eating

וַיֵּצֵא יָצוֹא וָשׁוֹב   And he went back and forth.

(lit.) He went forth, going forth and returning.

(3) Instead of emphasizing or complementing the main verb, the inf. absolute may be used to describe action on a par with the main verb and may be viewed thus as an uninflected substitute for a finite form:

אֶת־כָּל־זֶה רָאִיתִי וְנָתוֹן   All this have I seen and (I have) applied
אֶת־לִבִּי לְכָל־מַעֲשֶׂה...   (lit. given) my attention (lit. heart) to
every deed ...

(4) The use described in (3) gives an almost independent status to the infinitive. For reasons that are quite obscure, instances occur in which the inf. absolute is used instead of a finite verb, nor is it clearly dependent on any other verb in a given clause. Note the following imperative uses:

שָׁמוֹר אֶת־כָּל־הַמִּצְוָה   Observe the entire commandment.
זָכוֹר אֶת־הַיּוֹם הַזֶּה   Remember this day.
הָלוֹךְ וְקָרָאתָ בְאָזְנֵי יְרוּשָׁלַ͏ִם   Go and cry into the ears of Jerusalem.

130. The Numbers from 3 to 10.

The numbers from three to ten have two forms: a feminine in -āh which is used to modify *masculine* nouns and an endingless form used to modify *feminine* nouns:

	masc. modifier				*fem. modifier*			
	absolute		*construct*		*absolute*		*construct*	
three	שְׁלֹשָׁה	šəlōšāh	שְׁלֹשֶׁת	šəlṓšet	שָׁלֹשׁ	šālōš	שְׁלֹשׁ	šəlōš
four	אַרְבָּעָה	'arbā‘āh	אַרְבַּעַת	'arbá‘at	אַרְבַּע	'arba‘	אַרְבַּע	'arba‘
five	חֲמִשָּׁה	hămiššāh	חֲמֵשֶׁת	hămḗšet	חָמֵשׁ	hāmēš	חֲמֵשׁ	hămēš
six	שִׁשָּׁה	šiššāh	שֵׁשֶׁת	šḗšet	שֵׁשׁ	šēš	שֵׁשׁ	šēš
seven	שִׁבְעָה	šib‘āh	שִׁבְעַת	šib‘at	שֶׁבַע	šéba‘	שֶׁבַע	šéba‘
eight	שְׁמֹנָה	šəmōnāh	שְׁמֹנַת	šəmōnat	שְׁמֹנֶה	šəmōneh	שְׁמֹנֶה	šəmōneh
nine	תִּשְׁעָה	tiš‘āh	תִּשְׁעַת	tiš‘at	תֵּשַׁע	tēša‘	תֵּשַׁע	tēša‘
ten	עֲשָׂרָה	‘ăśārāh	עֲשֶׂרֶת	‘ăśéret	עֶשֶׂר	‘éśer	עֶשֶׂר	‘éśer

The absolute forms normally precede the noun, which is in the plural:

שֶׁבַע נָשִׁים seven women   שִׁבְעָה אֲנָשִׁים seven men
שֶׁבַע פָּרוֹת seven cows   שִׁבְעָה יָמִים seven days

The construct forms are used before the noun, which may be either definite or indefinite:

שְׁלֹשֶׁת אֲנָשִׁים three men   שְׁלֹשֶׁת הָאֲנָשִׁים the three men

Numbers may occur before collective nouns in the singular:

שִׁבְעָה בָקָר	seven (head of) cattle
שִׁבְעָה לֶחֶם	seven (loaves of) bread
שִׁבְעָה רֶכֶב	seven (units of) chariotry

131. Vocabulary 34.

NOUNS: קֵץ *qēṣ* (no pl.) end; מִקֵּץ *miqqēṣ* at the end of (usually + time word)

קָצֶה *qāṣeh* (no pl.) end, border, outskirts; מִקְצֵי *miqṣē* at the end of (+ time or place)

פָּרָה *pārāh* (pl. -ôṯ) cow, heifer

שָׂפָה *śāpāh* (dual שְׂפָתַיִם ; du. constr. שִׂפְתֵי) lip, edge; language

חָכָם *ḥāḵām* (pl. -îm) a wise person (also used as an adjective)

יְאֹר *yə'ōr* the Nile (usually with article); river (in general)

VERBS: [יָקַץ *yāqaṣ*] (יִיקַץ) to wake up (not attested in the perfect)

Exercises:

(a) Translate:

(8) הָעֵצִים הַנְּטוּעִים		(1) הָעָם הַנָּגוּף	
(9) הָאָסִיר אָסוּר		(2) הַכֹּהֲנִים הַהֲרוּגִים	
(10) הָעִבְרִים הַקְּרוּאִים		(3) הַכֵּלִים שְׁבוּרִים	
(11) הָעִיר הַבְּנוּיָה		(4) הַכֶּרֶם שָׂרוּף	
(12) הַשַּׁעַר סָגוּר		(5) הָרְשָׁעִים הָאֲרוּרִים	
(13) הַלּוּחוֹת שְׁבוּרִים		(6) הַדָּבָר הַכָּתוּב	
(14) הַפָּרָה הַשְּׁחוּטָה		(7) הַמִּצְרִי הַשָּׁלוּחַ	

(b) Give the Hebrew for the following orally:

1. six men (birds, vessels, women, maidservants, females)
2. three stones (images, masters)
3. five asses (horses, camels, altars)
4. eight prisoners (Canaanites, Egyptians, offerings)
5. the seven plagues, the seven cattle, the nine loaves of bread

(c) Translate:

(1) וַיֵּלֶךְ הָאִישׁ הָלוֹךְ וּבָכֹה

(2) רְאֵה רָאִיתִי אֶת־חַטַּאת עַמִּי

(3) הֲנָתוֹן תִּתֵּן לִי עֵזֶר

(4) זָכוֹר אֶת־יוֹם הַשַּׁבָּת

(5) עָשֹׂה נַעֲשֶׂה אֶת־נְדָרֵינוּ

(6) תִּשְׁמְעוּ אֶל־קוֹלִי וְשָׁמוֹר אֶת־מִצְוֹתַי

(7) שָׁבוֹת לֹא תִשְׁבְּתוּ מִמְּלַאכְתְּכֶם לִפְנֵי תֻמָּה

(8) הֲבוֹא נָבוֹא אֲנִי וְאִמְּךָ לְפָנֶיךָ

(9) יָצֹא הָאִישׁ יָצֹא וָשׁוֹב

(10) שָׁכוֹחַ לֹא תִשְׁכְּחוּ אֶת־דִּבְרֵי חַכְמֵיכֶם כָּל־יְמֵי חַיֵּיכֶם

(d) Write in Hebrew:

1. You shall surely remember these things until the end of your life.
2. We sat down weeping on the bank of the river.
3. When we raised our voice(s), he woke up and came near so that he could hear all that we (were) saying.
4. Are you wiser than we?
5. And at the end of three years he left us and returned to his (own) land.
6. At that time there was one language in all the earth.
7. Why have you withheld your help from me?

(e) Reading: Joseph as an Interpreter of Dreams

וַיְהִי בִּהְיוֹת יוֹסֵף בְּבֵית הָאֲסִירִים וַיִּפְתֹּר¹ חֲלוֹמוֹת סָרִיסֵי פַרְעֹה אֲשֶׁר הָיוּ אִתּוֹ שָׁם וַיְהִי כַּאֲשֶׁר פָּתַר לָהֶם כֵּן הָיָה.

וַיְהִי מִקֵּץ שְׁנָתַיִם וַיַּחֲלֹם פַּרְעֹה וְהִנֵּה הוּא עֹמֵד עַל־הַיְאֹר וְהִנֵּה מִן־הַיְאֹר עֹלֹת שֶׁבַע פָּרוֹת יְפוֹת מַרְאֶה וַתִּרְעֶינָה עַל־שְׂפַת הַיְאֹר וְהִנֵּה שֶׁבַע פָּרוֹת אֲחֵרוֹת עֹלוֹת אַחֲרֵיהֶן מִן־הַיְאֹר רָעוֹת מַרְאֶה וַתַּעֲמֹדְנָה אֵצֶל הַפָּרוֹת הַיָּפוֹת עַל־שְׂפַת הַיְאֹר וַתֹּאכַלְנָה הַפָּרוֹת רָעוֹת הַמַּרְאֶה אֶת־שֶׁבַע הַפָּרוֹת יְפוֹת הַמַּרְאֶה וַיִּיקַץ פַּרְעֹה.

וַיְהִי בַבֹּקֶר וַיִּשְׁלַח וַיִּקְרָא אֶל־כָּל־חַכְמֵי מִצְרַיִם וְלֹא יָכְלוּ לִפְתֹּר אֶת־חֲלוֹם פַּרְעֹה וַיֹּאמֶר סָרִיס פַּרְעֹה אֲשֶׁר הָיָה בְּבֵית הָאֲסִירִים אֶת־יוֹסֵף לֵאמֹר: הָיִיתִי בְּבֵית הָאֲסִירִים וְאִתִּי שָׁם נַעַר עִבְרִי וְהוּא פָּתַר לִי אֶת־חֲלוֹמִי וַיְהִי כַּאֲשֶׁר פָּתַר כֵּן הָיָה.

וַיִּשְׁלַח פַּרְעֹה וַיִּקְרָא אֶל־יוֹסֵף וַיֹּאמֶר אֵלָיו: חֲלוֹם חָלַמְתִּי וּפֹתֵר אֵין אֹתוֹ² וַאֲנִי שָׁמַעְתִּי עָלֶיךָ לֵאמֹר: תִּשְׁמַע³ חֲלוֹם לִפְתֹּר אֹתוֹ.

וַיַּעַן יוֹסֵף אֶת־פַּרְעֹה לֵאמֹר: אֱלֹהִים יַעֲנֶה⁴ אֶת־שְׁלוֹם פַּרְעֹה.

וַיְהִי אַחֲרֵי שָׁמְעוֹ אֶת־חֲלוֹם פַּרְעֹה וַיֹּאמֶר יוֹסֵף: אֵת־אֲשֶׁר הָאֱלֹהִים עֹשֶׂה הִגִּיד⁵ לְפַרְעֹה. שֶׁבַע הַפָּרוֹת הַטּוֹבֹת שֶׁבַע שָׁנִים שָׁבְעָ⁶ הֵנָּה וְשֶׁבַע הַפָּרוֹת הָרָעוֹת שֶׁבַע שְׁנֵי רָעָב הֵנָּה. הוּא הַדָּבָר אֲשֶׁר הָאֱלֹהִים עֹשֶׂה: הִנֵּה שֶׁבַע שָׁנִים בָּאוֹת, שָׂבָע⁶ גָּדוֹל בְּכָל־אֶרֶץ מִצְרָיִם וְקָמוּ שֶׁבַע שְׁנֵי רָעָב אַחֲרֵיהֶן.

Notes to the Reading:

1. פָּתַר to interpret
2. אֹתוֹ goes with פֹּתֵר: "one who can interpret it"
3. תִּשְׁמַע in the sense of "understand": "You know how to interpret a dream."
4. עָנָה in the rare sense "grant"
5. "he has told"
6. "satiety, fullness"

LESSON 35

132. Clauses joined with ⟨ֽ wə-.

One of the most striking features of Hebrew prose syntax is the relative rarity of subordinating conjunctions marking adverbial clauses as such. Instead, one finds almost interminable sequences of clauses connected only by a form of the conjunction *wə-* (and). A closer inspection of these sequences, however, has shown us that there is a great deal of differentiation in clause function signalled, not by variation of the conjunction, but by a variation of the word order within the clause or by a variation of the verbal form used immediately after the conjunction. Although there is some deviation from the general patterns summarized in the following discussion, the distinctions drawn here and in Lesson 55 should enable the reader to classify and understand the vast majority of sequences he will encounter.

There are two main types of clause relationships among those joined only with a form of the conjunction *wə-*:

(1) *conjunctive-sequential*, in which the second clause is temporally or logically posterior or consequent to the first, and

(2) *disjunctive*, in which the second clause may be in various relations, all non-sequential, with the first.

The major device in Hebrew for signalling the difference between conjunctive and disjunctive clauses is the type of word which stands immediately after the *wə-*:

> *wə-* (or *wa-*) + verb is conjunctive
> *wə-* + non-verb is disjunctive.

It follows from this definition that all non-verbal clauses (i.e. sentences with adverbial, adjectival, nominal, existential, or participial predicates) are essentially disjunctive when used as such within a narrative. Such clauses can be made part of the main sequential narrative only by being first transformed into verbal clauses with a punctual (finite) verb form. Negative clauses in which לֹא stands before the verb are disjunctive by definition.

The basic formulas of the conjunctive-sequential relationship are as follows: [Any verb describing an event as a unit and hence capable of being linked sequentially (either anterior or posterior) with other events on the time continuum will be referred to as punctual.]

(1) the narrative sequences:
    (a) punctual past tense: perfect + *wa* + (short) imperfect
    (b) punctual future
        punctual habitual   imperfect + *wə* + perfect   } § 98 above
    (c) non-verbal clause + *wə* + perfect (see below)
(2) the imperative sequences:
    (a) imperative + *wə* + perfect (§ 107 above)
    (b) imperative + *wə* + imperfect (or jussive or cohortative) (§ 107 above)

The many examples of these that have appeared in the exercises and readings should have made them familiar enough by now. A few words are necessary, however, on the sequence denoted as (1c). Because non-verbal clauses, especially those with participial predicates, may refer to the immediate future, a non-verbal clause so used may be continued with a converted perfect, in imitation of the more common type (1b):

אֲנִי נֹתֵן לְךָ אֶת־הַכֶּסֶף וְלָקַחְתָּ אֹתוֹ וְנָתַתָּ אֹתוֹ אֶל־אֲדֹנֶיךָ	I shall give you the money and you will take it and give it to your master.
אֲנַחְנוּ בָאִים הָעִירָה וְרָאִינוּ אֶת־הַבָּתִּים הַחֲדָשִׁים הַבְּנוּיִים שָׁם	We shall come to the city and see the new houses built there.
הוּא אִישׁ טוֹב וְעָשָׂה חֶסֶד עִמָּכֶם	He is a good man and will deal properly with you.

Semantic distinctions among disjunctive clauses are difficult to define because of overlapping. The categories given below cover most uses of this construction.

(a) *Contrastive*:

וַיָּשֶׁב אֶת־שַׂר הַמַּשְׁקִים עַל־מַשְׁקֵהוּ וְאֵת שַׂר הָאֹפִים תָּלָה	He returned the chief butler to his butlership, but he hanged the chief baker. (Gen. 40:21)
וַיְהִי רָעָב בְּכָל־הָאֲרָצוֹת וּבְכָל־אֶרֶץ מִצְרַיִם הָיָה לֶחֶם	There was famine in all the (other) lands, but in Egypt there was food. (Gen. 41:54)

[*163*]

(b) *Circumstantial,* where the disjunctive clause or clauses describe a situation or circumstance contemporary with or prior to the action of the preceding clause:

וַיִּמְצָאֵהוּ אִישׁ וְהִנֵּה תֹעֶה בַּשָּׂדֶה   And a man found him wandering lost in the field. (lit., [while] he [was] wandering lost ...) (Gen. 37:15)

וַיָּבֹא הַבַּיְתָה לַעֲשׂוֹת מְלַאכְתּוֹ וְאֵין אִישׁ מֵאַנְשֵׁי הַבַּיִת שָׁם בַּבָּיִת   And he came home to do his work, there being none of the household present. (Gen. 39:11)

It is difficult to distinguish between circumstantial usage of such clauses and

(c) *Explanatory or parenthetical* use, where disjunctive clauses break into the main narrative to supply information relevant to or necessary for the narrative. For example, in I Sam. 1:9, between the narrative clauses "Hannah arose ... and prayed" we find the explanatory disjunction

וְעֵלִי הַכֹּהֵן יֹשֵׁב עַל־הַכִּסֵּא עַל־מְזוּזַת הֵיכַל יהוה וְהִיא מָרַת נָפֶשׁ   (Now Eli the priest was sitting on the seat by the door post of the temple of Yahweh; and she (Hannah) was bitter of spirit)

The inserted information characterizes her mood at prayer and also explains how Eli happened to notice her. Likewise, In Gen. 29:16, the conversation between Jacob and Laban is interrupted with the clause

וּלְלָבָן שְׁתֵּי בָנוֹת...   (Now Laban had two daughters ...)

to explain the reference to Rachel given in the next clause belonging to the main narrative: "and he (Jacob) said, 'I will serve you seven years for your youngest daughter Rachel.'" These are but two examples selected at random from the hundreds of such instances.

(d) *Terminative or Initial,* indicating either the completion of one episode or the beginning of another. The following examples are taken from the beginnings of several chapters in Genesis; the chapter divisions often correspond to initial disjunctive clauses in the Hebrew:

וְהַנָּחָשׁ הָיָה עָרוּם...   Now the serpent was more subtle ... (3:1)

וְהָאָדָם יָדַע אֶת־חַוָּה...   Now the man knew Eve ... (4, 1)

וְשָׂרַי אֵשֶׁת אַבְרָם לֹא יָלְדָה לוֹ...   Now Sarah, the wife of Abram, had not borne him a child ... (16:1)

וַיהוה פָּקַד אֶת־שָׂרָה כַּאֲשֶׁר אָמָר...   Now the Lord attended Sarah as he had said ... (21:1)

It is interesting to note that a disjunction may be preceded by a temporal clause. In this case the disjunction must be understood as applying before the clause with וַיְהִי:

וַיְהִי אַחַר הַדְּבָרִים הָאֵלֶּה וְהָאֱלֹהִים   Now after these things, God tested
נִסָּה אֶת־אַבְרָהָם   Abraham (22:1)

Because a new episode may always be introduced, like a new paragraph, with no conjunction at all, such as

אַחַר הַדְּבָרִים הָאֵלֶּה הָיָה דְבַר יהוה   After these things the word of the Lord
אֶל־אַבְרָם   came to Abram (15:1)

we not unexpectedly find a mixing of the two styles:

וַיְהִי בִּימֵי אַמְרָפֶל ... עָשׂוּ מִלְחָמָה   In the days of Amraphel they made
war ... (14:1)

A third type of wə-clause, *conjunctive* but *non-sequential*, will be considered in a later lesson.

133. יֵשׁ and אֵין.

As predicators of existence and non-existence these two words approximate a verbal function in Hebrew, serving almost as tenseless forms of the verb "to be." It is hardly surprising, therefore, that these words are found inflected for number and gender by the addition of pronominal endings, rare in the case of יֵשׁ, but common with אֵין.

	SING.	PL.	SING.	PL.
1c			אֵינֶנִּי 'ênénnî	אֵינֶנּוּ 'ênénnû
2m	יֶשְׁךָ yeškā	יֶשְׁכֶם yeškem	אֵינְךָ 'ênəkā	אֵינְכֶם 'ênəkem
2f			אֵינֵךְ 'ênēk	
3m	יֶשְׁנוֹ yešnô		אֵינֶנּוּ 'ênénnû	אֵינָם 'ênām
3f			אֵינֶנָּה 'ênénnāh	

The rare inflected forms of יֵשׁ are found almost exclusively after the conjunction אִם (if), as in

אִם־יֶשְׁכֶם עֹשִׂים חֶסֶד   If you act properly ...

and may be regarded simply as optional replacements for the simple pronouns,

אִם־אַתֶּם עֹשִׂים חֶסֶד

The inflected forms of אֵין have a wider range of usage:

(a) Negative existential with nominal or pronominal subject:

אֵינֶנּוּ   he is not (he does not exist)
הַיֶּלֶד אֵינֶנּוּ   The boy is not (here).

Note that the inflected form is used regularly *after* a definite nominal subject. The quoted example is equivalent to אֵין הַיֶּלֶד.

(b) Negation of sentences with participial predicates (very common):

אֵינֶ֫נִּי כֹתֵב   I am not writing.

הָאֲנָשִׁים אֵינָם יֹדְעִים   The men do not know.

(c) More rarely אֵין alternates with לֹא in the negation of sentences with adjectival or adverbial predicates:

הָאִישׁ אֵינֶ֫נּוּ בַבַּ֫יִת   The man is not in the house.

הַבְּהֵמָה אֲשֶׁר אֵינֶ֫נָּה טְהֹרָה   the animal which is not ritually pure

134. Vocabulary 35.

NOUNS: אֹ֫כֶל *'ōkel* (w. suff. אָכְלִי ; no pl.) food

עֶרְוָה *'erwāh* (no pl.) shame, nakedness

ADJECTIVES: נָבוֹן *nābôn* intelligent, discerning (cf. בִּינָה)

כֵּן *kēn* honest, true

VERBS: יטב imperf. יִיטַב ; perfect not used. To go well, used impersonally with לְ , as in יִיטַב לִי It will go well with me.

רָעֵב *rā'ēb* (יִרְעַב) to be hungry

חָיָה *ḥāyāh* (יִחְיֶה) to live, be alive

קָרָה *qārāh* (יִקְרֶה) to meet, encounter, befall. This verb appears also as קָרָא *qārā'* (יִקְרָא); the forms of the two types are sometimes mixed up.

OTHER: רַק *raq* (adv.) only

Note on ordinals: eighth שְׁמִינִי ; ninth תְּשִׁיעִי ; tenth עֲשִׂירִי .

Exercises:

(a) Translate:

(1) קַח אֶת־הַלֶּ֫חֶם פֶּן־תִּרְעַב בַּדֶּ֫רֶךְ.

(2) נַעַזְבָה אֶת־הָעִיר וְנָ֫סְנוּ הָהָ֫רָה לְמַ֫עַן נִחְיֶה.

(3) וַיֵּ֫קֶר אֶת־שְׁנֵי הָאֲנָשִׁים וְהֵם עֹמְדִים עַל־שְׂפַת הַיְאֹר.

(4) תְּהִי עִם־אָחִ֫יךָ פֶּן־תִּקְרָא אֹתוֹ רָעָה בְּנָסְעוֹ הֵ֫נָּה.

(5) וַתֵּ֫לֶךְ הָאִשָּׁה אֶל־הַהֵיכָל וְהִיא בֹכָה וַתִּשָּׂא אֶת־עֵינֶ֫יהָ הַשָּׁמַ֫יְמָה וַתִּדֹּר נֶ֫דֶר לַיהוה.

(6) רָדְפוּ אַחֲרָיו וַיִּתְפְּשׂוּ אֹתוֹ וַיַּהַרְגוּ אֹתוֹ וְהוּא אֲחִי הַכֹּהֵן אֲשֶׁר בִּירוּשָׁלַ֫ם.

(7) לָ֫מָּה שָׁחַ֫טְתָּ אֶת־הַבָּקָר הַזֶּה וְהֵם אֵינָם לָךְ.

(8) יִיטַב לָעֲשִׁירִים וְהַדַּלִּים יֹאבֵ֫דוּ.

(9) קָרָה אֹתָ֫נוּ וַאֲנַ֫חְנוּ הֹלְכִים אֶל־הַמַּחֲנֶה וַיֹּ֫אמֶר אֵלֵ֫ינוּ כַּדְּבָרִים הָאֵ֫לֶּה.

(10) הָאֲנָשִׁים אֵינָם יֹדְעִים כִּי אֵינֵךְ אֲחוֹתִי.

(11) וַיָּ֫שֶׂם אֶת־הָרָקִיעַ בֵּין־הַמַּ֫יִם אֲשֶׁר עַל־הַשָּׁמַ֫יִם וּבֵין הַמַּ֫יִם אֲשֶׁר תַּ֫חַת הַשָּׁמַ֫יִם וְהָרָקִיעַ הוּא הַשָּׁמָ֫יִם.

(12) אֵין אִישׁ צַדִּיק בָּעִיר רַק רְשָׁעִים.

(13) אֵין מַ֫יִם בַּבּוֹר, רַק אֲבָנִים שָׁם.

(b) Reading: The Famine in Egypt and Canaan

וַיֹּאמֶר יוֹסֵף: וְעַתָּה יֵרֶא¹ פַרְעֹה אִישׁ נָבוֹן וְחָכָם וִישִׁיתֵת אֹתוֹ עַל־אֶרֶץ מִצְרָיִם וְיִקְבֹּץ הוּא
וְאֲנָשָׁיו אֶת־כָּל־אֹכֶל הַשָּׁנִים הַטּוֹבוֹת הַבָּאוֹת הָאֵלֶּה וְהָיָה הָאֹכֶל לְפִקָּדוֹן² לָאָרֶץ לְשֶׁבַע שְׁנֵי
הָרָעָב אֲשֶׁר תִּהְיֶינָה בְּאֶרֶץ מִצְרָיִם וְלֹא תֵאָבֵד הָאָרֶץ בָּרָעָב.

וַיִּיטַב הַדָּבָר בְּעֵינֵי פַרְעֹה וּבְעֵינֵי כָל־עֲבָדָיו וַיֹּאמֶר פַרְעֹה אֶל־יוֹסֵף: אֵין נָבוֹן וְחָכָם כָּמוֹךָ,
אַתָּה תִּהְיֶה עַל־בֵּיתִי וְעַל־עַמִּי, רַק הַכִּסֵּא אֶגְדַּל מִמְּךָ³, וַיֹּאמֶר פַרְעֹה אֶל־יוֹסֵף: רְאֵה נָתַתִּי
אֹתְךָ עַל־כָּל־אֶרֶץ מִצְרָיִם.

וַיְהִי אַחֲרֵי שֶׁבַע הַשָּׁנִים הַטּוֹבוֹת וַיְהִי רָעָב בְּכָל־הָאֲרָצוֹת וּבְכָל־אֶרֶץ מִצְרָיִם הָיָה לֶחֶם
וַתִּרְעַב כָּל־אֶרֶץ מִצְרַיִם וַיִּצְעַק הָעָם אֶל־פַּרְעֹה לַלֶּחֶם וַיֹּאמֶר פַּרְעֹה לְכָל־מִצְרַיִם: לְכוּ
אֶל־יוֹסֵף, אֶת־כָּל־אֲשֶׁר יֹאמַר לָכֶם תַּעֲשׂוּ, וְהָרָעָב הָיָה עַל־כָּל־פְּנֵי הָאָרֶץ וְכָל־הָאָרֶץ
בָּאוּ מִצְרַיְמָה לִקְנוֹת לֶחֶם וַיַּרְא יַעֲקֹב כִּי יֵשׁ לֶחֶם בְּמִצְרַיִם וַיֹּאמֶר יַעֲקֹב לְבָנָיו: הִנֵּה שָׁמַעְתִּי
כִּי יֵשׁ לֶחֶם בְּמִצְרַיִם, רְדוּ שָׁמָּה וּקְנוּ לָנוּ מִשָּׁם וְנִחְיֶה וְלֹא נָמוּת.

Notes to the Reading:

1. in the sense "choose"
2. "storage supply"
3. Supply "in regard to" before הַכִּסֵּא.

135. הִנֵּה.

The word הִנֵּה, traditionally translated as "behold," is very frequent in Hebrew prose and deserves special attention in translation. The retention of archaic expressions like "behold" even in the RSV merely points up the translators' refusal to come to grips with the meaning and syntactic functions of הִנֵּה in terms of modern English correspondents. There is, of course, some difficulty in this, but it is hoped that the following discussion will enable the reader to translate this word more accurately.

(1) The clearest and most basic use of הִנֵּה is as a predicator of existence. It differs from יֵשׁ in that it emphasizes the immediacy, the here-and-now-ness, of the situation. In this usage inflected forms are common:

	SINGULAR		PLURAL	
1c	הִנְנִי / הִנֵּ֫נִי	*hinənî (hinnénnî)*	הִנְנוּ / הִנֵּ֫נוּ	*hinənû (hinnénnû)*
2m	הִנְּךָ	*hinnəkā*	הִנְּכֶם	*hinnəkem*
2f	הִנֵּךְ	*hinnēk*	——	——
3m	הִנּוֹ	*hinnô*	הִנָּם	*hinnām*
3f	——	——	——	——

Examples:

הִנְנִי	Here I am. (Answer to question or address)
הִנֵּה הָאִישׁ	Here is the man.
הִנֵּה אִשְׁתְּךָ	Here is your wife.

[*168*]

(2) הִנֵּה may also be used to add this same nuance to sentences with adverbial, adjectival, or participial predicates. Thus, sentences such as אֲנִי בַבַּיִת become הִנְנִי בַבַּיִת I am here (now) in the house.

Examples:

הִנֵּה חָמִיךְ עֹלֶה תִמְנָתָה	Your father-in-law is now on his way up to Timnah.
הִנֵּה אָבִיךְ חֹלֶה	Your father is now ill.
הִנֵּה בִנְךָ בָּא אֵלֶיךָ	Your son is now coming to you.
הִנֵּה הָאָרֶץ לְפָנֶיךָ	The land is here before you.

It may also be prefixed to verbal sentences, adding to the vividness or importance of the fact stated:

הִנֵּה אֲנָשִׁים בָּאוּ הֵנָּה   Some men have just come here.

Most *hinnēh*-clauses occur in direct speech (this excludes *wəhinnēh*; see below) and serve to introduce a fact upon which a following statement or command is based. It becomes important, therefore, to consider each *hinnēh*-clause together with the type of clause that follows it, i.e. whether they stand in a conjunctive or disjunctive relationship. Among the most frequent conjunctive-sequential types are:

(1) *hinnēh*-CLAUSE + IMPERATIVE. The absence of *wə-* before the imperative marks this as a rather special construction. If desired, the *hinnēh*-clause may be subordinated in English.

הִנֵּה שִׁפְחָתֵךְ בְּיָדֵךְ עֲשִׂי־לָהּ...	Your handmaid is in your charge; do to her ... Or: *Since* your handmaid is etc. (Gen. 16:6)
הִנֵּה שָׁמַעְתִּי כִּי יֶשׁ־שֶׁבֶר בְּמִצְרָיִם רְדוּ־שָׁמָּה...	I have heard that there are rations in Egypt; go down there and ... (Gen. 42:2)

The semantic movement from one clause to the other is clear. Sometimes this can be made clear in the English by the subordination suggested; sometime the use of "so" or "therefore" in the second clause is recommended.

The imperative may be preceded by עַתָּה or וְעַתָּה:

הִנֵּה בַּעַל הַחֲלֹמוֹת... בָּא וְעַתָּה לְכוּ וְנַהַרְגֵהוּ	Here comes the dreamer. Come on, now, let's kill him. (Gen. 37:19)
הִנֵּה אַתָּה זָקַנְתָּ... עַתָּה שִׂימָה־לָּנוּ מֶלֶךְ...	You have grown old. So set a king over us ... (I Sam. 8:5)

(2) *hinnēh*-CLAUSE + CONVERTED PERFECT. This formula is an instance of type (1c) discussed in the previous lesson.

See p. 164

אֲנִי הִנֵּה בְרִיתִי אִתָּךְ וְהָיִיתָ לְאַב הֲמוֹן גּוֹיִם	My covenant is with you and you shall become father of a throng of nations ... (Gen. 17:4) Or: Because my covenant is (will be) ...

הִנֵּה יָמִים בָּאִים וְגָדַעְתִּי אֶת־זְרֹעֶךָ	Days are coming when I shall cut off your strength ... (I Sam. 2:31)

(3) *hinnēh*-CLAUSE + DISJUNCTIVE CLAUSE. There are several types of less frequent constructions under this heading, mostly conforming to the uses of the disjunctive relationship treated in the preceding lesson, but slightly modified by the initial *hinnēh*:

הִנֵּה בֵּרַכְתִּי אֹתוֹ ... וְאֶת־בְּרִיתִי אָקִים אֶת־יִצְחָק	Although I have blessed him (i.e. Ishmael), my covenant will I establish with Isaac ... (Gen. 17:20–21)
הִנֵּה הָאֵשׁ וְהָעֵצִים וְאַיֵּה הַשֶּׂה	Here are the fire and the wood, but where is the lamb? (Gen. 22:7)
הִנֵּה אָנֹכִי הוֹלֵךְ לָמוּת ... וְלָמָּה־זֶּה לִי בְּכֹרָה	Since I am practically dead, of what use to me is a birthright? (Gen. 25:32)

In a number of instances the use of a future disjunctive clause after *hinnēh* + participle seems to require that the participial clause be rendered in a completed sense:

הִנֵּה אָנֹכִי מֵת בְּקִבְרִי ... תִּקְבְּרֵנִי	When I have died, you shall bury me in my grave ... (Gen. 50:5)
הִנֵּה אֲנַחְנוּ בָאִים ... אֶת־תִּקְוַת חוּט ... תִּקְשְׁרִי	When we come..., you shall tie the thread ... (Jos. 2:18)

We have already noted the very frequent idiomatic use of וְהִנֵּה after רָאָה and other verbs of perception. וְהִנֵּה may also be used to introduce a circumstantial clause, sometimes without an explicit subject:

וַיָּבֹא אֶל־הָאִישׁ וְהִנֵּה עֹמֵד עַל־הַגְּמַלִּים	He came to the man while (he was) standing by the camels. (Gen. 24:30)
עוֹד שָׁאַר הַקָּטָן וְהִנֵּה רֹעֶה בַּצֹּאן	There remains yet the youngest, tending the sheep. (I Sam. 16:11)

136. הִנֵּה־נָא and נָא.

The particle נָא is frequently attached to imperatives, jussives, and cohortatives. It is traditionally known as a precative particle, translated as "please, I pray" or the like. In actual fact, however, there is little support for this rather vague rendering. The particle seems rather to denote that the command in question is a logical consequence, either of an immediately preceding statement or of the general situation in which it is uttered. As a modal particle its occurrence cannot be predicted; when it does occur, however, it would appear to show that the speaker regards his command as consequent upon his former statement or, as we have said, upon the context. It would seem natural therefore to find such a particle used in the clause following a *hinnēh* clause, because the *hinnēh* clause is precisely the kind of statement out of which an imperative emerges. This close relationship is signalled even more explicitly in Hebrew by appending נָא both to the *hinnēh* and to the following imperative:

הִנֵּה־נָא עֲצָרַנִי יהוה מִלֶּדֶת בֹּא־נָא אֶל־שִׁפְחָתִי	Because the Lord has prevented me from bearing a child, go to my handmaid ... (Gen. 16:2)
הִנֵּה נָא רָפָה הַיּוֹם לַעֲרֹב לִינוּ־נָא	Since the day has drawn to a close, spend the night here. (Judges 19:9)

Otherwise *hinnēh-nā'* conforms to the categories given for *hinnēh* alone. E.g.

הִנֵּה־נָא מָצָא עַבְדְּךָ חֵן... וְאָנֹכִי לֹא אוּכַל לְהִמָּלֵט	Even though your servant has found favor ..., I am nevertheless unable to escape ... (Gen. 19:19)
הִנֵּה־נָא מוֹשַׁב הָעִיר טוֹב... וְהַמַּיִם רָעִים	Even though the site of the city is good ..., the waters are bad ... (II Kings 2:19)

137. עוֹד and אַיֵּה.

In verbal sentences עוֹד is used as a simple adverb in the sense of "again, still, yet, once more":

יָשַׁב עוֹד וַיֹּאכַל	He sat down again and ate.
וַיַּחֲלֹם עוֹד חֲלוֹם אַחֵר	And he dreamed still another dream.

But עוֹד, like הִנֵּה, may be inflected and used as a predicator of existence, with the nuance of "to still be, to yet be."

	SING.		PLURAL	
1c	עוֹדִי/עוֹדֶנִּי	'ôḏî or 'ôḏénnî	———	
2m	עוֹדְךָ	'ôḏəḵā	———	
2f	עוֹדֵךְ	'ôḏāḵ	———	
3m	עוֹדֶנּוּ	'ôḏénnû	עוֹדָם	'ôḏām
3f	עוֹדֶנָּה	'ôḏénnāh	———	

Examples:

עוֹדֶנּוּ שָׁם	He is still there.
אַבְרָהָם עוֹדֶנּוּ עֹמֵד לִפְנֵי יהוה	Abraham is still standing before the Lord.
עוֹדֶנִּי חַי	I am still alive.
עוֹד יוֹסֵף חַי	Joseph is still alive.
עוֹד הָעָם רַב	The people are still too many.
הַעוֹד לָכֶם אָח	Do you have yet another brother?

These examples show clearly that עוֹד, like הִנֵּה, may be extended from purely existential predication to use in other types of non-verbal sentences.

A special use of עוֹד and בְּעוֹד is found in the temporal expressions

עוֹד חָמֵשׁ שָׁנִים	in yet five years, for five more years
בְּעוֹד שְׁלֹשֶׁת יָמִים	in yet three days, after three more days
בְּעוֹד הַיֶּלֶד חַי	while the boy was still alive
עוֹד מְעַט	in just a little while, shortly, soon

Such expressions were originally non-verbal sentences, first used circum-stantially:

there are still five years → there being still five years

and then incorporated as units into another clause, thus being reduced to phrase rather than clause status. בְּעוֹד would then be comparable to בְּ + the infinitive construct of הָיָה. עוֹד with a negative is translated "never again, no longer."

Occasionally אַיֵּה (where?) is found with subject suffixes similar to the preceding; attested forms are אַיֶּכָּה (2 m. s.), אַיּוֹ (3 m. s.), אַיָּם (3 m. pl.).

138. Vocabulary 36.

NOUNS: מְרַגֵּל *məraggēl* (pl. -îm) spy, scout

אֱמֶת *'ĕmét* (w. suff. אֲמִתִּי ; no pl.) truth

VERBS: בָּחַן *bāḥan* (יִבְחַן) to test, try, examine

OTHER: חַי *ḥay* ⎫ a form of חַי (living) or חַיִּים (life) used before proper
חֵי *ḥê* ⎬ nouns in an oath: חַי אֱלֹהִים as God lives, חֵי פַרְעֹה as
   ⎭ Pharaoh lives; cf. אִם below.

אִם *'im* (conj.) if; note the full oath formula: *ḥay/ḥê* X *'im* + imperf., where אִם has a negative force. E.g.

חֵי פַרְעֹה אִם תֵּצְאוּ מִזֶּה כִּי־אִם... As the Pharaoh lives, you shall *not* leave here unless ...

כָּל־ *kull*- all, every one of. Used with pronominal suffixes, in apposition: הָאֲנָשִׁים כֻּלָּם all of the men (lit. the men, all of them).

	SING.			PLURAL	
1c	——	_____		כֻּלָּנוּ	*kullánû*
2m	כֻּלְּךָ	*(kulləkā)*		כֻּלְּכֶם	*kulləkem*
2f	כֻּלֵּךְ	*kullēk, -āk*		——	_____
3m	כֻּלֹּה/וֹ	*kullōh, -ô*		כֻּלָּם	*kullām*
3f	כֻּלָּה	*kullāh*		——	_____

Exercises:

(a) Translate:

(1) אָבִיךָ עוֹדֶנּוּ חַי.

(2) וַיֹּאמֶר הַסָּרִיס: אַיֶּכָּה אֲדֹנִי.

(3) רוּץ נָא לִקְרָאתוֹ.

(4) אֵיפֹה נוּכַל לִמְצֹא אֹכֶל וְאֵין לֶחֶם בָּעִיר.

(5) שְׁמַע נָא אֶל־קוֹלִי וְתִהְיֶה אִישׁ נָבוֹן וְחָכָם.

(6) אֵינֶנִּי נָס הָהָרָה.

(7) קְנֵה לָנוּ אֹכֶל פֶּן־נִרְעַב.

(8) הִנֵּה אִשְׁתְּךָ קַח וָלֵךְ אֶל־אַרְצֶךָ.

(9) בָּנוּ עוֹד עִיר גְּדוֹלָה.

(10) הִנְנִי נֹתֵן לְךָ בִינָה וְחָכְמָה.

(11) הִנֵּה אָחִיךָ בָּרַח מֵהָעִיר רְדֹף אַחֲרָיו.

(12) הַאֵינְךָ יֹדֵעַ כִּי זֶה יוֹם הַשַּׁבָּת.

(b) Give the Hebrew for the following orally:

1. Our mother is still here in the house.
2. Here comes your brother.
3. I am not going to go up to the city.
4. There is still a fire in the mountains.
5. The men are not eating.
6. Where are the vessels which you fashioned?
7. We are not walking.
8. On the 9th day we rode to the end of the road.
9. Are you still hungry?
10. All of us were poor.

(c) Translate:

(1) הִנֵּה־נָא אָבִיךָ מֵת שׁוּב נָא אֶל־אַרְצְךָ וְאֶל־עַמֶּךָ.

(2) וַיֹּאמֶר הַמֶּלֶךְ אֶל־הַנָּבִיא: הִנֵּה־נָא דִּבְרֵי הַנְּבִיאִים הָאֲחֵרִים פֶּה אֶחָד טוֹב אֶל־הַמֶּלֶךְ יְהִיוּ נָא דְבָרֶיךָ כְּדִבְרֵיהֶם.

(3) הִנֵּה אִשְׁתְּךָ הִיא וְאֵיךְ אָמַרְתָּ כִּי אֲחוֹתְךָ הִיא.

(4) הִנֵּה הָאָרֶץ לְפָנֶיךָ שֵׁב בָּהּ בְּשָׁלוֹם.

(5) בְּעוֹד שְׁלֹשֶׁת יָמִים תֵּדַע כִּי אֱמֶת דְּבָרִי.

(6) הִנֵּה־נָא זָקַנְתִּי וְלֹא יָדַעְתִּי יוֹם מוֹתִי וְעַתָּה שְׁמַע נָא אֶל־קוֹלִי וְאֶתֵּן לְךָ בְרָכָה.

(7) הִנֵּה־נָא הָעִיר הַזֹּאת קְרֹבָה לָנוּס שָׁמָּה אִבָּרְחָה נָּא שָׁמָּה וְאֶחְיֶה.

(d) Write in Hebrew. Use *hinnēh*-clauses when possible.

1. Although our food is still plentiful (much), we cannot give you any of it.
2. Because your father has died, I shall send you to live (dwell) with your eldest (lit. great) brother.
3. Although I am here beside you, you cannot see me.
4. Now that you have come, sit down and eat with us.
5. Since we are sojourning here, let us tell them that we are rich so that it will go well with us.

6. Seeing that righteousness and truth have perished in the land, let us seek help from our God so that he will send us deliverance.

7. As the king lives, you shall not enter here before evening.

(e) Reading: Joseph Receives his Brothers in Egypt.

וַיֵּרְדוּ אֲחֵי יוֹסֵף עֲשָׂרָה לִקְנוֹת אֹכֶל מִמִּצְרָיִם וְאֶת־בִּנְיָמִין אֲחִי¹ יוֹסֵף לֹא שָׁלַח יַעֲקֹב אֶת־אֶחָיו כִּי אָמַר פֶּן תִּקְרָאֶנּוּ² רָעָה וַיָּבֹאוּ בְּנֵי יִשְׂרָאֵל בְּתוֹךְ הַבָּאִים מִצְרַיְמָה כִּי הָיָה הָרָעָב בְּאֶרֶץ כְּנָעַן.
וַיָּבֹאוּ אֲחֵי יוֹסֵף וַיִּשְׁתַּחֲווּ³ לוֹ אַפַּיִם אָרְצָה וַיַּרְא יוֹסֵף אֶת־אֶחָיו וַיַּכֵּר⁴ אֹתָם וְהֵם לֹא הִכִּירֻ⁵הוּ אֹתוֹ וַיֹּאמֶר אֲלֵיהֶם קָשׁוֹת⁶ לֵאמֹר: מֵאַיִן בָּאתֶם: וַיֹּאמְרוּ: מֵאֶרֶץ כְּנָעַן לִקְנוֹת אֹכֶל, וַיִּזְכֹּר יוֹסֵף אֶת־הַחֲלוֹמוֹת אֲשֶׁר חָלַם וַיֹּאמֶר אֲלֵיהֶם: מְרַגְּלִים אַתֶּם, לִרְאוֹת אֶת־עֶרְוַת הָאָרֶץ בָּאתֶם, וַיֹּאמְרוּ אֵלָיו: לֹא אֲדֹנִי, וַעֲבָדֶיךָ בָּאוּ לִקְנוֹת אֹכֶל, כֻּלָּנוּ בְּנֵי אִישׁ אֶחָד אֲנַחְנוּ, כֵּנִים אֲנַחְנוּ, לֹא הָיוּ עֲבָדֶיךָ מְרַגְּלִים, וַיֹּאמֶר אֲלֵיהֶם: לֹא, כִּי⁷ עֶרְוַת הָאָרֶץ בָּאתֶם לִרְאוֹת.

וַיֹּאמְרוּ: שְׁנֵי עָשָׂר⁸ עֲבָדֶיךָ אַחִים, אֲנַחְנוּ בְּנֵי אִישׁ אֶחָד בְּאֶרֶץ כְּנָעַן, וְהִנֵּה הַקָּטֹן אֶת־אָבִינוּ הַיּוֹם וְהָאֶחָד אֵינֶנּוּ.

וַיֹּאמֶר יוֹסֵף: הוּא⁹ אֲשֶׁר אָמַרְתִּי אֲלֵיכֶם לֵאמֹר מְרַגְּלִים אַתֶּם, בְּזֹאת אִבָּחֵן אֶתְכֶם, חֵי פַרְעֹה אִם תֵּצְאוּ מִזֶּה כִּי־אִם בְּבוֹא אֲחִיכֶם הַקָּטֹן הֵנָּה, שִׁלְחוּ מִכֶּם אֶחָד וְיִקַּח אֶת־אֲחִיכֶם וְאַתֶּם תֵּשְׁבוּ פֹה וְאֶת־דִּבְרֵיכֶם אֶבְחַן הַאֱמֶת¹⁰ אִתְּכֶם וְאִם לֹא, חֵי פַרְעֹה כִּי¹¹ מְרַגְּלִים אַתֶּם.

Notes to the Reading:

1. i.e. his full brother
2. תִּקְרָא אֹתוֹ =
3. "and they bowed down"
4. "and he recognized"
5. "they did not recognize"
6. Adjectives in the fem. pl. may be used adverbially: "harshly"
7. After a negative *kî* has a strong asseverative force: "but on the contrary, you *did* come etc."
8. "twelve"
9. הוּא is the predicate (here = "so, a fact"): the אֲשֶׁר clause is the subject.
10. הַ introduces an indirect question: "whether"
11. Note this frequent assertive use of כִּי: "As Pharaoh lives, you *are* spies."

LESSON 37

139. Derived Verbs.

All of the verbs studied in the preceding lessons belong to the conjugational type known as Qal, or the simple conjugation, since each consists analytically of an unaugmented root plus a stem pattern (perfect, imperfect, etc.). But in Hebrew, as in most languages, other verbs may be constructed from these same roots, mainly by the use of prefixal elements or by modification of the stem patterns. There are six important types of derived verbs (often called conjugations). Not all roots occur in all six forms, just as many roots are not employed as verbs in the Qal although they are well attested in nouns and adjectives. The six principal derived types are named by the Hebrew grammarians according to the form they would assume in the 3rd per. masc. sing. of the perfect with the root פעל :

נִפְעַל	Niphal	Lessons 37–39
פִּעֵל	Piel	Lessons 40–42
פֻּעַל	Pual	
הִפְעִיל	Hiphil	Lessons 43–49
הָפְעַל	Hophal	
הִתְפַּעֵל	Hithpael	Lesson 50

140. Niphal Verbs: Meaning.

Broadly speaking, Niphal verbs, characterized by an element *n-* prefixed to the root, are *medio-passive* in meaning. Because a theoretical discussion of

[*175*]

this term, by no means consistently employed in grammatical descriptions, would take us too far afield, we shall categorize these verbs on the basis of their translation value in English.

(1) *Incomplete passive:* The passive in English is a construction, not a category of verbal meaning. If a verb occurs in an active-transitive usage, such as

The students read the lesson,

there is a passive transformation to the corresponding

The lesson was read by the students.

By the incomplete passive we mean this same transformation minus the agent:

The lesson was read.

the use of which indicates that the speaker is not concerned with specifying the agent of the action. All Hebrew passives belong to this category; constructions with a specified agent are virtually non-existent. If the corresponding Qal verb is active-transitive, it is always possible to translate the Niphal verb as an incomplete passive:

Qal	*Niphal*	
כָּתַב אֶת־הַדָּבָר	נִכְתַּב הַדָּבָר	The word was written.
עָזַב אֶת־הָעִיר	נֶעֶזְבָה הָעִיר	The city was abandoned.
הָרַג אֶת־הָאִישׁ	נֶהֱרַג הָאִישׁ	The man was slain.

(2) *Middle.* Middle verbs in English are elusive because they pattern like active verbs and have the same form:

Active	*Middle*
He broke the window.	The window broke.
He stopped the car.	The car stopped.
He opened the door.	The door opened.

Unlike the incomplete passive construction, middle verbs are active in form, but the meaning (i.e. voice) is, in a sense, reversed: the object of the active verb has become the subject of the middle verb. Niphal verbs in Hebrew often correspond to middle verbs in English:

נִפְתַּח הַשַּׁעַר	The gate opened.
נִשְׁבַּר הַכְּלִי	The vessel broke.
נִקְבַּץ הָעָם	The people gathered.

(3) *Reflexive.* Reflexive verbs in English have an expressed object (the reflexive pronoun) which refers to the subject:

He saw himself in the water.
He washed himself.
He sold himself into slavery.

Niphal verbs often require this translation:

נִגְאַל   he redeemed himself
נִמְכַּר   he sold himself

(4) *Resultative*. More important than either of the two preceding categories is the Niphal verb in a resultative meaning. Essentially a stative verb, the resultative Niphal describes the state of its subject which has been produced by the verbal action named by the root:

Active	*Passive*	*Resultative*
פָּתַח to open	נִפְתַּח to be opened	נִפְתָּח to be open
שָׁבַר to break	נִשְׁבַּר to be broken	נִשְׁבָּר to be broken, to be in pieces

In English the equivalent of the resultative is so often formally the same as the passive that the distinction made here is difficult to grasp. In the passive *It was broken, was* is an auxiliary verb in the unit *was-broken*; in the resultative *It was broken, was* is the verb *to be* followed by an adjective/participle. One can see this difference most clearly by applying, for example, a transformation into present real:

passive: It is being broken.
resultative: It is broken.

Very frequently the resultative-stative has the nuance of potentiality:

רָאָה – נִרְאָה	: to see	to be seen	→	to be seeable, visible → to appear
יָרֵא – נוֹרָא	: to fear	to be feared	→	to be fearful, dreadful, terrible
אָכַל – נֶאֱכַל	: to eat	to be eaten	→	to be edible
בָּחַר – נִבְחַר	: to choose	to be chosen	→	to be choice, select, acceptable
אָהַב – נֶאֱהָב	: to love	to be loved	→	to be lovely, loveable
יָשַׁב – נוֹשָׁב	: to inhabit	to be inhabited	→	to be habitable
מָצָא – נִמְצָא	: to find	to be found	→	to be extant, to exist, (cf. se trouver)

These four categories have been defined on the basis of English. In Hebrew, however, they are one: the medio-passive as expressed by the Niphal form. Only a careful study of the context will enable the reader to decide among the various possibilities.

Some Niphal verbs have no Qal counterpart:

נִלְחַם	he fought	נִסְתַּר	he hid
נִמְלַט	he escaped	נִרְדָּם	he fell fast asleep

Others would appear to be denominative, although this is a rare use of the Niphal pattern: נִבָּא (for נִנְבָּא *) to prophesy, from נָבִיא, prophet.

141. Niphal Verbs: Stems and Inflection.

The Niphal verb is derived from a triliteral root by the prefixation of *n.* In the perfect the stem has the basic form נִכְתַּב *niktab,* which undergoes no unusual changes in inflection. The imperfect was originally of the form **yankatib,* which, with the assimilation of the *n,* became Hebrew יִכָּתֵב *yikkātēb.* The imperative and infinitive construct are based on the same stem as the imperfect, where the doubling of the first root consonant is the most striking characteristic of the type in general. The participle and infinitive absolute are based on the perfect.

ROOT TYPE	PERFECT		IMPERFECT		IMPERATIVE	
Regular	נִכְתַּב	*niktab*	יִכָּתֵב	*yikkātēb*	הִכָּתֵב	*hikkātēb*
III-gutt.	נִשְׁלַח	*nišlaḥ*	יִשָּׁלַח	*yiššālaḥ*	הִשָּׁלַח	*hiššālaḥ*
I-gutt.	נֶאֱמַן	*ne'ĕman*	יֵאָמֵן	*yē'āmēn*	הֵאָמֵן	*hē'āmēn*

	INF. CONSTR.		PARTICIPLE	
	הִכָּתֵב	*hikkātēb*	נִכְתָּב	*niktāb*
	הִשָּׁלַח	*hiššālaḥ*	נִשְׁלָח	*nišlāḥ*
	הֵאָמֵן	*hē'āmēn*	נֶאֱמָן	*ne'ĕmān*

Remarks:

(a) The only deviation from the regular pattern with roots III-gutt. is the replacement of *ē* with *a* in the imperfect and related forms.

(b) With roots I-gutt. (including א), the perfect usually has the pattern of נֶאֱמַן, with *e* in the preformative and *ĕ* after the guttural. In the imperfect and related forms the doubling of the first root consonant is replaced by a compensatory lengthening of the prefix vowel *i* to *ē*; this *ē* is unaltered in the inflection.

(c) The participle differs from the stem of the perfect only in the length of the stem vowel. As an adjective, the participle retains this vowel in inflection; e.g. the fem. נִכְתָּבָה *niktābāh,* as opposed to the verb, with reduction: נִכְתְּבָה *niktəbāh.*

	Regular		III-gutt.		I-gutt.	
PERFECT:	נִכְתַּב	*niktab*	נִשְׁלַח	*nišlaḥ*	נֶאֱמַן	*ne'ĕman*
	נִכְתְּבָה	*niktəbāh*	נִשְׁלְחָה	*nišləḥāh*	נֶאֶמְנָה	*ne'emnāh*

נִכְתַּבְתָּ	niktábtā	נִשְׁלַחְתָּ	nišláhtā	נֶאֱמַנְתָּ	ne'ĕmántā		
נִכְתַּבְתְּ	niktábt	נִשְׁלַחַתְּ	nišláht	נֶאֱמַנְתְּ	ne'ĕmánt		
נִכְתַּבְתִּי	niktábtî	נִשְׁלַחְתִּי	nišláhtî	נֶאֱמַנְתִּי	ne'ĕmántî		
נִכְתְּבוּ	niktəbû	נִשְׁלְחוּ	nišləhû	נֶאֶמְנוּ	ne'emnû		
נִכְתַּבְתֶּם	niktabtém	נִשְׁלַחְתֶּם	nišlahtém	נֶאֱמַנְתֶּם	ne'ĕmantém		
נִכְתַּבְתֶּן	niktabtén	נִשְׁלַחְתֶּן	nišlahtén	נֶאֱמַנְתֶּן	ne'ĕmantén		
נִכְתַּבְנוּ	niktábnû	נִשְׁלַחְנוּ	nišláhnû	נֶאֱמַנּוּ	ne'ĕmánnû		

IMPERFECT:	יִכָּתֵב	yikkātēb	יִשָּׁלַח	yiššālah	יֵאָמֵן	yē'āmēn
	תִּכָּתֵב	tikkātēb	תִּשָּׁלַח	tiššālah	תֵּאָמֵן	tē'āmēn
	תִּכָּתֵב	tikkātēb	תִּשָּׁלַח	tiššālah	תֵּאָמֵן	tē'āmēn
	תִּכָּתְבִי	tikkātəbî	תִּשָּׁלְחִי	tiššāləhî	תֵּאָמְנִי	tē'āmənî
	אֶכָּתֵב	'ekkātēb	אֶשָּׁלַח	'eššālah	אֵאָמֵן	'ē'āmēn
	יִכָּתְבוּ	yikkātəbû	יִשָּׁלְחוּ	yiššāləhû	יֵאָמְנוּ	yē'āmənû
	תִּכָּתַבְנָה	tikkātábnāh	תִּשָּׁלַחְנָה	tiššāláhnāh	תֵּאָמַנָּה	tē'āmánnāh
	תִּכָּתְבוּ	tikkātəbû	תִּשָּׁלְחוּ	tiššāləhû	תֵּאָמְנוּ	tē'āmənû
	תִּכָּתַבְנָה	tikkātábnāh	תִּשָּׁלַחְנָה	tiššāláhnāh	תֵּאָמַנָּה	tē'āmánnāh
	נִכָּתֵב	nikkātēb	נִשָּׁלַח	niššālah	נֵאָמֵן	nē'āmēn

IMPERATIVE:	הִכָּתֵב	hikkātēb	הִשָּׁלַח	hiššālah	הֵאָמֵן	hē'āmēn
	הִכָּתְבִי	hikkātəbî	הִשָּׁלְחִי	hiššāləhî	הֵאָמְנִי	hē'āmənî
	הִכָּתְבוּ	hikkātəbû	הִשָּׁלְחוּ	hiššāləhû	הֵאָמְנוּ	hē'āmənû
	הִכָּתַבְנָה	hikkātábnāh	הִשָּׁלַחְנָה	hiššāláhnāh	הֵאָמַנָּה	hē'āmánnāh

INF. CONSTR.	הִכָּתֵב	hikkātēb	הִשָּׁלַח	hiššālah	הֵאָמֵן	hē'āmēn
W. SUFF.	הִכָּתְבִי	hikkātəbî	הִשָּׁלְחִי	hiššāləhî	הֵאָמְנִי	hē'āmənî
	הִכָּתֶבְךָ	hikkātebkā	הִשָּׁלַחֲךָ	hiššālahăkā	הֵאָמֶנְךָ	hē'āmenkā
	etc.		etc.		etc.	

INF. (1)	נִכְתוֹב	niktôb	נִשְׁלוֹחַ	nišlô‎ᵃh	נַעֲבוֹר	na'ăbôr
ABSOLUTE (2)	הִכָּתוֹב	hikkātôb	הִשָּׁלוֹחַ	hiššālô‎ᵃh	הֵעֲבוֹר	hē'ăbôr

PARTICIPLE:	נִכְתָּב	niktāb	נִשְׁלָח	nišlāh	נֶאֱמָן	ne'ĕmān
	נִכְתָּבָה	niktābāh	נִשְׁלָחָה	nišlāhāh	נֶאֱמָנָה	ne'ĕmānāh
	נִכְתָּבִים	niktābîm	נִשְׁלָחִים	nišlāhîm	נֶאֱמָנִים	ne'ĕmānîm
	נִכְתָּבוֹת	niktābôt	נִשְׁלָחוֹת	nišlāhôt	נֶאֱמָנוֹת	ne'ĕmānôt

Remarks:

(1) The two forms of the infinitive absolute tend to pair off with the corresponding finite verb of the same general pattern:

הִשָּׁמוֹעַ יִשָּׁמַע   but   שָׁמוֹעַ יִשָּׁמַע

(2) The inf. absolute of נֶאֱמָן does not occur, and since its form could be disputed (more likely to have been נֶאֱמוֹן, with e because of the א) we have replaced it with the better attested type of נֶעֱבַר (to be crossed).

(3) The feminine participles singular may also be of the pattern נִכְתֶּבֶת, נֶאֱמֶנֶת, נִשְׁלַחַת.

142. Vocabulary 37.

NOUNS: נֶפֶשׁ *népeš* (w. suff. נַפְשִׁי etc.; pl. -*ôṯ*) soul, vital life-force; a person, living thing. With suffixes it is the equivalent of the intensive/reflexive pronoun: נַפְשִׁי myself, נַפְשְׁךָ yourself...

שַׂק *śaq* (pl. -*îm*) sack; sack-cloth (worn as a sign of mourning).

מִשְׁמָר *mišmār* (no pl.) place of confinement, jail; a guard unit.

מָלוֹן *mālôn* lodging-place, inn.

VERBS: אָשֵׁם *'āšēm* (יֶאְשַׁם) to be guilty; verbal adjective אָשֵׁם, guilty.

לָן *lān* (יָלִין) to spend the night.

נֶאֱמַן *ne'ĕman* (יֵאָמֵן) to be confirmed, verified, trustworthy.

נִשְׁאַר *niš'ar* (יִשָּׁאֵר) to be left over, remain, survive.

OTHER: לְבַדּ־ *ləḇadd-* w. suff.: alone, only. E.g. אֲנִי לְבַדִּי I alone, etc.

אֲבָל *'ăḇāl* (adv.) truly, indeed; however.

Note: The preposition בֵּין (between) has the following forms with pronominal suffixes:

בֵּינִי	*bênî*	בֵּינֵינוּ	*bênênû*	or	בֵּינוֹתֵינוּ	*bênôṯênû* (rare)
בֵּינְךָ	*bênəḵā*	בֵּינֵיכֶם	*bênêḵem*		——	
בֵּינֵךְ	*bênēḵ*	——			——	
בֵּינוֹ	*bênô*	בֵּינֵיהֶם	*bênêhem*	or	בֵּינוֹתָם	*bênôṯām* (rare)

Exercises:

(a) Punctuate the Niphal verbs fully and translate:

(1) נשבר הכלי.
(2) יאכל הבשׂר.
(3) נהרגו המרגלים.
(4) ישמעו דברי אמת.
(5) לא יכרת איש מעל הכסא.
(6) נשמע קול שירם.
(7) לא נחשׁך מאומה ממך.
(8) איך יבחן העם.
(9) אנחנו נשארנו לבדנו.
(10) יאמן דבר אלהים.

(11) תזכרו כלכם.
(12) אל־יכתב שׁמו בספר.
(13) אלה שׁמות הערים הנלכדות.
(14) וימכר יוסף בידי המצרים.
(15) חי אלהים אם־ישפך דם בהיותי פה.
(16) יתפשו הברחים.
(17) יחן את־הנבחרים.
(18) ידמו הנשארים.
(19) הפתחו השׁערים.
(20) תשׁארפנה הערים הנעזבות.

(b) Write in Hebrew:

1. And when their words were heard, we knew that they were guilty.
2. As God lives, you will not see your husband until the day of his death.
3. And in the evening he entered an inn and spent the night there.
4. Now that you have been chosen as our king, give us help so that we may slay our accursed enemies before our land is captured and our cities are burned.

5. They placed the food in their sacks and set out on the road.

6. Now that he has measured the field, go to him and ask him whether (hă-) he will sell it to us.

(c) Reading: Joseph and his Brothers in Egypt.

וַיֶּאֱסֹף יוֹסֵף אֶת־אֶחָיו אֶל־מִשְׁמָר שְׁלֹשֶׁת יָמִים וַיֹּאמֶר אֲלֵיהֶם בַּיּוֹם הַשְּׁלִישִׁי: זֹאת עֲשׂוּ וִחְיוּ,
אֶת־הָאֱלֹהִים אֲנִי יָרֵא, אִם־כֵּנִים אַתֶּם, אֲחִיכֶם אֶחָד יֵאָסֵר בְּבֵית מִשְׁמַרְכֶם וְאַתֶּם לְכוּ וְשׁוֹבוּ
אַרְצָה כְנַעַן עִם־הָאֹכֶל אֲשֶׁר קְנִיתֶם וְאֶת־אֲחִיכֶם הַקָּטֹן תִּקְחוּ מִשָּׁם וְהוּא יָבֹא אִתְּכֶם הֵנָּה
וְיֵאָמְנוּ דִבְרֵיכֶם וְלֹא תָמוּתוּ.

וַיֹּאמְרוּ אִישׁ אֶל־אָחִיו: אֲבָל אֲשֵׁמִים אֲנַחְנוּ עַל־אָחִינוּ¹ אֲשֶׁר רָאִינוּ צָרַת נַפְשׁוֹ וְלֹא שָׁמַעְנוּ,
עַל־כֵּן בָּאָה אֵלֵינוּ הַצָּרָה הַזֹּאת, וַיַּעַן רְאוּבֵן אֹתָם לֵאמֹר: הֲלֹא אָמַרְתִּי אֲלֵיכֶם לֵאמֹר אַל־
תֶּחֶטְאוּ בַיֶּלֶד וְלֹא שְׁמַעְתֶּם וְגַם־דָּמוֹ² הִנֵּה נִדְרָשׁ, וְהֵם לֹא יָדְעוּ כִּי שֹׁמֵעַ יוֹסֵף כִּי הַמֵּלִיץ³
בֵּינוֹתָם וַיִּסֹּב⁴ יוֹסֵף מֵעֲלֵיהֶם וַיֵּבְךְּ וַיָּשָׁב אֲלֵיהֶם וַיִּקַּח אֶת־שִׁמְעוֹן וַיֶּאֱסֹר אֹתוֹ לְעֵינֵיהֶם וַיִּתֵּן
לָהֶם אֶת־הָאֹכֶל אֲשֶׁר בָּאוּ מִצְרַיְמָה לִקְנוֹת וַיִּתֵּן לָהֶם גַּם־צֵדָה⁵ לַדֶּרֶךְ וַיָּשֶׂם אֶת־הַכֶּסֶף
אֲשֶׁר נָתְנוּ לוֹ בְּשַׂקֵּיהֶם וְהֵם לֹא יָדְעוּ וַיֵּלְכוּ מִשָּׁם לַעֲלוֹת אַרְצָה כְנַעַן.

וַיְהִי בַעֲלוֹתָם וַיָּלִינוּ בְמָלוֹן וַיְהִי כִּפְתֹחַ אֶחָד מֵהֶם אֶת־שַׂקּוֹ לָתֵת מֵהָאֹכֶל לַחֲמוֹרוֹ וַיַּרְא
אֶת־כַּסְפּוֹ וְהִנֵּה הוּא בְּפִי שַׂקּוֹ וַיֹּאמֶר אֶל־אֶחָיו: הִנֵּה כַסְפִּי בְּשַׂקִּי, וַיֵּרְאוּ וַיִּירְאוּ וַיֹּאמְרוּ אִישׁ
אֶל־אָחִיו לֵאמֹר: מַה־זֹּאת עָשָׂה אֱלֹהִים לָנוּ.

וַיָּבֹאוּ אֶל־יַעֲקֹב אֲבִיהֶם אַרְצָה כְנַעַן וַיַּגִּידוּ לוֹ אֶת־כָּל־הַקֹּרוֹת⁶ אֹתָם לֵאמֹר: אָמַר אֵלֵינוּ
הָאִישׁ אֲדֹנֵי הָאָרֶץ קָשׁוֹת וַיֹּאמֶר כִּי אֲנַחְנוּ מְרַגְּלִים וְכִי בָאנוּ לִרְאוֹת עֶרְוַת אַרְצוֹ וַנֹּאמֶר אֵלָיו:
כֵּנִים אֲנַחְנוּ, לֹא הָיִינוּ מְרַגְּלִים, וַיֹּאמֶר אֵלֵינוּ הָאִישׁ אֲדֹנֵי הָאָרֶץ: בְּזֹאת אֵדַע כִּי כֵנִים אַתֶּם,
אֲחִיכֶם הָאֶחָד יֵאָסֵר בְּבֵית הַמִּשְׁמָר וְאַתֶּם לְכוּ וְשַׁבְתֶּם אֶל־אַרְצְכֶם וּבוֹא יָבֹא אֲחִיכֶם הַקָּטֹן
אִתְּכֶם בְּרִדְתְּכֶם עוֹד אֵלַי, וְכֵן עָשִׂינוּ וְאֶת־אָחִינוּ שִׁמְעוֹן אָסְרוּ לְעֵינֵינוּ וַיָּשִׂימוּ אֹתוֹ בְּבֵית
הַמִּשְׁמָר.

וַיֹּאמֶר אֲלֵיהֶם יַעֲקֹב אֲבִיהֶם: אֹתִי שִׁכַּלְתֶּם,⁷ יוֹסֵף אֵינֶנּוּ וְשִׁמְעוֹן אֵינֶנּוּ וְאֶת־בִּנְיָמִן תִּקָּחוּ,
עָלַי הָיוּ כֻלָּנָה,⁸ וַיֹּאמֶר רְאוּבֵן אֶל־אָבִיו לֵאמֹר: אֶת־שְׁנֵי בָנַי תָּמִית⁹ אִם־לֹא יָשׁוּב בִּנְיָמִן
עִמִּי אֵלֶיךָ מִמִּצְרַיִם, תְּנָה אֹתוֹ עַל־יָדִי¹⁰ וְהוּא יָשׁוּב עִמִּי מִשָּׁם.

וַיֹּאמֶר יַעֲקֹב: לֹא יֵרֵד בְּנִי עִמָּכֶם כִּי אָחִיו מֵת וְהוּא לְבַדּוֹ נִשְׁאָר, אִם־תִּקְרָא אֹתוֹ רָעָה בַּדֶּרֶךְ
אֲשֶׁר תֵּלְכוּ בָהּ וְהוֹרַדְתֶּם¹¹ בְּיָגוֹן שְׁאֹלָה.

Notes to the Reading:

1. They are referring here to their earlier treatment of Joseph.
2. Prob. to be understood as "And now, moreover, (our penalty for shedding) his blood is to be exacted." דָּם is frequently used as the equivalent of the guilt (or punishment) involved in bloodshed.
3. מֵלִיץ an interpreter
4. סָבַב in the sense "turn oneself away"
5. "provisions"
6. fem. pl. = neuter pl. "the things which befell"

7. "you have bereaved"
8. A rare form, perhaps fem. pl., "everything".
9. "you may kill"
10. "in my charge"
11. Note that the apodosis (if... *then*) is not marked except by a con-junctive-sequential construction. יָגוֹן grief.

LESSON 38

143. Niphal Verbs: Stems and Inflection (continued).

Root Type	Perfect	Imperfect	Imperative	Inf. Construct
I-*Nun*	נִתַּן *nittan*	יִנָּתֵן *yinnātēn*	הִנָּתֵן *hinnātēn*	הִנָּתֵן *hinnātēn*
I-*Yodh*	נוֹלַד *nôlad*	יִוָּלֵד *yiwwālēd*	הִוָּלֵד *hiwwālēd*	הִוָּלֵד *hiwwālēd*
III-*Aleph*	נִקְרָא *niqrā'*	יִקָּרֵא *yiqqārē'*	הִקָּרֵא *hiqqārē'*	הִקָּרֵא *hiqqārē'*
III-*Hē*	נִבְנָה *nibnāh*	יִבָּנֶה *yibbāneh*	הִבָּנֵה *hibbānēh*	הִבָּנוֹת *hibbānôt*

Remarks:

(1) I-*Nun*. The assimilation of the first root consonant takes place in the perfect and participle: * nintan > nittan*. The stems and inflection are otherwise like those of the regular triliteral root. [Note: the assimilation of the stem-final *n* in the perfect of נִתַּן is proper only to this particular root; cf. the Qal perfect.]

(2) I-*Yodh*. Nearly all roots I-*Yodh* in Hebrew were originally I-*Waw*. The original *Waw* shows up clearly in the Niphal verbs. In the perfect an earlier * *nawlad* (root *yld < wld*) appears as נוֹלַד *nôlad* (he was born). In the imperfect and imperative the *n-* of the Niphal prefix is assimilated to the root *-w-* and a doubled *-ww-* results: יִוָּלֵד *yiwwālēd* (he will be born). Inflection is regular.

(3) III-*Aleph*. As expected, the stem vowel of the perfect is lengthened to *ā* before the quiescent א (cf. §52 etc.). Unlike the Qal perfect, however,

the stem vowel is replaced with ē before the 2nd and 1st person endings: e.g. *niqrē(')tā* (you were called). The full inflection is given below.

(4) III-*Hē*. The pattern of inflection learned for the Qal will hold for most of the verbs derived from roots III-*Hē*. In the Niphal perfect, however, the stem vowel before the 2nd and 1st person suffixes is regulary *ê*, not *î*. Contrast בָּנִיתִי and נִבְנֵיתִי (I was built). Just as in the Qal, the jussive or short form of the imperfect loses the final vowel: יִבָּנֶה → יִבָּן The inf. construct ends in -*ôt*, again like the Qal: הִבָּנוֹת, בְּנוֹת. Note the participle נִבְנֶה (cf. בֹּנֶה).

PERFECT:

נִתַּן	*nittan*	נוֹלַד	*nôlad*	נִקְרָא	*niqrā'*	נִבְנָה	*nibnāh*
נִתְּנָה	*nittənāh*	נוֹלְדָה	*nôlədāh*	נִקְרְאָה	*niqrə'āh*	נִבְנְתָה	*nibnətāh*
נִתַּתָּ	*nittáttā*	נוֹלַדְתָּ	*nôládtā*	נִקְרֵאתָ	*niqrē(')tā*	נִבְנֵיתָ	*nibnêtā*
נִתַּתְּ	*nittátt*	נוֹלַדְתְּ	*nôládt*	נִקְרֵאת	*niqrē(')t*	נִבְנֵית	*nibnêt*
נִתַּתִּי	*nittáttî*	נוֹלַדְתִּי	*nôládtî*	נִקְרֵאתִי	*niqrē(')tî*	נִבְנֵיתִי	*nibnêtî*
נִתְּנוּ	*nittənû*	נוֹלְדוּ	*nôlədû*	נִקְרְאוּ	*niqrə'û*	נִבְנוּ	*nibnû*
נִתַּתֶּם	*nittattem*	נוֹלַדְתֶּם	*nôladtém*	נִקְרֵאתֶם	*niqrē(')tem*	נִבְנֵיתֶם	*nibnêtem*
נִתַּתֶּן	*nittatten*	נוֹלַדְתֶּן	*nôladtén*	נִקְרֵאתֶן	*niqrē(')ten*	נִבְנֵיתֶן	*nibnêten*
נִתַּנּוּ	*nittánnû*	נוֹלַדְנוּ	*nôládnû*	נִקְרֵאנוּ	*niqrē(')nû*	נִבְנֵינוּ	*nibnênû*

IMPERFECT:

יִנָּתֵן	*yinnātēn*	יִוָּלֵד	*yiwwālēd*	יִקָּרֵא	*yiqqārē'*	יִבָּנֶה	*yibbāneh*
תִּנָּתֵן	*tinnātēn*	תִּוָּלֵד	*tiwwālēd*	תִּקָּרֵא	*tiqqārē'*	תִּבָּנֶה	*tibbāneh*
תִּנָּתֵן	*tinnātēn*	תִּוָּלֵד	*tiwwālēd*	תִּקָּרֵא	*tiqqārē'*	תִּבָּנֶה	*tibbāneh*
תִּנָּתְנִי	*tinnātənî*	תִּוָּלְדִי	*tiwwālədî*	תִּקָּרְאִי	*tiqqārə'î*	תִּבָּנִי	*tibbānî*
אֶנָּתֵן	*'ennātēn*	אִוָּלֵד	*'iwwālēd*	אֶקָּרֵא	*'eqqārē'*	אֶבָּנֶה	*'ebbāneh*
יִנָּתְנוּ	*yinnātənû*	יִוָּלְדוּ	*yiwwālədû*	יִקָּרְאוּ	*yiqqārə'û*	יִבָּנוּ	*yibbānû*
תִּנָּתַנָּה	*tinnātánnāh*	תִּוָּלַדְנָה	*tiwwāládnāh*	תִּקָּרֶאנָה	*tiqqāré(')nāh*	תִּבָּנֶינָה	*tibbānênāh*
תִּנָּתְנוּ	*tinnātənû*	תִּוָּלְדוּ	*tiwwālədû*	תִּקָּרְאוּ	*tiqqārə'û*	תִּבָּנוּ	*tibbānû*
תִּנָּתַנָּה	*tinnātánnāh*	תִּוָּלַדְנָה	*tiwwāládnāh*	תִּקָּרֶאנָה	*tiqqārē(')nāh*	תִּבָּנֶינָה	*tibbānênāh*
נִנָּתֵן	*ninnātēn*	נִוָּלֵד	*niwwālēd*	נִקָּרֵא	*niqqārē'*	נִבָּנֶה	*nibbāneh*

IMPERATIVE:

הִנָּתֵן	*hinnātēn*	הִוָּלֵד	*hiwwālēd*	הִקָּרֵא	*hiqqārē'*	הִבָּנֵה	*hibbānēh*
הִנָּתְנִי	*hinnātənî*,	הִוָּלְדִי	*hiwwālədî*	הִקָּרְאִי	*hiqqārə'î*	הִבָּנִי	*hibbānî*
	etc.		etc.		etc.		etc.

INF. CONSTRUCT:

הִנָּתֵן	*hinnātēn*	הִוָּלֵד	*hiwwālēd*	הִקָּרֵא	*hiqqārē'*	הִבָּנוֹת	*hibbānôt*

INF. ABSOLUTE:

נִתּוֹן	*nittôn*	[נוֹלוֹד	*nôlôd*]	נִקְרֹא	*niqrô'*	הִבָּנֵה	*hibbānēh*
						נִבְנֹה	*nibnōh*

PARTICIPLES:

נִתָּן nittān	נוֹלָד nôlāḏ	נִקְרָא niqrā'	נִבְנֶה nibneh
נִתָּנָה nittānāh	נוֹלָדָה nôlāḏāh	נִקְרָאָה niqrā'āh	נִבְנָה nibnāh
נִתֶּנֶת nitténet	נוֹלֶדֶת nôléḏet	נִקְרֵאת niqrē(')t	
נִתָּנִים nittānîm	נוֹלָדִים nôlāḏîm	נִקְרָאִים niqrā'îm	נִבְנִים nibnîm
נִתָּנוֹת nittānôt	נוֹלָדוֹת nôlāḏôt	נִקְרָאוֹת niqrā'ôt	נִבְנוֹת nibnôt

144. Niphal Verbs: Mixed Types.

The following are a sampling of verbs whose roots combine several of the characteristics described in the preceding paragraphs. The forms are all quite predictable from the types already given and thus require no comment.

I-*Waw* (*Yodh*) and III-gutt.:   PERF.:   נוֹדַע *nôḏa'*

I-*Waw* (*Yodh*) and III-*Aleph*:   נוֹרָא *nôrā'*

I-gutt. and III-*Hē*:   נַעֲשָׂה *na'ăśāh*

I-*Nun* and II-gutt. (root נחם)   נִחַם *niḥam*

IMPERF.:   יִוָּדַע *yiwwāḏa'*   IMPTV.:   הִוָּדַע *hiwwāḏa'*   *be known*

יִוָּרֵא *yiwwārē'*   הִוָּרֵא *hiwwārē'*   *be feared*

יֵעָשֶׂה *yē'āśeh*   הֵעָשֶׂה *hē'āśeh*   *be done*

יִנָּחֵם *yinnāḥēm*   הִנָּחֵם *hinnāḥēm*   *be sorry*

Note also the verb נִגַּשׁ *niggaš* (root נגשׁ). Only the perfect is a Niphal verb; in the imperfect the Qal form יִגַּשׁ is used.

145. Vocabulary 38.

NOUNS: רֹאשׁ *rō(')š* (pl. irreg. רָאשִׁים, see §34)   head, chief, top

פֶּתַח *pétaḥ* (w. suff. פִּתְחִי; pl. -îm)   an opening (of tent, house, wall etc.); also used as a prep.: at the opening of

טַף *ṭap* (no pl.)   a collective term for children; not used in construct

מְעַט *mə'aṭ* (no pl.)   a little; frequent in construct: מְעַט מַיִם a little water. Note מְעַט מְעַט little by little; בְּעוֹד מְעַט in a little while. Also used in a variety of idiomatic expressions with the basic meaning of slightness, smallness, unimportance.

עוֹלָם *'ôlām* (pl. -îm)   a word referring to a long duration of time, either past or future; thus, eternity, antiquity. Note the common phrases: לְעוֹלָם ,עַד־עוֹלָם forever. Frequent as the second element of a construct chain: יְמֵי עוֹלָם ancient days; בְּרִית עוֹלָם perpetual covenant.

VERBS: נוֹתַר *nôtar* (יִוָּתֵר) to be left, remain

נִלְחַם *nilḥam* (יִלָּחֵם) to fight (+ בְּ with)

נִחַם *niḥam* (יִנָּחֵם) to be sorry, repent; to be comforted

נִגַּשׁ *niggaš* (use Qal imperf. יִגַּשׁ) to approach (+ אֶל)

נִצַּב *niṣṣaḇ* (no imperf.) to station oneself, to stand; be stationed

נִפְלָא *niplā'* (יִפָּלֵא) to be wonderful, marvelous.

Exercises:

(a) Point the Niphal verbs fully and translate:

(1) נִגַּשְׁתִּי וְלֹא יָכֹלְתִּי לַעֲמֹד לְפָנָיו.   (13) אֵינֶנִּי אָשֵׁם, לֹא עָשִׂיתִי דָבָר.

(2) אֵיפֹה תָלִין הַלַּיְלָה.   (14) וַיִּבֶן לוֹ בָּיִת.

(3) מִי יִבָּחֵר לְרֹאשׁ הָעָם.   (15) נִחַמְתִּי עַל־הָרָעָה אֲשֶׁר עָשִׂיתִי.

(4) הֵם נִלְחָמִים אֵצֶל הַקִּיר.   (16) רָאִינוּ אֶת־מְלַאכְתּוֹ הַנִּפְלָאָה וַנֵּדַם.

(5) לֹא תִזָּכֵר בִּקְהַל הַצַּדִּיקִים.   (17) לָמָּה יֵעָשׂוּ הַדְּבָרִים הָאֵלֶּה.

(6) יֵאָסְפוּ מִקְצֵי הָאָרֶץ.   (18) וַיְהִי אַחֲרֵי הַמִּלְחָמָה וָאִוָּתֵר אֲנִי לְבַדִּי.

(7) לֹא יִוָּתֵר אִישׁ מֵהַפָּרָשִׁים.   (19) יִנָּתֵן לְךָ כֶּסֶף וְזָהָב.

(8) קְחוּ אֶת־הַסּוּסִים הַנּוֹתָרִים.   (20) יִוָּדַע שִׁמְךָ הַגָּדוֹל בְּכָל־הָאָרֶץ.

(9) תֶּן לִי מְעַט־לֶחֶם.   (21) וַיִּקֶן שָׁם בָּקָר.

(10) מִי הָאֲנָשִׁים הַנִּצָּבִים שָׁם.   (22) וַיִּשְׁמְעוּ דְבָרָיו וַיֵּאָמְנוּ.

(11) נִלְקְחוּ הָאֲנָשִׁים הַחוּצָה וַיֵּהָרְגוּ שָׁם.   (23) וַיְהִי מִקֵּץ אַרְבָּעָה יָמִים וַתֵּעָזֵב הָעִיר.

(12) יֵשְׁבוּ עַל־שְׂפַת הַנָּהָר עִם־טַפָּם.   (24) יִקָּרְאוּ הַדְּבָרִים הָאֵלֶּה בְּאָזְנֵי בְנֵיכֶם.

(b) Write in Hebrew:

1. There is a large hill between us and the camp.
2. The fruit will be taken to the house and eaten there.
3. The righteous shall be exalted (lit. raised up), but the wicked shall perish.
4. Countless men (lit. men, their number not existing) were slain near the wall.
5. Be consoled, my son; the sound of your distress has been heard and help will be given to you.
6. I was appointed (lit. stationed) to watch the women and the children.
7. A new city will be built for those who are left.

(c) Reading: Jacob and his Sons, after the First Trip to Egypt.

וְהָרָעָב כָּבֵד בָּאָרֶץ וַיְהִי כַּאֲשֶׁר כִּלּוּ הָאֹכֶל אֲשֶׁר נִקְנֶה בְמִצְרַיִם וַיֹּאמֶר יַעֲקֹב אֶל־בָּנָיו: שֻׁבוּ מִצְרַיְמָה וְקִחוּ מִשָּׁם מְעַט־אֹכֶל, וַיֹּאמֶר אֵלָיו יְהוּדָה לֵאמֹר: אָמַר הָאִישׁ אֵלֵינוּ, לֹא תִרְאוּ פָנַי בִּלְתִּי[1] אֲחִיכֶם אִתְּכֶם, אִם־יֶשְׁךָ שֹׁלֵחַ אֶת־אָחִינוּ אִתָּנוּ נֵרֵד וְנִקְנֶה לְךָ אֹכֶל וְאִם־אֵינְךָ שֹׁלֵחַ לֹא נֵרֵד כִּי אָמַר הָאִישׁ אֵלֵינוּ, לֹא תִרְאוּ פָנַי בִּלְתִּי אֲחִיכֶם אִתְּכֶם.

וַיֹּאמֶר יִשְׂרָאֵל: לָמָּה אֲמַרְתֶּם אֵלָיו כִּי עוֹד לָכֶם אָח, וַיֹּאמְרוּ: שָׁאוֹל שָׁאַל הָאִישׁ לָנוּ[2] לֵאמֹר: הַעוֹד אֲבִיכֶם חַי, הֲיֵשׁ לָכֶם אָח, וַנַּגֶּד־לוֹ עַל־פִּי הַדְּבָרִים הָאֵלֶּה, הֲיָדוֹעַ נֵדַע[3] כִּי יֹאמַר: אֲחִיכֶם יֵרֵד אִתְּכֶם.

וַיֹּאמֶר יְהוּדָה אֶל־יִשְׂרָאֵל אָבִיו: שִׁלְחָה הַנַּעַר אִתִּי וְנָקוּמָה וְנֵלֵכָה וְנִחְיֶה וְלֹא נָמוּת גַּם־

אֲנַחְנוּ גַם־אַתָּה גַם־טַפֵּנוּ, אִם־לֹא יָשׁוּב הַנַּעַר אֵלֶיךָ וְחָטָאתִי לְךָ⁴ כָּל־הַיָּמִים, וַיֹּאמֶר יַעֲקֹב: אִם־כֵּן, זֹאת עֲשׂוּ, קְחוּ אִישׁ מִנְחָה, וְכֶסֶף מִשְׁנֶה⁵ קְחוּ, וְאֶת־אֲחִיכֶם קְחוּ וְקוּמוּ שׁוּבוּ אֶל־הָאִישׁ וֵאלֹהִים יִתֵּן לָכֶם רַחֲמִים⁶ לִפְנֵי הָאִישׁ וְשִׁלַּח⁷ לָכֶם אֶת־אֲחִיכֶם וְאֶת־בִּנְיָמִין.

Notes to the Reading:

1. בִּלְתִּי unless
2. Note לְ in the sense "about" after שָׁאַל.
3. נֵדַע and יֹאמַר are imperfects used modally: "How were we to know that he would say".
4. "I shall be accountable (lit. sin against) to you".
5. "twice the (required) money"
6. "mercy, favor"
7. "and may he release"

(d) Reading: Psalm 24 : 7–10.

שְׂאוּ שְׁעָרִים רָאשֵׁיכֶם	שְׂאוּ שְׁעָרִים רָאשֵׁיכֶם
וּשְׂאוּ פִּתְחֵי עוֹלָם	וְהִנָּשְׂאוּ פִּתְחֵי עוֹלָם
וְיָבוֹא מֶלֶךְ הַכָּבוֹד:	וְיָבוֹא מֶלֶךְ הַכָּבוֹד:
מִי הוּא זֶה מֶלֶךְ הַכָּבוֹד	מִי¹ זֶה מֶלֶךְ הַכָּבוֹד
יהוה צְבָאוֹת	יהוה עִזּוּז² וְגִבּוֹר
הוּא מֶלֶךְ הַכָּבוֹד: סֶלָה³	יהוה גִּבּוֹר מִלְחָמָה:

Notes to the Reading:

1. See §82 (end).
2. A rare word: "mighty, powerful".
3. A frequent word at the close of verses or longer sections in the Psalms. Its meaning is unknown.

LESSON 39

146. Niphal Verbs: Stems and Inflection (concluded).

ROOT TYPE		PERFECT		IMPERFECT		IMPERATIVE	
Hollow	(כון)	נָכוֹן	*nāḵôn*	יִכּוֹן	*yikkôn*	הִכּוֹן	*hikkôn*
Geminate	(סבב)	נָסַב	*nāsaḇ*	יִסַּב	*yissaḇ*	הִסַּב	*hissaḇ*

	INF. CONSTRUCT		PARTICIPLE	
	הִכּוֹן	*hikkôn*	נָכוֹן	*nāḵôn*
	הִסֵּב	*hissēḇ*	נָסָב	*nāsāḇ*

As in the Qal, the two root types given above present the most striking deviation from the normal triliteral patterns of the preceding lessons. The retention of the stem vowel -ô- with the Hollow roots simplifies that paradigm, but attention must be called to the curious interchange of ô and û in pretonic syllables in the inflection of the perfect, where the stem vowel -ô- is added in the 1st and 2nd persons:

PERFECT:	נָכוֹן	*nāḵôn*	נָכֹונוּ	*nāḵônû*
	נָכֹונָה	*nāḵônāh*		
	נְכוּנֹותָ	*nəḵûnôṯā*	נְכוּנֹותֶם	*nəḵônôṯem*
	נְכוּנֹות	*nəḵûnôṯ*	נְכוּנֹותֶן	*nəḵônôṯen*
	נְכוּנֹותִי	*nəḵûnôṯî*	נְכוּנֹונוּ	*nəḵûnônû*
IMPERFECT:	יִכּוֹן	*yikkôn*	יִכֹּונוּ	*yikkônû*
	תִּכּוֹן	*tikkôn*	[תִּכֹּונֶֽינָה	*tikkônệnāh*]

	תִּכּוֹן *tikkôn*	תִּכּוֹנוּ *tikkônû*	
	תִּכּוֹנִי *tikkônî*	[תִּכּוֹנֶֽינָה *tikkônênāh*]	
	אִכּוֹן *'ikkôn*	נִכּוֹן *nikkôn*	
IMPERATIVE:	הִכּוֹן *hikkôn*	הִכּוֹנוּ *hikkônû*	
	הִכּוֹנִי *hikkônî*		
INF. CONSTRUCT:	הִכּוֹן *hikkôn*		
	הִכּוֹנִי *hikkônî* etc.		
PARTICIPLE:	נָכוֹן *nāḵôn*	נְכוֹנִים *nəḵônîm*	
	נְכוֹנָה *nəḵônāh*	נְכוֹנוֹת *nəḵônôt*	

The inf. absolute may have either the form נָכוֹן *nāḵôn* or הִכּוֹן *hikkôn*.

Niphal verbs from geminate roots are quite poorly attested and in many cases one cannot be certain that the form in question is indeed a Niphal and not a Qal verb. The 3rd pers. masc. sing. of the perfect, נָסַב (from an earlier *nasabb-)* resembles a Qal verb from a root נסב. The full inflection, however, shows that this resemblance is superficial and that the doubling of the second root consonant reappears when a vowel is added to the stem. Likewise in the imperfect יִסַּב confusion with other types is possible: this form could be from a root נסב (cf. יִגַּשׁ) or it could be a Qal variant (cf. יִתַּם for the more usual יִתֹּם). Some of the alternate forms that crop up are due to analogy. For example, the original pair יִמַּס – נָמַס was altered to נָמֵס – יִמַּס probably because יִמַּס was interpreted as a stative Qal verb (like יִכְבַּד) from a root נמס:

$$\text{יְכְבַּד is to כָּבֵד} \quad \text{as} \quad \text{יִמַּס is to נָמֵס.}$$

This mixing of Qal and Niphal forms, together with the relative rarity of these verbs, makes it quite impossible to decide which conjugation we are dealing with. The following selection of forms is a sufficient guide to the forms that will be met:

PERFECT:	נָסַב *nāsab*	or	נָסֵב *nāsēḇ*		
	נָסַּֽבָּה *nāsábbāh*	or	נָסֵּֽבָּה *nāsébbāh*		
	נְסַבּוֹת *nəsabbôṯā* etc.				
	נָסַּֽבּוּ *nāsábbû*	or	נָסֵֽבּוּ *nāsébbû*		
	נְסַבּוֹתֶם *nəsabbôṯem* etc.				
IMPERFECT:	יִסַּב *yissab* etc.	or	יִסֹּב *yissōḇ* etc.		
	תִּסַּֽבִּי *tissábbî* etc.	or	תִּסֹּֽבִּי *tissóbbî* etc.		
IMPERATIVE:	הִסַּב *hissab*	or	הִסֹּב *hissōḇ*		
	הִסַּֽבִּי *hissábbî* etc.	or	הִסֹּֽבִּי *hissóbbî* etc.		
INF. CONSTR.	הִסֵּב *hissēḇ*				
	הִסִּֽבִּי *hissibbî* etc.				
PARTICIPLE:	נָסָב *nāsāḇ*	נְסַבִּים *nəsabbîm*			
	נְסַבָּה *nəsabbāh*	נְסַבּוֹת *nəsabbôṯ*			

147. Vocabulary 39.

NOUNS: טֶבַח *ṭébaḥ* slaughtering

תְּחִלָּה *təḥillāh* beginning, first occasion (of some event)

צֵל *ṣēl* (w. suff. צִלִּי; pl. irreg. צְלָלִים) shade, shadow; fig., protection

יָמִין *yāmîn* the right; right hand or side (f.)

שְׂמֹאל *śəmō(')l* the left; יַד שְׂמֹאל the left hand or side (m.)

לֵב *lēḇ* (w. suff. לִבִּי; pl. -ôṯ) heart

VERBS: נָם *nām* (יָנוּם) to sleep

טָבַח *ṭāḇaḥ* (יִטְבַּח) to slaughter (animals for food)

רָחַץ *rāḥaṣ* (יִרְחַץ) to wash (tr. and intr.)

נָמֵס *nāmēs* (Niphal verb from root מסס; imperf. יִמַּס) to melt, dissolve

נָכוֹן *nāḵôn* (Niphal verb from root כון; imperf. יִכּוֹן) to be firm, fixed, secure, established

OTHER: יוֹמָם *yômām* (adv.) by day, in the daytime

Exercises:

(a) Translate:

(1) לֹא אִירָא לָנוּם בִּהְיוֹתְךָ אִתִּי.

(2) וַיְהִי בְּגִשְׁתֵּנוּ וַנֵּרֶא אֶת־רָאשֵׁי הֶהָרִים.

(3) וְנִרְאֲתָה עֶרְוָתְךָ וּבָשְׁתָּ.

(4) וְהָיָה בַבֹּקֶר וְלֹא יִוָּתֵר הֶעָנָן בַּשָּׁמָיִם.

(5) יִמַּס לִבָּם לִפְנֵי אֹיְבֵיהֶם.

(6) וַיְהִי בְּצֵאת הַשֶּׁמֶשׁ וַיָּנוּסוּ הַכּוֹכָבִים וְלֹא נִרְאוּ.

(7) תִּנָּחֲמוּ כִּי לֹא לְקַחְתֶּם אֶת־מִנְחָתִי.

(8) בְּטַח אֶל־יהוה בְּכָל־לִבְּךָ.

(9) כְּתֹב אֶת־דְּבָרַי עַל־לוּחַ לִבֶּךָ.

(10) יִכּוֹן מֶלֶךְ חָדָשׁ וְנָבוֹן עַל־הַכִּסֵּא.

(11) וַיְהִי בַּעֲשׂוֹתוֹ אֶת־הַמִּשְׁתֶּה וַיִּטְבַּח טֶבַח גָּדוֹל.

(12) אֱלֹהִים הוּא צוּרֵנוּ וְצִלֵּנוּ.

(13) הֲרָחַצְתָּ אֶת־אָזְנֶיךָ.

(14) וַיִּשְׁכַּב בְּצֵל הָעֵץ וַיִּנָם.

(15) הִנֵּה אֹיְבַי עַל־יְמִינִי וְעַל־שְׂמֹאלִי וַאֲנִי נְסַבּוֹתִי.

(16) וַיִּגְּשׁוּ אֵלָיו הַמַּלְאָכִים וְהוּא יֹשֵׁב פֶּתַח הַבָּיִת.

(17) תִּמָּלֵא הָעִיר דָּם עַל־פִּי דְבַר הַנָּבִיא.

(18) תֵּרָאֶינָה לָכֶם נִפְלָאוֹת.

(19) אֵין מִסְפָּר לַנִּלְחָמִים.

(b) Write in Hebrew:

1. Your hearts will be broken.
2. The city will be surrounded and its inhabitants will be taken captive.
3. On the right are the tombs of their fathers.

4. Seven men were stationed over him lest he escape.
5. There was only a little food left for us.
6. We washed our hands and feet before we sat down to eat.
7. The words of his law are established for ever.
8. When I heard his words, my heart melted within me and I was not able to stand.

(c) Reading: Joseph and his Brothers: the Second Trip to Egypt.

וַיִּקְחוּ הָאֲנָשִׁים אֶת־הַמִּנְחָה הַזֹּאת וּמִשְׁנֶה¹ כֶּסֶף לָקְחוּ בְיָדָם וְאֶת־בִּנְיָמִן וַיָּקֻמוּ וַיֵּרְדוּ מִצְרַיְמָה וַיַּעַמְדוּ לִפְנֵי יוֹסֵף וַיַּרְא יוֹסֵף אִתָּם אֶת־בִּנְיָמִן וַיֹּאמֶר לַאֲשֶׁר² עַל־בֵּיתוֹ הָבֵא³ אֶת־הָאֲנָשִׁים הַבַּיְתָה וּטְבֹחַ⁴ טֶבַח וְהָכֵן⁵ כִּי אִתִּי יֹאכְלוּ הָאֲנָשִׁים בַּצָּהֳרָיִם.

וַיַּעַשׂ הָאִישׁ כַּאֲשֶׁר אָמַר יוֹסֵף וַיִּירְאוּ הָאֲנָשִׁים כִּי הוּבָאוּ⁶ בֵּית יוֹסֵף וַיֹּאמְרוּ: עַל־דְּבַר הַכֶּסֶף הַשָּׁב בְּשַׂקֵּינוּ בַּתְּחִלָּה אֲנַחְנוּ מוּבָאִים⁷ לָקַחַת אֹתָנוּ לַעֲבָדִים וְאֶת־חֲמוֹרֵינוּ, וַיִּגְּשׁוּ אֶל־הָאִישׁ אֲשֶׁר עַל־בֵּית יוֹסֵף וַיֹּאמְרוּ אֵלָיו פֶּתַח הַבָּיִת: יָרֹד יָרַדְנוּ בַּתְּחִלָּה לִקְנוֹת אֹכֶל וַיְהִי כִּי בָאנוּ אֶל־הַמָּלוֹן וַנִּפְתְּחָה אֶת־שַׂקֵּינוּ וְהִנֵּה כֶסֶף אִישׁ בְּפִי שַׂקּוֹ וַנָּשֶׁב⁸ אֹתוֹ בְּיָדֵנוּ, לֹא יָדַעְנוּ מִי שָׂם כַּסְפֵּנוּ בְשַׂקֵּינוּ.

וַיֹּאמֶר הָאִישׁ אֲשֶׁר עַל־בֵּית יוֹסֵף: שָׁלוֹם לָכֶם, אַל־תִּירָאוּ, אֱלֹהֵיכֶם וֵאלֹהֵי אֲבִיכֶם נָתַן לָכֶם אֶת־הַכֶּסֶף הַהוּא, כַּסְפְּכֶם בָּא אֵלָי.

וַיּוֹצֵא⁹ אֲלֵיהֶם אֶת־שִׁמְעוֹן וַיָּבֵא¹⁰ הָאִישׁ אֶת־הָאֲנָשִׁים בֵּיתָה יוֹסֵף וַיִּתֶּן מַיִם וַיִּרְחֲצוּ רַגְלֵיהֶם וַיִּתֶּן אֹכֶל לַחֲמוֹרֵיהֶם וַיֵּשְׁבוּ שָׁם עַד־בּוֹא יוֹסֵף בַּצָּהֳרָיִם כִּי שָׁמְעוּ כִּי שָׁם יֹאכְלוּ לָחֶם.

Notes to the Reading:

1. "the double amount of silver"
2. אֲשֶׁר is used substantively: "the one who".
3. "bring"
4. A rare imperative with ō instead of the normal טְבַח.
5. "and make ready"
6. "they were brought"
7. "have been brought"
8. "and we have brought it back"
9. "and he brought out"
10. "and he brought"

(d) Reading: Psalm 121 (vocalization slightly altered):

(1) אֶשָּׂא עֵינַי אֶל־הֶהָרִים	מֵאַיִן יָבֹא עֶזְרִי:
(2) עֶזְרִי מֵעִם יְהוָה	עֹשֵׂה שָׁמַיִם וָאָרֶץ:
(3) אַל־יִתֵּן לַמּוֹט¹ רַגְלֶךָ	אַל־יָנוּם שֹׁמְרֶךָ:
(4) הִנֵּה לֹא יָנוּם וְלֹא יִישָׁן	שׁוֹמֵר יִשְׂרָאֵל:
(5) יְהוָה שֹׁמְרֶךָ	יְהוָה צִלְּךָ עַל־יַד יְמִינֶךָ:
(6) יוֹמָם הַשֶּׁמֶשׁ לֹא יַכֶּכָּה²	וְיָרֵחַ בַּלָּיְלָה:
(7) יְהוָה יִשְׁמָרְךָ³ מִכָּל־רָע	יִשְׁמֹר אֶת־נַפְשֶׁךָ:

(8) יְהוָה יִשְׁמֹר צֵאתְךָ וּבוֹאֶךָ   מֵעַתָּה וְעַד־עוֹלָם׃

Notes to the Reading:

1. Inf. constr. מוֹט with לְ: to totter; note נָתַן in the sense "to allow".
2. "will not smite (strike, kill) you"
3. – יִשְׁמֹר אֹתְךָ.

LESSON 40

148. Piel Verbs: Meaning.

Piel verbs are regularly distinguished by a doubling of the second root consonant and stem patterns quite distinct from those of the Qal. Because the root of a Piel verb may not always occur as a Qal verb, it is sometimes difficult to define the meaning of a Piel form by direct comparison. Following is listed a representative collection of Piel verbs classified in regard to the meaning that may be assigned to the Piel as a derived type, i.e. secondary to some other form in the language.

  a. *Factitive (transitivizing).* Perhaps the most consistent use of the Piel formation is to construct a verb with transitive active meaning from a root which appears in the Qal as an intransitive or stative verb. Such Piel verbs usually have a factitive meaning:

QAL (to be sound) → PIEL (to make sound)
QAL (to be great) → PIEL (to magnify)

Such a transformation of meaning may also be designated as causative, but we shall restrict this latter term to roots whose Qal verbs are transitive:

QAL (to learn) → PIEL (to teach, i.e. to cause to learn)

Examples:

	QAL			PIEL	
אָבַד	to perish		אִבַּד	*'ibbad*	to destroy
קַל	to be light, trivial		קִלֵּל	*qillēl*	to curse (make light of, treat as unimportant)
קָדֵשׁ	to be holy		קִדַּשׁ	*qiddaš*	to sanctify
שָׁלֵם	to be sound		שִׁלַּם	*šillam*	to make sound, whole; to recompense, reward
חָיָה	to live, be alive		חִיָּה	*ḥiyyāh*	to cause to live, let live
טָמֵא	to be unclean		טִמֵּא	*ṭimmē'*	to pollute
כָּלָה	to be at an end		כִּלָּה	*killāh*	to finish, complete, bring to an end
לָמַד	to learn		לִמַּד	*limmad*	to teach

In some instances the Qal verb is either transitive or intransitive, while the Piel verb is specifically transitive:

מָלֵא	to be full, fill		מִלֵּא	*millē'*	to fill
בָּעַר	to burn (tr. or intr.)		בִּעֵר	*bi'ēr*	to burn (tr.)

b. *Denominative.* When the Piel verb is closer in meaning to some noun or adjective than to the Qal verb (which in most of these cases does not exist), we may say that the Piel has a denominative function:

דָּבָר	word		דִּבֶּר	*dibber*	to speak
סֵפֶר	book, record		סִפֵּר	*sippēr*	to recount, narrate, tell a story
בְּרָכָה	blessing		בֵּרַךְ	*bēraḵ*	to bless
מִצְוָה	command		צִוָּה	*ṣiwwāh*	to command
זְמָרָה	music, song		זִמֵּר	*zimmēr*	to sing, make music
שָׁלוֹשׁ	three		שִׁלֵּשׁ	*šillēš*	to divide something into three parts; to do something for a third time
קִנְאָה	jealousy		קִנֵּא	*qinnē'*	to be jealous

c. *Intensive.* In several instances the Piel denotes a pluralization of the action named in the Qal. This may take on the nuance of an intensive, but the intensive force is difficult to discern in most occurrences. Many of the so-called intensive Piels seem more to be stylistic variants of the Qal verb (most likely denominative in origin) used in poetry, probably for variation rather than intensification.

d. *Unclassified.* In addition to the three preceding categories there are many Piel verbs whose origin is not clear. Some of these verbs could doubtlessly be placed in the above classifications if we had more data on the related Qal or nominal forms.

[194]

פֻּזַּר *pizzar* to scatter   בִּקֵּשׁ *biqqēš* to seek
גֵּרֵשׁ *gērēš* to drive away   מִהַר *mihar* to hurry, hasten

Awareness of the factitive-denominative-intensive function of the Piel, together with familiarity with a given root, will certainly assist the learner in mastering these new verbs, but because he will not be able to predict unerringly the meaning of a new Piel verb, they will all be listed in the vocabularies of the following lessons.

149. Piel Verbs: Stems and Inflection.

ROOT TYPE	PERFECT		IMPERFECT		IMPERATIVE	
Regular	גִּדֵּל	*giddēl*	יְגַדֵּל	*yəgaddēl*	גַּדֵּל	*gaddēl*
III-gutt.	שִׁלַּח	*šillaḥ*	יְשַׁלַּח	*yəšallaḥ*	שַׁלַּח	*šallaḥ*
II-gutt.	בֵּעֵר	*biʿēr*	יְבַעֵר	*yəbaʿēr*	בַּעֵר	*baʿēr*
	מֵאֵן	*mēʾēn*	יְמָאֵן	*yəmāʾēn*	מָאֵן	*māʾēn*

INF. CONSTRUCT		PARTICIPLE	
גַּדֵּל	*gaddēl*	מְגַדֵּל	*məgaddēl*
שַׁלַּח	*šallaḥ*	מְשַׁלֵּחַ	*məšallēªḥ*
בַּעֵר	*baʿēr*	מְבַעֵר	*məbaʿēr*
מָאֵן	*māʾēn*	מְמָאֵן	*məmāʾēn*

Remarks:

1. There are essentially only two stems, the perfect and the imperfect. As elsewhere, the imperative and inf. construct are predictable from the imperfect. The participle also resembles the imperfect, but with the prefix מְ *mə-*.

2. Piel verbs from roots III-gutt. deviate only in having *a* as the second stem vowel throughout, except in the participle.

3. Even in non-guttural verbs the stem vowel *a* instead of *ē* is found in the perfect; thus *giddēl* or *giddal*. The choice would appear to be optional. There are a few verbs, notably דִּבֶּר *dibber* (to speak) and כִּפֶּר *kipper* (to atone for), which have *e* instead of *ē* or *a* in the 3rd masc. sing. of the perfect.

4. Piel verbs from roots II-gutt. (including ר) fall into two classes:

(a) those with virtual doubling of the guttural in question (see בֵּעֵר above); the vocalization is the same as that of the regular verb; (b) those with compensatory lengthening of the vowel before the guttural (*i → ē, a → ā*; see מֵאֵן above). Before ר compensatory lengthening is the rule. The other gutturals may be treated in either way, as will be indicated in the vocabularies.

PERFECT:

גִּדֵּל	*giddēl*	שִׁלַּח	*šillaḥ*	בֵּעֵר	*biʿēr*	מֵאֵן	*mēʾēn*
גִּדְּלָה	*giddəlāh*	שִׁלְּחָה	*šilləḥāh*	בֵּעֲרָה	*biʿărāh*	מֵאֲנָה	*mēʾănāh*

[195]

גִּדַּלְתָּ *giddáltā*	שִׁלַּחְתָּ *šilláhtā*	בֵּעַרְתָּ *biʿárta*	מֵאַנְתָּ *mēʾántā*
גִּדַּלְתְּ *giddált*	שִׁלַּחְתְּ *šilláht*	בֵּעַרְתְּ *biʿárt*	מֵאַנְתְּ *mēʾánt*
גִּדַּלְתִּי *giddáltî*	שִׁלַּחְתִּי *šilláhtî*	בֵּעַרְתִּי *biʿártî*	מֵאַנְתִּי *mēʾántî*
גִּדְּלוּ *giddəlû*	שִׁלְּחוּ *šilləhû*	בֵּעֲרוּ *biʿărû*	מֵאֲנוּ *mēʾănû*
גִּדַּלְתֶּם *giddaltém*	שִׁלַּחְתֶּם *šillahtém*	בֵּעַרְתֶּם *biʿartém*	מֵאַנְתֶּם *mēʾantém*
גִּדַּלְתֶּן *giddaltén*	שִׁלַּחְתֶּן *šillahtén*	בֵּעַרְתֶּן *biʿartén*	מֵאַנְתֶּן *mēʾantén*
גִּדַּלְנוּ *giddálnû*	שִׁלַּחְנוּ *šilláhnû*	בֵּעַרְנוּ *biʿárnû*	מֵאַנּוּ *mēʾánnû*

IMPERFECT:

יְגַדֵּל *yəgaddēl*	יְשַׁלַּח *yəšallah*	יְבַעֵר *yəbaʿēr*	יְמָאֵן *yəmāʾēn*
תְּגַדֵּל *təgaddēl*	תְּשַׁלַּח *təšallah*	תְּבַעֵר *təbaʿēr*	תְּמָאֵן *təmāʾēn*
תְּגַדֵּל *təgaddēl*	תְּשַׁלַּח *təšallah*	תְּבַעֵר *təbaʿēr*	תְּמָאֵן *təmāʾēn*
תְּגַדְּלִי *təgaddəlî*	תְּשַׁלְּחִי *təšalləhî*	תְּבַעֲרִי *təbaʿărî*	תְּמָאֲנִי *təmāʾănî*
אֲגַדֵּל *ʾăgaddēl*	אֲשַׁלַּח *ʾăšallah*	אֲבַעֵר *ʾăbaʿēr*	אֲמָאֵן *ʾămāʾēn*
יְגַדְּלוּ *yəgaddəlû*	יְשַׁלְּחוּ *yəšalləhû*	יְבַעֲרוּ *yəbaʿărû*	יְמָאֲנוּ *yəmāʾănû*
תְּגַדֵּלְנָה *təgaddélnāh*	תְּשַׁלַּחְנָה *təšalláhnāh*	תְּבַעֵרְנָה *təbaʿérnāh*	תְּמָאֵנָּה *təmāʾénnāh*
תְּגַדְּלוּ *təgaddəlû*	תְּשַׁלְּחוּ *təšalləhû*	תְּבַעֲרוּ *təbaʿărû*	תְּמָאֲנוּ *təmāʾănû*
תְּגַדֵּלְנָה *təgaddélnāh*	תְּשַׁלַּחְנָה *təšalláhnāh*	תְּבַעֵרְנָה *təbaʿérnāh*	תְּמָאֵנָּה *təmāʾénnāh*
נְגַדֵּל *nəgaddēl*	נְשַׁלַּח *nəšallah*	נְבַעֵר *nəbaʿēr*	נְמָאֵן *nəmāʾēn*

IMPERATIVE:

גַּדֵּל *gaddēl*	שַׁלַּח *šallah*	בַּעֵר *baʿēr*	מָאֵן *māʾēn*
גַּדְּלִי *gaddəlî*	שַׁלְּחִי *šalləhî*	בַּעֲרִי *baʿărî*	מָאֲנִי *māʾănî*
גַּדְּלוּ *gaddəlû*	שַׁלְּחוּ *šalləhû*	בַּעֲרוּ *baʿărû*	מָאֲנוּ *māʾănû*
גַּדֵּלְנָה *gaddélnāh*	שַׁלַּחְנָה *šalláhnāh*	בַּעֵרְנָה *baʿérnāh*	מָאֵנָּה *māʾénnāh*

INFINITIVE CONSTRUCT:

גַּדֵּל *gaddēl*	שַׁלַּח *šallah*	בַּעֵר *baʿēr*	מָאֵן *māʾēn*
גַּדְּלִי *gaddəlî*	שַׁלְּחִי *šalləhî*	בַּעֲרִי *baʿărî*	מָאֲנִי *māʾănî*
גַּדֶּלְךָ *gaddelkā*	שַׁלַּחֲךָ *šallahăkā*	בַּעֶרְךָ *baʿerkā*	מָאֶנְךָ *māʾenkā*
גַּדֶּלֵךְ *gaddəlēk* etc.	שַׁלְּחֵךְ *šalləhēk* etc.	בַּעֲרֵךְ *baʿărēk* etc.	מָאֲנֵךְ *māʾănēk*

INFINITIVE ABSOLUTE:

גַּדּוֹל *gaddôl*	שַׁלּוֹחַ *šallôᵃh*	בַּעוֹר *baʿôr*	מָאוֹן *māʾôn*

PARTICIPLE:

מְגַדֵּל *məgaddēl*	מְשַׁלֵּחַ *məšallēᵃh*	מְבַעֵר *məbaʿēr*	מְמָאֵן *məmāʾēn*
מְגַדְּלָה *məgaddəlāh*	מְשַׁלְּחָה *məšalləhāh*	מְבַעֲרָה *məbaʿărāh*	מְמָאֲנָה *məmāʾănāh*
מְגַדְּלִים *məgaddəlîm*	מְשַׁלְּחִים *məšalləhîm*	מְבַעֲרִים *məbaʿărîm*	מְמָאֲנִים *məmāʾănîm*
מְגַדְּלוֹת *məgaddəlôt*	מְשַׁלְּחוֹת *məšalləhôt*	מְבַעֲרוֹת *məbaʿărôt*	מְמָאֲנוֹת *məmāʾănôt*

Remarks:

(1) After a *waw*-conversive the prefix *yə-* of the imperfect loses its vowel and the *y* is not doubled:

וַיְמָאֵן *way-mā-'ēn* (not: *way-yə-mā-'ēn*) and he refused

(2) The characteristic doubling of the middle radical is given up sometimes when it is followed by the vowel *ə*:

בִּקֵּשׁ *biqqēš* he sought but בִּקְשׁוּ *biqšû* they sought

יְבַקֵּשׁ *yəbaqqēš* he will seek but יְבַקְשׁוּ *yəbaqšû* they will seek

This loss of doubling never occurs with the consonants ב ג ד כ פ ת. Otherwise no clear rule can be formulated.

(3) The forms listed above and in the next lesson for the infinitive absolute are rather rare. More frequently the Piel infinitive construct is used as the infinitive absolute.

150. Vocabulary 40.

VERBS:

קִדֵּשׁ	*qiddēš*		to sanctify (cf. קָדוֹשׁ)
בָּעַר	*bā'ar*	(יִבְעַר)	to burn (tr. or intr.)
בִּעֵר	*bi'ēr*	(יְבַעֵר)	to burn (tr.), consume, remove completely
דִּבֶּר	*dibber*	(יְדַבֵּר)	to speak, talk (cf. דָּבָר)
בֵּרֵךְ	*bērēk*	(יְבָרֵךְ)	to bless (cf. בְּרָכָה) [Note וַיְבָרֶךְ]
בִּקֵּשׁ	*biqqēš*	(יְבַקֵּשׁ)	to seek
שִׁלַּח	*šillaḥ*	(יְשַׁלַּח)	to expel, send forth, let go
גֵּרֵשׁ	*gērēš*	(יְגָרֵשׁ)	to drive away [Note וַיְגָרֶשׁ]
נִאֵץ	*ni'ēṣ*	(יְנַאֵץ)	to spurn
מֵאֵן	*mē'ēn*	(יְמָאֵן)	to refuse
שֵׁרֵת	*šērēt*	(יְשָׁרֵת)	to serve, administer [Note וַיְשָׁרֶת]
OTHER:	אוֹ	*'ô*	(conj.)	or

Note the idiom: כְּ ... כְּ. Translation may vary with the context, but the implication is that the two items involved are in some way equal. E.g.

כָּמוֹךָ כְּפַרְעֹה You are the equal of the Pharaoh.
כָּמוֹךָ כָּמוֹנִי You and I are equal, are in the same predicament.

Exercises:

(a) Translate:

(1) וַיְגָרֶשׁ אֶת־הָאֲנָשִׁים פַּעֲמַיִם וְלֹא שָׁבוּ.
(2) נָאַצְתָּ אֶת־בְּרִיתִי וְאֶת־תּוֹרוֹתַי מֵאַנְתָּ לִשְׁמֹר.
(3) וַיְשָׁרֶת הַיֶּלֶד בְּהֵיכַל יהוה.
(4) וַיְבָרֶךְ אֹתוֹ כִּי הוּא מָצָא חֵן בְּעֵינָיו.

(5) יְבַקְשׁוּ אֶת־הָאֲשֵׁמִים וְשִׁלְּחוּ אֹתָם מִן־הָעִיר.

(6) אֲנִי לְבַדִּי אוּכַל לְבָרֵךְ אֹתְךָ.

(7) תִּשְׁמֹר אֶת־דְּבָרַי בְּלִבֶּךָ.

(8) מֵאֲנוּ לֶאֱכֹל אֶת־הַבְּהֵמוֹת הַטְּבוּחוֹת.

(9) אֶת־מִי אַתְּ תְּבַקְשִׁי.

(10) וַיְדַבְּרוּ אֵלָיו כַּדְּבָרִים הָאֵלֶּה.

(11) קוֹל שִׂמְחָה יִשָּׁמַע בָּאָרֶץ.

(12) וַיְקַדֵּשׁ אֶת־הָאֲנָשִׁים לִפְנֵי בוֹאָם בֵּית יהוה.

(13) מֵאֲנוּ לִרְדֹּף אַחֲרֵיהֶם.

(14) וַיְדַבֵּר אֵלַי עַל־הַמָּלוֹן אֲשֶׁר לָן בּוֹ הַלַּיְלָה.

(15) לֹא תֹאכַל אֶת־הַבָּשָׂר אֲשֶׁר בּוֹ נֶפֶשׁ חַיָּה.

(16) מֵאֲנָה לִרְחֹץ אֶת־הַבְּגָדִים.

(17) וַיְהִי כְּנוּמוֹ וַיְבַקְשׁוּ אֹתוֹ וַיַּהַרְגוּ אֹתוֹ.

(18) בַּיּוֹם הַהוּא יִמַּסּוּ הֶהָרִים וְהָיוּ כְמַיִם.

(19) תְּקַדֵּשׁ אֶת־הַנִּשְׁאָרִים כִּי נֶאֱמָנִים הֵם בְּעֵינַי.

(b) Give the Hebrew for the following orally:

1. Drive them away.
2. Do not spurn his words.
3. Why do you refuse to speak?
4. Are you looking for me?
5. Bless me.
6. I have sanctified you.
7. He did not want to serve.
8. They expelled us.
9. Let us bless them.
10. We sought them.

(c) Write in Hebrew:

1. They took the vessels with which they served and gave them to the priest.
2. The Pharaoh became angry and expelled them from his presence (lit. from before him).
3. He refused to sanctify them, for he knew that they were not honest men.
4. He sought his brothers there, for he did not know that they had travelled eastward.
5. You shall completely-remove the evil from your midst.
6. We drove the guilty men out of the congregation.
7. We could not refuse to spend the night there.

(d) Reading: Joseph and his Brothers: the Final Test.

After meeting with Joseph and obtaining the release of Simon through Benjamin's presence with them, the sons of Jacob set out again for Canaan with the provisions they had obtained in Egypt. Joseph had had a silver goblet planted in Benjamin's sack, and as soon as the brothers had begun the return journey, he sent his men after them to examine their baggage, find the goblet and accuse them of theft and treachery. Joseph then expressed his willingness to allow all the brothers except Benjamin to return home, but Judah stands up to this final test and delivers the following plea: (Gen. 44:18–26, vocalization slightly altered).

(18) וַיִּגַּשׁ אֵלָיו יְהוּדָה וַיֹּאמֶר בִּי‏[1] אֲדֹנִי, יְדַבֶּר־נָא עַבְדְּךָ דָבָר בְּאָזְנֵי אֲדֹנִי, וְאַל־יִחַר אַפְּךָ בְּעַבְדֶּךָ כִּי כָמוֹךָ כְּפַרְעֹה.

(19) אֲדֹנִי שָׁאַל אֶת־עֲבָדָיו לֵאמֹר הֲיֵשׁ לָכֶם אָב אוֹ אָח.

(20) וַנֹּאמֶר אֶל־אֲדֹנִי יֶשׁ־לָנוּ אָב זָקֵן וְיֶלֶד זְקֻנִים קָטָן וְאָחִיו מֵת וַיִּוָּתֵר הוּא לְבַדּוֹ לְאִמּוֹ וְאָבִיו אֲהֵבוֹ‏[2].

(21) וַתֹּאמֶר אֶל־עֲבָדֶיךָ הוֹרִידֻהוּ‏[3] אֵלַי וְאָשִׂימָה עֵינִי עָלָיו.

(22) וַנֹּאמֶר אֶל־אֲדֹנִי לֹא יוּכַל הַנַּעַר לַעֲזֹב אֶת־אָבִיו וְעָזַב‏[4] אֶת־אָבִיו וָמֵת.

(23) וַתֹּאמֶר אֶל־עֲבָדֶיךָ אִם לֹא יֵרֵד אֲחִיכֶם הַקָּטֹן אִתְּכֶם לֹא תֹסִפוּן‏[5] לִרְאוֹת פָּנָי.

(24) וַיְהִי כִּי עָלִינוּ אֶל־עַבְדְּךָ אָבִי וַנַּגֶּד‏[6] לוֹ אֵת־דִּבְרֵי אֲדֹנִי.

(25) וַיֹּאמֶר אָבִינוּ שֻׁבוּ שִׁבְרוּ‏[7] לָנוּ מְעַט־אֹכֶל.

(26) וַנֹּאמֶר לֹא נוּכַל לָרֶדֶת, אִם יֵשׁ אָחִינוּ הַקָּטֹן אִתָּנוּ וְיָרַדְנוּ‏[8] כִּי לֹא נוּכַל לִרְאוֹת פְּנֵי הָאִישׁ וְאָחִינוּ הַקָּטֹן אֵינֶנּוּ אִתָּנוּ.

Notes to the Reading:

1. A rare particle of entreaty: "Please, I beg you".
2. = אָהַב אֹתוֹ
3. "bring him down"
4. וְעָזַב ...וָמֵת a conditional sequence: "if he abandon... he would die".
5. "you will not (see) again"
6. "we told him"
7. "obtain (as rations or provisions)"
8. Note the apodosis after the אִם clause.

LESSON 41

151. Piel Verbs: Stems and Inflection (concluded).

ROOT TYPE	PERFECT		IMPERFECT		IMPERATIVE	
III-*Aleph*	מִלֵּא	*millē'*	יְמַלֵּא	*yəmallē'*	מַלֵּא	*mallē'*
III-*Hē*	עִנָּה	*'innāh*	יְעַנֶּה	*yə'anneh*	עַנֵּה	*'annēh*
Geminate	הִלֵּל	*hillēl*	יְהַלֵּל	*yəhallēl*	הַלֵּל	*hallēl*

	INF. CONSTRUCT		PARTICIPLE	
	מַלֵּא	*mallē'*	מְמַלֵּא	*məmallē'*
	עַנּוֹת	*'annôṯ*	מְעַנֶּה	*mə'anneh*
	הַלֵּל	*hallēl*	מְהַלֵּל	*məhallēl*

Remarks: So far as the stems are concerned, only verbs from roots III-*Hē* require special attention. The forms of these verbs conform to the patterns encountered in the Niphal and Qal: the perfect ends in -*āh*, the imperfect in -*eh*, the imperative in -*ēh*, and the infinitive construct in -*ôṯ*. In the inflection of these forms the only unpredictable feature is the prevalence of -*î*- over -*ê*- in the perfect, but -*ê*- is found in the first person singular as well: thus both עִנֵּיתִי and עִנִּיתִי

PERFECT:	מִלֵּא/מִלָּא	*millē'/millā'*	עִנָּה	*'innāh*	הִלֵּל	*hillēl*
	מִלְאָה	*millə'āh*	עִנְּתָה	*'innətāh*	הִלְלָה	*hiləlāh*
	מִלֵּאתָ	*millé(')ṯā*	עִנִּיתָ	*'innîṯā*	הִלַּלְתָּ	*hillálṯā*
	מִלֵּאת	*millé(')ṯ*	עִנִּית	*'innîṯ*	הִלַּלְתְּ	*hillált*
	מִלֵּאתִי	*millé(')ṯî*	עִנִּיתִי/עִנֵּיתִי	*'innîṯî/'innêṯî*	הִלַּלְתִּי	*hilláltî*
	מִלְאוּ	*millə'û*	עִנּוּ	*'innû*	הִלְלוּ	*hiləlû*

	מִלֵּאתֶם	millē(')tem	עִנִּיתֶם	'innîtem	הִלַּלְתֶּם	hillaltém
	מִלֵּאתֶן	millē(')ten	עִנִּיתֶן	'innîten	הִלַּלְתֶּן	hillaltén
	מִלֵּאנוּ	millē(')nû	עִנִּינוּ	'innînû	הִלַּלְנוּ	hillálnû
IMPERFECT:	יְמַלֵּא	yəmallē'	יְעַנֶּה	yə'anneh	יְהַלֵּל	yəhallēl
	תְּמַלֵּא	təmallē'	תְּעַנֶּה	tə'anneh	תְּהַלֵּל	təhallēl
	תְּמַלֵּא	təmallē'	תְּעַנֶּה	tə'anneh	תְּהַלֵּל	təhallēl
	תְּמַלְאִי	təmallə'î	תְּעַנִּי	tə'annî	תְּהַלְלִי	təhaləlî
	אֲמַלֵּא	'ămallē'	אֲעַנֶּה	'ă'anneh	אֲהַלֵּל	'ăhallēl
	יְמַלְאוּ	yəmallə'û	יְעַנּוּ	yə'annû	יְהַלְלוּ	yəhaləlû
	תְּמַלֶּאנָה	təmallé(')nāh	תְּעַנֶּינָה	tə'annênāh	תְּהַלֵּלְנָה	təhallélnah
	תְּמַלְאוּ	təmallə'û	תְּעַנּוּ	tə'annú	תְּהַלְלוּ	təhaləlû
	תְּמַלֶּאנָה	təmallé(')nāh	תְּעַנֶּינָה	tə'annênāh	תְּהַלֵּלְנָה	təhallélnāh
	נְמַלֵּא	nəmallē'	נְעַנֶּה	nə'anneh	נְהַלֵּל	nəhallēl
IMPERATIVE:	מַלֵּא	mallē'	עַנֵּה	'annēh	הַלֵּל	hallēl
	מַלְאִי	mallə'î	עַנִּי	'annî	הַלְלִי	haləlî
	מַלְאוּ	mallə'û	עַנּוּ	'annû	הַלְלוּ	haləlû
	מַלֶּאנָה	mallé(')nāh	עַנֶּינָה	'annênāh	הַלֵּלְנָה	hallélnāh
INF. CONSTR.:	מַלֵּא	mallē'	עַנּוֹת	'annôt	הַלֵּל	hallēl
	מַלְאִי	mallə'î etc.	עַנּוֹתִי	'annôtî etc.	הַלְלִי	halləlî etc.
INF. ABS.:	מַלֹּא	mallō'	עַנֹּה 〉 עַנֵּה 〉	'annōh 〉 'annēh 〉	הַלֹּל	hallōl
PARTICIPLE:	מְמַלֵּא	məmallē'	מְעַנֶּה	mə'anneh	מְהַלֵּל	məhallel
	מְמַלְּאָה	məmallə'āh	מְעַנָּה	mə'annāh	מְהַלְלָה	məhalləlāh
	מְמַלֵּאת	məmallē(')t			מְהַלֶּלֶת	məhallélet
	מְמַלְּאִים	məmallə'îm	מְעַנִּים	mə'annîm	מְהַלְלִים	məhalləlîm
	מְמַלְּאוֹת	məmallə'ôt	מְעַנּוֹת	mə'annôt	מְהַלְלוֹת	məhalləlôt

Piel verbs from roots I-*Yodh*, I-*Nun*, I-guttural are in no way irregular.
Piel verbs from Hollow roots are very rare.

152. Pausal Forms.

The text of the Hebrew Bible is divided into short groups of clauses known as verses. Each verse is usually subdivided into two parts, often of unequal length, the first of which is closed by the accent sign known as *'aṭnaḥ* (⌄) and the second by a sign similar to metheg called *sillûq* (ֽ), followed by *sôp̄ pāsûq* (:), marking the end of the verse. Each half of the verse is then subdivided into as many parts as the syntax demands, with each accentual unit receiving an accent mark. The accents fall into two main groups, conjunctive and disjunctive, the former being used when a word is closely bound syntactically with the following word and the latter elsewhere. The use of the various accents is very complex and will not be taken up in this book.

In the text of the reading selections we shall employ only *sillûq* (+ *sôp̄ pāsûq*). Clause divisions that are likely to cause difficulty will be marked by commas, but it should be noted that the comma does not appear in the original text.

Words standing at the end of the major verse divisions, and thus especially with *'aṭnaḥ* and *sillûq*, are said to be in pause because of the break in the recitation of the text at these points. Such words may have a vocalization slightly different from that of the normal context form. The following changes are the most frequent:

(a) $a \rightarrow \bar{a}$: כָּתָב (he wrote) for כָּתַב

(b) $e \rightarrow \bar{a}$ in some segholate nouns: קָבֶר (grave) for קֶבֶר

(c) If a word ends in the sequence -*əCv̆* the accent is usually retracted and the *ə* is replaced by the full vowel it corresponds to elsewhere in the paradigm:

$$כָּתְבָה \quad \rightarrow \quad כָּתְֿבָה \quad \text{she wrote}$$
$$כָּבְדָה \quad \rightarrow \quad כָּבֵֿדָה \quad \text{it (f.) was heavy}$$

The *ə* of the second person masc. sing. suffix -*əkā* is regularly replaced by *e*:

$$מַלְכְּךָ \quad \rightarrow \quad מַלְכֶּֿךָ \quad \text{your king}$$
$$סוּסְךָ \quad \rightarrow \quad סוּסֶֿךָ \quad \text{your horse}$$
$$שֹׁמְרְךָ \quad \rightarrow \quad שֹׁמֶרְךָ \quad \text{your keeper (note the change in the word structure)}$$

But the pausal forms of לְךָ and בְּךָ are לָךְ and בָּךְ, both of which are the same as the corresponding feminine form. Other prepositions have a similar change.

Because of printing difficulties, the pausal accents within a verse do not appear in the biblical texts accompanying the following lessons. Pausal forms, however, have been retained. The reader should be on the alert for their occurrence.

153. Vocabulary 41.

VERBS: צִוָּה *ṣiwwāh* (יְצַוֶּה juss. יְצַו) to command; charge; appoint. Examples:

וַיְצַו שֹׁפְטִים עֲלֵיהֶם   and he appointed judges over them

וַיְצַו אֶת־הָאֲנָשִׁים לָלֶכֶת   and he commanded the men to go

וַיְצַו אֹתָם לֵאמֹר...   and he commanded them, saying...

וַיְצַו אֹתָם בְּיַד מַלְאָכוֹ   and he handed them over to the charge of his messenger

הִלֵּל   *hillēl* (יְהַלֵּל) to praise. Note הַלְלוּיָהּ Halelujah. Praise Yah(weh).

כִּסָּה   *kissāh* (יְכַסֶּה juss. יְכַס) to cover, overwhelm

עִנָּה   *'innāh* (יְעַנֶּה juss. יְעַן) to oppress (cf. עָנִי)

סִפֵּר   *sippēr* (יְסַפֵּר) to tell, narrate (cf. סֵפֶר)

קִלֵּל   *qillēl* (יְקַלֵּל) to curse

עָרַב 'āraḇ (יַעֲרֹב) to stand as pledge for

קָשַׁר qāšar (יִקְשֹׁר) to bind ('eṯ + something + 'al [to] + something);
to band together, conspire ('al: against)

NOUNS: שֵׂיבָה śêḇāh   grey hair, old age

שְׁאֹל šə'ōl   Sheol, Hell, the residence of the dead

OTHER: אַךְ 'aḵ (adv.) surely, doubtlessly; but, however, only

עַד־הֵנָּה 'ad-hénnāh (adv.) until now

Exercises:

(a) Translate

(1) וַיְצַו אֹתָם לָתֵת מְעַט אֹכֶל לְטַפָּם.

(2) לָכְדוּ אֶת־רְכוּשׁ הַכְּנַעֲנִי וַיְבַעֲרוּ אֹתוֹ.

(3) שָׁמְעָה הָאָמָה קוֹל וַתִּפֹּל אַרְצָה וַתְּכַס אֶת־פָּנֶיהָ בְּיָדֶיהָ.

(4) וַיְצַו אֶת־הַנִּצָּבִים וַיִּגְּשׁוּ אֵלָיו.

(5) לֹא מֵאֵן לַעֲרֹב אֶת־הַיֶּלֶד וְלֹא מֵאֵן לִגְאֹל אֹתוֹ.

(6) שָׁלַח אֹתָם מֵאַרְצוֹ כִּי קָשְׁרוּ עָלָיו לַהֲרֹג אֹתוֹ וְלִבְחֹר אִישׁ אַחֵר לְרֹאשׁ הָעָם.

(7) וַיִּזְבַּח הַמֶּלֶךְ הָרָשָׁע אֶת־בִּתּוֹ הַקְּטַנָּה עַל־הַמִּזְבֵּחַ.

(8) וַיְסַפְּרוּ לוֹ אֶת־הַקֹּרוֹת אֹתָם בַּדֶּרֶךְ.

(9) עַד־הֵנָּה לֹא רָאִיתִי אֶת־יְשׁוּעַת עַמִּי.

(10) לָמָה תַּחְפֹּץ לְעַנּוֹת אֹתִי.

(11) אֲהַלְלָה אֹתְךָ מֵעַתָּה וְעַד־עוֹלָם.

(12) וַיְכַס אֶת־פָּנָיו בְּיָדָיו וַיֵּבְךְּ.

(13) אַל־תְּקַלְלוּ אֶת־הַנֹּתְנִים לָכֶם עֵזֶר.

(14) וָאֶבְרַח כִּי בִּקְשׁוּ אֹתִי לַהֲרֹג אֹתִי.

(15) זְכֹר נָא אֶת־הַבֹּטְחִים בְּךָ וְאַל־תְּנַאֵץ אֶת־דִּבְרֵיהֶם.

(16) וַיְצַו אֶת־בְּנוֹ בְּיַד הַנּוֹתָרִים כִּי הָיָה לָמוּת.

(b) Write in Hebrew:

1. He tied his donkey to a tree, lay down under the tree, and slept.
2. Let us curse them and the place from which they came.
3. I will stand as surety for you and your sons.
4. He will praise the Lord all the days of his life until he goes down to Sheol with grey hair.
5. It is not good to oppress the poor and not to give them food.
6. Darkness shall cover the earth on that day.
7. He drove us away from the well and we were not able to find water in an(y) other place.

(c) Reading: Judah's Plea to Joseph (concluded) Gen. 44:27–34.

(27) וַיֹּאמֶר עַבְדְּךָ אָבִי אֵלֵינוּ אַתֶּם יְדַעְתֶּם כִּי שְׁנַיִם יָלְדָה־לִּי אִשְׁתִּי:

(28) וַיֵּצֵא הָאֶחָד מֵאִתִּי וָאֹמַר אַךְ טָרֹף טֹרָף¹ וְלֹא רְאִיתִיו² עַד־הֵנָּה:

(29) וּלְקַחְתֶּם גַּם־אֶת־זֶה מֵעִם פָּנַי וְקָרָהוּ³ אָסוֹן⁴ וְהוֹרַדְתֶּם⁵ אֶת־שֵׂיבָתִי בְּרָעָה שְׁאֹלָה:

(30) וְעַתָּה כְּבֹאִי אֶל־עַבְדְּךָ אָבִי וְהַנַּעַר אֵינֶנּוּ אִתָּנוּ וְנַפְשׁוֹ קְשׁוּרָה בְנַפְשׁוֹ:

(31) וְהָיָה כִּרְאוֹתוֹ כִּי־אֵין הַנַּעַר וָמֵת וְהוֹרִידוּ עֲבָדֶיךָ אֶת־שֵׂיבַת עַבְדְּךָ אָבִינוּ בְּיָגוֹן שְׁאֹלָה:

(32) כִּי עַבְדְּךָ עָרַב אֶת־הַנַּעַר מֵעִם אָבִי לֵאמֹר אִם־לֹא אֲבִיאֶנּוּ אֵלֶיךָ וְחָטָאתִי לְאָבִי כָּל־הַיָּמִים:

(33) וְעַתָּה יֵשֶׁב־נָא עַבְדְּךָ תַּחַת הַנַּעַר עֶבֶד לַאדֹנִי וְהַנַּעַר יַעַל עִם־אֶחָיו:

(34) כִּי־אֵיךְ אֶעֱלֶה אֶל־אָבִי וְהַנַּעַר אֵינֶנּוּ אִתִּי פֶּן אֶרְאֶה בָרָע אֲשֶׁר יִמְצָא אֶת־אָבִי:

Notes to the Reading:

1. "he has surely been torn to pieces (by some wild animal)"
2. רְאִיתִי אֹתוֹ =
3. קָרָה אֹתוֹ =
4. "an accident"
5. "you will send down"
6. "and (we) will have sent down"
7. "sorrow"
8. "I shall bring him"
9. cf. note 8 p.199
10. פֶּן here = "except that"

Joseph, unable to continue his deception, revealed himself to his brothers, whom he forgave of their past crime against him. He caused Jacob and his entire family to be brought down to Egypt and settled them in the rich pasture land of the Nile Delta. Jacob died and was taken back to Canaan for burial in accordance with his wishes; Joseph was embalmed upon his death and his body placed in a sarcophagus for eventual burial in Canaan. After the death of Joseph there is a break in the traditional history until the story of Moses and a pharaoh "who knew not Joseph".

LESSON 42

154. The Pual.

Corresponding to every Piel verb there is a passive counterpart known as the Pual, characterized, like the Piel, by a doubling of the middle root consonant. The pattern of vowels is more or less consistent throughout, with *u* in the first stem syllable and *a* (when not reduced) in the second.

Piel	Pual		
גִּדֵּל	גֻּדַּל	*guddal*	he was magnified
בִּקֵּשׁ	בֻּקַּשׁ	*buqqaš*	he was sought
הִלֵּל	הֻלַּל	*hullal*	he was praised

Pual forms are relatively infrequent, being most often encountered in the participle, which functions as a passive to that of the Piel:

מְבֹרָךְ	*məḇōrāḵ*	being (having been) blessed
מְבֻקָּשׁ	*məḇuqqāš*	being (having been) sought

Attested stem forms are as follows:

Root Type	Perfect		Imperfect		Imperative	Inf. Construct		Participle	
Regular	גֻּדַּל	*guddal*	יְגֻדַּל	*yəguddal*	—	—		מְגֻדָּל	*məguddāl*
I-guttural	בֹּרַךְ	*bōrak*	יְבֹרַךְ	*yəḇōrak*	—	—		מְבֹרָךְ	*məḇōrāḵ*
II-*Aleph*	מֻלָּא	*mullā'*	יְמֻלָּא	*yəmullā'*	—	—		מְמֻלָּא	*məmullā'*
II-*Hē*	עֻנָּה	*'unnāh*	יְעֻנֶּה	*yə'unneh*	—	עֻנּוֹת	*'unnôṯ*	מְעֻנֶּה	*mə'unneh*

[205]

Remarks: With roots II-guttural virtual doubling is also attested, as in נֻחַם *nuḥam* (he was comforted) corresponding to the Piel verb נִחַם *niḥam* (to comfort); the more common form בֹּרַךְ shows compensatory lengthening of *u* to *ō*.

The lengthening of the final stem vowel in מֻלָּא should be an expected phenomenon by now, as should the conformity of the stem endings of verbs from roots III-*Hē* to those of the other verb types (Qal, Niphal, and Piel).

PERFECT:

גֻּדַּל *guddal*	בֹּרַךְ *bōrak*	מֻלָּא	עֻנָּה
גֻּדְּלָה *guddəlāh*	בֹּרְכָה *bōrəkāh*	מֻלְּאָה	עֻנְּתָה
גֻּדַּלְתָּ *guddáltā*	בֹּרַכְתָּ *bōráktā*	מֻלֵּאתָ	עֻנֵּיתָ
גֻּדַּלְתְּ *guddált*	בֹּרַכְתְּ *bōrakt*	מֻלֵּאת	עֻנֵּית
גֻּדַּלְתִּי *guddáltî*	בֹּרַכְתִּי *bōráktî*	מֻלֵּאתִי	עֻנֵּיתִי
גֻּדְּלוּ *guddəlû*	בֹּרְכוּ *bōrəkû*	מֻלְּאוּ	עֻנּוּ
גֻּדַּלְתֶּם *guddaltem*	בֹּרַכְתֶּם *bōraktem*	מֻלֵּאתֶם	עֻנֵּיתֶם
גֻּדַּלְתֶּן *guddalten*	בֹּרַכְתֶּן *bōrakten*	מֻלֵּאתֶן	עֻנֵּיתֶן
גֻּדַּלְנוּ *guddálnû*	בֹּרַכְנוּ *bōráknû*	מֻלֵּאנוּ	עֻנֵּינוּ

IMPERFECT:

יְגֻדַּל *yəguddal*	יְבֹרַךְ *yəbōrak*	יְמֻלָּא	יְעֻנֶּה
תְּגֻדַּל *təguddal*	תְּבֹרַךְ *təbōrak*	תְּמֻלָּא	תְּעֻנֶּה
תְּגֻדַּל *təguddal*	תְּבֹרַךְ *təbōrak*	תְּמֻלָּא	תְּעֻנֶּה
תְּגֻדְּלִי *təguddəlî*	תְּבֹרְכִי *təbōrəkî*	תְּמֻלְּאִי	תְּעֻנִּי
אֲגֻדַּל *ʾăguddal*	אֲבֹרַךְ *ʾăbōrak*	אֲמֻלָּא	אֲעֻנֶּה
יְגֻדְּלוּ *yəguddəlû*	יְבֹרְכוּ *yəbōrəkû*	יְמֻלְּאוּ	יְעֻנּוּ
תְּגֻדַּלְנָה *təguddálnāh*	תְּבֹרַכְנָה *təbōráknāh*	תְּמֻלֶּאנָה	תְּעֻנֶּינָה
תְּגֻדְּלוּ *təguddəlû*	תְּבֹרְכוּ *təbōrəkû*	תְּמֻלְּאוּ	תְּעֻנּוּ
תְּגֻדַּלְנָה *təguddálnāh*	תְּבֹרַכְנָה *təbōráknāh*	תְּמֻלֶּאנָה	תְּעֻנֶּינָה
נְגֻדַּל *nəguddal*	נְבֹרַךְ *nəbōrak*	נְמֻלָּא	נְעֻנֶּה

PARTICIPLE:

מְגֻדָּל *məguddāl*	מְבֹרָךְ *məbōrāk*	מְמֻלָּא	מְעֻנֶּה
מְגֻדָּלָה *məguddālāh*	מְבֹרָכָה *məbōrākāh*	מְמֻלָּאָה	מְעֻנָּה
מְגֻדֶּלֶת *məguddélet*	מְבֹרֶכֶת *məbōréket*	מְמֻלָּאִים	מְעֻנִּים
מְגֻדָּלִים *məguddālîm*	מְבֹרָכִים *məbōrākîm*	מְמֻלָּאוֹת	מְעֻנּוֹת
מְגֻדָּלוֹת *məguddālôt*	מְבֹרָכוֹת *məbōrākôt*		

Note: One occasionally finds *o* for *u* in the first stem syllable; e.g. כֻּסּוּ *kossû* (they were covered).

The passive represented by the Pual has no expressed agent:

סֻפַּר לוֹ הַדָּבָר   The matter was related to him.

Because this corresponds semantically to an active verb with an indefinite subject (somebody, one, they), it may be followed ("ungrammatically") by an object with אֶת־:

סֻפַּר לוֹ אֶת־הַדָּבָר   One recounted the matter to him.

A second construction peculiar to passive verbs is that in which a preposition is omitted before a specifying noun.

כֻּסּוּ הֶהָרִים צֵל   The mountains were covered with a shadow.

This probably has its origin in the following mixture of constructions:

(a) A verb like מָלֵא in its intransitive sense (to be full) regularly has a specifying noun without a preposition:

מָלֵא הַכְּלִי מַיִם   The vessel is full of water.

This is an old construction in Semitic and may be termed "historically correct".

(b) The corresponding transitive usage of מָלֵא employs the same construction:

מָלֵא אֶת־הַכְּלִי מַיִם   He filled the vessel with water.

(c) The Piel verb מִלֵּא being a transitive form only is used in two ways, first as a normal verb without reference to the above,

מִלֵּא אֶת־הַכְּלִי בְמַיִם   He filled the vessel with water.

or, as the equivalent of מָלֵא:

מִלֵּא אֶת־הַכְּלִי מַיִם   He filled the vessel with water.

(d) The Pual verb מֻלָּא may be regarded as a transformation of either of the two constructions given in (c):

מֻלָּא הַכְּלִי בְמַיִם   The vessel was filled with water.
מֻלָּא הַכְּלִי מַיִם

155. Proclisis, Retraction of Stress, and Conjunctive Daghesh.

There are several orthographic features of the Masoretic Text which, because of their frequency, must be noted at this point.

a. *Proclisis.* As was mentioned in our discussion of pause (§ 152), certain types of words stand in a syntactically conjunctive relationship.

Any word in this category may be made proclitic to the one that follows if the accentual pattern of the verse so demands. Proclisis is marked with *maqqēp̄* and is more or less the rule for the monosyllabic prepositions and particles ־אֶל, ־עַל, ־עַד, ־עִם, ־מִן, ־אִם, פֶּן and ־אַל (negative), though instances may be cited where these words are accentually distinct. Examples of other types of words in proclisis are:

לֹא־יָסוּר	he will not depart	נִמְצָא־חֵן	we shall find favor
אֲשֶׁר־נָתַן־לִי	which he gave to me	קְנֵה־אֹתָנוּ	buy us
כִּי־יָשִׁית	that he was placing	יֵשְׁבוּ־נָא	let them dwell now

The only important vowel changes before *maqqēp̄* are $\bar{e} \rightarrow e$ and $\bar{o} \rightarrow o$ in the final syllable of many words:

יִתֶּן־לִי	he will give to me
שְׁמָר־נָא	observe now

b. *Retraction of Stress (nəsîḡāh or nāsôḡ 'āḥôr).* There is a tendency, by no means consistently applied, to avoid two stressed syllables in succession, such as

תֹּאכַל לֶחֶם   you will eat bread.

Instead, one may find either proclisis תֹּאכַל־לֶחֶם in which the stress of the first word is surrendered completely, or retraction of the stress, in which the stress of the first word is moved back to the next full vowel (not ə):

תֹּאכַל לֶחֶם	your will eat bread
וַיִּהְיוּ שָׁם	and they were there

c. *Conjunctive Daghesh.* When a word ending in an unstressed *-ā(h)* or *-eh* is followed by one beginning with a stressed syllable, a daghesh may be placed in the first consonant of the second word:

הָיִיתָ לָּנוּ   you were for us

The absence of stress on the final *-ā(h)* or *-eh* of the first word may be

(1) normal, as in the preceding example;
(2) due to retraction, as in   יֵעָשֶׂה לוֹ   it was done for him;
(3) due to proclisis, as in   הָבָה־לָּנוּ   give to us.

The phonetic value of this daghesh is not certain.

156. Vocabulary 42.

VERBS:	זָעַק	*zā'aq*	(יִזְעַק)	a synonym (and doublet) of צָעַק to cry out
	סָר	*sār*	(יָסוּר)	to turn aside (from a given course), to depart, go away (all intransitive).
	חִלֵּל	*ḥillēl*	(יְחַלֵּל)	to defile, pollute, dishonor

כִּפֵּר *kipper* (יְכַפֵּר) to atone for, make atonement

נִחַם *niḥam* (יְנַחֵם) to comfort, console (cf. נִחַם Niphal)

שִׂמַּח *śimmaḥ* (יְשַׂמַּח) to gladden, cause to rejoice (cf. שִׂמְחָה, שָׂמַח)

NOUNS: חֹתֵן *ḥōtēn* father-in-law

לֶהָבָה *lehābāh* (constr. לֶהֶבֶת or לַבַּת; pl. -ôṯ) flame

נַעַל *ná'al* (pl. -îm) shoe, sandal (f.)

קֹדֶשׁ *qódeš* (pl. -îm) holiness, sacredness

עָוֹן *'āwōn* (pl. -ôṯ) guilt, iniquity; punishment

OTHER: מַדּוּעַ *maddûa'* (interrog. adv.) why? for what reason?

הֲלֹם *hălōm* (adv.) hither (a less frequent synonym of הֵנָּה)

PROPER NAMES: מֹשֶׁה *Mōšeh* Moses

מִדְיָן *Miḏyān* Midian, a land in northwestern Arabia.

יִתְרוֹ *Yiṯrô* Jethro, the father-in-law of Moses

חֹרֵב *Ḥōrēḇ* Mt. Horeb, an alternate name for Mt. Sinai, the location of which is disputed.

Exercises:

(a) Translate:

(1) מַדּוּעַ חִלַּלְתָּ אֶת־מְקוֹם קָדְשִׁי.

(2) וַיַּעַשׂ מֹשֶׁה כַּאֲשֶׁר צֻוָּה.

(3) טוֹב־לִי כִּי עֻנֵּיתִי לְמַעַן אֶזְכֹּר אֶת־תּוֹרָתֶךָ.

(4) כִּי אֲשֶׁר־לֹא סֻפַּר לָהֶם יִרְאוּ וַאֲשֶׁר לֹא שָׁמְעוּ יֶדָעוּ.

(5) מְבֹרָכָיו יִירְשׁוּ אֶת־הָאָרֶץ וּמְקֻלָּלָיו יִכָּרֵתוּ.

(6) שַׂמַּח נֶפֶשׁ עַבְדֶּךָ כִּי אֵלֶיךָ אֲדֹנִי נַפְשִׁי אֶשָּׂא.

(7) אִישׁ־אֹהֵב חָכְמָה יְשַׂמַּח אָבִיו.

(8) כְּאִישׁ אֲשֶׁר אִמּוֹ תְּנַחֲמֶנּוּ כֵּן אָנֹכִי אֲנַחֵם אֶתְכֶם וּבִירוּשָׁלַ‍ם תְּנֻחָמוּ:

(9) גָּדוֹל יהוה וּמְהֻלָּל מְאֹד בְּעִיר אֱלֹהֵינוּ הַר קָדְשׁוֹ.

(10) וַיִּפֹּל דָּוִד וְהַזְּקֵנִים מְכֻסִּים בַּשַּׂקִּים עַל־פְּנֵיהֶם.

(11) נִרְאָה אֵלַי בַּחֲלוֹם אַחֵר אַחֲרֵי הֵרָאֹתוֹ אֵלַי בַּתְּחִלָּה.

(12) קֶשֶׁר קָשַׁרְתִּי עַל־אֲדֹנִי וָאֶהֱרֹג אֹתוֹ.

(13) וַיֹּאמֶר קַיִן אֶל־יְהוָה גָּדוֹל עֲוֹנִי מִנְּשֹׂא. הִנֵּה גֵּרַשְׁתָּ אֹתִי מֵעַל פְּנֵי הָאֲדָמָה.

(14) אַל־תָּסוּר עַל־יָמִין אוֹ עַל־שְׂמֹאל.

(15) אֲכַסֶּה צִלֵּךְ.

(16) בֻּקְּשׁוּ הָאֲתֹנוֹת וְלֹא נִמְצָאוּ.

(17) עַד־הֵנָּה צַמְתִּי עַל־דְּבַר עֲוֹנִי הַגָּדוֹל לְמַעַן יְכֻפַּר.

(b) Write in Hebrew:

1. Because of the righteous (ones) I shall not send a flame of fire upon the city to consume it and its inhabitants.
2. Where did you put your shoes?
3. His father-in-law was an Egyptian priest.

4. If you touch the vessels in the temple you will pollute them.
5. They turned off the road and stayed (= dwelt) in an inn until morning.
6. She used to come to the river every day with her sister to wash clothes, and when the clothes had been washed, she would return to the city.
7. Why did you not receive the men who had been driven out of the city?

(c) Reading: Moses and the Burning Bush (Ex. 2:23–3:6)

(23) וַיְהִי בַיָּמִים הָרַבִּים הָהֵם וַיָּמָת מֶלֶךְ מִצְרַיִם וַיֵּאָנְחוּ¹ בְנֵי־יִשְׂרָאֵל מִן־הָעֲבֹדָה וַיִּזְעָקוּ וַתַּעַל שַׁוְעָתָם² אֶל־הָאֱלֹהִים מִן־הָעֲבֹדָה:

(24) וַיִּשְׁמַע אֱלֹהִים אֶת־נַאֲקָתָם³ וַיִּזְכֹּר אֱלֹהִים אֶת־בְּרִיתוֹ אֶת־אַבְרָהָם אֶת־יִצְחָק וְאֶת־יַעֲקֹב:

(25) וַיַּרְא אֱלֹהִים אֶת־בְּנֵי־יִשְׂרָאֵל וַיֵּדַע אֱלֹהִים:

(1) וּמֹשֶׁה הָיָה רֹעֶה אֶת־צֹאן יִתְרוֹ חֹתְנוֹ כֹּהֵן מִדְיָן וַיִּנְהַג⁴ אֶת־הַצֹּאן אַחַר⁵ הַמִּדְבָּר וַיָּבֹא אֶל־הַר הָאֱלֹהִים חֹרֵבָה:

(2) וַיֵּרָא מַלְאַךְ יהוה אֵלָיו בְּלַבַּת־אֵשׁ מִתּוֹךְ הַסְּנֶה⁶ וַיַּרְא וְהִנֵּה הַסְּנֶה בֹּעֵר בָּאֵשׁ וְהַסְּנֶה אֵינֶנּוּ אֻכָּל⁷:

(3) וַיֹּאמֶר מֹשֶׁה אָסֻרָה־נָּא וְאֶרְאֶה אֶת־הַמַּרְאֶה הַגָּדֹל הַזֶּה מַדּוּעַ לֹא־יִבְעַר הַסְּנֶה:

(4) וַיַּרְא יהוה כִּי סָר לִרְאוֹת וַיִּקְרָא אֵלָיו אֱלֹהִים מִתּוֹךְ הַסְּנֶה וַיֹּאמֶר מֹשֶׁה מֹשֶׁה וַיֹּאמֶר הִנֵּנִי:

(5) וַיֹּאמֶר אַל־תִּקְרַב הֲלֹם שַׁל⁸ נְעָלֶיךָ מֵעַל רַגְלֶיךָ כִּי הַמָּקוֹם אֲשֶׁר אַתָּה עוֹמֵד עָלָיו אַדְמַת־קֹדֶשׁ הוּא:

(6) וַיֹּאמֶר אָנֹכִי אֱלֹהֵי אָבִיךָ אֱלֹהֵי אַבְרָהָם אֱלֹהֵי יִצְחָק וֵאלֹהֵי יַעֲקֹב וַיַּסְתֵּר⁹ מֹשֶׁה פָּנָיו כִּי יָרֵא מֵהַבִּיט¹⁰ אֶל־הָאֱלֹהִים:

Notes to the Reading:

1. אנח Niphal: "to sigh"
2. שַׁוְעָה a cry
3. נְאָקָה a cry
4. נָהַג Qal: "to lead, drive"
5. In the sense: "to the edge of"
6. סְנֶה a bush
7. An irregular passive adjective: "consumed"
8. "Remove"
9. "and he hid"
10. "to look"

LESSON 43

157. Hiphil Verbs: Meaning.

Hiphil verbs are, for the most part, causatives of the corresponding Qal. The distinctive mark of this conjugational type is a prefixed *h-*, but because this is not present in the imperfect and the participle, one must rely also on vowel patterns to identify these forms and to distinguish them from the Qal. The meanings that can be assigned to the Hiphil may be grouped as follows:

a. *Causative*. From roots whose Qal verbs are transitive, the causative may be doubly transitive, i.e. with an object of the "causing" and an object of the verbal idea expressed by the root:

הִשְׁמִיעַ   he caused (someone) to hear (something)

הִשְׁמִיעַ אֶת־הָאִישׁ אֶת־דִּבְרֵי הַמֶּלֶךְ   he caused the man to hear the words of the king

More commonly, however, there is only one object. If the second object is omitted, the verbal idea is intransitive:

הִשְׁמִיעַ אֶת־הָאִישׁ   he caused the man to hear

It is better to seek a more idiomatic translation value in English, one that contains the force of the causative but requires no further object: "He informed (or notified) the man". If the first object is omitted, the verbal notion becomes passive in English:

הִשְׁמִיעַ אֶת־דִּבְרֵי הַמֶּלֶךְ   he caused the words of the king to be heard.

Here again, a more suitable translation can usually be found: "He announced (or made public) the words of the king".

A further example with הֶרְאָה (to cause to see):

כַּאֲשֶׁר הֶרְאָה אֹתְךָ בָּהָר   as he showed you on the mountain (no second object)

יַרְאֶה אֶת־כְּבוֹדוֹ   he will reveal his glory (no first object)

From roots whose Qal verbs are intransitive, Hiphil verbs are simply transitive. To this group belong the extremely frequent causatives from verbs of motion:

עָבַר	הֶעֱבִיר	to bring (take, lead, send) across
יָצָא	הוֹצִיא	to bring (take, lead, send) out
יָרַד	הוֹרִיד	to bring (take, lead, send) down
עָלָה	הֶעֱלָה	to bring (take, lead, send) up
שָׁב	הֵשִׁיב	to bring (take, lead, send) back
בָּא	הֵבִיא	to bring (take, lead, send) in, to, into

From roots stative in the Qal, Hiphil verbs often partially overlap with the Piel:

כִּבֵּד	to honor; (rarely) make heavy	הִכְבִּיד	to make heavy; (rarely) honor
קִדֵּשׁ	to sanctify, consecrate	הִקְדִּישׁ	to sanctify, consecrate
גִּדֵּל	to cause to grow; rear; magnify	הִגְדִּיל	*idem* + to do great things

b. *Permissive.* This is closely related to the causative meaning and can be decided only from context: E.g.

הֶרְאָה אֹתִי אֱלֹהִים גַּם־אֶת־זַרְעֶךָ   God has allowed me to see your children too.

c. *Stative* (or *intransitive*). A rather unusual use of the Hiphil is the formation of stative verbs from roots that are also stative in the Qal:

QAL		HIPHIL	
———		הִלְבִּן	to be white
קָרַב	to be near	הִקְרִיב	to be near, about to (do something)
רָחַק	to be distant	הִרְחִיק	to move or go to a distance

A subgroup of this type consists of verbs describing action or behavior:

יָטֹב	to be good	הֵיטִיב	to do well, get along well
רַע	to be wicked	הֵרַע	to act wickedly

These do constitute a translation problem since nearly all of them have a transitive causative meaning as well:

הִלְבִּין	to make white	הִרְחִיק	to remove, put away
הִקְרִיב	to bring near, presént	הֵיטִיב	to make (something) good

The causative value is the more frequent one.

d. *Denominative.* Like the Piel, the Hiphil is used to form verbs from roots attested (in a specialized meaning) in nouns:

אֹזֶן ear	הֶאֱזִין to give ear, to listen
עֶרֶב evening	הֶעֱרִיב to do something in the evening.

e. *Unclassified:* Many verbs of the Hiphil type cannot be placed in the preceding classification. As in the Piel, this is due mainly to our ignorance of the sources in the language from which they were derived. E.g.

הִשְׁקָה to water, give to drink (used as causative of שָׁתָה)
הִשְׁכִּים to do something early in the day
הִשְׁלִיךְ to throw, cast away
הִשְׁמִיד to annihilate, destroy

158. Hiphil Verbs: Stems and Inflection.

Root Type	Perfect	Imperfect	Jussive
Regular	הִשְׁמִיד *hišmîd*	יַשְׁמִיד *yašmîd*	יַשְׁמֵד *yašmēd*
I-*Nun*	הִגִּיד *higgîd*	יַגִּיד *yaggîd*	יַגֵּד *yaggēd*
I-Guttural	הֶעֱמִיד *heʿĕmîd*	יַעֲמִיד *yaʿămîd*	יַעֲמֵד *yaʿămēd*

Imperative	Inf. Construct	Infinitive Absol.	Participle
הַשְׁמֵד *hašmēd*	הַשְׁמִיד *hašmîd*	הַשְׁמֵד *hašmēd*	מַשְׁמִיד *mašmîd*
הַגֵּד *haggēd*	הַגִּיד *haggîd*	הַגֵּד *haggēd*	מַגִּיד *maggîd*
הַעֲמֵד *haʿămēd*	הַעֲמִיד *haʿămîd*	הַעֲמֵד *haʿămēd*	מַעֲמִיד *maʿămîd*

Remarks:

(a) The basic stem of the perfect has prefixed *hi-* and a long stem vowel *î*; this is replaced with *a* in inflection (see paradigm below). With roots I-*Nun*, the familiar assimilation takes place: **hingîd > higgîd*. With roots I-guttural (including א) the prefix is *he-*, with a secondary vowel after the guttural.

(b) In the imperfect only the vowel pattern identifies the form as a Hiphil verb. Note again the secondary vowel with roots I-guttural. The short imperfect (jussive) has *ē* as the stem vowel.

(c) The *h*-prefix appears also in the imperative and the infinitives, which have different stem vowels. The participle, like that of the Piel/Pual system, has prefixed *m-*.

Perfect:	הִשְׁמִיד *hišmîd*	הִשְׁמִידוּ *hišmîdû*
	הִשְׁמִידָה *hišmîdāh*	

	הִשְׁמַ֫דְתָּ	*hišmádtā*	הִשְׁמַדְתֶּם	*hišmadtem*
	הִשְׁמַ֫דְתְּ	*hišmádt*	הִשְׁמַדְתֶּן	*hišmadten*
	הִשְׁמַ֫דְתִּי	*hišmádtî*	הִשְׁמַ֫דְנוּ	*hišmádnû*

IMPERFECT:	יַשְׁמִיד	*yašmîd*	יַשְׁמִ֫ידוּ	*yašmîdû*
	תַּשְׁמִיד	*tašmîd*	תַּשְׁמֵ֫דְנָה	*tašmédnāh*
	תַּשְׁמִיד	*tašmîd*	תַּשְׁמִ֫ידוּ	*tašmîdû*
	תַּשְׁמִ֫ידִי	*tašmîdî*	תַּשְׁמֵ֫דְנָה	*tašmédnāh*
	אַשְׁמִיד	*'ašmîd*	נַשְׁמִיד	*našmîd*

JUSSIVE:	יַשְׁמֵד	*yašmēd*	וַיַּשְׁמֵד	*wayyašmēd*
	תַּשְׁמֵד	*tašmēd*	וַתַּשְׁמֵד	*wattašmēd*

COHORTATIVE:	אַשְׁמִ֫ידָה	*'ašmîdāh*	נַשְׁמִ֫ידָה	*našmîdāh*

IMPERATIVE:	הַשְׁמֵד	*hašmēd*	הַשְׁמִ֫ידוּ	*hašmîdû*
	הַשְׁמִ֫ידִי	*hašmîdî*	הַשְׁמֵ֫דְנָה	*hašmédnāh*

INFINITIVE CONSTRUCT:	הַשְׁמִיד	*hašmîd*		
	הַשְׁמִידִי	*hašmîdî*		
	הַשְׁמִידְךָ	*hašmîdəkā* etc.		

INFINITIVE ABSOLUTE:	הַשְׁמֵד	*hašmēd*		

PARTICIPLE	מַשְׁמִיד	*mašmîd*	מַשְׁמִידִים	*mašmîdîm*
	מַשְׁמִידָה	*mašmîdāh*	מַשְׁמִידוֹת	*mašmîdôt*

The paradigms of הִגִּיד and הֶעֱמִיד are the same as the preceding. In learning the paradigm of the Hiphil, the reader should note the vowel replacements (perfect: *î → a*; imperfect: *î → ē*) and the fact that the stem vowel *ē* does not occur in open syllables, while *î* occurs in all open stem syllables and in all final syllables except that of the jussive, the imperative, and the infinitive absolute.

One peculiarity should be mentioned in connection with the perfect of הֶאֱמִין and other Hiphil verbs from roots I-guttural: when used in a future sequence, the converted form, with the customary shift of stress, has *a* in the preformative syllable:

וְהַאֲמַנְתָּ֫ and you will believe
וְהַאֲמַנְתִּ֫י and I shall believe

A very rare alternate form for הֶאֱמִין is הַאֲמִין.

159. Vocabulary 43.

The following Hiphil verbs are derived from roots which have already occurred in this text. Note the meanings which are not completely predictable.

הֶאֱבִיד to destroy, kill (אָבַד) הֶעֱבִיר to lead (bring) across
הֶאֱמִין to believe, trust (נֶאֱמַן) הֶעֱמִיד to station, set up, appoint
הִגְדִּיל to magnify, make great (גָּדַל) הִקְרִיב to bring near, present

הַזְכִּיר to cause to remember or be re-   הַגִּישׁ to bring near (נגשׁ)
membered; to remind; to mention הַצִּיב to station, set up (נצב)
הֶחֱזִיק to seize, lay hold of (חזק)

VERBS:
  הִבִּיט *hibbîṭ* (root נבט) to look (at: אֶל, עַל); to look at (+dir.obj.)
  הִגִּיד *higgîd* (root נגד) to tell (something) (to: לְ)
  הִצִּיל *hiṣṣîl* (root נצל) to rescue, deliver
  הִשִּׂיג *hiśśîg* (root נשׂג) to reach, attain, overtake
  הִסְתִּיר *histîr* (root סתר) to hide, conceal (trans.)
  נִקְרָה *niqrāh* (imperf. יִקָּרֶה) ⎫
  נִקְרָא *niqrā'* (imperf. יִקָּרֵא) ⎭ to meet, encounter (+ בְּ, עַל, אֶל)

NOUNS:
  חָלָב *ḥālāb* (constr. irreg. חֲלֵב; no pl.) milk
  דְּבַשׁ *dəbaš* honey
  זֵכֶר *zéker* (w. suff. זִכְרִי; no pl.) remembrance, memorial
  אוֹת *'ôt* (pl. -ôt) sign, omen
  דּוֹר *dôr* (pl. -îm or -ôt) generation, corresponding period of time

ADJECTIVE: רָחָב *rāḥāb* broad, wide

Note: Hiphil verbs from roots whose Qal is unknown or little used often have a corresponding Niphal; in addition to נֶאֱמָן, נִצַּב, and נִגַּשׁ note

נִצַּל *niṣṣal* to be rescued   נִסְתַּר *nistar* to hide (oneself)

Exercises:

(a) Translate:

(1) וַיֶּאֱסַר מֹשֶׁה לְהַבִּיט אֶל־לַהֶבֶת הָאֵשׁ.
(2) תָּבוֹא וְהַאֲבַדְתָּ אֹתָם מִתַּחַת הַשָּׁמָיִם.
(3) מַדּוּעַ אֵינְכֶם מַאֲמִינִים בַּיהוה אֱלֹהֵיכֶם.
(4) וַיַּגִּידוּ לוֹ אֶת־כָּל־הַדְּבָרִים אֲשֶׁר שָׁמְעוּ בַּלָּיְלָה.
(5) וַיְהִי כְּהַשִּׂיגֵנוּ אֹתָם וַיִּזְעֲקוּ בְּקוֹל גָּדוֹל וַיַּסְתִּירוּ אֶת־פְּנֵיהֶם.
(6) וְהָיָה בְּהַזְכִּירָם אֶת־שִׁירֵי אֲבִיהֶם וּבָכוּ.
(7) הֶעֱבִיר אֹתָם אֶת־הַנָּהָר וַיַּקְרֵב אֹתָם הָעִירָה.
(8) הֶחֱזִיקָה אֶת־בִּגְדוֹ וְהוּא נָס הַחוּצָה.
(9) אַגְדִּיל אֶת־שִׁמְךָ הַקָּדוֹשׁ יוֹמָם וָלַיְלָה וְלֹא אֶשְׁכַּח אֶת־מִצְוֺתֶיךָ.
(10) אֵי־מִזֶּה אַתְּ תָּבֹאִי הֲלֹם וְאֶת־מִי אַתְּ מְבַקֶּשֶׁת פֹּה.
(11) אַל־תַּקְרִיבוּ אֶת־הַבְּהֵמָה פֶּן־תְּחַלְּלוּ אֶת־הַמָּקוֹם הַזֶּה.
(12) וַתַּסְתֵּר אֶת־הָאֲנָשִׁים פֶּן־יִמָּצְאוּ וְנֶהֱרָגוּ.
(13) הִזְכִּיר אֹתָנוּ אֶת־הָאוֹתוֹת אֲשֶׁר שָׁלַח אֵלֵינוּ.
(14) יַגְדִּיל אֶת־שֵׁם הַמַּאֲמִין בּוֹ.
(15) הַגֶּד־לוֹ כִּי־סָבְבוּ אֹתָנוּ אוֹיְבֵינוּ וְכִי אֵין מַצִּיל אֹתָנוּ בְּצָרָתֵנוּ.
(16) אָרוּר אַתָּה עַל־דְּבַר עֲוֺנְךָ הַגָּדוֹל הַזֶּה.
(17) תְּנִי אֶת־הֶחָלָב אֶל־גְּבִרְתֵּךְ לְמַעַן תִּשְׁתֶּה.

(b) Write in Hebrew:

1. The maidservant hid near the well.
2. Overtake him and tell him that we are returning to our city.
3. We were not able to rescue them.
4. Look at the mountains and tell me what you see there.
5. He will station his men by the road.
6. The man who meets you will tell you where I have hidden.
7. Why have you come to destroy us?
8. He hid the money so that no one could find it.

(c) Reading: Moses and the Burning Bush (concl.); Ex. 3:7-15.

(7) וַיֹּאמֶר יהוה רָאֹה רָאִיתִי אֶת־עֳנִי עַמִּי אֲשֶׁר בְּמִצְרָיִם וְאֶת־צַעֲקָתָם¹ שָׁמַעְתִּי מִפְּנֵי נֹגְשָׂיו² כִּי יָדַעְתִּי אֶת־מַכְאֹבָיו:³

(8) וָאֵרֵד לְהַצִּילוֹ⁴ מִיַּד מִצְרַיִם וּלְהַעֲלֹתוֹ⁵ מִן־הָאָרֶץ הַהִוא אֶל־אֶרֶץ טוֹבָה וּרְחָבָה אֶל־אֶרֶץ זָבַת⁶ חָלָב וּדְבָשׁ אֶל־מְקוֹם הַכְּנַעֲנִי וְהַחִתִּי⁷ וְהָאֱמֹרִי וְהַפְּרִזִּי וְהַחִוִּי וְהַיְבוּסִי:

(9) וְעַתָּה הִנֵּה צַעֲקַת בְּנֵי־יִשְׂרָאֵל בָּאָה אֵלָי וְגַם־רָאִיתִי אֶת־הַלַּחַץ⁸ אֲשֶׁר מִצְרַיִם לֹחֲצִים אֹתָם:

(10) וְעַתָּה לְכָה וְאֶשְׁלָחֲךָ⁹ אֶל־פַּרְעֹה וְהוֹצֵא¹⁰ אֶת־עַמִּי בְנֵי־יִשְׂרָאֵל מִמִּצְרָיִם:

(11) וַיֹּאמֶר מֹשֶׁה אֶל־הָאֱלֹהִים מִי אָנֹכִי כִּי אֵלֵךְ אֶל־פַּרְעֹה וְכִי אוֹצִיא¹¹ אֶת־בְּנֵי יִשְׂרָאֵל מִמִּצְרָיִם:

(12) וַיֹּאמֶר כִּי־אֶהְיֶה עִמָּךְ וְזֶה־לְּךָ הָאוֹת כִּי אָנֹכִי שְׁלַחְתִּיךָ¹² בְּהוֹצִיאֲךָ¹³ אֶת־הָעָם מִמִּצְרַיִם תַּעַבְדוּן אֶת־הָאֱלֹהִים עַל הָהָר הַזֶּה:

(13) וַיֹּאמֶר מֹשֶׁה אֶל־הָאֱלֹהִים הִנֵּה אָנֹכִי בָא אֶל־בְּנֵי יִשְׂרָאֵל וְאָמַרְתִּי לָהֶם אֱלֹהֵי אֲבוֹתֵיכֶם שְׁלָחַנִי¹⁴ אֲלֵיכֶם וְאָמְרוּ־לִי מַה־שְּׁמוֹ מָה אֹמַר אֲלֵהֶם:

(14) וַיֹּאמֶר אֱלֹהִים אֶל־מֹשֶׁה אֶהְיֶה אֲשֶׁר אֶהְיֶה¹⁵ וַיֹּאמֶר כֹּה תֹאמַר לִבְנֵי יִשְׂרָאֵל אֶהְיֶה שְׁלָחַנִי¹⁴ אֲלֵיכֶם:

(15) וַיֹּאמֶר עוֹד אֱלֹהִים אֶל־מֹשֶׁה כֹּה־תֹאמַר אֶל־בְּנֵי יִשְׂרָאֵל יהוה אֱלֹהֵי אֲבֹתֵיכֶם אֱלֹהֵי אַבְרָהָם אֱלֹהֵי יִצְחָק וֵאלֹהֵי יַעֲקֹב שְׁלָחַנִי¹⁴ אֲלֵיכֶם זֶה־שְּׁמִי לְעֹלָם וְזֶה זִכְרִי לְדֹר דֹּר:¹⁶

Notes to the Reading:

1. צְעָקָה   cry
2. נָגַשׂ   to drive, oppress
3. מַכְאֹב   pain
4. The suffix -ô is an object pronoun.
5. "to lead him (them) up"
6. זָב   to flow
7. The Hittites, the Amorites, the Perizzites, the Hivites, and the Jebusites; names of peoples occupying Palestine at that time.
8. לַחַץ oppression; לָחַץ to oppress
9. = וְאֶשְׁלַח אֹתְךָ
10. "and bring forth"

11. "I should bring forth"
12. = שָׁלַּחְתִּי אֹתְךָ
13. inf. construct of הוֹצִיא to bring forth
14. = שָׁלַח אֹתִי
15. A cryptic phrase, not fully understood.
16. "forever;" an idiomatic use of repetition for durational expression.

LESSON 44

160. Hiphil Verbs: Stems and Inflection (cont.).

Root Type	Perfect	Imperfect	Jussive	Imperative	Inf. Constr.	Participle
III-guttural	הִשְׁמִיעַ	יַשְׁמִיעַ	יַשְׁמַע	הַשְׁמַע	הַשְׁמִיעַ	מַשְׁמִיעַ
III-*Aleph*	הִמְצִיא	יַמְצִיא	יַמְצֵא	הַמְצֵא	הַמְצִיא	מַמְצִיא

Remarks: A guttural (other than א) in third root position affects only those forms which have *ē* in the final stem syllable of the corresponding non-guttural type. In the imperfect (fem. pl.), jussive, and imperative this is replaced by *a*. The paradigm is otherwise like that of הִשְׁמִיד except for the furtive *paṭaḥ* with the final guttural: הִשְׁמִיעַ, יַשְׁמִיעַ.

Imperfect	Jussive	Imperative
יַשְׁמִיעַ	יַשְׁמַע	הַשְׁמַע
תַּשְׁמִיעַ	תַּשְׁמַע	הַשְׁמִיעִי
...	...	הַשְׁמִיעוּ
תַּשְׁמַעְנָה	...	הַשְׁמַעְנָה

Hiphil verbs from roots III-*Aleph* have *ē(')* in the perfect before endings beginning with a consonant: הִמְצֵאתָ (just like the Niphal נִמְצֵאתָ, Piel מִלֵּאתָ, and the Pual מֻלֵּאתָ). All other forms are the same as those of הִשְׁמִיד except for the fem. pl. of the imperfect, where we find the usual *-ē(')nāh:* תִּמְצֶאנָה

Perfect	Imperfect	Imperative
הִמְצִיא	יַמְצִיא	הַמְצֵא
הִמְצִּיאָה	...	הַמְצִיאִי
הִמְצֵאתָ	תַּמְצֶאנָה	הַמְצִיאוּ
...	...	הַמְצֶאנָה

The verb הֶחֱטִיא combines the features of verbs I-guttural and III-*Aleph.*

161. More on the Numbers.

(a) The tens. Apart from *twenty,* which is expressed by the plural form of *ten,* namely עֶשְׂרִים, the tens are the plurals of the corresponding units:

שְׁלֹשִׁים	thirty	שִׁבְעִים	seventy
אַרְבָּעִים	forty	שְׁמֹנִים	eighty
חֲמִשִּׁים	fifty	תִּשְׁעִים	ninety
שִׁשִּׁים	sixty		

They may be used with either a singular noun (the more common usage) or a plural noun:

שְׁלֹשִׁים אִישׁ   or   שְׁלֹשִׁים אֲנָשִׁים   thirty men.

They may also be used as ordinals: בִּשְׁנַת אַרְבָּעִים in the fortieth year.

(b) Fractions are poorly attested. The expression for *half* (חֲצִי) is un-related to the number two. A *fourth* is רֶבַע or רֹבַע; a *fifth* is חֹמֶשׁ.

(c) In addition to the regular series of ordinals (רִאשׁוֹן, שֵׁנִי, שְׁלִישִׁי, etc.) there is a second type attested only by שִׁלֵּשׁ (third) and רִבֵּעַ (fourth). To judge from their limited use, they are more substantival than adjectival: "that which pertains to the third," etc.

(d) Adverbial multiplicatives are usually expressed with פַּעַם (once), פַּעֲמַיִם (twice), שָׁלוֹשׁ פְּעָמִים (three times), etc., but also attested are the forms שִׁבְעָתַיִם (sevenfold), אַרְבַּעְתַּיִם (fourfold).

(e) Most of the units have corresponding verbs (usually Piel) which have rather wide-ranging meanings: "to do something x-times; to divide into x-parts; to do something for an x time." Thus,

שָׁנָה   to repeat, do again
שִׁלֵּשׁ   to divide into three parts
רָבַע   to be square; [רִבַּע] to make square, and similarly for the others.

162. Vocabulary 44.

VERBS: הִשְׁמִיעַ   to cause to hear; to tell, to proclaim.

הִמְצִיא   to cause to find; to present (= cause to be found).

הֶחֱטִיא		to cause to sin, to lead into sin
הִצְלִיחַ		to make prosperous; to be prosperous
הִשְׁלִיךְ		to throw
הִשְׁמִיד		to destroy
הֶאֱרִיךְ		to lengthen (tr.); to be long (intr.)
זָבַח	(יִזְבַּח)	to sacrifice
גָּנַב	(יִגְנֹב)	to steal
רָצַח	(יִרְצַח)	to kill (with or without intent or premeditation)
NOUNS: מַטֶּה		(pl. -ôṯ) staff, rod; tribe
כַּף		(w. suff. כַּפִּי; dual כַּפַּיִם; pl. -ôṯ) palm or hollow of hand; sole
OTHER: הֵן		(adv.) a synonym of הִנֵּה; if

Exercises:

(a) Translate:

(1) יַשְׁמִידוּ אֶת־שַׁעֲרֵי עִירֵנוּ.

(2) וַיַּצְלַח יהוה אֶת־יוֹסֵף.

(3) צִוִּיתִי אֹתוֹ לְהַחֲזִיק אֶת־הַצְּלָמִים וּלְהַשְׁמִיד אֹתָם.

(4) הִשְׁלִיכוּ אֶת־אֲחִיהֶם בַּבּוֹר.

(5) גָּדוֹל עֲוֹנֵנוּ כִּי הֶחֱטָאנוּ אֹתוֹ.

(6) יַאֲרֵךְ יהוה אֶת־יְמֵי חַיֶּיךָ.

(7) הִשְׁמִיעוּ אֶת־כָּל־הָעָם אֶת־דְּבָרַי.

(8) יְבֹרַךְ הַמַּאֲמִין בּוֹ וְהַמְקַלֵּל אֹתוֹ יֹאבַד.

(9) אַצִּיל אֶת־הָעָם הַמְעֻנֶּה הַזֶּה.

(10) אַל־תַּחֲטִיא אֶת־רֵעֶךָ.

(11) לָמָה תִסָּתֵר מִמֶּנִּי.

(12) לֹא תַעֲנוּ אֶת־הַדַּלִּים.

(13) מִי גָנַב אֶת־הַלּוּחוֹת.

(14) הִשְׁלִיךְ אֶת־הַדָּג בַּיָּם.

(15) בֹּאוּ וְהַלְלוּ אֶת־יהוה אֱלֹהֵיכֶם.

(16) נַשִּׂיגָה־נָּא אֹתוֹ לִפְנֵי הַקָּרְאוֹ עַל־מַחֲנֵה אֹיְבֵינוּ.

(17) קָרַע אֶת־בְּגָדָיו וַיְכַס אֶת־רֹאשׁוֹ בַּשַּׂקִּים.

(18) זֶה אוֹת אַהֲבָתִי.

(19) קָם עַל־רֵעֵהוּ וַיִּרְצַח אֹתוֹ.

(20) אַל־תִּזְבְּחוּ אֶת־עוֹף הַשָּׁמַיִם.

(b) Give the Hebrew for the following orally:

1. 50 fish
2. 20 tablets
3. 30 stones
4. 40 days and 40 nights
5. 50 honest men
6. 90 garments
7. half of the milk.

(c) Write in Hebrew:

1. And when he had proclaimed the commandments of the Lord, he departed from their midst.

2. And when they destroy this city, you will be slain with the remaining inhabitants.

3. And when they told him about the enemies' army, his heart melted within him and he fled from before them.

4. Now that the Lord has made you prosperous, leave your place and come with us to be our king.

5. It is bad to steal and kill in this manner.

(d) Reading: Exodus 3:16–4:5.

(16) לֵךְ וְאָסַפְתָּ אֶת־זִקְנֵי יִשְׂרָאֵל וְאָמַרְתָּ אֲלֵהֶם יהוה אֱלֹהֵי אֲבֹתֵיכֶם נִרְאָה אֵלַי אֱלֹהֵי אַבְרָהָם יִצְחָק וְיַעֲקֹב לֵאמֹר פָּקֹד פָּקַדְתִּי אֶתְכֶם וְאֶת־הֶעָשׂוּי לָכֶם בְּמִצְרָיִם:

(17) וָאֹמַר אַעֲלֶה¹ אֶתְכֶם מֵעֳנִי מִצְרַיִם אֶל־אֶרֶץ הַכְּנַעֲנִי וְהַחִתִּי² וְהָאֱמֹרִי וְהַפְּרִזִּי וְהַחִוִּי וְהַיְבוּסִי אֶל־אֶרֶץ זָבַת³ חָלָב וּדְבָשׁ:

(18) וְשָׁמְעוּ לְקֹלֶךָ וּבָאתָ אַתָּה וְזִקְנֵי יִשְׂרָאֵל אֶל־מֶלֶךְ מִצְרַיִם וַאֲמַרְתֶּם אֵלָיו יהוה אֱלֹהֵי הָעִבְרִיִּים נִקְרָה עָלֵינוּ וְעַתָּה נֵלֲכָה־נָּא דֶּרֶךְ⁴ שְׁלֹשֶׁת יָמִים בַּמִּדְבָּר וְנִזְבְּחָה לַיהוה אֱלֹהֵינוּ:

(19) וַאֲנִי יָדַעְתִּי כִּי לֹא־יִתֵּן אֶתְכֶם מֶלֶךְ מִצְרַיִם לַהֲלֹךְ⁵ וְלֹא בְּיָד חֲזָקָה:⁶

(20) וְשָׁלַחְתִּי אֶת־יָדִי וְהִכֵּיתִי⁷ אֶת־מִצְרַיִם בְּכֹל נִפְלְאֹתַי אֲשֶׁר אֶעֱשֶׂה בְּקִרְבּוֹ וְאַחֲרֵי־כֵן יְשַׁלַּח אֶתְכֶם:

(21) וְנָתַתִּי אֶת־חֵן הָעָם־הַזֶּה בְּעֵינֵי מִצְרָיִם וְהָיָה כִּי תֵלֵכוּן לֹא תֵלְכוּ רֵיקָם:⁸

(22) וְשָׁאֲלָה אִשָּׁה מִשְּׁכֶנְתָּהּ⁹ וּמִגָּרַת בֵּיתָהּ כְּלֵי־כֶסֶף וּכְלֵי זָהָב וּשְׂמָלֹת וְשַׂמְתֶּם עַל־בְּנֵיכֶם וְעַל־בְּנֹתֵיכֶם וְנִצַּלְתֶּם¹⁰ אֶת־מִצְרָיִם:

(1) וַיַּעַן מֹשֶׁה וַיֹּאמֶר וְהֵן לֹא־יַאֲמִינוּ לִי וְלֹא יִשְׁמְעוּ בְּקֹלִי כִּי יֹאמְרוּ לֹא־נִרְאָה אֵלֶיךָ יהוה:

(2) וַיֹּאמֶר אֵלָיו יהוה מַזֶּה¹¹ בְּיָדֶךָ וַיֹּאמֶר מַטֶּה:

(3) וַיֹּאמֶר הַשְׁלִיכֵהוּ¹² אַרְצָה וַיַּשְׁלִכֵהוּ¹³ אַרְצָה וַיְהִי לְנָחָשׁ וַיָּנָס מֹשֶׁה מִפָּנָיו:

(4) וַיֹּאמֶר יהוה אֶל־מֹשֶׁה שְׁלַח יָדְךָ וֶאֱחֹז בִּזְנָבוֹ¹⁴ וַיִּשְׁלַח יָדוֹ וַיַּחֲזֶק בּוֹ וַיְהִי לְמַטֶּה בְּכַפּוֹ:

(5) לְמַעַן¹⁵ יַאֲמִינוּ כִּי־נִרְאָה אֵלֶיךָ יהוה אֱלֹהֵי אֲבֹתָם אֱלֹהֵי אַבְרָהָם אֱלֹהֵי יִצְחָק וֵאלֹהֵי יַעֲקֹב

Notes to the Reading:

1. "I shall lead (you) up"
2. The Hittites, the Amorites, the Perizzites, the Hivites, and the Jebusites.
3. זוּב to flow
4. "a journey (of three days)"
5. לַהֲלֹךְ a "regular" inf. construct of הָלַךְ
6. "except by a show of strength"
7. "and I shall smite"

8. רֵיקָם empty (adv.)
9. "from her neighbor;" fem. form of שָׁכֵן
10. נָצַל (Piel): to plunder, take spoil from
11. = מַה זֶּה
12. = הַשְׁלֵךְ אֹתוֹ
13. = וַיַּשְׁלֵךְ אֹתוֹ
14. זָנָב tail
15. The purpose clause fits only loosely with the preceding verses.

LESSON 45

163. Hiphil Verbs: Stems and Inflection.

With roots I-*Yodh* (originally I-*Waw*) the Hiphil verb has the same contraction to *ô* that was found in the Niphal.

Perfect	Imperfect	Jussive	Imperative	Inf. Construct	Participle
הוֹרִיד	יוֹרִיד	יוֹרֵד	הוֹרֵד	הוֹרִיד	מוֹרִיד
		וַיּוֹרֶד			(to lead down)

The inflection is perfectly regular: the syllable with *ô* is unchanged throughout, and the final stem syllable undergoes the changes given in the paradigm of הִשְׁמִיד Because the preformative syllable is open, the accent of the converted imperfect is regularly retracted, with *ē → e*: וַיּוֹלֶד.

The following verbs combine several inflectional peculiarities:

(a) I-*Yodh* and III-guttural:

הוֹדִיעַ	יוֹדִיעַ	וַיּוֹדַע / יוֹדַע	הוֹדַע	הוֹדִיעַ	מוֹדִיעַ	(cause to know)
הוֹשִׁיעַ	יוֹשִׁיעַ	וַיּוֹשַׁע / יוֹשַׁע	הוֹשַׁע	הוֹשִׁיעַ	מוֹשִׁיעַ	(deliver, save)
הוֹכִיחַ	יוֹכִיחַ	וַיּוֹכַח / יוֹכַח	הוֹכַח	הוֹכִיחַ	מוֹכִיחַ	(reprove)

(b) I-*Yodh* and III-*Aleph*:

הוֹצִיא	יוֹצִיא	וַיּוֹצֵא / יוֹצֵא	הוֹצֵא	הוֹצִיא	מוֹצִיא	(bring forth)

The Hiphil verb corresponding to Qal הָלַךְ is הוֹלִיךְ, as though from a root ילך.

The few verbs in Hebrew which are from roots originally I-*Yodh* have the Hiphil form הֵיטִיב (to treat well; root יטב). The *ê* is not reducible and the inflection is regular throughout.

164. The Numbers from 11–19.

The 'teens are formed by placing the unit before the word for ten, which has special forms differing from those already learned:

	Masculine Modifier	*Feminine Modifier*
eleven	אַחַד עָשָׂר	אַחַת עֶשְׂרֵה
	עַשְׁתֵּי עָשָׂר	עַשְׁתֵּי עֶשְׂרֵה
twelve	שְׁנֵים עָשָׂר	שְׁתֵּים עֶשְׂרֵה
	שְׁנֵי עָשָׂר	שְׁתֵּי עֶשְׂרֵה
thirteen	שְׁלֹשָׁה עָשָׂר	שְׁלֹשׁ עֶשְׂרֵה
fourteen	אַרְבָּעָה עָשָׂר	אַרְבַּע עֶשְׂרֵה
fifteen	חֲמִשָּׁה עָשָׂר	חֲמֵשׁ עֶשְׂרֵה
sixteen	שִׁשָּׁה עָשָׂר	שֵׁשׁ עֶשְׂרֵה
seventeen	שִׁבְעָה עָשָׂר	שְׁבַע עֶשְׂרֵה
eighteen	שְׁמֹנָה עָשָׂר	שְׁמֹנֶה עֶשְׂרֵה
nineteen	תִּשְׁעָה עָשָׂר	תְּשַׁע עֶשְׂרֵה

As with the tens (§161a), both singular and plural nouns occur with the numbers from 11 to 19. Nouns frequently itemized, such as אִישׁ, יוֹם, שָׁנָה, נֶפֶשׁ (in the sense of "person"), and שֵׁבֶט (tribe) are usually singular:

חֲמִשָּׁה עָשָׂר אִישׁ   fifteen men

חֲמֵשׁ עֶשְׂרֵה נֶפֶשׁ   15 persons (rem.: נֶפֶשׁ is fem.)

With other nouns the plural is regularly used.

165. Vocabulary 45.

VERBS: הוֹשִׁיב   to cause to dwell; to settle (someone in a place) (cf. יָשַׁב)

הוֹרִיד   to bring (lead, take) down (cf. יָרַד)

הוֹלִיד   to beget, engender (cf. יָלַד)

הוֹדִיעַ   to cause to know; to teach (someone); to declare or proclaim (something) (cf. יָדַע)

הוֹצִיא   to bring (lead, take) out (cf. יָצָא)

הוֹלִיךְ   to cause to go; to lead (cf. הָלַךְ)

הוֹסִיף   to do again; to continue doing something. Two constructions are frequent:

הוֹסִיף לָצוּם   he fasted again, continued to fast

הוֹסִיף וַיָּצָם   he fasted again, continued to fast

In the second construction the verbs are simply coordinated

in Hebrew. The verb may also have the meaning "to add"
but the actual translation value depends on the context:

וְהוֹסַפְתִּי עַל־יָמֶיךָ חֲמֵשׁ עֶשְׂרֵה שָׁנָה — I shall add to your days fifteen years

הוֹסַפְתָּ חָכְמָה... אֶל־הַשְּׁמוּעָה אֲשֶׁר שָׁמַעְתִּי — You are wiser than you are reputed to be. (lit.: You have added wisdom to the report I have heard.)

Note also the common phrase (exclamatory, asseverative):

כֹּה יַעֲשֶׂה לִי יהוה וְכֹה יוֹסִף — May God do thus for me, and even more so (if such-and-such is/is-not true).

הוֹשִׁיעַ — to save, deliver
הוֹכִיחַ — to reprove; to decide
קִנֵּא — to be jealous (אֶת־ or בְּ + person); to be zealous (לְ: for)

NOUNS:
פֶּסֶל — (pl. irreg. פְּסִילִים) idol, image
אֵל — (pl. -îm) god; God (w. or without article)
שָׁוְא — emptiness, vanity; לַשָּׁוְא in vain, for nothing
גֵּר — (pl. -îm) sojourner, resident alien
שׁוֹר — a head of cattle (a singular corresponding to the collective בָּקָר)

OTHER:
מִמַּעַל — (adv.) above; + לְ (=prep.)
מִתַּחַת — (adv.) below; + לְ (=prep.)

Exercises:

(a) Translate:

(1) אֶת־הָרְשָׁעִים הוֹשִׁיב בַּחֹשֶׁךְ וְאֶת־הַצַּדִּיקִים הוֹלִיךְ בְּאוֹר פָּנָיו.
(2) הוֹלִיךְ אֹתִי בְדַרְכֵי עֳנִי וְלֹא שָׁמַע לְקוֹלִי בְּקָרְאִי אֵלָיו.
(3) לֹא אוֹסִיף עוֹד לַעֲשׂוֹת חֶסֶד עִמָּכֶם.
(4) וַיּוֹדַע אֹתִי אֶת־הָאֹתוֹת וְאֶת־הַנִּפְלָאוֹת אֲשֶׁר יֵעָשׂוּ בַּיָּמִים הָהֵם.
(5) אֱלֹהִים הוּא הַמּוֹצִיא אֹתָנוּ מֵאֶרֶץ מְעַנֵּינוּ.
(6) וַיּוֹלֶד בֵּן לִזְקוּנָיו וְהַיֶּלֶד שִׂמַּח אֶת־לֵב אָבִיו עַד־קֵץ יָמָיו.
(7) וַיּוֹרֶד אֶת־אָבִיו וְאֶת־אֶחָיו מִצְרַיְמָה.
(8) הוֹשִׁיעָה אֹתָנוּ יהוה וּפְקָדָה אֹתָנוּ כַּאֲשֶׁר דִּבַּרְתָּ.
(9) לֹא אוֹכִיחַ אֶתְכֶם עַל־חַטַּאת בְּנֵיכֶם.
(10) הַגֶּשׁ־נָא אֶת־סִפְרִי וְאֶקְרָאָה אֵלֶיךָ אֶת־הַדְּבָרִים אֲשֶׁר בָּם.
(11) וְעָשִׂיתָ נָּא עִמָּדִי חֶסֶד וְהִזְכַּרְתָּ אֹתִי אֶל־פַּרְעֹה וְהוֹצֵאתָ אֹתִי מִבֵּית הָאֲסִירִים הַזֶּה.
(12) לַשָּׁוְא דִּבַּרְתִּי אֲלֵיכֶם כִּי לֹא שְׁמַעְתֶּם אֶת־דְּבָרִי.
(13) אַל־תִּתֵּן אֶת־הַגֵּרִים לָבוֹא הַהֵיכָל כִּי מְקוֹם קֹדֶשׁ הוּא.
(14) וַיִּבְחַר שְׁלֹשָׁה עָשָׂר אִישׁ וַיַּקְרֵב אֹתָם אֶל־הָעִיר.
(15) וַיְקַנְאוּ אֹתוֹ אֶחָיו כִּי אֲבִיהֶם אָהַב אֹתוֹ מִכָּל־אֶחָיו.
(16) לֹא תוֹסִיפוּ לִתְעוֹת כִּי אוֹדִיעַ לָכֶם אֶת־הַדָּרֶךְ.
(17) לֹא יָכֹלְנוּ לְנַחֵם אֹתָהּ אַחֲרֵי מוֹת אִישָׁהּ.

(b) Write in Hebrew:

1. He begot seventeen sons during his lifetime.

2. They settled the people in twelve small cities near the great river.

3. We defiled their holy place and brought out the fifteen large stones that they had set up there.

4. When he saw the flame of the fire, he ran out of the house without his clothes and shoes (= circum. clause: "and his clothes and shoes [were] not with him").

5. Now that my days on earth are finished, I charge these eighteen persons to you so that you may be a help and a comforter to them.

6. And after that he left the house of his father-in-law and set forth with this people as a sojourner in their midst.

(c) Reading: The Ten Commandments (Ex. 20:1–14):

(1) וַיְדַבֵּר אֱלֹהִים אֵת כָּל־הַדְּבָרִים הָאֵלֶּה לֵאמֹר:

(2) אָנֹכִי יהוה אֱלֹהֶיךָ אֲשֶׁר הוֹצֵאתִיךָ¹ מֵאֶרֶץ מִצְרַיִם מִבֵּית עֲבָדִים:²

(3) לֹא יִהְיֶה־לְךָ אֱלֹהִים אֲחֵרִים עַל־פָּנָי:

(4) לֹא תַעֲשֶׂה־לְךָ פֶסֶל וְכָל־תְּמוּנָה³ אֲשֶׁר בַּשָּׁמַיִם מִמַּעַל וַאֲשֶׁר בָּאָרֶץ מִתָּחַת וַאֲשֶׁר בַּמַּיִם מִתַּחַת לָאָרֶץ:

(5) לֹא־תִשְׁתַּחֲוֶה⁴ לָהֶם וְלֹא תָעָבְדֵם⁵ כִּי אָנֹכִי יהוה אֱלֹהֶיךָ אֵל קַנָּא⁶ פֹּקֵד עֲוֹן אָבֹת עַל־בָּנִים עַל־שִׁלֵּשִׁים⁷ וְעַל־רִבֵּעִים לְשֹׂנְאָי:

(6) וְעֹשֶׂה חֶסֶד לַאֲלָפִים⁸ לְאֹהֲבַי וּלְשֹׁמְרֵי מִצְוֹתָי:

(7) לֹא תִשָּׂא⁹ אֶת־שֵׁם־יהוה אֱלֹהֶיךָ לַשָּׁוְא כִּי לֹא יְנַקֶּה יהוה אֵת אֲשֶׁר־יִשָּׂא אֶת־שְׁמוֹ לַשָּׁוְא:

(8) זָכוֹר אֶת־יוֹם הַשַּׁבָּת לְקַדְּשׁוֹ:¹⁰

(9) שֵׁשֶׁת יָמִים תַּעֲבֹד וְעָשִׂיתָ כָּל־מְלַאכְתֶּךָ:

(10) וְיוֹם הַשְּׁבִיעִי שַׁבָּת לַיהוה אֱלֹהֶיךָ לֹא־תַעֲשֶׂה כָל־מְלָאכָה אַתָּה וּבִנְךָ־וּבִתֶּךָ עַבְדְּךָ וַאֲמָתְךָ וּבְהֶמְתֶּךָ וְגֵרְךָ אֲשֶׁר בִּשְׁעָרֶיךָ:

(11) כִּי שֵׁשֶׁת־יָמִים עָשָׂה יהוה אֶת־הַשָּׁמַיִם וְאֶת־הָאָרֶץ אֶת־הַיָּם וְאֶת־כָּל־אֲשֶׁר־בָּם וַיָּנַח¹¹ בַּיּוֹם הַשְּׁבִיעִי עַל־כֵּן בֵּרַךְ יהוה אֶת־יוֹם הַשַּׁבָּת וַיְקַדְּשֵׁהוּ:¹²

(12) כַּבֵּד אֶת־אָבִיךָ וְאֶת־אִמֶּךָ לְמַעַן יַאֲרִכוּן יָמֶיךָ עַל הָאֲדָמָה אֲשֶׁר יהוה אֱלֹהֶיךָ נֹתֵן לָךְ:

(13) לֹא תִרְצָח: לֹא תִנְאָף:¹³ לֹא תִגְנֹב: לֹא־תַעֲנֶה¹⁴ בְרֵעֲךָ עֵד¹⁵ שָׁקֶר:

(14) לֹא תַחְמֹד¹⁶ בֵּית רֵעֶךָ לֹא־תַחְמֹד אֵשֶׁת רֵעֶךָ וְעַבְדּוֹ וַאֲמָתוֹ וְשׁוֹרוֹ וַחֲמֹרוֹ וְכֹל אֲשֶׁר לְרֵעֶךָ:

Notes to the Reading:

1. = הוֹצֵאתִי אֹתְךָ
2. A plural noun used as an abstract: "bondage"
3. תְּמוּנָה "likeness"
4. "You shall (not) bow down"
5. = תַּעֲבֹד אֹתָם
6. קַנָּא (adj.) "jealous"
7. See §161c.
8. אֶלֶף "thousand"
9. נָשָׂא here = "to utter" (prob. in an oath); נִקָּה to absolve, regard as innocent
10. The suffix is objective.
11. "And he rested"
12. = וַיְקַדֵּשׁ אֹתוֹ

13. נָאַף "to commit adultery"

14. עָנָה בְּ "to testify against; to bring as testimony against"

15. עֵד "witness, testimony" שֶׁקֶר "falsehood"

16. חָמַד "to desire, covet"

166. Hiphil Verbs: Stems and Inflection (cont.).

The stems of Hiphil verbs from roots III-*Hē* are as follows:

Root Type	Perfect	Imperfect	Jussive	Imperative	Inf. Construct	Participle
III-*Hē*	הִרְבָּה	יַרְבֶּה	יֶ֫רֶב	הַרְבֵּה	הַרְבּוֹת	מַרְבֶּה
Also I-gutt.	הֶעֱלָה	יַעֲלֶה	יַ֫עַל	הַעֲלֵה	הַעֲלוֹת	מַעֲלֶה
Also I-*Yodh*	הוֹרָה	יוֹרֶה	יוֹר	הוֹרֵה	הוֹרוֹת	מוֹרֶה
Also I-*Nun*	הִכָּה	יַכֶּה	יַ֫ךְ	הַכֵּה	הַכּוֹת	מַכֶּה

Remarks: Note that the otherwise characteristic long vowel *î* of Hiphil verbs is not present in these forms. The stem endings and their inflection are virtually the same as that learned for all other verbs from roots III-*Hē* (cf. בָּנָה, נִבְנָה, עָנָה); only the beginning of the form marks it clearly as a Hiphil verb.

The inflection is given below only in abbreviated form because of the similarities to other verbs already mentioned. Note that in the perfect the stem vowel before the suffixes beginning with a consonant is either *ê* or *î*:

PERFECT: הִרְבָּה   IMPERFECT: יַרְבֶּה   IMPERATIVE: הַרְבֵּה
    הִרְבְּתָה   . . .   הַרְבִּי
    הִרְבֵּ֫יתָ)   תַּרְבִּי   הַרְבּוּ
    הִרְבִּ֫ית)   . . .   הַרְבֶּ֫ינָה
       etc.   תַּרְבֶּ֫ינָה
                 etc.

INFINITIVE CONSTRUCT: הַרְבּוֹתְךָ ,הַרְבּוֹתִי ,הַרְבּוֹת, etc.
INFINITIVE ABSOLUTE: הַרְבֵּה
PARTICIPLE: מַרְבֶּה מַרְבָּה מַרְבִּים מַרְבּוֹת

The verbs הֶעֱלָה ,הוֹרָה, and הִכָּה illustrate various combinations of root types. Their inflection is like that of הִרְבָּה.

The jussive forms, like those of the Qal verbs from roots III-*Hē*, show the loss of the final stem vowel *(-eh)* and the resultant secondary vowel: *yarbeh > *yarb > yéreḇ*. Hiphil verbs, then, are distinguished from Qal verbs only by having *é* and not *i* or *ē* in the first syllable of the jussive (and converted) form:

QAL: וַיִּ֫בֶן and he built   וַתֶּ֫רֶב and it (f.) grew numerous
HIPHIL: וַיֶּ֫בֶן and he caused to build   וַתֶּ֫רֶב and it (f.) caused to grow numerous

When the root is I-guttural as well, there is no distinction:

וַיַּ֫עַל   QAL: and he went up   or   HIPHIL: and he led up

Note that in the jussive form of הִכָּה (root נכה) the expected *yakk (<yakkeh)* becomes יַךְ *yak* by the regular loss of doubling at the end of a word. Compare the Qal verb יִטֶּה (he will extend), jussive יֵט.

Occasionally *e* is found instead of *i* in the preformative of the perfect:

הֶרְאָה   to cause to see
הֶגְלָה   to lead into exile

The infinitive absolute הַרְבֵּה (from הִרְבָּה to increase, cause to be numerous) is commonly used as an adverb "very, much," sometimes with an added מְאֹד:

וַתֵּבְךְּ הַרְבֵּה מְאֹד   and she wept very much

167. The Numbers from 21–99.

Because the tens are not inflected for gender, the combination of these with the units (21, 22, etc.) is not unduly complicated. The unit may precede or follow the ten, but agrees in gender with the modified noun, which is usually in the singular.

עֶשְׂרִים וְאֶחָד אִישׁ or	אֶחָד וְעֶשְׂרִים אִישׁ	21 men
שְׁלֹשִׁים וּשְׁנַ֫יִם אִישׁ or	שְׁנַ֫יִם וּשְׁלֹשִׁים אִישׁ	32 men
	אַרְבָּעִים וְשָׁלוֹשׁ אִשָּׁה	43 women
	חֲמִשִּׁים וְשֵׁשׁ נֶ֫פֶשׁ	56 persons

If the counted item is placed before the numeral it may be in the plural:

אֲנָשִׁים שְׁלֹשִׁים וְאֶחָד   31 men

168. Vocabulary 46.

VERBS:

הֶרְאָה   to cause to see; to show (cf. רָאָה)

הִכָּה   to strike, smite, kill (root נכה)

הוֹדָה   to give thanks. In the imperfect the *h* is sometimes anomalously retained: יוֹדֶה = יְהוֹדֶה. (root ידה)

הִשְׁקָה   to give water to, to cause to drink; used as the causative of שָׁתָה.

הוֹרָה   to shoot (arrows); to direct, teach (root ירה)

הֶעֱלָה   to lead (take, bring) up (cf. עָלָה)

גָּלָה   (יִגְלֶה) to uncover, reveal; to go into exile; גָּלָה אֶת־אָזְנִי he informed me.

הִגְלָה   to carry away into exile

לָמַד   (יִלְמַד) to learn

לִמֵּד   (יְלַמֵּד) to teach

רָבָה   (יִרְבֶּה) to be(come) numerous; to be great

הִרְבָּה   to increase (tr.); make numerous

NOUNS:

חֹק   (w. suff. חֻקִּי; pl. -*îm*) statute

חֻקָּה   (pl. -*ôṯ*) statute

מִשְׁפָּט   (pl. -*îm*) judgement; court decision

לֵבָב   (pl. -*ôṯ*) a synonym of לֵב heart.

Exercises:

(a) For each of the following jussive and converted forms first give the corresponding normal imperfect and then the perfect. Translate. E.g.

יֵרֶב ← יַרְבֶּה ← הִרְבָּה

(11) יַשֵּׂג	(6) יֵתַע	(1) וַיּוֹשֶׁב
(12) יְעַן	(7) יִגֶל	(2) יְקַר
(13) יוֹר	(8) יְכֵל	(3) וַיּוֹדַע
(14) וַיּוֹסֶף	(9) יַעַן	(4) יֵשְׁק
(15) יַךְ	(10) וַיּוֹשַׁע	(5) יַעַל

(b) Translate:

(1) וַיַּךְ אֶת־הַמִּצְרִי וַיַּהַרְג אֹתוֹ וַיִּקְבֹּר אֹתוֹ פֶּן־יִמָּצֵא.

(2) הוֹדוּ לוֹ, בָּרְכוּ אֶת־שְׁמוֹ, כִּי טוֹב יהוה, לְעוֹלָם חַסְדּוֹ.

(3) בָּאוּ אֶל־הָעַיִן לְמַעַן הַשְׁקוֹת אֶת־צֹאנָם.

(4) וְהוֹרֵיתִי אֶתְכֶם אֶת־הַדֶּרֶךְ הַטּוֹב וְהַיָּשָׁר.

(5) וְאַתָּה תַעֲלֶה אֶת־עַמִּי אַרְצָה כְנָעַן.

(6) וַיהוה גָּלָה אֶת־אֹזֶן הַנָּבִיא יוֹם אֶחָד לִפְנֵי בוֹא הַמֶּלֶךְ.

(7) יוֹדוּ שִׁמְךָ כִּי קָדוֹשׁ אַתָּה.

(8) גָּלָה כְבוֹד יִשְׂרָאֵל.

(9) לַמֵּד אֹתִי אֶת־חֻקֶּיךָ וְאֶהְיֶה לְאִישׁ צַדִּיק.

(10) מַדּוּעַ הִכִּיתָ אֶת־הַגֵּר לַהֲרֹג אֹתוֹ.

[229]

(11) לְכוּ וְנַהַרְגָה אֹתָם פֶּן־יִרְבּוּ וְנִלְחֲמוּ בָּנוּ.

(12) נָס הָעָם מִן־הַמִּלְחָמָה וְגַם־הַרְבֵּה נָפַל מִן־הָעָם.

(13) וַיְצַו אֹתָנוּ לַעֲשׂוֹת אֶת־כָּל־הַחֻקִּים הָאֵלֶּה.

(14) שָׁלַח אֶת־הָאִישׁ לִפְנֵיהֶם לְהוֹרוֹת אֹתָם אֶת־הַדֶּרֶךְ.

(15) יִשְׁמְעוּ וְלָמְדוּ לְיִרְאָה אֶת־יהוה.

(16) אַרְבֶּה אֹתְךָ עַל־פְּנֵי הָאָרֶץ וְהָיִיתָ לְעַם גָּדוֹל וְחָזָק.

(17) וְקִרְעוּ לְבַבְכֶם וְאַל־בִּגְדֵיכֶם וְשׁוּבוּ אֶל־יהוה אֱלֹהֵיכֶם.

(18) יהוה אֲשֶׁר עָשָׂה אֶת־מֹשֶׁה וַאֲשֶׁר הֶעֱלָה אֶת־אֲבֹתֵיכֶם מֵאֶרֶץ מִצְרָיִם.

(19) וַיֶּגֶל אֶת־יֹשְׁבֵי יְרוּשָׁלַ͏ִם אֶל־אֶרֶץ רְחוֹקָה.

(c) Write in Hebrew:

1. I shall give thanks to the Lord.
2. They led us into exile.
3. Teach me so that I may know your (m. s.) many wonders.
4. Deliver us from the hands of our enemies.
5. When he hears about this matter, he will be jealous.
6. You have served them in vain, for they will not give you help.
7. The Lord will reprove his people.

(d) Reading: Deuteronomy 6 : 1–9.

(1) וְזֹאת הַמִּצְוָה הַחֻקִּים וְהַמִּשְׁפָּטִים אֲשֶׁר צִוָּה יהוה אֱלֹהֵיכֶם לְלַמֵּד אֶתְכֶם לַעֲשׂוֹת בָּאָרֶץ אֲשֶׁר אַתֶּם עֹבְרִים שָׁמָּה לְרִשְׁתָּהּ:¹

(2) לְמַעַן תִּירָא אֶת־יהוה אֱלֹהֶיךָ לִשְׁמֹר אֶת־כָּל־חֻקֹּתָיו וּמִצְוֹתָיו אֲשֶׁר אָנֹכִי מְצַוֶּךָ² אַתָּה וּבִנְךָ וּבֶן־בִּנְךָ כֹּל יְמֵי חַיֶּיךָ וּלְמַעַן יַאֲרִכֻן יָמֶיךָ:

(3) וְשָׁמַעְתָּ יִשְׂרָאֵל וְשָׁמַרְתָּ לַעֲשׂוֹת אֲשֶׁר יִיטַב לְךָ וַאֲשֶׁר³ תִּרְבּוּן מְאֹד כַּאֲשֶׁר דִּבֶּר יהוה אֱלֹהֵי אֲבֹתֶיךָ לָךְ אֶרֶץ⁴ זָבַת חָלָב וּדְבָשׁ:

(4) שְׁמַע יִשְׂרָאֵל יהוה אֱלֹהֵינוּ יהוה אֶחָד:

(5) וְאָהַבְתָּ אֵת יהוה אֱלֹהֶיךָ בְּכָל־לְבָבְךָ וּבְכָל־נַפְשְׁךָ וּבְכָל־מְאֹדֶךָ:⁵

(6) וְהָיוּ הַדְּבָרִים הָאֵלֶּה אֲשֶׁר אָנֹכִי מְצַוְּךָ² הַיּוֹם עַל־לְבָבֶךָ:

(7) וְשִׁנַּנְתָּם⁶ לְבָנֶיךָ וְדִבַּרְתָּ בָּם בְּשִׁבְתְּךָ בְּבֵיתֶךָ וּבְלֶכְתְּךָ בַדֶּרֶךְ וּבְשָׁכְבְּךָ וּבְקוּמֶךָ:

(8) וּקְשַׁרְתָּם⁷ לְאוֹת עַל־יָדֶךָ וְהָיוּ לְטֹטָפֹת⁸ בֵּין עֵינֶיךָ:

(9) וּכְתַבְתָּם עַל־מְזוּזֹת⁹ בֵּיתֶךָ וּבִשְׁעָרֶיךָ:

Notes to the Reading:

1. The suffix is objective.
2. מְצַוֶּה אֹתְךָ =
3. Both אֲשֶׁר 's are used as compound relatives: "that which… and that (by) which…"
4. The phrase "a land flow-ing…" is rather loosely attached to what pre-cedes it.
5. מְאֹד is a noun here: "strength".
6. "You shall teach them"
7. וְקִשַׁרְתָּ אֹתָם =
8. "bands, frontlet-bands"
9. מְזוּזָה "door-post"

169. Hiphil Verbs: Stems and Inflection (cont.).

The Qal distinction between roots II-*Waw* (יָקוּם) and roots II-*Yodh* (יָשִׂים) is not maintained in the Hiphil verbs derived from these same roots. The forms given for הֵקִים (from the root of קָם) are standard.

Root Type	Perfect	Imperfect	Jussive	Imperative	Inf. Constr.	Participle
Hollow (II-Waw/Yodh)	הֵקִים	יָקִים	יָקֵם	הָקֵם	הָקִים	מֵקִים
Also III-gutt.	הֵנִיחַ	יָנִיחַ	יָנַח	הָנַח	הָנִיחַ	מֵנִיחַ
Also III-*Aleph*	הֵבִיא	יָבִיא	יָבֵא	הָבֵא	הָבִיא	מֵבִיא

Note that the participle has the same preformative vowel as the perfect. This stands in contrast to all other Hiphil verbs studied up to this point. The presence of a guttural (other than א) in final root position has the same effect it has in הִשְׁמִיעַ. For הָבִיא compare הִמְצִיא.

In the inflection of the perfect there are two distinct paradigms, one with the linking vowel -ô- and one without:

I   II

I		II	
הֵקִים	הֵקִֿימוּ	הֵקִים	הֵקִֿימוּ
הֵקִֿימָה		הֵקִֿימָה	
הֲקִימֿוֹתָ	הֲקִימוֹתֶם	הֲקִמְתָּ	הֲקַמְתֶּם
הֲקִימוֹת	הֲקִימוֹתֶן	הֲקִמְתְּ	הֲקַמְתֶּן
הֲקִימֿוֹתִי	הֲקִימֿוֹנוּ	הֲקִמְתִּי	הֲקִמְנוּ

Paradigm I is by far the more frequent.

The very common verb הֵבִיא (to bring; root בוא) is usually inflected according to paradigm II: הֵבִיא, הֵבִיאָה, הֵבֵאתָ, etc.

The imperfect and the remaining forms follow a single inflectional pattern; note the retraction of stress and the vowel replacement in the converted imperfect:

IMPERFECT:		JUSSIVE:		IMPERATIVE:
יָקִים יָקִימוּ		וַיָּ֫קֶם יָקֵם		הָקֵם
תָּקִים תְּקִימֶ֫ינָה		וַתָּ֫קֶם תָּקֵם		הָקִ֫ימִי
תָּקִים תָּקִ֫ימוּ				הָקִ֫ימוּ
תָּקִ֫ימִי תְּקִימֶ֫ינָה				⸻
אָקִים נָקִים				

INF. CONSTRUCT: הָקִים, הֲקִימִי, הֲקִימְךָ, etc.

INF. ABSOLUTE: הָקֵם

PARTICIPLE: מֵקִים, מְקִימָה, מְקִימִים, מְקִימוֹת

170. An Idiomatic Use of הָלַךְ.

In the example:

(a) וַיֵּ֫לֶךְ הָלוֹךְ וְאָכוֹל   And he walked along eating.

the inf. absolute הָלוֹךְ is used in accordance with the construction studied in §129 and may be taken as modifying or supplementing the main verb of the clause, with which it is cognate. But in

(b) וַיָּשֻׁ֫בוּ הַמַּ֫יִם הָלוֹךְ וָשׁוֹב   And the waters receded *gradually* (Gen. 8:3)

the idiomatic use of הָלוֹךְ is clear, since a literal translation is impossible. More explicitly, if the first of two infinitives absolute in the construction instanced above is הָלוֹךְ, there is a nuance of continuous or gradual action.

Closely related to this is a parallel use of the participle הֹלֵךְ; the basic idiom is:

subject + הֹלֵךְ + { a second participle / an adjective

(c) הַיָּם הֹלֵךְ וְסֹעֵר   The sea (was) growing more and more tempestuous.

(d) דָּוִד הֹלֵךְ וְגָדוֹל   David was growing more and more important.

Now, in transforming a participial clause into a verbal one, the usual result is (for past tense):

הָאִישׁ הֹלֵךְ →   וַיֵּ֫לֶךְ הָאִישׁ

The man is going.   The man went.

This same transformation was applied to the idiom cited in (c) and (d):

(e)   וַיֵּ֫לֶךְ הַיָּם הָלוֹךְ וְסָעֹר   The sea grew more and more tempestuous.

(f)   וַיֵּ֫לֶךְ דָּוִד הָלוֹךְ וְגָדוֹל   David grew more and more important.

The verb הָלַךְ is taken as the main verb and is repeated, now as an infinitive absolute in the manner of (b) above to express the idea of continuity. But although (e) and (f) correspond to (b) in construction, their meaning can be gained only from a knowledge of the idiom in (c) and (d): "the sea grew..." and *not* "the sea went..."; "David grew (or became)..." and *not* "David went...".

As a further example take the sentence:

(g)   וַתֵּ֫לֶךְ יַד בְּנֵי־יִשְׂרָאֵל הָלוֹךְ וְקָשָׁה עַל־מֶ֫לֶךְ כְּנַ֫עַן   (cf. Judges 4:24)

Assuming a basic idiomatic construction:

*(g)   יַד בְּנֵי־יִשְׂרָאֵל הֹלֶ֫כֶת וְקָשָׁה עַל־מֶ֫לֶךְ כְּנַ֫עַן

the obvious translation (and the correct one) of (g) is "The strength of the Israelites grew more and more severe against the king of Canaan."

These constructions, though not too frequent, are troublesome unless understood properly.

171. Vocabulary 47.

VERBS: זָנָה (יִזְנֶה) to be a prostitute; to act wantonly. זֹנָה a prostitute.

מִהַר (יְמַהֵר) to hurry; the inf. abs. מַהֵר is used as an adverb: quickly.

עָרַךְ (יַעֲרֹךְ) to arrange, set in order; draw up (in battle array).

הֶחֱרִים (יַחֲרִים) to destroy, exterminate (often as a religious act of banning).

הֵכִין (יָכִין) to make ready, prepare; establish (cf. נָכוֹן).

הֵבִין (יָבִין) to perceive, consider, understand; to cause to understand (cf. בִּינָה).

הֵסִיר (יָסִיר) to remove, take away, turn away (tr.) (cf. סָר).

נָח (יָנוּחַ) to rest; to settle down. There are two Hiphil verbs related to this Qal verb: (1) הֵנִיחַ (יָנִיחַ) to cause to rest, set at rest; (2) הִנִּיחַ (יַנִּיחַ) to set down, deposit, leave alone.

רָם (יָרוּם) to be high, lofty; הֵרִים (יָרִים) to lift up, lift off.

הֵשִׁיב (יָשִׁיב) to bring (lead, take) back (cf. שָׁב)

הֵבִיא (יָבִיא) to bring (cf. בָּא)

NOUNS: גַּג (w. suff. גַּגִּי; pl. ôṯ) roof

PROPER NAMES: יְהוֹשֻׁעַ בֶּן־נוּן Joshua, the son of Nun.

יְרִחוֹ Jericho, an important city at the lower end of the Jordan valley.

שִׁטִּים an unidentified site across the Jordan from Jericho, where the Israelites camped before crossing the river.

רָחָב Rahab, a prostitute in Jericho.

סִיחֹן Sihon, a king of Heshbon (east of the Jordan) whom, together with Og, king of Bashan, the Israelites defeated in their passage to Canaan.

עוֹג Og (see Sihon above).

Exercises:

(a) Translate:

(1) הָבֵא אֹתוֹ הֵנָּה.   (6) הָשֵׁב אֹתָם אֵלַי.

(2) הַנַּח אֹתוֹ שָׁם.   (7) הָנַח לָנוּ.

(3) הָסִירוּ אֹתוֹ מֵעַל הַשֻּׁלְחָן.   (8) הָרִימוּ אֶת־הָאֲבָנִים.

(4) הָבִינוּ לִי מְעַט לֶאֱכֹל.   (9) הָבִיאִי אֵלֵינוּ מַיִם וָלֶחֶם.

(5) הַבִּיחוּ אֶת־סְפָרַי פֹּה.   (10) מַהֲרוּ כִּי הֵמָּה רֹדְפִים אַחֲרֵינוּ.

(b) Negate each of the imperative sentences in (a): Ex. אַל־תָּבִיא (תָּבֵא) אֹתוֹ הֵנָּה

(c) Translate:

(1) הֵבֵאתִי אֶת־מִנְחָתִי.   (6) הֲרִימֹתִי אֶת־קוֹלִי וָאֵבְךְּ.

(2) הֵסִירוּ אֶת־פְּנֵיהֶם.   (7) הֵשִׁיב אֹתָנוּ אֶל־אַרְצֵנוּ.

(3) הֲכִינוֹתִי אֶת־הַבַּיִת לָכֶם.   (8) הֶחֱרִימוּ אֶת־עָרֵי הָאֹיְבִים.

(4) הִנַּחְנוּ אֶת־הַזָּהָב אֵצֶל הַכֵּלִים.   (9) עָרַכְנוּ אֶת־הָאֲבָנִים עַל־שְׂפַת הַנָּהָר.

(5) הֵבִין אֶת־דִּבְרֵי הַחֲכָמִים.   (10) מִהֲרָה לִקְרָאתִי.

(d) Convert each of the sentences in (c) to a sequential form: Ex. וָאָבִיא אֶת־מִנְחָתִי

(e) Translate:

(1) יהוה בַּשָּׁמַיִם הֵכִין כִּסְאוֹ.

(2) וְגַם אֶל־שֹׁפְטֵיהֶם לֹא שָׁמֵעוּ כִּי זָנוּ אַחֲרֵי אֱלֹהִים אֲחֵרִים.

(3) אֵיפֹה הִנַּחְתָּ אֶת־כְּלֵי הַמִּזְבֵּחַ.

(4) יִרְאֶה הָעָם בְּעֵינָיו וּבְאָזְנָיו יִשְׁמַע וּלְבָבוֹ יָבִין וְשָׁב אֵלַי.

(5) וַיְהִי כַהֲרִימוֹ אֶת־מַטֵּהוּ וַיָּדֹם הָעָם.

(6) מַדּוּעַ לֹא תָשִׁיב אֹתָנוּ אֶל־עִירֵנוּ וְאֶל־עַמֵּנוּ.

(7) סוּרוּ מִדֶּרֶךְ הָרְשָׁעִים וְשִׁמְרוּ אֶת־תּוֹרוֹתַי אֶת־חֻקּוֹתַי וְאֶת־מִצְוֹתַי לַעֲשׂוֹת אוֹתָן כָּל־יְמֵי חַיֵּיכֶם.

(8) אָז תָּבִין צֶדֶק וּמִשְׁפָּט כִּי תָבוֹא חָכְמָה בְלִבֶּךְ וְהָיִיתָ לְאִישׁ יָשָׁר.

(9) לֹא הֵבִינוּ אֶת־עֲצָתִי וְלֹא שָׁמְעוּ בְקוֹלִי.

(10) יַעַן אֲשֶׁר הֲרִימֹתִי אֹתְךָ מִתּוֹךְ הָעָם וָאֶתֵּן אֹתְךָ רֹאשׁ עַל־עַמִּי וָאֶתֵּן אִתְּךָ וְלֹא הָיִיתָ כְעַבְדִּי דָוִד אֲשֶׁר שָׁמַר אֶת־מִצְוֹתַי וַאֲשֶׁר הָלַךְ אַחֲרַי בְּכָל־לְבָבוֹ לַעֲשׂוֹת רַק הַיָּשָׁר בְּעֵינַי, וַתַּעַשׂ הָרַע בְּעֵינַי וְאוֹתִי הִשְׁלַכְתָּ אַחֲרֶיךָ הִנְנִי מֵבִיא רָעָה עַל־בֵּיתֶךָ וּבִעַרְתִּי אַחֲרֶיךָ עַד־תֻּמְּךָ.

(f) Translate into Hebrew:

1. He will give rest to his people when he has settled them in the new city.
2. I brought them to the place I had prepared for them and left them there.
3. Where did the men prepare the camp?
4. I shall go with you and give you rest.
5. Do not raise your voice lest they hear and come and slay us.
6. As he led us into exile, thus will he bring us back.
7. He will teach us many new songs so that we may give thanks to the Lord.

(g) Reading: Rahab and the Spies (Joshua 2 : 1–11).

(1) וַיִּשְׁלַח יְהוֹשֻׁעַ בִּן־נוּן מִן־הַשִּׁטִּים שְׁנַֽיִם אֲנָשִׁים מְרַגְּלִים חֶֽרֶשׁ¹ לֵאמֹר לְכוּ רְאוּ אֶת־
הָאָֽרֶץ וְאֶת־יְרִיחוֹ וַיֵּלְכוּ וַיָּבֹֽאוּ בֵּית־אִשָּׁה זוֹנָה וּשְׁמָהּ רָחָב וַיִּשְׁכְּבוּ־שָֽׁמָּה:

(2) וַיֵּאָמַר לְמֶֽלֶךְ יְרִיחוֹ לֵאמֹר הִנֵּה אֲנָשִׁים בָּֽאוּ הֵֽנָּה הַלַּֽיְלָה מִבְּנֵי יִשְׂרָאֵל לַחְפֹּר² אֶת־הָאָֽרֶץ:

(3) וַיִּשְׁלַח מֶֽלֶךְ יְרִיחוֹ אֶל־רָחָב לֵאמֹר הוֹצִֽיאִי הָאֲנָשִׁים הַבָּאִים אֵלַֽיִךְ אֲשֶׁר־בָּֽאוּ לְבֵיתֵךְ
כִּי לַחְפֹּר אֶת־כָּל־הָאָֽרֶץ בָּֽאוּ:

(4) וַתִּקַּח הָאִשָּׁה אֶת־שְׁנֵי הָאֲנָשִׁים וַתִּצְפְּנוֹ³ וַתֹּֽאמֶר כֵּן בָּֽאוּ אֵלַי הָאֲנָשִׁים וְלֹא יָדַֽעְתִּי
מֵאַֽיִן הֵֽמָּה:

(5) וַיְהִי הַשַּֽׁעַר לִסְגּוֹר בַּחֹֽשֶׁךְ וְהָאֲנָשִׁים יָצָֽאוּ לֹא יָדַֽעְתִּי אָֽנָה הָלְכוּ הָאֲנָשִׁים רִדְפוּ מַהֵר
אַחֲרֵיהֶם כִּי תַשִּׂיגוּם⁴:

(6) וְהִיא הֶעֱלָֽתַם⁵ הַגָּֽגָה וַתִּטְמְנֵם⁶ בְּפִשְׁתֵּי הָעֵץ⁷ הָעֲרֻכוֹת לָהּ עַל־הַגָּֽג:

(7) וְהָאֲנָשִׁים רָדְפוּ אַחֲרֵיהֶם דֶּֽרֶךְ⁸ הַיַּרְדֵּן עַל הַמַּעְבְּרוֹת⁹ וְהַשַּֽׁעַר סָגֽרוּ אַחֲרֵי כַּאֲשֶׁר יָצְֽאוּ
הָרֹדְפִים אַחֲרֵיהֶם:

(8) וְהֵֽמָּה טֶֽרֶם יִשְׁכָּבוּן וְהִיא עָלְתָה עֲלֵיהֶם עַל־הַגָּֽג:

(9) וַתֹּֽאמֶר אֶל־הָאֲנָשִׁים יָדַֽעְתִּי כִּי־נָתַן יהוה לָכֶם אֶת־הָאָֽרֶץ וְכִי נָפְלָה אֵימַתְכֶם עָלֵֽינוּ
וְכִי נָמֹֽגוּ¹⁰ כָּל־יֹשְׁבֵי הָאָֽרֶץ מִפְּנֵיכֶם:

(10) כִּי שָׁמַֽעְנוּ אֵת¹¹ אֲשֶׁר־הוֹבִישׁ¹² יהוה אֶת־מֵי יַם־סוּף¹³ מִפְּנֵיכֶם בְּצֵאתְכֶם מִמִּצְרָֽיִם וַאֲשֶׁר¹⁴
עֲשִׂיתֶם לִשְׁנֵי מַלְכֵי הָאֱמֹרִי¹⁵ אֲשֶׁר בְּעֵֽבֶר¹⁶ הַיַּרְדֵּן לְסִיחֹן וּלְעוֹג אֲשֶׁר הֶחֱרַמְתֶּם אֹתָם:

(11) וַנִּשְׁמַע וַיִּמַּס לְבָבֵֽנוּ וְלֹא קָֽמָה עוֹד רֽוּחַ בְּאִישׁ מִפְּנֵיכֶם כִּי יהוה אֱלֹֽהֵיכֶם הוּא אֱלֹהִים
בַּשָּׁמַֽיִם מִמַּֽעַל וְעַל־הָאָֽרֶץ מִתָּֽחַת:

(to be continued)

Notes to the Reading :

1. A difficult word, probably meaning "secretly"
2. חָפַר to dig, search out, explore
3. "and she hid them" (צָפַן to hide)
4. תַּשִּׂיגוּ אֹתָם = תַּשִּׂיגוּם
5. הֶעֱלִֽיתָ אֹתָם = הֶעֱלָֽתַם

6. "and she hid them" (טָמַן to hide)
7. "stalks of flax" lit. "flax (פִּשְׁתִּים) of the tree". Note that פִּשְׁתִּים is feminine
8. Often used thus without a preposition in the meaning "by way of"

9. "as far as the fords" (sing.
   מַעְבָּרָה)

10. "(they) have melted away"

11. אֶת marks the אֲשֶׁר clause as
    the object of שָׁמַ֫עְנוּ.

12. הוֹבִישׁ to dry up (root יבשׁ
    cf. יַבָּשָׁה)

13. יַם־סוּף The Red Sea; lit.
    "sea of reeds"

14. "that which"

15. Amorite

16. עֵ֫בֶר the other side

LESSON 48

172. Hiphil Verbs: Stems and Inflection (concluded).

Hiphil verbs from geminate roots have the following stems:

Root Type	Perfect	Imperfect	Converted Impf.	Imperative	Inf. Constr.
Geminate Also II/III-gutt.	הֵסֵב הֵרַע	יָסֵב יָרַע	וַיָּסֶב וַיָּרַע	הָסֵב הָרַע	הָסֵב הָרַע

	Inf. Abs.	Participle
	הָסֵב הָרֵעַ	מֵסֵב מֵרַע

Note the general (but not consistent) replacement of *ē* by *a* in the final stem syllable before a guttural. In inflection the *ē* appears before the guttural whenever the non-guttural counterpart has *i*:

PERFECT

הֵסֵב	הֵסֵבּוּ	הֵרַע	הֵרֵעוּ
הֵסֵבָּה		הֵרֵעָה	
הֲסִבּוֹתָ	הֲסִבּוֹתֶם	הֲרֵעוֹתָ	הֲרֵעוֹתֶם
הֲסִבּוֹת	הֲסִבּוֹתֶן	הֲרֵעוֹת	הֲרֵעוֹתֶן
הֲסִבּוֹתִי	הֲסִבּוֹנוּ	הֲרֵעוֹתִי	הֲרֵעוֹנוּ

[237]

IMPERFECT

יָסֵב	יָסֵבּוּ	יָרַע	יָרֵעוּ
תָּסֵב	תְּסֻבֶּינָה	תָּרַע	תְּרֵעֶינָה
תָּסֵב	תָּסֵבּוּ	תָּרַע	תָּרֵעוּ
תָּסֵבִּי	תְּסֻבֶּינָה	תָּרֵעִי	תְּרֵעֶינָה
אָסֵב	נָסֵב	אָרַע	נָרַע

IMPERATIVE

הָסֵב	הָסֵבּוּ	הָרַע	הָרֵעוּ
הָסֵבִּי	(הַסֻבֶּינָה)	הָרֵעִי	(הַרֵעֶינָה)

INF. CONSTRUCT

הָסֵב	הָרַע
הַסִבִּי	הָרֵעִי
הַסִבְּךָ	הָרֵעֶךָ

PARTICIPLE

מֵסֵב	מְסִבִּים	מֵרַע	מְרֵעִים
מְסִבָּה	מְסִבּוֹת	מְרֵעָה	מְרֵעוֹת

Deviant forms are attested, most frequently those showing a doubling of the first root consonant, such as יִסֹּב (for יָסֵב). Compare the similar confusion in Qal verbs from these same roots (§126).

173. Verbal Hendiadys and Related Idioms.

In the construction

וַיָּשָׁב וַיֵּבְךָ   and he wept again

the two verbs are simply coordinated, both having the form as required by the narrative sequence in which they occur, but in meaning the first serves to qualify the second and is best translated adverbially in English. The verbs most commonly used in this way in Hebrew are:

שָׁב   to do something again
הוֹסִיף   to do something again
הוֹאִיל   to do something willingly, voluntarily; to be content to do; the imperative is virtually equivalent to "please"
מִהַר   to do something quickly
הִשְׁכִּים   to do something early in the day
הִרְבָּה   to do something much or a lot

Examples:

וַיֹּסֶף אַבְרָהָם וַיִּקַּח אִשָּׁה   (Gen. 25:1) And Abraham took another wife.

לוּ הוֹאַלְנוּ וַנֵּשֶׁב בְּעֵבֶר הַיַּרְדֵּן	(Joshua 7:7) Would that we had been content to dwell on the other side of the Jordan.
וַיָּשָׁב וַיָּלֶן שָׁם	(Judges 19:7) And he again spent the night there.
וּמִהַרְתֶּם וְהוֹרַדְתֶּם אֶת־אָבִי הֵנָּה	(Gen. 45:13) And you shall quickly bring my father down here.
וְהִשְׁכַּמְתֶּם וַהֲלַכְתֶּם לְדַרְכְּכֶם	(Gen. 19:2) And early in the morning you will go on your way.

The two verbs may have no conjunction between them. This construction, termed asyndetic, is common with imperative, rare with narrative forms:

אָשׁוּבָה אֶרְעֶה צֹאנְךָ	(Gen. 30:31) I will again tend your sheep.
שׁוּב שְׁכַב	(I Sam. 3:5) Lie down again.
אוֹסִיף אֲבַקְשֶׁנּוּ עוֹד	(Prov. 23:35) I will again search for him.
כִּי הוֹאִיל הָלַךְ אַחֲרֵי־צָו	(Hosea 5:11) For he has willingly gone after filth.
הוֹאֵל קַח כִּכָּרָיִם	(II Kings 5:23) Be content to take two talents.
מָה רְאִיתֶם עָשִׂיתִי מַהֲרוּ עֲשׂוּ כָמוֹנִי	(Judges 9:48) What you have seen me do quickly do likewise.

Most of these same verbs may also occur with a following complementary infinitive usually with לְ:

כִּי יָשׁוּב יהוה לָשׂוּשׂ עָלֶיךָ	(Deut. 30:9) For the Lord will again rejoice over you.
וַיּוֹאֶל מֹשֶׁה לָשֶׁבֶת אֶת־הָאִישׁ	(Ex. 2:21) And Moses was content to stay with the man.
וַיְמַהֵר לַעֲשׂוֹת אֹתוֹ	(Gen. 18:7) And he quickly prepared it.
מַהֲרוּ לָלֶכֶת	(II Sam. 15:14) Go quickly.

The two verbs may function together in complementary usage after another verb:

לֹא יוּכַל ... לָשׁוּב לְקַחְתָּהּ	(Deut. 24:4) He will not be able to take her back again.

Rarely more than one may appear before the main verb:

וַיְמַהֲרוּ וַיַּשְׁכִּימוּ וַיֵּצְאוּ	(Joshua 8:14) And early in the morning they went forth quickly...

The verbs קָם and הָלַךְ, especially the former, are employed in a similar construction where a literal translation is awkward or impossible. וַיָּקָם so used seems to do little more than give a slight emphasis to the fact that some activity is about to begin, corresponding to English "then, thereupon;" the imperative often corresponds to "come, come now, so." E.g.

קוּם־נָא שְׁבָה (Gen. 27:19) Come now and sit... (hardly "arise and sit...").

קוּם עֲשֵׂה־לָנוּ אֱלֹהִים (Ex. 32:1) Come, make for us a god who...

174. Vocabulary 48.

VERBS: הֵרַע (root רעע) to injure, hurt (dir. obj. or with בְּ/לְ); to act wickedly, badly.

הֵסֵב (root סבב) to turn, turn away, turn around (all trans.); to cause to go around.

הֵחֵל (root חלל) to begin (usually followed by a complementary inf.).

הֵפֵר (root פרר) to break, vitiate, annul.

הִשְׁכִּים to do something early in the day (see §173).

הוֹאִיל to be willing or content to do something (see §173).

נִשְׁבַּע (Niphal) to swear (an oath); to promise (something) by an oath.

הִשְׁבִּיעַ (Hiphil) to cause to take an oath.

חִיָּה (Piel) to let live, to revive, restore to life.

הֶחֱיָה (Hiphil) idem (not used in the imperfect).

פָּגַע (יִפְגַּע) to meet, encounter (with dir. obj. or בְּ).

NOUNS: שְׁבוּעָה (pl. -ôt) oath

חוֹמָה (pl. -ôt) wall of a city.

דֶּלֶת (w. suff. דַּלְתִּי; dual דְּלָתַיִם; pl. דְּלָתוֹת) door (of house or room).

PREPOSITIONS: בְּעַד through. The translation of this preposition varies widely. After verbs of prayer or entreaty it has the meaning "for, on behalf of." Note its use with verbs of closing:

וַיִּסְגְּרוּ בַּעֲדָם and they shut themselves in

סָגַר יהוה בְּעַד רַחְמָה the Lord had closed up her womb

It also has the sense of "around, surrounding" as in

וְאַתָּה מָגֵן בַּעֲדִי You are a shield surrounding me.

עַל־יַד beside, in the company of, to the side of.

Exercises:

(a) Translate:

(6) וַיָּפֶר אֶת־בְּרִיתוֹ עִמִּי.	(1) הֲפֵרוֹתִי אֶת־מִצְוָתוֹ.
(7) יָחֵלּוּ לְהָבִין בְּדִבְרֵי אֲלֵיהֶם.	(2) לֹא נָתַן אֹתוֹ יהוה לְהָרַע עִמָּדִי.
(8) יָרֵעוּ דִבְרֵיהֶם כִּי יָרֵעוּ.	(3) וַיַּעַשׂ הַמֶּלֶךְ הָרַע בְּעֵינֵי יהוה
(9) הַחֵלּוֹנוּ לַעֲרֹךְ מִלְחָמָה.	וַיֵּרַע מִכֹּל אֲשֶׁר לְפָנָיו.
(10) וַיָּסֵב אֶת־עֵינָיו מֵהַמַּרְאֶה.	(4) הֵחֵלּוּ לִבְכּוֹת וְלִקְרֹעַ אֶת־בִּגְדֵיהֶם.
	(5) וַתָּחֶל לִזְנוֹת וּלְהָרַע.

(b) Translate into Hebrew using the constructions treated in §173.

1. and we shall bring again.
2. they were content to rest.
3. I arranged it quickly.
4. and early in the day he removed them.
5. and he struck him again.
6. and he prepared again.
7. and they quickly brought it.
8. be content to bring them back.

(c) Translate:

(1) וַיַּשְׁכֵּם וַיַּעֲמֹד עַל־יַד דֶּרֶךְ הַשָּׁעַר.

(2) וַיִּשְׁלַח הַמֶּלֶךְ לֵאמֹר לֵךְ פְּגַע־בּוֹ וְהִכִּיתָ אֹתוֹ וְיָמֹת.

(3) וְהָאִישׁ מִהַר וַיָּבֹא וַיַּגֵּד אֶת־הַדְּבָרִים לַכֹּהֵן.

(4) וְהָיָה בְסֻבֵּנוּ אֶת־הָעִיר וְנָפְלָה חוֹמָתָהּ.

(5) הִרְבָּה לַעֲשׂוֹת הָרַע בְּעֵינֵי יהוה.

(6) וַיָּבֹאוּ הַבַּיִת וַיִּסְגְּרוּ אֶת־הַדֶּלֶת בַּעֲדָם.

(7) וַיַּשְׁכֵּם דָּוִד הוּא וַאֲנָשָׁיו לָלֶכֶת בַּבֹּקֶר לָשׁוּב אֶל־הָאָרֶץ הַהִיא.

(8) בַּיּוֹם הַהוּא יְחַיֶּה אֶת־הַמֵּתִים וְלֹא יִהְיֶה עוֹד הַמָּוֶת.

(9) מַהֲרוּ לָלֶכֶת פֶּן־יְמַהֵר וְהִשִּׂיג אֹתָנוּ.

(10) הֲלֹא נִשְׁבַּעְתִּי לָכֶם כִּי אִלָּחֵם אִתְּכֶם. לָמָּה לֹא הֶאֱמַנְתֶּם אֶת־דִּבְרֵי שְׁבוּעָתִי.

(11) הוֹאַלְתָּ לְבָרֵךְ אֶת־בֵּית עַבְדְּךָ לִהְיוֹת לְעוֹלָם.

(12) וַתִּשָּׁבַע אַתֶּם כִּי לֹא יִרְצָחוּ אַתָּה וְאֶת־בֵּית אָבִיהָ.

(d) Reading: Joshua 2:12–24. Rahab and the Spies (concluded).

(12) וְעַתָּה הִשָּׁבְעוּ־נָא לִי בַּיהוה כִּי־עָשִׂיתִי עִמָּכֶם חָסֶד וַעֲשִׂיתֶם גַּם־אַתֶּם עִם־בֵּית אָבִי חֶסֶד וּנְתַתֶּם לִי אוֹת אֱמֶת:

(13) וְהַחֲיִתֶם אֶת־אָבִי וְאֶת־אִמִּי וְאֶת־אַחַי וְאֶת־אַחְיוֹתַי[1] וְאֵת כָּל־אֲשֶׁר לָהֶם וְהִצַּלְתֶּם אֶת־נַפְשֹׁתֵינוּ מִמָּוֶת:

(14) וַיֹּאמְרוּ לָהּ הָאֲנָשִׁים נַפְשֵׁנוּ תַחְתֵּיכֶם לָמוּת[2] אִם לֹא תַגִּידוּ אֶת־דְּבָרֵנוּ זֶה[3] וְהָיָה בְּתֵת־יהוה לָנוּ אֶת־הָאָרֶץ וְעָשִׂינוּ עִמָּךְ חֶסֶד וֶאֱמֶת:

(15) וַתּוֹרִדֵם בַּחֶבֶל[4] בְּעַד הַחַלּוֹן[5] כִּי בֵיתָהּ בְּקִיר הַחוֹמָה[6] וּבַחוֹמָה הִיא יוֹשָׁבֶת:

(16) וַתֹּאמֶר לָהֶם הָהָרָה לֵּכוּ פֶּן־יִפְגְּעוּ בָכֶם הָרֹדְפִים וְנַחְבֵּתֶם[7] שָׁמָּה שְׁלֹשֶׁת יָמִים עַד שֹׁב[8] הָרֹדְפִים וְאַחַר[9] תֵּלְכוּ לְדַרְכְּכֶם:

(17) וַיֹּאמְרוּ אֵלֶיהָ הָאֲנָשִׁים נְקִיִּם[10] אֲנַחְנוּ מִשְּׁבֻעָתֵךְ הַזֶּה אֲשֶׁר הִשְׁבַּעְתָּנוּ:

(18) הִנֵּה אֲנַחְנוּ בָאִים בָּאָרֶץ אֶת־תִּקְוַת חוּט הַשָּׁנִי הַזֶּה[11] תִּקְשְׁרִי בַּחַלּוֹן אֲשֶׁר הוֹרַדְתֵּנוּ[12] בוֹ וְאֶת־אָבִיךְ וְאֶת־אִמֵּךְ וְאֶת־אַחַיִךְ וְאֵת כָּל־בֵּית אָבִיךְ תַּאַסְפִי אֵלַיִךְ הַבָּיְתָה:

(19) וְהָיָה כֹּל אֲשֶׁר־יֵצֵא מִדַּלְתֵי בֵיתֵךְ הַחוּצָה דָּמוֹ בְרֹאשׁוֹ וַאֲנַחְנוּ נְקִיִּם וְכֹל אֲשֶׁר יִהְיֶה אִתָּךְ בַּבַּיִת דָּמוֹ בְרֹאשֵׁנוּ אִם־יָד תִּהְיֶה־בּוֹ:

(20) וְאִם־תַּגִּידִי אֶת־דְּבָרֵנוּ זֶה וְהָיִינוּ נְקִיִּם מִשְּׁבֻעָתֵךְ אֲשֶׁר הִשְׁבַּעְתָּנוּ:[13]

(21) וַתֹּאמֶר כְּדִבְרֵיכֶם כֶּן־הוּא וַתְּשַׁלְּחֵם[14] וַיֵּלֵכוּ וַתִּקְשֹׁר אֶת־תִּקְוַת הַשָּׁנִי בַּחַלּוֹן:

(22) וַיֵּלְכוּ וַיָּבֹאוּ הָהָרָה וַיֵּשְׁבוּ שָׁם שְׁלֹשֶׁת יָמִים עַד־שָׁבוּ הָרֹדְפִים וַיְבַקְשׁוּ הָרֹדְפִים בְּכָל־
הַדֶּרֶךְ וְלֹא מָצָאוּ:

(23) וַיָּשֻׁבוּ שְׁנֵי הָאֲנָשִׁים וַיֵּרְדוּ מֵהָהָר וַיַּעֲבֹרוּ וַיָּבֹאוּ אֶל־יְהוֹשֻׁעַ בִּן־נוּן וַיְסַפְּרוּ־לוֹ אֵת כָּל־
הַמֹּצְאוֹת¹⁵ אוֹתָם:

(24) וַיֹּאמְרוּ אֶל־יְהוֹשֻׁעַ כִּי־נָתַן יהוה אֶת־כָּל־הָאָרֶץ בְּיָדֵנוּ וְגַם־נָמֹגוּ¹⁶ כָּל־יֹשְׁבֵי הָאָרֶץ
מִפָּנֵינוּ:

Notes to the reading:

1. "my sisters"
2. "our lives in exchange for yours"
3. Note the absence of the article on זֶה.
4. וַתּוֹרֶד אֹתָם = וַתּוֹרִדֵם
5. חֶבֶל a rope
6. חַלּוֹן a window
7. נַחְבֵּאתֶם = נַחְבֵּתֶם from נֶחְבָּא to hide (oneself)
8. שֹׁב alternate inf. construct for שׁוּב
9. Take adverbially as "afterwards".
10. נָקִי innocent, guiltless. Verse 17 seems to be displaced; see vs. 20 below.
11. "this line of scarlet thread"
12. הוֹרַדְתְּ אֹתָנוּ = הוֹרַדְתֶּנוּ
13. הִשְׁבַּעַתְּ אֹתָנוּ = הִשְׁבַּעְתָּנוּ
14. וַתְּשַׁלַּח אֹתָם = וַתְּשַׁלְּחֵם
15. in the sense "befall"
16. "they have melted away"

175. The Hophal.

As in the Piel-Pual relationship, there is for each Hiphil verb a passive counterpart of the type called Hophal. The form is characterized by an *u*-vowel in the first stem syllable and *a* in the second. The exact nature of the first vowel depends on the root type, as is seen from the following synopsis:

Root Type	Hiphil Verb	Hophal		
	Perfect	Perfect	Imperfect	Participle
Regular	הִשְׁמִיד	הָשְׁמַד	יָשְׁמַד	מָשְׁמָד
I-gutt.	הֶעֱמִיד	הָעֳמַד	יָעֳמַד	מָעֳמָד
I-*Nun*	הִגִּיד	הֻגַּד	יֻגַּד	מֻגָּד
III-*Aleph*	הִמְצִיא	הָמְצָא	יָמְצָא	מָמְצָא
I-*Yodh*/*Waw*	הוֹרִיד	הוּרַד	יוּרַד	מוּרָד
III-*Hē*	הִבְנָה	הָבְנָה	יָבְנֶה	מָבְנֶה
Hollow	הֵקִים	הוּקַם	יוּקַם	מוּקָם
Geminate	הֵסֵב	הוּסַב	יוּסַב	מוּסָב

The following samples of their inflection will suffice for the remainder:

PERFECT

הָשְׁמַד	הָעֳמַד	הָבְנָה	הוּקַם
הָשְׁמְדָה	הָעֳמְדָה	(ho'om-) הָבְנְתָה	הוּקְמָה
הָשְׁמַדְתָּ...	הָעֳמַדְתָּ...	הָבְנֵית...	הוּקַמְתָּ...

IMPERFECT

... יִשָּׁמַד	יֵעָמַד	יִבָּנֶה	יוּקַם
... תָּשָּׁמְדִי	תָּעָמְדִי *(to'om-)*	תִּבָּנִי	תוּקְמִי
... תָּשָּׁמַדְנָה	תֵּעָמַדְנָה	תִּבָּנֶינָה	תוּקַמְנָה

PARTICIPLE

מָשְׁמָד	מָעֳמָד	מָבְנֶה	מוּקָם
מָשְׁמָדָה / מָשְׁמֶדֶת	מָעֳמָדָה / מָעֳמֶדֶת	מָבְנָה	מוּקָמָה / מוּקֶמֶת
מָשְׁמָדִים	מָעֳמָדִים	מָבְנִים	מוּקָמִים
מָשְׁמָדוֹת	מָעֳמָדוֹת	מָבְנוֹת	מוּקָמוֹת

As the passive of the Hiphil, the Hophal offers no problems in translation when the Hiphil is a simply transitive verb:

הִשְׁמִיד	he destroyed	הָשְׁמַד	he was destroyed
הִשְׁלִיךְ	he threw	הָשְׁלַךְ	he was thrown
הוֹרִיד	he brought down	הוּרַד	he was brought down

But when the Hiphil verb is capable of a double object construction, it is the causative portion of the meaning which is rendered passive in the Hophal:

הֶרְאָה אֶת־הָאִישׁ אֶת־הָאוֹר	He showed the man the light. (lit. he *caused the man* to see the light).
הָרְאָה הָאִישׁ אֶת־הָאוֹר	The man was shown the light. (lit. *the man was caused* to see the light).
הֶעֱבִיר אֶת־הָעָם אֶת־הַנָּהָר	He brought the people across the river.
הָעֳבַר הָעָם אֶת־הַנָּהָר	The people were brought across the river.

Or, when one of the two possible objects is omitted (cf. §157a):

הֶעֱבִיר אֶת־הָעָם	He led the people across.
הָעֳבַר הָעָם	The people were led across.
הֶרְאָה אֶת־הָאוֹר	He showed the light. (lit. he *caused the light* to be seen)
הָרְאָה הָאוֹר	The light was shown. (lit. *the light was caused* to be seen).

Note, too, the impersonal construction with the retention of אֵת (cf. §154 end):

הֻגַּד לוֹ אֶת־הַדְּבָרִים	He was told the words.

176. Vocabulary 49.

VERBS:	מָשַׁל	(יִמְשֹׁל)	to rule, have dominion over (obj. with בְּ)
	יָשַׁר	(יִישַׁר)	to be pleasing, agreeable
	קָצַף	(יִקְצֹף)	to be(come) angry (עַל against)
	שָׁכַן	(יִשְׁכֹּן)	to settle down, dwell
	חָזַק	(יֶחֱזַק)	to become strong, firm, hard
	הָגָה	(יֶהְגֶּה)	to mutter, roar, moan, sigh; to meditate, imagine

NOUNS: אַרְיֵה (no pl.) ⎫
        אֲרִי (pl. אֲרָיוֹת) ⎬ lion
        עֵת (w. suff. עִתִּי; pl. -îm or -ôṯ) time, appointed time (f.).
        גְּדִי (pl. גְּדָיִים; constr. גְּדָיֵי) kid
        עֵדָה (no pl.) congregation, assembly
        בָּחוּר (pl. irreg. בַּחוּרִים) young man

OTHER: עָרֵל (adj.) uncircumcised; (fig.) inept, deficient
        עַל־כֵּן (adv.) therefore

PROPER NAMES: שִׁמְשׁוֹן Samson

        תִּמְנָתָה Timnah (or Timnathah), a town held by the Philistines;
                  exact location unknown

        פְּלִשְׁתִּים The Philistines

Exercises:

(a) Transform each of the following sentences into the passive, replacing the Hiphil verb with the Hophal according to the example:

הֵבִיא אֶת־הָאִישׁ he brought the man → הוּבָא הָאִישׁ the man was brought

(1) הֵסִיר אֶת־הַכְּלִי מֵעַל הַמִּזְבֵּחַ.
(2) וַיַּכּוּ אֶת־הָאֲנָשִׁים.
(3) הוֹשִׁיב אֶת־הָעָם שָׁם.
(4) הוֹרִידָה אֶת־הָאֲנָשִׁים מִן־הַגָּג.
(5) הוֹצִיא אֶת־הָרְשָׁעִים חוּצָה.

(6) הֶעֱלָה אֶת־הַפָּרָה עַל־הַמִּזְבֵּחַ.
(7) הִגִּיד לוֹ אֶת־דִּבְרֵי הַסָּרִיס.
(8) הִשְׁלִיךְ אֶת־הָאִישׁ מֵעַל הַחוֹמָה.
(9) הִרְאֵיתִי אֶתְכֶם נִפְלָאוֹת רַבּוֹת.
(10) וַיָּבֵא אֹתוֹ אֶל־הַהֵיכָל.

(b) Translate:

(1) הֻצַּלְנוּ
(2) הָעָמְדוּ
(3) הֻגְּשָׁה
(4) הָאִישׁ הַמּוּבָא

(5) הָעָם הַמָּגְלֶה
(6) הוּסַרְתִּי
(7) יוּכְלוּ
(8) הָעָם הַמּוּשָׁב

(9) הָעָבְדוּ
(10) הָאֲנָשִׁים הַמֻּכִּים
(11) יוּסְרוּ
(12) הַבְּרִית הַמּוּפָרָה

(c) Translate:

(1) הַמָּשֹׁל תִּמְשֹׁל בָּנוּ.
(2) אֶתֵּן אֹתָהּ לַאֲשֶׁר יָשָׁר בְּעֵינָי.
(3) וַיְהִי כִּרְאוֹתוֹ אֶת־הָאֲנָשִׁים וַיִּקְצֹף עֲלֵיהֶם.
(4) חָזַק הָרָעָב בְּכָל־הָאָרֶץ בָּעֵת הַהִיא.
(5) כַּאֲרִי אֶרְדֹּף אַחֲרֵי שֹׂנְאַי וַעֲלֵיהֶם אֶהְגֶּה כַּאֲשֶׁר יֶהְגֶּה אַרְיֵה.
(6) וַיִּישַׁר הַדָּבָר בְּעֵינֵי הַמֶּלֶךְ.
(7) חִזְקוּ וְאַל־תִּירָאוּ כִּי אֲנִי אִתְּכֶם.
(8) וּבְתוֹרַת יהוה יֶהְגֶּה יוֹמָם וָלַיְלָה.
(9) אַל־תִּקְצֹף עָלַי אָבִי כִּי לֹא חָטָאתִי לָךְ.
(10) מָשַׁל יוֹסֵף בְּכָל־אֶרֶץ מִצְרַיִם.
(11) וַיֶּחֱזַק לֵב פַּרְעֹה וַיְמָאֵן לְשַׁלֵּחַ אֶת־הָעִבְרִיִּים.
(12) עַל־כֵּן לֹא יָקֻמוּ רְשָׁעִים בַּעֲדַת צַדִּיקִים.

(13) וְכֵן דִּבֶּר מֹשֶׁה אֶל־כָּל־עֲדַת יִשְׂרָאֵל.

(14) וַיִּטְבַּח אֶת־הַגְּדִי וַיָּשֶׂם אֹתוֹ מִנְחָה עַל־הַמִּזְבֵּחַ.

(d) Write in Hebrew:

1. The statute was annulled.
2. The work was begun but not finished.
3. He was made to swear that he would return early on the fourth day.
4. He fell from the wall and died.
5. He was taken outside the city and there was put to death (lit. was caused to die).
6. She stood beside the door until they had departed.

(e) Reading: Judges 14:1–10. Samson and the Riddle.

(1) וַיֵּרֶד שִׁמְשׁוֹן תִּמְנָתָה וַיַּרְא אִשָּׁה בְּתִמְנָתָה מִבְּנוֹת פְּלִשְׁתִּים:

(2) וַיַּעַל וַיַּגֵּד לְאָבִיו וּלְאִמּוֹ וַיֹּאמֶר אִשָּׁה רָאִיתִי בְתִמְנָתָה מִבְּנוֹת פְּלִשְׁתִּים וְעַתָּה קְחוּ אוֹתָהּ לִי לְאִשָּׁה:

(3) וַיֹּאמֶר לוֹ אָבִיו וְאִמּוֹ הַאֵין בִּבְנוֹת אַחֶיךָ וּבְכָל־עַמִּי אִשָּׁה כִּי אַתָּה הוֹלֵךְ לָקַחַת אִשָּׁה מִפְּלִשְׁתִּים הָעֲרֵלִים וַיֹּאמֶר שִׁמְשׁוֹן אֶל־אָבִיו אוֹתָהּ קַח־לִי כִּי־הִיא יָשְׁרָה בְעֵינָי:

(4) וְאָבִיו וְאִמּוֹ לֹא יָדְעוּ כִּי מֵיהוה הִיא¹ כִּי־תֹאֲנָה² הוּא־מְבַקֵּשׁ מִפְּלִשְׁתִּים וּבָעֵת הַהִיא פְּלִשְׁתִּים מֹשְׁלִים בְּיִשְׂרָאֵל:

(5) וַיֵּרֶד שִׁמְשׁוֹן וְאָבִיו וְאִמּוֹ תִּמְנָתָה וַיָּבֹאוּ עַד־כַּרְמֵי תִמְנָתָה וְהִנֵּה כְּפִיר³ אֲרָיוֹת שֹׁאֵג⁴ לִקְרָאתוֹ:

(6) וַתִּצְלַח⁵ עָלָיו רוּחַ יהוה וַיְשַׁסְּעֵהוּ⁶ כְּשַׁסַּע הַגְּדִי וּמְאוּמָה אֵין בְּיָדוֹ וְלֹא הִגִּיד לְאָבִיו וּלְאִמּוֹ אֵת אֲשֶׁר עָשָׂה:

(7) וַיֵּרֶד וַיְדַבֵּר לָאִשָּׁה וַתִּישַׁר בְּעֵינֵי שִׁמְשׁוֹן:

(8) וַיָּשָׁב מִיָּמִים לְקַחְתָּהּ⁷ וַיָּסַר לִרְאוֹת אֵת מַפֶּלֶת⁸ הָאַרְיֵה וְהִנֵּה עֲדַת דְּבֹרִים⁹ בִּגְוִיַּת¹⁰ הָאַרְיֵה וּדְבָשׁ:

(9) וַיִּרְדֵּהוּ¹¹ אֶל־כַּפָּיו וַיֵּלֶךְ הָלוֹךְ וְאָכֹל וַיֵּלֶךְ אֶל־אָבִיו וְאֶל־אִמּוֹ וַיִּתֵּן לָהֶם וַיֹּאכֵלוּ וְלֹא הִגִּיד לָהֶם כִּי מִגְּוִיַּת הָאַרְיֵה רָדָה¹² הַדְּבָשׁ:

(10) וַיֵּרֶד אָבִיהוּ אֶל־הָאִשָּׁה וַיַּעַשׂ שָׁם שִׁמְשׁוֹן מִשְׁתֶּה כִּי כֵן יַעֲשׂוּ הַבַּחוּרִים:

(to be concluded)

Notes to the Reading:

1. "that it (i.e. the situation) was the Lord's doing"
2. תֹּאֲנָה opportunity (for a quarrel)
3. כְּפִיר a young lion
4. שָׁאַג to roar
5. צָלַח to rush
6. שָׁסַע to rend, tear apart; "and he tore it apart"
7. The suffix is objective: "to take her"
8. מַפֶּלֶת carcass
9. דְּבוֹרָה (pl. -îm) bee(s)

[246]

10. גְּוִיָּה body
11. "and he scraped it"
12. "he had scraped"

LESSON 50

177. The Hithpael.

Relatively infrequent, Hithpael verbs are distinguished by the prefixal element *(h)it-* and the doubling of the second root consonant.

Root Type	Perfect	Imperfect	Imperative	Inf. Construct	Participle
Regular	הִתְגַּדֵּל	יִתְגַּדֵּל	הִתְגַּדֵּל	הִתְגַּדֵּל	מִתְגַּדֵּל
III-*Hē*	הִתְגַּלָּה	יִתְגַּלֶּה	הִתְגַּלֵּה	הִתְגַּלּוֹת	מִתְגַּלֶּה
Geminate	הִתְפַּלֵּל	יִתְפַּלֵּל	הִתְפַּלֵּל	הִתְפַּלֵּל	מִתְפַּלֵּל

In regard to formation the following points should be noted:

(a) With roots beginning with a sibilant (צ שׂ שׁ ז ס) there is regularly a metathesis of this consonant and the ת of the prefix: **hitšammēr* > הִשְׁתַּמֵּר. A further assimilation takes place, wherein **-zt-* > *-zd-*, as in **hitzakkēr* > **hiztakkēr* > הִזְדַּכֵּר; and **-ṣt-* > *-ṣṭ-* as in **hitṣaddēq* > **hiṣtaddēq* > הִצְטַדֵּק. Other assimilations occur sporadically, as in הִנַּבֵּא for more regular הִתְנַבֵּא.

(b) With geminate roots the doubling of the middle root consonant is often given up, as in the Piel verb, when preceding a *ə*: הִתְחַנְנוּ for הִתְחַנֵּנוּ.

(c) Roots II-gutt, show either compensatory lengthening or virtual doubling, as in the Piel. E.g. הִתְרָאָה but הִתְנַחֵם.

(d) The final stem syllable may have *a* instead of *ē*. This is normal before gutturals, optional elsewhere: הִתְוַדַּע, הִתְאַנַּף.

(e) With roots I-Waw/Yodh the original ו is sometimes preserved, as in הִתְוַכַּח (to argue) and הִתְוַדַּע (to make oneself known): contrast הִתְיַלֵּד (to declare or claim a pedigree) and הִתְיָעֵץ (to conspire against), both with י.

(f) Hollow roots seldom occur as Hithpael verbs.

(g) Vestiges of a closely related verb type without the doubling of the second root consonant occur sporadically, especially in the verb הִתְפָּקֵד (note the long ā and single ק).

Inflection is as follows:

PERFECT

הִתְגַּדֵּל	הִתְגַּדְּלוּ	הִתְגַּלָּה	הִתְגַּלּוּ	הִתְפַּלֵּל	הִתְפַּלְלוּ
הִתְגַּדְּלָה		הִתְגַּלְּתָה		הִתְפַּלְלָה	
הִתְגַּדַּלְתָּ	הִתְגַּדַּלְתֶּם	הִתְגַּלִּיתָ	הִתְגַּלִּיתֶם	הִתְפַּלַּלְתָּ	הִתְפַּלַּלְתֶּם
הִתְגַּדַּלְתְּ	הִתְגַּדַּלְתֶּן	הִתְגַּלִּית	הִתְגַּלִּיתֶן	הִתְפַּלַּלְתְּ	הִתְפַּלַּלְתֶּן
הִתְגַּדַּלְתִּי	הִתְגַּדַּלְנוּ	הִתְגַּלִּיתִי	הִתְגַּלִּינוּ	הִתְפַּלַּלְתִּי	הִתְפַּלַּלְנוּ

IMPERFECT

יִתְגַּדֵּל	יִתְגַּדְּלוּ	יִתְגַּלֶּה	יִתְגַּלּוּ	יִתְפַּלֵּל	יִתְפַּלְלוּ
תִּתְגַּדֵּל	תִּתְגַּדֵּלְנָה	תִּתְגַּלֶּה	תִּתְגַּלֶּינָה	תִּתְפַּלֵּל	תִּתְפַּלֵּלְנָה
תִּתְגַּדֵּל	תִּתְגַּדְּלוּ	תִּתְגַּלֶּה	תִּתְגַּלּוּ	תִּתְפַּלֵּל	תִּתְפַּלְלוּ
תִּתְגַּדְּלִי	תִּתְגַּדֵּלְנָה	תִּתְגַּלִּי	תִּתְגַּלֶּינָה	תִּתְפַּלְלִי	תִּתְפַּלֵּלְנָה
אֶתְגַּדֵּל	נִתְגַּדֵּל	אֶתְגַּלֶּה	נִתְגַּלֶּה	אֶתְפַּלֵּל	נִתְפַּלֵּל

IMPERATIVE

הִתְגַּדֵּל	הִתְגַּדְּלוּ	הִתְגַּלֵּה	הִתְגַּלּוּ	הִתְפַּלֵּל	הִתְפַּלְלוּ
הִתְגַּדְּלִי	הִתְגַּדֵּלְנָה	הִתְגַּלִּי	הִתְגַּלֶּינָה	הִתְפַּלְלִי	הִתְפַּלֵּלְנָה

INF. CONSTRUCT

הִתְגַּדֵּל	הִתְגַּלּוֹת	הִתְפַּלֵּל

PARTICIPLE

מִתְגַּדֵּל	מִתְגַּדְּלִים	מִתְגַּלֶּה	מִתְגַּלִּים	מִתְפַּלֵּל	מִתְפַּלְלִים
מִתְגַּדְּלָה	מִתְגַּדְּלוֹת	מִתְגַּלָּה	מִתְגַּלּוֹת	מִתְפַּלְלָה	מִתְפַּלְלוֹת
מִתְגַּדֶּלֶת				מִתְפַּלֶּלֶת	

Hithpael verbs are intransitive and often have a reflexive or reciprocal meaning in relation to their active counterparts of the Qal, Piel, or Hiphil type from the same root. The following is a representative list:

(a) Reflexive: הִתְקַדֵּשׁ to sanctify oneself (cf. קָדַשׁ; הִקְדִּישׁ)

הִתְגַּדֵּל to magnify oneself (cf. גָּדַל; הִגְדִּיל)

הִתְחַבֵּא to hide oneself

(b) Reciprocal: הִתְרָאָה to see one another (cf. רָאָה)

הִדַּבֵּר to converse (cf. דִּבֶּר)

(c) Indirect reflexive (i.e. to do something for one's self, for one's own benefit or to one's own detriment):

הִתְחַנֵּן to implore favor (cf. חָנַן)

הִתְפַּלֵּל to pray (see below)

הִצְטַיֵּד to supply oneself with provisions (cf. צַיִד provision)

(d) Iterative: הִתְהַלֵּךְ to walk back and forth; to go continually

(e) Denominative: הִתְנַבֵּא to prophesy (cf. נָבִיא)

הִתְאַנַּף to become angry (cf. אַף; root אנף)

Classification is often difficult, owing to the lack of data. The verb הִתְפַּלֵּל (to pray) offers a good example. One's first inclination is to regard it as denominative from תְּפִלָּה (prayer), to which it is most closely related in form and meaning. This is too simple an approach, however, since nouns of the type תְּפִלָּה (with prefixed *t*-) are often associated with Hithpael verbs in Hebrew and would appear to be derived from them and not vice versa. There is no Qal verb פָּלַל but there are several poorly attested nouns, such as פָּלִיל (referee, judge, arbiter), which suggest that there was a root verb (Qal) at one time in the meaning "to arbitrate, mediate" or the like. The Piel verb פִּלֵּל (to mediate, act as an arbiter for) is a denominative from פָּלִיל. The Hithpael verb, then, would have the force of a causative/indirect-reflexive: "to cause a mediation (by seeking or asking) for oneself." It would thus belong to the same category as הִתְחַנֵּן. It is obviously necessary to learn the exact nuance of a Hithpael verb as part of vocabulary acquisition.

178. Vocabulary 50.

VERBS:	הִתְפַּלֵּל	to pray
	הִתְחַנֵּן	to seek or implore favor
	הִתְחַבֵּא	to hide oneself
	נֶחְבָּא	(יֵחָבֵא) to hide oneself
	הִתְהַלֵּךְ	to walk back and forth; to go continually or constantly
	הִתְנַבֵּא	to prophesy
	נִבָּא	(יִנָּבֵא) to prophesy
	חָרַשׁ	(יַחֲרשׁ) to plow; to engrave
	פָּרַשׂ	(יִפְרשׂ) to spread out (trans.)
	סָפַר	(יִסְפֹּר) to count
NOUNS:	מַאֲכָל	(no pl.) food
	מָשִׁיחַ	one who has been anointed, the Messiah
	עֹז	(w. suff. עֻזִּי or עָזִּי) strength, might

תְּפִלָּה	(pl. -ôṯ) prayer	
עֵגֶל	(w. suff. עֶגְלִי; pl. -îm) calf	
עֶגְלָה	(pl. -ôṯ) heifer	

OTHER: עַז (adj.) strong, mighty (see §22)

לוּלֵי (conj.) unless, if not

כֹּה (adv.) thus (generally referring to what follows)

PROPER NAMES: אַשְׁקְלוֹן Ashkelon, an important Philistine city on the coast, about 12 miles north of Gaza.

Exercises:

(a) Translate:

(1) לָמָה הִתְחַבֵּאתֶם מִמֶּֽנִּי

(2) הִתְחַנֶּן אֵלַי וְחַנּֽוֹתִי אֹתְךָ

(3) הַבַּחוּרִים הַמִּתְהַלְּכִים בְּרַגְלָיו

(4) וַיָּֽחֶל לְהִתְנַבֵּא

(5) הִתְפַּלַּֽלְתִּי אֵלָיו וְלֹא שָׁמַע

(6) וַיִּתְחַבְּאוּ כִּי יָֽרְאוּ מְאֹד

(7) הִתְפַּלֵּל בַּעֲדִי

(8) מִי הַמִּתְנַבְּאִים

(9) נִשְׁמְעָה תְפִלָּתֶֽךָ

(10) אָבֹֽאָה עַל־בֵּיתֶֽךָ

(11) הֵחָבֵאִי

(b) Translate:

(1) אֲבָל אֲשֵׁמִים אֲנַ֫חְנוּ עַל־אָחִינוּ אֲשֶׁר רָאִינוּ צָרַת נַפְשׁוֹ בְּהִתְחַנְּנוֹ אֵלֵינוּ וְלֹא שָׁמָֽעְנוּ.

(2) וַיֻּגַּד לְדָוִד לֵאמֹר מְבַקֵּשׁ אָבִי לַהֲמִית אֹתְךָ וְעַתָּה הִשָּׁמֶר נָא בַּבֹּֽקֶר וְנַחְבֵּֽאתָ.

(3) וַהֲקִימֹֽתִי לִי כֹהֵן נֶאֱמָן, כַּאֲשֶׁר בִּלְבָבִי וּבְנַפְשִׁי יַעֲשֶׂה, וּבָנִֽיתִי לוֹ בַּֽיִת נֶאֱמָן וְהִתְהַלֵּךְ לִפְנֵי מְשִׁיחִי כָּל־הַיָּמִים.

(4) חַטַּאת יְהוּדָה חֲרוּשָׁה עַל־לֽוּחַ לִבָּם.

(5) וַיִּפְרְשׂוּ אֶת־שִׂמְלוֹתֵיהֶם עַל־הָאָ֫רֶץ וַיֵּשְׁבוּ עֲלֵיהֶן.

(6) וַיּוֹצֵא יהוה אֶת־אַבְרָם הַחֽוּצָה וַיֹּאמֶר הַבֶּט־נָא הַשָּׁמַ֫יְמָה וּסְפֹר הַכּֽוֹכָבִים, אִם־תּוּכַל לִסְפֹּר אֹתָם, וַיֹּֽאמֶר לוֹ כֹּה יִהְיֶה זַרְעֶֽךָ.

(7) וַיֵּט מֹשֶׁה אֶת־יָדוֹ עַל־הַיָּם וַיּֽוֹלֶךְ יהוה אֶת־הַיָּם בְּרוּחַ עַזָּה כָּל־הַלַּ֫יְלָה וַיָּ֫שֶׂם אֶת־הַיָּם לְיַבָּשָׁה.

(8) וַיִּפְרֹשׂ אֶת־כַּפָּיו אֶל־הַשָּׁמַ֫יִם וַיִּתְפַּלֵּל.

(9) וַיִּשְׁמְעוּ אֶת־קוֹל יהוה אֱלֹהִים מִתְהַלֵּךְ בַּגָּן וַיִּתְחַבֵּא הָאָדָם וְאִשְׁתּוֹ מִפְּנֵי יהוה אֱלֹהִים בְּתוֹךְ עֵץ הַגָּן.

(10) וָאֶתְחַנַּן אֶל־יְהוָֹה בָּעֵת הַהִוא לֵאמֹר אֲדֹנָי יֱהוִֹה אַתָּה הַחִלּֽוֹתָ לְהַרְאוֹת אֶת־עַבְדְּךָ אֶת־גָּדְלְךָ וְאֶת־יָדְךָ הַחֲזָקָה כִּי מִי אֵל בַּשָּׁמַ֫יִם וּבָאָ֫רֶץ אֲשֶׁר יַעֲשֶׂה כְמַעֲשֶׂיךָ וְכִגְבוּרֹתֶֽךָ.

(c) Write in Hebrew:

1. The lion was slain and his carcass (מַפֶּֽלֶת) was cast to the side of the road.
2. They searched all that evening but were not able to find the lost kid.
3. There was at that time no king ruling over Israel.
4. We were content to settle down there.
5. Be strong, therefore, and do not flee from your enemies.

6. The congregation will be destroyed.

7. There was no one prophesying in the land in those days.

(d) Reading: Judges 14:11–20. Samson and the Riddle.

(11) וַיְהִי כִּרְאוֹתָם אוֹתוֹ וַיִּקְחוּ שְׁלֹשִׁים מֵרֵעִים¹ וַיִּהְיוּ אִתּוֹ:

(12) וַיֹּאמֶר לָהֶם שִׁמְשׁוֹן אָחוּדָה־נָּא² לָכֶם חִידָה³ אִם־הַגֵּד תַּגִּידוּ אוֹתָהּ לִי שִׁבְעַת⁴ יְמֵי הַמִּשְׁתֶּה וּמְצָאתֶם וְנָתַתִּי לָכֶם שְׁלֹשִׁים סְדִינִים⁵ וּשְׁלֹשִׁים חֲלִפֹת⁶ בְּגָדִים:

(13) וְאִם־לֹא תוּכְלוּ לְהַגִּיד לִי וּנְתַתֶּם לִי שְׁלֹשִׁים סְדִינִים וּשְׁלֹשִׁים חֲלִיפוֹת בְּגָדִים וַיֹּאמְרוּ לוֹ חוּדָה חִידָתְךָ וְנִשְׁמָעֶנָּה⁷:

(14) וַיֹּאמֶר לָהֶם מֵהָאֹכֵל יָצָא מַאֲכָל וּמֵעַז יָצָא מָתוֹק⁸ וְלֹא יָכְלוּ לְהַגִּיד הַחִידָה שְׁלֹשֶׁת יָמִים:

(15) וַיְהִי בַּיּוֹם הַשְּׁבִיעִי וַיֹּאמְרוּ לְאֵשֶׁת שִׁמְשׁוֹן פַּתִּי⁹ אֶת־אִישֵׁךְ וְיַגֶּד־לָנוּ אֶת־הַחִידָה פֶּן־נִשְׂרֹף אוֹתָךְ וְאֶת־בֵּית אָבִיךְ בָּאֵשׁ הַלְיָרְשֵׁנוּ¹⁰ קְרָאתֶם לָנוּ הֲלֹא¹¹:

(16) וַתֵּבְךְּ אֵשֶׁת שִׁמְשׁוֹן עָלָיו וַתֹּאמֶר רַק שְׂנֵאתַנִי¹² וְלֹא אֲהַבְתָּנִי¹³ הַחִידָה חַדְתָּ לִבְנֵי עַמִּי וְלִי לֹא הִגַּדְתָּה וַיֹּאמֶר לָהּ הִנֵּה לְאָבִי וּלְאִמִּי לֹא הִגַּדְתִּי וְלָךְ אַגִּיד:

(17) וַתֵּבְךְּ עָלָיו שִׁבְעַת הַיָּמִים אֲשֶׁר־הָיָה לָהֶם הַמִּשְׁתֶּה וַיְהִי בַּיּוֹם הַשְּׁבִיעִי וַיַּגֶּד־לָהּ כִּי הֱצִיקַתְהוּ¹⁴ וַתַּגֵּד הַחִידָה לִבְנֵי עַמָּהּ:

(18) וַיֹּאמְרוּ לוֹ אַנְשֵׁי הָעִיר בַּיּוֹם הַשְּׁבִיעִי בְּטֶרֶם יָבֹא הַחַרְסָה¹⁵ מַה־מָּתוֹק מִדְּבַשׁ וּמֶה עַז מֵאֲרִי וַיֹּאמֶר לָהֶם לוּלֵא חֲרַשְׁתֶּם בְּעֶגְלָתִי לֹא מְצָאתֶם חִידָתִי:

(19) וַתִּצְלַח¹⁶ עָלָיו רוּחַ יהוה וַיֵּרֶד אַשְׁקְלוֹן וַיַּךְ מֵהֶם שְׁלֹשִׁים אִישׁ וַיִּקַּח אֶת־חֲלִיצוֹתָם¹⁷ וַיִּתֵּן הַחֲלִיפוֹת לְמַגִּידֵי הַחִידָה וַיִּחַר אַפּוֹ וַיַּעַל בֵּית אָבִיהוּ:

(20) וַתְּהִי אֵשֶׁת שִׁמְשׁוֹן לְמֵרֵעֵהוּ אֲשֶׁר רֵעָה¹⁸ לוֹ:

Notes to the Reading:

1. מֵרֵעַ companion

2. חָד (יָחוּד) to propound a riddle

3. חִידָה a riddle

4. Notice the temporal expression without a preposition: "*during* the seven days..."

5. סָדִין a linen garment

6. חֲלִיפָה a change (of clothing)

7. וְנִשְׁמַע אֹתָהּ = וְנִשְׁמָעֶנָּה

8. מָתוֹק sweet

9. פִּתָּה to lure, entice, beguile

10. הַלְיָרְשֵׁנוּ = הֲ + לְ + יִרַשׁ + suff. 1st pers. pl.: "have (you summoned us) in order to dispossess us?"

11. הֲלֹא probably a mistake for הֲלֹם, but it may be taken literally as an emphatically placed interrogative: "You've summoned us... haven't you?"

12. שְׂנֵאתָ אֹתִי = שְׂנֵאתַנִי

13. אָהַבְתָּ אֹתִי = אֲהַבְתָּנִי

14. הֱצִיקַתְהוּ "she harrassed (הֵצִיק) him"

15. An uncertain expression; probably "before the sun had set"

16. צָלַח to rush

17. חֲלִיצָה armor

18. רֵעָה to be a companion to, to be "best man"

179. The Qal Passive.

There are several forms, taken by the Masoretes as Pual or Hophal, which must rather be viewed as survivors of an obsolete passive of the Qal.

PERFECT	IMPERFECT	
לֻקַּח	יֻקַּח	to be taken
יֻלַּד	——	to be born
——	יֻתַּן	to be given

Isolated participial forms also occur: אֻכָּל (eaten, consumed), יִלּוֹד (born).

That these verbs are not true Pual or Hophal types is suggested (1) by the absence of a corresponding Piel or Hiphil active verb with the appropriate meaning, (2) by the absence of a מ -preformative on the few remaining participial forms, (3) by the irregular assimilation of the ל in יֻקַּח, a special feature of the Qal not found elsewhere, and (4) by the asymmetry of a Pual perfect and a Hophal imperfect. It is quite likely that a number of other Pual and Hophal verbs belong here, but assignment on the basis of meaning alone is precarious.

180. Polel, Polal, and Hithpolel.

In place of Piel, Pual, and Hithpael verbs from Hollow roots there is a derived system of verbs characterized by the reduplication of the final root consonant and *ô* in the first stem syllable:

	POLEL (active)	POLAL (passive)	HITHPOLEL (reflexive)
Perfect	קוֹמֵם	קוֹמַם	הִתְקוֹמֵם
Imperfect	יְקוֹמֵם	יְקוֹמַם	יִתְקוֹמֵם
Inf. Constr.	קוֹמֵם	——	——
Participle	מְקוֹמֵם	מְקוֹמָם	מִתְקוֹמֵם

Typical verbs are קוֹמֵם (to raise up), מוֹתֵת (to slay, kill), רוֹמֵם (to raise), כּוֹנֵן (to establish), and עוֹרֵר (to arouse) from the roots כון רום מות קום, and עור respectively. All verbs of this type are rare.

In the inflection of the perfect the distinction between the Polel and Polal is obscured:

POLEL	POLAL
קוֹמַם	קוֹמַם
קוֹמְמָה	קוֹמְמָה
קוֹמַ֫מְתָּ ...	קוֹמַ֫מְתָּ ...

Similar forms occur from geminate roots, as חוֹנֵן (to favor; root חנן) and סוֹבֵב (to encompass; root סבב).

181. Other Verb Types.

Biblical Hebrew has a number of verb types not belonging to those already treated. Most of these are so infrequent that a complete paradigm cannot be constructed for them. Given below, with the traditional name of the type, are a few examples.

POEL: similar to the Polel of the preceding paragraph but formed from regular triliteral roots. E.g. שֹׁרֵשׁ (imperf. יְשֹׁרֵשׁ; part. מְשֹׁרֵשׁ) to take root, a denominative from the noun שֹׁ֫רֶשׁ (root). Contrast the Piel verb שֵׁרֵשׁ (to root up, destroy the roots of).

PALAL: presumably from triliteral roots with reduplication of the final root consonant E.g. שַׁאֲנַן (to be at rest); אֻמְלַל (to be weary).

PILPEL: perhaps traceable to reduplicated biconsonantal (i.e. Hollow) roots. E.g. כִּלְכֵּל (imperf. יְכַלְכֵּל; inf. constr. כַּלְכֵּל; part. מְכַלְכֵּל) to sustain, support; גִּלְגֵּל (to roll).

The relatively frequent verb הִשְׁתַּחֲוָה formerly taken as a Hithpalel form of a root שחה is now known to be a Hishtaphel (i.e. prefix [*h*]*išt*-, root חוה). The attested forms of this verb are given below and should be learned. Its inflection is like that of other verbs from roots III-*Hē*.

PERF:		IMPERF:		IMPERATIVE:	
3 m.s.	הִשְׁתַּחֲוָה	3 m.s.	יִשְׁתַּחֲוֶה	2 f.s.	הִשְׁתַּחֲוִי
2 m.s.	הִשְׁתַּחֲוִ֫יתָ	3 m.pl.	יִשְׁתַּחֲווּ	2 m.pl.	הִשְׁתַּחֲווּ ·

3 m.pl. הִשְׁתַּחֲווּ		2 f.pl. תִּשְׁתַּחֲוֶ֫יןָ	
INF. CONSTRUCT: הִשְׁתַּחֲוֺת	JUSSIVE: יִשְׁתַּ֫חוּ		PARTICIPLE: מִשְׁתַּחֲוֶה

182. Final Remarks on the Numbers.

The numbers above 99 employ the following words:

		CONSTR.	DUAL	PL.	CONSTR.
hundred	מֵאָה	מְאַת	מָאתַ֫יִם	מֵאוֹת	מְאוֹת
thousand	אֶ֫לֶף	אֶ֫לֶף	אַלְפַּ֫יִם	אֲלָפִים	אַלְפֵי
ten thousand	רִבּוֹ רְבָבָה		רִבֹּתַ֫יִם	רְבָאוֹת	

Because the gender of מֵאָה is fem., modifiers have the masculine form:

שְׁלֹשׁ מֵאוֹת	300	אַרְבַּע מֵאוֹת	400

Whereas אֶ֫לֶף is masculine:

שְׁלֹ֫שֶׁת אֲלָפִים	3000	אַרְבַּ֫עַת אֲלָפִים	4000

There is a great deal of variety in the order and syntax of the higher numbers, but the following points will apply in most instances:

(a) מֵאָה is usually followed by a singular noun:

מֵאָה שָׁנָה	100 years	מֵאָה כֶּ֫סֶף	100 pieces of silver
מֵאָה רֶ֫כֶב	100 chariots		

The number may be in the construct:

מְאַת שָׁנָה	100 years	מְאַת כִּכָּר	100 talents

(b) אֶ֫לֶף, מָאתַ֫יִם, אַלְפַּ֫יִם are also followed by the singular noun, but plurals are attested:

מָאתַ֫יִם שָׁנָה	200 years	אֶ֫לֶף אִישׁ	1000 men
מָאתַ֫יִם כֶּ֫סֶף	200 pieces of silver	אֶ֫לֶף פְּעָמִים	1000 times
אַלְפַּ֫יִם אִישׁ	2000 men		
אַלְפַּ֫יִם סוּסִים	2000 horses		

(c) Compound numbers usually begin with the highest unit: x-thousand, y-hundred, and z. Only the final element (z) is affected by the gender of the noun being modified and will conform to the patterns already discussed (§§ 130, 161).

Note first the construction with אֶ֫לֶף:

שְׁלֹ֫שֶׁת אֲלָפִים	3000	עֶשְׂרִים וַחֲמִשָּׁה אֶ֫לֶף	25000
שְׁלֹ֫שֶׁת עָשָׂר אֶ֫לֶף	13000	מְאַת אֶ֫לֶף	100000
עֶשְׂרִים אֶ֫לֶף	20000	מָאתַ֫יִם אֶ֫לֶף	200000

Following is a selection of compound numbers illustrating normal usage. Study them and be sure their construction is clear.

מֵאָה (וּ)שְׁלֹשָׁה	103
מֵאָה (וּ)שְׁלֹשֶׁת עָשָׂר	113
מֵאָה (וּ)עֶשְׂרִים וּשְׁלֹשָׁה	123
מָאתַ֫יִם (וּ)שְׁלֹשָׁה	203
שְׁלֹשׁ מֵאוֹת (וּ)שְׁלֹשָׁה	303
אֶ֫לֶף (וּ)שְׁלֹשָׁה	1003
אֶ֫לֶף (וּ)מֵאָה (וּ)שְׁלֹשָׁה	1103
אֶ֫לֶף (וּ)מָאתַ֫יִם (וּ)שְׁלֹשָׁה	1203
שְׁלֹ֫שֶׁת אֲלָפִים (וּ)מָאתַ֫יִם (וּ)שְׁלֹשָׁה	3203
שְׁלֹ֫שֶׁת עָשָׂר אֶ֫לֶף	13000
עֶשְׂרִים וּשְׁלֹ֫שֶׁת אֶ֫לֶף	23000
מֵאַת אֶ֫לֶף	100000
מֵאָה וּשְׁלֹ֫שֶׁת אֶ֫לֶף	103000
מֵאָה (וּ)שְׁלֹ֫שֶׁת עָשָׂר אֶ֫לֶף	113000
שְׁלֹשׁ מֵאוֹת אֶ֫לֶף	300000
שְׁלֹשׁ מֵאוֹת (וּ)שְׁלֹ֫שֶׁת אֶ֫לֶף	303000
שְׁלֹשׁ מֵאוֹת (וּ)שְׁלֹ֫שֶׁת אֶ֫לֶף (וּ)שְׁלֹשׁ מֵאוֹת (וּ)שְׁלֹשִׁים (וּ)שְׁלֹשָׁה	303333

The words for ten-thousand are seldom used.

183. Vocabulary 51.

VERBS:	מוֹתֵת	to slay, kill (§ 180)
	כּוֹנֵן	to set up, establish (§ 180)
	עוֹרֵר	to arouse, stir up (§ 180)
	רוֹמֵם	to raise up, exalt (§ 180)
	הִשְׁתַּחֲוָה	to bow down (§ 181)
	הִתְיַצֵּב	to take one's stand, station oneself
	שָׁפַט	(יִשְׁפֹּט) to judge
	כָּחַד	(יִכַּחֵד) to hide, conceal
	פָּרַץ	(יִפְרֹץ) to break down, breach (a wall); to burst out suddenly (בְּ upon); to increase precipitously (in numbers, wealth etc.)

NOUNS:	אֲרוֹן	(w. art. הָאָרוֹן) the Ark of the temple, containing the tablets of the Law
	זֶ֫בַח	(w. suff. זִבְחִי; pl. -îm) sacrifice
	מֵאָה	hundred (see § 182)
	אֶ֫לֶף	thousand (see § 182)

ADVERB:	לָכֵן	therefore (usually introduces a divine judgement or declaration)

PROPER NAMES:	עֵלִי	Eli, the priest of the Lord at Shiloh to whom Samuel was entrusted.

Exercises:

(a) Give the Hebrew for the following numbers:

1. 3554	6. 7325	11. 100000
2. 1238	7. 5899	12. 220000
3. 9671	8. 2107	13. 460000
4. 8442	9. 4960	14. 587963
5. 7683	10. 10349	15. 666666

(b) Analyze and translate the following verbs:

(9) הִתְעוֹרַרְתֶּם	(5) מְכֹנְנִים	(1) מוֹתַתָּנוּ
(10) מוֹתַתִּי	(6) רוֹמַמְתָּ	(2) תִּתְכּוֹנְנִי
(11) הִתְרוֹמַמְתִּי	(7) יִתְמֹתְתוּ	(3) תְּעוֹרֵר
(12) הִשְׁתַּחֲווּ	(8) וַיִּשְׁתַּחוּ	(4) הִתְיַצְּבִי

(c) Translate:

(1) פָּרַץ יהוה אֶת־אֹיְבַי לְפָנַי.

(2) מִי אֲנִי כִּי אֶשְׁפֹּט אֶת־עַמְּךָ הַזֶּה.

(3) וְעוֹרַרְתִּי אֶת־אֲנָשַׁי עַל־אֹיְבַי.

(4) לֹא כִחַדְתִּי חַסְדְּךָ וַאֲמִתְּךָ מֵהָעֵדָה הַזֹּאת.

(5) וַיִּפְרְצוּ בְּחוֹמַת יְרוּשָׁלַ‍ִם.

(6) וְאֵין מִתְעוֹרֵר לִקְרֹא בְּשִׁמְךָ.

(7) יִשָּׁפְטוּ וְהִשָּׁמְדוּ מֵעַל הָאָרֶץ.

(8) וַיִּפְרֹץ הָאִישׁ מְאֹד מְאֹד.

(9) הַגֶּד־נָא לִי מֶה עָשִׂיתָ וְאַל־תְּכַחֵד מִמֶּנִּי.

(10) בָּעֵת הַהִיא יֻקַּח אֲרוֹן הַבְּרִית מִקִּרְבֵּנוּ.

(11) אָסְפָה שִׁבְעִים אִישׁ מִזִּקְנֵי יִשְׂרָאֵל וְלָקַחְתָּ אֹתָם וְהִתְיַצְּבוּ שָׁם עִמָּךְ.

(12) וַיִּזְבַּח יַעֲקֹב זֶבַח שָׁם.

(13) וַיֹּאמֶר אֵלָיו דָּוִד דָּמְךָ עַל־רֹאשֶׁךָ כִּי פִיךָ עָנָה בְךָ לֵאמֹר אָנֹכִי מוֹתַתִּי אֶת־מְשִׁיחַ יהוה.

(14) לֹא עַל־זְבָחֶיךָ אוֹכִיחַ אֹתָךְ.

(15) כּוֹנֵן יהוה אֶת־הָאָרֶץ עַל־הַנְּהָרוֹת אֲשֶׁר תַּחְתֶּיהָ.

(16) וַתִּקַּח הָאִשָּׁה בֵּית פַּרְעֹה.

(d) Write in Hebrew:

1. He was a just and righteous man and walked continually in the way of the Lord.

2. He will heed your prayer when you pray to him.

3. When they begin to prophesy in my name, do not listen to their words for they are evil men, going the way of the wicked.

4. They approached him and bowed down to the ground, for they feared him greatly.

5. This people will increase precipitously and prevail against us.

6. Our salvation is in his strength; he will not abandon us if we implore favor from (lit. to) him.

(e) Reading: Samuel and Eli (I Sam. 3:1–18).

(1) וְהַנַּעַר שְׁמוּאֵל מְשָׁרֵת אֶת־יהוה לִפְנֵי עֵלִי‏¹ וּדְבַר יהוה הָיָה יָקָר בַּיָּמִים הָהֵם אֵין חָזוֹן נִפְרָץ:‏²

(2) וַיְהִי בַּיּוֹם הַהוּא וְעֵלִי שֹׁכֵב בִּמְקוֹמוֹ וְעֵינָיו הֵחֵלּוּ כֵהוֹת‏³ לֹא יוּכַל לִרְאוֹת:

(3) וְנֵר‏⁴ אֱלֹהִים טֶרֶם יִכְבֶּה‏⁵ וּשְׁמוּאֵל שֹׁכֵב בְּהֵיכַל יהוה אֲשֶׁר־שָׁם אֲרוֹן אֱלֹהִים:

(4) וַיִּקְרָא יהוה אֶל־שְׁמוּאֵל וַיֹּאמֶר הִנֵּנִי:

(5) וַיָּרָץ אֶל־עֵלִי וַיֹּאמֶר הִנְנִי כִּי־קָרָאתָ לִּי וַיֹּאמֶר לֹא קָרָאתִי שׁוּב שְׁכָב וַיֵּלֶךְ וַיִּשְׁכָּב:

(6) וַיֹּסֶף יהוה קְרֹא עוֹד שְׁמוּאֵל וַיָּקָם שְׁמוּאֵל וַיֵּלֶךְ אֶל־עֵלִי וַיֹּאמֶר הִנְנִי כִּי קָרָאתָ לִי וַיֹּאמֶר לֹא קָרָאתִי בְנִי שׁוּב שְׁכָב:

(7) וּשְׁמוּאֵל טֶרֶם יָדַע אֶת־יהוה וְטֶרֶם יִגָּלֶה אֵלָיו דְּבַר יהוה:

(8) וַיֹּסֶף יהוה קְרֹא־שְׁמוּאֵל בַּשְּׁלִשִׁית‏⁶ וַיָּקָם וַיֵּלֶךְ אֶל־עֵלִי וַיֹּאמֶר הִנְנִי כִּי קָרָאתָ לִי וַיָּבֶן עֵלִי כִּי יהוה קֹרֵא לַנָּעַר:

(9) וַיֹּאמֶר עֵלִי לִשְׁמוּאֵל לֵךְ שְׁכָב וְהָיָה אִם־יִקְרָא אֵלֶיךָ וְאָמַרְתָּ דַּבֵּר יהוה כִּי שֹׁמֵעַ עַבְדֶּךָ וַיֵּלֶךְ שְׁמוּאֵל וַיִּשְׁכַּב בִּמְקוֹמוֹ:

(10) וַיָּבֹא יהוה וַיִּתְיַצַּב וַיִּקְרָא כְפַעַם־בְּפַעַם‏⁷ שְׁמוּאֵל שְׁמוּאֵל וַיֹּאמֶר שְׁמוּאֵל דַּבֵּר כִּי שֹׁמֵעַ עַבְדֶּךָ:

(11) וַיֹּאמֶר יהוה אֶל־שְׁמוּאֵל הִנֵּה אָנֹכִי עֹשֶׂה דָבָר בְּיִשְׂרָאֵל אֲשֶׁר כָּל־שֹׁמְעוֹ תְּצִלֶּינָה‏⁸ שְׁתֵּי אָזְנָיו:

(12) בַּיּוֹם הַהוּא אָקִים אֶל־עֵלִי אֵת כָּל־אֲשֶׁר דִּבַּרְתִּי אֶל־בֵּיתוֹ הָחֵל וְכַלֵּה:‏⁹

(13) וְהִגַּדְתִּי לוֹ כִּי־שֹׁפֵט אֲנִי אֶת־בֵּיתוֹ עַד־עוֹלָם‏¹⁰ בַּעֲוֺן אֲשֶׁר־יָדַע כִּי מְקַלְלִים לָהֶם‏¹¹ בָּנָיו וְלֹא כִהָה‏¹² בָם:

(14) וְלָכֵן נִשְׁבַּעְתִּי לְבֵית עֵלִי אִם־יִתְכַּפֵּר‏¹³ עֲוֺן בֵּית־עֵלִי בְּזֶבַח וּבְמִנְחָה עַד־עוֹלָם:

(15) וַיִּשְׁכַּב שְׁמוּאֵל עַד־הַבֹּקֶר וַיִּפְתַּח אֶת־דַּלְתוֹת בֵּית יהוה וּשְׁמוּאֵל יָרֵא מֵהַגִּיד אֶת־הַמַּרְאָה‏¹⁴ אֶל־עֵלִי:

(16) וַיִּקְרָא עֵלִי אֶת־שְׁמוּאֵל וַיֹּאמֶר שְׁמוּאֵל בְּנִי וַיֹּאמֶר הִנֵּנִי:

(17) וַיֹּאמֶר מָה הַדָּבָר אֲשֶׁר דִּבֶּר אֵלֶיךָ אַל־נָא תְכַחֵד מִמֶּנִּי כֹּה‏¹⁵ יַעֲשֶׂה־לְּךָ אֱלֹהִים וְכֹה יוֹסִיף אִם־תְּכַחֵד מִמֶּנִּי דָּבָר מִכָּל־הַדָּבָר אֲשֶׁר־דִּבֶּר אֵלֶיךָ:

(18) וַיַּגֶּד־לוֹ שְׁמוּאֵל אֶת־כָּל־הַדְּבָרִים וְלֹא כִחֵד מִמֶּנּוּ וַיֹּאמֶר יהוה הוּא הַטּוֹב בְּעֵינָיו יַעֲשֶׂה:

Notes to the Reading:

1. Note the series of disjunctive clauses giving the setting and explaining the circumstances of the narrative to follow.

2. חָזוֹן נִפְרָץ a frequent vision. Note the asyndetic אֵין clause: "there being no frequent vision."

3. כֵּהֶה weak (of the eyes)

4. נֵר light, lamp

5. כָּבָה to be extinguished, to go out (of a fire or light)

6. שְׁלִישִׁית fem. of the ordinal used adverbially: "for the third time."

7. An idiom: "as (he had) at the other times."

8. צָלַל to tingle. The form תְּצִלֶּינָה

[258]

is unusual; it looks like a Hiphil verb but is generally taken as a Qal.

9. Normal use of inf. absolutes (see § 129); translate: "from start to finish."

10. עָוֹן is in construct with אֲשֶׁר and hence with the whole following clause: "for the iniquity of (the fact that) he knew."

11. לָהֶם is reflexive here: "they were bringing a curse upon themselves."

12. כָּהָה to rebuke

13. אִם after a verb of swearing has a negative force: "I swear... that the iniquity... will not be expiated..."

14. מַרְאָה a vision

15. Cf. remarks under הוֹסִיף in § 165.

LESSON 52

184. The Verb with Object Suffixes.

A pronominal direct object may be suffixed directly to a verb rather than to the object marker אֵת (אֹתִי etc.):

רְאִיתִיהוּ – רָאִיתִי אֹתוֹ   I saw him.

הֲרָגָהּ – הָרַג אֹתָהּ   He killed her.

There is no difference in meaning between the two constructions, though there do appear to be stylistic preferences.

As with the noun, the major problem is to accommodate the proper form of the suffix to the proper form of the verbal stem. The following table shows the object suffixes as they appear after various types of stems:

	A. Post-consonantal, stressed		B. Post-vocalic, unstressed		C. Post-consonantal, unstressed	
1 c. s.	־ֵנִי	-ánî	־נִי	-nî	־נִי	-nî
2 m. s.	־ְךָ	–(ə)kā	־ךָ	–ḵā	־ְךָ	–ḵā
2 f. s.	־ֵךְ	–ēḵ	־ךְ	–ḵ	־ֵךְ	–eḵ
3 m. s.	־ֹו/־ֵהוּ	–ô or –áhû	־הוּ/־ו	–hû or –w	־הוּ/־ו	–hû or –:û
3 f. s.	־ָהּ	–āh	־הָ	–hā	־ָהּ	–:āh
1 c. pl.	־ֵנוּ	–ánû	־נוּ	–nû	־נוּ	–nû
3 m. pl.	־ָם	–ām	־ם	–m	־ָם	–am
3 f. pl.	־ָן	–ān	־ן	–n	־ֵן	–an

[260]

The use of object suffixes for the 2nd pers. pl. is so infrequent that we have omitted them from our table; they were presumably of the forms –*kem* and –*ken* after all types of stems.

185. Object Suffixes on the Perfect: 3rd pers. masc. sing.

שְׁמָרַ֫נִי	he observed me
שְׁמָרְךָ	he observed you (m.s.)
שְׁמָרֵךְ	he observed you (f.s.)
שְׁמָרוֹ or שְׁמָרָ֫הוּ	he observed him
שְׁמָרָהּ	he observed her
שְׁמָרָ֫נוּ	he observed us
שְׁמָרָם	he observed them (m.)
שְׁמָרָן	he observed them (f.)

The suffixes used are those given in column A of the preceding table. Because the suffixes are stressed, the propretonic vowel of the verbal stem is reduced to ə. In Piel verbs, however, where the propretonic syllable is closed or at least unchangeable, it is the pretonic vowel that is reduced: בִּקְשַׁ֫נִי he sought me. A further difference with Piel verbs is the change of ē to e before the suffix of the 2nd pers. masc. sing.: בִּקֶשְׁךָ he sought you. The following list includes all of the main types of Qal, Piel, and Hiphil verbs as they appear before the suffixes:

QAL	שָׁמַר	שְׁמָרַ֫נִי	שְׁמָרְךָ	שְׁמָרֵךְ · etc.
	עָזַב	עֲזָבַ֫נִי	עֲזָבְךָ	
	שָׁלַח	שְׁלָחַ֫נִי	שְׁלָחֲךָ	
	מָצָא	מְצָאַ֫נִי	מְצָאֲךָ	
	בָּנָה	בְּנַ֫נִי	בְּנְךָ	
	שָׂם	שָׂמַ֫נִי	שָׂמְךָ	
	סָבַב	סְבָבַ֫נִי	סְבָבְךָ	
	חָנַן	חַנַּ֫נִי	חַנְּךָ	
PIEL	בִּקֵּשׁ	בִּקְשַׁ֫נִי	בִּקֶשְׁךָ	
	שִׁלַּח	שִׁלְּחַ֫נִי	שִׁלַּחֲךָ	
	בֵּרַךְ	בֵּרְכַ֫נִי	בֵּרֶכְךָ	
	עִנָּה	עִנַּ֫נִי	עִנְּךָ	
HIPHIL	הִשְׁמִיד	הִשְׁמִידַ֫נִי	הִשְׁמִידְךָ	
	הִשְׁמִיעַ	הִשְׁמִיעַ֫נִי	הִשְׁמִיעֲךָ	
	הִמְצִיא	הִמְצִיאַ֫נִי	הִמְצִיאֲךָ	
	הֶעֱמִיד	הֶעֱמִידַ֫נִי	הֶעֱמִידְךָ	
	הֶעֱלָה	הֶעֱלַ֫נִי	הֶעֶלְךָ	
	הוֹרִיד	הוֹרִידַ֫נִי	הוֹרִידְךָ	
	הֵשִׁיב	הֱשִׁיבַ֫נִי	הֱשִׁיבְךָ	
	הֵסֵב	הֲסִבַּ֫נִי	הֲסִבְּךָ	

Remarks:

(1) Verbs from roots III-*Hē,* regardless of the conjugational type, have a shortened form before the suffix: הִגְלָה – הִגְלָ → עָנָה – עָנָ → בָּנָה – בָּנָ.

(2) A variation between *ĕ* and *ă* is found in the reduced syllable of verbs like הֵשִׁיב; thus either הֱשִׁיבַ֫נִי or הֱשִׁיבֹ֫נִי.

186. Object Suffixes on the Perfect: 2nd pers. masc. sing.

שְׁמַרְתַּ֫נִי	you observed me	שְׁמַרְתָּ֫נוּ	you observed us
שְׁמַרְתּוֹ / שְׁמַרְתָּ֫הוּ	you observed him	שְׁמַרְתָּם	you observed them (m.)
שְׁמַרְתָּהּ	you observed her	שְׁמַרְתָּן	you observed them (f.)

The endings are exactly the same as those of the 3rd pers. masc. sing. verb; it is convenient, therefore, to describe the stem change as שְׁמַרְתָּ → שְׁמַרְתָּ֫ (note the propretonic reduction) and to specify the suffixes of Column A above. Thus

Qal	שָׁמַ֫רְתָּ	שְׁמַרְתַּ֫נִי	שְׁמַרְתּוֹ	etc.
	עָזַ֫בְתָּ	עֲזַבְתַּ֫נִי	עֲזַבְתּוֹ	
	שָׁלַ֫חְתָּ	שְׁלַחְתַּ֫נִי	שְׁלַחְתּוֹ	
	מָצָ֫אתָ	מְצָאתַ֫נִי	מְצָאתוֹ	
	בָּנִ֫יתָ	בְּנִיתַ֫נִי	בְּנִיתוֹ	
	שַׂ֫מְתָּ	שַׂמְתַּ֫נִי	שַׂמְתּוֹ	
	סַבּ֫וֹתָ	סַבּוֹתַ֫נִי	סַבּוֹתוֹ	
Piel	בִּקַּ֫שְׁתָּ	בִּקַּשְׁתַּ֫נִי	בִּקַּשְׁתּוֹ	
	שִׁלַּ֫חְתָּ	שִׁלַּחְתַּ֫נִי	שִׁלַּחְתּוֹ	
	בֵּרַ֫כְתָּ	בֵּרַכְתַּ֫נִי	בֵּרַכְתּוֹ	
	עִנִּ֫יתָ	עִנִּיתַ֫נִי	עִנִּיתוֹ	
Hiphil	הִשְׁמַ֫דְתָּ	הִשְׁמַדְתַּ֫נִי	הִשְׁמַדְתּוֹ	
	הִשְׁמַ֫עְתָּ	הִשְׁמַעְתַּ֫נִי	הִשְׁמַעְתּוֹ	
	הִמְצֵ֫אתָ	הִמְצֵאתַ֫נִי	הִמְצֵאתוֹ	
	הֶעֱמַ֫דְתָּ	הֶעֱמַדְתַּ֫נִי	הֶעֱמַדְתּוֹ	
	הִרְאִ֫יתָ	הִרְאִיתַ֫נִי	הִרְאִיתוֹ	
	הֲשִׁיב֫וֹתָ	הֲשִׁיבוֹתַ֫נִי	הֲשִׁיבוֹתוֹ	
	הֲסִבּ֫וֹתָ	הֲסִבּוֹתַ֫נִי	הֲסִבּוֹתוֹ	
	הִפְר֫וֹתָ	הִפְרוֹתַ֫נִי	הִפְרוֹתוֹ	

Remarks:

Only the Hiphil verbs from roots I-gutt. require comment. We noted at the end of §158 that the converted perfect וְהַאֲמַנְתָּ has *a–ă* instead of the usual *e–ĕ,* as in הֶאֱמַנְתָּ. This same substitution is made where pronominal suffixes are added to the converted forms; thus:

הֶעֱמַדְתִּיךָ I stationed you → וְהַעֲמַדְתִּיךָ and I shall station you

It is interesting to note that the stress is the same in both of these forms, and that the substitution is morphologically rather than phonologically determined. There are, moreover, a few instances where this replacement is not made.

187. Vocabulary 52.

VERBS: מָאַס (יְמְאַס) to refuse, despise, reject

מָלַךְ (יְמְלֹךְ) to rule (עַל/בְּ over); to be/become king

קָצַר (יִקְצֹר) to reap, harvest

בָּלַע (יִבְלַע) to swallow

סָלַח (יִסְלַח) to pardon, forgive (+ לְ with person or thing)

מָרַד (יִמְרֹד) to rebel (עַל/בְּ against)

כָּשַׁל (יִכְשֹׁל) to stumble, totter

הֵעִיד (יָעִיד) to warn (בְּ)

NOUNS: מַעֲשֶׂה (pl. -îm) deed, act, work

זַיִת (pl. -îm) olive-tree, olive

שַׂר (pl. -îm) chief, officer

קָצִיר (no pl.) harvest, crop; time of harvest

גּוֹי (pl. -îm) people, nation; sometimes synonymous with עַם in referring to Israel, but more often used for non-Israelites.

PROPER NAMES: רָמָה Ramah, a town in the hill-country of Ephraim; home of Samuel.

Exercises:

(a) Transform the following according to the example and translate:

Ex. הָרַג אֹתִי → הֲרָגַ֫נִי he killed me

(11) שְׁכַחְתַּ֫נִי	(6) שְׁבָרֽתוֹ	(1) זְכַרְתָּם
(12) עֲזַבְתָּ֫הוּ	(7) קְבַצְתָּן	(2) שְׁפַטְתָּ֫נוּ
(13) אֲסָרֽךָ	(8) מְכָרֽךָ	(3) לְכַדְתַּ֫נִי
(14) בְּרָאָם	(9) גְּנָבָהּ	(4) סְגָרֽוֹ
(15) מְאָסֽהוּ	(10) גְּאָלֶ֫ךָ	(5) תְּפַשְׂתָּ֫הּ

(b) Transform the following according to the example and translate:

Ex. הֲרָגַ֫נִי → הָרַג אֹתִי

(11) שָׁתָה אֹתוֹ	(6) קָצַר אֹתוֹ	(1) אָחַז אֹתָהּ
(12) בָּזָה אֹתִי	(7) שָׂם אֹתְךָ	(2) נָגַֽפְתָּ אֹתוֹ
(13) רָאִיתָ אֹתָן	(8) שָׁלַחְתָּ אֹתִי	(3) נָשָׂא אֹתָ֫נוּ
(14) עָנִּיתָ אֹתוֹ	(9) בָּנִיתָ אֹתוֹ	(4) נָתַתְּ אֹתָ֫נוּ
(15) סָבַב אֹתָ֫נוּ	(10) קָנָה אֹתָהּ	(5) יָצַר אֹתָם

(c) Translate the following. Replace the nominal object with the appropriate pronoun, suffixed to the verb.

Ex. הַלֵּל אֶת־הַנָּבִיא → הַלְלוּ he praised him

(11) הֶעֱבִיר אֶת־הָעָם	(6) עִנָּה אֶת־הַדַּלִּים	(1) קִדֵּשׁ אֶת־הַשַּׂר
(12) הִגִּישׁ אֶת־הַלֶּחֶם	(7) צִוָּה אֶת־שָׂרָיו	(2) גֵּרֵשׁ אֶת־הַגּוֹיִם
(13) הוֹרִיד אֶת־הַמְרַגְּלִים	(8) כִּחֵד אֶת־הַמַּעֲשֶׂה	(3) בֵּרֵךְ אֶת־הַקָּצִיר
(14) הֶרְאָה אֶת־אוֹתוֹ	(9) הִזְכִּיר אֶת־שְׁמוֹ	(4) שִׁלַּח אֶת־הַמַּלְאָךְ
(15) הֶחֱיָה אֶת־הַמֶּלֶךְ	(10) הִקְרִיב אֶת־מִנְחָתוֹ	(5) נִאֵץ אֶת־הָאָדוֹן

(d) Transform the verbs of Exercise (c) to the 2nd pers. masc. sing. and add the object suffix of the 1st pers. pl. E.g. קִדֵּשׁ → קִדַּשְׁתָּ → קִדַּשְׁתָּנוּ

(e) Give the Hebrew for the following orally; use object suffixes when possible.

1. And he will gladden us.
2. And he will comfort them.
3. And you (m.s.) will cause them to swear.
4. And he will bring you back.
5. And you will take me up.
6. And he will strike him.
7. And you will save her.
8. And he will throw them.
9. And he will warn them.
10. And you will plant it.

(f) Write in Hebrew:

1. And when they rebelled against him, he became very angry and sent his men that they might put them to death.
2. But when they came to the city, they saw that the people had fled and had abandoned their houses, their property, their crops, and everything that belonged to them.
3. When the people saw the deeds that their chiefs had done, they rebelled against them and slew them.
4. Why should (=shall) I bow down before these idols of wood and stone? There is no breath of life in them, nor can they act in my behalf when I pray to them and call in their name.

(g) Reading: I Samuel 8:4-22. The Evils of Kingship:

(4) וַיִּתְקַבְּצוּ כֹּל זִקְנֵי יִשְׂרָאֵל וַיָּבֹאוּ אֶל־שְׁמוּאֵל הָרָמָתָה:

(5) וַיֹּאמְרוּ אֵלָיו הִנֵּה אַתָּה זָקַנְתָּ וּבָנֶיךָ לֹא הָלְכוּ בִּדְרָכֶיךָ עַתָּה שִׂימָה־לָּנוּ מֶלֶךְ לְשָׁפְטֵנוּ כְּכָל־הַגּוֹיִם:

(6) וַיֵּרַע הַדָּבָר בְּעֵינֵי שְׁמוּאֵל כַּאֲשֶׁר אָמְרוּ תְּנָה־לָּנוּ מֶלֶךְ לְשָׁפְטֵנוּ וַיִּתְפַּלֵּל שְׁמוּאֵל אֶל־יְהוָה:

(7) וַיֹּאמֶר יְהוָה אֶל־שְׁמוּאֵל שְׁמַע בְּקוֹל הָעָם לְכֹל אֲשֶׁר־יֹאמְרוּ אֵלֶיךָ כִּי לֹא אֹתְךָ מָאָסוּ כִּי־אֹתִי מָאֲסוּ מִמְּלֹךְ עֲלֵיהֶם:

(8) כְּכָל־הַמַּעֲשִׂים אֲשֶׁר־עָשׂוּ מִיּוֹם הַעֲלֹתִי אֹתָם מִמִּצְרַֹיִם וְעַד־הַיּוֹם הַזֶּה וַיַּעַזְבֻ֫נִי² וַיַּעַבְדוּ אֱלֹהִים אֲחֵרִים כֵּן הֵ֫מָּה עֹשִׂים גַּם־לָךְ:

(9) וְעַתָּה שְׁמַע בְּקוֹלָם אַךְ³ כִּי־הָעֵד תָּעִיד בָּהֶם וְהִגַּדְתָּ לָהֶם מִשְׁפַּט הַמֶּ֫לֶךְ אֲשֶׁר יִמְלֹךְ עֲלֵיהֶם:

(10) וַיֹּ֫אמֶר שְׁמוּאֵל אֵת כָּל־דִּבְרֵי יהוה אֶל־הָעָם הַשֹּׁאֲלִים מֵאִתּוֹ מֶֽלֶךְ:

(11) וַיֹּ֫אמֶר זֶה יִהְיֶה מִשְׁפַּט הַמֶּ֫לֶךְ אֲשֶׁר יִמְלֹךְ עֲלֵיכֶם אֶת־בְּנֵיכֶם יִקָּח וְשָׂם לוֹ בְּמֶרְכַּבְתּוֹ וּבְפָרָשָׁיו וְרָצוּ לִפְנֵי מֶרְכַּבְתּוֹ:

(12) וְלָשׂוּם⁴ לוֹ שָׂרֵי אֲלָפִים וְשָׂרֵי חֲמִשִּׁים וְלַחֲרֹשׁ חֲרִישׁוֹ⁵ וְלִקְצֹר קְצִירוֹ וְלַעֲשׂוֹת כְּלֵי־ מִלְחַמְתּוֹ וּכְלֵי רִכְבּוֹ:⁶

(13) וְאֶת־בְּנוֹתֵיכֶם יִקָּח לְרַקָּחוֹת⁷ וּלְטַבָּחוֹת וּלְאֹפוֹת:

(14) וְאֶת־שְׂדֽוֹתֵיכֶם וְאֶת־כַּרְמֵיכֶם וְזֵיתֵיכֶם הַטּוֹבִים יִקָּח וְנָתַן לַעֲבָדָיו:

(15) וְזַרְעֵיכֶם וְכַרְמֵיכֶם יַעְשֹׂר⁸ וְנָתַן לְסָרִיסָיו וְלַעֲבָדָיו:

(16) וְאֶת־עַבְדֵיכֶם וְאֶת־שִׁפְחוֹתֵיכֶם וְאֶת־בַּחוּרֵיכֶם הַטּוֹבִים וְאֶת־חֲמוֹרֵיכֶם יִקָּח וְעָשָׂה לִמְלַאכְתּוֹ:

(17) צֹאנְכֶם יַעְשֹׂר וְאַתֶּם תִּהְיוּ־לוֹ לַעֲבָדִים:

(18) וּזְעַקְתֶּם בַּיּוֹם הַהוּא מִלִּפְנֵי מַלְכְּכֶם אֲשֶׁר בְּחַרְתֶּם לָכֶם וְלֹא־יַעֲנֶה יהוה אֶתְכֶם בַּיּוֹם הַהוּא:

(19) וַיְמָאֲנוּ הָעָם לִשְׁמֹעַ בְּקוֹל שְׁמוּאֵל וַיֹּאמְרוּ לֹא כִּי אִם־מֶ֫לֶךְ יִהְיֶה עָלֵ֫ינוּ:

(20) וְהָיִ֫ינוּ גַם־אֲנַ֫חְנוּ כְּכָל־הַגּוֹיִם וּשְׁפָטָ֫נוּ מַלְכֵּ֫נוּ וְיָצָא לְפָנֵ֫ינוּ וְנִלְחַם אֶת־מִלְחֲמֹתֵ֫ינוּ:

(21) וַיִּשְׁמַע שְׁמוּאֵל אֵת כָּל־דִּבְרֵי הָעָם וַיְדַבְּרֵם⁹ בְּאָזְנֵי יהוה:

(22) וַיֹּ֫אמֶר יהוה אֶל־שְׁמוּאֵל שְׁמַע בְּקוֹלָם וְהִמְלַכְתָּ לָהֶם מֶ֫לֶךְ וַיֹּ֫אמֶר שְׁמוּאֵל אֶל־אַנְשֵׁי יִשְׂרָאֵל לְכוּ אִישׁ לְעִירוֹ:

Notes to the Reading:

1. The suffix is objective: "to judge us"
2. וַיַּעַזְבוּ אֹתִי = וַיַּעַזְבֻ֫נִי
3. אַךְ כִּי but, however
4. The infinitives can be taken gerundially, continuing the preceding sentence: "appointing (them) for him (self) as..."
5. חָרִישׁ land to be plowed
6. רֶ֫כֶב chariotry
7. רַקָּחָה perfumer; טַבָּחָה cook; אֹפָה baker (all feminine)
8. עָשַׂר to tithe, exact a tenth of
9. וַיְדַבֵּר אֹתָם = וַיְדַבְּרֵם

LESSON 53

188. Object Suffixes on the Perfect: 3rd pers. fem. sing.

The feminine ending -*āh* is replaced by -*āt* or -*at* before the pronominal suffixes, which have the forms given in Column C, §184:

שְׁמָרַ֫תְנִי	she observed me	שְׁמָרַ֫תְנוּ	she observed us
שְׁמָרָ֫תְךָ	she observed you (m.s.)		
שְׁמָרָ֫תֶךְ	she observed you (f.s.)		
שְׁמָרַ֫תְהוּ ‏)‏	she observed him	שְׁמָרָ֫תַם	she observed them (m.)
שְׁמָרַ֫תּוּ ‏(‏			
שְׁמָרַ֫תָּה	she observed her		

Peculiar features of this paradigm are (1) the restoration of the full vowel *ā* in pretonic positions, (2) the assimilation of -*at* + *hû* and -*at* + *hā* to -*áttû* and -*áttāh* respectively. A survey of extant forms:

QAL	שְׁמָרָה	שְׁמָרַ֫תְנִי	שְׁמָרַ֫תְךָ
	עֲזָבָה	עֲזָבַ֫תְנִי	עֲזָבַ֫תְךָ
	שְׁלָחָה	שְׁלָחַ֫תְנִי	שְׁלָחַ֫תְךָ
	רָאֲתָה	רָאַ֫תְנִי	רָאַ֫תְךָ
PIEL	בִּקְשָׁה	בִּקְשַׁ֫תְנִי	בִּקְשַׁ֫תְךָ
	עִנְּתָה	עִנַּ֫תְנִי	עִנַּ֫תְךָ
HIPHIL	הִשְׁמִ֫ידָה	הִשְׁמִידַ֫תְנִי	הִשְׁמִידַ֫תְךָ
	הֶרְאֲתָה	הֶרְאַ֫תְנִי	הֶרְאַ֫תְךָ
	הֶעֱלְתָה	הֶעֱלַ֫תְנִי	הֶעֱלַ֫תְךָ
	הֱשִׁ֫יבָה	הֱשִׁיבַ֫תְנִי	הֱשִׁיבַ֫תְךָ

189. Object Suffixes on the Remaining Forms of the Perfect.

These offer no new problems, other than the alterations in the form of the subject suffix:

    (a) The 2nd pers. fem. sing. ending *-t → -tî-*

    (b) The 2nd pers. masc. (and fem.?) pl. ending *-tem → -tû-*

All the remaining stems, then, end in a vowel, to which are added the suffixes of Column B, §184. Here is a representative sampling (cf. also the Exercises):

שְׁמַרְתִּ֫ינִי	you (f.s.) observed me
שְׁמַרְתִּים	you (f.s.) observed them
שְׁמַרְתִּ֫יךָ	I observed you (m.s.)
שְׁמַרְתִּיךְ	I observed you (f.s.)
שְׁמַרְתִּ֫ים	I observed them (m.)
שְׁמָר֫וּנִי	they observed me
שְׁמָר֫וּךְ	they observed you (f.s.)
שְׁמָר֫וּהוּ	they observed him
שְׁמָר֫וּם	they observed them
שְׁמַרְתּ֫וּנִי	you (pl.) observed me
שְׁמַרְתּ֫וּהוּ	you (pl.) observed him
שְׁמַרְנ֫וּךָ	we observed you (m.s.)
שְׁמַרְנ֫וּהוּ	we observed him

Note again (1) the shift of stress and resultant propretonic reduction; (2) the restoration of the full vowel in שְׁמָר֫וּהוּ etc.; (3) the possibility of confusion between the 2nd pers. fem. sing. and the 1st pers. com. sing. with *-tî-*.

QAL	שָׁמַ֫רְתִּי	שְׁמַרְתִּ֫יהוּ	שָׁמְרוּ	שְׁמָר֫וּהוּ
	עָזַ֫בְתִּי	עֲזַבְתִּ֫יהוּ	עָזְבוּ	עֲזָב֫וּהוּ
	מָצָ֫אתִי	מְצָאתִ֫יהוּ	מָצְאוּ	מְצָא֫וּהוּ
	רָאִ֫יתִי	רְאִיתִ֫יהוּ	רָאוּ	רָא֫וּהוּ
PIEL	בִּקַּ֫שְׁתִּי	בִּקַּשְׁתִּ֫יהוּ	בִּקְּשׁוּ	בִּקְּשׁ֫וּהוּ
	עִנִּ֫יתִי	עִנִּיתִ֫יהוּ	עִנּוּ	עִנּ֫וּהוּ
	בֵּרַ֫כְתִּי	בֵּרַכְתִּ֫יהוּ	בֵּרְכוּ	בֵּרְכ֫וּהוּ
HIPHIL	הִשְׁמַ֫דְתִּי	הִשְׁמַדְתִּ֫יהוּ	הִשְׁמִ֫ידוּ	הִשְׁמִיד֫וּהוּ
	הֶעֱלֵ֫יתִי	הֶעֱלֵיתִ֫יהוּ	הֶעֱלוּ	הֶעֱל֫וּהוּ
	הֲשִׁיבֹ֫ותִי	הֲשִׁיבוֹתִ֫יהוּ	הֵשִׁ֫יבוּ	הֲשִׁיב֫וּהוּ

190. A Group of Irregular Qal Verbs.

There are several Qal verbs which have *ē* or *i* in second stem syllable before the pronominal suffixes. Two of these יָרֵשׁ and שָׁאַל have unusual forms even in the 2nd pers. pl. of the non-suffixal paradigm: שְׁאֶלְתֶּם you asked; יְרִשְׁתֶּם

you inherited. Below, for reference, are the anomalous forms of the four important verbs of this type. Regular forms also occur in some instances.

אָהַב or אָהֵב	to love	3 m.s.	אֲהֵבְךָ	אֲהֵבוֹ	אֲהֵבָה
		3 f.s.	אֲהֵבָתְךָ	אֲהֵבַתְהוּ	
		3 m.pl.	אֲהֵבוּךָ	אֲהֵבוּנִי	
יָלַד	to bear	2 f.s.	יְלִדְתְּנִי		
		1 c.s.	יְלִדְתִּיךָ	יְלִדְתִּיהוּ	
יָרַשׁ	to inherit	2 m.s.	יְרִשְׁתָּה	יְרִשְׁתָּם	
		3 m.pl.	יְרֵשׁוּךָ	יְרֵשׁוּהוּ	
		2 m.pl.	יְרִשְׁתֶּם		
שָׁאַל	to ask	3 m.s.	שְׁאֵלְךָ		
		1 c.s.	שְׁאֵלְתִּיו	שְׁאֵלְתִּיהוּ	
		3 m.pl.	שְׁאֵלוּנוּ		
		2 m.pl.	שְׁאֵלְתֶּם		

191. Vocabulary 53.

VERBS: חָמַל (יַחְמֹל) to spare (+ inf.: to spare oneself the trouble/expense of doing something); to pity (+ עַל)

שִׁלֵּם (יְשַׁלֵּם) to restore, make good, recompense

מָשַׁח (יִמְשַׁח) to anoint

בָּזָה (יִבְזֶה) to despise

בָּקַע (יִבְקַע) to split

עָזַר (יַעֲזֹר) to help

רָפָא (יִרְפָּא) to cure, heal; P רִפֵּא idem.

NOUNS: כֶּבֶשׂ (pl. -îm) lamb (male)

כִּבְשָׂה (pl. -ôṯ) lamb (female)

חֵיק bosom

חֶרֶב (w. suff. חַרְבִּי; pl. -ôṯ) sword (f.)

OTHER: יַחְדָּו } (adv.) together, all together
יַחַד }

עֵקֶב אֲשֶׁר/כִּי (conj.) because

נֶגֶד (prep.) before, in front of; w. suff. נֶגְדִּי etc. Also לְנֶגֶד

אֶפֶס a rare syn. of אַיִן "non-existence"; אֶפֶס כִּי (conj.) except that, save that

PROPER NAMES: נָתָן Nathan, the prophet

אוּרִיָּה Uriah

חִתִּי Hittite (adj.)

Exercises:

(a) Transform the following according to the example and translate.

עֲזָרוּנִי → עָזְרוּ אֹתִי they helped me

(1) גֵּרְשׁוּם	(6) שְׁתִיתִיהוּ	(11) בֵּרַכּוּךְ
(2) מְכַרְנוּם	(7) קִדְּשׁוּנִי	(12) הֶעֱבִירוּם
(3) אֲחָזוּנִי	(8) לְכַדְתִּים	(13) הִזְכַּרְתּוּנִי
(4) זְכַרְתִּיךְ	(9) גְּנַבְנוּהוּ	(14) סְגַרְתִּיהוּ
(5) קְצַרְתֻּהוּ	(10) נְגַפְתֻּנִי	(15) גְּאַלְנוּךְ

(b) Transform the following according to the example and translate.

רְאִיתִיהוּ → רָאִיתִי אֹתוֹ I saw him *(accent moves)*

(1) תָּפַשְׂתִּי אֹתָן	(6) נָאֲצוּ אֹתוֹ	(11) עֲנָתָה אֹתָם
(2) שָׁלְחָה אֹתָנוּ	(7) צִוִּינוּ אֹתָם	(12) שְׁכֵחוּ אֹתָךְ
(3) עֲזָבֻנוּ אֹתָם	(8) הֵרְאוּ אֹתִי	(13) בָּזְנוּ אֹתוֹ
(4) מְשָׁחֻנוּ אֹתוֹ	(9) הוֹרִידָה אֹתָם	(14) הִגַּשְׁתִּי אֹתָהּ
(5) שָׁמְנוּ אֹתָם	(10) בָּנִיתִי אֹתָהּ	(15) בְּזָתָה אֹתִי

(c) Translate the following. Replace the object with the appropriate pronoun suffixed to the verb.

(1) עָזְבוּ אֶת־אֱלֹהֵיהֶם	(9) הוֹשַׁעְנוּ אֶת־הַשָּׂרִים
(2) שָׁבַרְתִּי אֶת־הַחֶרֶב	(10) נְטַעְתֶּם כְּרָמִים
(3) רָאִיתָ אֶת־עֶגְלֵיהֶם	(11) בָּקְעוּ אֶת־הָעֵצִים
(4) עִנּוּ אֶת־הָעָם	(12) נִחֲמוּ אֶת־הָאֲנָשִׁים
(5) אָסְרוּ אֶת־הַבַּחוּרִים	(13) קָבַצְתִּי אֶת־הַכְּבָשִׂים
(6) מָאֲסוּ אֶת־דְּבָרַי	(14) הֶעֱלִיתָ אֶת־הַיְלָדִים
(7) עֲזַרְנוּ אֶת־הַדַּלִּים	(15) שִׁלֵּם אֶת־הַכֶּסֶף
(8) לָקְחוּ אֶת־קְצִירֵנוּ	

(d) Write in Hebrew:

1. We shall continue to meet him.
2. They began to approach the city in the evening, before the gate had been closed.
3. At that time there was no place for us to settle in, so we continued travelling.
4. Even in this congregation there are unrighteous men who do not heed the word of the Lord and who take pleasure in nullifying his statutes.
5. Prophesy now to the people, for evil days are coming and they will not be able to hide themselves from the terror which is about to fall upon them.
6. Bow down before the one who has made you and give thanks to the one who has delivered you from your distress.

(e) Reading: II Samuel 12:1-15a

(1) וַיִּשְׁלַח יהוה אֶת־נָתָן אֶל־דָּוִד וַיָּבֹא אֵלָיו וַיֹּאמֶר לוֹ שְׁנֵי אֲנָשִׁים הָיוּ בְּעִיר אֶחָת אֶחָד
עָשִׁיר וְאֶחָד רָאשׁ²׃

(2) לְעָשִׁיר הָיָה צֹאן וּבָקָר הַרְבֵּה מְאֹד:

(3) וְלָרָשׁ אֵין־כֹּל כִּי אִם־כִּבְשָׂה אַחַת קְטַנָּה אֲשֶׁר קָנָה וַיְחַיֶּהָ³ וַתִּגְדַּל עִמּוֹ וְעִם־בָּנָיו יַחְדָּו מִפִּתּוֹ⁴ תֹאכַל וּמִכֹּסוֹ⁵ תִשְׁתֶּה וּבְחֵיקוֹ תִשְׁכָּב וַתְּהִי־לוֹ כְּבַת:

(4) וַיָּבֹא הֵלֶךְ⁶ לְאִישׁ הֶעָשִׁיר⁷ וַיַּחְמֹל לָקַחַת מִצֹּאנוֹ וּמִבְּקָרוֹ לַעֲשׂוֹת לָאֹרֵחַ הַבָּא לוֹ וַיִּקַּח אֶת־כִּבְשַׂת הָאִישׁ הָרָאשׁ וַיַּעֲשֶׂהָ⁸ לָאִישׁ הַבָּא אֵלָיו:

(5) וַיִּחַר־אַף דָּוִד בָּאִישׁ מְאֹד וַיֹּאמֶר אֶל־נָתָן חַי יהוה כִּי בֶן־מָוֶת⁹ הָאִישׁ הָעֹשֶׂה זֹאת:

(6) וְאֶת־הַכִּבְשָׂה יְשַׁלֵּם אַרְבַּעְתָּיִם¹⁰ עֵקֶב אֲשֶׁר עָשָׂה אֶת־הַדָּבָר הַזֶּה וְעַל אֲשֶׁר לֹא־חָמָל:

(7) וַיֹּאמֶר נָתָן אֶל־דָּוִד אַתָּה הָאִישׁ כֹּה אָמַר יהוה אֱלֹהֵי יִשְׂרָאֵל אָנֹכִי מְשַׁחְתִּיךָ לְמֶלֶךְ עַל־יִשְׂרָאֵל וְאָנֹכִי הִצַּלְתִּיךָ מִיַּד שָׁאוּל:

(8) וָאֶתְּנָה לְךָ אֶת־בֵּית אֲדֹנֶיךָ וְאֶת־נְשֵׁי אֲדֹנֶיךָ בְּחֵיקֶךָ וָאֶתְּנָה לְךָ אֶת־בֵּית יִשְׂרָאֵל וִיהוּדָה וְאִם־מְעָט וְאֹסִפָה לְּךָ כָּהֵנָּה וְכָהֵנָּה:¹¹

(9) מַדּוּעַ בָּזִיתָ אֶת־דְּבַר יהוה לַעֲשׂוֹת הָרַע בְּעֵינַי אֵת אוּרִיָּה הַחִתִּי הִכִּיתָ בַחֶרֶב וְאֶת־אִשְׁתּוֹ לָקַחְתָּ לְּךָ לְאִשָּׁה וְאֹתוֹ הָרַגְתָּ בְּחֶרֶב בְּנֵי עַמּוֹן:¹²

(10) וְעַתָּה לֹא־תָסוּר חֶרֶב מִבֵּיתְךָ עַד־עוֹלָם עֵקֶב כִּי בְזִתָנִי וַתִּקַּח אֶת־אֵשֶׁת אוּרִיָּה הַחִתִּי לִהְיוֹת לְךָ לְאִשָּׁה:

(11) כֹּה אָמַר יהוה הִנְנִי מֵקִים עָלֶיךָ רָעָה מִבֵּיתֶךָ וְלָקַחְתִּי אֶת־נָשֶׁיךָ לְעֵינֶיךָ וְנָתַתִּי לְרֵעֶיךָ וְשָׁכַב עִם־נָשֶׁיךָ לְעֵינֵי הַשֶּׁמֶשׁ הַזֹּאת:

(12) כִּי אַתָּה עָשִׂיתָ בַסָּתֶר¹³ וַאֲנִי אֶעֱשֶׂה אֶת־הַדָּבָר הַזֶּה נֶגֶד כָּל־יִשְׂרָאֵל וְנֶגֶד הַשָּׁמֶשׁ:

(13) וַיֹּאמֶר דָּוִד אֶל־נָתָן חָטָאתִי לַיהוה וַיֹּאמֶר נָתָן אֶל־דָּוִד גַּם־יהוה הֶעֱבִיר חַטָּאתְךָ לֹא תָמוּת:

(14) אֶפֶס כִּי־נִאֵץ נִאַצְתָּ אֶת־אֹיְבֵי¹⁴ יהוה בַּדָּבָר הַזֶּה גַּם הַבֵּן הַיִּלּוֹד¹⁵ לְךָ מוֹת יָמוּת:

(15) וַיֵּלֶךְ נָתָן אֶל־בֵּיתוֹ:

Notes to the reading:

1. אֶחָת pausal form of אַחַת
2. רָאשׁ (or רָשׁ) poor (adj.)
3. יְחַיֶּהָ = יְחַיֶּה אֹתָהּ
4. פַּת morsel
5. כֹּס or כּוֹס cup
6. הֵלֶךְ traveller
7. Note the construction לְאִישׁ הֶעָשִׁיר to the rich man, where the noun is in construct with the definite adjective.
8. וַיַּעַשׂ אֹתָהּ = וַיַּעֲשֶׂהָ
9. "deserving of/sentenced to death"
10. Note § 161 (d)

11. "and if (that were) too little, I would add unto you (i.e. increase your wealth and prestige) so much more"
12. בְּנֵי עַמּוֹן the Ammonites
13. בַּסָּתֶר secretly; סֵתֶר secret
14. אֹיְבֵי may have been inserted at an early date to prevent the verb נִאֵץ from having יהוה as its direct object. The word must be ignored in translation. נִאֵץ = inf. abs. (irreg.).
15. יִלּוֹד a rare type of verbal adjective: "born"

192. Object Suffixes on the Imperfect.

When the form of the imperfect ends in a consonant, the suffix -ē- or -en-
is added before the object pronoun; thus *yišmōr* + *ē/en* + *nî* → *yišmərénî/*
yišmərénnî (he will observe me). Because of various contractions, however,
it is simpler to learn the suffixed elements as a unit:

	(1)		(2)
1 c.s.	–ֶ֫נִּי	–énnî	–ֵ֫נִי	–énî
2 m.s.	–ֶ֫ךָּ	–ékkā	——	——
2 f.s.	——	——	–ֵ֫ךְ	–ék̲
3 m.s.	–ֶ֫נּוּ	–énnû	–ֵ֫הוּ	–éhû
3 f.s.	–ֶ֫נָּה	–énnāh	–ֶ֫הָ	–éhā
1 c.pl.	–ֶ֫נּוּ	–énnû	–ֵ֫נוּ	–énû
3 m.pl.	——	——	–ֵ֫ם	–ém
3 f.pl.	——	——	–ֵ֫ן	–én

Neither paradigm is complete in itself. Forms of either column may be used,
with no difference in meaning.

Excluding for the moment the imperfects of verbs from roots III-*Hē*,
we may distinguish those whose stem vowel is reducible (as in יִשְׁמֹר, יִשְׁמְרוּ),
which includes most Qal and Piel verbs, and those whose stem vowel is not
reducible, mainly Qal verbs from Hollow Roots and Hiphil verbs. When the
stem vowel is ō or ē, the same reduction takes place as in the main paradigm:

cf. יִשְׁמְרוּ (they will observe) and יִשְׁמְרֵנִי (he will observe me); יִתְּנוּ (they will give) and יִתְּנֵנִי (he will give me). But when the stem vowel is -a-, this is not reduced but lengthened to ā before the accented syllable of the suffix. Contrast יִשְׁמַע and יִשְׁמְעוּ with יִשְׁמָעֵנִי (he will hear me). Read carefully through the representative forms given below to be sure that this point is clear.

The imperfect plural forms in -û (e.g. תִּשְׁמְרוּ, יִשְׁמְרוּ) take the suffixes given in Column B, §184. But even in these forms the *a* vowel of the stem is restored.   Contrast

יִשְׁמְרוּ	יִשְׁמְרוּנִי	יִשְׁמְעוּ	יִשְׁמָעוּנִי.
יִשְׁמֹר	יִשְׁמְרֵנִי	יִשְׁמְרוּ	יִשְׁמְרוּנִי
יְלַמֵּד	יְלַמְּדֵהוּ	יְלַמְּדוּ	יְלַמְּדוּהוּ
יִשְׁמַע	יִשְׁמָעֵנִי	יִשְׁמְעוּ	יִשְׁמָעוּנִי
יַעֲזֹב	יַעַזְבֵנִי	יַעַזְבוּ	יַעַזְבוּנִי
יִמְצָא	יִמְצָאֵנִי	יִמְצְאוּ	יִמְצָאוּנִי
יֹאכַל	יֹאכְלֵהוּ	יֹאכְלוּ	יֹאכְלוּהוּ
תֵּלֵד	תֵּלְדֵהוּ	——	
יֵדַע	יֵדָעֵהוּ	יֵדְעוּ	יֵדָעוּהוּ
יָשִׂים	יְשִׂימֵהוּ	יָשִׂימוּ	יְשִׂימוּהוּ
יָסֹב	יְסֻבֵּהוּ	יָסֹבּוּ	יְסֻבּוּהוּ
יִתֵּן	יִתְּנֵנִי	יִתְּנוּ	יִתְּנוּנִי
יְבַקֵּשׁ	יְבַקְשֵׁנִי	יְבַקְשׁוּ	יְבַקְשׁוּנִי
יְשַׁלַּח	יְשַׁלְּחֵנִי	יְשַׁלְּחוּ	יְשַׁלְּחוּנִי
יְבָרֵךְ	יְבָרְכֵנִי	יְבָרְכוּ	יְבָרְכוּנִי
יַשְׁמִיד	יַשְׁמִידֵהוּ	יַשְׁמִידוּ	יַשְׁמִידוּהוּ
יַמְצִיא	יַמְצִיאֵהוּ	יַמְצִיאוּ	יַמְצִיאוּהוּ
יוֹרִיד	יוֹרִידֵהוּ	יוֹרִידוּ	יוֹרִידוּהוּ
יָקִים	יְקִימֵהוּ	יָקִימוּ	יְקִימוּהוּ
יָסֵב	יְסִבֵּהוּ	יָסֵבּוּ	יְסִבּוּהוּ

Row labels: QAL, PIEL, HIPHIL

The distinction between short (jussive, "converted") and normal imperfects is not retained before pronominal suffixes.

וַיַּשְׁמִידֵהוּ ← וַיַּשְׁמֵד אֹתוֹ   and he destroyed him

Note that the -a- in the final stem syllable of the Piel imperfects such as יְשַׁלַּח does not conform to the rule given above and is reduced: יְשַׁלְּחֵהוּ. Note also יֹאכְלֵהוּ.

The object suffix -kā (you, m.s.) may be added directly to the imperfect stem, in which ō → o and ē → e; a remains a; î remains î.

יִשְׁמָרְךָ	←	יִשְׁמֹר אֹתְךָ
יִתֶּנְךָ	←	יִתֵּן אֹתְךָ
יְבַקֶּשְׁךָ	←	יְבַקֵּשׁ אֹתְךָ

יְשַׁלַּח אֹתְךָ → יְשַׁלֵּחֲךָ (but note Qal יִשְׁלָחֶךָ)

יַשְׁמִיד אֹתְךָ → יַשְׁמִידְךָ

Verbs from roots III-*Hē* drop the final -*eh* before the suffixes:

QAL	יִבְנֶה / יִבֶן	יִבְנֵהוּ	יִבְנוֹ	יִבְנְךָ
PIEL	יְצַוֶּה / יְצַו	יְצַוֵּהוּ	יְצַוְּךָ	יְצַוְּךָ
HIPHIL	יַרְאֶה יַרְאֵהוּ	יַרְאֶךָּ	יַרְאֶךָּ	
	יַעֲלֶה יַעֲלֵהוּ	יַעֲלְךָ	יַעַלְךָ	

193. Object Suffixes on the Imperative.

The suffixes used are the same as those found with the imperfect. The general similarity with the imperfect is such that no new principles are involved in the attachment of the suffixes. The following examples should suffice:

QAL	שְׁמֹר	שָׁמְרֵנִי	שִׁמְרוּ	שָׁמְרוּנִי
	תֵּן	תְּנֵנִי	תְּנוּ	תְּנוּנִי
	שְׁמַע	שְׁמָעֵנִי	שִׁמְעוּ	שְׁמָעוּנִי
	מְצָא	מְצָאֵנִי	מִצְאוּ	מְצָאוּנִי
	בְּנֵה	בְּנֵהוּ	בְּנוּ	בְּנוּהוּ
	שִׂים	שִׂימֵהוּ	שִׂימוּ	שִׂימוּהוּ
	סֹב	סֻבֵּהוּ	סֹבּוּ	סֻבּוּהוּ
PIEL	בַּקֵּשׁ	בַּקְּשֵׁהוּ	בַּקְּשׁוּ	בַּקְּשׁוּהוּ
	שַׁלַּח	שַׁלְּחֵהוּ	שַׁלְּחוּ	שַׁלְּחוּהוּ
HIPHIL	הַשְׁמֵד	הַשְׁמִידֵהוּ	הַשְׁמִידוּ	הַשְׁמִידוּהוּ
	הַרְבֵּה	הַרְבֵּהוּ	הַרְבּוּ	הַרְבּוּהוּ
	הַעֲלֵה	הַעֲלֵהוּ	הַעֲלוּ	הַעֲלוּהוּ

194. Object Suffixes on the Infinitive Construct.

Because of the ambivalence of the infinitive with regard to voice, the subject suffixes learned in §115 may have an object value in translation. E.g. "he sought my killing" may refer to "my killing someone else" or "my being killed." In the first person singular the ambiguity may be resolved by employing -*énî* as object versus -*î* as subject: הָרְגֵנִי versus הָרְגִי In the third person singular masculine it is possible to use -*ô* as opposed to -*éhû* in this same way. In general, however, it is necessary to translate the infinitive plus pronominal suffix as the context demands. This is analogous, of course, to the situation when a noun follows: הָרֹג אִישׁ "killing a man" (objective) or "a man's killing (someone)" (subjective).

195. Vocabulary 54.

VERBS: הִטָּה (יַטֶּה) to turn aside, incline, thrust aside (all transitive)

פָּנָה (יִפְנֶה) to turn toward, turn (both trans. and intrans.)

נָטַשׁ (יִטּשׁ) to leave, forsake, abandon

חָשַׁב (יַחְשֹׁב) to think, devise, reckon, impute

NOUNS: תְּחִנָּה (pl. -ôṯ) supplication

צְדָקָה (pl. -ôṯ) righteousness, righteous act

מָטָר (pl. -ôṯ) rain

נַחֲלָה (pl. -ôṯ) property, possession, inheritance, portion

זְרוֹעַ (pl. -îm/-ôṯ) arm; (fig.) strength (usually fem.)

יִרְאָה fear; used also as the infinitive construct of יָרֵא (constr. יִרְאַת)

OTHER: נָכְרִי (adj.) foreign, strange; fem. נָכְרִיָּה

אָמְנָם) (adv.) truly, indeed
אֻמְנָם)

Exercises:

(a) Transform according to the example and translate.

Ex.   תִּשְׁמֹר אֹתָם → תִּשְׁמְרֵם   you shall observe them

(11) הַטֵּה אֹתוֹ   (6) רְפָא אֹתָם   (1) יַטֶּה אֹתָם
(12) גָּרֵשׁ אֹתָם   (7) מְשָׁחוּ אֹתוֹ   (2) יְמָאֲסוּ אֹתוֹ
(13) אַל־תְּקַלֵּל אֹתָה   (8) יְכַחֵד אֹתָם   (3) שַׁלֵּם אֹתָהּ
(14) שָׁרֵת אֹתוֹ   (9) תְּנַחֲמוּ אֹתָנוּ   (4) אַל־תִּטֹּשׁ אֹתִי
(15) אַל־תִּבְזֶה אֹתִי   (10) תִּמְצָא אֹתִי   (5) עֲזֹר אֹתָנוּ

(b) Transform according to the example and translate.

Ex.   שִׁמְרוּ אֹתוֹ → שְׁמָרוּהוּ   observe him

(11) שְׁלָחֹונִי   (6) יַחְשְׁבוּנִי   (1) הַעִידֵם
(12) וַיַּכֵּנִי   (7) יַגְדִּילֵם   (2) יַאֲרִיכֵם
(13) הִצַּלְיחֵנִי   (8) וַיּוֹרֵהוּ   (3) הוֹרִידֵהוּ
(14) וַיַּשְׁמִיעֵם   (9) וַיַּשִּׂיגֵנוּ   (4) יוֹלִיכֵךְ
(15) יִטְּשֹׁךְ   (10) הַאֲבִידֵם   (5) יִבְקָעֵם

(c) Translate the following. Replace the nominal object with the appropriate pronoun, suffixed to the verb. E.g. הֲרֹגֵהוּ → הֲרֹג אֶת־הָאִישׁ

(1) יִתֵּן לָנוּ מָטָר   (7) הָמֵת אֶת־שָׂרֵיהֶם
(2) שְׁמַע אֶת־תְּחִנָּתִי   (8) בַּעֵר אֶת־עָרֵיהֶם
(3) הָשֵׁב אֶת־הַנָּכְרִי   (9) אַל־תִּזְבַּח אֶת־הַכֶּבֶשׂ
(4) נָאֵץ אֶת־הָרְשָׁעִים   (10) יַשְׁלִיךְ אֶת־חַרְבּוֹ אַרְצָה
(5) הַשְׁמַע אֶת־הַגּוֹיִם   (11) תֵּן לִי אֶת־נַחֲלָתִי
(6) הַסְתֵּר אֶת־הַכֶּסֶף   (12) הַזְכֵּר אֶת־שְׁמוֹ

(15) נָטַע אֶת־הַזֵּיתִים   (13) הַזְכִּֽירוּ אֶת־מַעֲשֵׂיהֶם
(14) הָבֵא אֶת־הָאָרוֹן

(d) Write in Hebrew.

1. Let my supplication come before thee, O Lord.
2. He will continue to give rain upon the earth.
3. Who is that strange man the elders are speaking with?
4. Fear of him fell upon them and their hearts melted within them.
5. I shall walk in truth and righteousness all the days of my life.
6. The fear of the Lord is the beginning of wisdom.
7. Even the strong will fall before him.
8. Because you have slain his anointed one, you also shall die.
9. Have pity on the poor, for there is no other to help them.
10. I will not heed your prayers and your supplications.

LESSON 55

196. Conditional Sentences.

Any two clauses, the first of which states a real or hypothetical condition, and the second of which states a real or hypothetical consequence thereof, may be taken as a conditional sentence. Because conditional sentences entail a logical and (usually) temporal sequence, they form a natural subgroup related to the narrative sequences. Conditional sentences in Hebrew may be virtually unmarked; the translation of certain sets of clauses in a regular future narrative sequence often requires a conditional sentence in English:

> וְעָזַב אֶת־אָבִיו וָמֵת and if he leaves his father, he (i.e. his father) will die (Gen. 44:22)

> וְשָׁמַע שָׁאוּל וַהֲרָגָ֫נִי and if Saul hears (about it), he will kill me (I Sam. 16:2)

Many such occurrences are ambiguous, since a non-conditional translation can also be found. In a series of three or more clauses, it is only a matter of the translator's judgement where to end the protasis and begin the apodosis. In poetic, aphoristic, or legal styles an otherwise unmarked participial protasis is not infrequent:

> וּמַכֵּה אָבִיו וְאִמּוֹ מוֹת יוּמַת and if a man slays his father or his mother, he shall be put to death (Ex. 21:15)

> וְגֹנֵב אִישׁ וּמְכָרוֹ וְנִמְצָא בְיָדוֹ מוֹת יוּמַת and if a man kidnaps a man and sells

him, or (if) he is found in his hand,
he shall be put to death (Ex. 21:16)

These may also be translated non-conditionally as "Anyone who slays...
shall be put to death" etc.

Conditional sentences marked by a special conjunction "if" are of two
types: (1) those introduced by אִם, הֵן, or כִּי, which are real, fulfilled, or
fulfillable and (2) those introduced by לוּ (neg. לוּלֵי), which are unreal,
contrary-to-fact, unfulfillable.

Type (1). The protasis (the "if"-clause) may have a perfect, imperfect,
or participial predicate. It is difficult to maintain these distinctions in translation. The perfect sometimes has the value of the English perfect or (perhaps
over-correctly) of the future-perfect, but more often takes on the value of
the Hebrew imperfect in its general present-future function. Thus, although
one may make a valid distinction between

אִם מָצָאתִי חֵן...   if I have found favor...

אִם אֶמְצָא חֵן...   if I find favor (in the future)...

that same distinction becomes artificial if applied, e.g., to

אִם עָבַרְתָּ אִתִּי וְהָיִתָ עָלַי לְמַשָּׂא   If you cross over with me, you will be
a burden to me (II Sam. 15:33)

אִם־יַעַבְרוּ... אִתְּכֶם... וּנְתַתֶּם לָהֶם...   If they cross over with you, you shall
give them... (Num. 32:29).

Both protases refer to future events as conditions. It is always possible to
justify the use of the perfect in the protasis as representing a completed
action of accomplished state in the mind of the speaker. It is difficult within
Hebrew itself to predict the choice between the perfect and the imperfect in
the construction with the same meaning. Whatever the original distinction
was, it has become obscured in Hebrew of the biblical period, so that both
verbs will have, in general, the same range of translation values.

The apodosis corresponds closely to a clause in a present-future sequence:

wə + perfect (converted)
wə (optional) + non-verb + imperfect (disjunctive pattern)
wə + non-verbal clause
imperative

None of these offers any special problems in translation. The following
examples illustrate the more frequent combinations of the possible clause
types:

וְאִם־יָשַׁבְנוּ פֹה וָמָתְנוּ   And if we stay here, we shall die
(II Kings 7:4)

אִם לֹא הֲבִיאֹתִיו אֵלֶיךָ... וְחָטָאתִי לְךָ   If I do not bring him back to you...

I shall be accountable to you (Gen. 43:9)

אִם שָׁכַ֫חְנוּ שֵׁם אֱלֹהֵ֫ינוּ וַנִּפְרֹשׂ כַּפֵּ֫ינוּ לְאֵל זָר הֲלֹא אֱלֹהִים יַחֲקָר־זֹאת

If we forget the name of our God and extend our hands to a foreign god, will not God find this out? (Ps. 44:21)

וְהָיָה אִם־לֹא חָפַ֫צְתָּ בָּהּ וְשִׁלַּחְתָּהּ

And if you are not pleased with her, you shall send her forth (Deut. 21:14)

וְאִם־יִהְיוּ חֲטָאֵיכֶם כַּשָּׁנִים כַּשֶּׁ֫לֶג יַלְבִּ֫ינוּ

Even if your sins are as scarlet, they shall become as white as snow (Is. 1:18)

וְהָיָה אִם־אִישׁ יָבֹא וּשְׁאֵלֵךְ ... וְאָמַרְתְּ

And if a man comes and asks you... you shall say... (Judges 4:20)

A clause introduced by the particles הֵן, כִּי and אֲשֶׁר (cf. §70) may also be equivalent to the protasis of a conditional sentence.

It was pointed out in a previous lesson (cf. §138) that אִם has a negative translation value as part of an oath formula. The expression אִם לֹא has thus a positive value in the same context. DOUBLE NEGATIVE

חַי־אָ֫נִי ... אִם־לֹא כַּאֲשֶׁר דִּבַּרְתֶּם בְּאָזְנָ֑י כֵּן אֶעֱשֶׂה לָכֶם

As I live, I shall do to you as you have spoken into my ears (or: as you have confided in me) (Num. 14:28)

וַיִּשָּׁבַע מֹשֶׁה ... לֵאמֹר אִם־לֹא הָאָ֫רֶץ ... לְךָ תִהְיֶה לְנַחֲלָה

And Moses swore saying: "The land .....will be an inheritance for you... (Joshua 14:9)

Type (2). Contrary-to-fact conditional sentences introduced by לוּ are too infrequent to allow a meaningful analysis. Here are some typical examples:

לוּ יֶשׁ־חֶ֫רֶב בְּיָדִי כִּי עַתָּה הֲרַגְתִּיךְ

If there were a sword in my hand, I would surely now kill you (Num. 22:29)

לוּ חָכְמוּ יַשְׂכִּ֫ילוּ זֹאת

If they were wise, they would understand this (Deut. 32:29)

לוּ הַחֲיִתֶם אוֹתָם לֹא הָרַ֫גְתִּי אֶתְכֶם

If you had let them live, I would not kill you (Judges 8:19)

לוּ חָפֵץ יהוה לַהֲמִיתֵ֫נוּ לֹא־לָקַח מִיָּדֵ֫נוּ עֹלָה

If the Lord had wanted to kill us, he would not have received an offering from us (Judges 13:23)

לוּלֵי אֱלֹהֵי אָבִי ... הָיָה לִי כִּי־עַתָּה רֵיקָם שִׁלַּחְתָּ֫נִי

If the God of my father had not been on my side, you would have sent me away empty (Gen. 31:42)

The particle לוּ may also be used in the sense "would that" without a following apodosis:

וְלוּ הוֹאַלְנוּ וַנֵּשֶׁב בְּעֵבֶר הַיַּרְדֵּן   Would that we had been content to dwell on the other side of the Jordan (Joshua 7:7)

197. Concluding Remarks on Clause Sequences.

The syntax of Biblical Hebrew presents difficult and often insoluble problems. Given the unknown numbers of sources, writers, and editors that have had a hand in the formation of the text, together with the grammatical schools of the later traditionalists, we can never be sure how much reliance (grammatically speaking) we may place in the textus receptus and, consequently, how refined our analysis can be before becoming meaningless. The narrative sequences presented in this grammar are a good case in point. To maintain that these are the sole devices pertinent to the syntax of wa-clauses would be false in the face of the many obvious exceptions. But because most sequences can be reduced to these patterns there is certainly some value in regarding them as standard. The evolution of Hebrew toward the post-biblical type replaced most of the older converting sequences by simpler non-converting ones. Thus, a formal tendency directly opposed to an earlier one must have been a work in the latest redactions of the text before it achieved its fixed form. Certainly some of the inconsistencies in verbal usage and clause syntax are to be attributed to this influence.

(a) Further remarks on the present-future narrative sequence (1b–c). This sequence, characterized by a continuing series of converted perfects, may be led off by a variety of clause types; we have already mentioned leading clauses with verbal (imperfect) and non-verbal predicates. The verb הָיָה in a leading clause requires special consideration. By virtue of its double meaning "be/become" it may be used to describe a non-punctual past tense situation (e.g. "there was a famine in the land"). If a narrative sequence begins with a clause containing the verb הָיָה (or וַיְהִי), the real nature of the sequence is not clear until we reach a continuing verb. Contrast

הָיָה רָעָב בָּאָרֶץ וְיָרַד מִצְרַיְמָה...   There was a famine in the land and he used to go down to Egypt... (habitual)

הָיָה רָעָב בָּאָרֶץ וַיֵּרֶד מִצְרַיְמָה...   There was a famine in the land and he went down to Egypt (specific; punctual)

The leading clause of the present-future sequence may thus be redefined as comprising the formal subtypes:

(a) imperfect

(b) non-verbal clause (including those with participial predicates)

(c) conditional clauses, with perfect or imperfect finite verb in a present-future meaning

(d) the verb הָיָה in a non-punctual sense

all continued by *wə* + (converted) perfect.

(b) Conjunctive, non-converting sequences:

(1) perfect + *wə* + perfect (unconverted)

(2) imperfect + *wə* + imperfect (unconverted)

(3) imperative + *wə* + imperative

The third of these sequences has already been mentioned (§107) and is included here only because of its formal similarity. Sequences (1) and (2), however, are new and because they are by no means uncommon deserve some comment. They seldom occur in punctual narrative and are used mainly where there is a simple listing of clauses without an explicit expression of logical or temporal consecution; they may thus be defined as conjunctive but non-consecutive. But when they *are* used in a consecutive series it is usually to continue a disjunctive clause rather than in the main narrative. For example, suppose that in the main narrative a person has been mentioned about whom the writer wishes to supply additional information. Such information is usually introduced by a disjunctive formula (verb not first). It is often the case that this explanatory disjunction will continue for several clauses before the writer returns to the main narrative; it is in this type of sub-sequence that (1) and (2) are frequently met in a consecutive sense. Note, for example, I Sam. 23:20, concerning a certain Benayahu:

וְהוּא יָרַד וְהִכָּה אֶת־הָאֲרִי   and he is the one who went down and killed the lion...

Another use of sequences (1) and (2) above is an analog of the imperative + *wə* + cohortative sequence, in which the second clause is best translated as a purpose or result clause (cf. §107). Thus corresponding to a hypothetical (but normal) sequence of the type (1b):

הַרְחֶב לָנוּ וְנִפְרֶה בָאָרֶץ   Make room for us, so that we may be fruitful in the land

we have the statement of fact in Gen. 26:22:

כִּי־עַתָּה הִרְחִיב יהוה לָנוּ וּפָרִינוּ בָאָרֶץ   ....for now the Lord has made room for us to be fruitful in the land.

(c) Finally, note the unusual sequence occurring in each of the three passages outlined below as illustrations. We are dealing in each case with a punctual, habitual sequence. Circumstantial information about action which

[280]

is prior to the clause that will follow is introduced by *wa* + imperfect (converted), best rendered "and when he had done so-and-so..." Such clauses are conjunctive by definition, but because of their formal departure from the sequence in which they occur, they clearly mark an anticipatory temporal subordination.

Illustrative Passages

I Sam. 17:34–5. In this passage David describes his prowess as a shepherd. The sequence begins with the ambiguous verb הָיָה and is uniformly with converted perfects (1b), with the exception of וַיָּקָם which belongs to the peculiar type mentioned in the preceding paragraph. [In this and the following passages only the leading elements of each clause are given. Clauses irrelevant to the discussion at hand are omitted. Indentation indicates subordination or disjunction. The reader should compare our outlines with the original text.]

Hebrew	Translation	Note
רֹעֶה הָיָה עַבְדְּךָ	I (your servant) was a shepherd...	Note ambiguous *hāyāh*.
וּבָא הָאֲרִי	and (whenever) a lion would come	
וְנָשָׂא	and take	
וְיָצָאתִי	I would go out	
וְהִכִּתִיו	and strike	
וְהִצַּלְתִּי	and rescue	
וַיָּקָם	and when he attacked me	Anticipatory subordination
וְהֶחֱזַקְתִּי	I would grab him	Resumption of main sequence.
וְהִכִּתִיו	and beat him	
וַהֲמִיתִיו	and kill him	

Job 1:1–5:

Hebrew	Translation	Note
אִישׁ הָיָה	There was a man	Beginning of the main narrative; note ambiguous *hāyāh*.
וְהָיָה הָאִישׁ הַהוּא	and that man was	Continuation with *wəhāyāh* marks the sequence as type 1b (habitual).
וַיִּוָּלְדוּ	and when there was born to him	Anticipatory subordination, continued by two consecutive clauses.
וַיְהִי	and his herds had reached (the extent of)	
וַיְהִי	and he had become great	
וְהָלְכוּ	his sons used to go	Resumption of main narrative.
וְעָשׂוּ	and make	

[281]

וְשָׁלְחוּ	and send	
וְקָרְאוּ	and call	
וַיְהִי כִּי הִקִּיפוּ	and when the feast days had run their course	Another anticipatory subordination marked by *wa* + imperf. (converted), complicated by a temporal clause insertion with *kî*.
וַיִּשְׁלַח	and he had sent	
וַיְקַדְּשֵׁם	and had sanctified them	
וְהִשְׁכִּים	he would get up early	Resumption of main narrative.
וְהֶעֱלָה	and send up offerings	
כִּי אָמַר אִיּוֹב	for Job said	Simple subordination with *kî*.
אוּלַי חָטְאוּ	perhaps they have sinned	Quotation, beginning a secondary sequence (type 3a).
וּבֵרְכוּ	and "blessed"	
כָּכָה יַעֲשֶׂה	thus he used to do	Disjunction marking the end of the general introduction to the narrative.

Note the correct reversion to the imperfect in the final disjunction.

J Sam. 1:1–7.

1:1a	וַיְהִי אִישׁ אֶחָד	(and) there was a certain man	Beginning of main sequence, followed by four disjunctive non-verbal clauses (omitted here).
1:2b	וַיְהִי לִפְנִנָּה	(and) Peninah had children	Continuation of main sequence, still with the ambiguous *wayhî*.
1:3a	וְעָלָה הָאִישׁ הַהוּא	(and) that man used to go up	Continuation of main sequence, now clearly habitual, with the converted perfect.
1:4a	וַיְהִי הַיּוֹם	and when, on a given day	Anticipatory subordination, doubled here with a temporal clause.
	וַיִּזְבַּח	he had sacrificed	
	וְנָתַן	he would give	Continuation of main sequence.
	וּלְחַנָּה יִתֵּן	but to Hannah he would give	Disjunction for contrast. Note the correct reversion to the imperfect.
	וְכִעֲסַתָּה צָרָתָהּ	and her rival would vex	Main narrative.
	וְכֵן יַעֲשֶׂה	and thus he would do	End of main sequence, as marked by the disjunction.

At this point in the narrative the writer turns to the specific occasion of Hannah's encounter with Eli and employs the regular past-punctual sequence, beginning with the *wayyómer* of vs. 8.

[282]

198. Vocabulary 55.

VERBS:

כִּלְכֵּל (יְכַלְכֵּל)   to contain, sustain, support

שָׁבָה (יִשְׁבֶּה)   to lead into exile; N. passive

רִחַם (יְרַחֵם)   to be compassionate toward

הִבְדִּיל (יַבְדִּיל)   to divide, make a separation between

כִּלָּה (יְכַלֶּה)   to complete, bring to an end; + inf.: to finish doing

כָּרַע (יִכְרַע)   to bow down

אָנַף (יֶאֱנַף)   to become angry

פָּשַׁע (יִפְשַׁע)   to rebel, transgress (בְּ: against)

NOUNS:

רִנָּה   (no pl.) a cry of joy (less commonly, of supplication)

בַּרְזֶל   (no pl.) iron

פֶּשַׁע   (w. suff. פִּשְׁעִי; pl. -îm) transgression, sin

מְנוּחָה   (pl. -ôt) rest, resting-place

ADJ: בָּרוּךְ   blessed

PROPER NAME: שְׁלֹמֹה   Solomon

Reading: I Kings 8:22–30; 44–58: Solomon's Prayer.

(22) וַיַּעֲמֹד שְׁלֹמֹה לִפְנֵי מִזְבַּח יהוה נֶגֶד כָּל־קְהַל יִשְׂרָאֵל וַיִּפְרֹשׂ כַּפָּיו הַשָּׁמָיִם:[1]

(23) וַיֹּאמַר יהוה אֱלֹהֵי יִשְׂרָאֵל אֵין־כָּמֹוךָ אֱלֹהִים בַּשָּׁמַיִם מִמַּעַל וְעַל־הָאָרֶץ מִתָּחַת שֹׁמֵר הַבְּרִית וְהַחֶסֶד לַעֲבָדֶיךָ הַהֹלְכִים לְפָנֶיךָ בְּכָל־לִבָּם:

(24) אֲשֶׁר שָׁמַרְתָּ לְעַבְדְּךָ דָוִד אָבִי אֵת אֲשֶׁר־דִּבַּרְתָּ לֹו וַתְּדַבֵּר בְּפִיךָ וּבְיָדְךָ מִלֵּאתָ כַּיֹּום הַזֶּה:

(25) וְעַתָּה יהוה אֱלֹהֵי יִשְׂרָאֵל שְׁמֹר לְעַבְדְּךָ דָוִד אָבִי אֵת אֲשֶׁר דִּבַּרְתָּ לֹו לֵאמֹר לֹא־יִכָּרֵת לְךָ אִישׁ מִלְּפָנַי יֹשֵׁב עַל־כִּסֵּא יִשְׂרָאֵל רַק אִם־יִשְׁמְרוּ בָנֶיךָ אֶת־דַּרְכָּם לָלֶכֶת לְפָנַי כַּאֲשֶׁר הָלַכְתָּ לְפָנָי:

(26) וְעַתָּה אֱלֹהֵי יִשְׂרָאֵל יֵאָמֶן נָא דְבָרֶיךָ[2] אֲשֶׁר דִּבַּרְתָּ לְעַבְדְּךָ דָוִד אָבִי:

(27) כִּי הַאֻמְנָם יֵשֵׁב אֱלֹהִים עַל־הָאָרֶץ הִנֵּה[3] הַשָּׁמַיִם וּשְׁמֵי הַשָּׁמַיִם לֹא יְכַלְכְּלוּךָ אַף כִּי־הַבַּיִת הַזֶּה אֲשֶׁר בָּנִיתִי:

(28) וּפָנִיתָ[4] אֶל־תְּפִלַּת עַבְדְּךָ וְאֶל־תְּחִנָּתֹו יהוה אֱלֹהָי לִשְׁמֹעַ אֶל־הָרִנָּה וְאֶל־הַתְּפִלָּה אֲשֶׁר עַבְדְּךָ מִתְפַּלֵּל לְפָנֶיךָ הַיֹּום:

(29) לִהְיֹות עֵינֶיךָ[5] פְתֻחֹות אֶל־הַבַּיִת הַזֶּה לַיְלָה וָיֹום אֶל־הַמָּקֹום אֲשֶׁר אָמַרְתָּ יִהְיֶה שְׁמִי שָׁם לִשְׁמֹעַ אֶל־הַתְּפִלָּה אֲשֶׁר יִתְפַּלֵּל עַבְדְּךָ אֶל־הַמָּקֹום הַזֶּה:

(30) וְשָׁמַעְתָּ אֶל־תְּחִנַּת עַבְדְּךָ וְעַמְּךָ יִשְׂרָאֵל אֲשֶׁר יִתְפַּלְלוּ אֶל־הַמָּקֹום הַזֶּה וְאַתָּה תִּשְׁמַע אֶל־מְקֹום שִׁבְתְּךָ אֶל־הַשָּׁמַיִם וְשָׁמַעְתָּ וְסָלָחְתָּ:

(44) כִּי־יֵצֵא עַמְּךָ לַמִּלְחָמָה עַל־אֹיְבֹו בַּדֶּרֶךְ אֲשֶׁר תִּשְׁלָחֵם וְהִתְפַּלְלוּ אֶל־יהוה דֶּרֶךְ[6] הָעִיר אֲשֶׁר בָּחַרְתָּ בָּהּ וְהַבַּיִת אֲשֶׁר־בָּנִתִי לִשְׁמֶךָ:

(45) וְשָׁמַעְתָּ הַשָּׁמַיִם אֶת־תְּפִלָּתָם וְאֶת־תְּחִנָּתָם וְעָשִׂיתָ מִשְׁפָּטָם:

(46) כִּי יֶחֶטְאוּ־לָךְ כִּי אֵין אָדָם אֲשֶׁר לֹא־יֶחֱטָא וְאָנַפְתָּ בָם וּנְתַתָּם לִפְנֵי אֹויֵב וְשָׁבוּם שֹׁבֵיהֶם אֶל־אֶרֶץ הָאֹויֵב רְחֹוקָה אֹו קְרֹובָה:

(47) וְהֵשִׁיבוּ[7] אֶל־לִבָּם בָּאָרֶץ אֲשֶׁר נִשְׁבּוּ־שָׁם וְשָׁבוּ וְהִתְחַנְּנוּ אֵלֶיךָ בְּאֶרֶץ שֹׁבֵיהֶם לֵאמֹר חָטָאנוּ וְהֶעֱוִינוּ[8] רָשָׁעְנוּ:[9]

(48) וְשָׁבוּ אֵלֶיךָ בְּכָל־לְבָבָם וּבְכָל־נַפְשָׁם בְּאֶרֶץ אֹיְבֵיהֶם אֲשֶׁר־שָׁבוּ אֹתָם וְהִתְפַּלְלוּ אֵלֶיךָ דֶּרֶךְ אַרְצָם אֲשֶׁר נָתַתָּה לַאֲבֹותָם הָעִיר אֲשֶׁר בָּחַרְתָּ וְהַבַּיִת אֲשֶׁר־בָּנִיתִי לִשְׁמֶךָ:

(49) וְשָׁמַעְתָּ הַשָּׁמַיִם מְכוֹן¹⁰ שִׁבְתֶּךָ אֶת־תְּפִלָּתָם וְאֶת־תְּחִנָּתָם וְעָשִׂיתָ מִשְׁפָּטָם:

(50) וְסָלַחְתָּ לְעַמְּךָ אֲשֶׁר חָטְאוּ־לָךְ וּלְכָל־פִּשְׁעֵיהֶם אֲשֶׁר פָּשְׁעוּ־בָךְ וּנְתַתָּם לְרַחֲמִים¹¹ לִפְנֵי שֹׁבֵיהֶם וְרִחֲמוּם:

(51) כִּי־עַמְּךָ וְנַחֲלָתְךָ הֵם אֲשֶׁר הוֹצֵאתָ מִמִּצְרַיִם מִתּוֹךְ כּוּר¹² הַבַּרְזֶל:

(52) לִהְיוֹת עֵינֶיךָ פְּתֻחוֹת אֶל־תְּחִנַּת עַבְדְּךָ וְאֶל־תְּחִנַּת עַמְּךָ יִשְׂרָאֵל לִשְׁמֹעַ אֲלֵיהֶם בְּכֹל קָרְאָם אֵלֶיךָ:

(53) כִּי־אַתָּה הִבְדַּלְתָּם לְךָ לְנַחֲלָה מִכֹּל עַמֵּי הָאָרֶץ כַּאֲשֶׁר דִּבַּרְתָּ בְּיַד מֹשֶׁה עַבְדֶּךָ בְּהוֹצִיאֲךָ אֶת־אֲבֹתֵינוּ מִמִּצְרַיִם אֲדֹנָי יְהוִה:

(54) וַיְהִי כְּכַלּוֹת שְׁלֹמֹה לְהִתְפַּלֵּל אֶל־יְהוָה אֵת כָּל־הַתְּפִלָּה וְהַתְּחִנָּה הַזֹּאת קָם¹³ מִלִּפְנֵי מִזְבַּח יְהוָה מִכְּרֹעַ עַל־בִּרְכָּיו¹⁴ וְכַפָּיו פְּרֻשׂוֹת הַשָּׁמָיִם:

(55) וַיַּעֲמֹד וַיְבָרֶךְ אֵת כָּל־קְהַל יִשְׂרָאֵל קוֹל¹⁵ גָּדוֹל לֵאמֹר:

(56) בָּרוּךְ יְהוָה אֲשֶׁר נָתַן מְנוּחָה לְעַמּוֹ יִשְׂרָאֵל כְּכֹל אֲשֶׁר דִּבֵּר לֹא־נָפַל דָּבָר אֶחָד מִכֹּל דְּבָרוֹ הַטּוֹב אֲשֶׁר דִּבֶּר בְּיַד מֹשֶׁה עַבְדּוֹ:

(57) יְהִי יְהוָה אֱלֹהֵינוּ עִמָּנוּ כַּאֲשֶׁר הָיָה עִם־אֲבֹתֵינוּ אַל־יַעַזְבֵנוּ וְאַל־יִטְּשֵׁנוּ:

(58) לְהַטּוֹת לְבָבֵנוּ אֵלָיו לָלֶכֶת בְּכָל־דְּרָכָיו וְלִשְׁמֹר מִצְוֹתָיו וְחֻקָּיו וּמִשְׁפָּטָיו אֲשֶׁר צִוָּה אֶת־אֲבֹתֵינוּ:

Notes to the Reading:

1. Note הַשָּׁמַיִם in the sense "heavenward" and "in heaven" throughout this passage.
2. The plural form in the consonantal text is pointed as a singular.
3. The הִנֵּה should be correlated with the כִּי אַף: "Since even the heavens and the heavens' heavens cannot contain you, how much less this house which I have built."
4. וּפָנִיתָ continues the sequence of vs. 26.
5. Defectively spelled עֵינֶךָ in the original text.
6. Here in the sense "toward".
7. Idiomatic: "if they lay it to heart, consider it".
8. הֶעֱוָה to sin
9. רָשַׁע to act wickedly
10. מָכוֹן = מָקוֹם
11. Idiomatic: "and you make them an object of compassion".
12. כּוּר a furnace
13. The form קָם instead of וַיָּקָם marks this as the first main verb of a new sequence. Compare the discussion at the end of §132.
14. בִּרְכַּיִם (dual) knees
15. Adverbially: "in a loud voice".

A CLASSIFIED LIST OF NOUNS

The following list contains all the nouns appearing in this book, classified according to the vocalic pattern of the absolute singular. Nouns of a given pattern are included under a single number; differences in the inflected form, such as construct or plural, account for the further subdivisions. The principal forms are arranged as follows:

absolute singular	construct singular	singular with 1 pers. sing. suff.	absolute plural	construct plural

Other forms with pronominal suffixes are listed under the appropriate stem.

When an entry presents a virtually unique type, parentheses indicate a conjectured, but securely based form. E.g., (יַמִּי) "my sea" is not attested, but the form is reasonably certain because יַמָּהּ "her sea" is attested. The same suffixal forms are given for each noun for the sake of consistency.

Square brackets enclose conjectures which are probable, but not as firmly established as those just mentioned.

Dual forms may be found in §92.

I. Monosyllabic nouns with a normally changeable (reducible) long vowel or *a* (plural §34; constr. sing. §§73, 75; constr. plur. §§78–79; w. suff. §§85, 88, 96):

1a.	יָד	יַד / יֶדְכֶם	יָדִי / יָדֶ֫ךָ	יָדוֹת	יָדוֹת (יְדוֹתַי)	hand (f.)
1b.	דָּם	דַּם / דִּמְכֶם	דָּמִי / דָּמְךָ	דָּמִים (דָּמַי)	דְּמֵי (דְּמֵיכֶם)	blood
1c.	אָב	אֲבִי / אֲבִיכֶם	אָבִי / אָבִ֫יךָ	אָבוֹת	אֲבוֹת אֲבוֹתַי	father
1d.	אָח	אֲחִי / אֲחִיכֶם	אָחִי / אָחִ֫יךָ	אַחִים אַחַי אֶחָיו	אֲחֵי אֲחִיכֶם	brother
1e.	יָם / יָ֫מָּה	יַם / יָם	(יַמִּי)	יַמִּים	——	sea
2a.	עַם	עַם / עַמְּכֶם	עַמִּי / עַמְּךָ	עַמִּים עַמַּי	עַמֵּי / עַמְמֵי עַמֵּיכֶם	people

Also: אַף nose   חַיִּים lifetime   כַּף palm
    גַּן (ôt) garden   חַג (îm) festival   עַז mighty (adj.)
    דַּל poor (adj.)   טַף children   רַב numerous (adj.)
    חַי alive (adj.)   Note: With def. art.: הֶחָג הַגָּן הָעָם

2b.	שַׂר	שַׂר / שַׂרְכֶם	שָׂרִי / שָׂרְךָ	שָׂרִים שָׂרַי	שָׂרֵי שָׂרֵיכֶם	chief

Also: מַר bitter (adj.)   צַר (îm) adversary
    פַּר (îm) steer (הַפָּר)   רַע evil (adj.); wickedness (noun)

2c.	הַר הֶ֫רָה הָהָר	הַר / הַרְכֶם	הֲרָרִי / הֲרָרִי הֶהָרִם	הָרִים הָרֵי הֲרָרֶ֫יהָ	הָרֵי / הַרְרֵי	mountain
2d.	צַד	צַד / (צִדְכֶם)	(צִדִּי) / צִדְּךָ	צְדָדִים (צִדַּי)	צִדֵּי צִדֵּיכֶם	side
3a.	עֵץ	עֵץ / (עֶצְנֶם)	(עֵצִי) / עֵצְךָ	עֵצִים (עֵצַי)	עֲצֵי (עֲצֵיכֶם)	tree
3b.	גֵּר	גֵּר / גֵּרְכֶם	גֵּרִי / גֵּרְךָ	גֵּרִים גֵּרַי	גֵּרֵי גֵּרֵיכֶם	sojourner

Also: אֵל *(îm)* god   מֵת *(îm)* dead person

מֵעִים inward parts   רֵעַ *(îm)* companion

3c.	בֵּן	בֶּן־ / בֶּן־ (בִּנְכֶם)	בְּנִי בִּנְךָ	בָּנִים בָּנַי	בְּנֵי בְּנֵיכֶם	son
3d.	שֵׁם	שֶׁם־ / שֶׁם־ שִׁמְכֶם	שְׁמִי שִׁמְךָ	שֵׁמוֹת	שְׁמוֹת (שְׁמוֹתַי)	name
3e.	חֵץ	חֵץ (חִצְּכֶם)	חִצִּי חִצְּךָ חִצְּכֶם	חִצִּים חִצַּי	חִצֵּי חִצֵּיכֶם	arrow

Also: אֵם *(ôt)* mother   חֵן grace   קֵץ end

אֵשׁ fire   לֵב *(ôt)* heart   שֵׁן (du.) teeth

3f.	צֵל	צֵל	צִלִּי	צְלָלִים	צִלְלֵי	shadow
3g.	חֵטְא	(חֵטְא)	(חֶטְאִי)	חֲטָאִים חֲטָאַי	חֲטָאֵי חֲטָאֵיכֶם	sin

II. Monosyllabic nouns with a normally unchangeable long vowel (plural §34; constr. sing. §73; constr. plur. §§78–79; w. suff. §85):

4a.	שִׁיר	שִׁיר שִׁירְכֶם	שִׁירִי שִׁירְךָ	שִׁירִים שִׁירַי	שִׁירֵי שִׁירֵיכֶם	song

Also: קִיר *(ôt)* wall   רִיב *(îm, ôt)* quarrel

4b.	עִיר	עִיר (עִירְכֶם)	עִירִי עִירְךָ	עָרִים עָרַי	עָרֵי עָרֵיכֶם	city
4c.	אִישׁ	אִישׁ (אִישְׁכֶם)	אִישִׁי (אִישְׁךָ)	אֲנָשִׁים אֲנָשַׁי	אַנְשֵׁי (אַנְשֵׁיכֶם)	man
5a.	קוֹל	קוֹל קוֹלְכֶם	קוֹלִי קוֹלְךָ	קוֹלוֹת	קוֹלוֹת קוֹלוֹתַי	voice

אוֹר *(îm)* light   דּוֹר *(ôt)* generation   עוֹף fowl

אוֹת *(ôt)* sign   הוֹד splendor   עוֹר *(ôt)* hide

בּוֹר *(ôt)* cistern   טוֹב good (adj.)   צֹאן small cattle

גּוֹי *(îm)* people   כֹּחַ power   שׁוֹר *(îm)* head of cattle

Note: The once attested plural שְׁוָרִים represents a rare alternative in nouns of this type.

5b.	יוֹם	יוֹם	(יוֹמִי)	יָמִים	יְמֵי	day
		(יוֹמְכֶם)	יוֹמְךָ	יָמַי	יְמֵיכֶם	
5c.	רֹאשׁ	רֹאשׁ	רֹאשִׁי	רָאשִׁים	רָאשֵׁי	head
		רֹאשְׁכֶם	רֹאשְׁךָ	(רָאשַׁי)	רָאשֵׁיכֶם	
5d.	עֹז	עֹז / עָז־	עֻזִּי / עָזִּי	[עֻזִּים]	[עֻזֵּי]	might
		עֻזְּכֶם	עֻזְּךָ / עָזְּךָ			

Also: תֹּם / integrity   רֹב multitude

5e.	חֹק	חֹק / חָק־	חֻקִּי	חֻקִּים	חֻקֵּי / חִקְקֵי	statute
		חָקְכֶם	חֻקְּךָ			
6.	סוּס	סוּס	סוּסִי	סוּסִים	סוּסֵי	horse
		סוּסְכֶם	סוּסְךָ	סוּסֵי	סוּסֵיכֶם	

Also: לוּחַ *(ôt)* tablet   צוּר *(îm)* rock   רוּחַ *(ôt)* wind, spirit

III. Dissyllabic nouns with penultimate stress (the Segholates) and related rarer types (plur. §§19, 50; constr. sing. §§73, 75; constr. plur. 99; w. suff. §§99, 104).

7a.	מֶלֶךְ	מֶלֶךְ	מַלְכִּי	מְלָכִים	מַלְכֵי	king
			מַלְכְּךָ	מְלָכַי	מַלְכֵיכֶם	
			מַלְכְּכֶם			

Also:
- אֶבֶן *(îm)* stone   חֶסֶד *(îm)* kindness   עֶבֶד *(îm)* servant
- אֶלֶף *(îm)* thousand   חֶרֶב *(ôt)* sword   עֶצֶם *(îm/ôt)* bone
- אֶרֶז *(îm)* cedar   יֶלֶד *(îm)* boy   עֶרֶב evening
- אֶרֶץ *(ôt)* earth   כֶּסֶף *(îm)* silver   צֶלֶם *(îm)* image
- גֶּבֶר *(îm)* man   כֶּרֶם *(îm)* vineyard   קֶרֶן *(îm/ôt)* horn
- גֶּפֶן *(îm)* vine   לֶחֶם bread   רֶגֶל (du.; pl. *îm*) foot
- דֶּרֶךְ *(îm)* way   נֶפֶשׁ *(ôt)* soul   שֶׁמֶן *(îm)* oil

7b.	חֶדֶר	חֶדֶר / חֲדַר	(חַדְרִי)	חֲדָרִים	חַדְרֵי	room
			(חַדְרְךָ)	(חֲדָרַי)	(חַדְרֵיכֶם)	
			(חַדְרְכֶם)			

Similarly: הֶבֶל *(îm)* vanity

7c. קֶבֶר	קֶבֶר	קִבְרִי קִבְרְךָ קִבְרְכֶם	קְבָרִים קְבָרֵי	קִבְרֵי קִבְרֵיכֶם	grave

Also:
    גֶּשֶׁם *(îm)* rain   פֶּסֶל idol   שֶׁמֶשׁ *(ôṯ)* sun

    יֶתֶר remainder   צֶדֶק righteousness   שֶׁקֶל *(îm)* shekel

    כֶּבֶשׂ *(îm)* lamb   קֶרֶב midst   שֶׁקֶר *(îm)* deception

    נֶדֶר *(îm)* vow   רֶכֶב chariotry

    פֶּגֶר *(îm)* corpse   שֶׁבֶר *(îm)* breaking

8a. זֶרַע	זֶרַע	זַרְעִי זַרְעֲךָ זַרְעֲכֶם	סְלָעִים	(סַלְעִי)	seed rock

The following may belong here or to the next type (8b); evidence insufficient.

    פֶּסַח *(îm)* Passover   יֶרַח *(îm)* month   בֶּטַח trust

8b. זֶבַח	זֶבַח	זִבְחִי זִבְחֲךָ זִבְחֲכֶם	זְבָחִים זְבָחֵי	זִבְחֵי זִבְחֵיכֶם	sacrifice

Also:
    נֶגַע *(îm)* stroke   פֶּשַׁע *(îm)* transgression   פֶּתַח *(îm)* opening

9. נַעַר	נַעַר	נַעֲרִי נַעַרְךָ נַעַרְכֶם	נְעָרִים נַעֲרֵי	נְעָרַי נַעֲרֵיכֶם	young man

Also:
    בַּעַל *(îm)* master   פַּחַד (פַּחְדְּךָ) *(îm)* dread

    יַעַר *(îm)* woods   שַׁעַר *(îm)* gate

    נַחַל *(îm)* wadi

10a. סֵפֶר	סֵפֶר	סִפְרִי סִפְרְךָ סִפְרְכֶם	סְפָרִים סְפָרֵי	סְפָרַי סִפְרֵיכֶם	book

Also:
    עֵמֶק *(îm)* valley   שֵׁבֶט *(îm)* rod

				‖			
10b. עֶדֶר	עֵדֶר	עֶדְרִי עֶדְרְךָ עֶדְרְכֶם		‖	עֲדָרִים עֲדָרַי	עֶדְרֵי עֶדְרֵיכֶם	flock

Also:

חֵלֶב	*(îm)* fat	עֵזֶר	help
חֵלֶק	*(îm)* share	עֵשֶׂב	herbage
עֵגֶל	*(îm)* calf		

				‖			
11. קֹדֶשׁ	קֹדֶשׁ	קָדְשִׁי קָדְשְׁךָ קָדְשְׁכֶם		‖	קֳדָשִׁים / קָדָשִׁים קֳדָשַׁי / קָדָשַׁי	קָדְשֵׁי קָדְשֵׁיכֶם	holiness

Also:

אֹהֶל	*(îm)* tent	גֹּרֶן	*(ôt)* threshing floor	עֹרֶף	neck
אֹזֶן	(du.) ear	חֹדֶשׁ	*(îm)* month	צָהֳרַיִם	noon
אֹכֶל	food	חֹשֶׁךְ	darkness	שֹׁרֶשׁ	*(îm)* root
בֹּקֶר	morning	מָתְנַיִם	loins		

The plural forms of אֹהֶל (tent) show some irregularities:

אֹהָלִים	אֹהָלַי
בָּאֳהָלִים	אֹהָלֶיךָ
	אָהֳלֵיכֶם

				‖			
12a. אֹרַח	אֹרַח	אָרְחִי אָרְחֲךָ אָרְחֲכֶם		‖	אֳרָחוֹת (אָרְחוֹתֵיכֶם)	אָרְחוֹת	way
12b. רֹחַב	רֹחַב	רָחְבִּי רָחְבְּךָ רָחְבְּכֶם		‖	——	——	breadth

Also: תֹּאַר (w. suff. תָּאֳרוֹ or תָּאֲרוֹ) form

				‖			
13a. עַיִן	עֵין	עֵינִי עֵינְךָ עֵינְכֶם		‖	עֲיָנוֹת	עֵינוֹת	eye spring

Also: חַיִל *(îm)* strength   יַיִן wine

No.						English
13b.	זַיִת	זֵית	זֵיתִי זֵיתְךָ (זֵיתְכֶם)	זֵיתִים (זֵיתַי)	זֵיתַי זֵיתֵיכֶם	olive-tree

Also: אַיִל (îm) ram

No.						English
13c.	בַּיִת	בֵּית בֵּיתְכֶם	בֵּיתִי בֵּיתְךָ	בָּתִּים (בָּתַּי)	בָּתֵּי בָּתֵּיכֶם	house
14.	גַּי(א)	גֵּי(א)	—	גֵּאָיוֹת	(גֵּיאוֹת)	valley
15.	מָוֶת	מוֹת מוֹתְכֶם	מוֹתִי מוֹתְךָ	—	—	death

Also: אָוֶן trouble   תָּוֶךְ midst

No.			English
16.	שָׁוְא	not inflected	nothingness

IV. Dissyllabic nouns with a sometimes changeable ə in the first syllable and a changeable vowel in the second.

No.						English
17.	שְׁכֶם	שֶׁכֶם	שִׁכְמִי (שִׁכְמְךָ)	—	—	shoulder
18.	דְּבַשׁ	—	דִּבְשִׁי	—	—	honey
19.	שְׁאָר	שְׁאָר	—	—	—	remainder
20.	בְּאֵר	בְּאֵר	(בְּאֵרִי)	בְּאֵרוֹת	בְּאֵרוֹת	well
	זְאֵב	זְאֵב	(זְאֵבִי)	זְאֵבִים	זְאֵבֵי	wolf

V. Dissyllabic nouns with an unchangeable ə in the first syllable and an unchangeable long vowel in the second (plural §19; constr. sing. §73; constr. plur. §§78, 79; with suffixes §85).

No.						English
22.	בְּכוֹר	בְּכוֹר בְּכוֹרְכֶם	בְּכוֹרִי בְּכוֹרְךָ	בְּכוֹרִים בְּכוֹרֵי	בְּכוֹרַי בְּכוֹרֵיכֶם	first-born

Also: אֱלוֹהַּ *(îm)* god, God   חֲלוֹם *(ôt)* dream   רְחוֹב *(ôt)* street

אֲרוֹן (הָאָרוֹן) ark   חֲמוֹר *(îm)* ass   שְׂמֹאל left-hand

זְרוֹעַ *(ôt, îm)* arm   יְאֹר Nile

No.						English
23.	גְּבוּל	גְּבוּל	גְּבוּלִי	גְּבוּלִים	גְּבוּלֵי	boundary

Also: לְבוּשׁ clothing   כְּרוּב *(îm)* cherub   נְאֻם declaration
רְכוּשׁ property

24.	מְעִיל	(מְעִיל)	(מְעִילִי)	מְעִילִים	(מְעִילֵי)		robe

VI. Dissyllabic nouns with normally changeable vowels in both syllables (plural §19; constr. sing. §§73, 75; constr. plur. §§78, 79; with suffixes §85).

25a.	דָּבָר	דְּבַר	דְּבָרִי	דְּבָרִים	דִּבְרֵי		word
		דְּבַרְכֶם	דְּבָרְךָ	דְּבָרַי	דִּבְרֵיכֶם		

Also: בָּקָר large cattle   יָקָר precious (adj.)   רָשָׁע evil (adj.)
בָּשָׂר flesh   יָשָׁר just (adj.)   שָׁלָל booty
חָזָק strong (adj.)   מָטָר *(ôt)* rain

25b.	הָדָר	הֲדַר	הֲדָרִי	הֲדָרִים	הֲדָרֵי		splendor
		הֲדַרְכֶם	הֲדָרְךָ	הֲדָרַי	הֲדָרֵיכֶם		

Also: אָדָם man (-kind)   חָלָל slain (adj.)   קָהָל *(îm)* assembly
זָהָב gold   נָהָר *(ôt)* river   רָעָב hunger
חָדָשׁ new (adj.)   עָנָן *(îm)* cloud
חָכָם wise (adj.)   עָפָר *(ôt)* dust

25c.	פָּרָשׁ	(פָּרַשׁ)	(פָּרָשִׁי)	פָּרָשִׁים	(פָּרָשֵׁי)		horseman
		(פָּרַשְׁכֶם)	(פָּרָשְׁךָ)	פָּרָשַׁי	(פָּרָשֵׁיכֶם)		

Also: חָרָשׁ *(îm)* engraver

25d.	גָּמָל	גְּמַל	(גְּמַלִּי)	גְּמַלִּים	גְּמַלֵּי	camel
			(גְּמַלְּךָ)	(גְּמַלַּי)	(גְּמַלֵּיכֶם)	

25e.	חָלָב	חֲלֵב	חֲלָבִי	—	—	milk
			חֲלָבְךָ			

26a.	זָקֵן	זְקַן	זְקֵנִי	זְקֵנִים	זְקֵנַי / (זְקֵנֵי)	elder
		זְקַנְכֶם	זְקֵנְךָ	זְקֵנַי	זְקֵנֵיכֶם	

Also: כָּבֵד heavy (adj.)   שָׁלֵם complete (adj.)

שָׂמֵחַ glad (adj.)

שָׁכֵן *(îm)* neighbor

26b. חָצֵר | חֲצַר | חֲצֵרִי | חֲצֵרוֹת | חֲצֵרוֹת | courtyard

Also: עָרֵל uncircumcised (adj.)

26c. כָּתֵף | כְּתֵף | כְּתֵפִי | כְּתֵפוֹת | כְּתֵפוֹת | shoulder

Also: יָרֵחַ moon   יָרֵךְ (du.) thigh   עָרֵל uncircumcised (adj.)

26d. מָלֵא | מְלֵא | (מְלֵאִי) | מְלֵאִים | (מְלֵאֵי) | full (adj.)

Also: צָמֵא thirsty (adj.)   טָמֵא unclean (adj.)

26e. מָגֵן | מָגֵן | מָגִנִּי (מָגִנְּךָ) | מָגִנִּים (מָגִנֵּי) | מָגִנֵּי (מָגִנֵּיכֶם) | shield

27a. לֵבָב | לְבַב לְבַבְכֶם | לְבָבִי לְבָבְךָ | לְבָבוֹת | (לְבָבוֹת) | heart

Also: עֵנָב *(îm)* grapes   שֵׂעָר hair

27b. צֵלָע | צֵלַע צֶלַע | (צַלְעִי) | צְלָעִים | צְלָעוֹת | rib

VII. Dissyllabic nouns with a normally changeable long vowel in the first syllable and an unchangeable long vowel in the second (plural §19; constr. sing. §73; constr. plur. §§78–79; with suffixes §85).

28a. נָגִיד | נָגִיד נְגִידְכֶם | נְגִידִי נְגִידְךָ | נְגִידִים נְגִידֵי | נְגִידֵי נְגִידֵיכֶם | leader

Also: יָמִין right hand   נָשִׂיא *(îm)* prince

מָשִׁיחַ *(îm)* anointed one   עָשִׁיר rich (adj.)

נָדִיב noble (adj.)   פָּלִיט *(îm)* fugitive

פָּקִיד *(îm)* deputy   קָצִיר harvest

צָעִיר small (adj.)   שָׂעִיר *(îm)* he-goat

28b. סָרִיס | סָרִיס | (סְרִיסִי) | סָרִיסֵי/סְרִיסֵי סָרִיסִים | eunuch

29a. מָקוֹם | מְקוֹם מְקוֹמְכֶם | מְקוֹמִי מְקוֹמְךָ | מְקוֹמוֹת מְקוֹמֹתֵיכֶם | מְקוֹמוֹת | place

Also: אָדוֹן *(îm)* lord   לָשׁוֹן *(ôt)* tongue

גָּאוֹן majesty   עָוֹן *(ôt)* guilt

הָמוֹן roar   צָפוֹן north

כָּבוֹד glory   שָׁלוֹם *(îm)* welfare

29b. מָעוֹז	מָעוֹז	מָעֻזִּי	מָעֻזִּים	(מָעֻזֵּי)	refuge
30a. כָּתוּב	כָּתוּב כְּתֻבְכֶם	כְּתוּבִי כְּתוּבְךָ	כְּתוּבִים כְּתוּבֵיכֶם	כְּתוּבֵי כְּתוּבַי	written (adj.)

Here belong all Qal passive participles.

30b. בָּחוּר	——	——	בַּחוּרִים	בַּחוּרֵי	young man
30c. שָׁבוּעַ	שָׁבוּעַ	——	שָׁבוּעוֹת שָׁבוּעוֹתֵיכֶם	שָׁבוּעוֹת	week

VIII. Dissyllabic nouns ending in *-î* (§112).

31a. כְּלִי	כְּלִי	(כְּלִיִּי) כֶּלְיְךָ	כֵּלִים כֵּלַי	כְּלֵי כְּלֵיכֶם	vessel
פְּרִי	פְּרִי פְּרִיהֶם	פִּרְיִי פֶּרְיְךָ פֶּרְיְכֶם	——	——	fruit
שְׁבִי	שְׁבִי שֶׁבְיְכֶם	(שִׁבְיִי) שֶׁבְיְךָ שֶׁבְיָם	——	——	captivity
31b. חֲצִי	חֲצִי	(חֶצְיִי) (חֶצְיְךָ) חֶצְיוֹ	——	——	half
אֲרִי	——	——	אֲרָיוֹת/אֲרָיִים	——	lion

(Cf. also אַרְיֵה below)

31c. חֳלִי	——	(חָלְיִי)	חֳלָיִים	——	sickness
עֳנִי	עֳנִי	עָנְיִי (עָנְיְךָ) עָנְיָם	——	——	affliction

32. נָקִי   נְקִי   נְקִיֵּי | נְקִיִּם   נְקִיֵּי   innocent (adj.)

A subtype of 28a nearly always written defectively.

IX. Dissyllabic nouns with an unchangeable first syllable (closed or with an
unchangeable long vowel) and a changeable vowel (ā ē a) in the second
syllable (plural §25, constr. sing. §73, constr. plur. §§78–79, w. suff. §85):

33. מוֹשָׁב   מוֹשַׁב   מוֹשְׁבֵי | מוֹשָׁבִים   מוֹשְׁבֵי   dwelling place
      מוֹשַׁבְכֶם   מוֹשָׁבְךָ | מוֹשְׁבֵי   מוֹשְׁבֵיכֶם

Also: גּוֹרָל (ôṯ) lot   נוֹרָא dreadful (adj.)   שׁוֹפָר (ôṯ) shofar

      כּוֹכָב (îm) star   עוֹלָם (îm) eternity

34. הֵיכָל   הֵיכַל   הֵיכְלֵי | (הֵיכָלִים)   הֵיכְלֵי   palace
                                    הֵיכָלוֹת

Also: תֵּימָן   south (no pl.)

35. אֹיֵב   אֹיֵב   אֹיְבִי | אֹיְבִים   אֹיְבֵי   enemy
      אֹיִבְךָ | אֹיְבֵי   אֹיְבֵיכֶם
      אֹיִבְכֶם

Also: חֹתֵן   father-in-law   מוֹעֵד (îm) appointed time

      כֹּהֵן (îm) priest   סֹפֵר (îm) scribe

36. חֵרֵשׁ   ——   —— | חֵרְשִׁים   ——   deaf (adj.)

37. מִשְׁפָּט   מִשְׁפַּט   מִשְׁפָּטִי | מִשְׁפָּטִים   מִשְׁפְּטֵי   judgment

Also: מִגְדָּל (îm, ôṯ) tower   מִזְרָח east   מִשְׁכָּן (ôṯ) tabernacle

      מִגְרָשׁ (îm) pasture   מִסְפָּר (îm) number

      מִדְבָּר wilderness   מִקְדָּשׁ (îm) sanctuary

38. גַּנָּב   גַּנַּב   גַּנְּבִי | גַּנָּבִים   גַּנְּבֵי   thief

Also: מַאֲכָל food   מַעֲלָל (îm) deed   צַוָּאר (îm) neck

      מַלְאָךְ (îm) messenger   מַשָּׂא oracle   שַׁבָּת (ôṯ) Sabbath

Note the irregular presuffixal form of שַׁבָּת: שַׁבַּתּוֹ (his Sabbath).

39. אֶצְבַּע   אֶצְבַּע   (אֶצְבָּעִי) | אֶצְבָּעוֹת   אֶצְבְּעוֹת   finger

40. שֻׁלְחָן	שֻׁלְחַן	שֻׁלְחָנִי	שֻׁלְחָנוֹת	שֻׁלְחֲנוֹת	table
41a. עִוֵּר	—	—	עִוְרִים	—	blind

Also: פִּסֵּחַ (adj.) lame

41b. כִּסֵּא	כִּסֵּא	כִּסְאִי כִּסְאֲךָ	כִּסְאוֹת	(כִּסְאוֹת)	throne
41c. מִזְבֵּחַ	מִזְבַּח	מִזְבְּחִי	מִזְבְּחוֹת	מִזְבְּחוֹת	altar

X. Dissyllabic nouns with two unchangeable syllables (§50).

42. אֶבְיוֹן	אֶבְיוֹן	(אֶבְיוֹנִי)	אֶבְיוֹנִים	אֶבְיוֹנֵי	poor (adj.)

Also: עֶלְיוֹן high, lofty

43. גִּבּוֹר	גִּבּוֹר	(גִּבּוֹרִי)	גִּבּוֹרִים	גִּבּוֹרֵי	warrior

Also: מִזְמוֹר (îm) psalm

44. תַּחְתּוֹן	—	—	תַּחְתּוֹנִים	—	lower (adj.)

Also: אַחֲרוֹן latter (adj.)

45. תִּיכוֹן	—	—	תִּיכוֹנִים	—	inner (adj.)

Also: רִאשׁוֹן first (adj.)

46. צַדִּיק	צַדִּיק	(צַדִּיקִי)	צַדִּיקִים	צַדִּיקֵי	righteous person
47. עַמּוּד	עַמּוּד	(עַמּוּדִי)	עַמּוּדִים	עַמּוּדֵי	pillar

XI. Nouns ending in -eh and -ēh (§88, §116).

48a. פֶּה	פִּי	פִּי פִּיךָ (פִּיכֶם)	—	—	mouth
48b. שֶׂה	שֶׂה	שְׂיוֹ שְׂיֵהוּ	—	—	sheep/goat
49. שָׂדֶה	שְׂדֵה	שָׂדִי שָׂדְךָ	שָׂדוֹת	שְׂדוֹת	field

Also: יָפֶה (adj.) beautiful קָצֶה end

קָנֶה (îm, ôt) reed קָשֶׁה (adj.) hard, harsh

50. מִקְנֶה מִקְנֵה מִקְנִי / מִקְנֵי מִקְנֵיהוּ / מִקְנָיו (מִקְנִים) (מִקְנֵי) property

Also: מִשְׁתֶּה banquet

51. מַחֲנֶה מַחֲנֵה מַחֲנִי / מַחֲנֵי מַחֲנֵהוּ מַחֲנוֹת מַחֲנוֹת camp

Also: מַטֶּה (ôt) staff מַעֲשֶׂה (îm) deed מַרְאֶה appearance

52. אַרְיֵה — — — — lion

XII. Feminine nouns in -āh (plural §53; constr. sing. §76; constr. pl. §§78, 79; with suffixes §85).

53a. שָׁנָה שְׁנַת (שְׁנָתִי) שָׁנִים שְׁנֵי / שְׁנוֹת year

53b. צָרָה צָרַת צָרָתִי צָרוֹת צָרוֹת distress

Also: פָּרָה (ôt) heifer   Likewise participles of Qal verbs from

רָעָה (ôt) evil   hollow roots, like קָם שָׁם etc.

53c. בָּמָה — — בָּמוֹת בָּמֶתִי בָּמוֹתִי sacred high place

53d. שָׂפָה שְׂפַת (שְׂפָתִי) — — שְׂפָתַיִם שְׂפָתִי lip

53e. אָמָה (אֲמַת) אֲמָתִי אֲמָהוֹת אַמְהוֹת maidservant

54. עֵצָה עֲצַת עֲצָתִי עֵצוֹת עֵצוֹת counsel

Also: חֵמָה rage עֵדָה congregation

מֵאָה (ôt) hundred פֵּאָה corner

55. עוֹלָה עוֹלַת עוֹלָתִי עוֹלוֹת עוֹלוֹת burnt-offering

Also: חוֹמָה (ôt) wall טוֹבָה welfare תּוֹרָה (ôt) law, Law

No.						Meaning
56.	בִּינָה	בִּינַת	בִּינָתִי	——	——	understanding
57.	אַמָּה	(אַמַּת)	(אַמָּתִי)	אַמּוֹת	(אַמּוֹת)	cubit

Also: חַיָּה (ôṯ) wild beast

No.						Meaning
58a.	פִּנָּה	פִּנַּת	(פִּנָּתִי)	פִּנּוֹת	פִּנּוֹת	corner

Also: מִדָּה (ôṯ) measure

No.						Meaning
58b.	אִשָּׁה	אֵשֶׁת	אִשְׁתִּי	נָשִׁים	נְשֵׁי	woman
59.	חֻקָּה	חֻקַּת	חֻקָּתִי	חֻקּוֹת	חֻקּוֹת	statute
60a.	מַלְכָּה	מַלְכַּת	מַלְכָּתִי	מְלָכוֹת	מַלְכוֹת	queen
60b.	נַחֲלָה	נַחֲלַת	נַחֲלָתִי	נְחָלוֹת	נַחֲלוֹת	portion

Also: אַהֲבָה love   נַעֲרָה (ôṯ) girl

No.						Meaning
61a.	גִּבְעָה	גִּבְעַת	גִּבְעָתִי	גְּבָעוֹת	גִּבְעוֹת	hill

Also: יִרְאָה fear   שִׂמְחָה (ôṯ) joy   שִׁפְחָה (ôṯ) maidservant
מִנְחָה (ôṯ) gift   שִׂמְלָה (ôṯ) cloak

No.						Meaning
61b.	מִצְוָה	מִצְוַת	מִצְוָתִי	מִצְוֹת	מִצְוֹת	commandment
62.	חֶרְפָּה	חֶרְפַּת	חֶרְפָּתִי	חֲרָפוֹת	חֶרְפוֹת	reproach

Also: עֶגְלָה (ôṯ) heifer   עֶרְוָה nakedness

No.						Meaning
63.	חָכְמָה	חָכְמַת	חָכְמָתִי	חָכְמוֹת	(חָכְמוֹת)	wisdom
64a.	בְּרָכָה	בִּרְכַּת	בִּרְכָתִי	בְּרָכוֹת	בִּרְכוֹת	blessing

Also: צְדָקָה (ôṯ) righteousness   רְבָבָה myriad
קְלָלָה curse   שְׁמָמָה desolation

No.						Meaning
64b.	אֲדָמָה	אַדְמַת	אַדְמָתִי	עֲרָבוֹת	עַרְבוֹת	land/steppe
64c.	מְעָרָה	מְעָרַת	——	מְעָרוֹת	מְעָרוֹת	cave

[298]

No.	sing. abs.	sing. cstr.	sing. + suff.	pl. abs.	pl. cstr.	
64d.	מְלָאכָה	מְלֶאכֶת	מְלַאכְתִּי	(מַלְאָכוֹת)	מַלְאָכוֹת	task
65a.	נְבֵלָה	נִבְלַת	נִבְלָתִי נִבְלָתְךָ נִבְלָתוֹ	—	(נְבֵלוֹת)	corpse
65b.	שְׁאֵלָה	—	שָׁאֵלָתִי שְׁאֵלָתִי	—	—	request
65c.	בְּהֵמָה	בֶּהֱמַת	(בֶּהֶמְתִּי) בֶּהֶמְתְּךָ	בְּהֵמוֹת	בַּהֲמוֹת	beast
65d.	בְּרֵכָה	בְּרֵכַת	—	בְּרֵכוֹת	—	pond

Also fem. adj. and stative participles of the type כְּבֵדָה.

No.	sing. abs.	sing. cstr.	sing. + suff.	pl. abs.	pl. cstr.	
66.	עֲבוֹדָה	עֲבוֹדַת	עֲבוֹדָתִי	—	—	work
67.	תְּבוּאָה	תְּבוּאַת	תְּבוּאָתִי	תְּבוּאוֹת	תְּבוּאוֹת	product

Also: בְּתוּלָה *(ôt)* maiden   יְשׁוּעָה deliverance   תְּבוּנָה understanding

No.	sing. abs.	sing. cstr.	sing. + suff.	pl. abs.	pl. cstr.	
68.	תְּפִלָּה	תְּפִלַּת	תְּפִלָּתִי תְּפִלַּתְכֶם	תְּפִלוֹת	תְּפִלוֹת	prayer

Also: מְגִלָּה *(ôt)* scroll   תְּהִלָּה praise   תְּחִנָּה supplication

מְסִלָּה *(ôt)* highway   תְּחִלָּה beginning

No.	sing. abs.	sing. cstr.	sing. + suff.	pl. abs.	pl. cstr.	
69.	אֲחֻזָּה	אֲחֻזַּת	אֲחֻזָּתִי	—	—	possession
70.	מַמְלָכָה	מַמְלֶכֶת	מַמְלַכְתִּי	מַמְלְכוֹת	מַמְלָכוֹת	kingdom

Also: אַלְמָנָה *(ôt)* widow

No.	sing. abs.	sing. cstr.	sing. + suff.	pl. abs.	pl. cstr.	
71.	מֶרְכָּבָה	מֶרְכֶּבֶת	(מֶרְכַּבְתִּי)	מַרְכְּבוֹת	מַרְכָּבוֹת	chariot
72.	מִשְׁפָּחָה	מִשְׁפַּחַת	מִשְׁפַּחְתִּי	מִשְׁפְּחוֹת	מִשְׁפָּחוֹת	family

Also: מִלְחָמָה (מִלְחֶמֶת) war

No.	sing. abs.	sing. cstr.	sing. + suff.	pl. abs.	pl. cstr.	
73.	תּוֹעֵבָה	תּוֹעֲבַת	—	תּוֹעֲבוֹת	תּוֹעֵבוֹת	abomination
	—			תּוֹלְדוֹת	(תּוֹלְדוֹת)	history

XIII. Feminine Nouns in -*t* (plural §62; with suffixes §111).

74.	בַּת	בַּת	בִּתִּי	בָּנוֹת	בְּנוֹת	daughter
75.	עֵת	עֵת	עִתּוֹ	עִתִּים / עִתּוֹת	(עִתַּי) / (עִתּוֹת)	time
76.	אֱמֶת	——	אֲמִתְּךָ	——	——	truth
77.	דֶּלֶת	דֶּלֶת	(דַּלְתִּי)	דְּלָתוֹת	דַּלְתוֹת	door

Also: קֶשֶׁת bow

#						English
78.	דַּעַת	דַּעַת	דַּעְתִּי	——	——	knowledge
79.	נְחֹשֶׁת	נְחֹשֶׁת	נְחֻשְׁתִּי	——	——	bronze (fetter)
80.	(מוֹלֶדֶת)	מוֹלֶדֶת	מוֹלַדְתִּי	——	——	kindred
81.	מִשְׁמֶרֶת	מִשְׁמֶרֶת	מִשְׁמַרְתִּי	מִשְׁמָרוֹת	מִשְׁמְרוֹת	office

Also: תִּפְאֶרֶת beauty

#						English
82.	חַטָּאת	חַטַּאת	חַטָּאתִי	חַטָּאוֹת	חַטֹּאות	sin
83a.	חֲנִית	(חֲנִית)	(חֲנִיתִי)	חֲנִיתִים	(חֲנִיתַי)	spear

Also probably the following (insufficient attestation):

בְּרִית pact   אַחֲרִית close   שְׁבִית captivity

#						English
83b.	מִצְרִית	(מִצְרִית)	מִצְרִיתִי	מִצְרִיּוֹת	(מִצְרִיּוֹת)	Egyptian (fem.adj)

Also the many other fem. adj. ending in -*ît*, such as שְׁלִשִׁית third,

for which we have not made separate classifications.

#						English
84.	עֵדוּת	——	——	——	עֵדְוֺת	testimony
85.	מַלְכוּת	מַלְכוּת	מַלְכוּתִי	מַלְכֻיּוֹת	——	kingdom
86.	אָחוֹת	אֲחוֹת	אֲחוֹתִי	(אֲחָיוֹת)	(אֲחָיוֹת)	sister

XIV. Masculine nouns in *-āh*.

87.	לַ֫יְלָה	——	——		לֵילוֹת	לֵילוֹת	night
88.	פֶּחָה	פַּחַת	(פֶּחָתִי)		פַּחֲוֺת/פַּחוֹת	פַּחֲוֺת/פַּחוֹת	governor

Appendix B

QAL VERBS: THE PRINCIPAL PARTS
ACCORDING TO ROOT TYPES

The following is a classified list of all the Qal verbs appearing in this grammar. Under the heading "imperfect" are included: (1) the normal imperfect, (2) the jussive (if it differs from the preceding), and (3) the converted imperfect. Under "imperative": (1) the 2nd pers. masc. sing., (2) the 2nd pers. fem. sing., and (3) the "emphatic" form of the 2nd pers. masc. sing. in *-āh*. Under "inf. constr.": (1) the free (unbound) form of the infinitive construct, and (2) the inf. construct with the suffix of the 1st person singular. Under "other": (1) the active participle, (2) the passive participle, and (3) the infinitive absolute, in that order. The numbers in parentheses refer to the paragraphs of the grammar where the full paradigms of the form in question may be found. Minor deviations from the given type are indicated in parentheses.

Perfect	*Imperfect*	*Imperative*	*Inf. Construct*	*Other*

1. Triliteral roots with no phonetic peculiarities (called Regular or Sound).

	Perfect	Imperfect	Imperative	Inf. Construct	Other
1a.	כָּתַב (43)	יִכְתֹּב (90)	כְּתֹב (102)	כְּתֹב (114)	כֹּתֵב (26)
		וַיִּכְתֹּב	כִּתְבִי	כָּתְבִי	כָּתוּב (128)
			כָּתְבָה		כָּתוֹב

גָּנַב	to steal	פָּרַץ to break out
דָּרַךְ	to tread	פָּרַשׂ to spread

[302]

דָּרַשׁ to seek, inquire		קָבַץ to gather		
זָכַר to remember		קָבַר to bury		
כָּרַת to cut		קָצַף to become angry		
כָּשַׁל to stumble		קָצַר to harvest		
כָּתַב to write		קָשַׁר to bind together		
לָכַד to capture		רָדַף to pursue		
מָכַר to sell		שָׂרַף to burn		
מָלַךְ to rule		שָׁבַר to break		
מָרַד to rebel		שָׁבַת to cease, rest		
מָשַׁךְ to drag		שָׁכַן to dwell		
מָשַׁל to rule		שָׁמַר to observe		
סָגַר to close		שָׁפַט to judge		
סָפַר to count		שָׁפַךְ to pour		
פָּקַד to attend to		תָּפַשׂ to catch hold of		

	Perfect	*Imperfect*	*Imperative*	*Inf. Construct*	*Other*
1b.	לָמַד (43)	יִלְמַד (94) וַיִּלְמַד	לְמַד (102) לִמְדִי {לִמְדָה לְמַדָה}	לְמֹד (114) {לָמְדִי לִמְדִי}	לָמֵד (26) לָמוּד (128) לָמוֹד
	לָמַד to learn			שָׁכַב to lie down	
	רָכַב to ride				
1c.	קָרַב (43)	יִקְרַב (94) וַיִּקְרַב	קְרַב (102) קִרְבִי קָרְבָה	קְרֹב (114) קָרְבִי	——— ——— קָרוֹב
	גָּדַל to be big			קָרַב to approach	
	לָבַשׁ to dress				
1d.	כָּבֵד (87)	יִכְבַּד (94) וַיִּכְבַּד	כְּבַד (102) כִּבְדִי	{כְּבֹד (114) כְּבַד} כִּבְדִי	——— ——— כָּבוֹד
	זָקֵן to be old			רָעֵב to be hungry	
	טָהֵר to be pure			שָׁפֵל to be low	
	כָּבֵד to be heavy				
1e.	קָטֹן	יִקְטַן (94) וַיִּקְטַן	(קְטַן)	(קְטֹן) (87)	——— ——— קָטוֹן

(to be small)

2. Roots II/III-guttural; II/III-*Aleph*

	Perfect	Imperfect	Imperative	Inf. Construct	Other
2a.	בָּחַר (48)	יִבְחַר (94) וַיִּבְחַר	בְּחַר (102) בַּחֲרִי	בְּחֹר (114) בָּחֳרִי	בֹּחֵר (35) בָּחוּר (128) בָּחוֹר

בָּחַר	to choose		פָּעַל	to do
בָּחַן	to test		צָחַק	to laugh
בָּעַר	to burn		צָעַק	to cry out
גָּאַל	to redeem		רָחַץ	to wash
גָּעַר	to rebuke		שָׂחַק	to laugh
זָעַק	to cry out		שָׁאַל	to ask
מָאַס	to reject		שָׁחַט	to slaughter

	Perfect	Imperfect	Imperative	Inf. Construct	Other
2b.	שָׁמַע (48)	יִשְׁמַע (94) וַיִּשְׁמַע	שְׁמַע (102) שִׁמְעִי שָׁמְעָה) שִׁמְעָה (	שְׁמֹעַ (114) שָׁמְעִי) שִׁמְעִי (	שֹׁמֵעַ (35) שָׁמוּעַ (128) שָׁמוֹעַ

בָּטַח	to trust		פָּשַׁע	to rebel, err
בָּלַע	to swallow		פָּתַח	to open
בָּקַע	to split		קָרַע	to tear
בָּרַח	to flee		רָצַח	to kill
זָבַח	to sacrifice		שָׂבַע	to be sated
כָּרַע	to bow down		שָׂמַח	to rejoice
מָשַׁח	to anoint		שָׁכַח	to forget
סָלַח	to pardon		שָׁלַח	to send
פָּגַע	to meet		תָּקַע	to thrust, blow
שָׁמַע	to hear			

	Perfect	Imperfect	Imperative	Inf. Construct	Other
2c.	מָצָא (52)	יִמְצָא (95) וַיִּמְצָא	מְצָא (102) מִצְאִי מְצָאָה	מְצֹא (114) מָצְאִי	מֹצֵא (35) מָצוּא (128) מָצוֹא (128)

בָּרָא	to create		קָרָא	to call
מָצָא	to find		רָפָא	to heal

	Perfect	Imperfect	Imperative	Inf. Construct	Other
2d.	מָלֵא (87)	יִמְלָא (95) וַיִּמְלָא	מְלָא (102) מְלִאי	מְלֹא (114)	—— —— מָלוֹא (128)

מָלֵא	to be full		שָׂנֵא	to hate

3. Roots I-guttural (not I-*Aleph*)

	Perfect	*Imperfect*	*Imperative*	*Inf. Construct*	*Other*
3a.	עָמַד (48)	יַעֲמֹד (103) וַיַּעֲמֹד	עֲמֹד (103) עִמְדִי עִמְדָה	עֲמֹד (114) עָמְדִי	עֹמֵד (26) עָמוֹד (128) עָמוֹד (128)

הָפַךְ	to overturn			חָשַׂךְ	to withhold (יַחְשֹׂךְ)
הָרַג	to kill			עָבַד	to serve
הָרַס	to break down (tr.) (also יֶהֱרַס)			עָבַר	to cross
חָגַר	to gird (יַחְגֹּר)			עָזַב	to abandon
חָלַם	to dream			עָזַר	to help (also יַעְזֹר)
חָמַל	to spare			עָמַד	to stand
חָקַר	to explore (also יַחְקֹר)			עָרַב	to give as pledge
חָרַשׁ	to plow			עָרַךְ	to arrange
חָשַׁב	to reckon (יַחְשֹׁב)				

	Perfect	*Imperfect*	*Imperative*	*Inf. Construct*	*Other*
3b.	חָזַק (48)	יֶחֱזַק (103) וַיֶּחֱזַק	חֲזַק (103) חִזְקִי	חֲזַק (114) חֶזְקִי	—— —— חָזוֹק (128)

הָדַר	to honor (יֶהְדַּר)			חָזַק	to be strong
חָדַל	to cease (יֶחְדַּל)				

	Perfect	*Imperfect*	*Imperative*	*Inf. Construct*	*Other*
3c.	חָטָא (52)	יֶחֱטָא (103) וַיֶּחֱטָא	—— ——	חֲטֹא (114) חָטְאִי	חֹטֵא (35) ——

(to sin)

	Perfect	*Imperfect*
3d.	חָפֵץ (48)	יַחְפֹּץ (103)

(to take pleasure in)

4. Roots I-*Aleph*

	Perfect	*Imperfect*	*Imperative*	*Inf. Construct*	*Other*
4a.	אָסַר (48)	יֶאְסֹר (108) וַיֶּאְסֹר	אֱסֹר (108) אִסְרִי אִסְרָה	אֱסֹר (114) אָסְרִי	אֹסֵר (26) אָסוֹר (128) אָסוֹר (128)

אָסַף	to collect, gather			אָסַר	to bind, take captive

	Perfect	*Imperfect*	*Imperative*	*Inf. Construct*	*Other*
4b.	אָכַל (48)	יֹאכַל (108) וַיֹּאכַל	אֱכֹל (108) אִכְלִי אִכְלָה	אֱכֹל (114) אָכְלִי	אֹכֵל (26) אָכוֹל (128) אָכוֹל (128)

אָבַד to perish   אָכַל to eat

אָחַז to seize (יֶאֱחֹז or יֹאחֵז)   אָמַר to say (וַיֹּאמֶר)

	Perfect	Imperfect	Imperative	Inf. Construct	Other
4c.	(48) אָהַב	(108) יֶאֱהַב	(108) אֱהַב	(114) אַהֲבָה	(35) אֹהֵב
	אָהֵב	יֹאהַב	——	אַהֲבָתִי	(128) אָהוּב

אָהַב to love   אָשֵׁם (יֶאְשַׁם) to be guilty

5. Roots I-*Nun*

	Perfect	Imperfect	Imperative	Inf. Construct	Other
5a.	(43) נָפַל	(118) יִפֹּל	(118) נְפֹל	(118) נְפֹל	(26) נֹפֵל
		וַיִּפֹּל	נִפְלִי	נָפְלִי	(128) (נָפוּל)
			נִפְלָה		(128) נָפוֹל

נָגַף to strike   נָפַל to fall

נָדַר to vow   נָצַר to guard

נָטַשׁ to forsake

	Perfect	Imperfect	Imperative	Inf. Construct	Other
5b.	(43) נָגַע	(118) יִגַּע	(118) גַּע	(118) גַּעַת	(35) נֹגֵעַ
		וַיִּגַּע	גְּעִי	גַּעְתִּי	(128) נָגוּעַ
			גְּעָה	נְגֹעַ	(128) נָגוֹעַ
				נָגְעִי	

נָגַע to touch   נָסַע to set out

נָטַע to plant

	Perfect	Imperfect	Imperative	Inf. Construct	Other
5c.	(52) נָשָׂא	(118) יִשָּׂא	(118) שָׂא	(118) שְׂאֵת	(35) נֹשֵׂא
		וַיִּשָּׂא	שְׂאִי	שְׂאֵתִי	(128) נָשׂוּא
			שְׂאָה		(128) נָשׂוֹא

(to raise up)

	Perfect	Imperfect	Imperative	Inf. Construct	Other
5d.	(49) נָתַן	(118) יִתֵּן	(118) תֵּן	(118) תֵּת	(26) נֹתֵן
		וַיִּתֵּן	תְּנִי	תִּתִּי	(128) נָתוּן
			תְּנָה		(128) נָתוֹן

(to give)

	Perfect	Imperfect	Imperative	Inf. Construct	Other
5e.	(48) לָקַח	(118) יִקַּח	(118) קַח	(118) קַחַת	(35) לֹקֵחַ
		וַיִּקַּח	קְחִי	קַחְתִּי	(128) לָקוּחַ
			קְחָה		(128) לָקוֹחַ

(to take)

6. Roots I-*Yodh*

	Perfect	Imperfect	Imperative	Inf. Construct	Other
6a.	יָשַׁב (43)	יֵשֵׁב (120)	שֵׁב (120)	שֶׁבֶת (120)	יַשֵּׁב (26)
		וַיֵּשֶׁב	שְׁבִי	שִׁבְתִּי	
			שְׁבָה		יָשׁוֹב (128)

יָרַד to go down   יֵשֵׁב to dwell
יָלַד to bear (a child)

6b.	יָדַע (48)	יֵדַע (120)	דַּע (120)	דַּעַת (120)	יִדַּע (35)
		וַיֵּדַע	דְּעִי	דַּעְתִּי	יָדוּעַ (128)
			דְּעָה		יָדוֹעַ (128)

(to know)

6c.	יָצָא (52)	יֵצֵא (120)	צֵא (120)	צֵאת (120)	יֻצָּא (35)
		וַיֵּצֵא	צְאִי	צֵאתִי	
			צְאָה		יָצוֹא (128)

(to go forth)

6d.	יָרַשׁ (43)	יִירַשׁ (120)	רֵשׁ (120)	רֶשֶׁת (120)	יֻרַשׁ (26)
		וַיִּירַשׁ		רִשְׁתִּי	יָרוֹשׁ (128)
					יָרוֹשׁ (128)

יָשַׁר to be upright   יָרַשׁ to inherit
יָעַץ to advise

6e.	יָשֵׁן (87)	יִישַׁן (120)	——		יְשֹׁן (120)	
(to sleep)					

6f.	יָרֵא (87)	יִירָא (120)	יְרָא (102)		
(to fear)					

6g.	יָצַר (43)	יְצַר/ (118)	——	——	יֵצֶר (26)
		יִצֹּר			
		וַיִּיצֶר/וַיִּצֶר			

(to fashion)

6h.	יָצַק (43)	יִצֹּק/צַק (118)	יְצֹק/צַק (118)	צֶקֶת (120)	
		וַיִּצֹק			

(to pour)

	Perfect	Imperfect	Imperative	Inf. Construct	Other
6i.	יָכֹל (87)	יוּכַל (120)	———	יְכֹלֶת	

(to be able)

	Perfect	Imperfect	Imperative	Inf. Construct	Other
6j.	הָלַךְ (48)	יֵלֵךְ (120) וַיֵּלֶךְ	לֵךְ (120) לְכִי לְכָה	לֶכֶת (120) לֶכְתִּי	הֹלֵךְ (26) הָלוֹךְ (128)

(to go, walk)

7. Hollow Roots (II-*Waw*/*Yodh*)

	Perfect	Imperfect	Imperative	Inf. Construct	Other
7a.	קָם (64)	יָקוּם (124) יָקֹם וַיָּקָם	קוּם (124) קוּמִי קוּמָה	קוּם (124) קוּמִי	קָם (64) ——— קוֹם (128)

גָּר	to sojourn	פָּץ	to be scattered
מָל	to circumcise	צָם	to fast
נָח	to rest (וַיָּנַח)	צָר	to besiege (וַיָּצַר)
נָם	to sleep	קָם	to arise
נָס	to flee	רָם	to be high
סָר	to turn aside (וַיָּסַר)	רָץ	to run
עָר	to arouse oneself	שָׁב	to return

	Perfect	Imperfect	Imperative	Inf. Construct	Other
7b.	שָׂם (64)	יָשִׂים (124) יָשֵׂם וַיָּשֶׂם	שִׂים (124) שִׂימִי שִׂימָה	שׂוּם/שִׂים (124) שׂוּמִי	שָׂם (64) שִׂים (128) שׂוּם (128)

גָּל	to rejoice	שָׂם	to put, place
דָּן	to judge	שָׁר	to sing
לָן	to spend the night	שָׁת	to set, place

	Perfect	Imperfect	Imperative	Inf. Construct	Other
7c.	מֵת (87)	יָמוּת (124) יָמֹת וַיָּמָת	מוּת (124)	מוּת (124)	מֵת (87) ——— מוֹת (128)

(to die)

	Perfect	Imperfect	Imperative	Inf. Construct	Other
7d.	בּשׁ (87)	יֵבשׁ (124)	בּשׁ (124)		

(to be ashamed)

	Perfect	Imperfect	Imperative	Inf. Construct	Other
7e.	בָּא (64)	יָבֹא (124) וַיָּבֹא	בֹּא (124) בֹּאִי בֹּאָה	בֹּא (124) בֹּאִי	בָּא (64) בֹּא (128)

(to come)

8. Roots III-Hē

	Perfect	Imperfect	Imperative	Inf. Construct	Other
8a.	בָּנָה (57)	יִבְנֶה (122) יִבֶן וַיִּבֶן	בְּנֵה (122) בְּנִי	בְּנוֹת (122) בְּנוֹתִי	בֹּנֶה (41) בָּנוּי (128) בָּנֹה (128)

בָּזָה	to despise	קָנָה	to acquire
בָּכָה	to weep (וַיֵּבְךְּ)	קָרָה	to meet
בָּנָה	to build	רָאָה	to see (וַיַּרְא)
גָּלָה	to reveal; go into exile	רָבָה	to be many
זָנָה	to be a harlot	רָעָה	to pasture (וַיִּרַע)
כָּלָה	to be done, finished	שָׁבָה	to take captive
פָּדָה	to ransom	שָׁתָה	to drink (וַיֵּשְׁתְּ)
פָּנָה	to turn toward	תָּלָה	to hang
		תָּעָה	to wander lost

	Perfect	Imperfect	Imperative	Inf. Construct	Other
8b.	עָלָה (57)	יַעֲלֶה (122) יַעַל וַיַּעַל	עֲלֵה (122) עֲלִי	עֲלוֹת (122) עֲלוֹתִי	עֹלֶה (41) עָלֹה (128)

הָרָה	to conceive	עָנָה	to answer
חָנָה	to camp	עָשָׂה	to do, make
עָלָה	to ascend, go up		

	Perfect	Imperfect	Imperative	Inf. Construct	Other
8c.	חָזָה (57)	יֶחֱזֶה (122) יֶחַז וַיֶּחַז	חֲזֵה (122) חֲזִי	חֲזוֹת (122) חֲזוֹתִי	חֹזֶה (41) חָזוּי (128) חָזֹה (128)

הָגָה	to mutter, meditate	חָזָה	to see
הָמָה	to roar	חָרָה	to be angry

	Perfect	Imperfect	Imperative	Inf. Construct
8d.	הָיָה (57)	יִהְיֶה (122) יְהִי וַיְהִי	הֱיֵה (122) הֱיִי	הֱיוֹת (122) הֱיוֹתִי לִהְיוֹת

הָיָה	to be	חָיָה	to live

	Perfect	Imperfect
8e.	אָבָה (57)	יֹאבֶה (122) יֹאב

אָבָה	to be willing	אָפָה	to bake

	Perfect	Imperfect	Imperative	Inf. Construct	Other
8f.	נָטָה (57)	יִטֶּה (122) יֵט וַיֵּט	נְטֵה (122)	נְטוֹת (122)	נֹטֶה (41) נָטוּי (128)

(to stretch forth)

9. Geminate Roots (a sampling of major types only; for details see §126).

	Perfect	Imperfect	Imperative	Inf. Construct	Other
9a.	סָבַב (68)	יָסֹב/יִסֹּב (126) וַיָּסָב	סֹב (126) סֹבִּי	סֹב (126) סָבִּי	סֹבֵב (26) סָבוּב (128) סָבוֹב (128)

(to surround, go around)

	Perfect	Imperfect	Imperative	Inf. Construct	Other
9b.	אָרַר (68)	יָאֹר (126)	אֹר (126)	——	אָרוּר (128)

(to curse)

	Perfect	Imperfect	Imperative	Inf. Construct	Other
9c.	תַּם (87)	יֵתַם (126)	——	תֻּמִּי תֹּם (126)	

רַע to be bad   תַּם to be finished, completed

קַל to be light, contemptible

Appendix C

THE DERIVED CONJUGATIONS: A SYNOPSIS*

	Niphal	Piel	Pual	Hiphil	Hophal	Hithpael
1. Sound Triliteral Roots	(141)	(149)	(154)	(158)	(175)	(178)
Perfect	נִכְתַּב	כָּתַב	כָּתַּב	הִכְתִּיב	הָכְתַּב	הִתְכַּתֵּב
Imperfect	יִכָּתֵב	יְכַתֵּב	יְכֻתַּב	יַכְתִּיב	יָכְתַּב	יִתְכַּתֵּב
Jussive	יִכָּתֵב	יְכַתֵּב	יְכֻתַּב	יַכְתֵּב	יָכְתַּב	יִתְכַּתֵּב
Imperative	הִכָּתֵב	כַּתֵּב	——	הַכְתֵּב	——	הִתְכַּתֵּב
Inf. Construct	הִכָּתֵב	כַּתֵּב	——	הַכְתִּיב	——	הִתְכַּתֵּב
Inf. Absolute	נִכְתֹּב	כַּתֹּב	כֻּתֹּב	הַכְתֵּב	הָכְתֵּב	הִתְכַּתֵּב
Participle	נִכְתָּב	מְכַתֵּב	מְכֻתָּב	מַכְתִּיב	מָכְתָּב	מִתְכַּתֵּב
2. Roots I-guttural (excluding I-*Aleph*)	(141)	(149)	(154)	(158)	(175)	(178)
Perfect	נֶעֱמַד	עִמַּד	עֻמַּד	הֶעֱמִיד	הָעֳמַד	הִתְעַמֵּד
Imperfect	יֵעָמֵד	יְעַמֵּד	יְעֻמַּד	יַעֲמִיד	יָעֳמַד	יִתְעַמֵּד
Jussive	יֵעָמֵד	יְעַמֵּד	יְעֻמַּד	יַעֲמֵד	יָעֳמַד	יִתְעַמֵּד
Imperative	הֵעָמֵד	עַמֵּד	——	הַעֲמֵד	——	הִתְעַמֵּד
Inf. Construct	הֵעָמֵד	עַמֵּד	——	הַעֲמִיד	——	הִתְעַמֵּד
Inf. Absolute	נַעֲמֹד	עַמֹּד	עֻמֹּד	הַעֲמֵד	הָעֲמֵד	הִתְעַמֵּד
Participle	נֶעֱמָד	מְעַמֵּד	מְעֻמָּד	מַעֲמִיד	מָעֳמָד	מִתְעַמֵּד

* The same root is used to illustrate all the conjugations of a given root type, regardless of whether it is attested in that particular form or not. References are to paragraphs in the body of the grammar where the complete paradigms may be found.

[311]

	Niphal	Piel	Pual	Hiphil	Hophal	Hithpael
3. Roots II-guttural	(141)	(149)	(154)	(158)	(175)	(178)
Perfect	נִבְרַךְ	בֵּרַךְ	בֹּרַךְ	הִבְרִיךְ	הָבְרַךְ	הִתְבָּרֵךְ
Imperfect	יִבָּרֵךְ	יְבָרֵךְ	יְבֹרַךְ	יַבְרִיךְ	יָבְרַךְ	יִתְבָּרֵךְ
Jussive	יִבָּרֵךְ	יְבָרֵךְ	יְבֹרַךְ	יַבְרֵךְ	יָבְרַךְ	יִתְבָּרֵךְ
Imperative	הִבָּרֵךְ	בָּרֵךְ	——	הַבְרֵךְ	——	הִתְבָּרֵךְ
Inf. Construct	הִבָּרֵךְ	בָּרֵךְ	——	הַבְרִיךְ	——	הִתְבָּרֵךְ
Inf. Absolute	נִבְרֹךְ	בָּרֵךְ	——	הַבְרֵךְ	הָבְרֵךְ	הִתְבָּרֵךְ
Participle	נִבְרָךְ	מְבָרֵךְ	מְבֹרָךְ	מַבְרִיךְ	מָבְרָךְ	מִתְבָּרֵךְ
4. Roots III-guttural (excluding III-*Aleph*)	(141)	(149)	(154)	(160)	(175)	(178)
Perfect	נִשְׁמַע	שִׁמַּע	שֻׁמַּע	הִשְׁמִיעַ	הָשְׁמַע	הִשְׁתַּמַּע
Imperfect	יִשָּׁמַע	יְשַׁמַּע	יְשֻׁמַּע	יַשְׁמִיעַ	יָשְׁמַע	יִשְׁתַּמַּע
Jussive	יִשָּׁמַע	יְשַׁמַּע	יְשֻׁמַּע	יַשְׁמַע	יָשְׁמַע	יִשְׁתַּמַּע
Imperative	הִשָּׁמַע	שַׁמַּע	——	הַשְׁמַע	——	הִשְׁתַּמַּע
Inf. Construct	הִשָּׁמַע	שַׁמַּע	——	הַשְׁמִיעַ	——	הִשְׁתַּמַּע
Inf. Absolute	נִשְׁמוֹעַ	שַׁמֵּעַ	——	הַשְׁמֵעַ	הָשְׁמֵעַ	——
Participle	נִשְׁמָע	מְשַׁמֵּעַ	מְשֻׁמָּע	מַשְׁמִיעַ	מָשְׁמָע	מִשְׁתַּמֵּעַ
5. Roots III-*Aleph*	(143)	(151)	(154)	(160)	(175)	(178)
Perfect	נִמְצָא	מִצֵּא	מֻצָּא	הִמְצִיא	הָמְצָא	הִתְמַצֵּא
Imperfect	יִמָּצֵא	יְמַצֵּא	יְמֻצָּא	יַמְצִיא	יָמְצָא	יִתְמַצֵּא
Jussive	יִמָּצֵא	יְמַצֵּא	יְמֻצָּא	יַמְצֵא	יָמְצָא	יִתְמַצֵּא
Imperative	הִמָּצֵא	מַצֵּא	——	הַמְצֵא	——	הִתְמַצֵּא
Inf. Construct	הִמָּצֵא	מַצֵּא	——	הַמְצִיא	——	הִתְמַצֵּא
Inf. Absolute	נִמְצֹא	מַצֹּא	——	הַמְצֵא	——	——
Participle	נִמְצָא	מְמַצֵּא	מְמֻצָּא	מַמְצִיא	מָמְצָא	מִתְמַצֵּא
6. Roots I-*Nun*	(143)	(149)	(154)	(158)	(175)	(178)
Perfect	נִפַּל	נִפֵּל	נֻפַּל	הִפִּיל	הֻפַּל	הִתְנַפֵּל
Imperfect	יִנָּפֵל	יְנַפֵּל	יְנֻפַּל	יַפִּיל	יֻפַּל	יִתְנַפֵּל
Jussive	יִנָּפֵל	יְנַפֵּל	יְנֻפַּל	יַפֵּל	יֻפַּל	יִתְנַפֵּל
Imperative	הִנָּפֵל	נַפֵּל	——	הַפֵּל	——	הִתְנַפֵּל
Inf. Construct	הִנָּפֵל	נַפֵּל	——	הַפִּיל	הֻפַּל	הִתְנַפֵּל
Inf. Absolute	נִפֹּל	נַפֵּל	——	הַפֵּל	הֻפֵּל	הִתְנַפֵּל
Participle	נִפָּל	מְנַפֵּל	מְנֻפָּל	מַפִּיל	מֻפָּל	מִתְנַפֵּל
7. Roots I-*Waw*/*Yodh*	(143)	(149)	(154)	(163)	(175)	(178)
Perfect	נוֹשַׁב	יִשֵּׁב	יֻשַּׁב	הוֹשִׁיב	הוּשַׁב	הִתְיַשֵּׁב
Imperfect	יִוָּשֵׁב	יְיַשֵּׁב	יְיֻשַּׁב	יוֹשִׁיב	יוּשַׁב	יִתְיַשֵּׁב
Jussive	יִוָּשֵׁב	יְיַשֵּׁב	יְיֻשַּׁב	יוֹשֵׁב	יוּשַׁב	יִתְיַשֵּׁב

	Niphal	Piel	Pual	Hiphil	Hophal	Hithpael
Imperative	הִוָּשֵׁב	יַשֵּׁב	—	הוֹשֵׁב	—	הִתְיַשֵּׁב
Inf. Construct	הִוָּשֵׁב	יַשֵּׁב	—	הוֹשִׁיב	הוּשַׁב	הִתְיַשֵּׁב
Inf. Absolute	—	יַשֵּׁב	—	הוֹשֵׁב	—	הִתְיַשֵּׁב
Participle	נוֹשָׁב	מְיַשֵּׁב	מְיֻשָּׁב	מוֹשִׁיב	מוּשָׁב	מִתְיַשֵּׁב

8. Roots II-*Waw*/*Yodh* (Hollow)

	Niphal (146)	Piel	Pual	Hiphil (169)	Hophal (175)	Hithpael
Perfect	נָקוֹם	—	—	הֵקִים	הוּקַם	—
Imperfect	יִקּוֹם	—	—	יָקִים	יוּקַם	—
Jussive	יִקּוֹם	—	—	יָקֵם	יוּקַם	—
Imperative	הִקּוֹם	—	—	הָקֵם	—	—
Inf. Construct	הִקּוֹם	—	—	הָקִים	הוּקַם	—
Inf. Absolute	נָקוֹם	—	—	הָקֵם	—	—
Participle	נָקוֹם	—	—	מֵקִים	מוּקָם	—

9. Roots III-*Hē*

	Niphal (143)	Piel (151)	Pual (154)	Hiphil (166)	Hophal (175)	Hithpael (178)
Perfect	נִבְנָה	בִּנָּה	בֻּנָּה	הִבְנָה	הָבְנָה	הִתְבַּנָּה
Imperfect	יִבָּנֶה	יְבַנֶּה	יְבֻנֶּה	יַבְנֶה	יָבְנֶה	יִתְבַּנֶּה
Jussive	יִבָּן	יְבַן	—	יֶבֶן	—	יִתְבַּן
Imperative	הִבָּנֵה	בַּנֵּה	—	הַבְנֵה	—	הִתְבַּנֵּה
Inf. Construct	הִבָּנוֹת	בַּנּוֹת	בֻּנּוֹת	הַבְנוֹת	—	הִתְבַּנּוֹת
Inf. Absolute	נִבְנֹה	בַּנֹּה	—	הַבְנֵה	הָבְנֵה	—
Participle	נִבְנֶה	מְבַנֶּה	מְבֻנֶּה	מַבְנֶה	מָבְנֶה	מִתְבַּנֶּה

10. Geminate Roots

	Niphal (146)	Piel (151)	Pual (154)	Hiphil (172)	Hophal (175)	Hithpael (178)
Perfect	נָסַב	סִבֵּב	סֻבַּב	הֵסֵב	הוּסַב	הִסְתַּבֵּב
Imperfect	יִסַּב	יְסַבֵּב	יְסֻבַּב	יָסֵב	יוּסַב	יִסְתַּבֵּב
Jussive	יִסַּב	יְסַבֵּב	יְסֻבַּב	יָסֵב	יוּסַב	יִסְתַּבֵּב
Imperative	הִסַּב	סַבֵּב	—	הָסֵב	—	הִסְתַּבֵּב
Inf. Construct	הִסֵּב	סַבֵּב	—	הָסֵב	—	הִסְתַּבֵּב
Inf. Absolute	הִסּוֹב	—	—	הָסֵב	—	הִסְתַּבֵּב
Participle	נָסָב	מְסַבֵּב	מְסֻבָּב	מֵסֵב	מוּסָב	מִסְתַּבֵּב

CHRONOLOGICAL TABLE

Patriarchal Period, as reflected in the traditional accounts of Genesis	c. 1900–1500 B. C.
The Exodus	c. 1280
The Conquest of Canaan	c. 1250–1200
The Period of the Judges	c. 1200–1020
Reign of Saul	c. 1020–1000
Reign of David	c. 1000–961
Reign of Solomon	c. 961–922
Division into the Kingdoms of Judah and Israel	922
Fall of Samaria (cap. of Israel) to Assyria	722
Fall of Jerusalem (cap. of Judah) to Babylon	587/6
The Babylonian Exile	587–538
Post-Exilic Period (Persian domination)	538–332
Beginning of Greek Rule (with Alexander)	332

Appendix E

BRIEF BIBLIOGRAPHY

DICTIONARIES

F. Brown, S. R. Driver, C. A. Briggs: *Hebrew and English Lexicon of the Old Testament.* Oxford, 1907 (corrected impression, 1952).

W. Gesenius, F. Buhl: *Hebräisches und aramäisches Handwörterbuch über das Alte Testament.* 17th edition, Berlin, 1915.

K. Feyerabend: *Langenscheidt's Pocket Hebrew Dictionary to the Old Testament.* 13th edition, New York, 1961.

GRAMMARS

W. Gesenius, E. Kautzsch, A. E. Cowley: *Hebrew Grammar.* Oxford, 1910.

G. Bergsträsser: *Hebräische Grammatik,* Leipzig, 1918. Reissued in Hildesheim, 1962.

TEXT AND VERSIONS

B. J. Roberts: *The Old Testament Text and Versions.* Cardiff, 1951.

F. M. Cross: *The Ancient Library of Qumran.* New York, 1958.

Biblia Hebraica, ed. by R. Kittel and others. 3rd edition, Stuttgart, 1937.

HISTORY AND ARCHAEOLOGY

W. F. Albright: *Archaeology and the Religion of Israel.* Baltimore, 1946.

J. Bright: *A History of Israel.* Philadelphia, 1959.

R. de Vaux: *Ancient Israel, Its Life and Institutions.* New York, 1961.

HEBREW-ENGLISH GLOSSARY

Verbs are listed according to the root. Conjugational types are abbreviated as follows:

Q	qal	H	hiphil
N	niphal	Ho	hophal
P	piel	Ht	hithpael
Pu	pual	Po	polel

All other words are listed alphabetically as they appear.
References of the types A1c and B3c refer to the Appendices A and B respectively.
All other references are to paragraphs in the grammar.

א

אָב (-ôṯ) father, ancestor (A1c)

אָבַד (יֹאבַד) to perish, be destroyed (B4b); H הֶאֱבִיד to destroy, kill

אָבָה (יֹאבֶה) to be willing (B8e)

אֲבָל truly, indeed; however

אֶבֶן (îm) stone (f.) A7a

אַבְרָהָם Abraham

אַבְרָם Abram = Abraham

אָדָם Adam; man; mankind (80)

אֲדָמָה earth, ground, soil (A64b)

אָדוֹן (îm) lord, master (A29a)

אָהַב (יֶאֱהַב) to love (B4c)

אַהֲבָה love (A60b)

אוֹ or

אוֹר (îm) light (A5a)

אוּרִיָּה Uriah

אוֹת (ôṯ) sign, omen (A5a)

אָז then, at that time

אֹזֶן (du. אָזְנַיִם) ear (f.) A11

אָח (אַחִים) brother (A1d)

[316]

אֶחָד one (m.)

אָחוֹת sister (f.) A86

אָחַז (יֹאחֵז) to seize, grasp, take hold of (108, B4b)

אַחֵר (אֲחֵרִים) other; fem. אַחֶרֶת, pl. אֲחֵרוֹת

אַחַר after (prep.); afterwards

אַחֲרֵי after (prep.); + אֲשֶׁר after (conj.); + כֵּן afterwards

אַחַת one (f.)

אֵי־מִזֶּה from what place, from which?

אֹיֵב (îm) enemy (A35)

אַיֵּה where?

אֵיךְ/אֵיכָה how? in what manner?

אֵימָה dread, terror (cf. A55, 56)

אֵין there is not, are not

אֵיפֹה where?

אִישׁ (אֲנָשִׁים)man, husband (A4c)

אַךְ surely, doubtlessly; but, however

אָכַל (יֹאכַל) to eat (B4b)

אֹכֶל food (A11)

אֶל to, toward

אֵל (îm) god; God (A3b)

אֵלֶּה these; 40

אֱלֹהִים gods; God (59; cf. A22)

אֶלֶף (îm) thousand (181; A7a)

אִם if

אֵם (אִמּוֹת) mother (f.) A3e

אָמָה (אֲמָהוֹת) maidservant, fem. slave (A54e)

(אמן) N. נֶאֱמַן to be confirmed, verified, trustworthy; H. הֶאֱמִין to believe, trust

אָמְנָם surely, indeed

אָמַר (יֹאמַר) to say (B4b)

אֱמֶת truth (A76)

אָנָה whither?

אֲנַחְנוּ we (81)

אֲנִי I (81)

אָנֹכִי I (81)

אָסִיר (îm) prisoner (A28a)

אָסַף (יֶאֱסֹף) to gather (B4a)

אָסַר (יֶאֱסֹר) to bind, take prisoner (B4a)

אַף (du. אַפַּיִם) nose, face; anger (A2a)

אֶפֶס + כִּי except that, save that (conj.)

אֵצֶל near, beside, by (A10b)

אַרְבַּע four (f.)

אַרְבָּעָה four (m.)

אַרְבָּעִים forty

אֲרוֹן ark (of the covenant); w. art. הָאָרוֹן (A22)

אָרוּר accursed (A30a)

אֲרִי (אֲרָיוֹת) lion (cf. A31b)

אַרְיֵה lion (A52)

(ארך) H. הֶאֱרִיךְ to be long; to lengthen

אָרַר (יָאֹר) to curse (B9b)

אֶרֶץ (ôt) earth, land (f.) A7a

אֵשׁ fire (f.) A3e

אִשָּׁה (נָשִׁים) woman, wife (A58b)

אָשֵׁם (יֶאְשַׁם) to be guilty; (adj.) guilty

אַשְׁקְלוֹן Ashkelon

אֲשֶׁר who, which, that (rel. pron.); that, since, because (conj.)

אֵת/אֶת־ dir. obj. marker

אֵת/אֶת־ with, together with

אַתְּ you (f.s.) 81

אַתָּה you (m.s.) 81

אָתוֹן (ôt) she-ass, donkey (f.) A29a

אַתֶּם you (m.pl.) 81

אֶתְמוֹל yesterday

אַתֵּן you (f.pl.) 81

אַתֵּנָה you (f.pl.) 81

ב

בְּ in, with (instrumental); (+ inf.) when, while

בְּאֵר (ôt) well, pit (A20a)

בֶּגֶד (îm) garment (A7c)

(בדד) לְבַד־ alone, only; 142

בְּהֵמָה (ôt) beast, animal;
80 (A65c)

(בוא) בָּא (יָבוֹא) to come, enter
(B7e); H. to bring

(בין) H. הֵבִין to perceive, consider, understand; to
make understand

בּוֹר (ôt) pit, cistern (A5a)

(בוש) בֹּשׁ (יֵבוֹשׁ) to be ashamed
(B7d)

בָּזָה (יִבְזֶה) to despise (B8a)

בָּחוּר (îm) young man (A30b)

בָּחַן (יִבְחַן) to test, try, examine
(B2a)

בָּחַר (יִבְחַר) to choose (obj.
with בְּ) B2a

בָּטַח (יִבְטַח) to trust, rely (B2a)

בֵּין between; 47

בִּינָה understanding, perceptiveness (A56)

בַּיִת (בָּתִּים) house (A13c)

בָּכָה (יִבְכֶּה) to weep, mourn
(B8a)

בָּלַע (יִבְלַע) to swallow (B2b)

בִּלְתִּי not(negates infinitive; 115)

בֵּן (בָּנִים) son (A3c)

בָּנָה (יִבְנֶה) to build (B8a);
H. caus., N. pass.

בַּעֲבוּר for the sake of, because of

בְּעַד through; around;
on behalf of; 174

בְּעֵינֵי in the eyes of, in the
opinion of

בַּעַל (îm) lord, master, husband, owner; 121 (A9)

בָּעַר (יִבְעַר) to burn (tr. and
intr.) B2a; P. to burn
(tr.), consume com-
pletely

בֶּצַע profit, advantage; מַה־בֶּצַע
what profit is there?
(A8b)

בָּקַע (יִבְקַע) to split (B2b)

בֹּקֶר morning (A11)

בָּקָר (large) cattle (coll.)

(בקש) P. בִּקֵּשׁ to seek

בָּרָא (יִבְרָא) to create (B2c);
N. pass.

בְּרִית covenant, treaty (A83)

בָּרַח (יִבְרַח) to flee (B2b)

(ברך) P. בֵּרַךְ to bless

בְּרָכָה (ôt) blessing (A64a)

בָּשָׂר flesh, meat; כָּל־בָּשָׂר
mankind (A25a)

בַּת (בָּנוֹת) daughter (A74)

ג

גָּאַל (יִגְאַל) to redeem (B2a);
N. pass.

גִּבּוֹר (îm) warrior, hero;
+ חַיִל idem (A43)

גִּבְעָה (ôt) hill (A61a)

גְּבֶרֶת mistress, lady (cf. A81)

גָּדוֹל big, great (A29a)

גָּדַל (יִגְדַּל) to be(come) great,
big; to grow up (B1c);
H. to magnify, make
great

גְּדִי (גְּדָיִים) kid (A31a)

(גור) גָּר (יָגוּר) to sojourn, dwell
(B7a)

(גיל) גָּל (יָגִיל) to rejoice (B7b)

גָּלָה (יִגְלֶה) to reveal, uncover;
go into exile (B8a); N.
pass.; H. to carry away
into exile

גִּלְעָד Gilead

גַּם also, too, even

גָּמָל (גְּמַלִּים) camel (A25d)

גַּן (גַּנּוֹת) garden; הַגָּן, §21
(A2a)

גָּנַב (יִגְנֹב) to steal (B1a)

גָּעַר (יִגְעַר) to rebuke (B2a)

גֵּר (îm) sojourner, resident alien (A3b)

(גרש) P. גֵּרֵשׁ to drive away

ד

דָּבָר (îm) word, thing, matter, affair; עַל־דְּבַר because of, for the sake of

(דבר) P. דִּבֶּר to speak, talk

דְּבַשׁ honey (A18)

דָּג (îm) fish (cf. A1a, 1b)

דָּגָה fish (coll.) A53a

דָּוִד David

דּוֹר (îm, ôt) generation (A5a)

דּוֹתָן Dothan

(דין) דָּן (יָדִין) to judge (B7b)

דַּל poor; §22 (A2a)

דֶּלֶת (du. דְּלָתַיִם; pl. ôt) door (A77)

דָּם (îm) blood (A1b)

(דמם) דַּם (יִדֹּם) to be silent, astonished (B9a, c)

דֶּרֶךְ (îm, ôt) road, way (m. or f.) A7a

דָּרַשׁ (יִדְרֹשׁ) to inquire, seek, require (B2a)

ה

הַ הָ הֶ the def. art.; §14, 18, 21

הַ הֲ interrog. marker

הָב (defective verb) give! come! let's...! 119

הֶבֶל Abel

הָגָה (יֶהְגֶּה) to mutter, moan, roar; meditate, imagine (B8c)

הוּא he; that

הוּא = היא ; see 87

הִיא she, it; that

הָיָה (יִהְיֶה) to be, become (B8d)

הֵיכָל (îm) palace, temple (A34)

הָלַךְ (יֵלֵךְ) to go, walk; H. הוֹלִיךְ to cause to go, lead; Ht. to walk back and forth, to go continually (B6j)

(הלל) P. הִלֵּל to praise; הַלְלוּיָהּ Halelujah, Praise Yah(weh)

הֲלֹם hither

הֵם they; those

הֵן if

הִנֵּה see §135–6

הֵנָּה they (f.); those (f.)

הֵנָּה hither, to this place, here

הַר (הָרִים) mountain (A2c)

הָרַג (יַהֲרֹג) to slay, kill; N. pass. (B3a)

הָרָה (יַהֲרֶה) to become pregnant, conceive (B8b)

ו

וְ and; 17

ז

זֹאת this (f.); 40

זָבַח (יִזְבַּח) to sacrifice (B2b)

זֶבַח (îm) sacrifice (A8b)

זֶה this (m.); 40

זָהָב gold (A25a)

זַיִת (îm) olive, olive-tree (A13b)

זָכַר (יִזְכֹּר) to remember; N. pass.; H. to mention, cause to remember (B1a)

זֵכֶר remembrance, memorial (A10a)

זָכָר (îm) male (A25a)

זָנָה (יִזְנֶה) to be(come) a prostitute, harlot; זֹנָה a harlot (B8a)

זָעַק (יִזְעַק) = צָעַק to cry out (in distress) B2a

זָקֵן (יִזְקַן) to be(come) old; (adj.) old (B1d)

זָקֵן (îm) old man, elder
(of city) A26a

זְקֻנִים (pl.) old age (cf. A23, 30a)

זְרוֹעַ (îm, ôṯ) arm; fig. strength
(A22)

זֶ֫רַע seed, offspring, progeny
(A8a)

ח

(חבא) N. נֶחְבָּא to hide (intr.);
Ht. הִתְחַבֵּא to hide (intr.)

חָדַל (יֶחְדַּל) to cease, stop; 117
(B3b)

חָדָשׁ new (A25b)

חַוָּה Eve

(חוה) Hišt. הִשְׁתַּחֲוָה to bow down,
humble oneself

חוֹמָה (ôṯ) city-wall (A55)

חוּץ outside; הַח֫וּצָה, ח֫וּצָה (to
the) outside; מִחוּץ לְ
outside (prep.)

חָזַק (יֶחֱזַק) to be(come) strong,
firm, hard; (adj.) idem
(B3b)

חָטָא (יֶחֱטָא) to sin (לְ against);
H. to lead into sin (B3c)

חַטָּאת (חַטָּאוֹת) sin (A82)

חַי living, alive; as-lives
(in oath), 138 (A2a)

חָיָה (יִחְיֶה) to live, be alive
(B8d); P. חִיָּה to let live,
revive, restore to life;
H. הֶחֱיָה, same as P.

חַיָּה (ôṯ) animal, living thing
(A57)

חַ֫יִל (חֲיָלִים) army; strength;
גִּבּוֹר חַ֫יִל warrior (A13a)

חַיִּים life, lifetime (cf. A2a)

חֵיק bosom (cf. A3b)

חָכָם wise; wise man (A25b)

חָכְמָה wisdom (A63)

חָלָב milk (cf. A25b)

חֲלוֹם (ôṯ) dream (A22)

(חלל) H. הֵחֵל to begin

(חלל) P. חִלֵּל to defile, pollute,
dishonor

חָלַם (יַחֲלֹם) to dream (B3a)

חֲמוֹר (îm) he-ass, donkey (A22)

חֲמִישִׁי fifth

חָמַל (יַחְמֹל) to spare (B3a)

חָמֵשׁ five (f.)

חֲמִשָּׁה five (m.)

חֲמִשִּׁים fifty

חֵן grace, favor (A3e)

חָנַן (יָחֹן) to favor, be gracious
toward (B9a); Ht. הִתְחַנֵּן
to seek or implore favor

חֶ֫סֶד (îm) kindness, mercy,
proper conduct

חָפֵץ (יַחְפֹּץ) to take delight in;
to desire (B3d)

חֲצִי half (A31b)

חֹק (îm) statute (A5d)

חֻקָּה (ôṯ) statute (A59)

חֶ֫רֶב (ôṯ) sword (f.) A7a

חֹרֵב (Mt.) Horeb

חָרָה (יֶחֱרֶה) to become enraged,
angry (B8c); used im-
personally with לְ or
with אַף

(חרם) H. הֶחֱרִים to destroy, exterminate (often as a
religious act)

חָרַשׁ (יַחֲרשׁ) to plow; engrave
(B3a)

חָשַׂךְ (יַחְשֹׂךְ) to withhold, keep
back for oneself (B3a)

חָשַׁב (יַחְשֹׁב) to think, devise,
reckon, impute (B3a)

חֹ֫שֶׁךְ darkness

חִתִּי Hittite

חֹתֵן father-in-law (A35)

ט

טָבַח (יִטְבַּח) to slaughter (B2b)

טֶ֫בַח a slaughtering (A8b)

טוֹב good (A5a)

טַף children (coll.) A2a

טֶרֶם before, not yet; בְּטֶרֶם idem; 121

י

(יאל) H. הוֹאִיל to be willing, content (173)

יְאֹר The Nile; river

יַבָּשָׁה dry ground (cf. A70)

יָד (du. áyim; pl. ôṯ) hand, side (f.) A1a

(ידה) H. הוֹדָה to give thanks

יָדַע (יֵדַע) to know (B6b); H. to make known, teach, declare

יְהוּדָה Judah

יהוה Yahweh, "Jehovah," the Lord (59)

יוֹם (pl. יָמִים) day; כַּיּוֹם, הַיּוֹם today (A5b)

יוֹמָם by day, in the daytime

יוֹסֵף Joseph

יַחַד together

יַחְדָּו together

(יטב) יִיטַב to go well with (לְ) B6d

(יכח) H. הוֹכִיחַ to reprove; to decide

יָכֹל (יוּכַל) to be able; to prevail against (לְ) B6i

יָלַד (יֵלֵד) to bear (a child); N. pass.; H. to beget, engender (B6a)

יֶלֶד (pl. îm) boy (A7a)

יָם (pl. יַמִּים) sea; יָמָּה seaward, westward (A1e)

יָמִין the right hand (f.) A28a

(יסף) H. הוֹסִיף to add; to do something again; to continue doing something

יָפֶה beautiful, handsome (A49)

יַעַן because (+ inf.); יַעַן אֲשֶׁר because

יַעֲקֹב Jacob

יָצָא (יֵצֵא) to go out, to go forth (B6c); H. caus.

(יצב) Ht. הִתְיַצֵּב to take one's stand, to station oneself

יָצַר (יִיצֶר) to form, fashion (B6g)

(יקץ) יִיקַץ to wake up (B6d)

יָקָר precious (A25a)

יָרֵא (יִירָא) to be afraid (of: מִפְּנֵי, מִן) B6f.; N. to be dreadful, terrible

יִרְאָה fear (A61a)

יָרַד (יֵרֵד) to go down, descend (B6a); H. caus.

יְרוּשָׁלַ͏ִם Jerusalem

(ירה) H. הוֹרָה to shoot (arrows); to direct, teach

יָרֵחַ the moon

יָרַשׁ (יִירַשׁ) to inherit (B6d); to dispossess

יִשְׂרָאֵל Israel

יֵשׁ there is, are

יָשַׁב (יֵשֵׁב) to sit, dwell (B6a); H. caus.

יְשׁוּעָה (pl. ôṯ) salvation, deliverance (A67)

יִשְׁמְעֵאלִים Ishmaelites

יָשֵׁן (יִישַׁן) to sleep (B6e)

(ישע) H. הוֹשִׁיעַ to save, deliver

יָשַׁר (יִישַׁר) to be pleasant, agreeable (B6d)

יָשָׁר just, upright (A25a)

(יתר) N. נוֹתַר to be left, remain

יִתְרוֹ Jethro

כ

כְּ like, as; (+ inf.) when, as

כַּאֲשֶׁר as, according as

כָּבֵד (יְכְבַּד) to be (come) heavy,

important, serious;
(adj.) idem (B1d)

כָּבוֹד glory, honor (A29a)

כֶּבֶשׂ (îm) lamb (m.) A7c

כִּבְשָׂה (ôṯ) lamb (f.) A61a

כֹּה thus, as follows

כֹּהֵן (îm) priest (A35)

כּוֹכָב (îm) star (A33)

(כון) N. נָכוֹן to be firm, fixed,
established; H. הֵכִין to
prepare, establish; Po.
כּוֹנֵן to set up, establish

(כחד) P. כִּחֵד to hide, conceal

כִּי because, since; for; that;
כִּי אִם unless, except
that, but rather

כַּיּוֹם today, this day

כֹּל/כָּל־ all, each, every; presuffixal כָּל־ 138; כָּל־אֲשֶׁר
everything which (cf.
A5d)

כָּלָה (יִכְלֶה) to be depleted,
finished, at an end
(B8a); P. to finish,
bring to an end

כְּלִי (îm) vessel, utensil (A31a)

כֵּן thus, so; עַל־כֵּן therefore;
לָכֵן therefore

כֵּן honest, true (A3b)

כְּנַעַן Canaan

כְּנַעֲנִי Canaanite

כִּסֵּא (ôṯ) throne (A41b)

(כסה) P. כִּסָּה to cover, overwhelm

כֶּסֶף silver, money (A7a)

כַּף (du. כַּפַּיִם; pl. ôṯ) palm or
hollow of hand, sole of
foot (A2a)

(כפר) P. כִּפֶּר to atone for, make
atonement

כֶּרֶם (îm) vineyard (A7a)

כָּרַת (יִכְרֹת) to cut (B1a); כָּרַת
בְּרִית to make a treaty

כַּשְׂדִּים Chaldaeans

כָּשַׁל (יִכָּשֵׁל) to stumble (B1a)

כָּתַב (יִכְתֹּב) to write (B1a)

כְּתֹנֶת or כֻּתֹּנֶת (ôṯ) tunic (A79)

ל

לְ to, for

לֹא not, no

לֵאמֹר "saying" (used to mark a
direct quote)

לֵב (ôṯ) heart (A3e)

לֵבָב (ôṯ) heart (A27a)

לְבַד־ see (בדד)

לָבָן Laban

לֶהָבָה (ôṯ) flame (cf. A71)

לוּחַ (ôṯ) tablet (A6)

לוֹט Lot

לוּלֵא/לוּלֵי unless, if not

לֶחֶם bread, food (A7a)

(לחם) N. נִלְחַם to fight

לַיְלָה night; at night (A87)

(לין) לָן (יָלִין) to spend the night
(B7b)

לָכַד (יִלְכֹּד) to capture (B1a)

לָכֵן therefore

לָמַד (יִלְמַד) to learn (B1b); P.
לִמַּד to teach

לָמָה why? (לָמָה 74 before ע ה ח)

לְמַעַן so that, in order that

לִפְנֵי before, in front of, in the
presence of

לָקַח (יִקַּח) to take (B5e); N.
pass.

לִקְרַאת toward, against, to meet
(125)

מ

מְאֹד very, much

מֵאָה (ôṯ) hundred; 181

מֵאַיִן from where?

מַאֲכָל food (A38)

מְאוּמָה anything; w. neg. nothing
(A67)

(מאן) P. מֵאֵן to refuse

מָאַס (יִמְאַס) to refuse, despise (B2a)

מְגוּרִים (pl.) sojourning, residence (A30a)

מַגֵּפָה (ôt) plague, stroke (cf. A73)

מִדְבָּר wilderness (A37)

מָדַד (יָמֹד) to measure (B9a)

מַדּוּעַ why?

מִדְיָן Midian

מַה what?

(מהר) P. מִהַר to hurry; מַהֵר quickly

מָוֶת death (A15)

(מות) (יָמוּת) מֵת to die (B7c); H. הֵמִית to kill; Po. מוֹתֵת to kill

(מול) (יָמוּל) מָל to circumcise (B7a)

מִזְבֵּחַ (ôt) altar (A41c)

מַחֲנֶה (ôt) camp (A51)

מַטֶּה (ôt) staff, rod; tribe (A51)

מָטָר rain (A25a)

מִי who?

מַיִם (pl.) water

מָכַר (יִמְכֹּר) to sell (B1a)

מָלֵא (יִמְלָא) to be full, filled (B2d); (adj.) idem; P. מִלֵּא to fill

מַלְאָךְ (îm) messenger, angel (A38)

מְלָאכָה occupation, work (A64d)

מָלוֹן lodging place (A29a)

מִלְחָמָה (ôt) battle, war (A72)

מֶלֶךְ (îm) king, ruler (A7a)

מָלַךְ (יִמְלֹךְ) to rule, be(come) king (B1a)

מִמַּעַל above (adv.); (+ לְ) above (prep.)

מִן from; some of

מִנְחָה (ôt) offering (A61a)

(מסס) N. נָמֵס to melt

מִסְפָּר number; אֵין מִסְפָּר לְ is/

אַנְשֵׁי are innumerable; מְסְפָּר a few men (A37)

מְעַט a little; מְעַט מְעַט little by little; עוֹד מְעַט in a little while

מַעֲשֶׂה (îm) deed, act, work (A51)

מָצָא (יִמְצָא) to find (B2c); N. נִמְצָא to be extant; H. הִמְצִיא to present

מִצְוָה (ôt) commandment (A61b)

מִצְרִי Egyptian; fem. מִצְרִית

מִצְרַיִם Egypt; מִצְרַיְמָה toward Egypt

מָקוֹם (ôt) place (A29a)

מִקְנֶה cattle, property (A50)

מַרְאֶה appearance (A51)

מְרַגֵּל (îm) spy, scout (P. participle)

מָרַד (יִמְרֹד) to rebel (B1a)

מֶרְכָּבָה (ôt) chariot (A71)

מֹשֶׁה Moses

מָשַׁח (יִמְשַׁח) to anoint (B2b)

מָשַׁל (יִמְשֹׁל) to rule, have dominion (over: בְּ) B1a

מִשָּׁם from there; thence

מִשְׁמָר place of confinement, jail (A37)

מִשְׁפָּט (îm) judgement, court decision; manner (A37)

מִשְׁתֶּה banquet (A50)

נ

נָא particle used after imperative, jussive, or cohortative; 102, 105

(נאץ) P. נִאֵץ to spurn

(נבא) N. נִבָּא, Ht. הִתְנַבֵּא to prophesy

נָבוֹן intelligent, discerning (A29a)

(נבט) H. הִבִּיט to look at (עַל ,אֶל)

נָבִיא (îm) prophet (A28a)

נֶגֶב the Negev, (הַנֶּגְבָּה) toward the Negev, Southward

נֶגֶד before, in front of (cf. A7b)

(נגד) H. הִגִּיד to tell

נָגַע (יִגַּע) to touch, strike (B5b)

נָגַף (יִגֹּף) to strike, smite (B5a)

(נגש) N. נִגַּשׁ (יִגַּשׁ) to approach; H. הִגִּישׁ to bring near

נֶדֶר or נֵדֶר (îm) vow (A7c, 10a)

נָדַר (יִדֹּר) to vow (B5a)

נָהָר (ôt) river (A25b)

(נוח) נָח (יָנוּחַ) to rest, settle down (B7a); H. הֵנִיחַ to set at rest; H. הִנִּיחַ to set down, deposit, leave alone

(נום) נָם (יָנוּם) to sleep (B7a)

(נוס) נָס (יָנוּס) to flee (B7a)

נַחֲלָה property, possession, inheritance, portion (A60b)

(נחם) N. נִחַם (יִנָּחֵם) to be sorry, repent, be comforted; P. נִחַם (יְנַחֵם) to comfort, console

נֶחְמָד pleasant (A39)

נָחָשׁ (îm) snake (A25b)

נָטָה (יִטֶּה) to extend; pitch (tent); turn aside (intr.) B8f.; H. הִטָּה to turn or thrust aside, to incline (tr.)

נָטַע (יִטַּע) to plant (B5b)

נָטַשׁ (יִטֹּשׁ) to leave, forsake, abandon (B5a)

(נכה) H. הִכָּה to strike, smite, slay

נָכְרִי foreign, strange

נָסַע (יִסַּע) to set out, travel, journey (B5b)

נַעַל (îm) shoe, sandal (f.) A9

נַעַר (îm) young man, attendant (A9)

נָפַל (יִפֹּל) to fall (B5a); H. הִפִּיל caus.

נֶפֶשׁ (ôt) soul, person, living thing; life; (+ pron. suff.) self (A7a)

(נצב) N. נִצַּב to station oneself, stand; H. הִצִּיב to station, set up

(נצל) N. נִצַּל to be rescued, saved; H. הִצִּיל to deliver, rescue

נְקֵבָה female (A65a)

נָשָׂא (יִשָּׂא) to raise, lift up (B5c); N נִשָּׂא pass.

(נשג) H. הִשִּׂיג to reach, attain, overtake

נָתַן (יִתֵּן) to give, set, put, allow (B5d)

נָתָן Nathan

ס

סָבַב (יָסֹב) to surround, go around (B9a); H. הֵסֵב to turn away, to turn around (tr.), cause to go around

סָגַר (יִסְגֹּר) to close (B1a)

סוּס (îm) horse (A6)

(סור) סָר (יָסוּר) to turn aside (intr.), to depart (B7a); H. הֵסִיר to remove, take away, turn away

סָלַח (יִסְלַח) to pardon (B2b)

סֵפֶר (îm) book, writing (A10a)

סָפַר (יִסְפֹּר) to count (B1a); P. סִפֵּר to tell, narrate

סָרִיס (סָרִיסִים) eunuch, officer (A28b)

(סתר) N. נִסְתַּר to hide (intr.); H. הִסְתִּיר to hide (tr.)

ע

עֶבֶד (îm) servant, slave (A7a)

עָבַד (יַעֲבֹד) to work, serve, till (ground) B3a

עֲבוֹדָה work, task, servitude (A66)

עָבַר (יַעֲבֹר) to cross; to transgress (B3a); H. הֶעֱבִיר caus.

עִבְרִי Hebrew; fem. עִבְרִיָּה

עֵגֶל (îm) calf (m.) A10b

עֶגְלָה (ôt) heifer (A62)

עַד to, as far as, by; (+ inf.) until; עַד־אֲשֶׁר until; עַד־הֵנָּה until now; עַד־עוֹלָם forever

עֵדָה congregation, assembly (A54)

עֵדֶר (îm) flock, herd (A10b)

עוֹד again, still, yet

(עוד) H. הֵעִיד to warn, protest

עוֹלָם (îm) eternity; עַד־עוֹלָם, לְעוֹלָם, forever (A33)

עָוֹן (ôt) guilt, iniquity, punishment (A29a)

עוֹף birds, fowl (coll.) A5a

(עור) Po. עוֹרֵר to arouse, stir up

עַז strong, mighty (A2a)

עֹז strength (A5e)

עָזַב (יַעֲזֹב) to abandon (B3a)

עָזַר (יַעֲזֹר) to help (B3a)

עֵזֶר help, assistance (A10b)

עַיִן (du. עֵינַיִם) eye; spring, well (f.) A13a

עִיר (עָרִים) city (f.) A4b

עַל on, upon, over, against, concerning; עַל־דְּבַר for the sake of, because of; עַל־יַד beside, in the company of, to the side of; עַל־כֵּן therefore; עַל־פְּנֵי on the surface of, up against

עָלָה (יַעֲלֶה) to ascend, go up (B8b); H. הֶעֱלָה caus.

עֵלִי Eli

עִם with, together with

עַם (îm) people, nation (A2a)

עָמַד (יַעֲמֹד) to stand (B3a); H. הֶעֱמִיד to station, set up, appoint

עֵמֶק (îm) valley, lowland (A10a)

עָנָה (יַעֲנֶה) to answer (B8b); P. עִנָּה to oppress

עֳנִי affliction (A32a)

עָנָן (îm) cloud (A25b)

עֵץ (îm) tree, wood (A3a)

עֵצָה counsel, advice (A54)

עֵקֶב אֲשֶׁר/כִּי + because

עֶרֶב evening

עָרַב (יַעֲרֹב) to stand as pledge for (B3a)

עֶרְוָה shame, nakedness (A62)

עָרַךְ (יַעֲרֹךְ) to arrange, set in order; draw up (in battle array) B3a

עָרֵל uncircumcised; (fig.) deficient, inept

עֵשֶׂב grass, herbage (coll.) A10b

עָשָׂה (יַעֲשֶׂה) to do, make, act, bring about (B8b)

עֲשִׂירִי tenth; fem. עֲשִׂירִית

עֶשֶׂר ten (f.)

עָשָׂר -teen (m.)

עֲשָׂרָה ten (m.)

עֶשְׂרֵה -teen (f.)

עֶשְׂרִים twenty

עָשִׁיר rich (A28a)

עֵת (îm, ôt) time (f.) A75

עַתָּה now, then, (and) so then

פ

פָּגַע (יִפְגַּע) to meet, encounter (בְּ/אֶת־) B2b

פָּדָה (יִפְדֶּה) to ransom (B8a)

פֶּה mouth; עַל־פִּי, כְּפִי according to; כְּפִי אֲשֶׁר

according as; פֶּה אֶחָד unanimous, in agreement (A48a)

פֹּה here

פּוֹטִיפַר Potiphar

(פלא) N. נִפְלָא to be wonderful, marvelous

(פלל) Ht. הִתְפַּלֵּל to pray

פְּלִשְׁתִּים the Philistines

פֶּן lest, so that not

פָּנָה (יִפְנֶה) to turn (toward) (tr. & intr.) B8a

פָּנִים (pl.) face; לִפְנֵי before, in the presence of; מִפְּנֵי, מִלִּפְנֵי from before; עַל־פְּנֵי on the surface of, up against. 100, 101 (A89)

פֶּסֶל (פְּסִילִים) idol, image (A7c/28a)

פַּעַם (îm) time; פַּעֲמַיִם twice (A9)

פָּקַד (יִפְקֹד) to keep one's promise to; to pay attention to; to visit; to appoint; to pass in review (B1a)

פָּרָה (ôt) cow, heifer (A53b)

פְּרִי fruit (A31a)

פַּרְעֹה Pharaoh

פָּרַץ (יִפְרֹץ) to break down, breach, burst (out) B1a

(פרר) H. הֵפֵר to annul, cancel

פָּרַשׂ (יִפְרֹשׂ) to spread (out) (tr.) B1a

פָּרָשׁ (פָּרָשִׁים) horseman (A25c)

פָּתַח (יִפְתַּח) to open (B2b)

פֶּתַח (îm) opening (A8b)

צ

צֹאן small cattle (sheep and goats) cf. A5c

צָבָא (ôt) army, host (A25e)

צַדִּיק righteous (A46)

צֶדֶק righteousness (A7c)

צְדָקָה (ôt) righteousness, righteous act (A64a)

צָהֳרַיִם noon (cf. A12b)

(צוה) P. צִוָּה to command, charge, appoint 153

(צום) צָם (יָצוּם) to fast (B7a)

(צור) צָר (יָצוּר) to besiege, confine (B7a)

צוּר (îm) rock, cliff; (fig.) support, defense (A6)

צֵל (צְלָלִים) shade, shadow, protection (A3f)

(צלח) H. הִצְלִיחַ to make prosperous; to be prosperous

צֶלֶם (îm) image, likeness (A7a)

צֵלָע (îm, ôt) rib, side (A27b)

צָעִיר small, young (A28a)

צָעַק (יִצְעַק) to cry out (in distress) B2a

צָרָה (ôt) distress, trouble (A53b)

ק

קָבַץ (יִקְבֹּץ) to gather; Ht. to gather (intr.)

קֶבֶר (îm) grave, sepulchre (A7c)

קָבַר (יִקְבֹּר) to bury, inter (B1a)

קָדוֹשׁ holy

קֶדֶם east; קֵדְמָה eastward; מִקֶּדֶם לִ to the east of (cf. A7b)

קֹדֶשׁ (îm) holiness (A11)

(קדשׁ) P. קִדֵּשׁ to sanctify

קָהָל assembly, congregation (A25b)

קוֹל (ôt) voice, sound (A5a)

(קום) קָם (יָקוּם) to arise (B7a); H. הֵקִים to establish, set up

קָטֹן small, little, unimportant; also קָטָן (cf. A25d)

קַיִן Cain

קִיר (ôt) wall (A4a)

(קלל) קַל (יֵקַל) to be light, of little importance (B9c); P. קִלֵּל to curse

(קנא) P. קִנֵּא to be jealous (of: בְּ/אֶת); to be zealous (for: לְ)

קָנָה (יִקְנֶה) to acquire, purchase (B8a)

קֵץ end; מִקֵּץ at the end of (A3e)

קָצֶה end, border; מִקְצֵי at the end of (A49)

קָצִיר harvest, crop; time of harvest (A28a)

קָצַף (יִקְצֹף) to be(come) angry (against: עַל) B1a

קָצַר (יִקְצֹר) to reap, harvest (B1a)

קָרָא (יִקְרָא) to call, name, summon, declare, read; (+ אֶל) to call unto; (+ לְ) to summon (B2c)

קָרָא (יִקְרָא) a common variant of קָרָה

קָרַב (יִקְרַב) to be near, draw near, approach (B1c); H. הִקְרִיב to bring near, present

קֶרֶב midst, interior; בְּקֶרֶב in, within, inside of (A7c)

קָרָה (יִקְרֶה) to meet, encounter, befall (person usually object) B8a; N. נִקְרָה idem (person usually subject; object with עַל/אֶל/בְּ)

קָרוֹב near, close (to: אֶל) A29a

קָרַע (יִקְרַע) to rend, tear (B2b)

קָשֶׁה difficult, hard, harsh (A49)

קָשַׁר (יִקְשֹׁר) to bind; to band together, conspire (B1a)

ר

רָאָה (יִרְאֶה) to see (B8a); N. נִרְאָה to appear; H. הֶרְאָה to show

רְאוּבֵן Reuben

רֹאשׁ (רָאשִׁים) head, top, chief

רִאשׁוֹן first (A45)

רַב much, many, numerous (A2a)

רָבָה (יִרְבֶּה) to be(come) numerous, great (B8a); H. הִרְבָּה to make numerous, great; to do (something) much

רְבִיעִי fourth; fem. רְבִיעִית

רֶגֶל (du. רַגְלַיִם) foot (f.); בְּרַגְלֵי in the following of, belonging to (A7a)

רָדַף (יִרְדֹּף) to pursue, chase, persecute (+ אַחֲרֵי) B1a

רוּחַ (ôt) spirit, wind, soul

(רום) רָם (יָרוּם) to be high, lofty (B7a); H. הֵרִים to lift up, off; Po. רוֹמֵם to raise up

(רוץ) רָץ (יָרוּץ) to run (B7a)

רָחָב broad, wide (A25b)

רָחוֹק distant, far; מֵרָחוֹק at a distance, from afar; of old (A29a)

רָחֵל Rachel

רָחַץ (יִרְחַץ) to wash (B2a)

רֵיק empty, worthless, idle (cf. A3b)

רָכַב (יִרְכַּב) to ride (B1b)

רְכוּשׁ (moveable) property (A23)

רֶמֶשׂ creeping things (coll.)

רֵעַ (îm) friend, companion (A3b)

רַע evil, bad, wicked (A2b)

רָעָב famine (A25b)

רָעֵב (יִרְעַב) to be(come) hungry (B2a); (adj.) idem (A26)

רֹעֶה (îm) shepherd (Qal part. act.)

רָעָה (יִרְעֶה) to tend flocks, shepherd (B8a)

(רעע) רַע (יֵרַע) to be bad, wicked (B9d); H. הֵרַע to injure, to act wickedly

רָפָא (יִרְפָּא) to heal, cure (B2c)

רָצַח (יִרְצַח) to kill (B2b)

רַק only

רָקִיע firmament (A28a)

רָשָׁע evil, bad, criminal (A25a)

שׂ

שָׂדֶה (ôṯ) field (A49)

(שים) שָׂם (יָשִׂים) to put, place; to make (x) into (y) B7b

שֵׂיבָה old age, grey hair (cf. A56)

שְׂמֹאל left (hand); north (cf. A22)

שָׂמַח (יִשְׂמַח) to rejoice (B2b); P. שִׂמַּח to gladden

שִׂמְחָה (ôṯ) joy (A61a)

שִׂמְלָה (ôṯ) cloak, outer garment (A61a)

שָׂנֵא (יִשְׂנָא) to hate (B2d)

שָׂפָה (du. שְׂפָתַיִם) lip; language; edge (A53d)

שַׂק (îm) sack (-cloth) A2a

שַׂר (îm) chief, leader (A2b)

שָׂרַף (יִשְׂרֹף) to burn (tr.) B1a; N. to burn (intr.)

שׁ

שָׁאַל (יִשְׁאַל) to ask, inquire, request (B2a)

שְׁאֹל Sheol

(שאר) N. נִשְׁאַר to be left over, remain, survive

שָׁבָה (יִשְׁבֶּה) to take captive (B8a)

שְׁבוּעָה (ôṯ) oath (A67)

שְׁבִיעִי seventh; fem. שְׁבִיעִית

(שבע) N נִשְׁבַּע to swear; H. הִשְׁבִּיע to cause to swear

שֶׁבַע seven (f.)

שִׁבְעָה seven (m.)

שִׁבְעִים seventy

שָׁבַר (יִשְׁבֹּר) to break, smash (B1a)

שָׁבַת (יִשְׁבֹּת) to cease, rest (B1a)

שַׁבָּת (שַׁבָּתוֹת) sabbath (f.) cf. A82

שָׁוְא emptiness, vanity; לַשָּׁוְא in vain (A16)

(שוב) שָׁב (יָשׁוּב) to return, go/ come back (B7a); H. הֵשִׁיב to bring back

שׁוֹר (îm) a head of cattle (A5a [note])

שָׁחַט (יִשְׁחַט) to slaughter (an animal) B2a

שִׁיר (îm) song (A4a)

(שיר) שָׁר (יָשִׁיר) to sing (B7b)

(שית) שָׁת (יָשִׁית) to put, place, set (B7b)

שָׁכַב (יִשְׁכַּב) to lie down (B1b)

שָׁכַח (יִשְׁכַּח) to forget (B2b)

שְׁכֶם Shechem

(שכם) H. הִשְׁכִּים to do something early in the day 173

שָׁכַן (יִשְׁכֹּן) to settle down, dwell (B1a)

שָׁלוֹם peace, well-being, health; שָׁאַל לְשָׁלוֹם לְ to ask about someone (A29a)

שְׁלִישִׁי third; fem. שְׁלִישִׁית

שָׁלַח (יִשְׁלַח) to send (B2b); P. שִׁלַּח to expel, send forth, let go

שֻׁלְחָן (ôṯ) table (A40)

(שלך) H. הִשְׁלִיךְ to throw

(שלם) P. שִׁלֵּם to restore, make good, recompense

שָׁלֹשׁ three (f.)

שְׁלֹשָׁה three (m.)

שְׁלֹשִׁים	thirty	(שרת)	P. שֵׁרֵת to serve, administer
שֵׁם	(ôt) name (A3d)	שֵׁשׁ	six (f.)
שָׁם	there, in that place; שָׁמָּה thither, to that place	שִׁשָּׁה	six (m.)
(שמד)	H. הִשְׁמִיד to destroy	שִׁשִּׁי	sixth
שְׁמוּאֵל	Samuel	שִׁשִּׁים	sixty
שָׁמַיִם	heaven(s)	שָׁתָה	(יִשְׁתֶּה) to drink
שְׁמִינִי	eighth; fem. שְׁמִינִית	שְׁתַּיִם	two (f.)
שָׁמֵם	(יִשַּׁם) to be desolated, appalled (B9c); (adj.) idem		

ת

שְׁמֹנֶה	eight (f.)
שְׁמֹנָה	eight (m.)
שְׁמֹנִים	eighty
שָׁמַע	(יִשְׁמַע) to hear; heed, listen to (לְקוֹל + לְ/בְּ); B2b; N. pass.; H. הִשְׁמִיעַ to tell, declare, proclaim
שָׁמַר	(יִשְׁמֹר) to watch, keep, observe (B1a)
שֶׁמֶשׁ	sun (A7c)
שִׁמְשׁוֹן	Samson
שָׁנָה	(îm) year (A53a)
שֵׁנִי	second; fem. שֵׁנִית
שְׁנַיִם	two (m.)
שַׁעַר	(îm) gate (A9)
שִׁפְחָה	(ôt) maidservant, fem. slave (A61a)
שָׁפַט	(יִשְׁפֹּט) to judge (B1a)
שֹׁפֵט	(îm) judge (A35)
שָׁפַךְ	(יִשְׁפֹּךְ) to pour, shed (blood) B1a
שָׁפֵל	(יִשְׁפַּל) to be(come) low (B1d); H. הִשְׁפִּיל to lay low, abase
(שקה)	H. הִשְׁקָה to give water to, cause to drink

תֹּאַר	form, appearance (A12b)
תָּוֶךְ	midst; בְּתוֹךְ in the midst of; מִתּוֹךְ from the midst of (A15a)
תּוֹלְדוֹת	(pl.) history, genealogy (A73)
תּוֹרָה	(ôt) law, Law (A55)
תְּחִלָּה	beginning, first occasion (A68)
תְּחִנָּה	(ôt) supplication (A68)
תַּחַת	under; instead of; מִתַּחַת beneath (adv.), (+ לְ) idem (prep.)
תָּלָה	(יִתְלֶה) to hang (B8a)
תְּמוֹל	yesterday
(תמם)	תַּם (יִתַּם) to be finished, at an end; to finish (doing something) B9c
תִּמְנָתָה	Timnah, Timnathah
תָּעָה	(יִתְעֶה) to wander lost (B8a)
תְּפִלָּה	(ôt) prayer (A68)
תָּפַשׂ	(יִתְפֹּשׂ) to seize, grab (B1a)
תְּשִׁיעִי	ninth; fem. תְּשִׁיעִית
תֵּשַׁע	nine (f.)
תִּשְׁעָה	nine (m.)
תִּשְׁעִים	ninety

ENGLISH-HEBREW GLOSSARY

A

a: (see §14)

abandon, to: נָטַשׁ, עָזַב

abase, to: הִשְׁפִּיל

Abel: הֶבֶל

able, to be: יָכֹל

above (prep.): עַל; (adv.) מִמַּעַל

Abraham: אַבְרָהָם

according as: כַּאֲשֶׁר

according to: כְּפִי, עַל־פִּי, לְפִי, כְּ

accursed: אָרוּר

acquire, to: קָנָה

act, to: עָשָׂה; to – – wickedly: הֵרַע

act: מַעֲשֶׂה

Adam: אָדָם

add, to: הוֹסִיף

administer, to: שֵׁרֵת

advantage: בֶּצַע

advice: עֵצָה

afar; from – –: מֵרָחוֹק

affair: דָּבָר

affliction: עֳנִי, צָרָה

afraid: יָרֵא; to be – –: יָרֵא

after (prep.): אַחַר, אַחֲרֵי
   (conj.): אַחֲרֵי אֲשֶׁר

afterwards: אַחֲרֵי־כֵן, אַחַר

again: עוֹד; to do – –: שָׁב, הוֹסִיף

against: עַל

agreeable; to be – –: יָשַׁר

alive: חַי; to be – –: חָיָה

all: כָּל־, כֹּל

alone: לְבַד־

also: גַּם

altar: מִזְבֵּחַ

although: see §§135–136

and: וְ

angel: מַלְאָךְ

anger: אַף

angry, to be(come): חָרָה; he became – –: קָצַף; חָרָה לוֹ

animal: בְּהֵמָה, חַיָּה

annul, to: הֵפֵר

anoint, to: מָשַׁח

answer, to: עָנָה

another: אַחֵר

anything: מְאוּמָה; anything + adj.: כֹּל + adj.

appalled, to be: שָׁמֵם

appear, to: נִרְאָה

appearance: מַרְאֶה

appoint, to: שָׂם, צִוָּה, פָּקַד

appointed, to be: נִצָּב

approach, to: הִקְרִיב, קָרַב, נִגַּשׁ

arise, to: קָם

ark: אֲרוֹן

arm: זְרוֹעַ

army: צָבָא, חַיִל

around: בַּעַד

arouse, to: עוֹרֵר

arrange, to: עָרַךְ

as: כְּ + inf., כַּאֲשֶׁר; as X lives: חַי

ascend, to: עָלָה

ashamed, to be(come): בֹּשׁ

ask, to: שָׁאַל

ass: (m) חֲמוֹר; (f) אָתוֹן

assembly: עֵדָה, קָהָל

assistance: עֵזֶר

astonished, to be(come): דָּם

atone for, to: כִּפֶּר

attain, to: הִשִּׂיג

attend to, to: פָּקַד

B

bad: רָשָׁע, רַע

bad, to be: רַע

band together, to: קָשַׁר

bank: שָׂפָה

banquet: מִשְׁתֶּה

battle: מִלְחָמָה

be, to: הָיָה

bear (child), to: יָלַד

bear witness, to: הֵעִיד

beast: חַיָּה, בְּהֵמָה

beautiful: יָפֶה

because: יַעַן, כִּי, יַעַן אֲשֶׁר + inf., עֵקֶב כִּי/אֲשֶׁר,

because of: עַל־דְּבַר, בַּעֲבוּר

become, to: הָיָה (לְ +)

befall, to: נִקְרָא, קָרָא, קָרָה

before (prep.): נֶגֶד, לִפְנֵי; (conj.) לִפְנֵי + inf., (בְּ)טֶרֶם

beget, to: הוֹלִיד

begin, to: הֵחֵל

beginning: תְּחִלָּה

behalf; on – – of: בְּעַד

believe, to: הֶאֱמִין

belong, to: use אֲשֶׁר לְ (§72) or
    בְּרַגְלֵי (§93)

below: (prep.) תַּחַת; (adv.) מִתַּחַת

beside: עַל־יַד, אֵצֶל

besiege, to: צָר

better: comparative of "good"

between: בֵּין

big: גָּדוֹל

big, to be(come): גָּדַל

bind, to: קָשַׁר

birds: עוֹף

bless, to: בֵּרַךְ

blessing: בְּרָכָה

blood: דָּם

book: סֵפֶר

border: קָצֶה

bosom: חֵיק

bow down, to: הִשְׁתַּחֲוָה

boy: נַעַר, יֶלֶד

bread: לֶחֶם

break, to: הֵפֵר, שָׁבַר

break down, to: פָּרַץ

bring, to: הִקְרִיב, הֵבִיא

bring about, to: עָשָׂה

bring across, to: הֶעֱבִיר

bring back, to: הֵשִׁיב

bring down, to: הוֹרִיד

bring near, to: הִגִּישׁ, הִקְרִיב

bring out, to: הוֹצִיא

bring up, to: הֶעֱלָה; (= rear): גָּדַל

broad: רָחָב

brother: אָח

build, to: בָּנָה

burn, to: (intr.) בָּעַר, שָׂרַף
    (tr.) בִּעֵר, שָׂרַף

burst out, to: פָּרַץ

bury, to: קָבַר

but: אֲבָל, אַךְ, וְ

but rather: כִּי־אִם

by (= near, at): אֵצֶל

C

Cain: קַיִן

calf: עֶגְלָה, עֵגֶל

call, to: קָרָא

camel: גָּמָל

camp: מַחֲנֶה

can: יָכֹל

Canaan: כְּנַעַן

captive, to take: שָׁבָה, לָכַד

capture, to: לָכַד

cattle: (large) בָּקָר; (small) צֹאן; a
    head of – –: שׁוֹר; (as property):
    מִקְנֶה

cease, to: חָדַל, שָׁבַת

chariot: מֶרְכָּבָה

chase, to: רָדַף

chief: שַׂר, רֹאשׁ

children: בָּנִים, טַף

choose, to: בָּחַר

circumcise, to: מָל

cistern: בּוֹר

city: עִיר

cliff: צוּר

cloak: שִׂמְלָה

close (adj.): קָרוֹב; to be – –: קָרַב

close, to: סָגַר

cloud: עָנָן

come, to: בָּא; see also "to go"

come back, to: שָׁב

come to an end, to: תַּם, כָּלָה

comfort, to: נִחַם be – – ed: נֻחַם;

commandment: מִצְוָה

command, to: צִוָּה

commit (a sin), to: חָטָא

companion: רֵעַ

conceal, to: הִסְתִּיר, כִּחֵד

conceive, to: הָרָה

concerning: עַל

confine, to: צָר

confirmed, to be: נֶאֱמַן

congregation: עֵדָה, קָהָל

consider, to: חָשַׁב

console, to: נִחַם; be – – ed: נֻחַם

conspire, to: קָשַׁר

consume, to: אָכַל; be ––ed: בָּעַר, נֶאֱכַל

content, to be: הוֹאִיל

continue (doing something), to: הוֹסִיף

counsel: עֵצָה

count, to: סָפַר

countless: = without number

covenant: בְּרִית

cover, to: כִּסָּה

cow: פָּרָה

create, to: בָּרָא

creeping things: רֶמֶשׂ

criminal (adj.): רָשָׁע

crop: קָצִיר

cross, to: עָבַר

cry (= weep), to: בָּכָה

cry out, to: זָעַק, צָעַק

cure, to: רָפָא

curse, to: אָרַר

cut, to: כָּרַת

D

darkness: חֹשֶׁךְ

daughter: בַּת

David: דָּוִד

day: יוֹם; by – –: יוֹמָם

daytime; in the – –: יוֹמָם

dead: מֵת

death: מָוֶת

deed: מַעֲשֶׂה

defence: צוּר

defile, to: חִלֵּל

decide, to: הוֹכִיחַ

declare, to: הוֹדִיעַ, קָרָא

deliver, to: הוֹשִׁיעַ

deliverance: יְשׁוּעָה

depart, to: סָר

depleted, to be(come): כָּלָה

deposit, to: הִנִּיחַ

descend, to: יָרַד

descendants: זֶרַע

desert: מִדְבָּר

desire, to: חָפֵץ

desolated, to be(come): שָׁמֵם

despise, to: בָּזָה, מָאַס

destroy, to: הֶאֱבִיד, הִשְׁמִיד, הֶחֱרִים

destroyed, to be: אָבַד

die, to: מֵת

difficult: קָשֶׁה

discerning: נָבוֹן

dishonor, to: חִלֵּל

distance; at a – –: מֵרָחוֹק

distant: רָחוֹק

distress: עֳנִי, צָרָה

do, to: עָשָׂה; to – – early in the day: הִשְׁכִּים

do again, to: שָׁב, הוֹסִיף

donkey: (m) חֲמוֹר; (f) אָתוֹן

door: דֶּלֶת

draw near, to: נִגַּשׁ, קָרַב

draw up (for battle), to: עָרַךְ

dread: אֵימָה

dream: חֲלוֹם; to – –: חָלַם

drink, to: שָׁתָה; cause to – –: הִשְׁקָה

drive away, to: גֵּרֵשׁ

dry ground: יַבָּשָׁה

dwell, to: שָׁכַן, יָשַׁב, גָּר; cause to – –: הוֹשִׁיב

E

each: כֹּל, אִישׁ (see §123)

ear: אֹזֶן

earth: אֲדָמָה, אֶרֶץ

east: קֶדֶם; to the – – of: מִקֶּדֶם לְ

eat, to: אָכַל

edge: שָׂפָה

Egypt: מִצְרַיִם; Egyptian: מִצְרִי

eight: שְׁמֹנָה, שְׁמֹנֶה

eighty: שְׁמֹנִים

Eli: עֵלִי

elder: זָקֵן; (= older) use: גָּדוֹל

emptiness: שָׁוְא

empty: רֵיק

encounter, to: נִקְרָא ,נִקְרָה ,קָרָא ,קָרָה

end: קֵץ ,קָצֶה; at the − − of: מִקְצֵי ,מִקֵּץ;
    to be at an − −: כָּלָה ,תַּם

enemy: אֹיֵב

engender, to: הוֹלִיד

enter, to: בָּא

entire: כֹּל

establish, to: הֵכִין; be − −ed: נָכוֹן

eternity: עוֹלָם

Eve: חַוָּה

even (adv.): גַּם

evening: עֶרֶב

every: כֹּל; everything (which):
    כֹּל אֲשֶׁר (§66)

evil (adj.): רָשָׁע ,רַע

evil (noun): רָעָה ,רַע

evil, to be(come): רַע

exalt, to: רוֹמֵם ,הֵרִים ,נָשָׂא

except (that): אֶפֶס כִּי ,כִּי־אִם

expel, to: שִׁלַּח

extend, to: שָׁלַח ,נָטָה .

exterminate, to: הֶחֱרִים ,בִּעֵר

eye: עַיִן; in the − −s of: בְּעֵינֵי

F

face: פָּנִים

fall, to: נָפַל

famine: רָעָב

far: רָחוֹק; as − − as: עַד

fashion, to: יָצַר

fast, to: צָם

father: אָב

father-in-law: חֹתֵן

favor: חֵן; to seek − −: הִתְחַנֵּן

fear: יָרְאָה

female: נְקֵבָה

few: מִסְפָּר (§86); אֲחָדִים (pl. of אֶחָד)

field: שָׂדֶה

fifth: חֲמִישִׁי

fifty: חֲמִשִּׁים

fight, to: נִלְחַם

filled = to be full

find, to: מָצָא

finish, to: כִּלָּה

finished, to be: תַּם ,כָּלָה

fire: אֵשׁ

firm: חָזָק; to be(come) − −: נָכוֹן ,חָזַק

firmament: רָקִיעַ

first: רִאשׁוֹן

fish: דָּגָה ,דָּג

five: חֲמִשָּׁה ,חָמֵשׁ

flame: לֶהָבָה

flee, to: נָס ,בָּרַח

flesh: בָּשָׂר

flock: עֵדֶר

following; in the − − of: בְּרַגְלֵי

food: לֶחֶם

foot: רֶגֶל

for: (prep.) לְ ,בְּעַד; (conj.): כִּי

foreign: נָכְרִי

forever: עַד־עוֹלָם ,לְעוֹלָם

forget, to: שָׁכַח

form: תֹּאַר

form, to: יָצַר

forsake, to: נָטַשׁ ,עָזַב

forty: אַרְבָּעִים

four: אַרְבָּעָה ,אַרְבַּע

fourth: רְבִיעִי

fowl: עוֹף

friend: רֵעַ

from: מִן

front; in − − of: נֶגֶד ,לִפְנֵי

fruit: פְּרִי

full: מָלֵא; to be(come)− −: מָלֵא

G

gain: בֶּצַע

garden: גַּן

garment: בֶּגֶד

gate: שַׁעַר

gather, to קָבַץ

genealogy: תּוֹלְדוֹת

generation: דּוֹר

give, to: נָתַן

give birth to, to: יָלַד

gladden, to: שִׂמַּח

glory: כָּבוֹד

go, to: הָלַךְ; to cause to – –: הוֹלִיךְ; to – – continuously: הִתְהַלֵּךְ

go around, to סָבַב

go back, to: שָׁב

go down, to: יָרַד

go forth, to: יָצָא

go up, to: עָלָה

go well with, to: יִיטַב

god: אֵל

God: אֵל, אֱלֹהִים

gold: זָהָב

good: טוֹב; to make – – (as compensation): שִׁלֵּם

grab, to: תָּפַשׂ

grace: חֵן

gracious; to be – – toward: חָנַן

grasp, to: הֶחֱזִיק, אָחַז

grass: עֵשֶׂב

grave: קֶבֶר

great: גָּדוֹל; to become – –: גָּדַל; to make – –: הִגְדִּיל

grey hair: שֵׂיבָה

ground: אֲדָמָה; dry – –: יַבָּשָׁה; onto the – –: אַרְצָה

grow fond of, to: (מָצָא חֵן בְּעֵינֵי)

grow up, to: גָּדַל

guard, to: שָׁמַר, נָצַר

guilt: עָוֹן

guilty, to be: אָשֵׁם

H

half: חֲצִי

hand: יָד

handsome: יָפֶה

hang, to: תָּלָה

hard: חָזָק; (= difficult): קָשֶׁה

harsh: קָשֶׁה

harvest, to: קָצַר

harvest: קָצִיר

hate, to: שָׂנֵא

he: הוּא

head: רֹאשׁ

heal, to: רָפָא

health: שָׁלוֹם

hear, to: שָׁמַע

heart: לֵבָב, לֵב

heaven(s): שָׁמַיִם

heavy: כָּבֵד; to be – –: כָּבֵד

Hebrew: עִבְרִי

heed, to: שָׁמַע (+ בְּ/לְ; בְּ/לְקוֹל)

heifer: פָּרָה, עֶגְלָה

help, to: עָזַר

help: עֵזֶר

herbage: עֵשֶׂב

herd: עֵדֶר

here: פֹּה see also §135

hide, to: (tr.) כִּחֵד, הִסְתִּיר; (intr.) הִתְחַבֵּא, נֶחְבָּא, נִסְתַּר

high, to be: רָם

hill: גִּבְעָה

history: תּוֹלְדוֹת

hither: הֵנָּה, הֲלֹם

Hittite: חִתִּי

holiness: קֹדֶשׁ

honest: כֵּן

honey: דְּבַשׁ

honor: כָּבוֹד

horse: סוּס

horseman: פָּרָשׁ

host: צָבָא

house: בַּיִת

how?: אֵיכָה

however: אֲבָל, אַךְ

hundred: מֵאָה

hunger: רָעָב

hungry, to be: רָעֵב

hurry, to: מִהַר

hurt, to: הֵרַע

husband: אִישׁ

I

I: אָנֹכִי, אֲנִי
idle: רֵיק
idol: פֶּסֶל, צֶלֶם
if: הֵן, אִם; if not: לוּלֵי, לוּלֵא
image: צֶלֶם
important: כָּבֵד
in: בְּ
indeed: אָמְנָם, אֲבָל
inherit, to: יָרַשׁ
inheritance: נַחֲלָה
iniquity: עָוֹן
injure, to: הֵרַע
inn: מָלוֹן
innumerable: אֵין מִסְפָּר לְ
inquire, to: שָׁאַל, דָּרַשׁ
inside: בְּקֶרֶב, בְּתוֹךְ
instead of: תַּחַת
intelligent: נָבוֹן
Israel: יִשְׂרָאֵל
is (see "to be")
it: הִיא, הוּא

J

Jacob: יַעֲקֹב
jail: מִשְׁמָר
jealous, to be: קִנֵּא
Jerusalem: יְרוּשָׁלַ͏ִם
Joseph: יוֹסֵף
journey, to: נָסַע
joy: שִׂמְחָה
Judah: יְהוּדָה
judge, to: שָׁפַט; judge: שֹׁפֵט
just: יָשָׁר

K

kid: גְּדִי
kill, to: מוֹתֵת, הֶאֱבִיד, רָצַח, הָרַג
king: מֶלֶךְ; to be(come) – –: מָלַךְ
know, to: יָדַע

L

lamb: כִּבְשָׂה, כֶּבֶשׂ
land: אֲדָמָה, אֶרֶץ
language: שָׂפָה
law (Law) תּוֹרָה
lead, to: הוֹלִיךְ
lead across, to: הֶעֱבִיר
lead into sin, to: הֶחֱטִיא
leave, to: נָטַשׁ, עָזַב
leave alone, to: הִנִּיחַ
left, to be: נוֹתַר, נִשְׁאַר
left hand: שְׂמֹאל
left over, to be: נוֹתַר
lengthen, to: (tr.) הֶאֱרִיךְ
lest: פֶּן
lie down, to: שָׁכַב
life: נֶפֶשׁ, חַיִּים
lifetime: חַיִּים
lift up, to: הֵרִים, נָשָׂא
light: אוֹר
like (prep.): כְּ
likeness: צֶלֶם
lion: אַרְיֵה, אֲרִי
lip: שָׂפָה
listen to, to (see "obey")
little: קָטָן, קָטֹן; a little: מְעַט; in a little while: עוֹד מְעַט; little by little מְעַט מְעַט
live, to: חָיָה, חָיָה; to let – –: הֶחֱיָה
living (adj.): חַי
lodging-place: מָלוֹן
lofty, to be: רָם
long, to be: הֶאֱרִיךְ
look at, to: הִבִּיט
lord: בַּעַל, אָדֹן
Lord: יהוה
Lot: לוֹט
love: אַהֲבָה
love, to: אָהַב
low, to be(come): שָׁפֵל; to lay – –: הִשְׁפִּיל

M

magnify, to: הִגְדִּיל

maidservant: שִׁפְחָה, אָמָה

make, to: עָשָׂה; to – – a treaty:
כָּרַת בְּרִית

male: זָכָר

man: אָדָם, אִישׁ; young – –: בָּחוּר, נַעַר
old – –: זָקֵן

mankind: אָדָם, כָּל־בָּשָׂר

manner; in this – –: כֹּה, כֵּן

many: רַב

marvelous, to be: נִפְלָא

master: בַּעַל, אָדֹן

matter: דָּבָר

measure, to: מָדַד

meat: בָּשָׂר

meditate, to: הָגָה

meet, to: קָרָה, קָרָא; see also לִקְרַאת
פָּגַע (§ 125);

melt, to: נָמֵס

mention, to: הִזְכִּיר

memorial: זֵכֶר

messenger: מַלְאָךְ

midst; in the – – of: בְּתוֹךְ; from the
– – of: מִתּוֹךְ

might: עֹז, זְרוֹעַ

mighty: עַז

milk: חָלָב

mistress: גְּבֶרֶת

money: כֶּסֶף

month: חֹדֶשׁ

moon: יָרֵחַ

morning: בֹּקֶר

Moses: מֹשֶׁה

mother: אֵם

mountain: הַר

mourn, to: בָּכָה

mouth: פֶּה

much: (adj.) רַב; (adv.) מְאֹד, הַרְבֵּה

N

name: שֵׁם

name, to: קָרָא

narrate, to: סִפֵּר, הִגִּיד

Nathan: נָתָן

nation: עַם

near: (prep.) אֵצֶל; (adj.) קָרוֹב

near, to be: קָרַב

Negev: נֶגֶב

new: חָדָשׁ

night: לַיְלָה

Nile, the: יְאֹר

nine: תֵּשַׁע, תִּשְׁעָה

ninety: תִּשְׁעִים

none = no one, not one (cf. §65 end);
use negative with verb or predicate

noon: צָהֳרַיִם

north: שְׂמֹאל, צָפוֹן

nose: אַף

not: לֹא; there is – –: אֵין

not yet: (בְּ)טֶרֶם

now: עַתָּה; see also §135

number: מִסְפָּר

numerous: רַב

O

oath: שְׁבוּעָה

obey, to: שָׁמַע בְּ/לְקוֹל

observe, to: שָׁמַר

occupation: מְלָאכָה

offering: מִנְחָה

officer: שַׂר, סָרִיס

offspring: זֶרַע

olive (-tree): זַיִת

old: זָקֵן; old man: idem

old age: זְקוּנִים, שֵׂיבָה

omen: אוֹת

on: עַל, בְּ

one: אֶחָד, אַחַת

only: רַק, לְבַד־

open, to: פָּתַח

opening: פֶּתַח

opinion; in the – – of: בְּעֵינֵי

oppress, to: עִנָּה

or: אוֹ

order; in – – that: לְמַעַן

other: אַחֵר

outside: חוּץ, (הַ)חוּצָה; outside of: מִחוּץ לְ

overtake, to: הִשִּׂיג

overwhelm, to: כִּסָּה

own, to: (use idiom for possession with לְ)

owner: בַּעַל

P

palace: הֵיכָל

palm: כַּף

pardon, to: סָלַח

peace: שָׁלוֹם

people: עַם, גּוֹי

perceive, to: הֵבִין

perceptiveness: בִּינָה

perform, to: עָשָׂה

perish, to: אָבַד

permitted, it is not – –: אֵין לְ (+ inf.)

persecute, to: רָדַף

person: נֶפֶשׁ, אִישׁ

Pharaoh: פַּרְעֹה

Philistines: פְּלִשְׁתִּים

pit: בּוֹר

pitch (tent), to: נָטָה

place: מָקוֹם

place, to: נָתַן, שָׂם, שָׁת, הֶעֱמִיד, הִצִּיב

plague, to: נָגַף

plague: מַגֵּפָה

plant, to: נָטַע

pleasant: נֶחְמָד

pleased with, to be: x was pleased with y = y found favor in the eyes of x

pleasing, to be: יָשַׁר

pledge; to stand as – – for: עָרַב

plow, to: חָרַשׁ

portion: נַחֲלָה

pollute, to: חִלֵּל

poor: דַּל

pour, to: שָׁפַךְ

praise, to: הִלֵּל

pray, to: הִתְפַּלֵּל

prayer: תְּפִלָּה

precious: יָקָר

pregnant, to become: הָרָה

prepare, to: הֵכִין

presence; in the – – of: נֶגֶד, לִפְנֵי

present, to: הֵבִיא, הִקְרִיב, הִמְצִיא

prevail, to: יָכֹל

priest: כֹּהֵן

prisoner: אָסִיר

proclaim, to: קָרָא, הוֹדִיעַ

profit: בֶּצַע

progeny: זֶרַע

property: רְכוּשׁ, מִקְנֶה, נַחֲלָה

prophesy, to: נִבָּא, הִתְנַבֵּא

prophet: נָבִיא

prosperous, to make: הִצְלִיחַ; to be – –: הִצְלִיחַ

prostitute; to be(come) a – –: זָנָה

prostitute: זֹנָה

protection: צוּר

protest, to: הֵעִיד

punishment: עָוֹן

purchase, to: קָנָה

pursue, to: רָדַף

put, to: שָׁת, שָׂם

put forth, to: שָׁלַח

Q

quickly: מַהֵר

R

rain: מָטָר

raise, to: נָשָׂא, הֵרִים, רוֹמֵם; (= to rear) גִּדֵּל

ransom, to: פָּדָה

read, to: קָרָא

ready; to make – –: הֵכִין

reap, to: קָצַר

rebel, to: מָרַד

rebuke, to: גָּעַר

reckon, to: חָשַׁב

recompense, to: שִׁלֵּם

redeem, to: גָּאַל

refuse, to: מֵאֵן, מָאַס

rejoice, to: שָׂמַח; cause to – –: שִׂמַּח

remain, to: (= stay) יָשַׁב; (= be left over): נִשְׁאַר, נוֹתַר

remember, to: זָכַר

remembrance: זֵכֶר

remind, to: הִזְכִּיר

remove, to: הֵסִיר

remove completely, to: בִּעֵר

rend, to: קָרַע

repent, to: נִחַם

reprove, to: הוֹכִיחַ

request, to: שָׁאַל, דָּרַשׁ

require, to: דָּרַשׁ

rescue, to הִצִּיל; to be – – ed: נִצַּל

residence: מְגוּרִים

rest, to: נָח, שָׁבַת; cause to – –: הֵנִיחַ

restore, to: שִׁלֵּם

return, to: שָׁב

revive, to: הֶחֱיָה, חָיָה

rib: צֵלָע

rich: עָשִׁיר

ride, to: רָכַב

right hand: יָמִין

righteous: צַדִּיק

righteousness: צְדָקָה, צֶדֶק

river: נָהָר

road: דֶּרֶךְ

rock: צוּר

rod: מַטֶּה

roof: גַּג

rule, to: מָלַךְ, מָשַׁל

run, to: רָץ

S

Sabbath: שַׁבָּת

sack: שַׂק; sack-cloth: idem

sacrifice, to: זָבַח

sacrifice: זֶבַח

sake; for the – – of: עַל־דְּבַר, בַּעֲבוּר

salvation: יְשׁוּעָה

Samuel: שְׁמוּאֵל

sanctify, to: הִקְדִּישׁ, קִדֵּשׁ

sandal: נַעַל

save, to: הִצִּיל, הוֹשִׁיעַ

say, to: דִּבֶּר, אָמַר

sea: יָם; seaward: יָמָּה

second: שֵׁנִי

secure, to be: נָכוֹן

see, to: רָאָה

seed: זֶרַע

seek, to: דָּרַשׁ, בִּקֵּשׁ

seize, to: הֶחֱזִיק, אָחַז

self: נֶפֶשׁ (+ suffix)

sell, to: מָכַר

send, to: שָׁלַח

send forth, to: שִׁלַּח

servant: עֶבֶד

serve, to: עָבַד

serious: כָּבֵד; to be – –: כָּבֵד

serpent: נָחָשׁ

servitude: עֲבוֹדָה

set, to: שָׁת, שָׂם, נָתַן

set at rest, to: הֵנִיחַ

set down, to הִנִּיחַ

set in order, to: עָרַךְ

set out, to: נָסַע

set up, to: הִצִּיב, הֶעֱמִיד

settle, to: (tr.) הוֹשִׁיב

settle down, to: שָׁכַן, נָח

seven: שִׁבְעָה, שֶׁבַע

seventh: שְׁבִיעִי

seventy: שִׁבְעִים

shade: צֵל

shadow: צֵל

shame: עֶרְוָה

she: הִיא

Shechem: שְׁכֶם

shed (blood), to: שָׁפַךְ

shepherd: רֹעֶה; to – –: רָעָה
Sheol: שְׁאֹל
shoe: נַעַל
side: יָד; at/to the – – of: עַל־יַד
sign: אוֹת
silent, to be: דָּם
silver: כֶּסֶף
since: see §135; (= because): כִּי
sinful: רָשָׁע ,רַע
sing, to: שָׁר
sin: חַטָּאת
sin, to: חָטָא: cause to – –: הֶחֱטִיא
sister: אָחוֹת
sit, to: יָשַׁב
six: שֵׁשׁ ,שִׁשָּׁה
sixth: שִׁשִּׁי
sixty: שִׁשִּׁים
sky: שָׁמַיִם
slaughter, to: שָׁחַט ,טָבַח
slaughtering: טֶבַח
slave: (m) עֶבֶד; (f) שִׁפְחָה ,אָמָה
slay, to: מוֹתֵת ,רָצַח ,הָרַג
sleep, to: נָם ,יָשֵׁן
small: צָעִיר ,קָטָן ,קָטֹן
smash, to: שָׁבַר
snake: נָחָשׁ
so that: לְמַעַן + imperf. or inf.; so that...not: פֶּן
soil: אֲדָמָה
sojourn, to: גָּר
sojourner: גֵּר
sojourning: מְגוּרִים
sole: כַּף
some (of): מִן
son: בֵּן
song: שִׁיר
sorry, to be: נִחַם
soul: רוּחַ ,נֶפֶשׁ
sound: קוֹל
south: יָמִין
spare, to: חָמַל
speak, to: דִּבֶּר
spend the night, to: לָן

split, to: בָּקַע
spread (out), to: פָּרַשׂ
spring: בְּאֵר ,עַיִן
spurn, to: נָאַץ ,מָאַס
spy: מְרַגֵּל
staff: מַטֶּה
stand, to: נִצַּב ,עָמַד; to take one's– –: הִתְיַצֵּב
star: כּוֹכָב
station, to: הִצִּיב ,הֶעֱמִיד; to – – one-self: הִתְיַצֵּב ,נִצַּב; to be – – ed. נִצַּב
steal, to: גָּנַב
still (adv.): עוֹד
stone: אֶבֶן
stop, to: חָדַל ,שָׁבַת
strange: נָכְרִי
strength: עֹז ,חַיִל
strike, to: הִכָּה
stroke: נֶגַע
strong: עַז ,חָזָק to be(come) – –: חָזַק
stumble, to: כָּשַׁל
surround, to: סָבַב
summon, to: קָרָא לְ
sun: שֶׁמֶשׁ
supplication: תְּחִנָּה
support (fig.): צוּר
surely: אָמְנָם ,אֲבָל
surety: (see pledge)
surface; on the – – of: עַל־פְּנֵי
survive, to: נוֹתַר ,נִשְׁאַר
swallow, to: בָּלַע
swear, to: נִשְׁבַּע; to make – –: הִשְׁבִּיעַ
sword: חֶרֶב

T

table: שֻׁלְחָן
tablet: לוּחַ
talk, to: דִּבֶּר
task: עֲבוֹדָה ,מְלָאכָה
take, to: לָקַח
take across, to: הֶעֱבִיר
take away, to: הֵסִיר

take captive, to: שָׁבָה ,לָכַד

take hold of, to: תָּפַשׂ ,אָחַז

take prisoner, to: אָסַר ,לָכַד

take pleasure in, to: חָפֵץ

teach, to: לִמֵּד

tear, to: קָרַע

tell, to: הִגִּיד

temple: הֵיכָל

ten: עֲשָׂרָה ,עֶשֶׂר

tend (flocks), to: רָעָה

terror: אֵימָה

test, to: בָּחַן

that (conj.): כִּי

that (rel.): אֲשֶׁר

the: see §§14, 18, 21

then (at that time): אָז

then (and – –): וְ; (and) so then: וְעַתָּה

thence: מִשָּׁם

there: שָׁם

therein = "in it" or "in them"

there is/are: יֵשׁ

there is/are not: אֵין

therefore: לָכֵן ,עַל־כֵּן

thing: מְאוּמָה ,דָּבָר

think, to: חָשַׁב

third: שְׁלִישִׁי

three: שְׁלֹשָׁה ,שָׁלֹשׁ

thirty: שְׁלֹשִׁים

thousand: אֶלֶף

throne: כִּסֵּא

through: בְּעַד

throw, to: הִשְׁלִיךְ

thrust aside, to: הִטָּה

thus: כֹּה ,כֵּן

till, to: עָבַד ,חָרַשׁ

time: עֵת ,פַּעַם

time; at that – –: אָז

to: אֶל ,לְ

today: כַּיּוֹם ,הַיּוֹם

together: יַחְדָּו ,יַחַד

together with: אֵת ,עִם

too (= also): גַּם

too: see § 31

top: רֹאשׁ

touch, to: נָגַע

toward: עַד ,לִקְרַאת ,אֶל

travel, to: נָסַע

transgress, to: עָבַר

treaty: בְּרִית

tree: עֵץ

tribe: מַטֶּה

trouble: צָרָה ,עֳנִי

true: כֵּן

truly: אָמְנָם ,אֲבָל

trust, to: בָּטַח ,הֶאֱמִין

trustworthy, to be: נֶאֱמַן

truth: אֱמֶת

tunic: כֻּתֹּנֶת ,כְּתֹנֶת

turn around, to: סָבַב

turn aside, to: סָר ,נָטָה; (tr.) הִטָּה

turn away, to: (tr.) הֵסֵב ,הֵסִיר

turn toward, to: פָּנָה

two: שְׁתַּיִם ,שְׁנַיִם

twice: פַּעֲמַיִם

U

unanimous: פֶּה אֶחָד

uncircumcised: עָרֵל

under: תַּחַת

understand, to: הֵבִין

understanding: בִּינָה

unimportant: קָטֹן

unless: לוּלֵא ,כִּי אִם

until: עַד

until now: עַד־הֵנָּה

up against: עַל־פְּנֵי

up to: עַד

upon: עַל

upright: יָשָׁר

utensil: כְּלִי

V

vain; in – –: לַשָּׁוְא

valley: עֵמֶק

vanity: שָׁוְא

verified, to be: נֶאֱמַן

very: הַרְבֵּה ,מְאֹד

vessel: כְּלִי

vineyard: כֶּרֶם

visit, to: פָּקַד

voice: קוֹל

vow: נֶדֶר

vow, to: נָדַר

W

wake up, to: יִיקַץ

walk, to: הָלַךְ; to – – back & forth: הִתְהַלֵּךְ

wall: קִיר

wander about lost, to: תָּעָה

want to, to: אָבָה ,חָפֵץ

war: מִלְחָמָה

warn, to: הֵעִיד

warrior: גִּבּוֹר

wash, to: רָחַץ

watch, to: נָצַר ,שָׁמַר

water: מַיִם

we: אֲנַחְנוּ

weep, to: בָּכָה

well: בּוֹר ,בְּאֵר

west: יָם westward: יָמָּה

when: בְּ/כְּ + inf.

whence: מֵאַיִן

where?: אֵיפֹה ,אַיֵּה

which: אֲשֶׁר

while: בְּ/כְּ + inf.

whither: אָנָה

who?: מִי

who (rel.): אֲשֶׁר

whole: כֹּל

why?: מַדּוּעַ ,לָמָה ,לָמָּה

wicked: רָשָׁע ,רַע

wide: רָחָב

wife: אִשָּׁה

wilderness: מִדְבָּר

willing, to be: הוֹאִיל ,אָבָה

wisdom: חָכְמָה

wise: חָכָם

with: אֵת ,עִם ,בְּ

withhold, to: חָשַׂךְ

without; use אֵין

write, to: כָּתַב

woman: אִשָּׁה

wonderful, to be: נִפְלָא

wood: עֵץ

word: דָּבָר

work: מַעֲשֶׂה ,עֲבוֹדָה ,מְלָאכָה; עָשָׂה ,עָבַד

worse: (comp. of "bad")

worthless: רֵיק

Y

year: שָׁנָה

yesterday: אֶתְמוֹל

yet: עוֹד

you: אַתֵּנָה ,אַתֵּן ,אַתֶּם ,אַתְּ ,אַתָּה

young: בָּחוּר ,נַעַר; – – man: צָעִיר

Z

zealous, to be: קִנֵּא

INDEX

References are to the numbered paragraphs.
For the location of verb forms and paradigms see the table at the end of the Index.

Root Type:	Regular		I-gutt.	II-gutt.	III-gutt.	I-Aleph	III-Aleph	I-Nun	I-Yodh/Waw	III-Hē	Hollow	Geminate
QAL:												
perfect	43;	(st.87)	48	48	48	48	52	43	43	57	64,87	68,87
imperfect	90;	(st.94)	103	94	94	108	95	118	120	122	124	126
imperative	102		103	102	102	108	102	118	120	122	124	126
jussive, cohort.	106		108	106	106	108	106	118	120	122	124	126
inf. construct	114		114	114	114	114	114	118	120	122	124	126
inf. absolute	128		128	128	128	128	128	128	128	128	128	128
participle active	26		26	35	35	26	35	26	26	41	64	26
participle passive	128		128	128	128	128	128	128	128	128	128	128
NIPHAL	141		141	141	141	141	143	143	143	143	146	146
PIEL	149		149	149	149	149	151	149	149	151	—	151
PUAL	154		154	154	154	154	154	154	154	154	—	154
HIPHIL	158		158	158	160	158	160	158	163	166	169	172
HOPHAL	175		175	175	175	175	175	175	175	175	175	175
HITHPAEL	178		178	178	178	178	178	178	178	178	178	178

QAL PASSIVE 179
POLEL, POLAL, HITHPOLEL 180
PERFECT of נָתַן 49
IMPERFECT of הָלַךְ 120; חָקָה 118; יָכֹל 120
QAL PERFECTS with irregularities 190